Neanderthals on the Edge

Neanderthals on the Edge

*Papers from a conference marking the 150th anniversary
of the Forbes' Quarry discovery, Gibraltar*

Edited by
C. B. Stringer, R. N. E. Barton and J. C. Finlayson

Oxbow Books
2000

Published by
Oxbow Books, Park End Place, Oxford OX1 1HN

ISBN 1 84217 015 5

This book is available direct from
Oxbow Books, Park End Place, Oxford OX1 1HN
(Phone: 01865-241249; Fax: 01865-794449)

and

The David Brown Book Company
P.O. Box 511, Oakville, CT 06779
(Phone: 860-945-9329; Fax: 860-945-9468)

and

via our website
www.oxbowbooks.com

Printed in Great Britain at
The Short Run Press, Exeter

Foreword

The Hon. Keith Azopardi, Deputy Chief Minister and Minister with responsibility for Heritage, Gibraltar

1998 was a very special year for Gibraltar. It was the year when we celebrated the 150th anniversary of the discovery of the famous Gibraltar skull. We had been planning these events for some time and we were very fortunate in having the support of the Natural History Museum in London and, particularly, that of Professor Christopher Stringer. It was through his efforts that we were able to see the return of the skull to Gibraltar where it was exhibited in the Gibraltar Museum for four months during the summer.

The culmination of the events commemorating the anniversary was the "Gibraltar and the Neanderthals" conference. We were delighted to host this as part of the Government of Gibraltar's annual Calpe series of historical conferences which aim at highlighting the many varied facets of Gibraltar's unique heritage. The conference managed to gather a very unique group of leading specialists and the papers in this volume reflect the state of our knowledge and of the role played by Gibraltar and the southern Iberian Peninsula in a crucial period of human evolution. I am grateful to everyone who helped to make the Conference such a success, particularly the organisers, Dr Nick Barton, Professor Chris Stringer and Dr Clive Finlayson.

The work in Gibraltar carries on. The excavations at Gorham's and Vanguard Caves as well as explorations at other sites continue and the Government of Gibraltar is fully behind this research through sponsorship and logistical support. We are also keen to support the Gibraltar Museum's initiative of making Gibraltar a major centre for research and discussion of matters relating to Neanderthals. As part of this commitment I have now agreed to sponsor another conference along these lines in 2001. I hope that Calpe 2001 can live up to the expectations created after the very successful 1998 conference.

To understand our future we must strive to understand our past. It is only if we realise this that we will really be able to define the meaning of progress. The publication of this volume will, I hope, make a small contribution towards that enormous task.

Contents

Foreword v

List of contributors ix

1   Neandertal Landscapes – A Preview
     by William Davies, John Stewart and Tjeerd H. van Andel 1

2   A Mediterranean Perspective on the Middle/Upper Palaeolithic Revolution
     by Ofer Bar-Yosef 9

3   The Mousterian in Mediterranean France: A Comparative Perspective
     by Carolyn C. Szmidt 19

4   Late Neandertals in the South West of France and the Emergence of the Upper Palaeolithic
     by Jean-Philippe Rigaud 27

5   Châtelperronian Chronology and the Case for Neanderthal/Modern Human 'Acculturation'
     in Western Europe
     by Paul Mellars 33

6   The Transition from the Final Acheulian to the Middle Palaeolithic in the South of the Iberian Peninsula
     by F. Giles Pacheco, A. Santiago Perez, J. M^a. Gutierrez Lopez, E. Mata Almonte
     and L. Aguilera Rodriguez 41

7   Middle Palaeolithic Technocomplexes and Lithic Industries in the Northwest of the Iberian Peninsula
     by J. A. Cano Pan, F. Giles Pacheco, E. Aguirre, A. Santiago Perez, F. J. Gracia Prieto,
     E. Mata Almonte, J. M^a. Gutierrez Lopez and O. Prieto Reina 49

8   Mousterian Hearths at Abric Romaní, Catalonia (Spain)
     by Ignasi Pastó, Ethel Allué and Josep Vallverdú 59

9   The Late Middle Palaeolithic in the Northeast of the Iberian Peninsula
     by Manuel Vaquero and Eudald Carbonell 69

10   Continuity Patterns in the Middle-Upper Palaeolithic Transition in Cantabrian Spain
     by Victoria Cabrera, Anne Pike-Tay, Mercedes Lloret and Federico Bernaldo de Quiros 85

11   The Middle-Upper Palaeolithic Transition in Portugal
     by Luis Raposo 95

12   The Ebro Frontier: A Model for the Late Extinction of Iberian Neanderthals
     by João Zilhão 111

13   Bajondillo Cave (Torremolinos, Malaga, Andalucia) and the Middle-Upper Palaeolithic Transition
      in Southern Spain
      by Miguel Cortés Sánchez 123

14   Gibraltar and the Neanderthals1848–1998
      by Chris Stringer 133

15   The Southern Iberian Peninsula in the Late Pleistocene: Geography, Ecology and Human Occupation
      by Clive Finlayson and Francisco Giles Pacheco 139

16   AMS Radiocarbon and Luminescence Dating of Gorham's and Vanguard Caves, Gibraltar,
      and Implications for the Middle to Upper Palaeolithic Transition in Iberia
      by P. B. Pettitt and R. M. Bailey 155

17   Results of the Current Program of ESR Dating of Gorham's Cave Teeth from the Gibraltar Museum
      by V. Volterra, H. P. Schwarcz and W. J. Rink 163

18   ESR, OSL and U-Series Chronology of Gorham's Cave, Gibraltar
      by W. J. Rink, J. Rees-Jones, V. Volterra and H. Schwarcz 165

19   The Taphonomy of Pleistocene Caves, with particular reference to Gibraltar
      by Yolanda Fernández-Jalvo and Peter Andrews 171

20   Geoarchaeological Investigation of Sediments from Gorham's and Vanguard Caves, Gibraltar:
      Microstratigraphical (Soil Micromorphological and Chemical) Signatures
      by Richard I. Macphail and Paul Goldberg with a contribution by Jöhan Linderholm 183

21   A Review of the Quaternary Mammals of Gibraltar
      by Andrew P. Currant 201

22   Charcoal and Charred Seed Remains from Middle Palaeolithic Levels at Gorham's
      and Vanguard Caves
      by Rowena Gale and Wendy Carruthers 207

23   Mousterian Hearths and Shellfish: Late Neanderthal Activities on Gibraltar
      by Nick Barton 211

24   Provenancing of Mousterian Cherts
      by V. Volterra, R. G. V. Hancock, C. B. Stringer, R. N. E. Barton
      and L. G. Vega Toscano 221

25   The 'Robusticity Transition' Revisited
      by Erik Trinkhaus 227

26   Investigation of Neanderthal Morphology with Computer-Assisted Methods
      by M. S. Ponce de León, C. P. E. Zollikofer, R. D. Martin and C. B. Stringer 237

27   CT Reconstruction and Analysis of the Le Moustier 1 Neanderthal
      by J. L. Thompson and B. Illerhaus 249

28   Heterochrony and the Human Fossil Record: Comparing Neandertal and Modern Human
      Craniofacial Ontogeny
      by Frank L'Engle Williams 257

List of Contributors

L. AGUILERA RODRIGUEZ
Museo municipal de El Puerto de Santa Maria
C/Pagador 1
11500 El Puerto de Santa Maria
Càdiz
Spain

E. AGUIRRE
Museo Nacional de Ciencias Naturales
Centro Superior de Invesigaciones Científicas (C.S.I.C)
José Gutiérrez Abascal 2
28006 madrid
Spain

ETHEL ALLUÉ
Area de Prehistòria
Universitat Rovira i Virgili
Unitat Associada al CSIS
Plaça Imperial Tàrraco 1
43005 Tarragona
Spain

TJEERD H. VAN ANDEL
Department of Earth Science
Godwin Institute for Quaternary Research
Cambridge University
Downing Street
Cambridge CB2 3EQ

PETER ANDREWS
Department of Palaeontology
Natural History Museum
London SW7 5BD

R. M. BAILEY
Research Laboratory for Archaeology
and the History of Art
University of Oxford
6 Keble Road
Oxford OX1 3QJ

NICK BARTON
Department of Anthropology
Oxford Brookes University
Headington
Oxford OX3 0BP

OFER BAR-YOSEF
Harvard University Department of Anthropology
Peabody Museum
11 Divinity Avenue
Cambridge, MA 02138
USA

FEDERICO BERNALDO DE QUIROS
Area de Prehistoria
Univesidad de León
León 24071
Spain

VICTORIA CABRERA
Departamento de Prehistoria e Historia Antigua
U.N.E.D.
28040 Madrid
Spain

J. A. CANO PAN
Departamento de Prehistoria
Universidad de Santiago 1
15703 Santiago de Compostela
Spain

EUDALD CARBONELL
Universitat Rovira Virgili
Departament de Geografia i Història
Area de Prehistòria
Plaça Imperial Tàrraco 1
43005 Tarragona
Spain

WENDY CARRUTHERS
Sawmills House
Castellau
Llantrisant
Mid-Glamorgan
South Wales CF72 8LQ

MIGUEL CORTÉS SÁNCHEZ
Area de Prehistoria
Facultad de Filosofía y Letras
Universidad de Córdoba
Plaza del Cardenal Salazar s/n
14071 Córdoba
Spain

ANDREW P. CURRANT
Department of Palaeontology
Natural History Museum
London SW7 5BD

WILLIAM DAVIES
McDonald Institute for Archaeological Reasearch and Godwin
Institute for Quaternary Research
Cambridge University
Downing Street
Cambridge CB2 3ER

YOLANDA FERNÁNDEZ-JALVO
Museo Nacional de Ciencias Naturales
Dept. Paleobiologia
José Gutierrez Abascal 2
28006 Madrid
Spain

CLIVE FINLAYSON
The Gibraltar Museum
18–20 Bomb House Lane
PO Box 939
Gibraltar

Rowena Gale
Folly Cottage
Chute Cadley
Andover SP11 9EB

F. Giles Pacheco
Museo Municipal de El Puerto de Santa Maria
C/Pagador 1
11500 El Puerto de Santa Maria
Càdiz
Spain

Paul Goldberg
Department of Archaeology
Boston University
675 Commonwealth Avenue
Boston, MA 02215
USA

F. J. Gracia Prieto
Dpto. de Estructura y Propiedades de los Materiales
Facultad de Ciencias del Mar.
Campus Universitario de Puerto Real
Universidad de Càdiz
Spain

J. M. Gutierrez Lopez
Museo Municipal de El Puerto de Santa Maria
C/Pagador 1
11500 El Puerto de Santa Maria
Càdiz
Spain

R. G. V. Hancock
SLOWPOKE Reactor Facility
Univeristy of Toronto
Toronto
Ontario
Canada

B. Illerhaus
Bundesanstalt für Materialforschung und -prüfung
Unter den Eichen 87
D-12205 Berlin
Germany

Frank L'Engle Williams
Department of Anthropology
Machmer Hall
University of Massachusetts
Amherst, MA 01003
USA

Jöhan Linderholm
Institute of Archaeology
University of Umeå
Sweden

Mercedes Lloret
Departamento de Prehistoria e Historia Antigua
U.N.E.D.
28040 Madrid
Spain

Richard I. Macphail
Institute of Archaeology
University College
London

Robert D. Martin
Anthrologisches Institut und Museum
Universität Zürich-Irchel
8057 Zürich
Switzerland

E. Mata Almonte
Museo Municipal de El Puerto de Santa Maria
C/Pagador 1
11500 El Puerto de Santa Maria
Càdiz
Spain

Paul Mellars
Department of Archaeology
Downing Street
Cambridge CB2 3DZ

Ignasi Pastó
Area de Prehistòria
Universitat Rovira i Virgili
Unitat Associada al CSIS
Plaça Imperial Tàrraco 1
43005 Tarragona
Spain

P. B. Pettitt
Research Laboratory for Archaeology
and the History of Art
University of Oxford
Oxford OX1 3QJ

Anne Pike-Tay
Anthropology Department
Vassar College
Poughkeepsie, NY 12601
USA

Marcia S. Ponce de León
Anthropologisches Institut und Museum
Universität Zürich-Irchel
8057 Zürich
Switzerland
and
MultiMedia Laboratorium
Institut für Informatik
Universität Zürich-Irchel
8057 Zürich
Switzerland

O. Priento Reina
Dpto de Estructura y Propiedades de los Materiales
Facultad de Ciencias del Mar
Campus Universitario de Puerto Real
Universidad de Càdiz
Spain

Luís Raposo
Museu Nacional de Arqueologia
Praça do Império
1400 Lisbon
Portugal

Julie Rees-Jones
School of Geography and Geology
McMaster University
Hamilton, Ontario
Canada L8S 4MI

JEAN-PHILIPPE RIGAUD
Insitut de Préhistoire et de Géologie du Quaternaire
Université Bordeaux 1
France

W. JACK RINK
School of Geography and Geology
McMaster University
Hamilton
Ontario
Canada L8S 4MI

A. SANTIAGO PEREZ
Museo Municipal de El Puerto de Santa Maria
C/Pagador 1
11500 El Puerto de Santa Maria
Càdiz
Spain

HENRY SCHWARCZ
School of Geography and Geology
McMAster University
Hamilton
Ontario
Canada L8S 4MI

JOHN STEWART
McDonald Institute for Archaeological Reasearch and Godwin
Institute for Quaternary Research
Cambridge University
Downing Street
Cambridge CB2 3ER

CHRIS STRINGER
Department of Palaeontology
Natural History Museum
London SW7 5BD

CAROLYN C. SZMIDT
Department of Archaeology
University of Cambridge
Cambridge CB2 3DZ

ERIK TRINKHAUS
Department of Anthropology
Washington University
St. Louis, MO 63130
USA
and
U.M.R. 5809 de C.N.R.S.
Laboratoire d'Anthropologie
Université de Bordeaux I
Avenue des Facultés
33405 Talence
France

JENNIFER L. THOMPSON
Department of Anthropology
University of Nevada
Las Vegas 4505, Maryland Parkway
Box 455012
Las Vegas, Nevada 89154–5503
USA

MANUEL VAQUERO
Universitat Rovira i Virgili
Departament de Geografia i Història
Area de Prehistòria
Plaça Imperial Tàrraco 1
43005 Tarragona
Spain

JOSEP VALLVERDÚ
Area de Prehistòria
Universitat Rovira i Virgili
Unitat Associada al CSIS
Plaça Imperial Tàrraco 1
43005 Tarragona
Spain

L. G. VEGA TOSCANO
Departimiento Prehistorico
Universidad Complutense 28040
Madrid
Spain

VITO VOLTERRA
Department of Anthropology
McMaster University
Hamilton
Ontario
Canada L8S 4MI

JOÃO ZILHÃO
Instituto Português de Arqueologia
Av. da India 136
P-1300 Lisboa
Portugal

CHRISTOPH P. E. ZOLLIKOFER
Anthropologisches Institut und Museum
Universität Zürich-irchel
8057 Zürich
Switzerland
and
MultiMedia Laboratorium
Institut für Informatik
Universität Zürich-Irchel
8057 Zürich
Switzerland

1

Neandertal Landscapes – A Preview

William Davies, John Stewart and Tjeerd H. van Andel

Introduction: A major historical event

A few events in human prehistory have been true turning points. The appearance of the first hominids is one of these; the spread of ancient humans (*Homo erectus*) from Africa northward into Europe and eastward into Asia, another. The question of how, why and under what conditions both developments took place is the subject of much speculation, but the palaeo-environmental data needed to underpin those speculations is sparse and ill-defined. Arguably of equal impact is the entry of modern human beings into Europe and the subsequent demise of their predecessors, the Neandertals: the time when two co-existing human species were reduced to a single one.

This momentous event is often, explicitly or implicitly, set against the harsh, bleak background of a fully glacial landscape where the great Fennoscandian ice-sheets were separated from the smaller but nonetheless forbidding ice-caps of Pyrenees, Alps and mountain ranges farther east by a vast, cold tundra poor in resources. Although those conditions apply to less than one tenth of the duration of the last glacial period, the image has become deeply rooted in the archaeological literature. In reality, the climate of the middle pleniglacial (60–25 ka) was far less hostile and its landscape in the main much less barren than is widely assumed. Recent work, exemplified by Broglio (1996), Gamble (1993), Hublin (1998), Kozlovski (1996), Kuhn (1996), Mellars (1996a, b), Miskovsky (1992), and Stiner (1994), displays a growing awareness of the moderate conditions prevailing during much of the last glacial interval. However, the true nature of palaeo-environments of the time and of their temporal variations remains as nebulous as its significance in terms of human resources.

It is also often forgotten that even during a full glacial maximum the summers were long, the sun stood high, and growing days were more numerous between 35° and 55°

N latitude than in the present Arctic, so that conditions, biomes and resources were not comparable to those of northern Canada and Norway or Siberia today. In fact, it is virtually certain that many of the mid-glacial biomes have no modern analogues. Nor does a widely held conviction – that the low tree pollen percentages of European mid-latitudes indicate severe cold – deserve the semi-axiomatic status that it appears to have acquired.

This point deserves elaboration. An early suggestion that uniformitarianism cannot be straightforwardly applied to the understanding of the major biomes of NW Europe during the late Pleistocene came from a diverse temperate insect fauna found at Upton Warren (UK) by Coope (1977), associated with a flora apparently completely lacking in trees.

Mammalian workers have also argued strongly against the idea that the mid-glacial vegetation covering much of Europe was a barren tundra. On the contrary, the environment commonly known as 'steppe-tundra' (or 'mammoth steppe') is regarded by them as having been extremely rich, with a high carrying capacity that was able to sustain the abundant megafauna of the period (Lister & Sher 1995; Guthrie 1990).

Not only were there large extinct herbivore species such as mammoth (*Mammuthus primigenius*), woolly rhino (*Coelodonta antiquus*) and giant deer (*Megaloceros giganteus*), but some of the species which survived into the Holocene were much larger. These include both mammals and bird species such as brown bear (*Ursus arctos*), wild cat (*Felis sylvestris*), and the ptarmigan and willow grouse (*Lagopus* spp.) (Kurtén 1968; Lister 1987; Stewart in press).

The other striking characteristic of this environment from the point of view of vertebrates was the mixture of species. Communities with no modern analogues were prevalent, with combinations of species found today in

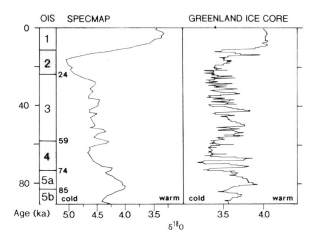

Figure 1.1: Left: Oxygen isotope-based ($\delta^{18}o$) calendrical chronology of the last 80 ka. Small numbers are boundary ages (Martinson et al. 1987) of oxygen isotope stages (OIS). This SPECMAP curve (Imbrie et al. 1984) is a record of the waxing and waning of the global ice sheet. Right: Dansgaard/ Oeschger events: the numerous clusters of brief, major climate excursions recorded in Greenland ice cores (GRIP Members 1993: Fig.1) contrast sharply with the more stable mild climate suggested by SPECMAP.

more northern latitudes (or higher altitudes) together with others which today inhabit drier continental areas as well as some biomes normally associated with more temperate climes. For example, during the mid-pleniglacial reindeer (*Rangifer tarandus*) can be found in western Aquitaine together with chamois (*Rupicapra rupicapra*), steppe ass (*Equus hydruntinus*) and wild boar (*Sus scrofa*) (Delpech 1993).

The climate of the middle last glacial

The stratigraphy of the middle and late Pleistocene has long been burdened by a surfeit of local and regional units that tend to lack convincing continent-wide correlations. These units are gradually being replaced with the basic time-scale called SPECMAP (Imbrie *et al.* 1984) which rests on a global oceanic oxygen isotope stratigraphy calibrated with the orbital cycles of the earth. SPECMAP offers a calendrical time-scale (Martinson *et al.* 1987) divided into oxygen isotope stages (OIS) and substages (Figure 1.1: left side). Moreover, being based on the ratio of stable oxygen isotopes ^{18}O and ^{16}O in ocean water (usually given as the deviation $\delta^{18}O$ of an arbitrary standard), it indicates the volume of water removed from the oceans and stored as ice on the continents as this increases and decreases over time. It is therefore often seen in terms of warmer and colder climates.

The SPECMAP curve, so interpreted, clearly shows a climate of intermediate warmth between the initial (OIS-4) and final (OIS-2) maxima of the last glacial period. The climate of this interval, being relatively mild, slowly

deteriorates between 60 ka and 25 ka as is recorded by a gradual increase in the global continental ice volume (Figure 1.1: left side).

The relative mildness of OIS-3 is misleading, however, as new data from Greenland ice cores GRIP and GISP2 (Dansgaard *et al.* 1993; Grootes *et al.* 1993) have recently demonstrated. These cores have a time resolution which is much higher than that of the slowly settling ocean sediments on which SPECMAP is based. For the entire last interglacial/glacial cycle, the ice core record displays numerous warm excursions (Dansgaard/Oeschger events) that were up to 7 °C above the intervening cold spells, and at times only 2 °C below the local Holocene average, whereas the cold spells themselves reached temperatures close to those of the last glacial maximum. During OIS-3 (Figure 1.1: right side), the warm events tended to last a few millennia and cold spells some centuries, while the transitions from one into the other were very sharp, sometimes taking less than a century (Figure 1.1: right side). The same sharp events are displayed in ocean cores from the North Atlantic and can be seen in sediment records from north-western Europe to the eastern Mediterranean.

This unstable, bipolar climate contrasts sharply with the previous image of a long, stable mid-glacial pause implied by the OIS-3 oxygen isotope record. Clearly, the impact of the often brief but sharp climate fluctuations on the landscape may have been dramatic and is likely to have affected human affairs in the middle and early Upper Palaeolithic to some degree. How can we test this possibility?

The frequency distribution of a set of archaeological dates, if large, can serve as a proxy for population density variations (Rick 1987) and, when compared with the OIS-3 climatic history, might reveal a correspondence between Palaeolithic climate and human history that would encourage further study. The ice core climate events, however, are on a near-calendrical time scale, whereas the bulk of Palaeolithic archaeological dates are in uncalibrated ^{14}C years. Fortunately, calibration of the latter has come recently within reach (Laj *et al.* 1996; Kitigawa & van der Plicht 1998; van Andel 1998; Voelker *et al.* 1998). Figure 1.2 shows the result of the comparison, based on a set of more than 300 carefully chosen dates for European archaeological sites of the Middle and Upper Palaeolithic (van Andel 1998). Almost two thirds of the dates are clustered within only two warm events, suggesting that further study of the relations between climate and climate changes and the archaeological record might bear fruit.

Mid-Palaeolithic palaeo-environments of Europe

To explore the potential of an integrated palaeo-environmental archaeological study of the middle pleniglacial, a provisional synthesis using existing data of the

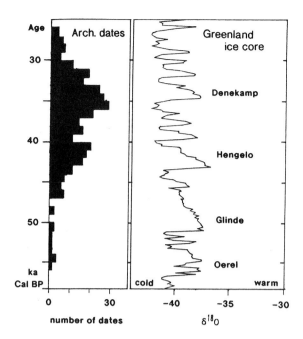

Figure 1.2: Frequency distribution of a set of 306 calendrical dates (U/Th, TL, ESR and calibrated ^{14}C) from late Middle and early Upper Palaeolithic sites (see van Andel 1998 for sources, data selection and ^{14}C calibration) compared with the Greenland ice core climatic record (GRIP Members 1993: Fig.1).

climate and landscape of Europe between 60 and 25 ka cal could be useful and was prepared for that purpose by van Andel & Tzedakis (1996). The resulting images are both general and speculative, but they do illustrate the opportunity as well as the problems associated with the task of setting Palaeolithic humans in the context of their landscapes. The synthesis rests predominantly on pollen data from long sediment cores (Figure 1.3), supplemented by a small range of other palaeo-environmental data. For details, the methods and the sources see van Andel and Tzedakis (1996).

In North America a significant ice advance *c*. 110 ka initiated the last glacial interval, accompanied by a drop of sea-level to about –80 m, as compared to *c*. –120 m during the final glacial maximum. This drop was due almost entirely to a build-up of Antarctic, North American and Greenland ice-caps, because in Europe the glaciation started slowly as two cold phases separated by warmer ones preceded the first true ice advance from *c*. 70–60 ka (OIS-4) which probably did not cross the Baltic. In fact, the role of the Fennoscandian ice-caps remained minor until the onset of the last glacial maximum (K. Lambeck, pers. com. 1998). Global sea-level remained at -80 m until *c*. 25 ka and thus did not expose anything like the large coastal plains of the final glacial maximum (OIS-2) in the North Sea, the Atlantic shore and the Mediterranean. Moreover, it was only towards the end of OIS 4 (74–59 ka) that extensive open vegetation (tundra or steppe)

appeared north of the Pyrenees and Alpine ranges.

The mid-pleniglacial (OIS-3) climate slowly declined as each of the four successive main warm events (Figure 1.2), while maintaining about the same mean annual temperature, was shorter than its predecessor. At same time, the intervening cold phases evolved to clusters of brief, alternating, colder and slightly milder events.

The presence of events significantly warmer than the mean values for OIS-3 has been confirmed by studies of Coleoptera in a few long cores from France (Guiot 1990; Ponel 1995). In the Massif Central (Guiot *et al.* 1989) those events, lasting several millennia, had an annual mean temperature of *c*. 7 °C against a present value of 11 °C and precipitation of 500–600 mm (Figure 1.4), while the intervening cold events had annual mean temperatures of 0–2 °C, similar to those of the late OIS 4 glacial advance, and were much drier. Mean July temperatures of 20–22 °C based on pollen or 16–18 °C on pollen and beetles combined were reported by Guiot *et al.* (1993) from two warm events at *c*. 32–36 and 40–43 ka at Grande Pile in the Vosges, north-eastern France. Also, Coope *et al.* (1998) show that in the Thames valley the summer temperature was close to the present value at the same time that pollen and plant macrofossils indicate a tundra with some birch and pine.

Clearly, for much of Stage 3 the climate conditions were considerably less severe than is usually assumed, not only in the Mediterranean but also north of the Alps. These warm, moist intervals, lasting several thousand years, were certainly long enough to affect significantly the vegetation and wildlife, and so potentially the human beings that depended on them.

Provisional reconstruction of warm and cold events

The main warm events of northern Europe, the Oerel, Glinde, Hengelo and Denekamp interstadials, are reflected in arboreal pollen excursions both north and south of the Alps, but more ephemeral events are seen only in Mediterranean record. This is evident when comparing continuous pollen sequences from France at Grande Pile with Valle di Castiglione in Italy (Figure 1.5), or from Lagaccione, Vico and Straciacappa (Follieri *et al.* 1997) and Monticchio (Watts *et al.* 1996) with those of the Massif Central in France (Reille & de Beaulieu, 1990a).

Other differences exist between north and south. In France, warm, moist events display an increase in conifers (pine and spruce) and birch at the same time that deciduous woodland of oak, hazel, elm, lime and beech expand in Italy. Diversity within tree refugia is illustrated at Monticchio where two long warm/moist events, probably equivalents of the Glinde and Hengelo events, contain a tree sequence which, on a small scale, resembles the succession in southern Europe during the last interglacial. On the other hand, brief warm and moist events show a

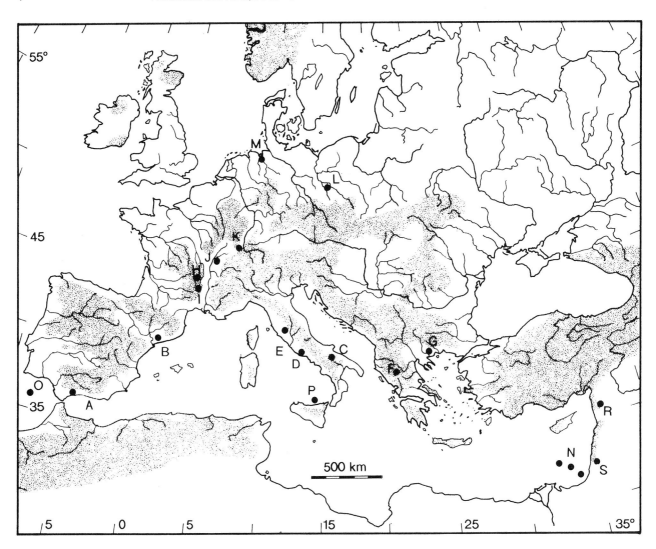

Figure 1.3: Data points for the reconstruction of European OIS 3 landscapes. A– Padul; B– Banyoles; C– Monticchio; D– Valle di Castiglione; E– Vico; F– Ioannina; G– Tenaghi Philippn; H–. Bouchet; I– Ribains; J– Les Echets; K– Grande Pile; L– Samerberg; M– Oer l; N– SE Mediterranean; O– NW Africa; P– Tyrrhenian Sea; R– Ghab valley, Syria; S– Lake Huleh, Israel. Mountainous regions are shaded. See van Andel and Tzedakis (1996) for sources.

quasi-synchronous expansion of tree populations. North of the Alps there is no succession of tree species, because all warm events have only conifers. Farther north, in the North European Plain, pollen records of warm/moist events point only to shrub tundra.

These temporal and geographic variations are well enough established (van Andel & Tzedakis 1998) to permit a rough reconstruction of European vegetation patterns during the warm and moist Hengelo event and the cold, dry phase that preceded it (Figure 1.6). During the Hengelo, arctic vegetation covered Scandinavia (Donner 1995) and shrub tundra with juniper, dwarf birch and willow spread across northern Germany and the Low Countries (Behre 1989), interspersed with spruce in the eastern Baltic (Liivrand 1991). France and the north Alpine foreland had an open pine, spruce and birch parkland that lacked other deciduous trees (Grüger 1989; de Beaulieu & Reille 1984, 1992a, 1992b; Reille & de Beaulieu 1990).

South of the mountains the mixed pine and deciduous oak parkland was found in Catalunya (Perez-Obiol & Juliá 1994) in warm phases, while a richer deciduous woodland with hazel, oak, beech, lime and elm occurred in central Italy (Follieri *et al.* in press; Leroy *et al.* 1996; Watts *et al.* 1996) and northern Greece (Wijmstra 1969; Tzedakis 1994). Mediterranean open woodland of deciduous and evergreen oak with pine and juniper extended from southern Spain (Pons & Reille 1988; Carrión 1992) to southern Greece.

The cold, dry interval that preceded the Hengelo was similar to OIS-4 except for a much-reduced Fenno-Scandinavian icecap (van Andel & Tzedakis 1996). Immediately south of the ice limit, a polar desert with at best a low, patchy plant cover formed the transition to the tundra/steppe farther south. South of the mountains the reduction in tree pollen percentage implies a sparse, discontinuous tree cover, but the herbaceous vegetation

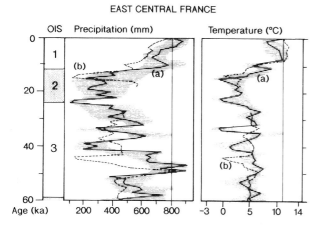

Figure 1.4: Precipitation and temperature history for OIS 3 from a long pollen core at Les Echets, eastern Massif Central, France (Guiot et al. 1989). Shading indicates confidence limits of estimates. Calendrical time-scale (non-linear) added.

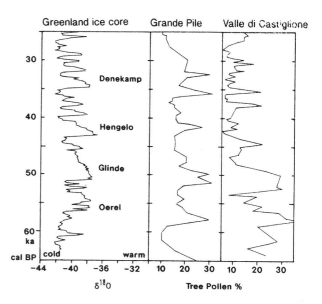

Figure 1.5: OIS 3 climate oscillations displayed by the δ^{18}o record of the GRIP ice core (Greenland: GRIP Members 1993) and arboreal pollen percentages from Valle di Castiglione (Italy: Follieri et al. in press),) and Grande Pile (Vosges, France: de Beaulieu and Reille 1992).

of grasses, (indicating a precipitation of 300 mm/yr dominating over *Artemisia*, which tolerates 100 mm/yr ; Rossignol-Strick 1995) was different from OIS-4. The vast, less dry grass steppe of OIS-3 cold events offered a much richer resource base for human beings.

The Stage 3 Project

At first sight, the landscape reconstructions of Figure 1.6 suggest that we have fair knowledge of the climatic conditions and landscapes that accompanied the unstable climate which existed when anatomically modern humans replaced the Neanderthals. On closer inspection, however, the lack of geographic precision and the absence of essential details are only too obvious, as are the qualitative nature of the climate descriptions and the vague definitions of the landscape units. Clearly, if we wish to specify the conditions under which the human genus was reduced from two to only one species and assess the role that climate changes may or may not have played in this event, much higher geographic resolution and more detailed definitions of the landscape units are essential.

Objectives

Therefore, in 1996 the Godwin Institute of Quaternary Research at Cambridge University established the **Stage 3 Project** in order to attempt to answer two fundamental archaeological questions.

– How can the palaeo-environmental units that are used to describe glacial landscapes be adequately related to the resources required and exploited by Middle and early Upper Palaeolithic human beings?

– To what degree, if at all, do the Middle and early Upper Palaeolithic events reflect the continuously

changing climatic and environmental conditions of the mid-pleniglacial?

These questions cannot be addressed without significant advances in our understanding of the nature and history of the environments of the mid-pleniglacial interval, which are required to answer the following questions:

– What were the climatic conditions and environments of the middle pleniglacial and how did they vary in space and time?

– What was the impact in Europe of the large and rapid climate oscillations observed recently in Greenland ice cores?

Thus the specific objectives of the Stage 3 Project are the following:

– To model the climates and landscapes of a typically 'warm' and typically 'cold' climate excursion for Europe and the adjacent North Atlantic Ocean and Mediterranean Sea, *c.* 45 ka to 30 ka.

– To equip the palaeoclimatic and landscape simulations with mammalian resources relevant to Middle and early Upper Palaeolithic hunter-gatherers, and compare the results to the spatial and temporal distribution of human beings.

Fulfilling these objectives

The preliminary studies discussed above justify the use of existing data in the traditional mode of synthesising a large multi-disciplinary data set, determining whether the results make sense geologically and, if necessary, repeating the process with more data. How might one proceed from

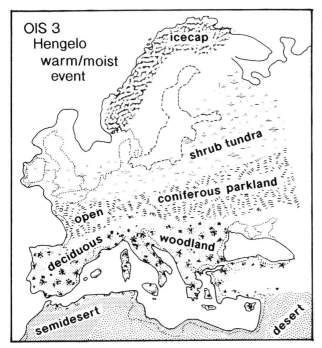
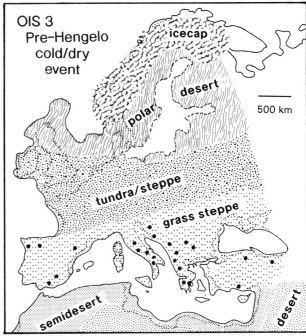

Figure 1.6: Europe during OIS 3: Left: sketch map of the Hengelo (c. 43–40 ka) warm/moist event; Right: the preceding cold/dry event (45 ka). Fennoscandian icecap modified from Andersen and Mangerud (1989) based on ^{14}C dates in Donner (1996). The coastline for the Hengelo event is the –70 m isobath and –85 m for the cold/dry event (Lambeck 1995). Shores of the Baltic are approximate. Black dots indicate tree refugia.

assembling databases to the construction of climate, landscape and human land-use simulations? Since it was clear that a method capable of yielding geographically detailed, quantitative results amenable to validation by suitably reserved other data was required, we chose climate modelling. This was because climate models may also be rigorously validated with real data.

The ability of palaeoclimate models to perform the desired functions depends on their spatial resolution. By good fortune, a novel approach allowing high-resolution modelling was made available to us by Professor Eric Barron at Pennsylvania State University (USA) which replaces the usual global circulation model (GCM) with its output grid spacing of 4.5° latitude and 7.5° longitude with a 'nested' strategy. The GCM provides the lateral boundary conditions, such as solar energy input, earth orbital parameters, polar ice-sheets, atmospheric CO_2 level and sea surface temperatures to a regional circulation model (RCM). As the simulation steps through the seasonal cycle over many years, the GCM continuously provides global winds, air pressure, moisture and temperature and other variables at the boundaries of an RCM with parameters selected for high-resolution simulation on a fine output grid, in our case 60x60 km, and equipped with appropriate key variables such as isostatically compensated topography, shorelines, ice sheet dimensions, sea surface temperatures and sea-ice limits.

An evolving methodology

The initial *modus operandi*, adopted at a Godwin Institute Conference on Oxygen Isotope Stages in 1996, was simplicity itself, being directly derived from the approach used with great success by the famous CLIMAP Project (CLIMAP 1976). It differed from its predecessor only because, rather than creating new data, it envisaged the use of the largest and most diverse existing input database possible, on which iterative modelling experiments would be based, tested for sensitivity to variations in input parameters, and validated with a data set kept in reserve for that specific purpose.

However, in the course of the first two years it became clear that the more effective and far simpler approach was to minimise the amount of input data and maximise the data used for the testing and validation of the output. As a result the present round of climate simulations rests on an input base of relief, ice-sheet dimensions and resulting isostatically compensated topography, sea surface temperatures and sea-ice limits for a nested GCM/RCM model (GENESIS 2.0; Thompson & Pollard 1997). Rather than using the pollen data as input for the simulation of the plant cover, the climate output of the RCM coupled to the biodynamic model BIOME3 (Prentice *et al.* 1992; modified by Haxeltine & Prentice 1996) simulates in the form of functional units the vegetation pattern appropriate for the modelled climate. As climate is strongly affected by the type of vegetation, a number of reiterations is needed to create climate/vegetation equilibria. The final simulation is then rigorously verified with pollen spectra that represent local warm and cold phase floras rendering the resulting simulations quite robust. In this way correlation problems inherent in the use of interpretations of pollen cores for input are much reduced, and the consequences of the inevitable emphasis on the weakest part of direct input of vegetation patterns, i.e. their boundaries, is eliminated.

Having gained insight into the benefits of an inverse use of data in modelling experiments, the Project team is now considering whether the same approach can be devised for the mammalian fauna, using vegetation and climate simulations to predict the distribution of large mammals, in particular those likely to have been important resources for human beings. This might allow us to use a simple and, we hope, non-controversial archaeological database focussed mainly, but not entirely, on the distribution in space and time of archaeological sites, to relate climate, landscape and resources to the presence or absence of human beings, and to test the significance of the archaeological information.

Organisation

The near-complete reliance on existing data enables the Project to dispense with major funding and to use a volunteer-based team with the highly diverse range of expertise required for the provision of databases and the interpretation of the simulations. Thus the Project relies on contributions of some 30 expert contributors from 13 countries on three continents, many of them of high international standing, who contribute their skill, energy, time and data to a degree and in a measure that is convenient to each. Their reward is free access to the entire body of data and simulations for their own research interests. The group is held together by a co-ordinator at Cambridge University through an e-mail network, one annual, and a few special-purpose workshops.

Conclusion: What we expect to achieve

The Stage Three Project is, at the time of writing in late 1998, at the mid-point of its planned 4–year life. When it is completed in late 2000 or early 2001, we hope to have achieved the following:

- Enhanced insight into a climatic state that is curiously intermediate between glacial and interglacial conditions.

- An appreciation of the downwind consequences of the climatic instability evidenced in Greenland ice cores that might lead to a better understanding of their forcing factors and to the consequences of the eastward change from maritime to continental conditions.

- A temporally and spatially specific palaeoenvironmental backdrop to the events that led to the dominance of modern humans and the demise of the Neanderthals.

- A proven high-resolution modelling method that might revitalise palaeoclimatology, a subject that today appears to stagnate somewhat in its application of global models to problems that require more detail.

- A flexible operating mode for an interdisciplinary research project based on electronic communication, one that does not require a large, grant-supported organisation with its associated time-consuming funding, costly management demands and tendency to exclusivity.

References

Andersen, B.G. & Mangerud, J. (1989). The last interglacial-glacial cycle in Fennoscandia. *Quat. Internat.* **3–4**, 21–29.

Behre, K.-E. (1989). Biostratigraphy of the last glacial period in Europe. *Quat. Sci. Rev.* **8**, 25–44.

Broglio, A. (1996). The appearance of modern humans in Europe: the archaeological evidence from the Mediterranean. *XIII Int. Cong. Prehist. Protohist. Sci., Forli, Italy, Coll.* **5**, 237–249.

Carrión, J.S. (1992). A palaeoecological study in the western Mediterranean area: the Upper Pleistocene pollen record from Cova Benito (Alicante, Spain). *Palaeogeo. Palaeoclim. Palaeoeco.* **92**, 1–14.

CLIMAP Project Members (1976). The surface of the Ice-age earth. *Science* **191**, 1131–1137.

Coope, G.R. (1977). Fossil coleopteran assemblages as sensitive indicators of climatic change during the Devensian (Last) cold stage. *Phil. Trans. R. Soc.* B. **280**, 313–340.

Coope, G.R., Gibbard, P.L., Hall, A.R., Preece, R.C., Robinson, J.E. & Sutcliffe, A.J. (1997). Climatic and environmental reconstructions based on fossil assemblages from Middle Devensian (Weichselian) deposits of the River Thames at South Kensington, central London. *Quat. Sci. Rev.* **16**, 1163–1196.

de Beaulieu, J.L. & Reille, M. (1984). A long upper Pleistocene pollen record from Les Echets near Lyon, France. *Boreas* **13**, 111–132.

de Beaulieu, J.L. & Reille, M. (1992a). Long Pleistocene pollen sequences from the Velay Plateau (Massif Central, France), 1. Ribains Maar. *Veget. Hist. Archaeobot.* **1**, 223–242.

de Beaulieu, J.L. & Reille, M. (1992b). The climatic cycle at Grande Pile (Vosges, France): a new pollen profile. *Quat. Sci. Rev.* **11**, 431–438.

Delpech, F. (1993). The Fauna of the Early Upper Paleolithic: Biostratigraphy of Large Mammals and Current Problems in Chronology. In (H. Knecht, A. Pike-Tay & R. White, Eds.). *Before Lascaux: the Complex Record of the Early Upper Paleolithic.* Ann Arbor, MI: CRC Press.

Donner, J. (1995). *The Quaternary of Scandinavia.* Cambridge: Cambridge University Press.

Follieri, M., Magri, D. & Sadori, L. (1988). 250,000–year pollen record from Valle di Castiglione (Roma). *Pollen et Spores* **30**, 329–356.

Follieri, M, Giardini, M, Magri, D, & Sadori, L. (in press). Palynostratigraphy of the last glacial period in the volcanic region of Central Italy, *Quat. Int.*

Gamble, C. (1993). People on the move: Interpretations of regional variation in Palaeolithic Europe. In (J. Chapman & P. Dolukhanov, Eds.) *Cultural transformations and interactions in eastern Europe*, pp. 36–55. Avebury: Aldershot.

GRIP (Greenland Ice-core Project) Members. (1993). Climate instability during the last interglacial period recorded in the GRIP ice core. *Nature* **364**, 203–207.

Grootes, P.M., Stuiver, M., White, J.W., Johnsen, S. & Jouzel, J.

(1993). Comparison of oxygen isotope records from the GISP2 and GRIP Greenland ice cores. *Nature*, **366**, 552–554.

Grüger, E. (1989). Palynostratigraphy of the last interglacial/glacial cycle in Germany. *Quat. Int.* **3–4**, 69–79.

Guiot, J. (1990). Methodology of the last climatic cycle reconstruction in France from pollen data. *Palaeogeo. Palaeoclim. Palaeoeco.* **80**, 44–69.

Guiot, J., de Beaulieu, J.L., Cheddadi, R., David, F., Ponel, P. & Reille, M. (1993). The climate in western Europe during the last glacial/interglacial cycle derived from pollen and insect remains. *Palaeogeo. Palaeoclim. Palaeoeco.* **103**, 73–94.

Guiot, J. Pons, A., de Beaulieu, J.L. & Reille, M. (1989). A 140,000-year continental climate reconstruction from two European pollen records. *Nature* **338**, 309–313.

Guthrie, R.D. (1990). *Frozen Fauna of the Mammoth Steppe: the Story of Blue Babe.* Chicago: University of Chicago Press.

Haxeltine, A. & Prentice, I.C. (1996). BIOME3: An equilibrium terrestrial biosphere model based on ecophysiological constraints, resource availability and competition among plant functional types. *Glob. Biogeochem. Cycles* **10**, 603–628.

Hublin, J.-J. 1998. Climatic changes, paleogeography and the evolution of the Neandertals. In (T. Akazawa, K. Aoki & O. Bar-Yosef, Eds.) *Neandertals and Modern Humans in Western Asia,* pp. 295–310. New York: Plenum Press.

Imbrie, J., Hays, J.D., Martinson, D.G., McIntyre, A.C., Mix, A.,C., Morley, J.J., Pisias, N.G., Prell, W.L. & Shackleton, N.J. 1984. The orbital theory of Pleistocene climate: support from a revised chronology of the marine ä¹⁸O record. In (A.L. Berger, J. Imbrie, J.D. Hays, G.J. Kukla & B. Saltzman, Eds.) *Milankovitch and Climate,* pp. 269–306. Dordrecht: Reidel.

Kitigawa, H. & van der Plicht, J. (1998). Atmospheric radiocarbon calibration to 45,000 yr B.P.: Late glacial fluctuations and cosmogenic isotope production. *Science* **279**, 1187–1190.

Kozlowski, J. K. (1996). Cultural context of the last Neandertals and early modern humans in central-eastern Europe. *XIII Int. Cong. Prehist. Protohist. Sci., Forli, Italy, Coll.* **5**, 205–218.

Kuhn, S.L. (1995). *Mousterian Lithic Technology: An Ecological Perspective.* Princeton NJ: Princeton University Press.

Kurtén, B. (1968). *Pleistocene mammals of Europe.* London: Weidenfeld and Nicolson.

Laj, C., Mazaud, A. & Duplessy, J.-C. (1996). Geomagnetic intensity and ¹⁴C abundance in the atmosphere and ocean during the past 50 kyr. *Geophys. Res. Lett.* **23**, 2045–2048.

Lambeck, K. (1995). Late Devensian and Holocene shorelines of the British Isles and North Sea from models of glacio-hydro-isostatic rebound. *J. Geol. Soc. London* **152**, 437–448.

Leroy, S.A.G., Giralt, S., Francus, P. & Seret, G. (1996). The high sensitivity of the palynological record in the Vico Maar lacustrine sequence (Latium, Italy) highlights the climatic gradient through Europe for the last 90 ka. *Quat. Sci. Rev.* **15**, 189–202.

Liivrand, E. (1991). *Biostratigraphy of the Pleistocene Deposits in Estonia and Correlations in the Baltic Region.* Stockholm: University of Stockholm, Dept. Quat. Geol. Rpt **19**, Stockholm.

Lister, A.M. (1987). Giant deer and giant red deer from Kent's Cavern, and the status of *Strongyloceros spelaeus* Owen. *Trans. Proc. Torquay nat. Hist. Soc.* **91**, 189–198.

Lister, A.M. & Sher, A.V. (1995). Ice cores and Mammoth extinction. *Nature,* **378**, 23–24.

Martinson, D., Pisias, N.G., Hays, J.D., Imbrie, J., Moore Jr., T.C. & Shackleton, N.J. (1987). Age dating and the orbital theory of the Ice Ages: Development of a high-resolution 0–300,000 year chronostratigraphy. *Quat. Res.* **27**, 1–29.

Mellars, P.A. (1996a). *The Neanderthal Legacy: An Archaeological Perspective from Western Europe.* Princeton NJ: Princeton University Press.

Mellars, P.A. (1996b). Models for the dispersion of anatomically modern populations across Europe: Theoretical and archaeological perspectives. *XIII Int. Congr. Prehist. Protohist. Sci., Forli, Italy, Coll.* **5**, 225–236.

Miskovsky, J.-C. (Ed.) (1992). Les applications de la géologie à la reconnaissance de l'environnement de l'homme fossile. *Mém. Soc. Géol. France, New Series.* **160**.

Pérez-Obiol, R. & Juliá, R. (1994). Climatic change on the Iberian Peninsula recorded in a 30,000–year pollen record from Lake Banyoles. *Quat. Res.* **41**, 91–97.

Ponel, P. (1995). Rissian, Eemian and Würmian coleoptera assemblages from the Grande Pile (Vosges, France). *Palaeogeo. Palaeoclim. Palaeoeco.* **114**, 1–41.

Pons, A. & Reille, M. (1988). The Holocene and upper Pleistocene pollen record from Padul (Granada, Spain): a new study. *Palaeogeo. Palaeoclim. Palaeoeco.* **66**, 243–263.

Prentice, I.C., Cramer, W., Harrison, S.P., Leemans, R., Monserud, R.A. & Solomon, A.M. (1992). A global biome model based on plant physiology and dominance, soil properties and climate. *J. Biogeog.* **19**, 117–134.

Prentice, I.C., Guiot, J., Huntley, B., Jolly, D. & Cheddadi, R. (1996). Reconstructing biomes from palaeo-ecological data: a general method and its application to European pollen data at 0 and 6 ka. *Clim. Dynam.* **12**, 185–194.

Reille, M. & de Beaulieu, J.L. (1990). Pollen analysis of a long upper Pleistocene continental sequence in a Velay Maar (Massif Central, France). *Palaeogeo. Palaeoclim. Palaeoeco.* **80**, 35–48.

Rossignol-Strick, M. (1995). Sea-land correlation of pollen records in the eastern Mediterranean for the glacial-interglacial transition: biostratigraphy versus radiometric time-scale. *Quat. Sci. Rev.* **14**, 893–915

Stewart, J.R. (in press). Intraspecific variation in modern and Quaternary European *Lagopus. Smithsonian Contrib. Paleobio.,* **89**.

Stiner, M.C. (1994). *Honor among thieves – A zooarchaeological study of Neandertal sociology.* Princeton NJ: Princeton University Press.

Thompson, S.L. & Pollard, D. (1997). Greenland and Antarctic mass balances for present and doubled atmospheric CO_2 from the GENESIS version-2 global climate model. *J. Climat.* **10**, 8712–8900.

van Andel, T.H. (1998). Middle and Upper Palaeolithic environments and the calibration of ¹⁴C dates beyond 10,000 BP. *Antiquity* **72**, 26–33.

van Andel, T.H. & Tzedakis, P.C. (1996). Palaeolithic landscapes of Europe and Environs, 150,000–25,000 years ago. *Quat. Sci. Rev.* **15**, 481–500.

van Andel, T.H. & Tzedakis, P.C. (1998). Priority and opportunity: Reconstructing the European Middle Palaeolithic climate and landscape. In (J. Bayley Ed.) *Science in Archaeology: An Agenda for the Future,* pp. 37–46. London: English Heritage.

Voelker, A.H., Santhein, M., Grootes, P., Erlenkeuser, H., Laj. C., Mazaud, A., Nadeau, M.-J. & Schleicher, M. (1998). Correlation of marine ¹⁴C ages from the Nordic Seas with GISP2 Isotope record: implications for radiocarbon calibration beyond 25 kyr. *Radiocarbon* (in press).

Watts, W.A., Allen, J.R.M. & Huntley, B. (1996). Vegetation history and palaeoclimate of the last glacial period at Lago Grande di Monticchio, southern Italy. *Quat. Sci. Rev.* **15**, 133–153.

2

A Mediterranean Perspective on the Middle/Upper Palaeolithic Revolution

Ofer Bar-Yosef

The nature of technological revolutions

The history of humankind has witnessed several major socio-economic transitions. Scholars continue to disagree on their precise number and the relative importance of the host of cultural expressions that warrant the label 'revolution'. The transition from the Middle to the Upper Palaeolithic is a case in point. While the majority of archaeologists regard it as a revolutionary transition (Oakley 1961; Pfeiffer 1982; White 1982; Gilman 1984; Mellars 1989; 1996a), a few consider that the available evidence does not justify this definition (Lindly and Clark 1990; Clark 1997). A similar, two-sided approach, is also presented in writings concerning the transition from foraging to cultivation and the domestication of plants and animals (compare Braidwood 1975; Bar-Yosef and Meadow 1995; Harris 1996b; Smith 1997 with Rindos 1984). This dichotomy of interpretation resembles arguments raised by historians who studied the Industrial Revolution (Landes 1998).

Past revolutions are always evaluated on their outcome. Gradualists see even the most dramatic cultural and socio-economic transition as a slow process that began at some point in time, but took hundreds or even thousands of years to be completed. In contrast, those who view the change as radical and relatively rapid, try to find out 'when' and 'where' this beginning took place. The successful completion of the initial phase of a major socio-economic transition often culminates in reaching 'a point of no return', at least in the region where the revolution occurred. This region is seen as the core area. Once the major changes have occurred, and a new socio-economic system has emerged, people around the core area find it almost impossible to maintain the previous mode of life.

Each of the elements mentioned here, such as 'when', 'where', and 'people', is succinctly defined. Otherwise, the sweeping assertions would remain as a 'Just So' story.

While an in-depth discussion of these issues is beyond the scope of this paper, clarification of the terms directly employed in the process of interpreting the transition from the Middle to the Upper Palaeolithic is both necessary and possible.

Setting the timing of an historical event or a reasonably well-defined short-term process is essential. In the first case, the year or the decade can be ascertained. Defining the age limits of a process requires the configuration of three numbers. The first and second define the onset and the termination of the process. In other words, it means pinpointing 'when' the process began and 'when' the change reached completion. The third number is rather elusive, but is directly related to the number of human generations that were involved in or witnessed the change. This measurable timespan provides us with the human dimension, allowing us to create scenarios and test hypotheses in an effort to discover whether the technology that initiated the change was enjoyed, accepted, rejected or modified by the people it affected, and how this happened relative to their social concepts and biological needs. For the Neolithic revolution this can be accomplished via radiocarbon dates, which, with the correction implied by the calibration curve, can limit each end of the time span to within 100–200 years.

Unfortunately, the Middle/Upper Palaeolithic revolution is not well defined by the available physical dating techniques. This period, which we place in the Mediterranean basin around 50 ka to 35 ka, is partially recorded by current radiocarbon techniques, which can be calibrated (*c.f.* van Andel 1998 and references therein) and in part by TL, ESR and several other methods (e.g. Aitken 1990; Wagner 1998). This means that the standard deviation is commonly around 800–1,600 years and therefore possibly implies the involvement of a very large number of human generations. If each generation in the Palaeolithic was about 20 years, then the total length ranges from 40–80 generations, even if the revolution occurred within a much shorter time span.

In addition, there are a number of taphonomic problems that plague the dated samples. Foremost is the contextual relationship between an excavated assemblage and the charcoal fragments collected during the digging process (Bar-Yosef 1993; Bar-Yosef *et al.* 1996). Second is the contextual relationship between a TL-dated burnt piece in a Mousterian layer and the entire lithic assemblage. Third, the original location of an ESR-dated animal tooth needs to be evaluated on the same grounds. Essentially, the role of burrowing animals, dripping water and other natural disturbances in Levantine caves is not well understood, as was demonstrated in a recent report (Goldberg and Bar-Yosef 1998). Even a cursory review of dating reports demonstrates these uncertainties (Grün and Stringer 1991; Mercier *et al.* 1995). Resolving taphonomic complications requires tight co-operation between archaeologists and the dating scientists. It also demands detailed publications that include drawings of the archaeological sections of the site on which the published dates are clearly marked (Bar-Yosef *et al.* 1996). Following such procedures allows others to evaluate the validity of the published radiometric readings.

I turn now to the 'where' issue. The geographic location in which a socio-economic transition is archaeologically documented is often a well-defined region and can be referred to as the *core area*. When a larger territory is concerned, one may identify, as did the historians of the Industrial Revolution in Britain, *peripheries* within the core area. Identifying the core area responds to the question of 'where' the change began. As similar phenomena are well-dated in neighbouring regions, it becomes feasible to trace the nature of interactions between the core area and the peripheries. These are often variable and include the diffusion of techniques and products, the effects of migration (or colonisation), and the long distance effects of cultural impacts, which could be interpreted as due to acculturation or the results of cultural contacts.

The third major element in characterising a prehistoric revolution is the 'people'. Using this term, or some other synonym such as 'social unit' or 'social entity', we avoid the debates among social anthropologists concerning the terminologies of 'band', 'macro-band', 'tribe', and 'dialectical tribe'. These terms are considered inadequate for describing non- or pre-industrial societies. Detailed reconstruction of social rankings, especially in the remote past, is seen as a futile exercise, given the structural variability of societies (Kuper 1988). To avoid the daunting task of attempting to recreate prehistoric societies on paper, simplified terminology is preferred, unless an archaeologically testable hypothesis can be put forward and either verified or falsified.

Analogies

In order to facilitate the study of the Middle to the Upper Palaeolithic transition, it has already been proposed in several papers that the available models for the origins of agro-pastoral societies, or what is commonly known as the Neolithic Revolution, can provide building blocks for constructing and testing alternative models (Bar-Yosef 1992; 1994a; 1998a). There are undoubtedly several advantages to using our current knowledge of the processes involved in the Neolithic Revolution in the examination of the dramatic changes that occurred some 50 to 35 ka in the circum-Mediterranean world.

First, the Neolithic Revolution was the achievement of a single human species, namely our own, *Homo sapiens sapiens*. Second, the archaeological records indicate a direct relationship between Western Asia, Europe and North Africa. Third, there is a large body of data concerning the transition from foraging to cultivation that was gathered from a well-defined geographic region, where temporal and spatial trajectories are clearly demonstrated. The following is a brief description, as a fuller presentation was recently published (Bar-Yosef 1998a). A necessary addition at this point is to remind ourselves that both revolutions began among hunter-gatherers. The first caused a change from the Middle Palaeolithic foraging ways of life to Upper Palaeolithic ones, and the question remains – what was the nature of that change? In the second, foragers shifted their subsistence strategy from harvesting in wild stands to organised cultivation in fields. Thus, the end result was a society with an altered economic base. The reader might justifiably wonder if this analogy is valid. My response is yes, because it is hypothesised that the basic principles are the same, namely that a technological change results in a new socio-economic system, to paraphrase a palaeontologist (Ward 1997).

In examining a cultural change among hunter-gatherers, we should consult the ethnographic literature for information concerning the relationships between ecology, technology, social organisation, degree of mobility and cosmology of various groups. The economic aspects, which are better preserved among the archaeological remains, are directly affected by the nature, distribution, predictability, reliability, and accessibility of resources, which together determine the carrying capacity of a given territory (Binford 1980; 1983; Bettinger 1991; Kelly 1995 and references therein; Rocek and Bar-Yosef 1998). For any given population, social alliances with neighbouring groups increase the overall size of exploitable territory and create a buffer zone for seasons of scarcity. Hence, the nature of mobility (often a mixture of residential and logistical moves) affects the overall group size and/or its mating system, and therefore has consequences concerning the optimal size of territory required to ensure long-term biological survival. Foragers, in the past, were involved in long distance migrations. This, at least, is one of the common explanations for the shift from the Dorset to the

Thule culture in the Arctic; the debates concerning this particular cultural change are not much different from those concerning the MP/UP transition (Fitzhugh 1994; Odess 1998 and references therein). Relying blindly on studies of historically recent foragers without examining their past may result in importing naïve analogies into archaeology. We need to remind ourselves that the hunter-gatherers we know are those who historically survived beyond the farming lands. In these marginal regions, at least as seen from the viewpoint of the dominant cultures, foragers were probably subject to additional adaptations.

For the purpose of a generalised analogy with the Mediterranean basin, we turn to groups that have inhabited 'Mediterranean-type' regions. Environments somewhat similar to those of the Mediterranean are found in southern Australia, southern Africa and California. In these regions, densities of hunter-gatherers were estimated to be among the highest in each continent (Lourandos 1997). Territories were much smaller than those occupied by foragers in temperate, desert or arctic belts. Under such circumstances, the interactions and boundaries between groups were maintained through communal feasts, ceremonies and exchange. Conflicts, as expected from the pattern of seasonality that characterises the Mediterranean climate, arose in cases of prolonged droughts, which repeatedly caused diminishing yields of fruits and seeds, fat-depleted mammals and reduced numbers of docile small animals such as tortoise, resulting in social and economic stresses.

Phases of the Neolithic Revolution

Figuring out the when and where of a prehistoric cultural transition is not easy, but the Neolithic Revolution has the advantage that the timescale is based on radiocarbon dates. With AMS dates, a standard deviation of less than 100 years, and the new calibration curves, we reach a commendable resolution. Unfortunately however, due to periods of excessive production of ^{14}C, especially at the Pleistocene-Holocene boundary, the onset of intentional cultivation can not yet be precisely determined.

As a step towards employing the lessons learned from research on the Neolithic Revolution, the relevant evidence is summarised here. General overviews and interpretations can be found in a large number of publications (Bar-Yosef and Belfer-Cohen 1992; Bar-Yosef and Meadow 1995; Smith 1995 (second edition); van Andel and Runnels 1995; Harris 1996a; Hillman 1996; Sherratt 1997; Bar-Yosef 1998a, b), and are briefly enumerated here:

1. The climatic crisis of the Younger Dryas (c. 11 ka – 10.3 ka), lasting about 1,300±70 years in calibrated dates (Mayewski and Bender 1995), caused major environmental deterioration, which undoubtedly had an impact on the subsistence strategies of the Late Natufian populations in the Near East and their contemporaries. It is suggested that the cultivation of cereals and pulses was the outcome of this period of stress in the western portion of the Fertile Crescent, which at the time was the main nuclear area for the dense natural growth of cereals. Other populations, although the evidence is rather scanty, chose different solutions. Some became sedentary foragers such as in Hallan Äemi in south east Anatolia (Rosenberg et al. 1995), while others increased their mobility.

2. Population growth in early sedentary (or semi-sedentary) villages led to the onset of active emigration (Ammerman and Cavalli-Sforza 1984; van Andel and Runnels 1995). The process of establishing new communities in arable lands was facilitated by the wetter and gradually increasingly warmer conditions of the early Holocene. These circumstances also favoured the wider geographic dispersal of the progenitors of wild cereals. Thus, the present day distribution, as recorded by Harlan and Zohary (1966; see also Zohary and Hopf 1994) does not reflect the situation during the Younger Dryas.

3. Increased levels of sedentism and greater reliability of food supplies have biological effects. A drop in the age of menarche and a longer period of fertility for better-fed women, promoted a population increase (Bentley 1996). Large villages (from the very early Neolithic, known as the PPNA) became viable biological units and reduced the need to travel substantial distances to find a mate, as was common among foragers. The sense of ownership and territoriality also reached a different level. All these changes caused the emergence of new and more complex levels of social alliances, supported by re-designed cosmologies (Cauvin 1997).

4. The domestication of animals (goats, sheep, cattle and pigs) took place in the context of farmer-hunter villages, within the PPNB. The domestication of goat and sheep most likely first occurred in the hilly flanks of the Taurus/Zagros region, where these animals had been hunted for many millennia and local inhabitants were familiar with their behaviour.

5. The inevitable expansion of Early Neolithic communities was initially orientated northward from the Levantine Corridor into Anatolia, while eastward, the new economy was transmitted to the Zagros foothills, from Kurdistan in the north to Khuzistan in the south, probably without major displacement of human communities. In this area, the lithic tradition of manufacturing microlithic artefacts continued from the Late Palaeolithic through the Neolithic, when in Anatolia, at least in part, the Levantine technology was adopted.

6. The Neolithic economy spread throughout the Mediterranean basin during the period 9 ka to 7 ka via coastal navigation and inland movement through the Danube valley (Renfrew 1987; Piazza et al. 1995). The processes of demic diffusion and acculturation were largely responsible for the "Neolithisation" of Europe and the exact mechanism of how this happened is, in each case, open to debate (Donahue 1992).

7. Eastward expansions of Neolithic subsistence systems reached beyond the Caspian and into the Indus Valley within 1,500 radiocarbon years. Surprisingly, however, it apparently took about 2,000 radiocarbon years for agriculture to penetrate into the Nile valley (by c. 7 ka c.f. Wetterstrom 1998), although it lies within only one week's walk southwards from the Jordan Valley. This discrepancy is perhaps explained if one keeps in mind that the Nile delta is constantly sinking and thus the earliest sites had possibly disappeared under a very thick alluvial mantle.

In conclusion, the current evidence confirms that the core area of the Neolithic Revolution was in the Levantine Corridor, where intentional cultivation began. The ensuing socio-economic changes forged new interaction spheres within the region. The transmission of information along exchange routes and the establishment by colonists of new villages on arable lands marked the move into Europe and the Mediterranean islands. The lessons learned from the Neolithic Revolution lead us to several assertions concerning humans and their behaviour. First, that competition for resources is part and parcel of human behaviour, whether individuals or groups. Second, when one group increases its number, it will encroach onto its neighbours' territories. Third, foragers on the move may ignore the presence of others, kill them, or live in peace and intermarry. All such forms of relationships are known from ethnographic records and the history of humankind. If earlier revolutions had a somewhat similar or at least comparable structure, then we should certainly be able to trace the course of the changes over time. The lessons learned raise a series of issues relevant to an understanding of the Middle to Upper Palaeolithic revolution.

The Middle to Upper Palaeolithic Transition

The majority of scholars who have written about the Middle to Upper Palaeolithic transition do indeed consider it to be a revolution (Marshack 1972; White 1982; Gilman 1984; Gamble 1986; Mellars 1989; Stringer and Gamble 1993; Mellars 1996a, b; Mithen 1996; White 1997). However, there are others (Clark 1997; Straus 1997), who view this transition as merely a gradual change occurring on a regional scale.

As I have expressed before, I view the Middle to Upper Palaeolithic transition in Western Asia, Europe and North Africa as a true technological and cultural revolution (Bar-Yosef 1992; 1994b; 1996; 1998a). These changes occurred within and by a population referred to as the Cro-Magnons, a definition that follows what scholars of the Neolithic call the Near Eastern Neolithic farmers, who colonised parts of Europe. This is not seen as a closed society, but rather as a mixture of colonisers, who, as mentioned above, could interact with local inhabitants, be they Neandertals (in Europe) or early AMH (in North Africa).

The first and principal lesson to be learned from the study of the Neolithic Revolution is that this too began in a core area. No specific region in Europe, as shown by the dating of EUP, can be considered as that core area. Therefore, comparing European Neanderthal archaeological remains with those of the Cro-Magnons is irrelevant to the study of the original revolution, because it occurred elsewhere. Only by locating and investigating the core area can we speculate on the causes and early phases of this revolution. Cro-Magnons succeeded in inhabiting Europe, which had been occupied by the Neandertals for hundreds of thousands of years, as the result of being active colonisers.

There are several proposals for the location of the core area. Some place it in East Africa (Klein 1995; Ambrose 1998), while others suggest the Levant (Sherratt 1997). None of these regions has produced sufficiently complete archaeological evidence and human fossils (Clark 1992; Deacon 1992; Foley and Lahr 1997; Akazawa et al. 1998; Ambrose 1998; Van Peer 1998). The nuclear and molecular evidence indicates that the emergence of Anatomically Modern Humans (AMH) took place some 300–100 ka in sub-Saharan Africa (Ruvolo 1996; 1997; Harpending et al. 1998) and was followed by dispersals into Eurasia. What this means in archaeological terms is that the AMH manufactured Middle Palaeolithic (also called MSA) lithic assemblages. There is no easy way to identify these forefathers from amongst the other groups. It also means that at least 50 ka were needed for AMH to evolve culturally before we witness the cultural change of the Middle to Upper Palaeolithic Revolution, unless Klein's proposal for an additional neurological change around that date (50 ka) is accepted. The fossil evidence does not, so far, support his suggestion. A good example is that of the early Modern Humans who reached western Asia by 110–90 ka ago (the Skhul-Qafzeh group, also known as Proto-Cro-Magnons), producing essentially the same Mousterian industries as others. They differed in their intentional burials, use of red ochre, and the collection of a few marine shells for an as yet unknown purpose (Bar-Yosef 1989; papers in Akazawa et al. 1998). Another example of the achievements of early AMH is the successful reaching of Australia by about 60 ka (Roberts et al. 1990). Perhaps it is no accident that this move to Australia occurred immediately after the invasion of the Neandertals into the Levant some 60,000 ka.

AMH were present in North Africa during the Middle Palaeolithic, in Gebel Irhoud (Hublin 1992), the Aterian deposits at Mughâret el 'Aliya and Dar es Sultan (Minugh-Purvis 1993), in Haua Fteah in Libya (McBurney 1967) and in Egypt (Van Peer 1998; Vermeersch et al. 1998). Therefore, if the current molecular and nuclear evidence is correct, this means that the Middle/Upper Palaeolithic Revolution took place within *one* social entity and spread through the Mediterranean basin, possibly in the same way that the Neolithic Revolution did. This contention, which is not new, is currently supported by the east-west dates for the onset of the Upper Palaeolithic across both

Europe and North Africa, as well as by certain observations of lithic industries (Fig. 2.1; Otte and Keeley 1990; Straus 1996).

Stating my views, I admit that the archaeological evidence, as it currently stands, is amenable to several interpretations, and with every new or old proposal certain questions should be answered:

Did the transition from the Middle to the Upper Palaeolithic mark a technological change? Was it the result of a new social structure, or only a suite of technological innovations within the original society? Who were the people responsible for the cultural transition from the Middle to the Upper Palaeolithic? Does this transition reflect the emergence of modern behaviour? Does it reflect the appearance of language as we know it today? Can we use western European cave art as an indicator of the emergence of language? Could the Neandertals have produced the same kind of stone tools, beads and bone tools as the Cro-Magnons?

The Middle/Upper Palaeolithic cultural transition might have been, but was not necessarily produced by a population biologically different from other human populations. The innovative guys were not necessarily inherently smarter than their contemporaries. Instead, I suggest that the population which started this revolution, due to as yet unknown circumstances, succeeded in improving its technical skills, was able to achieve better returns on hunting and gathering forays, and had reached higher fertility and infant survival rates (Bentley *et al.* 1993; Bentley 1996). This population consequently re-organised its social structure and created a better means of communication. Such a population, as history demonstrates, would tend to expand rapidly. Employing this approach eliminates the need to view phylogenetic factors as the sole essential triggers for change at a particular time, and draws our attention to socio-economic factors.

The east-west trend, mentioned above and known from previous publications (Otte and Keeley 1990) is exemplified by the currently available dates (Fig. 2.1). The early Upper Palaeolithic (EUP) cultural manifestions appeared around 50–45 ka in East Africa, if the evidence published by Ambrose (1998) is accepted in full. In the Levant, Level 1 at Boker Tachtit yielded an age of 47–46 ka (Marks 1983; 1993). Kebara cave, where the early Emiran industry is missing, produced a series of radiocarbon readings around 43–42 ka (Bar-Yosef *et al.* 1996; for possible calibration see Kitagawa and van der Plicht 1998; van Andel 1998). The late Mousterian in Crimea is dated to *c.* 38–33 ka (Marks and Chabai 1998). The chronological information on this crucial stage in the Trans-Caucasian region (Meshveliani 1989) is poor and it is quite possible that the Mousterian prevailed into later times (*c.* 35 ka). EUP sites in south east and central Europe include Bacho-Kiro and Temnata caves in Bulgaria (43–38 ka, with a 45 ka TL date) and the Bohunician in Moravia (dated to 38 ka, see Svoboda and Simán 1989). One may even speculate that despite the great distance between the

Bohunician and Boker Tachtit Levels 1–2 assemblages (the so-called Transitional Industry, or Emiran in the Levant), their similarity means that they were actually produced by the bearers of the same technological tradition. Unfortunately, the early Upper Palaeolithic in Anatolia and the Balkans south of Bulgaria is yet poorly known (Kozlowski 1998).

Mapping the time of change in North Africa is also far from clear. A recent summary (Van Peer 1998) indicates that the time of the transition in north east Africa is not radiometrically well-established. In Haua Fteah cave (Libya) the interpolated date for the transition is around 35–30 ka (McBurney 1967). The situation in the Maghreb is not well documented. The latest dates for the Aterian could be around 25 ka or slightly earlier, perhaps around 35–30 ka (Tillet 1989; Wengler 1997; Cremaschi *et al.* 1998).

In Western Europe, the evidence from France, the Pyrenees and northern Italy produces dates of 40/38–35 ka. However, most of the Iberian peninsula south of the Ebro Valley continued to be inhabited by the Neandertals until at least till 27 ka (Hublin *et al.* 1995; Straus 1996; d'Errico *et al.* 1998; Raposo and Cardoso 1998; Zilhao, this volume).

In summary, the Middle/Upper Palaeolithic transition across the Mediterranean basin is an intriguing phenomenon. The traditional approach, which tended to rely solely on the Franco-Cantabrian province, should be recognised as describing the situation within a limited geographic area, which needs to be fitted into a much larger geographic puzzle. The proposal that cave art is a sign of modern language (supposedly a tool that provided the Cro-Magnons with an advantage while taking over Europe), was a resort for those who refused to look hard into the details of the archaeological records, or to admit that language origin is a question that cannot be resolved with the evidence at hand. It is not surprising that for different reasons Humphrey (1988) reached similar conclusions. He demonstrated that cave art is similar to the drawings of an autistic child, therefore supporting the hypothesis that there is no need for the presence of modern language. Humphrey's mistake was that he did not examine other signs for the use of language among humans, as expressed, for example in the designs of variable *chaînes opératoires* which require the learned knowledge of *savoir faire*. In addition, I have elsewhere reminded the reader (Bar-Yosef 1998a) that the EUP contexts in other parts of the Eurasian continent (such as in central and eastern Europe, and Western Asia) did not reveal the same richness of bone and antler objects and cave art known from France and Spain.

The Nature of the Middle/Upper Palaeolithic Revolution

The most debated issue here concerns the nature of the transition. It requires examining globally the variable

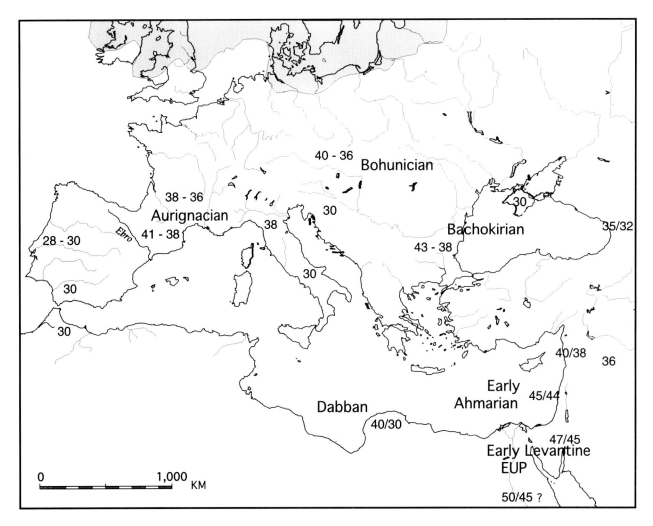

Figure 2.1: Map illustrating the east-west trend in the dating of Upper Palaeolithic Sites in the Mediterranean and Central Europe.

aspects of Mousterian foragers' lifeways. Only in Europe, where at least one ancient DNA sample showed that Neandertals were a different species or sub-species from the incoming Cro-Magnons, can one employ the fact of biological difference to explain the transition. In other areas, such as North Africa, the technological and social revolution was carried out by the Cro-Magnons, originally a population of AMH. If the early AMH were not replaced by the Cro-Magnons, then the change may have occurred as adaptation through cultural contact, acculturation or extermination. Therefore, the most plausible explanation needs to take into account all aspects of human life, namely, technology, social organisation, subsistence, settlement pattern (or degree of mobility), adaptations to cold climate (in temperate Europe), and past demographics (Bar-Yosef 1994a; Table 2), including reproduction.

If we examine the inhabitants of the tropical or subtropical core area and its margins, we may conclude that they were characterised by the following aspects (these would effectively define the Late Mousterian in such a region):

1. A low degree of residential and logistical mobility, especially in the well- watered, resource-rich areas, caused by a sufficient amount of both food and raw material sources and increasing competition between groups (Kuhn and Stiner 1998).

2. The seasonal exploitation of resources in marginal areas, such as steppic environments, semi-deserts and high altitudes, enhanced logistical strategies (Baumler and Speth 1993; Henry 1998).

3. A low degree of regionalisation in cultural attributes except perhaps under boundary conditions.

4. Simple technologies for food acquisition, including hafted or wooden spears; the use of hafted knives and scraping tools (Boâda *et al.* 1998; Shea 1998).

5. Simple clothing, requiring minimal maintenance.

6. The gathering and processing of selected plant resources, and small docile animals, perhaps mostly by women and children.

7. A low level of symbolic behaviour, including burials and the use of red ochre.

The MP/UP revolution was successful, as is seen from the outcome. What triggered it leaves room for numerous speculations. One is the additional biological change as proposed by Klein (1995) that could be interpreted as mastering modern language, or the capacity for modern culture (Lieberman 1989; Whallon 1989). Another would be a rapid environmental deterioration within the almost over-populated core area, that forced a shift in food acquisition techniques, in social and logistical organisation, and possibly in means of communication. Whatever triggered the revolution, the results were as follows:

1. Improved subsistence strategies with new technologies, perhaps the invention of spear throwers (atlatl) or even the simple bow.
2. Improved clothing, especially of the kind needed in northern latitudes (Jelinek 1994).
3. Improved gathering and transport devices – basketry (?), early fibres, and composite objects where wood, hide, fibre, bone and antler were used in variable fashions.
4. Use of grinding-stones for food processing (Solecki and Solecki 1983; Wright 1994).
5. A change in the raw materials exploited, including antler and bone, and special hard rocks.
6. Long distance procurement of raw materials (e.g., Roebroeks et al. 1988).
7. Improved systems of long-distance, inter-group communication and referential signs (e.g., drums, markings on rocks or trees).

The results could be identified as short or long term. The short-term results include increased survival rates of newborns, prolonged survival for the elders in the group and thus better record-keeping of environmental changes and location of resources, better planning depth of subsistence strategies, and changes in the intensity of symbolic behaviour reflected in new expressions of self-awareness, intra- and inter-societal attitudes, rituals, conflict control and so on.

The long-term results were the selective advantages of forming long-distance social alliances, increasing the rate of technological adaptation to specific regional environments (e.g., the formation of regional cultures identified by their tool kits), an overall population increase, and the resulting migrations.

Conclusion

The interpretation adopted in this paper views the transition from the Middle to the Upper Palaeolithic as a techno-logical revolution, which resulted in numerous social and economic changes. This was a revolution expressed in various archaeological aspects such as blade production (an old invention that came back fully-blown and probably much improved in its core reduction strategy), and the invention of new hunting and trapping devices. The spread of the Cro-Magnons in Eurasia and across North Africa was in some regions fast, in others very slow. Local foragers either survived for some time (perhaps for the longest in Iberia and also the northwest Maghreb), adapted the new-comers' technology, or became extinct. For European archaeologists, the demise of the Neandertals is a crucial issue. From an east Mediterranean viewpoint, the Neandertals were the losers. Even if they were biologically different from the Cro-Magnons, this says nothing about their capabilities. Their long-term survival through glacial cycles in temperate Europe (it was easier for the Mediterranean Neandertals) and the Castel-perronian material manifestions indicate that they were able people. They were not the only losers, however. There were others who gave up, such as those in North Africa, morphologically defined as anatomically modern humans. It is the sign of a powerful revolution when the change occurs, beginning in a core area and sweeping into the peripheries.

References

Aitken, M.J. (1990). *Science-based Dating in Archaeology*. New York: Longman.

Ambrose, S.H. (1998). Late Pleistocene human population bottle-necks, volcanic winter, and differentiation of modern humans. *Journal of Human Evolution*. **34**(6), 623–651.

Ammerman, A.J. & Cavalli-Sforza, L.L. (1984*). The Neolithic Transition and the Genetics of Populations in Europe*. Princeton: Princeton University Press.

Bar-Yosef, D.E. (1989). Late Paleolithic and Neolithic marine shells in the Southern Levant as cultural markers. In (C.F. Hayes, Ed) *Shell Bead Conference,* pp. 169–174. Rochester, New York: Rochester Museum and Science Center.

Bar-Yosef, O. (1992). Middle Paleolithic human adaptations in the Mediterranean Levant. In (T. Akazawa, K. Aoki and T. Kimura, Eds) *The Evolution and Dispersal of Modern Humans in Asia,* pp. 189–216. Tokyo: Hokusen-Sha.

Bar-Yosef, O. (1993). Site formation processes from a Levantine viewpoint. In (P. Goldberg, D.T. Nash & M.D. Petraglia, Eds.) *Formation Processes in Archaeological Context*, pp. 11–32. Madison: Prehistory Press.

Bar-Yosef, O. (1994a). The contributions of southwest Asia to the study of the origin of modern humans. In (M.H. Nitecki & D.V. Nitecki, Eds) *Origins of Anatomically Modern Humans*, New York: Plenum Press.

Bar-Yosef, O. (1994b). Form, function and numbers in Neolithic lithic studies. In (H.G. Gebel & S.K. Kozlowski, Eds) *Neolithic Chipped Stone Industries of the Fertile Crescent: Proceedings of the First Workshop on PPN Chipped Lithic Industries*, pp. 5–14. Berlin: Ex Oriente.

Bar-Yosef, O. (1996). The Middle/Upper Palaeolithic Transition: A View from the Eastern Mediterranean. In (E. Carbonell & M. Vaquero, Eds.) *The Last Neandertals, the First Anatomically Modern Humans* pp. 79–94. Tarragona: Universitat Rovira i Virgili.

Bar-Yosef, O. (1998a). On the Nature of Transitions: the Middle to Upper Palaeolithic and the Neolithic Revolution. *Cambridge Archaeological Journal* **8**(2), 141–63.

Bar-Yosef, O. (1998b). The Natufian Culture in the Levant-Threshold to the Origins of Agriculture. *Evolutionary Anthropology* **6**.

Bar-Yosef, O., Arnold, M., Belfer-Cohen, A., Goldberg, P., Housely,

R., Laville, H., Meignen, L., Mercier, N., Vogel, J.C. & Vandermeersch, B. (1996). The dating of the Upper Paleolithic layers in Kebara Cave, Mount Carmel. *Journal of Archaeological Science* **23**, 297–306.

Bar-Yosef, O. & Belfer-Cohen, A. (1992). From foraging to farming in the Mediterranean Levant. In (A.B. Gebauer & T.D. Price, Eds) *Transitions to Agriculture in Prehistory*, pp. 21–48. Madison: Prehistory Press.

Bar-Yosef, O., & Meadow, R.H. (1995). The Origins of Agriculture in the Near East. In (T.D. Price & A.B. Gebauer, Eds) *Last Hunters, First Farmers: New Perspectives on the Prehistoric Transition to Agriculture,* pp. 39–94. Santa Fe: School of American Research Press.

Baumler, M.F. & Speth, J.D. (1993). A Middle Paleolithic assemblage from Kunji Cave, Iran. In (D.I. Olszewski and H.L. Dibble, Eds) *The Paleolithic Prehistory of the Zagros-Taurus,* pp. 1–74. Philadelphia: The University Museum, University of Pennsylvania.

Bentley, G.R. (1996).How did prehistoric women bear "Man the Hunter"? Reconstructing fertility from the archaeological record. In (R.P. Wright, Ed) *Gender and Archaeology,* pp. 23–51. Philadelphia: University of Pennsylvania.

Bentley, G.R., Jasienska, G. & Goldberg, T. (1993). 'Is the fertility of agriculturalists higher than that of nonagriculturalists?' *Current Anthropology* **34**, 778–785.

Bettinger, R.L. (1991). *Hunter-Gatherers: archaeological and evolutionary theory.* New York: Plenum Press.

Binford, L.R. (1980). Willow Smoke and Dogs' Tails: Hunter-Gatherer Settlement Systems and Archaeological Site Formation. *American Antiquity.* **45**, 4–20.

Binford, L.R. (1983). *In Pursuit of the Past: Decoding the Archaeological Record* London: Thames and Hudson.

Boâda, E., Connan, J., & Muhesen, S. (1998). Bitumen as Hafting Material on Middle Paleolithic Artifacts from the El Kowm Basin, Syria. In (T. Akazawa, K. Aoki and T. Kimura, Eds) *The Evolution and Dispersal of Modern Humans in Asia,* pp. 181–204.Tokyo: Hokusen-Sha.

Braidwood, R.J. (1975). *Prehistoric Men* Glenview, Illinois: Scott, Freeman and Co.

Cauvin, J. (1997). *Naissance des divinités, naissance de l'agriculture.* Second Edition. Paris: CNRS.

Clark, G.A. (1997). The Middle-Upper Paleolithic transition in Europe: An American perspective. *Norw. Arch. Rev.* **30**, 25–53.

Clark, J.D. (1992). The earlier Stone Age/ Lower Palaeolithic in North Africa and the Sahara. In (F. Klees and R. Kuper, Eds) *New Light on the Northeast African Past,* pp. 5: 18–37, Kîln: Heinrich Barth Institut. 5: 18–37.

Cremaschi, M., Di Lernia, S., & Garcea, E.A.A. (1998). Some insights on the Aterian in the Libyan Sahara: Chronology, Environment, and Archaeology. *African Archaeological Review.* **15** (4), 261–286.

d'Errico, F., Zilhão, J., Julien, M., Baffier, D. & Pelegrin, J. (1998). Neanderthal acculturation in Western Europe? A critical review of the evidence and its interpretation. *Current Anthropology* **39** (Supplement), S1–S44.

Deacon, H.J. (1992). Southern Africa and modern human origins. *Philosophical Transactions of the Royal Society* **337** (1280), 177–183.

Donahue, R.E. (1992). Desperately seeking Ceres: A critical examination of current models for the transition to agriculture in Mediterranean Europe. In (A. B. Gebauer & T. D. Price Eds) *Transitions to Agriculture in Prehistory,* pp.73–80. Madison: Prehistory Press.

Fitzhugh, W.W. (1994). Staffe Island1 and the Northern Labrador Dorset-Thule Succession. In (D. Morrison & J.-L. Pilon) *Threads of Arctic Prehistory: Papers in Honour of William E. Taylor,*

Jr. pp. 239–268. Hull, Ontario: Canadian Museum of Civilization. Mercury Series No. 149.

Foley, R. and M.M. Lahr (1997). Mode 3 technologies and the evolution of modern humans. *Cambridge Archaeological Journal* **7**(1), 3–36.

Gamble, C. (1986). *The Palaeolithic Settlement of Europe.* Cambridge: Cambridge University Press.

Gilman, A. (1984). Explaining the Upper Palaeolithic revolution. In (E. Springs, Ed) *Marxist Perspectives in Archaeology,* pp. 115–126. Cambridge: Cambridge University Press.

Goldberg, P. & Bar-Yosef, O. (1998). Site Formation Processes in Kebara and Hayonim Caves and Their Significance in Levantine Prehistoric Caves. In (T. Akazawa, K. Aoki and T. Kimura, Eds) *The Evolution and Dispersal of Modern Humans in Asia,* pp. 107–125. Tokyo: Hokusen-Sha.

Grün, R., & Stringer, C.B. (1991). Electron spin resonance dating and the evolution of modern humans. *Archaeometry* **33**(2), 153–199.

Harlan, J.R., & Zohary, D. (1966). Distribution of wild wheat and barley. *Science.* **153**, 1074–1080.

Harpending, H., Batzer, M., Gurven, M., Jorde, L., Rogers A., and Sherry, S. (1998). Genetic traces of ancient demography. *Proc. of the National Academy of Science USA.* **95**, 1961–1967.

Harris, D.R. (1996). The Origins and Spread of Agriculture and Pastoralism in Eurasia: an overview. In (D.R. Harris, Ed.) *The Origins and Spread of Agriculture and Pastoralism in Eurasia,* pp. 552–573. London, UCL Press).

Henry, D.O. (1998). Intrasite Spatial Patterns and Behavioral Modernity: Indications from the Late Levantine Mousterian Rockshelter of Tor Faraj, Southern Jordan. In (T. Akazawa, K. Aoki and T. Kimura, Eds) *The Evolution and Dispersal of Modern Humans in Asia,* pp. 127–142. Tokyo: Hokusen-Sha.

Hillman, G. (1996). Late Pleistocene changes in wild plant-foods available to hunter-gatherers of the Northern Fertile Crescent: Possible preludes to cereal cultivation. In (D. R. Harris, Ed.) *The Origins and Spread of Agriculture and Pastoralism in Eurasia,* pp. 159–203. London, UCL Press.

Hublin, J.J. (1993). Recent human evolution in Northwestern Africa. *Origin of Modern Humans and the Impact of Chronometric Dating,* **1993**, 118–131.

Hublin, J.J., Ruiz, C.B., Lara, P.M., Fontugne, M., & Reyss, J.M. (1995). The Mousterian site of Zafarraya (Andalucia, Spain): Dating and implications on the Paleolithic peopling process of Western Europe. *Comptes Rendus de l'Acadmie des Sciences, série IIz,* **321**, 931–937.

Humphrey, N.K. (1988). The social function of intellect. In (R.W. Byrne and A. Whiten, Eds.) *Machiavellian Intelligence: Social Expertise and the Evolution of Intellect in Monkeys, Apes, and Humans,* pp. 13–26. Oxford: Clarendon Press.

Jelinek, A.J. (1994). Hominids, energy, environment, and behavior in the Late Pleistocene. In (M.H. Nitecki and D.V. Nitecki, Eds.) *Origins of Anatomically Modern Humans,* pp. 67–92. New York: Plenum Press.

Kelly, R. (1995). *The Foraging Spectrum: Diversity in Hunter-Gatherer Lifeways.* Washington: Smithsonian Institution Press.

Kitagawa, H., & van der Plicht, J. (1998). Atmospheric radiocarbon calibration to 45,000 yr B.P.: Late glacial fluctuations and cosmogenic isotope production. *Science.* **279**, 1187–1190.

Klein, R. G. (1995). Anatomy, behavior, and modern human origins. *Journal of World Prehistory.* **9**(2), 167–198.

Kozlowski, J.K. (1998). The Middle and the Early Upper Paleolithic around the Black Sea In (T. Akazawa, K. Aoki and T. Kimura, Eds) *The Evolution and Dispersal of Modern Humans in Asia,* pp. 461–482. Tokyo: Hokusen-Sha.

Kuhn, S.L., & Stiner, M.C. (1998). The earliest Aurignacian of Riparo Mochi (Liguria, Italy). *Current Anthropology.* **39** (Supplement), S175–S189.

Kuper, A. (1988). *The Invention of Primitive Society: Transformations of an Illusion.* London: Routledge.

Landes, D.S. (1998). *The wealth and poverty of nations: why some are so rich and some so poor.* New York: W. W. Norton.

Lieberman, P. (1989). The origins of some aspects of human language and cognition. In (P. Mellars & C. Stringer, Eds.), *The Human Revolution: Behavioural and Biological Perspectives on the Origins of Modern Humans,* pp. 391–414. Edinburgh: Edinburgh University Press.

Lindly, J.M. & Clark, G.A. (1990). Symbolism and modern human origins. *Current Anthropology.* 31(3), 233–262.

Lourandos, H. (1997). *Continent of Hunter-Gatherers: New Perspectives in Australian Prehistory.* Cambridge Univ. Press.

Marks, A. (1983). *Prehistory and Paleoenvironments in the Central Negev, Israel, Volume III.* Dallas, USA: Southern Methodist University Press.

Marks, A. (1993). The Early Upper Paleolithic: The view from the Levant. In (H. Knecht, A. Pike-Tay and R. White, Eds.) *Before Lascaux: The Complete Record of the Early Upper Paleolithic,* pp. 5–22. Boca Raton: CRC Press.

Marks, A.E. and V.P. Chabai (eds.), (1998). The Middle Paleolithic of Western Crimea, Vol. 1. The Paleolithic of Crimea, I. (Liége, ERAUL).

Marshack, A. (1972). *The roots of civilization; the cognitive beginnings of man's first art, symbol, and notation.* New York: McGraw-Hill.

Mayewski, P.A. & Bender, M. (1995). The GISP2 ice core record – Paleoclimate highlights. *Reviews of Geophysics,* Supplement July. 1287–1296.

McBurney, C.B.M. (1967). *The Haua Fteah (Cyrenaica) and the Stone Age of the South-East Mediterranean.* Cambridge: Cambridge University Press.

Mellars, P. (1989). Technological changes at the Middle-Upper Palaeolithic transition: Economic, social and cognitive perspectives. In (P. Mellars & C. Stringer, Eds), *The Human Revolution: Behavioural and Biological Perspectives on the Origins of Modern Humans,* pp. 338–365. Edinburgh: Edinburgh University Press.

Mellars, P. (1996a). *The Neanderthal Legacy: An Archaeological Perspective from Western Europe.* Princeton University Press.

Mellars, P. (1996b). Symbolism, language, and the Neanderthal mind. In (P. Mellars & K. Gibson, Eds), *Modelling the Early Human Mind,* pp. 15–32. Cambridge: McDonald Institute of Archaeological Research

Mercier, N., Valladas, H., Joron, J.L., Schiegl, S., Bar-Yosef, O. and Weiner, S. (1995). Thermoluminescence dating and the problem of geochemical evolution of sediment – a case study. The Mousterian levels at Hayonim. *Israel Journal of Chemistry.* 35, 137–141.

Meshveliani, T. (1989). About the early stages of the Upper Paleolithic cultures in western Georgia. *Newsletters of the State Museum of Georgia.* 40–B, 13–31.

Minugh-Purvis, N. (1993). Reexamination of the immature hominid maxilla from Tangier, Morocco. *American Journal of Physical Anthropology* 92, 449–461.

Mithen, S. (1996). *The Prehistory of the Mind: A Search for the Origins of Art, Religion, and Science.* London: Thames and Hudson.

Oakley, K.P. (1961). *Man the Tool-Maker.* London: (Trustees of the British Museum).

Odess, D. (1998). The Archaeology of Interaction: Views from Artifact Style and Material Exchange in Dorset Society. *American Antiquity* 63(3), 417–435.

Otte, M. & L.H. Keeley. (1990). The impact of regionalisation on the Palaeolithic studies. *Current Anthropology* 31(5), 577–582.

Pfeiffer, J.E. (1982). *The Creative Explosion: An Inquiry into the Origins of Art and Religion.* New York: Harper and Row.

Piazza, A., Rendine, S., Minch, E., Menozzi, P., Mountain J., and Cavalli-Sforza, L.L.(1995). Genetics and the origin of European languages. *Proc. of the National Academy Science USA* 92, 5836–5840.

Raposo, L. & Cardoso, J.L. (1998). *O Sîto do Paleolítico Médio da Conceição, Alcochete.* Lisboa: Centro de Estudos e Monitorização Ambiental [CEMA].

Renfrew, C. (1987). *Archaeology and Language: The Puzzle of Indo-European Origins.* Cambridge University Press.

Rindos, D. (1984). *The Origins of Agriculture: An Evolutionary Perspective.* New York: Academic Press.

Roberts, R.G., Jones, R. & Smith, R.A. (1990). Thermoluminescence dating of a 50,000 year old human occupation site in northern Australia. *Nature.* 345, 153–6.

Rocek, T.R. and O. Bar-Yosef (Eds.) (1998). *Seasonality and Sedentism: Archaeological Perspectives from Old and New World Sites.* Peabody Museum Bulletin 6 (Cambridge, Peabody Museum of Archaeology and Ethnology).

Roebroeks, W., Kolen, J. & E. Rensink. (1988). Planning depth, anticipation and the organization of Middle Palaeolithic technology: The "Archaic Natives meet Eve's Descendents". *Helinium.* XXVIII, 17–34.

Rosenberg, M., Nesbitt, R.M., Redding, R.W. & Strasser, T.F. (1995). Hallan Çemi Tepesi: some preliminary observations concerning early Neolithic subsistence behaviors in eastern Anatolia. *Anatolica* 21, 1–12.

Ruvolo, M. (1996). A new approach to studying modern human origins: Hypothesis testing with coalescence time distributions. *Molecular Phylogenetics and Evolution.* 5(1), 202–219.

Ruvolo, M. (1997). Genetic diversity in hominoid primates. *Annual Review of Anthropology.*

Shea, J.J. (1998). Neandertal and Early Modern Human Behavioral Variability: A Regional-Scale Approach to Lithic Evidence for Hunting in the Levantine Mousterian. *Current Anthropology.* 39 (Supplement, June 1998), S45–S78.

Sherratt, A. (1997). Climatic cycles and behavioural revolutions: The emergence of modern humans and the beginning of farming. *Antiquity* 71, 271–287.

Smith, B.D. (1995). *The Emergence of Agriculture.* New York: Scientific American Library.

Smith, B.D. (1997). The initial domestication of Cucurbita pepo in the Americas 10,000 years ago. *Science.* 276, 932–934.

Solecki, R.L. & Solecki, R.S. (1983). Late Pleistocene-Early Holocene cultural traditions in the Zagros and the Levant. In (T.C. Young, Jr., P.E.L. Smith and P. Mortensen, Eds), *The Hilly Flanks and Beyond,* pp. 123–137. Chicago: The Oriental Institute.

Straus, L.G. (1996). Continuity or rupture; convergence or invasion; adaptation or catastrophe; mosaic or monolith: views on the Middle to Upper Paleolithic transition in Iberia. In (E. Carbonell & M. Vaquero, Eds.)*The Last Neandertals, the First Anatomically Modern Humans* pp. 203–218. Tarragona: Universitat Rovira i Virgili.

Straus, L.G. (1997). The Iberian situation between 40,000 and 30,000 BP in light of European models of migration and convergence. In (G.A. Clark & C.M. Willermet, Eds), *Conceptual Issues in Modern Humans Origins Research,* pp. 235–252. New York: Aldine de Gruyter.

Svoboda, J., & Simán, K. (1989). The Middle-Upper Paleolithic transition in southeastern Central Europe (Czechoslovakia and Hungary*). Journal of World Prehistory.* 3, 283–322.

Tillet, T. (1989). L'Atérien saharien: Essaie sur le comportement d'une civilisation paléolithique face à l'accroissement de l'aridité. *Bulletin Soc. Géol. Fr.* 5, 91–97.

van Andel, T. (1998). Middle and Upper Palaeolithic environments and the calibration of 14C dates beyond 10,000 BP. Antiquity 72(275), 26–33.

van Andel, T. & Runnels, C.N. (1995). The earliest farmers in Europe. *Antiquity* **69**(264), 481–500.

Van Peer, P. (1998). The Nile Corridor and the Out-of-Africa model: An examination of the archaeological record. *Current Anthropology.* 39.

Vermeersch, P.M., Paulissen, E., Stokes, S., Charlier, C., Van Peer, P., Stringer, C., & Lindsay, W. (1998). A Middle Palaeolithic burial of a modern human at Taramsa Hill, Egypt. *Antiquity.* **72**(277), 475–484.

Wagner, G.A. (1998). *Age Determination of Young Rocks and Artifacts: Physical and Chemical Clocks in Quaternary Geology and Archaeology.* Berlin: Springer Verlag.

Ward, P.D. (1997). *The Call of Distant Mammoths: Why the Ice Age Mammals Disappeared.* New York: Copernicus.

Wengler, L. (1997). La Transition du Moustérien à l'Atérien. *L'Anthropologie* **101**, 448–81.

Wetterstrom, W. (1998). The Origins of Agriculture in Africa: with particular reference to Sorghum and Pearl Millet. *Review of Archaeology.* **19**(2).

Whallon, R. (1989). Elements of Cultural change in the Later Palaeolithic. In (P. Mellars & C. Stringer, Eds), *The Human Revolution: Behavioural and Biological Perspectives on the Origins of Modern Humans,* pp. 433–454. Edinburgh: Edinburgh University Press.

White, R. (1982). Rethinking the middle/upper paleolithic transition. *Current Anthropology.* **23**(2), 169–176, 187–192.

White R. (1997). Substantial acts: From materials to meaning in Upper Paleolithic representation. In (M.W. Conkey, O. Soffer, D. Stratmann & N.G. Jablonski, Eds*), Beyond Art: Pleistocene Image and Symbol*, pp. 93–121. San Francisco: Memoirs of the California Academy of Sciences, 23.

Wright, K.I. (1994). Ground stone tools and hunter-gatherer subsistence in southwest Asia: Implications for the transition to farming. *American Antiquity.* **59**(2), 238–263.

Zohary, D. & Hopf, M. (1994). *Domestication of Plants in the Old World.* Oxford, Clarendon Press.

3

The Mousterian in Mediterranean France: A Comparative Perspective

Carolyn C. Szmidt

Introduction

Many models and hypotheses regarding Neanderthal behaviour have been developed based on the extensive Mousterian data set of south-western France. In fact, the topic of Mousterian variability, an issue which thirty years later is still largely unresolved, was first played out in this region (Binford 1973; Binford & Binford 1966;1969; Bordes & de Sonneville Bordes 1970; Dibble 1987; 1988a; 1988b; Dibble & Rolland 1992; Mellars 1970; 1992; Rolland 1981; 1990).

This paper focuses on the Mousterian of an adjacent region, that of south eastern France (also referred to as Mediterranean France). This region encompasses the administrative areas of Provence, Languedoc-Roussillon and part of Rhône-Alpes and is delimited by the Massif Central and the Alps to the north, the Alps to the east, the Pyrénées to the west and the Mediterranean Sea to the south. One of the main geographic features of this region is the River Rhône, which runs along a north-south axis and divides the Mediterranean region into Provence to the east and Languedoc-Roussillon and the *département* of Ardèche to the west.

The purpose of this paper is to present a few preliminary patterns, obtained from an initial comparative examination of the lithic data from 43 Mousterian sites in Mediterranean France. This forms part of on-going doctoral research in which the patterns in the lithic, faunal, raw material and environmental data from this region are being analysed and integrated together to examine broad spatial and chronological patterns in Neanderthal behaviour within the region of Mediterranean France and between Mediterranean and south-western France.

The large body of data from south-western France provides a solid base from which comparisons can be made to the archaeological data, and in particular from the patterns, found in other regions, such as those of Medi-terranean France. This does not imply that the patterns of behaviour exhibited by Neanderthals in south-western France should necessarily apply elsewhere. On the contrary, this is the very assumption that should be tested by examining both the differences and the similarities between the 'classic' region and other regions.

Three types of patterns will be presented and discussed in this paper: those which demonstrate a contrast between Mediterranean and south-western France (Figures 3.1a and 3.1b); those which show the heterogeneity of patterns within Mediterranean France (Figures 3.2 and 3.3) and those which show similarities between this region and the 'classic' region (Figures 3.4 and 3.5).

Criteria for assemblage selection

In deciding which assemblages to include in this analysis, the main criterion used was the availability of at least a few basic Bordes typological and technological indices (Bordes 1950a; 1950b; 1953; 1992; Bordes & Bourgon 1951). Standardisation of this sort was deemed to be necessary if appropriate comparisons were to be feasible. Also, Mellar's (1996:4) definition of the 'Mousterian' was adopted, being defined as the period between 115ka and 35ka. This corresponds to Oxygen Isotope Stages 5d to 3 inclusive in the deep sea core marine record, and Würm I and II (or *Würm ancien* as it is often referred to in older literature) of the Alpine sequence (Valladas *et al.* 1987).

A total of 43 sites, representing 73 assemblages, have been included in the research presented here. Sites which are currently under investigation (Aubesier, Combette, Moula, Payre, Crouzade, Ramandils) have not been included, unless they were excavated by previous researchers, in which case the earlier excavations are included, where appropriate. The sites used in this study

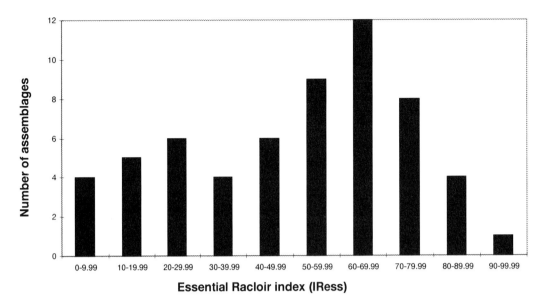

Figure 3.1a: Overall distribution of racloir frequencies in Mediterranean France (n=59). The sites included in this paper are: 1) Provence: Murée, Plaine de Sirène, Sainte-Maxime, Pié-Lombard, Adaouste, Tonneau, Breuil, Michelles, Rigabe, Saint-Loup, Sauzade, Aubésier, Bérigoule, Coquillade,Peyrards, Pied de Sault, Sablons, Trécassats; 2) Ardèche: Figuier, Maras, Moula, Néron, Oullins, Ranc de l'Arc, Ranc Pointu; 3) Languedoc-Roussillon: Balauzière, Baumasse d'Antonègue, Bézal de Souvignargues, Bourgade, Brugas, Calmette, Cayla, Crouzade, Esquicho-Grapaou, Hortus, Ioton, mas d'Espanet, Ramandils, Roquette, Rouziganet, Tournal and Verrerie. The data used in the graphs have been obtained from publications about the sites. The reader is invited to consult the bibliography for exact sources. The number of assemblages, n, varies between graphs because not all the indices examined were calculated and published for every assemblage.

are listed in Figure 3.1a. Some of these assemblages were recovered from older excavations and some published statistics may have been based on relatively small assemblages, therefore some caution is required. Given that the aim of this study is to identify broad patterns in the data, however, it is unlikely that a small percentage of unreliable data will significantly alter the overall patterns. Some sites have not been dated by chronometric dating techniques, therefore it is possible that their assemblages are older than the dates mentioned above. Assemblages referred to as 'Mousterian' by their excavators were included regardless of whether they were dated by chronometric dating techniques, sedimentological or faunal analysis etc.

Differences between Mediterranean and south-western France

One difference between Mediterranean and south-western France is the frequency distribution of the Esssential Racloir Index (IRess). Figure 3.1a shows the distribution of this index in the former region and Figure 3.1b in the latter. As can be seen, the multimodal pattern of IRess produced by the south-western French assemblages is not the pattern produced by the Mediterranean assemblages.

The data from the south-western French assemblages were replotted into ranges of tens to make Figure 3.1b, rather than in the original ranges of fives presented by Bordes (Bordes & de Sonneville-Bordes 1970: Figure 15).

This was done in an attempt to see whether the multimodality in the IRess index was created artificially by the narrowness of the ranges in which the data were originally plotted. Plotting data in a histogram in small ranges has the effect of increasing the number of categories plotted, thereby exaggerating small differences between assemblages and hence possibly leading to an artificial multimodal pattern.

When a slightly more significant difference of 10 % between categories is used, as in Figure 3.1b, the pattern in the racloir index in the south-western French assemblages remains multimodal (although with fewer categories). This is contrasted, however, by the IRess histogram of the Mediterranean assemblages (Figure 3.1a), which displays one main peak, or mode.

A similar histogram to that of Figure 3.1a has been produced by Rolland (Rolland 1981: 24, Figure 3; and reproduced with six added assemblages in Dibble & Rolland 1992: 7, Figure 1.1). Although the histograms produced by Rolland are also based on assemblages from Mediterranean France, the graphs are different from the one produced here in that the majority (59%) 'of the assemblages in Figure 3.1a fall between IRess values of 40 and 80, with the modal catedory being the range 60 to 70, as compared with Rolland's graphs, in which the majority of the IRess values fall between values of 30 and 70, with the modal category being the range 50 to 60. In other words, the concentration of values and the actual

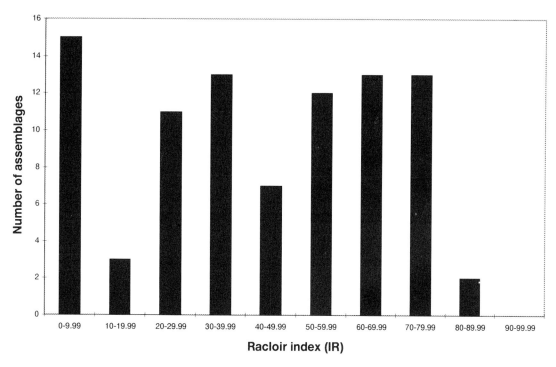

Figure 3.1b: Distribution of the Racloir index in Southwestern France (n=88) (redrawn from Bordes & de Sonneville-Bordes 1970, in groups of tens, than five's). In the publication of which Figure 3.1b is based (Bordes & Sonneville-Bordes 1970:69, Figure 15), the authors refer to the 'Scraper index' as the one being plotted and giving rise to the multimodal pattern. In an earlier publication (Bordes 1953:459, Figure 1f), though, the author plotted the Essential racloir index (based on a smaller sample of assemblages) which also gave rise to a multimodal pattern.

modal category in the histogram presented here are shifted to the right (more left-skewed) compared to the ones presented by Rolland. This dissimilarity could be due to differences in assemblages selected for inclusion in the histogram. It is not clear which assemblages were used by Rolland to produce his histograms since he did not provide a list of the included assemblages in either publication (1981; Dibble and Rolland 1992). In one publication (1981), however, he cites three references as those from which the data were taken. These references have also been used here, but given that the numbers of assemblages in Rolland's graphs were larger, it is possible that he included sites referred to as 'late Acheulian' or Rissian, which were not included in this study. If this is the case, then this may indicate, very interestingly, that this lack of multimodality extends further back in time.

The difference between the IRess histograms of south-western and Mediterranean France is an important contrast between the regions since it is primarily this multimodality which led Bordes (Bordes 1953; Bordes and de Sonneville-Bordes 1970) to separate the Mousterian into *faciès*, the meaning of which have been the source of debate for the last thirty years leading to cultural (Bordes 1981; Bordes & Bourgon 1951; Bordes & de Sonneville Bordes 1970), functional (Binford 1973; Binford & Binford 1966;1969), reduction (Dibble 1987; 1988a; 1988b; Dibble & Rolland 1992), environmental (Rolland 1981; 1990) and chrono-logical (Mellars 1970; 1992) hypotheses.

The lack of multimodality does not, in itself, necessarily mean that the various Mousterian facies are absent from Mediterranean France; after all, the facies were also defined based on technological and other typological characteristics (Bordes 1981; Bordes & de Sonneville Bordes 1970). Once again, however, Mediterranean France provides a contrast to south-western France in that the MTA is completely lacking from the former region (Combier 1990: 270–1). This is not simply an arbitrary typological difference if, as Mellars (1992: 39; 1996: 325–6, 414) has argued, the MTA represents the final Mousterian facies, and a precursor to the Châtelperronian (also absent from Mediterranean France (Combier 1990: 270–1)) in south-western France. This difference may reflect variations in late Neanderthal behaviour between the two regions and may have important implications regarding the interaction of the final Neanderthals with the anatomically modern *Homo sapiens* when the latter arrived in Mediterranean France.

Also, the particular spatial distribution of other Mousterian facies within Mediterranean France is notable in that Provence has very few Denticulate and Quina Mousterian assemblages, whilst these exist in higher proportion west of this region. If, as Rolland (1981: 35; 1990: 367) suggests, racloir-rich (i.e. including Quina Mousterian) and Denticulate assemblages tend to be produced in highly contrasting climatic conditions (severe *versus* milder conditions, respectively), the virtual lack of

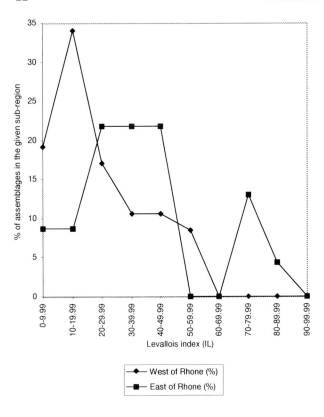

Figure 3.2: Frequency of the Levallois index east and west of the Rhone river, showing a difference between these two sub-regions of Mediterranean France (n=70).

these two facies is particularly interesting and deserves further consideration.

Heterogeneity of patterns within Mediterranean France

As the last point illustrates, the patterns within Mediterranean France are not necessarily homogeneous throughout the region, but can exhibit spatial differences. For instance, the frequency of use of the Levallois technique (as indicated by the Levallois index, IL) varies within Mediterranean France. When the Levallois index is plotted in ranges (Figure 3.2), one can see that the Levallois method, overall, is used more frequently east of the Rhône river (in Provence) than west of it, with more than half of the assemblages west of the river having values below 20, whilst in the east, more than half of the assemblages have IL values above 30. In fact, the IL ranges from the two sides of the Rhône are virtually mirror images of each other, i.e. a range of the Levallois index that is high in the east is low in the west and *vice versa*.

Interestingly, sites with particularly elevated levels of the IL index in Provence are all located in a region rich in flint sources, some of which are of very high quality for flaking (Texier & Wilson 1994: 136–7). The possibility of there being a link between high levels of Levallois use

and regions of high quality, quantity and size of raw material has been made by others for south-western French assemblages (Bordes 1950a: 411; Mellars 1992: 35; 1996: 89; Morala & Turq 1991). This does not mean that the Levallois technique will automatically be practised whenever such conditions exist, though, as demonstrated by the fact that in the same region in Provence, there are assemblages with lower levels of Levallois use (site of Trécassats, some levels at Peyrards) indicating that raw material, by itself, is by no means sufficient in explaining the distribution of IL values. Also, conversely, it has been shown (Jaubert & Farizy 1995), in the Garonne Basin (south-western France), for example, that high levels of Levallois use can be produced in regions with raw material of poor quality and small size. Simply, the conditions above make the Levallois method more feasible and increase the possibility of producing large amounts of Levallois flakes.

The overall frequency distribution of the IL index in Provence, shown in Figure 3.2, is radically different from the IL frequency distribution pattern obtained by Rolland (1988: 165, Figure 9.1) for a large sample of Western European Mousterian assemblages. In it, he demonstrates that the distribution pattern for the larger region of Western Europe resembles an 'exponential pattern', in other words, that the higher the Levallois index is, the fewer assemblages there are bearing that value. Based on this frequency distribution, Rolland (1988: 164) concludes that "Levallois flaking was a relatively 'improbable' event (...)". The assemblages from Provence, however, indicate that the Levallois technique was much more frequently used in that particular region of Western Europe.

This example demonstrates the value of looking for patterns at different geographical scales of analysis, the larger scale in this case reflecting broad patterns which could be compared to the patterns obtained from other broad regions of Europe or the Near East and the smaller scale bringing out the variability of the larger region and the particular distinctiveness of one of its microcosms which may otherwise have gone unnoticed.

A second aspect which is heterogeneous within Mediterranean France is the relationship between the Levallois index and the proportion of blades (ILam). In Provence, the frequency of use of the Levallois technique correlates quite well with the proportion of blades, not only in the high Levallois/high blade relationship, but also in mid- and even low values of these indices, as Figure 3.3 illustrates. West of the Rhône, however, medium and high IL values are nearly exclusively associated with low ILam values. What is consistent throughout Mediterranean France, however, is that, on both sides of the Rhône, the number of blades is never high when the Levallois index is low.

The relationship between IL and ILam is not necessarily one to be expected. Careful re-fitting of cores at a number of sites in Belgium and northern France has shown that blades were sometimes made using non-Levallois methods

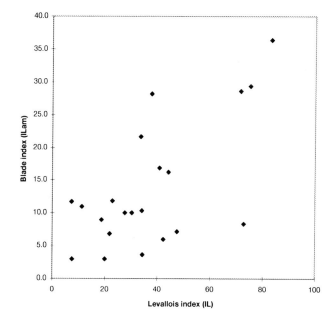

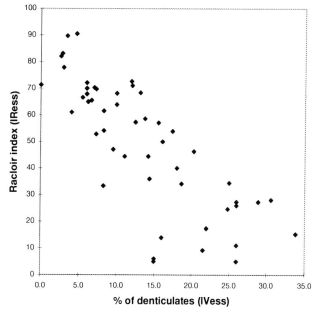

Figure 3.3: Scatter plot showing the relationship between Levallois and blade indices in Provence (n=21).

Figure 3.4: Scatter plot showing the relationship between racloirs and denticulates in assemblages from Mediterranean France (n=50).

during the Middle Palaeolithic in addition to the more common Levallois methods used (Boëda 1988; Révillion 1993; 1995). In Mediterranean France, though, it does not seem that in those cases in which numerous blades were produced, the Neanderthals adopted a non-Levallois technique to make them, since such assemblages would have appeared as dots in the, currently empty, upper left-hand corner of Figure 3.3.

Similarities between Mediterranean and south-western France

Despite having very different patterns in their racloir frequency distributions, one relationship which seems to be similar between Mediterranean and south-western France is the quite strong and highly significant negative correlation between the percentage of racloirs and that of denticulates (Spearman's rank correlation coefficient = -0.83, p<0.01), as Figure 3.4 illustrates. Not only does this pattern hold for the Mediterranean region as a whole, but it is also the kind of trend seen when only sites from Provence are used, despite it being an area with a number of unique patterns compared to the rest of the Mediterranean zone, as demonstrated above. This is a similar pattern to that obtained by Dibble (1988b: 183) based on assemblages from south-western France and the pattern seen specifically at the site of Combe Grenal (Jelinek 1988: 202, Figure 11.1, 207, Figure 11.5). In fact, Dibble (1988b: 186, 190) believes that this is the main source of variability in Mousterian assemblages in south-western France.

Another similarity between Mediterranean France and south-western France is represented by the relationship between the IL index and the proportion of specific racloir types. Figure 3.5 shows the Levallois index plotted against the relative proportion of transverse racloirs to transverse and lateral racloirs (transverse ÷ (transverse + lateral)). The scatter plot illustrates that, overall, there is a general negative relationship between Levallois use and the proportion of transverse racloirs (Spearman's r= -0.66, p<0.01). In other words, high quantities of transverse racloirs are not found with high levels of Levallois use. The same pattern is found in south-western French assemblages, as demonstrated by Mellars (1996: 105, Figure 4.7).

This could indicate that despite possible cultural differences between Mediterranean and south-western France, the production of certain types of racloirs may be linked more fundamentally to constraints imposed by technology. The type of racloir produced may be linked to the original shape of the flake and given that the Levallois method tends to produce flakes whose longest edge is parallel to the axis of the flake, Levallois flakes would tend to lead to the production of lateral (rather than transverse) racloirs if Neanderthals generally chose to retouch the longest edge of a flake (Bordes & de Sonneville-Bordes 1970: 61; Geneste 1989: 83).

Conclusion

The data presented have focused on indices developed under the Bordes system of typology. There has been a

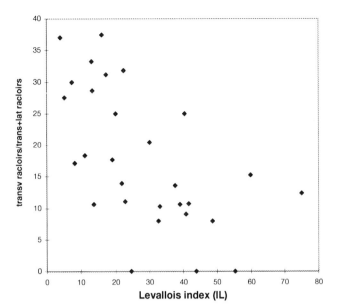

Figure 3.5: Scatter plot showing the relationship between the Levallois index and the relative frequency of transverse versus lateral racloirs in Mediterranean France (n=29).

in the environment between regions and random effects may account, at least in part, for apparent cultural similarities. Likewise, environmental, faunal or raw material differences between regions may mask actual cultural similarities. It is only once these factors have been taken into account that one can begin to address Neanderthal behavioural variability, aspects which are currently being considered and investigated as part of this larger research project.

Acknowledgements

I wish to thank my supervisor, Professor P.A. Mellars, for his comments and more generally for his constant support and good advice. Research for my Ph.D., from which this article stems, would not be possible without the following awards, for which I am extremely grateful: a Commonwealth Scholarship, a Social Sciences and Humanities Research Council of Canada Doctoral Fellowship, a Pelham Roberts Bursary from Newnham College, an O.R.S. Award (UK) and a Cambridge Commonwealth Trust award. Finally, I wish to express my warmest thanks to all those who have helped me along the way.

tendency in more recent years to focus instead on the production sequence of the lithics, or *chaîne opératoire*, rather than on detailed typology *per se* (Kuhn 1995; Texier & Francisco-Ortega 1995). Nevertheless, the indices used are fundamental ones which refer to technological and typological parameters which are broadly still in use.

The basic division of racloirs and denticulates is still contrasted, some believing in fact that these are the main divisions in the Middle Palaeolithic (Dibble 1988b; Dibble and Rolland 1992). The IRess index, in grouping the multitude of scraper types into one category, avoids the issue of the possible redundancy and arbitrary nature of the subdivisions within the racloirs that some researchers (Dibble 1987: 36; 1988b: 182; Kuhn 1995; Rolland 1990: 365) have pointed out and tried to reduce. In addition, the quantity of Levallois use and blades are still considered to be important issues, as demonstrated by the fact that these concepts have been defined more precisely and refined into finer categories (Boëda 1988; 1993; Révillion 1993; 1995). These recent subdivisions and their precision do not diminish or negate the value of the indices developed by Bordes, but instead build on them by adding another dimension of variability which would also be valuable to investigate in relation to the parameters included here.

The various patterns presented here show a complex interplay of homogeneity and heterogeneity between, and within, regions. It must be stated, however, that patterns of similarity between regions do not necessarily demonstrate a fundamental or intrinsic Neanderthal norm of behaviour shared between groups. External factors, such as availablity or lack of access to raw material, similarities

References

Bazile, F. & Meignen, L. (1974). Le gisement moustérien de Rouziganet (Gard). *Bulletin de la Société Préhistorique Française* **71**, 170–175.

Binford, L.R. (1973). Interassemblage variability-the Mousterian and the 'functional' argument. In (C. Renfrew, Ed.) *The Explanation of Culture Change: Models in Prehistory*, pp. 227–254. London: Duckworth.

Binford, L.R. & Binford, S.R. (1966). A preliminary analysis of functional variability in the Mousterian of Levallois facies. In (J.D. Clark & F.C. Howell, Eds) *Recent Studies in Paleoanthropology*, American Anthropologist special publication 68 No.2, Part 2, pp. 238–295.

Binford, S.R. & Binford, L.R. (1969). Stone tools and human behavior. *Scientific American* **220**, 70–84.

Boëda, E. (1988). Le concept laminaire: rupture et filiation avec le concept Levallois. In (M. Otte, Ed.) *L'Homme de Néandertal*. Volume 8, *La Mutation*, pp. 41–59. Liège: Etudes et Recherches Archéologiques de l'Université de Liège.

Boëda, E. (1993). *Le Concept Levallois: Variabilité des Méthodes*. Centre de Recherches Archéologiques, Monographie 9. Paris: Centre National de la Recherche Scientifique

Bonifay, E. (1964–65). Moustérien et prémoustérien de la grotte de Rigabe (Artigues, Var). *Quartär* **15–16**, 61–78.

Bordes, F. (1950*a*). L'évolution buissonante des industries en Europe occidentale. Considérations théoriques sur le Paléolithique ancien et moyen. *L'Anthropologie* **54**, 393–420.

Bordes, F. (1950*b*). Principes d'une méthode des techniques de débitage et de la typologie du Paléolithique ancien et moyen. *L'Anthropologie* **54**, 19–34.

Bordes, F. (1953). Essai de classification des industries "moustériennes". *Bulletin de la Société Préhistorique Française* **50**, 457–466.

Bordes, F. (1981). Vingt-cinq ans après: le concept moustérien revisité. *Bulletin de la Société Préhistorique Française* **78**, 77–87.

Bordes, F. (1992). *Leçons sur le Paléolithique: Tome 2: Paléolithique en Europe*. Paris: Centre National de la Recherche Scientifique.

Bordes, F & Bourgon, M. (1951). Le complexe moustérien: Moustériens, Levalloisien et Tayacien. *L'Anthropologie* **55**, 1–23.

Bordes, F. & Sonneville-Bordes, D de. (1970). The significance of variability in Palaeolithic assemblages. *World Archaeology* **2**, 1–73.

Brugal, J.-P., Francisco-Ortega, I., Jaubert, J. & Texier, P.-J. (1994). Diversité et complémentarité des principaux gisements Vauclusiens: les industries lithiques: Bérigoule. In (J. Buisson-Catil, Ed.) *Le Paléolithique Moyen en Vaucluse: À la Rencontre des Chasseurs Néandertaliens de Provence Nord-Occidentale*, pp. 91–100. Avignon: Notices d'Archéologie Vauclusienne 3.

Brugal, J.-P., Jaubert, J. & Texier, P.-J. (1989). Découverte d'un site moustérien de plein-air en Vaucluse (Bérigoule, Murs). *Bulletin de la Société Préhistorique Française* **86**, 69–71.

Combier, J. (1967). Le Paléolithique de l'Ardèche dans son cadre paléoclimatique. *Institut de Préhistoire de l'Université de Bordeaux Mémoire* **4**, 1–462.

Combier, J. (1990). De la fin du Moustérien au Paléolithique supérieur-Les données de la région rhodanienne. In (C. Farizy, Ed.) *Paléolithique Moyen Récent et Paléolithique Supérieur Ancien en France*, pp. 267–277. Nemours: Mémoires du Musée de Préhistoire d'Ile-de-France 3.

Defleur, A. (1988). Le Moustérien de l'abri Moula (Soyons, Ardèche). *Travaux du Laboratoire d'Anthropologie et de Préhistoire des Pays de la Méditerranée Occidentale*, 127–138.

Defleur, A. (1989–1990). Le Moustérien de l'abri Moula (Soyons, Ardèche). *Bulletin de la Société d'Étude des Sciences Naturelles de Vaucluse*, 59–85.

Defleur, A., Onoratini, G. & Crégut-Bonnoure, E. (1989). Découverte de niveaux moustériens dans la grotte de l'Adaouste (Jouques, Bouches-du-Rhône). *Bulletin de la Société Préhistorique Française* **86**, 76–78.

Defleur, A., Valladas, H., Radulescu, C., Combier, J. & Arnold, M. (1990). Stratigraphie et datation carbone-14, en spectrométrie de masse par accélérateur, du Moustérien récent de 'abri du Ranc de l'Arc (Ardèche, France). *Comptes Rendus de l'Académie des Sciences* **311**, 719–724.

Defleur, A., Bez, J.-F., Crégut-Bonnoure, E., Desclaux, E., Onoratini, G., Radulescu, C., Thinon, M. & Vilette, P. (1994). Le niveau moustérien de la grotte de l'Adaouste (Jouques, Bouches-du-Rhône): Approche culturelle et paléoenvironnements. *Bulletin du Musée d'Anthropologie Préhistorique de Monaco* **37**, 11–48.

Defleur, A., Bez, J.-F., Crégut-Bonnoure, E., Fontugne, M., Jeannet, M., Magnin, F., Talon, B., Thinon, M. & Combier, J. (1994). Industrie, biostratigraphie, restes humains et datation du gisement moustérien de la Baume Néron (Soyons, Ardèche). *Comptes Rendus de l'Académie des Sciences* **318**, 1409–1414.

Dibble, H.L. (1987). Reduction sequences in the manufacture of Mousterian implements of France. In (O. Soffer, Ed.) *The Pleistocene Old World: Regional Perspectives*, pp. 33–45. London: Plenum Press.

Dibble, H.L. (1988*a*). The interpretation of Middle Paleolithic scraper reduction patterns. In (M. Otte, Ed.) *L'homme de Néandertal*. Volume 4, *La Technique*, pp. 49–58. Liège: Etudes et Recherches Archéologiques de l'Université de Liège.

Dibble, H.L. (1988*b*). Typological aspects of reduction and intensity of utilization of lithic resources in the French Mousterian. In (H.L. Dibble & A. Montet-White, Eds) *Upper Pleistocene Prehistory of Western Eurasia*, pp. 181–197. Philadelphia: The University Museum Monograph 54.

Dibble, H.L. & Rolland, N. (1992). On assemblage variability in the Middle Paleolithic of western Europe: History, perspectives and a new synthesis. In (H.L. Dibble & P.A. Mellars, Eds) *The Middle Paleolithic: Adaptation, Behavior and Variability*, pp.

1–28. Philadelphia: The University Museum Monograph 72.

Escalon de Fonton, M. & Lumley, H. de (1960). Le Paléolithique moyen de la grotte de Rigabe (Artigues, Var). *Gallia Préhistoire* **3**, 1–39.

Geneste, J.-M. (1989). Économie des ressources lithiques dans le Moustérien du sud-ouest de la France. In (M. Otte, Ed.) *L'Homme de Néandertal*. Volume 6, *La Subsistance*, pp. 75–97. Liège: Etudes et Recherches Archéologiques de l'Université de Liège.

Jaubert, J. & Farizy, C. (1995). Levallois debitage: exclusivity, absence or coexistence with other operative schemes in the Garonne Basin, south-western France. In (H.L. Dibble & O. Bar-Yosef, Eds) *The Definition and Interpretation of Levallois Technology*, pp. 227–248. Madison: Prehistory Press Monographs in World Archaeology 23.

Jelinek, A.J. (1988). Technology, typology, and culture in the Middle Paleolthic. In (H.L. Dibble & A. Montet-White, Eds) *Upper Pleistocene Prehistory of Western Eurasia*, pp. 199–212. Philadelphia: The University Museum Monograph 54.

Kuhn, S. (1995). *Mousterian Lithic Technology: An Ecological Perspective*. Princeton: Princeton University Press.

Lumley-Woodyear, H. de (1969). Le Paléolithique inférieur et moyen du Midi Méditerranéen dans son cadre géologique (Ligurie-Provence). Vème supplément à *Gallia Préhistoire*, Tome 1. Paris: Centre National de la Recherche Scientifique.

Lumley-Woodyear, H. de (1971). Le Paléolithique inférieur et moyen du Midi Méditerranéen dans son cadre géologique (Bas-Languedoc-Roussillon-Catalogne). Vème supplément à *Gallia Préhistoire*, Tome 2. Paris: Centre National de la Recherche Scientifique.

Lumley, H. de (1972) (Ed). La grotte de l'Hortus (Valflaunès, Hérault): Les chasseurs néandertaliens et leur milieu de vie. Elaboration d'une chronologie du Würmien II dans le Midi méditerranéen. *Etudes Quaternaires Mémoire* **1**, 1–668.

Lumley, H. de (1976). Les civilisations du Paléolithique moyen en Provence. In (H. de Lumley, Ed.) *La Préhistoire Française: Civilisations Paléolithiques et Mésolithiques de la France* (Tome 1:3), pp. 989–1004. Paris: Centre National de la Recherche Scientifique.

Meignen, L. (1976). Le site moustérien charentien de Ioton (Beaucaire-Gard): Étude sédimentologique et archéologique. *Bulletin de l'Association Française pour l'Étude du Quaternaire*, 3–17.

Meignen, L. (1981). L'abri moustérien du Brugas à Vallabrix (Gard). *Gallia Préhistoire* 24, 239–253.

Meignen, L. & Coularou, J. (1981). *Le Gisement Paléolithique Moyen La Roquette (Conqueyrac, Gard): Étude Archéologique*. Centre de Recherches Archéologiques: notes internes **26**, 1–19.

Mellars, P.A. (1970). Some comments on the notion of "functional variability" in stone-tool assemblages. *World Archaeology* **2**, 74–89.

Mellars, P.A. (1992). Technological change in the Mousterian of southwest France. In (H.L. Dibble & P.A. Mellars, Eds) *The Middle Paleolithic: Adaptation, Behavior and Variability*, pp. 29–43. Philadelphia: The University Museum Monograph 72.

Mellars, P.A. (1996). *The Neanderthal Legacy: An Archaeological Perspective from Western Europe*. Princeton: Princeton University Press.

Moncel, M.-H. (1996). Le Moustérien de la Baume d'Oullins (Ardèche): Fouilles Jean Combier. *Bulletin de la Société Préhistorique Française* 93, 169–172.

Moncel, M.-H. (1996). Le Moustérien de la grotte du Ranc Pointu (Ardèche): Fouilles René Gilles et Jean Combier. *Bulletin de la Société Préhistorique Française* 93, 164–168.

Morala, A. & Turq, A. (1991). Relations entre matières premières lithiques et technologie: l'exemple du Paléolithique entre Dordogne et Lot. In *25 Ans d'Etudes Technologiques en*

Préhistoire. XI ème Rencontres internationales d'archéologie et d'histoire d'Antibes, pp.159–168. Juan-les-Pins: APDCA.

Olson, C.L. (1988). *Statistics: Making Sense of Data*. Dubuque: William C. Brown.

Révillion, S. (1993). Question typologique à propos des industries laminaires du Paléolithique moyen de Seclin (Nord) et de Saint-Germain-des-Vaux/Port Racine (Manche): Lames levallois ou lames non Levallois? *Bulletin de la Société Préhistorique Française* **90**, 269–273.

Révillion, S. (1995). Technologie du débitage laminaire au Paléolithique moyen en Europe septentrionale: état de la question. *Bulletin de la Société Préhistorique Française* **92**, 425–441.

Rolland, N. (1981). The interpretation of Middle Palaeolithic variability. *Man* (New Series) **16**, 15–42.

Rolland, N. (1988). Observations on some Middle Paleolithic time series in southern France. In (H.L. Dibble & A. Montet-White, Eds) *Upper Pleistocene Prehistory of Western Eurasia*, pp. 161–180. Philadelphia: The University Museum Monograph 54.

Rolland, N. (1990). Middle Palaeolithic socio-economic formations in Western Eurasia: An explanatory survey. In (P.A. Mellars, Ed.) *The Emergence of Modern Humans: An Archaeological Perspective*, pp. 347–388. Edinburgh University Press.

Tavoso, A. (1987*a*). Le Moustérien de la grotte Tournal. *Cypsela* **VI**, 161–174.

Tavoso, A. (1987*b*). Le remplissage de la grotte Tournal à Bize-Minervois (Aude). *Cypsela* **VI**, 23–35.

Texier, P.-J. (1974). L'industrie moustérienne de l'abri Pié-Lombard (Tourettes-sur-Loup, Alpes-Maritimes). *Bulletin de la Société Préhistorique Française* **71**, 429–448.

Texier, P.-J. & Francisco-Ortega, I. (1995). Main technological and typological characteristics of the lithic assemblage from Level 1 at Bérigoule, Murs-Vaucluse, France. In (H.L. Dibble & O. Bar-Yosef, Eds) *The Definition and Interpretation of Levallois Technology*, pp. 213–226. Madison: Prehistory Press Monographs in World Archaeology 23.

Texier, P.-J. & Wilson, L. (1994). La récolte des matériaux lithiques. In (J. Buisson-Catil, Ed.) *Le Paléolithique Moyen en Vaucluse: À la Rencontre des Chasseurs Néandertaliens de Provence Nord-Occidentale*, pp. 133–138. Avignon: Notices d'Archéologie Vauclusienne 3.

Valladas, H., Chadelle, J.-P., Geneste, J.-M., Joron, J.L., Meignen, L. & Texier, P.-J. (1987). Datations par la thermoluminescence de gisements moustériens du sud de la France. *L'Anthropologie* **91**, 211–226.

4

Late Neandertals in the South West of France and the Emergence of the Upper Palaeolithic

Jean-Philippe Rigaud

Introduction

Indisputable anatomical differences mark the taxonomic distinction between Neandertals and *Homo sapiens sapiens,* and for some of our colleagues a number of these differences indicate the behavioural limitations of Neandertals. For example, constraints on locomotion might have made various technical activities difficult or impossible, and there may also have been physiological constraints in communication and abstract conceptualisation. One of the consequences of this way of thinking is an automatic assumption on the part of the majority of prehistorians and palaeoanthropologists for an association between Neandertals and Mousterian cultures and between anatomically modern humans and the Upper Palaeolithic.

Until the late 1960's, the great majority of prehistorians considered the Châtelperronian as one of the first Upper Palaeolithic cultures. Referred to as the 'Lower Perigordian' in south west France by the Peyrony and Bordes school, the Châtelperronian was seen as 1) being clearly different from the Aurignacian, with which it was frequently associated stratigraphically, and 2) providing some phylogenetic origins for the Perigordian culture (i.e. the Gravettian of the Perigord). Outside this 'Perigord-centric' point of view we must remember that for some prominent prehistorians in the mid- 20th century, the Châtelperronian was without doubt an Upper Palaeolithic culture both technologically and typologically because it was associated with anatomically modern humans (Peyrony 1943). At the same time, F.Bordes (1968) went even further in assuming that anatomically modern humans could have been responsible for the Mousterian of Acheulean Tradition type B. For technological and typological reasons the MATb was, in his view, the starting-point of the Châtelperronian, but this was also because no Neandertal remains had been found in association with an MTAb assemblage (Bordes 1968).

The Châtelperronian legacy

The discovery at St. Césaire of Neandertal remains associated with a lithic assemblage (Lévêque & Vandermeersch 1980) contradicted the Bordian model, and, with almost no resistance, prehistorians accepted the new evidence. Châtelperronian industries were the ultimate (last?) expression of Mousterian technology, augmented by a specific Châtelperronian *chaîne opératoire* for the production of Châtelperronian points (Pelegrin 1995). It is worth stressing that since the St. Césaire discovery some prehistorians have attempted to move the MP/UP dividing line further towards the Aurignacian because they thought that Cro Magnon man was responsible for the early Aurignacian, a point which is by no means well established. From the moment of the St. Césaire discovery, the Châtelperronian was no longer regarded as an UP culture but became a type of upgraded epi-Mousterian, directly or indirectly influenced by *Homo sapiens sapiens.* The Châtelperronian *châine opératoire* is in fact a system of production of specific laminar blanks used for Châtelperronian points but also for end-scrapers, burins, etc. In fact, blade technology in the Châtelperronian did not represent a real innovation in Mousterian production methods since it had already appeared earlier in the Mousterian of the Levant and in the north and east of France (Meignen 1994; Tuffreau 1984 ; Revillon & Tuffreau 1994). A more sophisticated technological analysis will probably show that a degree of variability exists between these different laminar industries but it is clear, in any case, that the concept of the blade as a blank was not unknown to the Neandertals. Typology reveals exactly the same independence of development between Châtelperronian and Aurignacian. The 'Aurignaco-Perigordian synthetotype' proposed by Laplace (1970), which proposes a common origin of the Aurignacian and Châtelperronian, is represented by industries of a mixed character (or 'polymorphism' according to Laplace) in which the carinated and bladelet tools (i.e. Dufour) of the Aurignacian are also found with Châtelperronian points. In fact, we now know these are the result of mixing between several originally distinct assemblages by natural or human agents. Based on modern excavation in undisturbed contexts, only distinctive Aurignacian and Châtelperronian industries have been brought to light – neither having the mixed nor polymorphic characteristics at the heart of Laplace's synthetotype. Frequently, Mousterian artefacts have been recorded within Châtelperronian assemblages (e.g. by Arambourou and Jude 1964 ; Bordes 1968 ; Sonneville-Bordes 1960). Such results had been explained in different ways: Laville (1981) considered that they were the result of geological phenomena (mainly solifluction and cryoturbation) which had mixed archaeological horizons. For archaeologists like Bordes (1968) it confirmed a cultural continuity between the Mousterian (MAT b) and the Châtelperronian.

How do we interpret the presence and meaning of typologically Mousterian artefacts in the Châtelperronian? Are they 'Mousterian souvenirs' as Bordes claimed? Can we take their abundance as an indication of the 'techno-typological evolution'of an industry that was initially Mousterian and then evolved towards the Upper Palaeolithic?

To evaluate the risk of contamination within Châtelperronian assemblages I have listed: 1) Châtelperronian assemblages rich in typological Mousterian artefacts, and 2) Châtelperronian assemblages poor in typological Mousterian artefacts, and these are further subdividied according to the presence or absence of an underlying Mousterian cultural layer in the same stratigraphical sequence.

From Table 4.1 it is clear 1) that Châtelperronian assemblages overlying a Mousterian horizon are rich in technical and typological Mousterian artefacts, 2) where two Châtelperronian horizons overlie a Mousterian horizon, the upper Châtelperronian horizon is poor in Mousterian artefacts, 3) where there is no underlying Mousterian, the Châtelperronian has very few Mousterian artefacts, and 4) there is no Châtelperronian assemblage with numerous Mousterian artefacts which is not in contact with a Mousterian assemblage.

While these observations cannot be used for rejecting, as contaminated, all Châtelperronian assemblages associated with Mousterian, they nevertheless should make us think more warily about checking the homogeneity of such examples and developing more critical forms of analysis. At St. Césaire, according to Guilbaud, Backer and Lévêque (1994), the spatial organisation of the Châtelperronian occupation level reveals internal differentiation. In the sheltered area, in association with the Neandertal skeleton, small tools and flakes, backed points, backed blades and blade cores are more numerous than in the open area where there is a predominance of large tools and flakes, large scrapers, foliate pieces and a biface. The finds content

Table 4.1: Stratigraphic sequences for sites in S.W. France.

	Stratigraphic sequences with Mousterian & Châtelperronian	Stratigraphic sequences with only Châtelperronian
Châtelperronian with numerous techno-typogical Mousterian artefacts	Arcy/Cure (Renne) Trou de la Chèvre lower La Ferrassie Saint Césaire La Roche à Quinçay lower Combe-Saunière Grotte XVI	
Châtelperronian with few techno-typological Mousterian artefacts	Grotte des Fées Trou de la Chèvre upper La Roche à Quinçay upper	Grotte du Loup Les Cottés Fontenioux Le Basté Les Tambourets Canaule II La Côte

of the sheltered area seems to be technically and typologically more Upper Palaeolithic-looking than the unsheltered area where Mousterian-like artefacts are dominant.

The faunal assemblage from the unsheltered space has a majority of bovine remains, while reindeer are more common in the sheltered part. According to the authors : 'This view, however, cannot rule out the possibility that the materials were deposited sequentially in time' (Guilbaud *et al., op.cit.*). A serious re-evaluation of the archaeological assemblages is clearly needed.

The contemporaneity of Châtelperronian and Aurignacian cultures and the hypothesis of acculturation

In order to explain the Neandertals' novel tendency to produce laminar blanks, a new typological repertory, and a developed bone, antler and ivory technology, some archaeologists have proposed acculturation processes between the Châtelperronian Neandertals and Aurignacian newcomers (Mellars 1989; Demars & Hublin 1989). But for this to be so, acculturation implies: 1) the contemporaneous existence of Aurignacian and Châtelperronian populations in the same geographical area, and 2) evidence

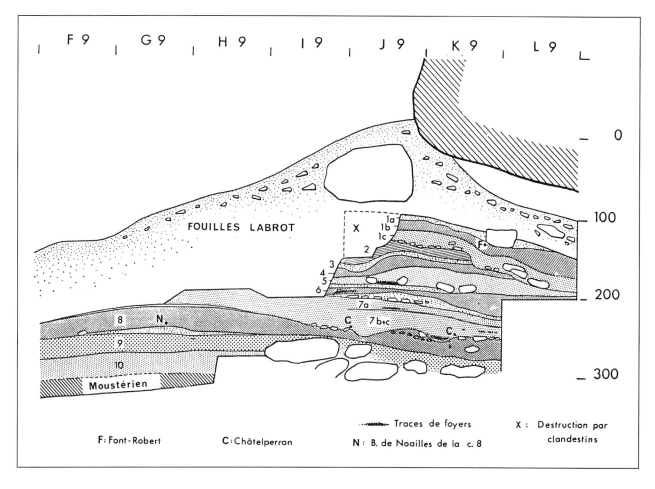

Figure 4.1: Stratigraphic section of Roc de Combe (after Bordes & Labrot, 1967). Layer 10: Castelperronian; Layer 9: Aurignacian; Layer 8: Castelperronian; Layer 7: (a,b,C) Aurignacian.

of sharing or borrowing of techniques, behaviours or symbols.

Interstratification

The contemporaneity of Aurignacian and Châtelperronian cultures has been shown by the apparent interstratification of both cultures at le Piage (Champagne & Espitalié 1967) and at Roc de Combe (Bordes & Labrot 1967). However, in the light of more recent work on site formation processes and lithic analysis these ideas must be viewed with some caution.

At Le Piage, Champagne and Espitalié (1981) as well as Laville (1981) mentioned 'difficulties in following the continuity of certain deposits' and Laville introduced the possibility of disturbances caused by the retriggering of the karstic activity. At the same time, Pelegrin and Demars have reported Aurignacian intrusions within the Châtelperronian lithic assemblage (Pelegrin 1995; Demars 1990). For this reason some archaeologists, myself included, think that the interstratification of the Aurignacian and the Châtelperronian at Le Piage is highly suspect and that the homogeneity and independence of these archaeological horizons should be tested – by refitting studies, for example (Bordes, J.-G. 1998).

At Roc de Combe (Figure 4.1) a careful reading of Borde's and Labrot's preliminary report (Bordes and Labrot 1967) shows that sedimentological phenomena elements might be responsible for the contamination of the archaeological assemblages :

1) The occupants of the Aurignacian Layer 7 dug a pit into the underlying Châtelperronian Layer 8. Fragments of Châtelperronian points were found in Layer 7, near the pit, and some Dufour bladelets must have been intrusive into Layer 8 (*op. cit.* p. 23)

2) There is a Noailles burin in Layer 8 (*op. cit.* p.23)

3) According to F. Bordes 'During the excavations it was almost impossible to separate Layer 10 from Layer 9' (*op. cit.* p.27)

4) In the cave, Layer 7 (Aurignacian) was subdivided into three sub-levels (a,b,and c) but such a distinction was not possible outside the cave.

5) At the entrance of the cave, Layer 7 sat above Layer 8, the underlying Layer 9 was unexcavated. Outside the cave, Layer 8 lay on Layer 9 but nowhere is there a stratigraphical profile showing the complete sequence from Layer 10 to Layer 7. The 'identification' of Layer 8 outside the cave plays a key rôle in making

the correlation between the stratigraphic layers inside and outside the cave possible – and consequently the reconstruction of virtually the whole archaeological sequence of Roc de Combe. Outside the cave the sediment of Layer 8 (a yellow sand) is almost indentical to the sediment of Layers 9 and 10 – making the indentification and separation of these stratigraphical units difficult. In addition, we must bear in mind the possibility of the type of contamination and mixing mentioned above. If Layer 8 cannot be used as a secure link for correlating the sequence inside and outside the cave, we could propose a very different reading of the Roc de Combe's stratigraphy: with, outside the cave, a superposition of the Aurignacian (Layer 9) above the Châtelperronian (Layer 10), and, at the entrance of the cave, the Châtelperronian (Layer 8) underlying the Aurignacian (Layer 7).

Moreover, various discrepancies in the ^{14}C dates from Roc de Combe caused Hedges, Houseley, Lawn and Bronk (1990) to suspect some form of pollution or disturbance in the sediment sequence.

For all these reasons the interstratification of Roc de Combe is in my opinion highly doubtful. This is not a criticism of the competence of the site excavators – on the contrary, it reflects an improvement in our analytical methods, made possible by their original work. Such an issue has to be checked by using different techniques, and especially by looking at refitting stratigraphical boundaries, as J.-G. Bordes has shown in his work on the lithic assemblages from Caminade (1998).

^{14}C chronology

Further argument concerning the contemporaneity of the Châtelperronian and the Aurignacian is based on the record of ^{14}C dates. As may be seen in Table 4.2, there is some agreement between Aurignacian and Châtelperronian dates at a broad regional scale, but it is not enough to prove that there was contact between them. If we accept the contemporary nature of the Châtelperronian and Aurignacian as a working hypothesis, is there any evidence for acculturation? A comparative analysis of the Châtelperronian and Aurignacian blade production by Pelegrin (1995) shows some significant technical differences between the two groupings, and, as such, does not support the idea of any technical influences.

In the 'MATb/Châtelperronian' distribution area (south west and east-central France) there is no archaic Aurignacian (older than 38ka); the earliest Aurignacian occupation in this area is dated around 37ka. A 'Châtelperronian province', initially isolated from the new Aurignacian culture, therefore appears to be a plausible alternative model which would explain the absence of technological and typological influences. This model is also compatible with the radiometric data at the regional scale.

Table 4.2: Radiometric dates for Castelperronian and Aurignacian cultures in France.

CHÂTELPERRONIAN	Age (years)
Roc-de-Combe c10	38 000±2000 Oxa 1443
Grotte XVI c.B	38 100±1670 Tucs
Arcy/Cure 14C	33 860±250
Les Cottés 14C	33 300±500
AURIGNACIAN	
Pataud c 14	34 250±675 GrN 4507
Pataud c 14	33 300±760 GrN 4610
Pataud c 14	33390±410 GrN 4720
Flageolet 1 c.XI	33 800±1800 Oxa 598
Flageolet 1 c.XI	34 300±1100 GifA 95559
Roc-de-Combe c 7b	33 400±100 Oxa 1262
Roc-de-Combe c 7c	34 800±1200 Oxa 1263
Caminade D2I	34 140±990 GifA 97187
Caminade F	35 400±1100 GifA 97186
Caminade G	37 200±1500 GifA 97185
Castanet	34 800±1100 GifA 97312
Castanet	35 200±1100 GifA 97313

Conclusions

The transition from MTAb to Châtelperronian is poorly documented because we do not yet have the quality or number of assemblages to track such a rapid and major transformation. This is why we have to be very critical of the data, and particularly in interpreting the meaning of the archaeological evidence: site formation processes and excavation techniques have to be taken into consideration when an evaluation of the integrity of the archaeological record is undertaken.

Despite such an apparently pessimistic outlook, I would suggest, as a working hypothesis, the following scenario for the emergence of the Upper Palaeolithic in the south west of France: following a procedure which has yet to be defined more precisely, the Mousterian of Acheulean Tradition type B, in becoming Châtelperronian, developed a laminar technology as a basis for the production of new types of tools which had a very important influence on techniques of subsistence, essentially on hunting strategies (Rigaud 1998), but also upon symbolic expression. Such a transformation occurred in an MAT/Châtelperronian province independently of the Aurignacian technology, which arrived in this area only after the Châtelperronian apogee. In this way, the peopling of western Europe by *Homo sapiens sapiens* was completed several millennia after their arrival in Cantabria and Catalona.

References

Arambourou, R. & Jude, P.E. (i964). *Le gisement de la Chèvre à Bourdeilles*. Dordogne: Périgueux, 132 p.

Bordes, F. (1968). La Question Périgordienne. In *La Préhistoire problèmes et tendances*. Paris: CNRS, pp. 59–70.

Bordes, J.-G. (1998). l'Aurignacien 0 en Périgord : analyse des données. Un exemple d'application d'une méthode de quantification des remontages d'intérêt stratigraphique : Caminade est,

Layer G. *Diplôme d'Etudes approfondies, Université Bordeaux 1, 1998 manuscript.*

Bordes, F. & Labrot, J. (1967). La stratigraphie du Roc de Combe (Lot) et ses implications. *Bulletin de la Sociètè Préhistorique Française.* **64**, 15–28.

Champagne, F. & Espitalié, R. (1967). La stratigraphie du Piage: note préliminaire. *Bulletin de la Société Préhistorique Française.* **64**, 29–34.

Champagne, F. & Espitalié R. (1981). Le Piage, site préhistorique du Lot. Paris, *Mémoire de la Société Préhistorique Française.* **15**, 205p.

Demars, P.-Y. & Hublin J.-J. (1989). La transition neandertaliens/ Homme de type moderne en Europe occidentale; aspects paléontologiques et culturels. In (M. Otte, Ed) *L'Homme de Néandertal, Vol. 7: L'extinction,* pp. 23–27. Liège: ERAUL.

Demars, P.-Y. (1990). Les interstratifications entre Aurignacien et Châtelperronien à Roc de Combe et au Piage (Lot). Approvisionnement en matières premières et position chronologique. In (C. Farizy, Ed) *Paléolithique moyen récent et Paléolithique supérieur ancien en Europe. Actes du Colloqe international de Nemours 9–11 mai 1988. Mémoire du Musée d'Ile de France, n°3,* pp. 235–239. Nemours: APRAIF.

Guilbaud, M., Backer A., & Lévêque F. (1994). Technological differentiation associated with the Saint Césaire neandertal. *Préhistoire Européenne.* **6**,187–196.

Laplace (G.) 1970. Les niveaux Aurignaciens et l'hypothèse du synthétotype. In *l'Homme de Cro-magnon,* pp. 141–164, Centre de Recherche Anthropologique, préhistorique et ethnographique. Conseil de la recherche en Algérie, Paris, Arts et Métiers graphiques.

Laville, H. (1981). Les dépôts paléolithiques du Piage à Fajoles (Lot), signification climatique et chronologie. In (F. Champagne & R. Espitalié, Eds) *Le Piage, site préhistorique du Lot,* pp.147–157. Paris: Mémoire de la Société Préhistorique française, n° 15, 205p.

Lévêque, F. & Vandermeersch, B. (1980). Découverte de restes humains dans un niveau castelperronien à Saint Césaire (Charente Maritime). *Comptes rendus de l'Académie des Sciences de Paris,* Série **2**, 291: 187–189.

Meignen, L. (1994). Le Paléolithique moyen au Proche Orient : Le Phénomène laminaire. Les industries laminaires au Paléolithgique moyen. *Actes de la table ronde Villeneuve d'Ascq, 1991 CNRS Ed. Dossiers de Documentation Archéologique,* **18**, 125–160.

Mellars, P. (1989). Technological changes across the Middle-Upper Palaeolithic transition: Economic, social and cognitive perspectives. In (P. Mellars and C.Stringer, Eds.), *The Human Revolution,* pp. 339–365. Princeton University Press.

Pelegrin, J. (1995). *Technologie lithique: une méthode appliquée à l'étude de deux séries du Périgordien ancien: Roc de Combe Layer 8, La Côte niveau III.* Doctoral diss. University of Peru.

Peyrony, D. (1943). Le gisement du Roc de Combe Capelle. *Bulletin de la Société Historique et Archéologique du Périgord.* 158–172.

Revillon, S. & Tuffreau, A. (1994).Valeur et signification du débitage laminaire des séries lithiques du gisement paléolithique de Seclin (Nord). In (CNRS, Ed) *Les industries laminaires au Paléolithique moyen.* pp. 19–44. *Actes de la table ronde Villeneuve d'Ascq, 1991. Dossiers de Documentation Archéologique, n° 18.*

Sonneville-Bordes, D. de, (1960). *Le Paléolithique supérieur en Périgord.* Bordeaux. Delmas, 558 p.

Tuffreau, A. (1984). Le débitage de lames dans le Paléolithique inférieur et moyen de la France septentrionale. *Préhistoire de la Pierre Taillée,* 2. *IIIe table ronde de technologie lithique meudon-bellevue, Octobre 1982. Cercle de Recherches et d'Etudes Préhistorique, p.* 53.

5

Châtelperronian Chronology and the Case for Neanderthal/Modern Human 'Acculturation' in Western Europe

Paul Mellars

Introduction

With the recent confirmation that the European Neanderthals became extinct without leaving any discernible descendants (Krings *et al.* 1997) there has been renewed interest in the mechanisms by which this process of population replacement of the Neanderthal by anatomically modern humans took place and, in particular, the extent of any contact or interaction between the two populations. Most recent opinion has favoured the view that in many parts of Europe there was a prolonged period of around 5000 years of coexistence between the two populations (probably within separate but adjacent territories) and that this is reflected in a substantial degree of 'acculturation' in the archaeological records of the final Neanderthal populations as reflected for example by the presence of bone and ivory tools, personal ornaments and extensive use of red ochre in the 'Châtelperronian' levels at Arcy-sur-Cure in Central France (Harrold 1989; Demars 1990; Graves 1991; Stringer & Gamble 1993; Djindjian 1993; Kozlowski 1993; Hublin *et al.* 1996; Mellars 1989, 1998).

Recently this view has been challenged by d'Errico *et al.* (1998) who argue instead for an extremely rapid replacement of the Neanderthal by anatomically modern populations in most areas of Europe, with apparently no discernible evidence for contact, behavioural interaction or 'acculturation' between the two groups. This view in turn has radical implications for the nature of the social and cognitive contrasts between the two populations and for the demographic or other mechanisms by which the Neanderthals became extinct (Zubrow 1989; Mellars 1998). The aim of the present paper is to review the available data on the chronology of the final Neanderthal populations in western France and the adjacent areas of northern Spain, and to reassess the available evidence for the extent of the chronological overlap between the late Neanderthal and early anatomically modern populations (see also Mellars 1999).

Archaeological context

There is now fairly general agreement on the basic patterns of the archaeological and associated human skeletal records associated with the transition from Neanderthal to anatomically modern populations in western Europe. The situation is most clearly reflected and best documented in the extensively researched areas of France and northern Spain. Here it is generally accepted that the earliest archaeological traces of anatomically modern populations are represented by the so called 'Aurignacian' industries – industries which are clearly intrusive in western Europe, and show evidence for a whole range of behavioural innovations which are not found in the preceding Middle Palaeolithic or Mousterian industries – including the extensive use of bone, antler and ivory implements, perforated animal teeth and other forms of personal ornamentation, long distance trading of decorative sea shells, and the earliest evidence of several forms of both representational and abstract art and musical instruments (Djindjian 1993; Kozlowski 1993; Mellars 1992; Gambier 1993; White 1993). These industries have recently been dated at a number of sites in both northeastern and northwestern Spain (L'Arbreda, Abric Romaní, Reclau Viver and El Castillo) by both radiocarbon-accelerator and uranium-series dating to around 38–40 ka in radiocarbon terms (Bischoff *et al.* 1989, 1994; Hedges *et al.* 1994; Cabrera-Valdés *et al.* 1996).

Recent debate has focused on the significance and chronology of the so-called Châtelperronian industries. These industries occur over broadly the same geographical range as the Aurignacian industries (principally in central and western France, with rare outliers in northern Spain) but reveal a technology which contrasts sharply with that of the Aurignacian and is clearly rooted in the immediately preceding late Neanderthal Mousterian technologies of the same region – specifically those of the 'Mousterian of Acheulian tradition' group (Harrold 1989; Mellars 1989,

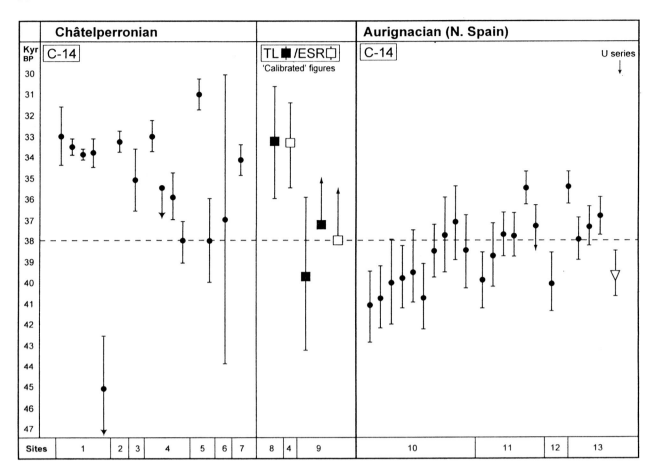

Figure 5.1: Absolute age determinations for Châtelperronian sites in southwest France and northern Spain, and for early Aurignacian sites in northern Spain. Note that the thermoluminescence (TL), electron spin resonance (ESR) and uranium series dates have been 'calibrated' to radiocarbon terms by the subtraction of 3,000 years as implied by the calibration studies of Bard et al. (1990, 1993) and Laj et al. (1996) The 'younger than' dates for the Châtelperronian level at Le Moustier are based on the TL and ESR ages for the underlying Mousterian levels on the site. It will be seen that while virtually all the dates for the Châtelperronian levels are younger than 38 ka, most of the dates for Spanish early Aurignacian levels lie between 38 and 40 ka. Note that if the discrepancy between radiocarbon and 'absolute' dates were greater than 3,000 years, this would make the TL and ESR dates for the Châtelperronian levels even younger than those shown here. The sites are as follows: 1. Arcy-sur-Cure; 2. Les Cottés; 3. Camiac; 4. Combe-Saunière; 5. Roc-de-Combe; 6. Cueva Morín; 7. Labeko Kova; 8. Saint-Césaire; 9. Le Moustier; 10. El Castillo; 11. L'Arbreda; 12. Reclau Viver; 13. Abric Romaní. For further details of samples and dates, see Table 5.1.

1996, 1998; Pelegrin 1995; d'Errico *et al.* 1998). Skeletal discoveries at both Saint-Césaire in western France and Arcy-sur-Cure in central France reveal beyond doubt that the Châtelperronian was manufactured by typically Neanderthal hominids (Lévêque & Vandermeersch 1980; Hublin *et al.* 1996). Significantly, however, many of the Châtelperronian industries show a number of typically Upper Palaeolithic features, analogous to those of the Aurignacian, including increased use of blade technology, some typically Upper Palaeolithic stone tool forms (notably end scrapers and burins) and in at least one well documented site (the Grotte du Renne at Arcy-sur-Cure) carefully shaped bone and ivory tools and a range of animal tooth pendants (Leroi-Gourhan & Leroi-Gourhan 1965; Baffier & Julien 1990; Pelegrin 1995; d'Errico *et al.* 1998).

The central issue is whether these characteristically Upper Palaeolithic features in the late Neanderthal Châtel-perronian industries were simply 'copied' or 'borrowed' from contemporaneous and adjacent Aurignacian popul-ations, or whether they reflect a totally independent, autonomous invention of Upper Palaeolithic technology and related 'symbolic' expression among the final Neanderthal populations of western Europe (d'Errico *et al.* 1998: 36). Clearly, the chronological relationship of the Châtelperronian to the Aurignacian is fundamental and pivotal to this debate.

In view of the apparently clear and undisputed evidence that typically Aurignacian industries were being produced in northern Spain by c. 40 ka (radiocarbon dated), the whole of the present issue hinges on whether the Châtelperronian industries are essentially contemporaneous with the early Aurignacian industries – as most recent workers have assumed – or whether they are entirely earlier than the Aurignacian, as recently argued by d'Errico *et al*. The purpose of what follows is to show that the totality of the current chronological evidence strongly favours the former view, and conflicts with the hypothesis of a clear chronological separation between the two technologies.

1. From the pattern of radiocarbon dates dates displayed in Figure 5.1, it is immediately clear that the available dates for Châtelperronian levels in France and northern Spain are almost entirely younger than 40 ka, and are concentrated mainly between 38 and 33 ka – with dates within this range now available for 16 separate samples from seven different sites. A number of new AMS radiocarbon dates recently secured by the Oxford radiocarbon laboratory for the Châtelperronian levels at the rock shelter site of Combe-Saunière in the Isle valley (Dordogne) of southwest France confirm this pattern (Mellars *et al*., n.d.) including one measurement produced by the 'tripeptide' extraction technique, which has been developed specifically to eliminate contamination effects by recent, intrusive carbon (Van Klinken *et al*. 1994). The only measurement which departs strikingly from this pattern is the single date of 45.1±2.8 ka based on a single bone fragment from the middle Châtelperronian level (level IX) at Arcy-sur-Cure. This measurement is more than 10 ka older than six other radiocarbon measurements (by both conventional and AMS dating) for the Châtelperronian levels on the site and, as the radiocarbon laboratory has already suggested (Hedges *et al*. 1994), almost certainly represents a stratigraphically misplaced sample derived from the underlying Mousterian levels on the site. The contrast between these dates for the Châtelperronian and the available dates for early Aurignacan levels in northern Spain is clearly apparent from Figure 5.1. While all except one of the 16 dates for Châtelperronian levels are younger than 38.5 ka, 11 of the 21 dates for the Spanish early Aurignacian levels lie between 38.5 and 41 ka – a pattern which clearly supports the view that the appearance of the Aurignacian technology in western Europe, and the seemingly associated appearance of anatomically modern populations, precedes most if not all the known occurrences of Châtelperronian industries in this region.

2. Absolute age measurements by other dating methods fully support this conclusion (see Table 5.1, Figure 5.1). Here it must be recalled that there is now clear evidence that radiocarbon dates in the 30–40 ka age span substantially underestimate the true (calendrical) ages of samples in comparison with those of other chronometric methods, as a result of the enrichment of the 14C component of the atmosphere over this

Table 5.1: Absolute age measurements for Châtelperronian and early Aurignacian levels in France and northern Spain.

CHÂTELPERRONIAN: C14 Dates

Arcy-sur-Cure (Grotte du Renne)

Layer VIII	GrN-1736	33,500±400	Vogel & Waterbolk 1963
"	GrN-1742	33,860±250	"
"	Ly-2163	33,000±1400	Delibrias & Fontugne 1990
Layer IX	OxA-3465	45,100±2800	Hedges *et al*. 1994
Layer X	OxA-3464	33,820±720	"
"	GrN-4251	25,500±380	Vogel & Waterbolk 1967
"	GrN-4216	24,500±360	"

Les Cottés

Layer G	GrN-4333	33,300±500	Vogel & Waterbolk 1967

Camiac

Layer D	Ly-1104	35,100±1500	Delibrias & Fontugne 1990; Guadelli & Laville 1990

Combe Saunière

Layer X	OxA-6503	35,900±1100	Mellars *et al*. n.d.
	(tripeptide)	38,100±1000	"
	OxA-6504	33,000±900	"

Roc-de-Combe

Layer X	OxA-1264	31,000±750	Hedges *et al*. 1990
"	OxA-1443	38,000±2000	"

Brassempouy

Layer 2g	Gif-8172	31,690±810	Bon *et al*. 1998

Cueva Morín

Layer 10	SI-951	36,950±6777	Harrold 1989

Labeko Kova

Châtel-perronian	Ua-3324	34,215±1265	Barandiarán Maetzu 1996

CHÂTELPERRONIAN: TL/ESR Dates

Saint-Césaire (TL)

Layer EJOP sup.		33,700±5400	Mercier *et al*. 1991, 1993
		35,600±4600	"
		36,600±5000	"
		36,600±4900	"
		37,400±5200	"
		38,200±5300	"
	Average:	36,300±2700	"

Combe-Saunière (ESR)

Layer X (Châtelperronian)	36,400±2500 (average)	Mellars *et al*. n.d.

Le Moustier (TL/ESR)

Layer K (Châtelperronian) (TL)	42,600±3700 (average)	Valladas *et al*. 1986
Layer J (Mousterian) (TL)	40,300±2600 (average)	"
Layer I (Mousterian) (TL)	40,900±5000 (average)	"
Layer H (MTA Type B) (TL)	42,500±2000 (average)	"
Layer H (MTA Type B)(ESR)	41,000±2600 (average)	Mellars & Grün 1991

Table 5.1: continued

AURIGNACIAN: Northern Spain

El Castillo

Layer 18b1	AA-2406	38,500±1800	Cabrera-Valdés and Bischoff 1989	
Layer 18b2	AA-2407	37,700±1800	"	
"	OxA-2473	37,100±2200	Hedges *et al.* 1994	
"	OxA-2474	38,500±1300	"	
"	OxA-2475	40,700±1600	"	
Layer 18c	OxA-2476	40,700±1500	"	
"	OxA-2477	41,100±1700	"	
"	AA-2405	40,000±2100	"	
"	OxA-2478	39,800±1400	"	
"	GifA-89147	39,500±2000	Cabrera-Valdés *et al.* 1996	

L'Arbreda

Layer H	AA-3779	37,700±1000	Bischoff *et al.* 1989
"	AA-3780	37,700±1000	"
"	AA-3781	39,900±1300	"
"	AA-3782	38,700±1200	"
"	OxA-3729	37,340±820	Hedges *et al.* 1994
"	OxA-3730	35,480±820	"

Reclau Viver

Layer III	OxA-3727	40,000±1400	Hedges *et al.* 1994

Abric Romaní

Layer A	AA-8037A	35,400±810	Bischoff *et al.* 1994
"	AA-8037B	37,900±1000	"
"	AA-7395	37,290±990	"
"	AA-6608	36,740±920	"
"	U- series	42,600±1100	"

AURIGNACIAN: Southwest France

La Rochette

Layer 7	GrN-4362	36,000±450	Vogel & Waterbolk 1967

La Ferrassie

Layer K6	Gif-4279	>35,000	Delibrias & Fontugne 1990
"	GrN-5751	33,220±570	"

Combe-Saunière

Layer VIII	OxA-6507	34,000±850	Mellars *et al.* n.d.

Roc-de-Combe

Layer 7b	OxA-1262	33,400±1100	Hedges *et al.* 1990
Layer 7c	OxA-1263	34,800±1200	"

Abri Pataud

Layer 12	GrN-4327	33,000±500	Vogel & Waterbolk 1967
Layer 14	GrN-4507	34,250±675	"
"	GrN-4720	33,330±410	"
"	GrN-4610	33,300±760	"

Le Flagéolet

Layer XI	OxA-598	33,800±1800	Mellars *et al.* 1987

period – probably by a factor of around 3000–4000 years (Bard *et al.* 1990, 1993; Laj *et al.* 1996). When this displacement is taken into account, all of the available dates for Châtelperronian levels by these other (non-radiocarbon) dating methods point to the same chronological pattern as that of the radiocarbon dates (see Table 5.1). A series of six thermolumin-

escence dates on burnt flint samples from the upper Châtelperronian layer (associated with the partial Neanderthal skeleton) at Saint-Césaire ranged between 33.7±5.4 ka and 38.2±5.3 ka in 'uncalibrated' terms, and converge on a central figure of around 36.3±2.7 ka (Mercier *et al.* 1991). Translated into radiocarbon terms this is equivalent to a 14C age of around 33.3±3 ka. Similarly, a series of six ESR measurements on animal teeth recently obtained for the Châtelperronian levels at Combe-Saunière centre once again on *c.* 36.4±2.5 ka – again equivalent to *c.* 33.4±3 ka in radiocarbon terms (Mellars *et al.* n.d.). Equally if not more significant is the TL dating of the Mousterian levels which clearly underlie the Châtelperronian levels at Saint-Césaire to *c.* 40 ka (*c.* 37 ka radiocarbon) and the dating of similar late Mousterian levels at Le Moustier (by both TL and ESR techniques) to *c.* 40–41 ka (*c.* 37–38 ka radiocarbon) (Mercier *et al.* 1991; Valladas *et al.* 1986; Mellars & Grün 1991). Unless all of these these mutually consistent age determinations, by two different dating methods, are grossly underestimating the true ages of the associated archaeological levels, they confirm that the whole of the time span of the Châtelperronian industries at least in the 'classic' region of south-western France must be younger than *c.* 38–40 ka in radiocarbon terms. Certainly, this dating leaves little scope for pushing the whole of the Châtelperronian – including the long stratified sequences at Quinçay, Arcy-sur-Cure and elsewhere to before 40 ka in radiocarbon terms, as the dating proposed recently by d'Errico *et al.* would imply.

3. As a further, direct confirmation of the same pattern it should be recalled that three and possibly four separate sites in France and northern Spain have been reported to show a direct interstratification of Châtelperronian and early Aurignacian occupations in the same stratigraphic succession – at Le Piage and the Roc-de-Combe in the Lot region of southwestern France, El Pendo in Cantabria, and probably at Châtelperron itself in northern Burgundy (Demars 1996; White 1998). Unless all of these sequences have been subjected to some strange geological disruptions, they provide further unmistakable evidence of a significant chronological overlap between the time ranges of the Châtelperronian and Aurignacian industries in these regions. It should be recalled that exactly the same conclusion was drawn over 15 years ago by Leroyer and Leroi-Gourhan (1983) on the basis of the climatic and palaeobotanical associations of the two groups of industries (see also Leroyer 1988).

4. Finally, it is interesting to compare the available radiocarbon and other age measurements for the earliest Aurignacian levels in northern Spain with those from the adjacent areas of southwestern France. As shown in Figure 5.2 this points clearly to a rather

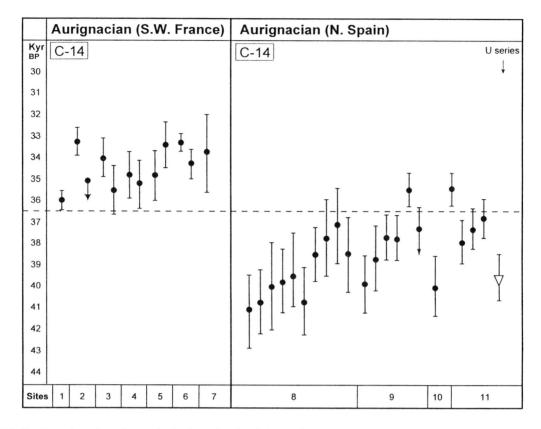

Figure 5.2: Radiocarbon dates for early Aurignacian levels in southwest France (left) and northern Spain (right). The sites are as follows: 1. La Rochette; 2. La Ferrassie; 3. Combe-Saunière; 4. Abri Castanet; 5. Roc-de-Combe; 6. Abri Pataud; 7. Le Flagéolet; 8. El Castillo; 9. l'Arbreda; 10. Reclau Viver; 11. Abric Romaní. For further details of samples and dates, see Table 5.1. Provisional unpublished dates for the Abri Castanet were kindly provided by J. Pelegrin, R. White, H. Valladas and N. Mercier.

later appearance of Aurignacian technologies – and presumably the associated anatomically modern populations – in southwestern France than in northern Spain, with dates for the earliest Aurignacian in the former area centering on *c*. 34–36 ka, while those in the latter area centre on 38–40 ka. The possible reasons for the delayed penetration of anatomically modern populations into the southwest French region have been discussed elsewhere, and were probably related partly to different climatic and ecological conditions in the two areas and (above all) to the exceptionally high population densities of the later Neanderthal populations in the southwest French region, clearly implied by the exceptionally high concentration of late Mousterian sites in this region (Mellars 1996, 1998). It is precisely in this region that we also find the densest concentration of Châtelperronian sites – approximately 90 percent of the known Châtelperronian occurrences (d'Errico *et al.* 1998; Pelegrin 1995). This confirms that this was indeed one of the latest regions of survival of the final Neanderthal populations in Europe, and suggests that the ability of the two populations to coexist over a period of apparently several thousand years was

largely due to the occupation of ecologically discrete territories – though probably with occasional episodes of interpenetration of the two territories in response to short term ecological or demographic fluctuations, as the occasional cases of interstratification of Châtelperronian and Aurignacian levels at the three sites referred to above would imply.

Conclusions

From the totality of the dating evidence discussed above – including the results of the new radiocarbon and ESR dating at Combe-Saunière and other sites – there can be no serious doubt that the time ranges of the Châtelperronian and early Aurignacian industries in France and northern Spain overlapped by a period of several thousand years, implying a similar overlap between the final Neanderthal and earliest, intrusive anatomically modern populations in these areas. The most important implication of this dating is that it leaves entirely open the possibility that the appearance of a range of distinctively 'modern' behavioural features among the late Neanderthal populations of western Europe – including the presence of simple bone and ivory tools and perforated pendants at Arcy-sur-

Cure was the product of some form of contact and interaction between the two populations, regardless of whether we refer to this as 'acculturation', or by some other term. The alternative is that after a period of around 200,000 years of typically Middle Palaeolithic technology and behaviour, the local Neanderthal populations in western Europe independently, coincidentally and almost miraculously 'invented' these distinctive features of Upper Palaeolithic technology at almost exactly the same time as anatomically and behaviourally modern populations are known to have been expanding across Europe (Kozlowski 1993; Mellars 1992; Gambier 1993; d'Errico et al. 1998: 36). It should be recalled here that we are speaking of not just one or two Upper Palaeolithic features, but a range of around ten or a dozen behavioural innovations, including increased blade technology, abundant and typical forms of end scrapers and burins, several forms of bone or ivory points, regularly notched bones, several forms of perforated or grooved pendants (including a preferential use of fox canine teeth for pendants), bone tubes, ivory rings, and liberal use of powdered red ochre scattered across living areas (d'Errico et al. 1998). In purely statistical terms, the entirely independent evolution of all these features would seem to demand an extraordinary degree of convergent and coincidental cultural development – in scientific terms perhaps not the most economical hypothesis. Certainly if the independent-development hypothesis were substantiated, this would have profound implications for our understanding of both the social and cognitive dimensions of Neanderthal populations, and of the entire processes by which typically 'modern' behavioural patterns emerged (cf. Bar-Yosef 1998).

There are of course several different ways in which various forms of contact and interaction between the intrusive anatomically modern and resident Neanderthal populations could be visualized (Graves 1991; d'Errico et al. 1998; Mellars 1998) and these allow for a range of different perspectives on the relative cognitive and intellectual capacities of the two populations. If we allow for the prolonged period of genetic separation of the Neanderthal and modern lineages implied by the recent DNA evidence (Krings et al. 1997), the possibility of some significant divergences in neurological structures between the two populations can hardly be ruled out. One could also argue that the survival of the Aurignacian and Châtelperronian industries as clearly identifiable and sharply separated technological traditions over a period of several thousand years must imply some fundamental barrier to communication and interbreeding between the two groups, which prevented their total assimilation and integration over this span of time. This would be fully consistent with recent suggestions that the Neanderthal and anatomically modern humans were biologically separate species (Stringer & McKie 1996), and also with the mitochnodrial DNA evidence for the clear genetic differences between the two groups (Krings et al. 1997).

At the same time it implies a very high degree of adapation of the Neanderthal groups to the specific environments of western Europe – which is hardly surprising in view of the 200,000 years or so of essentially continuous Neanderthal occupation in the area under a range of fluctuating environmental conditions (Stringer & Gamble 1993; Mellars 1996). Clearly, the issues of chronology discussed above are central to all of the current debates over the character of the final Neanderthal populations in Europe, their relationships to the incoming anatomically modern populations, and their eventual demise.

References

Baffier, D. & Julien, M. (1990). L'outillage en os des niveaux châtelperroniens d'Arcy-sur-Cure. In (C. Farizy, Ed.) *Paléolithique moyen récent et Paléolithique supérieur ancien en Europe*, pp. 329–34. Nemours: A.P.R.A.I.F. (Mémoires du Musée de Préhistoire d'Ile de France, no. 3).

Bar-Yosef, O. (1998). On the nature of transitions: the Middle to Upper Palaeolithic and the Neolithic revolution. *Cambridge Archaeological Journal* 8, 141–163.

Barandiarán Maetzú, I. (1996). Le Paléolithique supérieur au Pays Basque et dans le bassin de l'Ebre (1990–1995). In (M. Otte, Ed.) *Le Paléolithique Supérieur Européen: Bilan Quinquennial 1991–1996* , pp. 319–322. Liege: ERAUL.

Bard, E., Hamelin, B., Fairbanks, R.G. & Zindler, A. (1990). Calibration of the 14C timescale over the past 30,000 years using mass spectrometric U-Th ages from Barbados corals. *Nature* 354, 405–410.

Bard, E., Arnold, M., Fairbanks, R.G. & Hamelin, B. (1993). 230Th-234U and 14C ages obtained by mass spectrometry on corals. *Radiocarbon* 35, 191–199.

Bischoff, J.L., Ludwig, K., Garcia, J.F., Carbonell, E., Vaquero, M., Stafford, T. & Jull, A. (1994). Dating of the basal Aurignacian sandwich at Abric Romaní (Catalunya, Spain) by radiocarbon and uranium-series. *Journal of Archaeological Science* 21, 541–551.

Bischoff, J.L., Soler, N., Maroto, J. & Julia,R. (1989). Abrupt Mousterian/Aurignacian boundary at ca. 40 ka bp: accelerator 14C dates from l'Arbreda Cave (Catalunya, Spain). *Journal of Archaeological Science* 16, 563–576.

Bon, F., Ferrier, C., Gambier, D. & Gardère, P. (1998). Gisement de Brassempouy (Landes): les recherches de 1995 à 1997, bilan et perspectives. *Bulletin de la Société Borda*, 203–222.

Cabrera-Valdés, V. & Bischoff, J.L. (1989). Accelerator 14C dates for early Upper Palaeolithic (basal Aurignacian) at El Castillo Cave (Spain). *Journal of Archaeological Science* 16, 577–584.

Cabrera-Valdés, V., Valladas, H., Bernaldo de Quiros, F. & Gomez, M.H. (1996). La transition Paléolithique moyen-Paléolithique supérieur a El Castillo (Cantabrie): nouvelles datations par le carbone-14. *Comptes Rendus de l'Académie des Sciences de Paris* 322 (Ser. IIa) 1093–1098.

Delibrias, G. & Fontugne, M. (1990). Datations des gisements de l'Aurignacien et du Moustérien en France. In (C. Farizy, Ed.) *Paléolithique moyen récent et Paléolithique supérieur ancien en Europe*, pp. 39–42. Nemours: A.P.R.A.I.F. (Mémoires du Musée de Préhistoire d'Ile de France, no. 3).

Demars, P.Y. (1990). Les interstratifications entre Aurignacien et Châtelperronien à Roc-de-Combe et au Piage (Lot): approvisionnement en matières premières et position chronologique. In (C. Farizy, Ed.) *Paléolithique Moyen Récent et Paléolithique Supérieur Ancien en Europe*, pp. 235–240. Nemours: A.P.R.A.I.F. (Mémoires du Musée de Préhistoire d'Ile de France, no. 3).

Demars, P.Y. (1996). Demographie et occupation de l'espace au Paléolithique supérieur et au Mésolithique en France. *Préhistoire Européenne* **8**: 3–26.

D'Errico, F., Zilhao, J., Julien, M., Baffier, D. & Pelegrin, J. (1998). Neanderthal acculturation in western Europe? A critical review of the evidence and its interpretation. *Current Anthropology* **39**, S1–S44.

Djindjian, F. (1993). Les origines du peuplement Aurignacien en Europe. In (L. Banesz & J.K. Kozlowski, Eds.) *Aurignacien en Europe et au Proche Orient* , pp. 136–154. Bratislava: Acts of 12th International Congress of Prehistoric and Protohistoric Sciences.

Gambier, D. (1993). Les hommes modernes du debut du Paléolithique supérieur en France: bilan des données anthropologiques et perspectives. In (V. Cabrera-Valdés, Ed.) *El Origen del Hombre Moderno en el Suroeste de Europa*, pp. 409–430. Madrid: Universidad Nacional de Educacion a Distancia.

Graves, P. (1991). New models and metaphors for the Neanderthal debate. *Current Anthropology.* **32**, 513–541.

Guadelli, J.-L. & Laville, H. (1990). L'environnement climatique de la fin du Moustérien à Combe-Grenal et à Camiac. Confrontation des données naturalistes et implications. In (C. Farizy, Ed.) *Paléolithique moyen récent et Paléolithique supérieur ancien en Europe*, pp. 43–48. Nemours: A.P.R.A.I.F. (Mémoires du Musée de Préhistoire d'Ile de France, no. 3).

Harrold, F.B., (1989). Mousterian, Châtelperronian, and Early Aurignacian in Western Europe: continuity or discontinuity? In (P. Mellars & C. Stringer, Eds.) *The Human Revolution: behavioural and biological perspectives on the origins of modern humans*, pp. 677–713. Princeton University Press.

Hedges, R.E.M, Housley, R.A., Law, I.A. & Bronk, C.R. (1990). Radiocarbon dates from the Oxford AMS system: Archaeometry datelist 10. *Archaeometry* **32**, 101–108.

Hedges, R.E.M, Housley, R.A., Bronk-Ramsey, C. & Van Klinken, G.J. (1994). Radiocarbon dates from the Oxford AMS system: Archaeometry datelist 18. *Archaeometry* **36**, 337–374.

Hublin, J-J., Spoor, F., Braun, M., Zonneveld, F. & Condemi, S. (1996). A late Neanderthal associated with Upper Palaeolithic artefacts. *Nature* **381**, 224–226.

Kozlowski, J.K. (1993). L'Aurignacien en Europe et au Proche Orient. In (L. Banesz & J.K. Kozlowski, Eds.) *Aurignacien en Europe et au Proche Orient*, pp. 283–291. Bratislava: Acts of 12th International Congress of Prehistoric and Protohistoric Sciences.

Krings, M., Stone, A., Schmitz, R.W., Krainitzki, H., Stoneking, M. & Paabo, S. (1997). Neandertal DNA sequences and the origin of modern humans. *Cell* **90**, 19–30.

Laj, C., Mazaud, A. & Duplessy, J-C. (1996). Geomagnetic intensity and 14 C abundance in the atmosphere and ocean during the past 50 kyr. *Geophysical Research Letters* **23**, 2045–2048.

Leroi-Gourhan, Arl. & Leroi-Gourhan, A. (1965). Chronologie des grottes d'Arcy-sur-Cure. *Gallia-Préhistoire* 7, 1–64.

Leroyer, C. (1988). Des occupations castelperroniennes et aurignaciennes dans leur cadre chrono-climatique. In (M. Otte, Ed.) *L'Homme de Néandertal*, vol. 8., pp. 103–108. Etudes et Recherches Archéologiques de l'Université de Liège 35.

Leroyer, C. & Leroi-Gourhan, A. (1983). Problèmes de chronologie: le castelperronien et l'aurignacien. *Bulletin de la Société Préhistorique Française* **80**, 41–44.

Lévêque, F. & Vandermeersch, B. (1980). Découverte de restes humains dans un niveau castelperronien à Saint-Césaire (Charente-Maritime). *Comptes Rendus de l'Académie des Sciences de Paris* (series 2) 291, 187–189.

Mellars, P.A. (1985). The ecological basis of social complexity in the Upper Paleolithic of southwestern France. In (T.D. Price & J.A. Brown, Eds.) *Prehistoric Hunter-gatherers: the emergence of cultural complexity*, 271–297. Orlando: Academic Press.

Mellars, P.A. (1989). Major issues in the emergence of modern humans. *Current Anthropology* **30**, 349–385.

Mellars, P.A. (1992). Archaeology and the population-dispersal hypothesis of modern human origins in Europe. In (M.J. Aitken, C.B. Stringer & P.A. Mellars, Eds.) *The Origin of Modern Humans and the Impact of Chronometric Dating*, pp. 225–234. London: Royal Society (Philosophical Transactions of the Royal Society, series B, 337, no. 1280).

Mellars, P.A. (1996). *The Neanderthal Legacy: an archaeological perspective from Western Europe.* Princeton University Press.

Mellars, P.A. (1998). The impact of climatic changes on the demography of late Neanderthal and early anatomically modern populations in Europe. In (T. Akazawa, K. Aoki & O. Bar-Yosef, Eds.) *Neandertals and Modern Humans in Western Asia*, pp. 493–507. New York: Plenum.

Mellars, P.A. (1999). The Neanderthal problem: replies to d'Errico and colleagues. *Current Anthropology* **40** (in press).

Mellars, P.A., Bricker, H.M., Gowlett, J.A.J. & Hedges, R.E.M. (1987). Radiocarbon accelerator dating of French Upper Palaeolithic sites. *Current Anthropology* **28**, 128–133.

Mellars, P. and Grün, R. (1991). A comparison of the electron spin resonance and thermoluminescence dating methods: the results of ESR dating at Le Moustier (France). *Cambridge Archaeological Journal* **1**, 269–276.

Mellars, P.A., Zhou, L.P., Pettitt, P., Hedges, R.E.M. & Geneste, -M. (n.d.). Electron spin resonance and radiocarbon-accelerator dating of Combe-Saunière, Dordogne. In preparation.

Mercier, N., Valladas, H., Joron, J-L., Reyss, J-L., Lévêque, F. & Vandermeersch B. (1991). Thermoluminescence dating of the late Neanderthal remains from Saint-Césaire. *Nature* **351**, 737–739.

Mercier, N., Valladas, H., Joron, J-L., & Reyss, J-L. (1993). Thermoluminescence dating of the prehistoric site of La Roche à Pierrot, Saint-Césaire. In (F. Lévêque, M.A. Backer and M. Gilbaud, Eds.) *Context of a late Neandertal*, pp. 15–22. Madison: Prehistory Press.

Pelegrin, J. (1995). *Technologie lithique: Le Châtelperronien de Roc-de-Combe (Lot) et de la Côte (Dordogne).* Paris: CNRS.

Stringer, C. & Gamble, C. (1993). *In Search of the Neanderthals: solving the puzzle of human origins.* London: Thames & Hudson.

Stringer, C.B. & McKie, R. 1996. *African Exodus: the origins of modern humanity.* London: Jonathan Cape.

Valladas, H., Geneste, J-M., Joron, J-L. & Chadelle, J-P. (1986). Thermoluminescence dating of Le Moustier (Dordogne, France). *Nature* **322**, 452–454.

Van Klinken, G.J., Bowles, A.D. & Hedges, R.E.M. (1994). Radiocarbon dating of peptides isolated from contaminated fossil bone collagen by collagenase digestion and reversed-phase chromatography. *Geochimica et Cosmochimica Acta* **58**, 2543–2551.

Vogel, J.C. & Waterbolk, H.T. (1963). Groningen radiocarbon dates IV. *Radiocarbon* **5**, 163–202.

Vogel, J.C. & Waterbolk, H.T. (1967). Groningen radiocarbon dates VII. *Radiocarbon* **9**, 107–155.

White, R. (1993). Technological and social dimensions of "Aurignacian age" body ornaments across Europe. In (H. Knecht, A. Pike-Tay and R. White, Eds.) *Before Lascaux: the complex record of the early Upper Paleolithic.*, pp. 277–300. Boca Raton: CRC Press.

White, R. (1998). Comment on F. d'Errico et al. 'Neanderthal acculturation in western Europe? A critical review of the evidence and its interpretation'. *Current Anthropology* **39**, S30–S32.

Zubrow, E. (1989). The demographic modeling of Neanderthal extinction. In (P. Mellars & C. Stringer, Eds.) The Human Revolution: behavioural and biological perspectives on the Origins of modern humans, pp. 212–231. Princeton Univ. Press.

6

The Transition from the Final Acheulian to the Middle Palaeolithic in the South of the Iberian Peninsula

F. Giles Pacheco, A. Santiago Perez, J. Mª. Gutierrez Lopez, E. Mata Almonte & L. Aguilera Rodriguez

Introduction

The chronological framework of this paper is the final Middle Pleistocene (Riss and Riss/Würm Interglacial) to the beginning of the Upper Pleniglacial, covering Oxygen Isotope Stages 7, 6 and 5 between 250 and 70 Ka, (Shackleton & Opdyke 1973).

A palaeoanthropological problem within this time-frame is the question of the relationship between technological changes and biological replacement. The recent discoveries at TD6 and the Sima de los Huesos at Atapuerca have led to the proposal of the species *Homo antecessor* as the last common ancestor of the Neanderthals and Modern Humans, in an evolutionary line that would pass from *Homo heidelbergensis* and the fossils of the Sima de los Huesos to "classical Neanderthals" (Arsuaga & Martínez 1998; Carbonell *et al.* 1995).

The discussion about technological change has meant that the late Acheulian complexes, featuring bifacial macro-tools ("Mode 2" of Clark 1969) and their replacement by morphotechnical assemblages of high variability, features of the Middle Palaeolithic (Mode 3), have taken precedence over any other kind of consideration. In recent years we have witnessed a crisis of culturalist approaches to the study of the traditional typologies. The Logic-Analytical Conceptual System has been developed, defining the hypothesis of changes in the Technical Operating System by transfer or substitution (Carbonell *et al.* 1992; Carbonell *et al.* 1996).

The model of use of fluvial areas, interpreted in a post-Acheulian sense, (as distinct from the "classical" Middle Palaeolithic) has been proposed for the south of the Iberian Peninsula. The lack of long and well-dated sequences, especially in the west of Iberia, makes any generalisation difficult.

Studies of the economical and settlement systems are equally fraught with difficulties but some behavioural patterns can nevertheless be elucidated. For example, subsistence exploitation of middle and high mountain biotopes, as a result of marked seasonal movements, seems clear. The continuity of opportunistic exploitation of the carcasses of large size animals, as well as the evidence of hunting activity based on horses, deer and bovids, with some specialization in caprines in the high mountainous areas, must be highlighted. The general occupation of the coast adds to these observations although a quantification of the dietary contribution of the resources inthese areas is still required (Cortés *et al.* 1996).

Geographical Framework

The groups of sites examined cover large orographic areas with a diversity of ecological conditions and a variety of climate and altitudes, which influenced occupation patterns during the last Interglacial. We present a macrospatial distribution of technocultural evidence within the geographical context of the southern region of the Iberian Peninsula (Figure 6.1). This region is defined by continental areas and coastal belts, within the climatic patterns of the warm thermo- and meso- Mediterranean zone, between 0–600m above sea level in the Depressions of the Guadalquivir and Guadalete rivers and the Odiel and Tinto rivers on the Atlantic area; between 700 and 2000 m above sea level in the Betic System and Intrabetic Depression; and the Penibetic System – the mountain range on the Mediterranean coast from Gibraltar to Almería.

The archaeological record of the last interglacial (Early Upper Pleistocene), which coincides with Isotope Stage 5e, is characterised by a diversity of occupation patterns in the south of the Iberian Peninsula, not only on the Atlantic side but also in the Mediterranean area (Figure

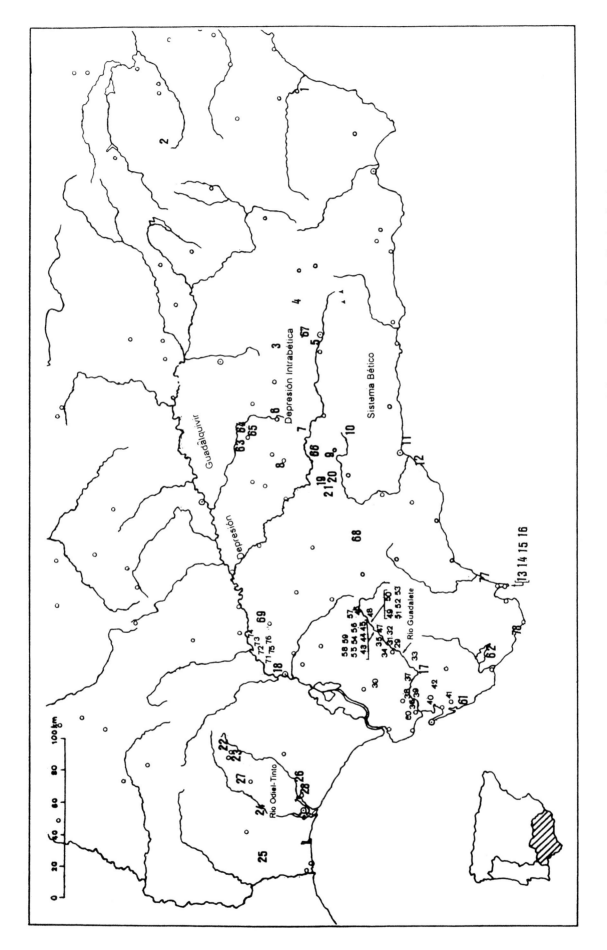

Figure 6.1: Proposed distribution of Late Acheulian and Middle Palaeolithic sites in the southern Iberian Peninsula.

6.1). This diversity, around which the technocultural evidence of the Middle Palaeolithic develops, is characterised by well-defined territorial units: cultural complexes within the sequential areas of the large Atlantic fluvial basins (Guadalquivir, Guadalete, Odiel, Tinto) and the Intrabetic Depressions (Antequera, Granada, Baza), based on the exploitation of the ecosystem within the fluvial basin (raw materials for the production of artefacts, hunting and forest resources, *etc.*). The sites are located on valley and lower-valley tracks (0 and 600 m above sea level). The *chaînes opératoires* of these occupations are defined by areas of collection and initial transformation of artefacts; areas of subsequent transformation and production; and production and butchering areas. The sites are: Majarromaque, (Guadalete), and La Solana del Zamborino (Guadiz-Baza Depression).

Sites On Fluvial Terraces

Guadalquivir Basin (10–200m above sea level): Tarazona II, Morilla (T-XIV), Guadajoz (T-XV), Carmona area, Arroyo del Rubio, Santiche, Los Graneros (Díaz del Olmo *et al.* 1993). (Figure 6.1).

Odiel Tinto Basin (10–100 m above sea level): Los Grillitos, La Dehesa, Graveras del Apeadero, el Monturrio (Castiñeira *et al.* 1989).

Guadalete Basin (10–100m above sea level): red soil levels at Medina Lake, Arcos-Bornos, T3, Bornos Dam, Almarda Stream, La Laguna, Alcornocalejos, Vega de Albardén, Torrecera, Dehesa del Boyal (Giles *et al.* 1993;1996).

Mediterranean area (400–600m above sea level): Cuenca Alta, Yedra Strean, Ventorrillo del Cojo (Medina *et al.* 1992).

Sites on *glacis* (10–200m above sea level), La Arenosa, La Escalera III, Matavaca, Hacienda Siret, Cortijo del Novillero (Giles *et al.* 1993; in press, a).

Peripheral fluvial basin techno-complexes, characterised by the concentration and transformation of raw materials. This pattern was detected in *glacis* formations very close to the hills near the basin (100 and 600m above sea level). It is probably linked to the transverse movements of "Mousterian" groups within the fluvial biogeographic framework.

Lacustrine Areas

Los Tollos Lake (Giles *et al.* 1992), La Janda Lake (Giles & Saez 1980; Ramirez *et al.* 1989). (Figure 6.1)

Middle Palaeolithic technocomplexes: Levallois Technical Operating Themes typically occur in inland lacustrine areas between 50 and 400m above sea level. The difference between the fluvial and lacustrine patterns is due to the environmental and resource constraints. They were occupied seasonally and the sites did not provide raw materials; therefore morphotypes of the sites are categorised according to the final production stage of artefacts.

In the Middle Palaeolithic, "open-air" fluvial depression patterns are highly homogeneous within the technological Middle Palaeolithic context, and are characterised by a balanced production of Positive Bases and Negative Base Second Generation (NB2G), scrapers, notches, and denticulates (see Carbonell *et al.* 1992: 1996).

Betic System

The sites in the Betic System act generally within the context of a technocultural evolution (Figure 6.1) evidenced by the production of "progressive" Indirect Technical Operative Themes in the technotypological order of the so-called "classic Mousterian" and are highly homogeneous. The Hora Cave and the Angel Cave area are exceptions and present an initial Riss-Würm industry with a "Late Acheulian" tradition of Direct Operating Themes.

The occupation pattern is categorised by habitation of caves, Cariguela Cave, Marmoles Cave (Cordoba) (Asquerino 1988), Murcielagos Cave (Cordoba) (Gavilán *et al.* 1994) and open-air sites like Llanos de la Sima (Villaluenga del Rosario, Cádiz (Giles *et al.* in press, b)), (Figure 6.2, numbers 1, 2 & 4).

The Intrabetic System: Mediterranean coastline. This represents the latest habitation of caves by the Neanderthal populations in Europe. The technotypological parameters develop during the Upper Pleniglacial Würm, with evidence of Early Upper Palaeolithic industries (see Zafarraya Cave (Medina *et al.* 1986), El Bajondillo (Malaga) (Baldomero *et al.* 1991);(Cortés & Simon, 1997), Gorham's Cave (Gibraltar) (Waechter 1964)). They have a certain homogeneity until the end of Würm II.

Chronological Data

The "transitional" Late Acheulian for the fluvial-lacustrine systems with terrace-*glacis* development in the Guadalquivir and Guadalete Depressions, occupies the levels of the complexes of the lower terraces T12 (Guadalquivir), T3 for the Guadalete, according to the data established by the geomorphological and chrono-sedimentary dynamics as well as the palaeomagnetic correlative datings. The Middle Palaeolithic techno-complexes with Levallois Indirect Operational Themes occupy terraces 13 and 14 of the Guadaquivir River, T3 and T2 of red soils in the Guadalete River. They comprise the transitional period between the Middle and Upper Pleistocene from 170–100 ka to 50ka. (Díaz del Olmo *et al.* 1993). The "transitional" Late Acheulian for the fluvial-lacustrine systems with terrace-*glacis* development in the Guadalquivir and Guadalete Depressions, occupies the levels of the complexes of the lower terraces T12 (Guadalquivir), T3 for the Guadalete, according to the data established by the geomorphological and chrono-sedimentary dynamics

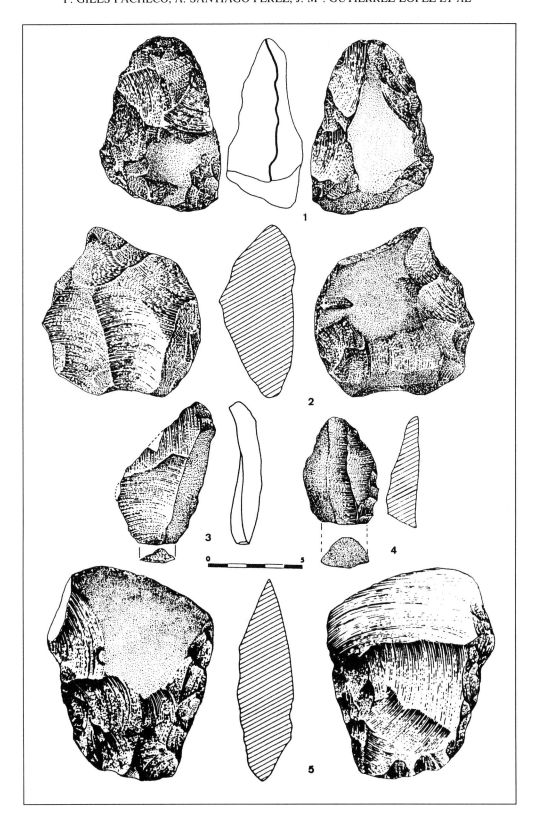

Figure 6.2: Late Acheulian Technical Complex: 1– Direct TOT. Bifacial Negative Base 1st. Generation (NB1G); 2– Centripetal recurrent NB1G Bifacial; 3– Positive Base (PB); 4– NB2G; 5– NB2G; 1,2 & 4– Llanos de la Sima (Villaluenga, Cádiz); 3– Guadalquitón/Borondo (San Roque, Cádiz); 5– Arroyo Pasada Blanca-Hozgarganta (Jerez de la Frontera, Cádiz).

as well as the paleomagnetic correlative datings. The Middle Palaeolithic techno-complexes with Levallois Indirect Operational Themes occupy terraces 13 and 14 of the Guadaquivir River, T3 and T2 of red soils in the Guadalete River. They comprise the transitional period between Middle and Upper Pleistocene from 170–100 ka to 50ka. (Díaz del Olmo *et al.* 1993).

Processes associated with the Riss-Würm chronology can be found in the Carigüela Betic area (episode 5e-5a) in levels XII and XI.

For the Mediterranean Intrabetic coastal area there are various deposits in the Gibraltar area, showing old sea level limits.

The most continuous and best dated and characterised level is the one associated with Isotope Stage 5c (Tyrrhenian II) in the Mediterranean Sea and Ouljiense in the Atlantic area. The Ouljiense episode can be referred to this whole area because no *Strombus bubonius*, characteristic of the Tyrrhenian cycle, have been detected.

This deposit is usually related to an aeolian deposit whose maximum development can be seen in Trafalgar. The marine deposit has been dated by Th/U to 107±2 ka. In Gibraltar (Gorham's Cave), it has not been possible to date a similar deposit because it represents an open geochemical system. Thus, it has only been possible to ascertain a minimum limit which guarantees that this sample is older than 78±(?) ka. Associated with, and sealing it, is an archeological series which comprises the Middle and Upper Palaeolithic. Between La Línea and Punta Acebuche, in the Getares inlet, there is also a marine deposit with an associated cemented dune whose maximum height is 3–4m. This deposit is observed near Tarifa and can be correlated with the + 15, + 11 and + 8 m levels already described. The + 11 m deposit from Tarifa has been dated by Th/U to 100±2 ka, confirming the age provided by Bruckner and Radtke (1985). It may be associated with those found between + 6–8m, between Punta Paloma and Punta Camarinal (Lario 1996).

The corresponding Mediterranean Tyrrhenian-II, which we associate with the high sea level limit, occurred in Isotope Substage 5c and has been dated by Th/U in Gibraltar (Europa Point). Since it has functioned as a geochemical open system, it cannot be dated accurately. The lower limit could be in >92.5±1 ka, which has been confirmed by the isotope dating of the stalagmite crust covering this deposit (76±2 Ka). Its position with respect to the following level (+10 m) leads us to situate this episode in Isotope Substage 5e. This episode could correspond to the one found in the east of Tarifa where the + 18 m level has been dated to 122,6±2,6 ka, correlating it with the deposits in Tarifa at +21 m (Hoyos *et al.* 1994).

Above this deposit, in Gibraltar (Europa Point), there is a deposit at + 10 m dated to 177±3,5 ka, linking it to the Mediterranean Tyrrhenian I episode, or to Isotope Substage 7a. This is the only deposit that can be accurately ascribed to this cycle. The correlation with other sites is only an assumption based on the situation of the deposit with respect to the next one (52, correlated with Tyrrhenian -II). The oldest deposits are assigned to the ages provided by Zazo (1989) and Zazo and Goy (1989).

Raw Materials And Provisioning Sources

The industrial complex in the Andalusian Middle and Upper Pleistocene is characterised by the differential provisioning of the rocks coming from the environment. The structure of the raw materials has an influence on the later development of segments within the Technical Operative Chains, (Giles *et al.* 1993; Gutiérrez *et al.* 1994; Santiago & Mata, in press.).

In the Andalusian sites, the raw materials selected for the production of the lithic industry consist mainly of quartzite, limestone, flint, sandstone and, to a lesser extent, protoquartzite and quartz. The preferential selection of these resources makes it possible to ascertain the morphological differences of the Acheulian complexes and the transitional industries of the Middle Palaeolithic in the Andalusian area.

The relationship between provisioning, rock sources and exploitation areas of the different geomorphological environments of Andalusia, spanning the entire Middle Pleistocene (Early & Middle Acheulian) takes place in the large fluvial environments of the region (Giles *et al.*, 1989; Giles *et al.* 1990; Giles *et al.* 1993; Santiago & Mata, in press). The regional chronostratigraphic sequence is represented by the sites on terraces of the Low Guadalquivir fluvial basin, and in the basins of the Guadalete and Tinto rivers extending to the closest fluvial networks. Here, the lithic detrital material exploited for manufacture consist mainly of quartz-like elements and gravel of a granitic nature, as is the case in the Guadalquivir and Tinto rivers. In the sites located in the Guadalete Basin, the main component is of calcareous elements typical of the Subbetic area.

With respect to the exploitation of the siliceous deposits, from the Upper Acheulian and spanning the entire Middle Palaeolithic, the occupation areas diversify towards lacustrine areas (La Solana del Zamborino in the Guadix-Baza Depression) and the mountainous area of the Betic Range (Hora Cave, Angel Cave, Carigüela Cave, the mountain track of the Genil and the Hozgarganta rivers). During the Upper Acheulian there is a selective use of flint which becomes exclusively used during the Middle and Upper Palaeolithic, when hardly any evidence of other lithologies can be found, (Giles *et al.* 1993; Santiago & Mata, in press.).

Technology

Middle Palaeolithic or Mode 3 (Clark 1969) represents an evolutionary phase within the technological development of human groups, characterised mainly by the generalisation of the exploitation of cores oriented to the morphological predetermination of items (Levallois

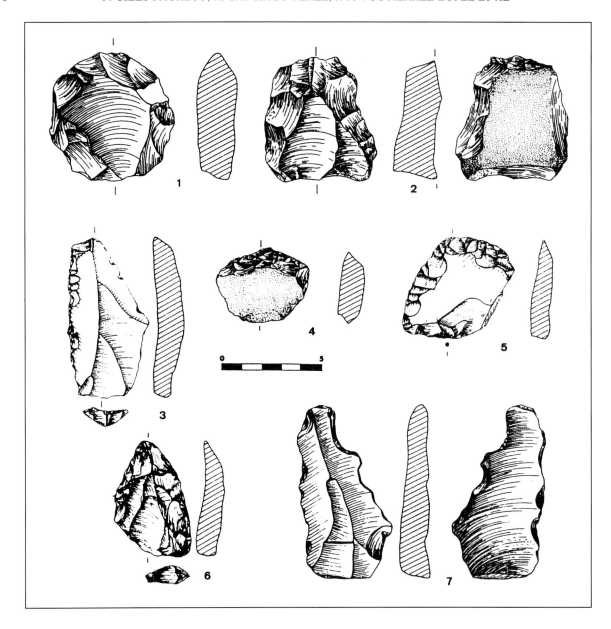

Figure 6.3: Middle Palaeolithic Technical Complex: 1 & 2– Preconfigured NB1Gs; 3, 4, 5 & 6– NB2G; 7– NB2G; 1 & 7– T-5 of the Guadalete River (Bornos, Cádiz); 2 & 4– Glacis of Las Arenosas (San José del Valle, Cádiz); 3, 5 & 6– Glacis of La Escalera-3 (Arcos de la Frontera, Cádiz).

technique), as well as a better use of raw materials and exploitabilty.

The transition can be analysed with respect to lithic items from the Late Upper Acheulian at open air occupations in fluvial environments such as the Guadalquivir and Guadalete rivers, lacustrine environments such as Solana de Zamborino (Botella *et al.* 1976) and in caves such as Las Grajas (Benito del Rey 1976), Horá (Botella *et al.* 1986) and Angel in the Intrabetic Depressions (Cortés *et al.* 1996). The industrial complexes with bifaces and cleavers are made more diverse by an increased presence of scrapers and denticulates. In Atlantic Andalusia, from the Guadalquivir (T-13/14), (Vallespí *et al.* 1993),

Guadalete (T-6), (Giles *et al.*, 1993) and Tinto-Odiel fluvial sequences, (Castiñeira *et al.* 1989). an indeterminate, post-Acheulian-like Middle Palaeolithic has been identified. It can be differentiated from the classic Mousterian, which is more usually linked with cave occupation in mountainous areas (Vallespí 1987). The differentiation of technical operational chains according to the type of occupation would be a consequence of strategies different from those of environment use, showing a better knowledge and control of available resources provided by it.

In terms of the lithic assemblages themselves, no changes have been observed with respect to the Acheulian

(Mode 2) regarding the simultaneous handling of various raw materials. A preference for flint during the Middle Palaeolithic has been observed, however. Limestone in the Guadalete occupation zones, and quarzite in the Guadalquivir area, were the materials preferentially used for macrolithic tools. Technical and morphological changes favoured the predominance of flint as the most productive material (Santiago & Mata, in press.).

In the Middle Palaeolithic *chaîne opératoire*, the abundance of base exploitation modes with centripetal extraction is important (Giles *et al.* in press.). On the other hand the selection of certain tabular-shaped rocks allows for a directional exploitation mode where the natural plane becomes the percussion plane. The Direct Technical Operational Themes (bifaces, trihedrals), characteristic of fluvial Acheulian assemblages, transfer their potential to other positive base morphologies (Figures 6.2 & 6.3). The application of the Levallois technique results in scarce and highly preconfigured items, and is related to the limited number of standarised shapes that appear in Mousterian lithic groups: convex scrapers and Mousterian points, whose shape variability is similar to the bifaces of the Late Acheulian. In the category of second generation negative bases there is a predominance of scrapers, denticulates, notches and abrupts. Equally important are the non-retouched items. The occurrence of wooden handles would provide information on the functionality of certain lithic items without a specific morphology. Despite the diversity of Middle Palaeolithic finds, the *chaîne opératoire* is currently considered to be highly homogeneous.

References

Asquerino Fernández, M.D. (1988). Cueva de los Mármoles (Priego de Córdoba). Avance de las campañas de excavación 1982/1986. *IFIGEA*, **III–IV**, 239–249. Córdoba.

Arsuaga, J.L. & Martínez, I. (1998). *La especie elegida*. Madrid.

Baldomero Navarro, A, Ferrer Palma, J.E. & Marques Merelo, I. (1991). Excavaciones de urgencia en el Bajondillo (Torremolinos, Málaga). *Anuario Arqueológico de Andalucía/1989*. **III**. Actividades de urgencia. 357–359. Sevilla.

Bruckner, H. & Radtke, U. (1985). Neue Erkenntnisse zum marinen Quartär an Spaniens Mittelmeerküste. *Kieler Geogr. Schrifgten*, **62**, 49–71.

Carbonell, E., Mosquera, M., Ollé, M., Rodríguez, X.P., Sala, R., Vaquero, M. & Verges J.M. (1992). New elements of the Logical Analytic System. *Cahier Noir*, **6**. Tarragona.

Carbonell, E., Bermúdez de Castro, J. Mª., Arsuaga, J.L., Diez, C., Rosas, A., Cuenca-Bescós, G., Sala, R., Mosquera, M. & Rodríguez X.P. (1995). Lower Pleistocene Hominids and artifacts from Atapuerca-TD6 (Spain). *Science*. **269**, 826–830.

Carbonell, E., Giralt, S., Marquez, B., Martín, A., Mosquera, M., Ollé, A., Rodriguez, X.P., Sala, R., Vaquero, M., Verges, J.M. & Zaragoza, J. (1996). The Litho-Technical Assemblage of the Sierra de Atapuerca in the frama of the European Middle Pleistocene. In (J.Mª Bermúdez, J.L. Arsuaga & E. Carbonell, Eds.) *Workshop Human Evolution in Europe and the Atapuerca evidence*, pp. 445–533.

Castiñeira Sanchez, J.M., Alvarez García, G., García Rincón, J.M.,

Gomez Toscano, F., Martín Gomez, J. & Rodríguez Vidal, J. (1989). Evidencias Paleolíticas en las terrazas de los ríos Tinto-Odiel (Huelva). In (F. Díaz del Olmo & J. Rodríguez, Eds.) *El Cuaternario en Andalucía Occidental*. AEQUA Monografías, **1**, 59–66. Huelva.

Clark, G. (1969). *World Prehistory. A new outline*. Cambridge University Press 2nd Ed.

Cortés Sanchez, M., Muñoz Vivas, V.E., Sanchidrián Torti, J.L. & Simón Vallejo, M.D. (1996). *El Paleolítico en Andalucía*. Córdoba.

Cortés, M. & Simon, M.D. (1997) La cueva del Bajondillo (Torremolinos, Málaga). In (J.Mª Fullola, & N.Soler, Eds.) *El Món mediterrani després del Pleniglacial (18.000–12.000 BP)*. *Serie Monografía*, **17**. Museo d'Arqueología de Catalunya. Girona.

Díaz del Olmo, F., Vallespí, E. & Baena Escudero, R. (1993). Formaciones cuaternarias y secuencia paleolítica en el Bajo Guadalquivir. *Investigaciones arqueológicas en Andalucía* (1985–1992). Proyectos. 193–210. Huelva.

Hoyos, M., Lario, J., Goy, J.L., Zazo, C., Dabrio, J.C., Hillaire-Marcel, C., Silva, P., Somoza, L. & Bardají, T. (1994). Sedimentación kárstica: Procesos morfosedimentarios en la zona del estrecho de Gibraltar. In (J. Rodríguez, F. Díaz del Olmo, C. Finlayson & F. Giles, Eds.) *Gibraltar during the Quaternary* pp. 36–48. AEQUA Monografías, **2**. Sevilla.

Gavilán Ceballos, B. & Vera Rodriguez, F.C. (1993). Breve avance sobre los resultados obtenidos en la excavación de urgencia en la Cueva de los Murciélagos de Zuheros (Córdoba). *Antiqvitas*, **3**, 23–30.

Giles, F. & Saez, A. (1980). Prehistoria de la Laguna de la Janda: Nuevas aportaciones. *Boletín del Museo de Cádiz*, **I**. 7–18.

Giles, F., Santiago, A., Gutiérrez, J.M., Mata, E. & Aguilera, L. (1989). El poblamiento paleolítico en el valle del río Guadalete. In (F. Díaz del Olmo & J. Rodríguez, Eds.) *El Cuaternario en Andalucía Occidental*, pp. 43–57. AEQUA Monografías, **1**: Sevilla.

Giles, F., Gutiérrez, J.M., Santiago, A., Mata, E. & Aguilera, L. (1992). Secuencia paleolítica del valle del Guadalete. Primeros resultados. *Revista de Arqueología*. **135**. pp. 16–26.

Giles, F., Gutiérrez, J.M., Mata, E., Santiago, A. & Gracia, F.J. (1993). Secuencia fluvial y paleolítica del río Guadalete (Cádiz). Resultados de las investigaciones hasta 1993. *Investigaciones arqueológicas en Andalucía* (1985–1992). Proyectos, 211–227.

Giles, F., Mata, E., Gutiérrez, J.M. & Santiago, A. (1995). El Pleistoceno de la Depresión Bornos-Villamartín. *Raña*. **18**, 73–74.

Giles, F., Gutiérrez, J.M., Mata, E. & Santiago, A. (1996). Laguna de Medina, Bassin du Fleuve Guadalete (Cádiz, Espagne). Un gisement Acheuléen Ancien dans le cadre des premiéres occupations humaines de la Péninsule Ibérique. *L'Anthropologie*. **100**, 4, 507–528.

Giles, F., Santiago, A., Mata, E., Aguilera, L & Gutiérrez, J.M. (in press, a). Prospecciones Arqueológicas Superficiales en la cuenca del río Guadalete (Cádiz). Análisis geocronológicos y sedimentológicos. 6ª Campaña (1994): Villamartín-Puerto Serrano. *Anuario Arqueológico de Andalucía*.

Giles, F., Santiago, A., Gutiérrez, J.M., Mata, E., Aguilera, L & Prieto, O. (in press, b). Ocupación humana en el Pleistoceno Superior Inicial en la Sierra de Grazalema. Registro Geo-arqueológico de los Llanos de la Sima y Llanos de Republicano (Villaluenga del Rosario, Cádiz). AEQUA-GAC, FAE.

Gutiérrez, J.M., Santiago, A., Giles, F., Gracia, F.J. & Mata, E. (1994). Areas de transformación de recursos líticos en glacis de la Depresión de Arcos de la Frontera. II *Reunión Nacional de Geoarqueología*, 1992, I.T.G.E.-AEQUA, 305–316.

Lario, J. (1996). Ultimo y presente interglacial en el área de conexión atlántico-mediterráneo (sur de España). Variaciones del nivel del mar. Paleoclima y Paleambientes. *Ph.D. Dissertattion*. Universidad Complutense Madrid.

Medina Lara, F. & Barroso Ruiz, C. (1992). Estudio tecno-tipológico del yacimiento lítico de superficie de Cuarterones (Villanueva del Rosario, Málaga). Proyecto: Los yacimientos líticos de superficie del Alto Valle del Guadalhorce (Málaga, España). Bases para el estudio integral del poblamiento prehistórico de la zona. Segunda campaña. 1990. *Anuario Arqueológico de Andalucía* /1990. **II**. Actividades Sistemáticas, 50–58.

Medina Lara, F., Barroso Ruiz, C., Sanchidrian Torti, J.L. & Ruiz Bustos, A. (1986). Avance al estudio de los niveles musterienses de la cueva del Boquete de Zafarraya, Alcaucín, Málaga. (Excavaciones de 1981–83). *Actas del Congreso Homenaje a Luis Siret (1934–1984)*, 79–83.

Ramirez Delgado, J.R., Fernández-Llebrez Butler, C. & Mateos Alonso, V. (1989). Aproximación al estudio del Cuaternario de la laguna de La Janda (Cádiz). In (F. Díaz del Olmo & J. Rodríguez, Eds.): *El Cuaternario en Andalucía Occidental*. AEQUA Monografías, **1**, 103–112.

Santiago, A. & Mata, E. (e.p.). Bases metodológicas para el estudio de los recursos líticos de la cuenca fluvial del río Guadalete utilizados durante el Paleolítico. In *III Congreso Nacional de Geoarqueología, Santiago de Compostela, 1995. Cuaternario y Geomorfología*. AEQUA y SEG, Zaragoza.

Shackleton, N.J. & Opdyke, N.D. (1973). Oxygen isotope and paleomagnetic stratigraphy of ecuatorial Pacific core V28-238. Oxygen isotope temperatures on a 105 and 106 year time scale. *Quaternary research*. **3**, 39–55.

Vallespí E. (1987). Un bifaz achelense del tramo Subbético exterior occidental (Los Corrales, Sevilla). *Anuario Arqueológico de Andalucía/* 1985. **III**. Actividades de urgencia, 288–290.

Vega Toscano, L.G. (1988). El Paleolítico Medio del sureste español y Andalucía oriental. *Serie Tesis Doctorales*, Universidad Complutense. Madrid.

Waechter, J. d'A (1964). The excavation of Gorham's Cave. Gibraltar, 1951–1954. *Bulletin of the Institute of Archaeology*. University of London, **4**, 189–221.

Zazo, C. (1989). Los depósitos marinos cuaternarios en el Golfo de Cádiz. In (F. Díaz del Olmo & J. Rodríguez, Eds.) *El Cuaternario en Andalucía Occidental*, pp. 113–122. AEQUA Monografías **1**: Sevilla.

Zazo, C. & Goy, J.L. (1989). Sea-level changes in the Iberian Peninsula during the last 200.000 years. In (D.B. Scott *et al.* Eds.) *Late Quaternary sea-level correlation and applications*, pp. 27–39. Kluwer Academic.

Appendix 1. List of sites in Figure 6.1.

1. Cueva Zájara II (Cuevas del Almanzora, Almería).
2. Cueva Umbría de Fuentesnuevas (Orce, Granada).
3. Cueva Horá (Darro, Granada).
4. Cueva de la Carigüela (Piñar, Granada).
5. Cueva Colomera (Atarfe, Granada).
6. Cueva de los Mármoles (Priego de Córdoba, Córdoba).
7. Cueva de los Murciélagos (Zuheros, Córdoba).
8. Cueva del Angel (Lucena, Córdoba).
9. Cueva de las Grajas (Archidona, Málaga).
10. Cueva del Boquete de Zafarraya (Alcaucín, Málaga).
11. Complejo Humo (Málaga).
12. Cueva Bajondillo (Torremolinos, Málaga).
13. Gorham's Cave (Gibraltar)
14. Devil's Tower (Gibraltar).
15. Forbe's Quarry (Gibraltar).
16. Genista 1 (Gibraltar).
17. Majarromaque (Jerez de la Frontera, Cádiz).
18. Tarazona 2.
19. Alto valle del rio Guadalhorce (Villanueva del Rosario, Málaga).
20. Ventorrillo del Cojo (Villanueva del Rosario, Málaga).
21. Cuarterones (Villanueva del Rosario, Málaga).
22. La Dehesa (Escacena del Campo, Huelva).
23. Rio Chanza (Escacena del Campo, Huelva).
24. El Grillito (Gibraleón, Huelva).
25. La Barca (Cartaya, Huelva).
26. La Dehesa (Lucena del Puerto, Huelva).
27. Gravera del Apeadero (Niebla, Huelva).
28. El Mentidero (Palos de Moguer, Huelva).
29. Cueva del Higueral de Valleja (Arcos de la Frontera, Cádiz).
30. Laguna de los Tollos (El Cuervo, Cádiz).
31. La Escalera 1 (Arcos de la Frontera, Cádiz).
32. La Escalera 2 (Arcos de la Frontera, Cádiz).
33. La Arenosa (San José del Valle, Cádiz).
34. El Santiscal (Arcos de la Frontera, Cádiz).
35. Pantano de Bornos (Bornos, Cádiz).
36. El Tesorillo (Jeréz de la Frontera, Cádiz).
37. Gravera del Torno (El Torno, Cádiz).
38. Lomopardo (Jeréz de la Frontera, Cádiz).
39. Laguna de Medina. Niveles de suelos rojos (Medina, Cádiz).
40. Finca de las Yegüas (Puerto Real, Cádiz).
41. Puente de Hierro (San Fernando, Cádiz).
42. La Laguna (Villamartín, Cádiz).
43. Cruce de las Cabezas (Villamartín, Cádiz).
44. Laguna Estación (Villamartín, Cádiz).
45. Almendrillo-Cortijo de Picas (Villamartín, Cádiz).
46. Cortijo de las Gateras (Villamartín, Cádiz).
47. Soledad (Bornos, Cádiz).
48. Higuerón (Villamartín-Puerto Serrano, Cádiz).
49. Carpintero (Puerto Serrano, Cádiz).
50. Rancho de Gachas (Puerto Serrano, Cádiz).
51. Glacis de las Cerillas (Puerto Serrano, Cádiz).
52. Pelarranas (Puerto Serrano, Cádiz).
53. El Coto (Puerto Serrano, Cádiz).
54. Hacienda Siret (Puerto Serrano, Cádiz).
55. Hacienda Siret-Corte de la Carretera (Puerto Serrano, Cádiz).
56. Arroyo de Matavaca (Puerto Serrano, Cádiz).
57. Cortijo de la Perdiz, Norte (Villamartín, Cádiz).
58. Cortijo de la Mediana (Villamartín, Cádiz).
59. Cortijo del Novillero (Villamartín, Cádiz).
60. Venta Alta (El Puerto de Santa María, Cádiz).
61. Carretera La Barrosa (Chiclana, Cádiz).
62. Laguna de la Janda (Tahivilla).
63. Cerro de las Viñas (Priego, Córdoba).
64. El Monte (Priego, Córdoba).
65. Cueva-sima Cholones (Priego, Córdoba).
66. Cueva de Belda (Cuevas de San Marcos, Málaga).
67. Abrigo del Pantano de Cubillas (Granada).
68. Alto Corbones (Puebla de Cazalla, Sevilla).
69. Bajo Corbones (Carmona, Sevilla).
70. El Saltillo (Sevilla).
71. Arroyo El Rubio (Carmona).
72. Morillo (Carmona, Sevilla).
73. Arroyo Graneros (Sevilla).
74. Arroyo Las Pipas (Sevilla).
75. Arroyo Los Espartales (Sevilla).
76. Ribera del Huezman (Sevilla).
77. San Roque (Guadalquitón-Borondo, Cádiz).
78. Punta del Almirante (Algeciras, Cádiz).
79. La Barrosa (Chiclana, Cádiz).

7

Middle Palaeolithic Technocomplexes and Lithic Industries in the Northwest of the Iberian Peninsula

J. A. Cano Pan, F. Giles Pachecho, E. Aguirre, A. Santiago Perez, F. J. Gracia Prieto, E. Mata Almonte, J. Mª. Gutierrez Lopez and O. Prieto Reina

Introduction

Complexes of lithic industries whose Technical Operative Themes correspond to the Middle Palaeolithic by their position in the stratigraphy have been identified, for the first time, in the Palaeolithic techno-cultural sequence of the middle to late Pleistocene in the north-west of the Iberian peninsula (Figure 7.1), (Cano *et al.* 1997). These are distributed in fluvial environments: the low and middle Miño river basins and in karstic environments in caves in eastern Galicia.

This paper reports on part of the results obtained in the course of the investigation programme named "The First Human Societies of Galicia: Archaeology and Society During the Pleistocene in Southern Galicia" (XUGA 21003b-95) financed by Dirección Xeral de Universidades e Investigación of Xunta de Galicia.

Regional Background

In a revision of the Palaeolithic in Galicia (Breuil & Zbyszewski 1942; Cano 1993) one of the most notable features is the confusion which existed until recently, concerning the definition and systematic description of the same assemblages (Senin 1995; 1996). This lack of consistency led some investigators to believe that in Galicia there had been a "cultural" survival from the Lower Palaeolithic to the Upper Palaeolithic (Aguirre 1964; Butzer 1967; Cano 1991a, 1991b).

This view was not arrived at arbitrarily, but was based on the absence of archaeological correlations with existing Middle Palaeolithic collections from the Iberian Peninsula or elsewhere in Europe, as well as a lack of Upper Palaeolithic evidence. This fact, together with the surprising

C-14 dates of 26.7 + 3.6/-2.5 ka and 18± 0.3 ka for the archaeological site of Budiño (Aguirre 1964; Butzer 1967), favoured the concept of long-term "cultural" continuity throughout the Palaeolithic in Galicia (Cerqueiro 1996).

In this context, it is understandable that the non-documented phases of the Middle and Upper Palaeolithic were filled with groups of odd artefacts, and in some areas their absence was attributed to geological factors. For example, the absence of artefacts dating after the Riss-Würm interglacial – 'Mousterian' and 'post-Mousterian'– in the terraces of the Miño River was explained by faulting and tectonic movements that caused the most modern terraces in the Miño to be located under its present course (Álvarez & Bouza 1949).

In an attempt to fill the gaps in the Palaeolithic, a number of authors have attributed a series of archaeological sites, such as those of the south-west coast of Pontevedra or that of Manilos in Ferrol, to the Middle Palaeolithic. However, this interpretation has now been discarded (Cano 1991a; 1991b).

Another problem is that raised by the archaeological sites of Budiño (Pontevedra) and A Piteira (Toén, Orense) whose ascription to the Middle Palaeolithic, although not without its problems, could be more reliable. J. Vidal (1982) located in Budiño, in Horizon A of Level II of Locus I, a group of artefacts which he provisionally related to the "Mousterian" (unpublished). Later on, in 1991 and 1992, a prolonged 'rescue' project was carried out which included surveying and excavation. However, to date, none of the problems raised by this site have been answered (Cerqueiro 1996).

V. Rodríguez (1976) considered that the artefacts in

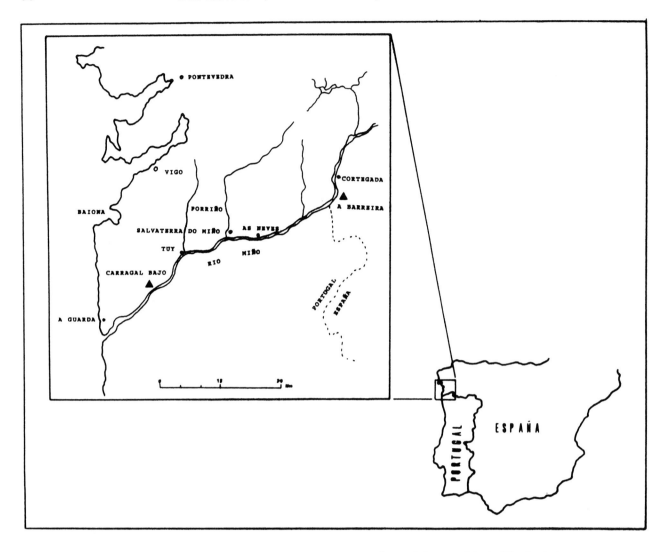

Figure 7.1: Location of A Barreira (Pontedeva, Cortegada) and Carragal Bajo (Tomiño) sites.

the A Piteira archaeological site (Toén, Orense), belonged to a 'Mousterian of Levallois facies', or perhaps a 'Mousterian of Acheulian tradition', although subsequently the site has been interpreted as an accumulation of artefacts in secondary position whose most important component would be Lower Palaeolithic (Cano 1991a).

The quaternary deposits of the lower valley of the Miño River

The valley of the Miño presents a section whose characteristics differ largely from those of the other upper sections. It begins in the vicinity of Caldelas, where the valley progressively opens out, from a previously narrow section about 3 kilometres wide, into a wider valley averaging between 4–5 km, until the mouth of the river (Figure 7.2).

This whole tract is about 40 km long and along its course numerous terrace levels are developed on both sides of the river. The Spanish riverbank is slightly wider than the Portuguese side; however, the levels of fluvial terraces here appear very degraded, which vastly hinders their study (Nonn & Medus 1963).

Historically, the lower tracts of the Miño terraces have been studied by numerous authors, both in the Spanish part as well as the Portuguese (Lautensach 1945; Feio 1948; Teixeira 1949 and 1952; Nonn 1967; Butzer 1967 among others).

In the course of the present work a detailed cartographic survey has been carried out by means of geomorphologic photo-interpretation, using various detailed maps, and has been completed with altimetrical work in the field and the laboratory, working from large scale maps. This study has allowed us to identify up to 8 terrace levels, along the whole valley of the Miño River on the Spanish side. The alimetric data, compared with that established by other authors, is as follows:

–   Terrace T8, corresponds to the maximum height reached by the terraces of the Miño in the whole of this section.

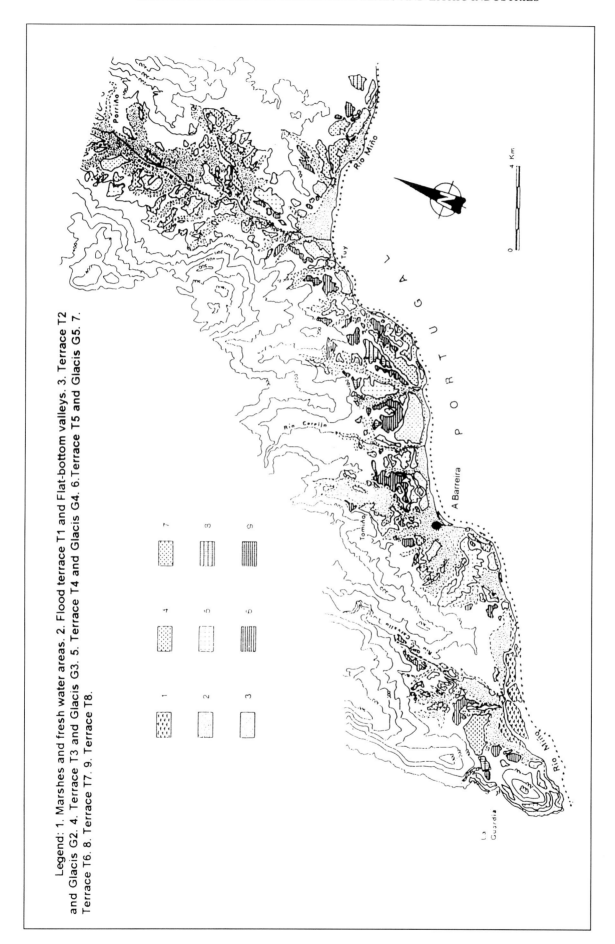

Legend: 1. Marshes and fresh water areas. 2. Flood terrace T1 and Flat-bottom valleys. 3. Terrace T2 and Glacis G2. 4. Terrace T3 and Glacis G3. 5. Terrace T4 and Glacis G4. 6. Terrace T5 and Glacis G5. 7. Terrace T6. 8. Terrace T7. 9. Terrace T8.

Figure 7.2: Schematic geomorphological map of the Quaternary fluvial levels of the lower valley of Miño river, on the Spanish side.

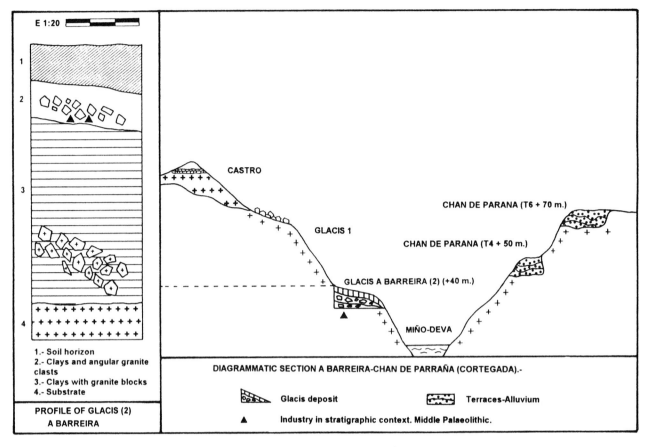

Figure 7.3: A Barreira tranverse diagram.

– Terrace T7 appears as very isolated sections in Caldelas, Curras, Taborda and Tomiño.

– Terrace T6 is notable in extent and continuity in the tract of Caldelas-Baldranes, Tuy, Amorin and Tomiño.

– Terrace T5 appears as small sections in numerous areas of the valley, especially down-river from Tuy up to the vicinity of Tomiño, where it develops into a *glacis*-terrace of complex character.

– Terrace T4 covers a considerable area. It is widespread and prominent in Volta Moura (the area connecting with the valley of the Louro), appearing in Piñeiro, Tomiño and Monte Seo.

– Terrace T3 is much more modest in development than the previous terraces. It appears in Baldranes, Amorin, Tomiño and Goyan.

– Terrace T2 appears repeatedly in the surroundings of Tuy, as well as in Carragal and Forcadela. In general it shows good continuity, appearing in practically all sectors of the valley, from Guillarey to the point of Santa Tecla.

– Terrace T1 constitutes the flood plain. In general it descends towards the mouth of the river, as Butzer (1967) already pointed out, although this tendency is not completely clear nor homogeneous.

Stratigraphic connection and Palaeolithic sequence

In the last few years, a sounding has been made in a cave in the east of Galicia, Cova Eiros (Triacastela, Lugo)(Cano & Vázquez 1986), which was well known for the large quantity of *Ursus spelaeus* remains found there. This sounding documented the presence of archaeological levels, namely IV and V, which still awaits dating, but which have been assigned to the Middle Palaeolithic based on the characteristics of the lithic artefacts.

The following proposed sequence (Cano *et al.* 1997), is based on the stratigraphic interpretation of the different systems of terrace complexes (it is, at the moment, provisional, pending the completion of the study of all the lithics located in the deposit):

– There are clear indications of lithic industry in the complexes of higher terraces, T8 Peteira, Consello de Tuy; T7 Tomiño, football field, Chan de Vide, Consello de Setado, in T7 and T5 (Lower Pleistocene).

– Acheulian technocomplexes (uncertain) in the levels of medium terraces, T4 Mounts de Seo (Tuy) (Early Pleistocene).

– "Classic" or Iberian Acheulian technocomplexes

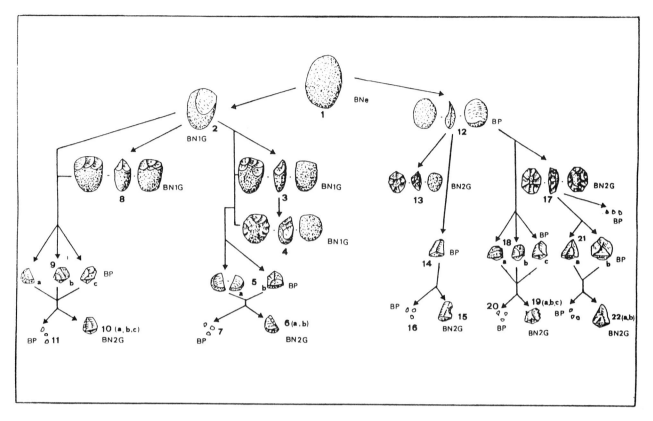

Figure 7.4: Structural morpho-genetic matrix of A Barreira.

(Vallespí & Díaz del Olmo 1996), with Direct Technical Operating System and Indirect Technical Operating System in the complexes of medium-low terraces, T3 in the whole area of the basin between La Guardia-Tuy and Salvaterra do Miño (Middle Pleistocene).

– Middle Palaeolithic.

The Palaeolithic cultural sequence disappears at the beginning of the complex of the low terraces Carragal Bajo T2 (Figure 7.2) and Tomiño-A Barreira (Orense) at the end of the Middle Pleistocene and beginning of the Upper Pleistocene. The fluvial deposits are more complex-alternating deposits of bars of medium and high energy with muds and flood clays, typical of alluvial complexes with large meanders. Chronologically, these terraces embrace the transition from Middle to Upper Pleistocene, the Upper Pleistocene and the Pleistocene-Holocene interface. Technologically, in this sequence all the structural categories are represented, with the Indirect Technical Operative Themes predominating. These industrial groups belong to characteristic technical complexes of the Middle Palaeolithic, with features and characteristics of the centripetal Levallois groups, both for obtaining PB types and for shaping of NB2G (see below).

For the first time, new technocomplexes belonging to the Middle-Upper Pleistocene can be incorporated within the geoarcheological sequence of the La Guardia-Tuy area, supported by the traverse profiles of the area of Salvaterra do Miño. This is a new contribution to the knowledge of the Palaeolithic settlement in the southern Galicia. The technologies are indistinguishable from the technology of other traditional groups of the Middle Palaeolithic in the Iberian Peninsula. The presence of clear indications of lithic industries in the high terraces, of the Lower Pleistocene and Middle-Lower Pleistocene have also been noted.

Middle Palaeolithic *châine opératoire* of the A Barriera site.

The different technocomplexes of Palaeolithic industries recorded in the river deposits of the stretch between the municipalities of Salvaterra do Miño and Cortegada add new results to the already established Palaeolithic sequence in the southern part of Galicia. The morphotechnic analysis of these sets, via the application of the Logical Analytical System criteria (Carbonell *et al.* 1992) allows us to characterise the structure of the different categories which make up the *châines opératoires*, starting with the collection and selection of raw materials, and their morphotechnic links. In this sense, it is useful to highlight the differential exploitation of quartzites, mainly re-presented in the river deposits of the stretch studied, over

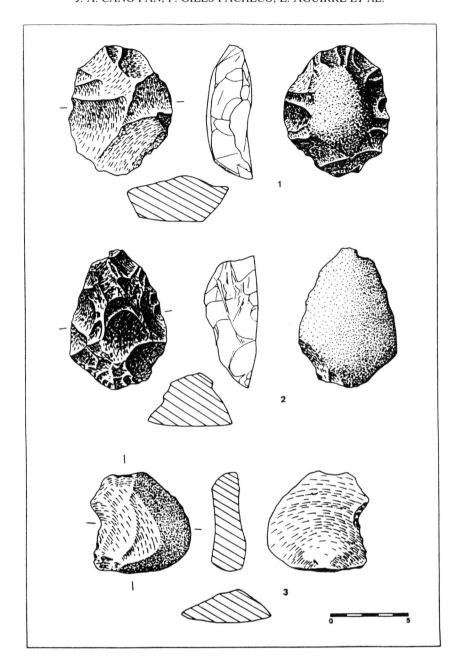

Figure 7.5: 1– Carragal Bajo. Bifacial NB1G; 2– Carragal Bajo. Unifacial NB1G; 3– A Barreira NB2G.

other lithologies (granitic gravels and quartz), which are less common.

The proposed interpretation is a first approach to the *châine opératoire* of the Middle Palaeolithic in Galicia using several archaeological sites of the river Miño and fundamentally based on the site of A Barreira (Cortegada)(Figure 7.3).

The raw material used is mainly quartzite pebbles (1), although quartz pebbles are also used in good number and some quartz blocks.

The *châine opératoire* (Figure 7.4), is structured in two directions:

A– This is the main one. Mixed methods of obtaining a Negative Base of First Generation (NB1G) (production and shaping), Positive Base (PB) and Negative Base of Second Generation (NB2G) starting from the Positive Bases that are obtained from NB1G (5). This is the sequence implied for NB1G with a configuration plane (3 and 4), PB with platform of cortical interaction and usually with cortical surfaces in the upper plane or dorsal face (5a,5b).

In a very few cases, NB1G with two or more planes of configuration (8), the PB can have cortical interaction Platforms (9a) although there are also interaction Platforms

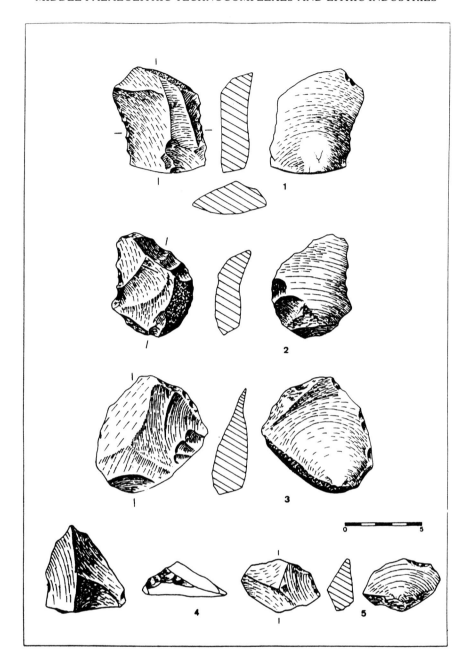

Figure 7.6: 1–2. A Barreira NB2G; 3–4–5. Carragal Bajo PB.

which are non-cortical, but not prepared (9b,9c) and they may (9a,9b) or may not have (9c) fringes in the upper plane or dorsal face. The PBs of sequence A will serve to obtain NB2G (6a,6b,10a,10b,and 10c), and produce PB2G in turn.

B– The supports are Positive Base which have had their outer surfaces removed (1st generation mostly) and are of good size (12). These bases will follow two transformation processes:

    B1– The plane of interaction constitutes the upper plane or dorsal face, the inferior plane or ventral face being the plane of configuration. The type

of transformation of the base is centripetal horizontal, giving as a result NB1G production, with a tendency to conical morphology (13). The PB is characterised by having cortical interaction platforms and non-cortical dorsal faces (14) that will also serve as supports for NB2G (15).

B2– In this transformation sequence, an outlying interaction plane must first be prepared, with a type of conical transformation, for which the interaction plane will be the ventral face and the configuration plane, the dorsal face. The resulting PB is characterised by having non-cortical interaction platforms and dorsal faces with or without cortical surfaces (18a, 18b, 18c), these bases can also be transformed into NB2G (19). Later on, this interaction plane is used for a centripetal transformation on a horizontal plane, a NB1G production with predetermined morphology (17) from which PBs of pre -determined morphology are obtained, characterised by the bi- or multifaceted interaction platforms and without cortical surfaces on the dorsal face (21a, 21b). It would also be possible to turn these PBs into NB2G. (22a,22b)(Figure 7.6).

Carragal Bajo (Tomiño) and A Barreira Cortegada). The complex of low terraces and *glacis*.

Main characteristics:

- Open-air sites in river system deposits.
- The archaeological context is limited to a specific undisturbed area of deposit.
- The deposits (terraces, *glacis*), occupy an area of 500 to 1000 m², in which all the processes of production are found, offering a morphotechnic matrix which can be assigned to Mode 3 (Middle Palaeolithic).
- Use of autochthonous raw materials.
- Consequently, the sites can be characterised as source areas of raw materials, of production and final shaping of artefacts.
- Lithic production of Levallois technical operatives themes for the production of Positive Bases.
- Occupation by groups of hunter-gatherers during the first stages of Oxygen Isotope Stage 3.
- From an anthropological point of view, the techno-culture of these sites could be assigned to groups of Neanderthals that occupied the coast and the interior, using the river systems as lines of communication, habitat and use of natural resources in general.

Conclusion

This project on the Pleistocene of southern Galicia constitutes a new approach to the study of the Palaeolithic of the north west Iberian Peninsula. For the first time, the topics within a short- and long-term programmme have been investigated by an integrated team of specialists in Quaternary science and by historians.

Our findings show that it is necessary to discard the idea that the Palaeolithic in Galicia has no exact equivalent, either chronologically or technologically, elsewhere in the rest of the Iberian Peninsula or in the rest of Western Europe.

The Palaeolithic settlement in the fluvial basin of the Miño river represents a chronological and sequential model similar to that of the rest of the large fluvial systems of the Iberian Peninsula (Giles *et al.* 1996), such as the Tajo

(Santonja 1996), the Cantabrian zone Guadiana (Santonja & Pérez González 1984), Guadalquivir (Vallespí 1988) and Guadalete (Giles *et al.* 1989; 1990; 1993). The results of new fieldwork on the structural formations T2 of the Miño identify the existence of technocomplexes characterised by Indirect Technical Operative Theme (T.O.T.) techniques, with methods of preshaping attributed to the Middle Palaeolithic, or Mode 3, according to nomenclature of Clark (1969).

This contribution can be added to the panorama of new discoveries of Palaeolithic sites in the northwestern area of the Iberian Peninsula.

References

Aguirre, E. (1964). Las Gándaras de Budiño. Porriño (Pontevedra). *Excavaciones Arqueológicas en España*. **31**. Madrid. Servicio Nacional de Excavaciones.

Álvarez Blázquez, J.M. & Bouza Brey, F. (1949). Industrias paleolíticas de la comarca de Tuy. *Cuadernos de Estudios Gallegos*. IV. **13**, 201–250.

Breuil, H. & Zbyszewski, G. (1942). Contributión a l'étude des industries paléolithiques du Portugal et de leurs rapports avec la Geologie du Quaternaire. *Comunicações dos Serviços Geológicos de Portugal*. I. **23**, 319–369.

Butzer, K.W. (1967). Geomorphology and stratigraphy of the Paleolithic site of Budiño. *Eiszeifalter und Gegenwart*. Band **18**. 31–12. pp. 82–103. Ohringen/Würt.

Cano Pan, J.A. (1991a). *Las industrias líticas talladas en la costa de La Guardia a Baiona*. Excma. Diput. Prov. de A Coruña: A Coruña.

Cano Pan, J. A. (1991b). O Paleolítico Inferior en Galicia. Larouco. 1. *Revista da Historia Primitiva*. Tradicións Orais e Patrimonio Cultural de Galicia. pp. 13–22.

Cano Pan, J.A. (1993). Análisis Historiográfico del Paleolítico en Galicia. In (J.G.Beramendi, Ed). *Galicia e a Historiografía*. Tórculo Edicións. Santiago de Compostela.

Cano Pan, J.A.; Giles Pacheco, F.; Aguirre Enríquez, E.; Gracia Prieto, J.; Santiago Pérez, A.; Mata Almonte, E.; Gutiérrez López, J.Mª.; Díaz del Olmo, F.; Baena Escudero, R. & Borja Barrera, F. (1997). Evolución del Pleistoceno en la cuenca baja del Miño, sector La Guardia-Tuy. Secuencia de los primeros poblamientos humanos y registro arqueológico.In (J. Rodríguez Vidal, Ed) *Cuaternario Ibérico*, pp. 201–212. AEQUA: Huelva.

Cano Pan, J.A. & Vázquez Varela, J.M. (1986). Nuevas aportaciones al estudio de las industrias líticas del Suroeste de Galicia. La prospección de 1984. *Studia Zamorensia Histórica*. **7,** 13–22.

Carbonell, E., Mosquera, M., Ollé, M., Rodríguez, X. P., Sala, R., Vaquero, M. & Verges, J.Mª. (1992). New elements of the Logical Analytic System. First International Meeting on Technical Systems to Configure Lithic objects of Scarce Elaboration. *Cahier Noir*. **6**.

Cerqueiro Landín, D. (1996). As Gándaras de Budiño: Prehistoria e Historia. In (R. Fábregas, Ed.). *Os primeiros poboadores de Galicia: O Paleolítico*, pp. 47–73. Cadernos do Seminario de Sargadelos. **73**. Edicios do Castro: A Coruña.

Clark, G. (1969). *World Prehistory. A new outline*. Cambridge University Press 2nd Edition.

Feio, M. (1948). Notas Geomorfológicas. II – Emtorno da interpretaçao dos terraços do Rio Minho. *Bol. Soc. Geol. Portugal*. **VII**, I-II.

Giles, F., Santiago, A., Gutiérrez, J.Mª., Mata, E. & Aguilera, L. (1989). El poblamiento paleolítico en el valle del río Guadalete. In (J. Rodríguez Vidal & F. Díaz del Olmo, Eds.). *El Cuaternario en Andalucía Occidentla,* pp. 43–57. AEQUA Monografías. **1**: Sevilla.

Giles, F., Santiago, A., Gutiérrez, J.Mª., Mata, E. & Aguilera, L. (1990). Aproximación a un complejo técnico del Pleistoceno medio en la cuenca baja del río Guadalete. Casa del Palmar del Conde, Jerez de la Frontera, Cádiz. XI Reunió de Paleolitistes Espanyols. *Xábiga.* **6**, 83–97.

Giles, F., Gutiérrez, J.Mª., Mata, E., Santiago, A. & Gracia, F.J. (1993). Secuencia fluvial y paleolítica del río Guadalete (Cádiz). Resultados de las investigaciones hasta 1993. In *Investigaciones Arqueológicas en Andalucía,* pp. 211–227. 1985–1992. Proyecto. VI Jornadas de Arqueología Andaluza. enero 1993: Huelva.

Giles, F., Gutiérrez, J.Mª., Mata, E. & Santiago, A. (1996). Laguna de Medina, bassin du fleuve Guadalete (Cádiz, Espagne). Un gisement Acheuléen Ancien dans le cadre des premières occupations humaines de la Péninsule Ibérique. *L'Anthropologie.* **100**, 4, 507–528.

Gracia Prieto, F.J. (in press). Los depósitos cuaternarios del valle bajo del Miño. *Cuaternario y Geomorfología.* AEQUA-S.E.G.

Lautensach, H. (1945). Formaçao dos terraços interglaciários do norte de Portugal e suas relaçoes com os problemas da época glaciária. *Publ. Soc. Geol. de Portugal.*

Nonn, H. (1967). Les terrasses du rio Minho inferior. Localisation et étude sédimentologique. *Rev. Geomorph. Dyn.* **XVII**, 97–106.

Nonn, H. & Medus, J. (1963). Primeros resultados geomorfológicos y palinológicos referentes a la cuenca de Puentes de García Rodríguez (Galicia). *Not. y Com. del Inst. Geol. y Min. de España.* **71**, 87–94.

Santonja, M. (1996). The Lower Paleolithic in Spain: sites, raw material and occupation of the land. In (N.Moloney, L. Raposo, & M. Santonja, Eds.). *Non-Flint Stone Tools and the Paleolithic Occupation of the Iberian Peninsula.* pp 151–165. B.A.R. International Series **649**: Oxford.

Santonja, M. & Pérez González, A. (1984). Las industrias paleolíticas de La Maya I en su ámbito regional. *Excavaciones Arqueológicas en España.* **135**.

Senin Fernández, L.J. (1995). *A investigación do Paleolítico en Galicia. Revisión bibliográfica.* Ediciós do Castro. Sada-A Coruña.

Senin Fernández, L.J. (1996). Historia da investigación do Paleolítico galego. In (R. Fábregas, Ed): *Os primeiros poboadores de Galicia: O Paleolítico,* pp. 25–45). Cadernos do Seminario de Sargadelos **73**: A Coruña.

Teixeira, C. (1949). Plages anciennes et terrasses fluviatiles du littoral du Nord-Ouest de la Péninsule Ibérique. *Bol. Ms. e Lab. Min. e Geol.* Univ. Lisboa. **17**, 3–18.

Teixeira, C. (1952). Os terraços da parte portuguesa do rio Minho. *Comm. Ser. Geol. Portugal.* **XXXIII**.

Vallespí, E. (1988). Paleolítico Medio de aspecto postachelense en la Depresión inferior del Guadalquivir. *Homenaje al Prof. E. Ripoll Perelló. Espacio, Tiempo y Forma.* Serie 1. Prehistoria. **I**, 85–91.

Vallespí E. & Diaz del Olmo, F. (1996). Industries in quarzite and the beginning of the use of flint in the Lower and Middle Paleolithic sequence of the Bajo Guadalquivir. In (N. Moloney, L. Raposo & M. Santonja, Eds.). *Non-Flint Stone Tools and the Paleolithic Occupation of the Iberian Peninsula,* pp. 151–165.. B.A.R. International Series **649**. Oxford.

Vidal Encinas, J.M. (1982). Las Gándaras de Budiño: balance preliminar de dos campañas de excavaciones (1980–1981). In *In Memoriam Alfredo Garcia Alen,* pp. 91–113. Museo de Pontevedra **XXXVI**. Pontevedra.

8

Mousterian Hearths at Abric Romaní, Catalonia (Spain)

Ignasi Pastó, Ethel Allué and Josep Vallverdú

Introduction

The control of fire has modified hominid behaviour irreversibly. The use of fire provides light and warmth and can be extended to other components necessary for subsistence (Wandsnider 1997). The earliest use of fire will always be the subject of debate due to the nature of archaeological records and their interpretations.

It seems instructive to study the use of fire from a holistic perspective as a multifaceted adaptative tool (Straus 1989). For example: how the different uses of fire were incorporated in the human adaptive system, how it affected the structure of the living floors and how it modified some earlier behaviour. From this point of view Abric Romaní has yielded numerous fireplaces which reflect a considerable capacity for organisation and planning on the part of the humans living there.

At Abric Romaní the human use of fire is evident. We have found burned patches on the ground surface which vary in colour from dark brown to black. They are associated with other remains derived from fire use, such as ashes, charcoal and faunal remains with different degrees of burning and fracturing. In Abric Romaní the difference between thermal alteration and the other natural alterations, such as oxidation caused by moss growth, manganese or guano is quite clear.

Abric Romaní is a rockshelter (Figures 8.1 and 8.2) formed within a 90 m limestone cliff in the town of Capellades, located 45 km north-west of Barcelona (41° 32′ N Lat., 1° 41′ E Long.). The platform underlying the town of Capellades is formed by peat and travertine deposits and corresponds to present and ancient springs. A travertine drip has developed from the upper part of the cliff leading to the formation of many rockshelters. This location, known as *Cinglera del Capelló*, was intensively inhabited by Middle and Upper Palaeolithic hominids due to its geographical position and the abundance of water.

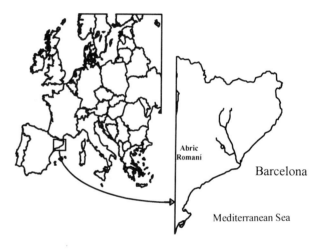

Figure 8.1: Geographical situation of Abric Romaní, near Barcelona, Spain.

Today, the water is still used for various purposes, although redistribution of fresh water and human pressure on the environment has decreased the encrusting capacity of the water. Other sites forming part of *Cinglera del Capelló* are Abric Agut and Abric de la Consagració.

The lithostratigraphic sequence is 17 m deep (Figure 8.3) and includes 27 archaeological levels ranging from 39.1±1.5 to 70.2±2.6 ka (U-Th Series). The Abric Romaní travertine deposit is well dated to the Middle to Upper Palaeolithic transition (Bischoff *et al.* 1988; 1994), and preserves reliable palaeonvironmental data from this period in a nonglaciated area under the influence of the Mediterranean Sea (Burjachs and Julià 1994).

All the occupation levels are Mousterian except the uppermost level A, which is Aurignacian. The archaeological levels document several occupation floors, both

Figure 8.2: General view of Cinglera del Capelló.

individual and as palimpsests buried quickly by processes of rapid sedimentation. The ongoing excavations, by a team from the Universitat Rovira i Virgili, began in 1989 and are being carried out with the purpose of exposing a maximum surface area to understand, as completely as possible, the synchronic nature of the occupation of the floors. The excavated surface area (25 by 225 m²) varies in the different levels, according to previous excavations.

Archaeological Remains

The lithic industry is characterised by an overwhelming predominance of flint as a raw material. Other rocks used, such as quartz, quartzite and limestone, are less well represented. Most of the raw material is derived from the immediate vicinity of the site. The most abundant morphotypes are denticulates and unretouched artifacts (Vaquero 1997). There also flaked bones and bones used as percussors (Aïmene 1998).

In terms of the faunal remains the number of herbivore bones is greater than carnivores. Moreover, herbivores are characterised by a predominance of *Equus caballus* and *Cervus elaphus*. Other species include *Equus asinus*, *Sus scrofa*, *Bos* sp., *Capra pyrenaica* and *Rupricapra rupricapra*, together with the punctuated occasional appearance of remains assigned to two large herbivores, *Rhinocerotidae* sp and *Elephas* sp.

The taphonomic analysis shows that carnivore activity had little impact on the accumulation of the animal bones. The identified taxa through the stratigraphic sequence generally occur in non-anthropic contexts; and they include *Canis lupus*, *Vulpes vulpes*, *Crocuta crocuta*, *Felis sylvestris* and *Lynx pardina*. Since the rockshelter is a source of water, it is likely that carnivores were naturally attracted by such a locality. However, some of the bone fragments show carnivore marks, posterior to anthropic ones. It is probable, therefore, that the nature of the site, the intense anthropic activities as well as the thermal treatment of bones deterred more than very occasional carnivore activity (Lupo 1995).

The state of preservation of the archaeobotanical remains is good. Numerous charcoal fragments, wooden artefacts and a number of wood pseudomorphs have been recovered. The charcoal fragments were sampled mostly from the hearths and/or their peripheries. The anthracological analysis shows a prevalence of *Pinus sylvestris/ nigra*. The exploitation of conifers is attested in all the levels analysed by our team, indicating the existence of these trees near the site, revealing recurrent pine wood collection by the occupants of the rockshelter. The palynological record also shows high percentages of conifers in all levels (Burjachs and Julià 1994)

In level H (*c.* 45 ka) three wooden planks were found (Carbonell and Castro-Curel 1992). One is of oval shape and was made of *Juniperus* sp. while the other two specimens were made with *Pinus* sp. The morphology, the association with burned bones, and especially the spatial relationship with hearths of the charred wood remains suggests a domestic use in connection with food processing activities (Figure 8.4).

In level I (*c.* 46 ka) an important number of wood pseudomorphs were found fossilised as a consequence of

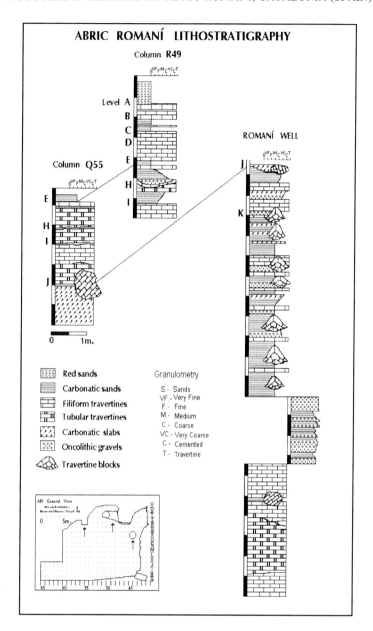

Figure 8.3: Lithostratigraphical sequence at Abric Romaní showing the levels excavated up to 1997.

a rapid travertine process (Castro-Curel and Carbonell 1995). For instance, a 3.5 m long by 45 cm wide tree trunk with broken parts of roots and branches was found lying on an inclined plane. Small residues of wood tissue were still preserved. The analysis indicates that this was a large pine specimen, most probably carried intentionally into the rockshelter. Level K preserves another large pseudomorph lying on the living floor. These remains possibly reflect stockpiling of wood and/or use of wood as benches near the hearths.

Also in level I, pseudomorphs of three long sticks, overcrossing above a large hearth suggest the existence of a tripod. In addition, a large number of wood imprints with the shape of tree branches were also recorded near several hearths.

In level J (*c.* 50 ka), a long pseudomorph of a cylindrical branch with a point fashioned at one end was recovered (Carbonell and Vaquero 1998). This piece was reproduced with a plaster cast (Jover 1994). The Scanning Electron Microscope studies of the point replica have confirmed the presence of characteristic striae produced by lithic instruments used in woodworking. This object was probably a digging stick.

Finally, in both levels I and K (*c.*52 ka), negatives of small wood flakes were recovered, some of which had charred ends. These remains reflect woodworking activities contemporaneous with the living floor. Some denticulated lithic flakes at the site also show microscopic evidence of woodworking activities.

These exceptional wooden remains, clearly associated

Figure 8.4: Wooden plank recovered from level H close to the small basin hearth.

Figure 8.5: View of Hearth Area from level K during excavation task.

Figure 8.6: Isolated flat hearth from level H.

Figure 8.7: Portion of level J displaying a long-term occupation floor with several hearths and abundant refitting faunal and lithic remains.

Figure 8.8: View of level K hearths close to the wall in a well-protected area of the shelter.

Figure 8.9: Hearthstone close to flat hearth in level J.

with human activities, reflect the importance of wood resources in the daily life of the Mousterian inhabitants.

Hearths

The ideal sedimentary conditions at Abric Romaní have permitted the preservation of hearths as well as the activities associated with them. In many cases, the hearths can be described as individual Hearth Units, whereas in some other cases they are treated as Hearth Areas because of their close association.

The first objective of the field work on the hearths was to excavate, document and sample them in optimum conditions. The following details were logged using a standardised index card:

1. Location of the fireplace in relation to the undisturbed burned ground surface and the horizontal delimitation of the perimeter. If there was an overlap, no total combustion area was delimited.
2. An identification name was assigned for further documentation, excavation and other analyses.
3. Initial observations on the hearth, including three-dimensional location in the rockshelter, directly associated finds and the sedimentary matrix. Also included were the drawing and photographic records.
4. Excavation of a quarter or a half of the fireplace depending on the state of concretion. The purpose was to have longitudinal and transverse cross-sections for stratigraphic description and definitive site drawings and pictures.
5. A range of different sampling techniques. According to the individual case, a micromorphological sample, samples of mixed ashes in the sediment, burned sediment and burned blocks from the hearths' interiors were sampled for analysis.

Hearths can be either tightly clustered or more dispersed. The number, different types and spatial distribution of the hearths within the shelter are related to the physical constraints of each living floor as well as the intensity of occupation (Figure 8.5).

The specific character and sizes of the Abric Romaní hearths are governed by the range and level of intensity of human activity, and are directly related to the sedimentary features. So, on the one hand, levels with travertine platforms and natural basins have hearths which are are flat without previous preparation or are situated in the depressions.On the other hand, in the terrigenous levels hearth variability and intensity is greater. There are three size groups ranging from 10–40 cm, 40–100 cm and 100–140 cm diameter.

In levels H and I, interpreted as recurrent short-term occupations with several stop-over episodes, flat hearths without associated blocks are dominant (Figure 8.6). Hearths are mostly found in natural basins. This is a consequence of the type of occupation and the characteristics of the ground relief. The latter creates small concave

surfaces between larger convex structural platforms. Based on the characteristics of the habitable space, the hearths conform to a mosaic (level H) or a cluster (level I) distribution pattern. Unlike other levels, there is little spatial correlation between the remains associated with the hearths and the structure of the occupation. Accordingly, the occupations of these levels do not present any defined spatial axis other than the one given by individual hearths.

On the other hand, level J comprises several long term occupations. It contains a large number of flat hearths, both isolated and overlapping. There are also many hearths with blocks and flagstones and complex hearth areas which are difficult to isolate in the field. The spatial distribution of the hearths is structured in various areas across the entire occupation surface. The large number of finds (hearths, charcoals, faunal and lithic remains) makes it difficult to identify a unique spatial distribution pattern for this level (Figure 8.7).

Level K presents a diversity of small flat hearths, with and without associated blocks, situated at the far end of the wall. There are also large hearth areas next to the wall in a well protected area of the shelter. The hearths so far excavated in level L are flat. As in level K, these hearths are arranged in parallel rows between the wall and the drip-line (Figure 8.8).

Discussion

The composition and variability of hearths is related to the intensity of occupation in each level. In the light of this, there is an optimisation of the internal resources of the shelter in the short-term occupations, with flat hearths lacking structure, in natural basins or following the natural relief of the platforms. In contrast, the long-term occupations reflect a greater accommodation of space, with a deliberate arrangement of internal elements of the shelter as well as a greater variability and intensity of hearths. In these cases, we find allochthonous elements such as large limestone blocks that were brought into the site for their use as hearthstones. Moreover, we see elements of the shelter itself within the hearths, including stalagmite fragments and small crystallised flagstones. these latter all occurring in a non-natural sedimentary context. We may infer that the Romani inhabitants recognised the refractory properties of these materials and deliberately incorporated them (Figures 8.9 and 8.10) within the hearth structures.

Fuel is an important item which implies gathering and hearth processing activities. In Abric Romaní, wood was the major fuel used for fire maintenance. Pine wood was probably collected from nearby the shelter. It is known that pine wood was available and locally abundant. However, the use of other wood sources cannot be ruled out. The length of occupation is also another important factor that influences the choice of fuel and therefore the variability in the anthracological record.

Figure 8.10: Charred flagstone from level K find inside a flat hearth.

Considerable quantities of burnt bones with differing degrees of burning have been recovered from the hearths and their surrounding areas. Most of them are small fragments. We do not regard this as a product due to the palimpsest event, since there are differences in the representation of burnt bones and other artefacts (lithic artifacts or gastropod shells) which we believe were burnt more randomly.

We cannot be sure if these bones were burnt during the process of cleaning activities, during food preparation (cooking) or whether bone was a complementary type of fuel. With the exception of level J, there is no certain evidence of cleaning activities and wood is considered to be the major fuel for hearths. The comparative quantification of the burnt bones and charcoal fragments will in the future provide further data to help us answer these questions.

If the burnt bones were the result of cooking activities it may not be possible to demonstrate this fully because we usually recover only the final bone waste which comprises the smallest fractions and therefore consists of mainly unidentifiable fragments. To evaluate the cooking processes we will have to consider butchery cut marks (Cáceres 1998), and especially fracture patterns on the long bones to determine whether thermal treatment occurred before fracturing.

Up to 1997, the large sample of hearths at Abric Romaní included 120 excavated units, 60 of which are now completely documented. They have been described, drawn in both horizontal plan and vertical cross-section. At the same time, we have taken into account micromorphological samples, burnt sediment and charcoals, as well as archaeological remains associated with the hearths. The evidence from Abric Romaní allows us to clarify the rôle of fire and the various methods of utilisation by Mousterian peoples, as well as enabling us to reconstruct some of their behavioural activities. The latter includes the collection of firewood and the thermal treatment of vegetal and animal resources. Overall, the hearths at Abric Romaní contribute to our knowledge of Mousterian pyrotechnology.

Acknowledgments

The present project is supported by Generalitat de Catalunya and Ajuntament de Capellades and especially the sponsorship of Tallers Gràfics Romanyà Valls S.A. We thank all the members of the excavation team, and Rolf Quam and Carolina Mallol for their help and especially Professor M. Sahnouni for the English translation.

References

Aïmene, M. (1998). Les différents aspects de l'activité anthropique du niveau E de l'Abric Romaní (Barcelone, Espagne). In (J.-P. Brugal, L. Meignen & M. Patou-Mathis, Eds) *Économie préhistorique: les comportements de subsistance au Paléolithique*, pp. 193–203., Actes des Rencontres, 23–25 octobre 1997. Sophia Antipolis, APDCA.

Bischoff, J., Julià, R. & Mora, R. (1988). Uranium series dating of the Mousterian occupation at the Abric Romaní, Spain. *Nature* **332**, 68–70.

Bischoff, J., Ludwig, K., Garcia, J.F., Carbonell, E., Vaquero, M., Stafford, Th.W.Jr. and Jull, A.J.T. (1994). Dating of the basal Aurignacian Sandwich at Abric Romaní (Catalunya, Spain) by Radiocarbon and Uranium-Series. *Journal of Archaeological Science.* **21,** 541–551.

Burjachs, F. & Julià, R. (1994). Abrupt Climatic Changes during the Last Glaciation Based on Pollen Analysis of the Abric Romaní, Catalonia, Spain. *Quaternary Research* **42**, 308–315.

Cáceres, I. (1998). Le niveau I de l'Abri Romaní (Barcelone, Espagne): séquence d'intervention des différents agents et processus taphonomiques. In (J.-P. Brugal, L. Meignen and M. Patou-Mathis, Eds), *Économie préhistorique: les comportaments de subsistance au Paléolithique.* pp. 173–180. Actes des Rencontres, 23–25 octobre 1997. APDCA: Sophia Antipolis.

Carbonell, E. & Castro-Curel, Z. (1992) Palaeolithic Wooden Artefacts from the Abric Romaní (Capellades, Barcelona, Spain). *J. of Archaeol. Sc.* **19**, 707–719.

Castro-Curel, Z. & Carbonell, E. (1995). Wood Pseudomorphs From level I at Abric Romaní, Barcelona, Spain. *J. of Field Archaeol.* **22**, 376–384.

Carbonell, E & Vaquero, M. (1998). Behavioral Complexity and Biocultural Change in Europe Around Forty Thousand Years Ago. *J. of Anthropol. Res.* **54**, 373–397.

Jover, A. (1994). The Application of PEG 4000 for the Preservation of Palaeolithic Wooden Artifacts. *Studies in Conservation* **39**, 193–198.

Lupo, K.D. (1995). Hadza Bone Assemblages and Hyena Attrition: An Ethnographic Example of the Influence of Cooking and Mode of Discard on the Intensity of Scavenger Ravaging. *J. of Anthropol. Archaeol.* **14**, 288–314.

Straus, L.G. (1989). On Early Hominid use of Fire. *Curr. Anthrop.* **30**, 488–491.

Vaquero, M. (1997). *Tecnología Lítica y Comportamiento Humano: Organización de las activitades técnicas y cambio diacrónico en el paleolítico medio del Abric Romaní (Capellades, Barcelona).* Tarragona, Spain. Ph.D. diss., Universitat Rovira i Virgili.

Wandsnider, L. (1997). The Roasted and the Boiled: Food Composition and Heat Treatment with Special Emphasis on Pit-Hearth Cooking. *J. of Anthropol. Archaeol.* **16**, 1–48.

9

The Late Middle Palaeolithic in the Northeast of the Iberian Peninsula

Manuel Vaquero and Eudald Carbonell

This paper gives a general view of the Late Middle Palaeolithic in the north east of the Iberian Peninsula. Recent evidence has allowed us to specify the chronology of some sites (Table 9.1). It seems reasonable to deal with the final moments of the Middle Palaeolithic as a specific issue. The background to this topic is the appearance of the Upper Palaeolithic and its anthropological and cultural implications. We will identify the aspects directly related to this cultural change at the end of the paper.

In recent years north-eastern Iberia has become a key area for understanding the Middle/Upper Palaeolithic transition in Europe. Some of the earliest dates for the European Upper Palaeolithic have been obtained here, at sites such as Arbreda Cave, Abric Romaní and Reclau Viver Cave. From this point of view, the study of the final Middle Palaeolithic is especially important. We have only chosen those sites that, according to radiometric data and palaeo-environmental studies, can be placed in the Late Middle Palaeolithic. We have interpreted the archaeological record from a behavioural perspective for two interrelated reasons. Firstly, only in this way can we deal with the cultural processes that are involved in the formation of archaeological sites, and secondly, because the behavioural domain is the background to most questions pertaining to the Middle/Upper Palaeolithic boundary.

Since the discovery of Abric Romaní in 1909, many sites in the north east of the Iberian Peninsula have been attributed to the Middle Palaeolithic. However, many of these sites present different problems which limit their contribution to a synthesis centred on human behaviour in a precise chronological and environmental context. Surface collections are numerous (e.g. the sites of La Selva or La Femosa), as well as the sites excavated without adequate methodology or stratigraphic control (e.g. Bóvila Sugranyes, Cova del Gegant, Cova del Muscle). Other sites were excavated many years ago and in general have

only provided typological data. Finally, for some sites no work is published or there is no chronological data, and they cannot reliably be placed in the final stages of the Middle Palaeolithic. Consequently, the sites that can be used in this synthesis are scarce and are mainly from excavations carried out in recent years. They are as follows:

Abric Romaní (Capellades). This is located over one of the natural passages between the Prelitoral Depression and the Ebro Depression, at 317m above sea level. The site was discovered by Amador Romaní in 1909 and has been excavated at different times during this century. The last phase of excavations started in 1983 and these are still in progress. The known stratigraphy is almost 20m in depth, although the measurements have not yet arrived at the bottom of the sequence. The sedimentary sequence is mainly composed of travertine layers, although other sedimentary processes have also been recorded, such as the falling of blocks from the roof of the shelter and the formation of clay deposits. 27 archaeological levels have been identified, but only the uppermost 10 have been excavated. Most of the archaeological levels correspond to the Middle Palaeolithic, except the uppermost one (level A) which has been attributed to the Early Upper Palaeolithic. A series of U/Th dates places the sequences between 40 and 70ka. Palynological analyses have shown the succession of five climatic phases, between the final moments of the OIS 5 and the Hengelo Interstadial (Bischoff *et al.* 1988; Burjachs and Julià 1994; Carbonell *et al.* 1994).

Arbreda Cave (Serinyà). This is located in the Banyoles-Besalú lacustrine basin. After an initial excavation carried out by J.M. Corominas in 1972–73, the main work started in 1975 and is still in progress. The stratigraphic sequence is 11m thick and contains Holocene and Pleistocene layers. Two sedimentary segments have

Table 9.1: Dates from the Late Middle Palaeolithic and Early Upper Palaeolithic in the NE of the Iberian Peninsula.

Middle Palaeolithic

Site	Level	Date (kyr BP)	Method	Lab No.	Source
Roca dels Bous	R3	38.8 ± 1.2	[14]C AMS	AA-6481	1
	S1	> 46.9	[14]C AMS	AA-6480	1
Ermitons Cave	IV	36.43 ± 1.8	Conv. [14]C	CSIC-197	2
	IV	33.19 ± 0.6	[14]C AMS	OxA-3725	2
Arbreda Cave	I	39.4 ± 1.4	[14]C AMS	AA-3776	3
	I	34.1 ± 0.7	[14]C AMS	AA-3777	3
	I	41.4 ± 1.6	[14]C AMS	AA-3778	3
	I	44.56 ± 2.4	[14]C AMS	OxA-3731	2
	Basal MP	83.0 +10.7/-8.7	Pa/U		4
	Basal MP	85.1 +38.2/-26.7	Th/U		4
	Basal MP	89.1 +36.8/-24.3	Ra/U		4
Banyoles		45.0 ± 4.0	U-Series		5
Abric Romaní	Travert.	43.8 ± 1.5	U-Series		6
	Travert.	46.3 ± 1.5*	U-Series		7
	Travert.	42.7 ± 1.3*	U-Series		7
	B	43.5 ± 1.2	[14]C AMS	NZA-2312	7
	Travert.	43.4 ± 1.5	U-Series		6
	Travert.	45.6 ± 3.5*	U-Series		6
	Travert.	43.2 ± 1.1*	U-Series		6
	Travert.	44.4 ± 0.2*	U-Series		6
	D	40.6 ± 0.9	[14]C AMS	NZA-2313	8
	E	43.2 ± 1.1	[14]C AMS	NZA-2314	8
	H	44.5 ± 1.2	[14]C AMS	NZA-2315	8
	Travert.	46.5 ± 1.7*	U-Series		6
	Travert.	48.0 ± 1.6	U-Series		6
	Travert.	49.3 ± 1.6	U-Series		6
	Travert.	50.4 ± 0.5*	U-Series		6
	Travert.	52.3 ± 0.6*	U-Series		6
	Travert.	52.2 ± 1.6	U-Series		6
	Travert.	54.5 ± 0.5*	U-Series		6
	Travert.	54.2 ± 1.1*	U-Series		6
	Travert.	56.8 ± 3.2*	U-Series		6
	Travert.	58.6 ± 1.2*	U-Series		6
	Travert.	60.0 ± 1.4*	U-Series		6
	Travert.	59.2 ± 1.1*	U-Series		6
	Travert.	70.2 ± 2.6	U-Series		9
Cova 120		57.9 +6.8/-6.5	U-Series		10
Gabasa	e	46.5 +4.4/-2.8	Conv. [14]C	GrN-12809	11

Table 9.1: continued

Early Upper Palaeolithic

Site	Level	Date (kyr BP)	Method	Lab No.	Source
Arbreda	H	37.7 ± 1.0	^{14}C AMS	AA-3779	3
	H	37.7 ± 1.0	^{14}C AMS	AA-3780	3
	H	39.9 ± 1.3	^{14}C AMS	AA-3781	3
	H	38.7 ± 1.2	^{14}C AMS	AA-3782	3
	H	37.34 ± 1.0	^{14}C AMS	OxA-3729	2
	H	35.48 ± 0.8	^{14}C AMS	OxA-3730	2
	H	> 33.5	Conv. ^{14}C	Beta-46690	12
Reclau Viver	B	30.19 ± 0.5	^{14}C AMS	OxA-3726	2
	A	40.0 ± 1.4	^{14}C AMS	OxA-3727	2
Mollet		33.78 ± 0.7	^{14}C AMS	OxA-3728	2
Abric Romaní	Travert.	40.8 ± 1.5*	U-Series		6
	Travert.	39.4 ± 1.5	U-Series		6
	Travert.	42.9 ± 1.6	U-Series		6
	Travert.	39.1 ± 1.5	U-Series		6
	Travert.	44.4 ± 1.6*	U-Series		7
	Travert.	41.8 ± 0.8*	U-Series		7
	Travert.	36.3 ± 1.3	Conv. ^{14}C		7
	A	37.29 ± 0.9	^{14}C AMS	AA-7395	7
	A	35.4 ± 0.8	^{14}C AMS	AA-8037A	7
	A	37.9 ± 1.0	^{14}C AMS	AA-8037B	7
	A	36.59 ± 0.6	^{14}C AMS	NZA-231 1	7

* Average

Sources: 1. Terradas *et al.* 1993; 2. Maroto *et al.* 1996; 3. Bischoff *et al.* 1989; 4. Yokoyama *et al.* 1987; 5. Julià & Bischoff 1991; 6. Bischoff *et al.* 1988; 7. Bischoff *et al.* 1994; 8. Vaquero 1997; 9. Burjachs & Julià 1994; 10. Agustí *et al.* 1991; 11. Utrilla & Montes 1993; 12. Soler & Maroto 1993.

been identified in the Pleistocene sequence. The upper one is mainly composed of clays and blocks; the Upper Palaeolithic and the latest Middle Palaeolithic levels have been documented in this sequence. The lower one entirely corresponds to the Middle Palaeolithic and is formed by clayey and sandy layers that show important disturbance processes. Middle Palaeolithic levels have been dated between 40 and 85ka. Palynological studies indicate that the latest Middle Palaeolithic occupations are placed in an interstadial context correlated with the Moershoofd-Hengelo complex (Burjachs & Renault-Miskovsky 1992; Maroto *et al.* 1996; Soler & Maroto 1987; Yokoyama *et al.* 1987).

120 Cave (Sales de Llierca, La Garrotxa). This is located in the Alta Garrotxa Massif, in the Pre-Pyrenees, at 460m above sea level. It is a small cave and was excavated between 1985 and 1989. Four Pleistocene archaeological levels (IV-VII) have been documented; except for levels IV and V, archaeological remains are very scarce. Palaeoenvironmental studies indicate a cold climate, although some mild species typical of this region survived. A carbonated layer above level IV was dated at around 57ka (Agustí *et al.* 1991).

Ermitons Cave (Sales de Llierca, La Garrotxa). The Ermitons Cave is also situated in the Alta Garrotxa Massif, near the 120 Cave. Archaeological excavations were carried out between 1970 and 1971. A 3m thick stratigraphic sequence has been documented. Among the six archaeological levels identified, three of them correspond to the Middle Palaeolithic. The Pleistocene strata are characterised by the predominance of clay and gravels, with some blocks having fallen from the ceiling and roofs of the cave.

Gabasa Cave (Huesca). This cave is situated in the Mesozoic formations of the Pre-Pyrenees, at 740m above sea level. The excavations carried out between 1984 and 1994 revealed a fairly homogeneous sedimentary deposit, mainly formed by a clayey matrix with many limestone blocks and pebbles. Seven archaeological levels have been identified, all of them attributed to the Middle Palaeolithic (Blasco 1997; Blasco *et al.* 1996; Hoyos *et al.* 1992; Montes 1988; Utrilla & Montes 1993).

Roca dels Bous (Sant Llorenç de Montgai, La Noguera). This site is located on the banks of the river Segre, at the boundary between the Pre-Pyrenees and the Ebro Depression. The Quaternary deposits are 20m thick, and are mainly formed by fluviatile and slope formation processes. For the moment, only the two uppermost archaeological levels (S1 and R3) have yielded useful data (Terradas *et al.* 1993; Jordá *et al.* 1994).

All the sites selected are caves or rockshelters. This is due to preservation phenomena, but also to the historical development of archaeological research. Cave sites have traditionally been preferred to open-air locations. Although some Middle Palaeolithic open-air sites have been documented, they are generally surface findings that lack a precise stratigraphical context. The chronology of other sites with a stratigraphical context has not been defined accurately enough to place them reliably in the late Middle Palaeolithic. These sites have therefore only provided some isolated lithic remains, which largely restricts their behavioural significance. To interpret these findings geoarchaeological work to reconstruct regional palaeo-environmental sequences needs to be done. Nevertheless, the open-air sites may be relevant in the future, especially in areas such as the Ebro valley or the Camp de Tarragona, where the appearance of caves and rockshelters is restricted because of the geomorphological context. Available data suggest that the Camp de Tarragona could have recorded an important Middle Palaeolithic occupation. The sites of the Reus area (e.g. Bóvila Sugranyes) (Vilaseca 1952) and the Francolí valley (e.g. Mas Blanc, Vinyes Grans) (Gabarró *et al.* 1995) therefore suggest that this kind of occupation was a fundamental aspect of the settlement systems.

Few human remains have been recovered in this area. Only two premolars, two molars, one phalanx and a fragment of clavicle have been found in Gabasa (Montes 1988: 236–7), and three molars and one premolar from the Abric Agut (Lumley 1973: 551–8). The dental pieces of Gabasa were found in level F and attributed to *Homo sapiens Neanderthalensis*. The dental pieces of the Abric Agut are, according to M.-A. de Lumley (1973), typically Neanderthal.

The most significant finding, but also the most controversial, is the Banyoles mandible (Maroto & Soler 1993). It was discovered in 1887 in the travertine formations around Lake Banyoles. Although the precise stratigraphical context and place of the finding is not known, some authors (Maroto & Soler 1993: 36–7) have suggested an approximate location. The first far-reaching study of the mandible was published by M.-A. de Lumley (1973), who attributed it to a female individual with disparate traits. Some were archaic or evolved, but others were Neanderthal. The mandible was finally attributed to the Ante-Neanderthals, and placed in the Riss-Würm interglacial or earlier. This phylogenetic attribution was widely accepted, although some radiometric datings did not completely support this chronology (Berger & Libby 1966; Yokoyama *et al.* 1987). The new U/Th dates from the travertine on the mandible (Julià & Bischoff 1991) have reinforced this contradiction. The date of 45±4ka is supported by the datings of the travertine sequence where the mandible was found and

tends to locate it in the late Middle Palaeolithic. If this chronology is accepted, the mandible's mixture of traits takes on a new significance. Nevertheless, the contradiction between anatomical and chronological studies does not provide an easy answer if we take into account the context of its discovery and the lack of a precise stratigraphical origin.

Geographical distribution

From a geomorphological point of view, there are three main units in the north east of the Iberian Peninsula: the Ebro valley, the Pyrenees and the Mediterranean System (Figure 9.1).

The **Pyrenees** are a 435 km-long range of mountains which extend from the Gulf of Gascony to the Mediterranean. With altitudes higher than 3,000m, they separate the Iberian Peninsula from continental Europe. From a geological point of view, they are made up of two units: a) the Axial Zone, in the middle of the range, where Palaeozoic materials predominate and the highest altitudes are found, and b) the Pre-Pyrenees, north and south of the Axial Zone, formed of Mesozoic materials, and where two ranges are identified (the Interior Range and the Exterior Range) which are separated by the Pre-Pyrenean Middle Depression. The fluvial courses (Noguera Pallaresa, Noguera Ribagorzana, Segre, *etc*) are the natural passages between the different geomorphological units, especially between the Pre-Pyrenean Middle Depression and the Ebro Depression. The Pre-Pyrenees are one of the main areas of site concentrations, especially after the work of recent years. Sites such as Roca dels Bous, Gabasa, Ermitons Cave and 120 Cave are located in these formations.

The **Ebro Depression** had its origin in an inland sea stretching from the Pyrenees to the north east border of the Meseta. In this sedimentary basin, continental and marine materials were deposited during the Oligocene and the Miocene. Except at the edges of the basin, where Tertiary materials were often folded in contact with other structural units, tabular forms tend to predominate. Although surface findings are frequent, sites in primary stratigraphical context are scarce, particularly in the central part of the Depression. None of the selected sites is fully located in this unit, although some of them are in the contact with other structural units (Pyrenees, Mediterranean System).

The **Mediterranean System** is a set of NE-SW trending topographical features, parallel to the Mediterranean coast. From east to west, there are three major units: a) the Littoral Range, b) the Pre-Littoral Depression, and c) the Pre-Littoral Range, features which were deformed by Alpine folding and faulting. In the north, the ranges are formed mainly of Palaeozoic materials, whereas Mesozoic terrains predominate in the south. The Pre-Littoral Depression is a sedimentary basin that was mainly infilled during the Miocene. Rivers flow through these features in a NW-SE

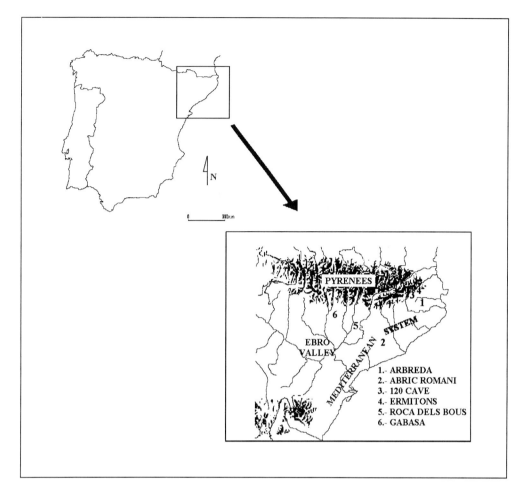

Figure 9.1: Map indicating the main geomorphological units and sites mentioned in the text.

direction and have been the preferred natural passages between the coastal areas and the interior regions. Abric Romaní is located in one of these passages. Next to Abric Romaní, another site of similar chronology, Abric Agut, is located. Few results of the archaeological excavations at the Abric Agut have been published (González *et al.* 1998), but they have provided some of the few human remains documented in the north east of the Peninsula.

Outside the Mediterranean System, but within the littoral and pre-littoral units, we should mention the Ampurdán Fossa. This was formed by the subsidence of a Hercynian block that created a terrestrial sedimentary basin during the Mio-Pliocene. It is bordered by a set of faults that separate it from the surrounding ranges. This depression is drained by the Ter and Fluvià rivers, the fault delimiting the western border of the depression forming Lake Banyoles. Near to this lake, one of the most important groups of sites is located, including the Arbreda, Reclau Viver and Mollet Caves. In this zone, the Banyoles mandible was also found.

Palaeoenvironment

The main data for reconstructing Middle Palaeolithic climatic conditions are provided by sites with long temporal sequences, such as Abric Romaní. With this site we have been able to reconstruct the climatic events recorded between 70 and 40 ka. The final moments of this period are also recorded in the palynological sequence of Arbreda Cave. Palynological analysis of Abric Romaní (Burjachs & Julià 1994) has shown five climatic zones between 70 and 40 ka. (Figure 9.2):

Zone 1 (70.2–65.5 ka). This corresponds to the base of the sequence and presents two warm phases characterised by high percentages of arboreal pollen, including thermophilous taxa such as *Quercus* and *Olea-Phyllyrea*. Between them, a cold period is characterised by the expansion of Poaceae. This zone correlates with the Isotopic Stages 20 and 19 of the Summit sequence and the short, warm episodes recorded in the Grande Pile between the Saint Germain II interstadial and the OIS 4.

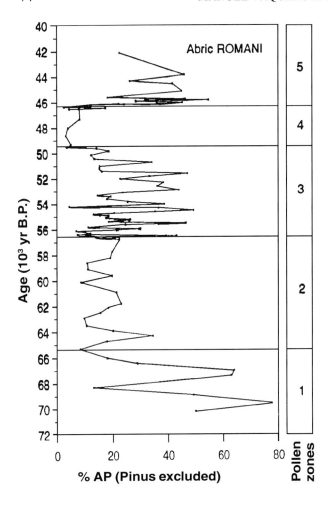

*Figure 9.2: Arboreal pollen percentages (*Pinus *excluded) from Abric Romaní sequence (From Burjachs & Julià 1994).*

Zone 2 (65.5–56.8 ka). This is characterised by a cold and humid climate with short intervals of warmer conditions. The percentage of AP is low and the Poaceae and *Artemisia* predominate. This zone would correspond to OIS 4. The short, warm episodes seem to take place at regular intervals of *c.* 2.3 ka.

Zone 3 (56.8–49.5 ka). This phase shows frequent climatic fluctuations at intervals of *c.* 1.0 ka. In the short, mild periods, thermophilous taxa developed and there was an increase in humidity. It is characterised by the dominance of Poaceae, *Artemisia* and *Pinus*, whereas in the warm periods taxa such as *Juniperus, Quercus, Olea-Phillyrea, Rhamnus*, Fabaceae and Escrofulariaceae developed.

Zone 4 (49.5–46.2 ka). This is a cold and dry phase, with low AP and a dominance of steppic vegetation (Asteraceae, Poaceae and *Artemisia*). It is the coldest period of the Abric Romaní sequence, although there was a progressive deterioration of climate in the final period of the previous phase.

Zone 5 (46.2–40.8 ka). This corresponds to the

uppermost sequence and shows a climatic warming of interstadial type. It began with an expansion of pioneer taxa (*Juniperus* and *Pinus*), followed by an increase in *Quercus* and *Olea-Phillyrea*. It correlates with the Hengelo Interstadial. At the top of this sequence, the first Upper Palaeolithic occupations are documented.

The base of Arbreda's pollen diagram corresponds to the final part of the Middle Palaeolithic and the Early Upper Palaeolithic (Burjachs & Renault-Miskovsky 1992). There is a light progression of the arboreal pollen from bottom to top, including taxa such as holm oak and *Olea-Phillyrea* at the top of the sequence. As for the herbaceous taxa, a small progression of Poaceae has been documented at the bottom, then a decrease in this taxon and an increase in Asteraceae, while the percentage of *Artemisia* falls slightly. These data indicate a period of mild climate which correlates with the interstadials of the Moershoofd-Hengelo complex.

Cultural evidence

Lithic operating chains

On the whole, lithic raw materials have a local origin, although a percentage of remains from distant sources is always found. The lithic record tends therefore to reflect the provenance of the environment in which each site is located. Quartz and quartzite are the most frequent raw materials in northern sites (Arbreda, 120 Cave, Ermitons), except in the archaeological unit R3 of Roca dels Bous and the Gabasa site, where flint is more common. The use of flint tends to increase as one moves southward and it is the predominant raw material in Abric Romaní, although its percentage varies within the sequence. In this site, there is an increasing tendency to use flint and this has also been documented in Roca dels Bous. In Abric Romaní, the lowest part of the sequence excavated so far shows a greater variability in the provisioning strategies, and quartz and limestone reach high percentages. In the upper levels, the percentage of flint substantially increases, and reaches values above 90%, which indicates a preferential selection of this raw material. In any case, data provided by Abric Romaní indicate that provisioning strategies are not simply a reflection of the local resources. Rather, they show a conscious selection between different options. Quartz and limestone are the most abundant materials in the surrounding area but flint is preferred, even though the most abundant sources are at least 5 km distant from the site.

Sidescrapers and denticulates are the most common retouched artifacts in lithic assemblages. Sidescrapers are dominant in most sites: level I of Arbreda Cave, Ermitons, Roca dels Bous, Gabasa and 120 Cave. Only in Abric Romaní are denticulates the most frequent retouched artifact, with percentages higher than 90% in some occupation levels (Figure 9.3).

The knapping strategies documented in the Iberian fall within the range of variability defined by the Levallois and discoidal methods. The Levallois method has been

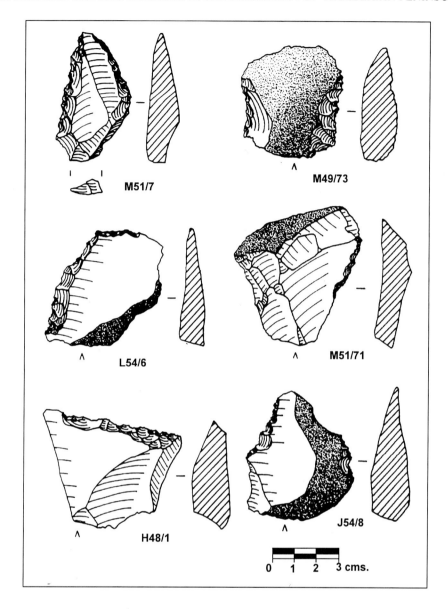

M51/7

M49/73

L54/6

M51/71

H48/1

J54/8

0 1 2 3 cms.

Figure 9.3: Retouched artifacts from the level Jb of Abric Romaní.

seen in level I of Arbreda Cave (Maroto *et al.* 1996: 222) but, because the industry is based on quartz, it is sometimes difficult to observe the technical criteria characteristics of this knapping method. Levallois reduction strategy has been also documented as the dominant method in Ermitons Cave and in 120 Cave, although in this site the polyhedric cores are more frequent. It is virtually absent in other sites, such as Gabasa, where formless, polyhedric and discoid cores are dominant. The discoid method also predominates in Roca dels Bous. Nevertheless, the two methods share most of their technical criteria and the distinctive criteria are defined by continuous variables, so it is often difficult to attribute certain artifacts technically.

In view of these problems, it seems reasonable to draw up analytical methods for defining the continuity between both strategies, disregarding the initial typological classification that divides the spectrum of morphological variability into discrete categories. The operatory field concept, defined by Michel Guilbaud (1995), allows us to articulate the different technical criteria in a wide techno-logical context, where the morphological differences and technical decisions can achieve a meaning. In Abric Romaní, the hierarchical organisation of knapping surfaces and the core symmetry are the criteria that can structure the variability of reduction strategies in both the synchronic and diachronic levels. From these criteria we can observe a central space of variability, where different technical options are located. The symmetry and hierarchical organisation of these options are different. In this morpho-technical field, we can also define a peripheral space, where some secondary technical options, developed from the morphologies created in the central space, are located.

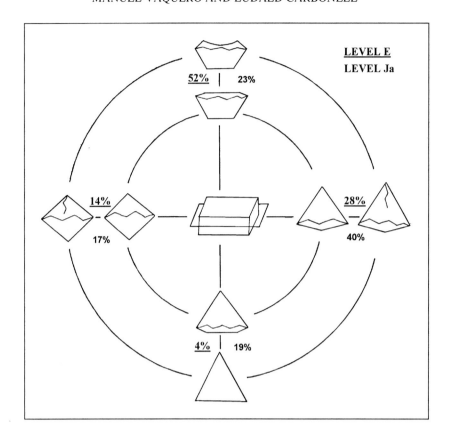

Figure 9.4: Morphotechnical field from the levels E and Ja of Abric Romaní.

Archaeological levels E and Ja are representative of two different technical phases within the Abric Romaní sequence. Comparing these levels can provide a good example of the different ways of articulating the space of variability (Figure 9.4).

– The lowermost levels of the sequence excavated so far (*c.* 45–50ka), and especially level Ja, are characterised by the dominance of unhierarchical methods (Figure 9.5), although there is a wide spectrum of variability. In this spectrum, no single technical option is clearly dominant.

– The uppermost levels (*c.* 43–45ka), represented by level E, show a predominance of the hierarchical and asymmetric method, providing morphologies similar to those defined for the Levallois method (Figure 9.6). The other technical options documented in the lower levels are still present, although their percentages are very low.

These differences in the organisation of the same morphotechnical field suggest that variability in Middle Palaeolithic reduction strategies is not only due to the choice between two clearly different reduction methods, but is also reflected in the structure of the variability field as a whole. We can see the diachronic meaning of these differences if we analyse the correlation between this change in knapping methods and those noted in other phases of the operating chain. From this correlation, two technical periods can be distinguished in the Abric Romaní sequence which differ in raw material provisioning strategies, reduction sequences and retouching of artifacts.

a) The first technical period corresponds to the lower levels. The wide spectrum of morphotechnical variability defined by knapping methods is also observed in raw material provisioning. Although flint is the raw material most frequently used, high percentages of other materials, such as quartz and limestone, are documented. In this context, denticulates are virtually the only retouched artifact represented.

b) The uppermost part of the sequence shows a more restrictive choice between the different options defined by the morphotechnical field. This restriction also extends to raw material provisioning strategies. Flint is practically the only raw material used in the knapping sequences. Some flake characteristics, such as the increase in the number of facetted platforms and concave ventral surfaces, indicate that these changes are related to criteria involving a higher technical competence, a greater control of reduction sequence and a more careful management of the production process. Retouch sequences show a significant increase in the percentage of sidescrapers, although denticulates are still the most frequent artifact.

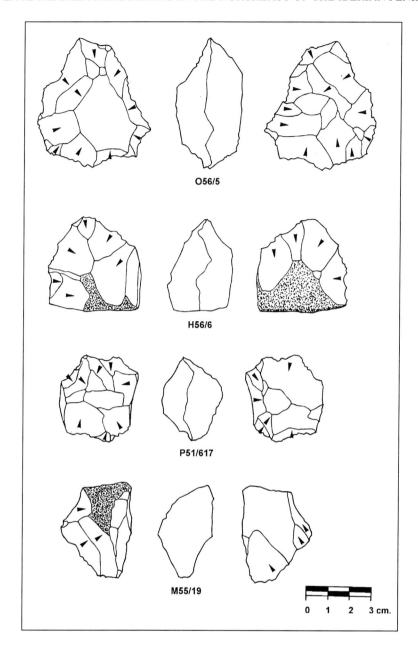

O56/5

H56/6

P51/617

M55/19

0   1   2   3 cm.

Figure 9.5: Cores from the level Ja of Abric Romaní.

Variability in the morphotechnical domain also extends to the spatial and temporal organisation of the operating chains and the ways of provisioning lithic resources. In general terms, it must be stressed that the transport of artifacts is one of the most important factors in lithic assemblage variability and has a fundamental rôle in interpreting the type and function of occupation events. The operating chain can be spatially divided in different ways. The technical form of transport can also be very diverse: unworked nodules, cores, flakes, retouched artifacts. Different strategies can be found in the same occupation level, as in Gabasa, where there has been transport of retouched artifacts, but the first stages of the reduction sequence are also well represented (Montes

1988: 139). Nevertheless, the spectrum of variability is sometimes more restricted and different technological facies can be defined, as those pointed out by Jean-Michel Geneste (1988, 63) for the Middle Palaeolithic of south west France. In Abric Romaní, different occupation levels show different strategies of transport. These differences may be related to other variables that reflect the intensity of occupation. Levels H, I and Ja are good examples of this pattern, especially if we compare the different provisioning strategies for the same raw material (Figure 9.7).

a)   In level H, a preferential transport of retouched artifacts and large flakes is documented. The technical

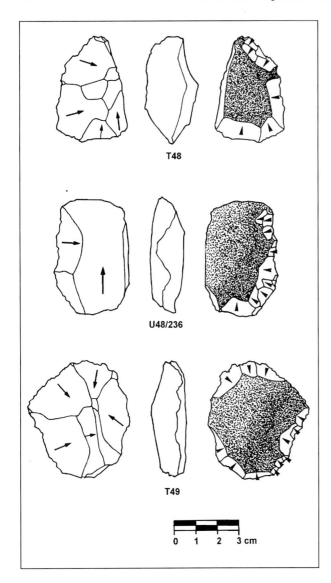

Figure 9.6: Cores from level E of Abric Romaní.

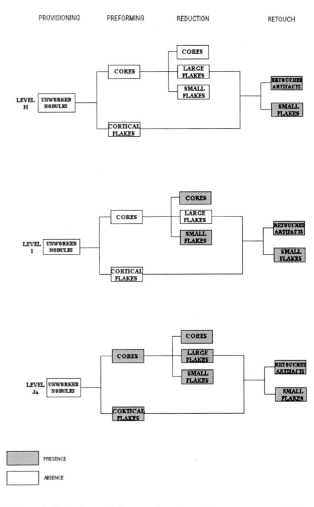

Figure 9.7: Differential organisation of the operatory chain of flint in the levels H, I and Ja of Abric Romaní, indicating the morphotechnical categories documented in the lithic assemblages.

processes carried out at the site are therefore limited to the retouching or resharpening of these supports.

b) Level I also shows the provisioning strategy noted earlier, but now some partially reduced cores are carried into the shelter. The lastest stages of the reduction sequences are developed inside the shelter, but the initial phases are absent.

c) Finally, level Ja, in addition to the two strategies noted above, shows some knapping sequences that take place entirely inside the shelter. This suggests that some unworked nodules or very slightly reduced cores were brought to the site.

Faunal resources

Red deer (*Cervus elaphus*), horse (*Equus caballus*), goat (*Capra pyrenaica*) and a large bovid are the most common herbivorous species in the north western Middle Palaeolithic sites. The frequency of each species depends on the

geographical setting of the sites. Thus, in the mountain environment goats are dominant, as in Ermitons (Maroto 1984–85; Maroto *et al.* 1996) and 120 Cave, although in the latter site the human origin of faunal remains is not clear (Agustí *et al.* 1991). Other sites show a wider spectrum of species. At Gabasa, horse, red deer, goat and *Rupicapra rupicapra* are the most common species, although taphonomical evidence suggests that only horse and red deer were mainly taken to the site by humans (Blasco 1997: 211). Horse and red deer are also the main species in all the archaeological levels of Abric Romaní (Carbonell *et al.* 1996: 399).

An important contribution by carnivores to the formation of faunal assemblages has been noted at different sites. As we pointed out earlier, both humans and carnivores brought goat remains to Ermitons and 120 Caves. This use of caves by humans and carnivores has also been documented in Gabasa (Blasco 1997) and Arbreda Cave, where taphonomical studies indicate that both agents carried herbivore remains to the site. In Arbreda Cave,

cave bear (*Ursus spelaeus*) is the dominant species. At Gabasa, spatial analysis of bone remains indicates that the activities of each agent tend to be located in different parts of the site. Human presence is related to the butchering of horse and red deer, whereas carnivores were mainly responsible for the presence of goat remains (Blasco *et al.* 1996; Blasco 1997). At Abric Romaní, on the other hand, the bulk of the faunal record was brought to the site by humans, as is clearly indicated by the scarcity of carnivore remains and the low percentage of gnaw marks.

A reconstruction of faunal provisioning strategies has been proposed for Abric Romaní. This shows different strategies according to animal size (Aïmene *et al.* 1996; Carbonell *et al.* 1996: 401–5). The small and medium-sized animals (red deer and goat) are represented by the presence of all their anatomical parts, except ribs, vertebrae and phalanges. By contrast, large animals (horse, large bovid and rhinoceros) are only represented by cranial and limb bones, while the axial skeleton and the distal ends of limb bones are missing. This suggests selective transport, or the *schlepp effect*:: large animals were partially processed before their transport to the shelter, leaving behind the less meaty anatomical parts. Resources carried to the site show intense exploitation, including the systematic breakage of long bones to obtain marrow. Sometimes the use of bone resources ended with the retouching of artifacts through direct percussion.

Vegetal resources

Lithics and animals were not the only resources exploited by humans during the Middle Palaeolithic. Evidence from several sources suggests that vegetal resources played an important rôle in subsistence strategies. In addition to the data provided by use-wear studies, which reveal widespread woodworking, direct proof of wooden artifacts associated with archaeological levels has been found in recent years. Because of the special characteristics of its sediments, Abric Romaní is the site that proves the exploitation of vegetal resources most emphatically.

The use of wood seems to be linked to two different domains of activity. On the one hand, wooden artifacts have been documented that suggest an intentional sharpening by humans. These artifacts were first recorded in level H (*c.* 45ka), where three carbonised objects, associated with hearths, were recovered. Two of them were oval and around 30 x 20 cm. The third artifact was rectangular and 55 x 20cm (Figure 9.8). On the other hand, different archaeological levels have yielded the travertine casts of pointed wooden artifacts. The best preserved is from level Ja, has a cylindrical section and is 100 cm long.

Besides the production of artifacts, several unmodified wooden elements have been found in Abric Romaní. As with the pointed artifacts noted earlier, only the travertine casts were recorded. These elements were found especially in level I, and may correspond to the accumulation of

firewood for supplying hearths. A 3.5m long pine trunk was also recovered in this level. The use of vegetal resources can also be proved by anthracological analysis. Pine (*Pinus sylvestris*) is the most common species at level I of the Arbreda Cave; some mild taxa are also documented, but in low percentages. The predominance of pine is also the main characteristic of the anthracological record of Abric Romaní sequence (Carbonell *et al.* 1996).

Settlement patterns

In principle, the function of sites is related to their geographical setting. In an environmental context, three types of locations can be distinguished from the sites selected in this paper:

a) Some sites are located in strategic natural passages that connect different geographical units. This is true of Abric Romaní and certain Pre-Pyrenean sites (Gabasa, Roca dels Bous). The setting of Roca dels, in a natural corridor between the Ebro Depression and the Pre-Pyrenean Depression, would allow control of the seasonal movements of the herbivore herds (Jordà *et al.* 1994: 42). A similar function has been attributed to the Gabasa site; its location and the characteristics of the faunal record suggested specialisation in hunting activities (Blasco *et al.* 1996).

b) Other sites are located in central places, from where it is possible to gain access to different geographical units and environments. Among these sites, Abreda Cave is the most characteristic, since it is located a short distance from river, lacustrine, mountain and plain ecosystems.

c) Finally, some sites are located within very specific ecosystems, which suggest the exploitation of a very limited array of resources. The sites in the Alta Garrotxa massif (Ermitons and 120 Cave) are located in ecosystems where mountain resources clearly predominate. Moreover, they are outside the main natural passages. From this point of view, Ermitons Cave has been characterised as a sporadic shelter for seasonal hunting. It must be taken into account that goat is the sole macromammal usable in this setting (Maroto *et al.* 1996: 237). The 120 Cave occupations have also been interpreted as short and episodic visits, although hunting as the main function has been rejected (Agustí *et al.* 1991).

Nevertheless, geographical location does not seem to be a determinant factor in site function. The best example is Abric Romaní, where different types of occupation appear during the sequence. These occupations varied both in length of occupation and size of group. They can be distinguished by criteria such as the size of surface area occupied, intrasite mobility, the interrelation between different areas, and the patterns of secondary refuse.

We have few data about the intrasite spatial patterns in the north eastern Middle Palaeolithic. Some sites do not show any clear spatial pattern, while others lack spatial

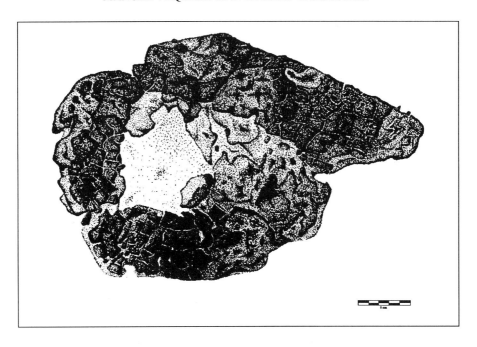

Figure 9.8: Wooden artifact from level H of Abric Romaní.

analyses or have not been excavated following criteria which allow organisation patterns to be reconstructed. Nevertheless, some data are available. Thus, level G of Gabasa indicates that human occupations were restricted to a limited part of the cave; as mentioned earlier, in this site human and carnivore activities tend to be spatially separated (Blasco *et al.* 1996).

Hearths played a central role in settlement strategies, judging by their recurrent appearance in certain sites such as Abric Romaní. Many combustion structures have been documented in the archaeological layers so far excavated, especially in those levels which record the highest occupation intensities such as level Ja, where over 50 hearths have been identified. They mainly show a flat cross-section and lack any element delimiting the combustion area.

Two types of strategies have been documented from spatial data in Abric Romaní, although they could be considered as the ends of a continuous spectrum of variability. These patterns are especially observed when analysing the spatial distribution of lithic remains.

a) Short-term occupations. These are restricted to small areas and their archaeological record resembles the accumulation model around hearths defined ethnographically. Although several of these accumulations can be found in the same archaeological level, refits suggest that they correspond to different occupation episodes. This kind of occupation has been documented in level I and is similar to that described in other Middle Palaeolithic sites (Pettitt 1997). There is no documentation of secondary accumulation processes or intentional artifact transport between different areas. Hearths show little variability and are always flat. Lithic operating chains were only partially developed in the shelter, and resources were carried as retouched artifacts, large flakes or highly reduced cores. Faunal processing activities were mainly limited to the consumption of resources transported from other occupation sites. Some of these occupations can be interpreted as short stops during the movements of small groups.

b) Long-term occupations. These extend over most of the site and show interzonal transport and secondary refuse remains. Hearths are characterised by more intense combustion processes and also show greater variability. Some lithic operating chains are entirely documented in the site, and, together with the transport patterns observed in short-term occupations, some unworked nodules were carried into the shelter. As well as consumption, activities related with faunal resources included carcass processing. These characteristics suggest longer occupations, and by larger groups, than in the previous type. Spatial distribution of lithic remains is the result of different factors, including:

   – The functional specialisation of certain areas, mainly related with to the use of unworked limestone cobbles.
   – The location of knapping activities, which seems to be linked to the setting of hearths, and corresponds to a preferentially occupied area. Most lithic remains obtained during such sequences were left on the spot, which allows accurate reconstruction of the knapping areas.
   – The disposal of larger refuse in peripheral areas,

outside the preferentially occupied zone. These kinds of secondary accumulations have been widely described in ethnoarchaeological contexts.

- The movement of certain artifacts, especially cores and retouched objects, across the site. Some reduction sequences became segmented between different areas, and certain locations could be distinguished as the confluence point of different operating chains, where long-distance intentional transport is mainly documented.

The Middle/Upper Palaeolithic transition

The first evidence of the Upper Palaeolithic in the north east of the Iberian Peninsula comes from the two principal sites in the zone, which contain long Middle Palaeolithic sequences: Arbreda Cave and Abric Romaní. Also, Reclau Viver Cave, near Arbreda Cave, only shows Upper Palaeolithic levels. At these sites, the Early Upper Palaeolithic has been dated at around 40ka (Table 9.1), thus providing some of the earliest dates obtained in Europe, and are similar to those from the Castillo Cave, in Northern Iberia, and some sites in Eastern Europe (Bacho Kiro, Temnata). The lithic assemblages located in these Early Upper Palaeolithic levels have been attributed to the first stages of the Aurignacian complex. No archaeological level containing transitional industries similar to the Châtelperronian have been found, although the appearance of four Châtelperron points in level I of the Arbreda Cave must be noted (Maroto *et al.* 1996: 222).

In general terms, sites documenting late Middle Palaeolithic and Early Upper Palaeolithic occupations in the same sequence (Arbreda and Abric Romaní) show a clear discontinuity from technical and typological points of view. The first Aurignacian occupations show a well-developed blade technology, and the underlying Middle Palaeolithic indicates no diachronic trend towards the production of blades. There is a similar discontinuity with the strategies of artifact retouch. These transformations came with changes in lithic raw material provisioning, which are especially clear in Arbreda Cave, where the systematic use of flint is seen for the first time, while quartz was the predominant raw material in all of the Middle Palaeolithic sequence. As far as retouched artifacts are concerned, the Early Aurignacian of Arbreda, Abric Romaní and Reclau Viver are characterised by the dominance of Dufour bladelets, retouched blades, end-scrapers and burins.

Besides this clear discontinuity from a technological perspective, the Early Upper Palaeolithic shows other cultural features that are generally associated with its appearance in Europe. Bone industry is well represented in the Reclau Viver and Arbreda Cave, and perforated shells and teeth have been found in Abric Romaní and Arbreda. In Abric Romaní, an assemblage of perforated fish vertebrae was found. However, other data indicate changes in settlement patterns. So, the bone record of the

Arbreda Cave shows less incidence of carnivore marks than that of the Middle Palaeolithic. This suggests a change in the use of the cave, possibly as a result of longer occupations during the Upper Palaeolithic.

Some scholars argue that certain Middle Palaeolithic sites have lithic assemblages showing evidence of influence by Upper Palaeolithic technical criteria. This influence would coincide in time with the appearance of the first Upper Palaeolithic occupations in other sites, such as Arbreda and Abric Romaní. Julià Maroto has pointed out, therefore, that the high percentage of Upper Palaeolithic tools in the Middle Palaeolithic assemblage of Ermitons Cave could reflect a process of acculturation. According to Blasco *et al.* (1996: 293), the increase in the proportion of *débordant* flakes in the Late Middle Palaeolithic of Gabasa (levels A+C) could also be related with the passage to the Upper Palaeolithic. Although we think that these technological arguments cannot be used to sustain the acculturation argument (*débordant* flakes are one of the main characteristics of some Middle Palaeolithic reduction strategies), these interpretations support the late dates provided by the Middle Palaeolithic of Ermitons (Table 9.1) and the sedimentological analysis of the Gabasa stratigraphy.

Nevertheless, the late survival of Middle Palaeolithic in NE Iberia is not as clear as in the centre and south of the Peninsula. At Gabasa, the location of the uppermost part of the sequence in the Würm III has been made through sedimentological analyses, but is in disagreement with a date of 46ka for level E. Moreover, the palaeoclimatic sequence provided by sedimentology is not in keeping with the results of pollen and microfaunal analyses (Hoyos *et al.* 1992). In Ermitons Cave, a previous conv. ^{14}C date located level IV around 36ka, three thousand years older than the new ^{14}C AMS date, although in general AMS dates tend to be older. Nevertheless, the sample dated by ^{14}C AMS has a more reliable stratigraphic origin than the sample previously dated.

In any case, these data suggest that a late survival of Middle Palaeolithic groups in certain areas of NE Iberia must be seriously considered. If the dating of Ermitons level IV is accepted, the Middle Palaeolithic survived in the Pre-Pyrenean area 7ka after the appearance of the Upper Palaeolithic in the Arbreda, Reclau Viver and Abric Romaní. It must be stressed that the Arbreda and Reclau Viver sites are only 20km from the Ermitons Cave. This suggests a long coexistence on a regional scale, but not in the framework of the same ecological niche. Sites suggesting a late survival of Middle Palaeolithic populations are located in mountain areas, out of the main natural corridors that connect this part of the Iberian Peninsula with the rest of Europe. In contrast, the Early Upper Palaeolithic is located in the littoral and prelittoral formations, which would be occupied first if the new human groups came from the European continent. Therefore, the differential distribution of the Early Upper Palaeolithic did not have only a latitudinal expression, marked by the *Ebro frontier*, but was also reflected at the scale of the different ecosystems existing in the same geographical area.

Conclusions

From a behavioural point of view, the different analytic domains that we have showed are characterised by a clear *variability*. This variability indicates the capability of human groups to confront different environments and modify their behaviour accordingly. In principle, behavioural changes could be connected with this variability of the ecosystem, which includes mountain habitats, characterised by a limited array of resources, as well as strategical settings that allow access to different economical areas. Such variability can be also observed in settlement and intra-site organisation patterns. Despite the scarcity of data, some evidence, like that from Abric Romaní, indicates that occupation processes are not characterised by a stereotyped pattern, but show variability trends according to different criteria. Contrary to the opinions of some authors (Mellars 1996; Pettitt 1997), short-term occupation events around a hearth are not the only kind of settlement identified for the Middle Palaeolithic. Some factors, widely documented in ethnographic contexts, such as functional specialisation, spatial articulation and secondary refusal, played an important role in occupation strategies. These changes in spatial organisation patterns may be related with different kinds of occupation events, defined by occupation length and group size. Some archaeological levels may be interpreted as short-term camps by small groups which covered a small area, while other levels seem to reflect longer occupations and larger groups that needed wider areas.

It seems reasonable to assume that some of these variations had an *intentional* character. Some scholars have suggested that variability in the archaeological record, especially in lithics, could be closely linked with environmental factors that demanded a specific answer from humans. The availability of raw materials and climatic conditions could have affected occupation length and the intensity of artefact use and would be the main causes of assemblage variability. The human answer to environmental changes would not be based on the intentional variation of technical criteria, but on how intensely some unchanged technical criteria were applied. Differential repetition in the use of these criteria would be the main reason for the changes in the morphology of lithic artifacts. Our evidence, especially from Abric Romaní archaeological record, indicates that changes between occupation levels correspond to variations in technical criteria that are reflected in the technical system as a whole, from the provisioning of raw materials to the sharpening of artifacts.

As several workers have stressed, planning depth can be a useful concept for interpreting Middle Palaeolithic behavioural patterns. It has ben used as a criterion for defining a clear boundary between Middle and Upper

Palaeolithic behaviour (Binford 1989; Mellars 1996). According to this argument, many of the changes documented in the Middle/Upper Palaeolithic boundary can be explained by a significant increase in planning depth. Lithic data have provided the best evidence to support this point of view. Transport strategies could indicate whether the place and moment of artifact use have been anticipated. Moreover, the criteria of artifact shaping would reflect the degree of anticipation in the form-function adaptation. From this point of view, it is difficult to deny that there is some anticipation of needs during the Middle Palaeolithic. Transport of lithic resources has been well documented in different sites, and is a main factor in assemblage variability. Nevertheless, most authors agree that such anticipation is a well-established fact, but argue that the problems arise with the temporal depth of planning. However, temporal depth is characterised by a continuous variation, so it does not seems logical that this criterion could give a qualitative boundary between different human groups.

In any case, it must be stressed that the anticipation of needs was not a marginal aspect of Middle Palaeolithic behavioural strategies. Rather, it played a recurrent role in Neanderthal adaptations. The spatial and temporal breakage of lithic operatory chains is a good example of the central role of planning in resource management, regardless of the length of time or distance involved in such anticipation. The increase in long-term planning during the Upper Palaeolithic cannot be used as a criterion for defending differences in the cognitive capabilities of Neanderthals and anatomically modern humans. The problem underlying this controversy is the difficulty in establishing a clear link between material culture and the biological constitution of humans, and, above all, for separating the biologically determined changes from those caused by economical and social development, which are well documented throughout the human history.

References

Agustí, B., Alcalde, G., Güell, A., Juan-Muns, N., Rueda, J.M. & Terradas, X. (1991). La cova 120, parada de caçadors-recollectors del paleolític mitjà. *Cypsela*, **IX**: 7–20.

Aïmene, M., Cáceres, I., Huguet, R., Ibáñez, N., Rosell, J. & Saladié, P. (1996). Procesos de aprovechamiento de la fauna en el Abric Romaní (Capellades, Barcelona). In (G. Meléndez, M.F. Blasco & I. Pérez, Eds) *II Reunión de Tafonomía y fosilización*, pp. 19–26. Zaragoza: Institución Fernando el Católico.

Berger, R. & Libby, W.F. (1966). UCLA Radiocarbon Dates V. *Radiocarbon*, **8**: 480.

Binford, L.R. (1988). Isolating the transition to cultural adaptations: an organizational approach. In (E. Trinkaus, Ed.) *The Emergence of Modern Humans. Biocultural adaptations in the later Pleistocene*, pp. 18–41. Cambridge: Cambridge University Press.

Bischoff, J.L., Julià, R. & Mora, R. (1988). Uranium-series dating of the Mousterian occupation at Abric Romaní, Spain. *Nature*, **332**: 68–70.

Bischoff, J.L., Ludwig, K., García, J.F., Carbonell, E., Vaquero, M., Stafford, T.W. & Jull, A.J.T. (1994). Dating of the Basal

Aurignacian Sandwich at Abric Romaní (Catalunya, Spain) by Radiocarbon and Uranium-Series. *Journal of Archaeological Science*, **21**: 541–51.

Bischoff, J.L., Soler, N., Maroto, J. & Julià, R. (1989). Abrupt Mousterian/Aurignacian Boundary at c. 40 ka: Accelerator ¹⁴C dates from L'Arbreda Cave (Catalunya, Spain). *Journal of Archaeological Science*, **16**: 563–76.

Blasco, M.F. (1997). In the pursuit of game: the Mousterian cave site of Gabasa 1 in the spanish Pyrenees. *Journal of Anthropological Research*, **53**: 177–217.

Blasco, F., Montes, L. & Utrilla, P. (1996). Deux modèles·de strategie occupationelle dans le Moustérien tardif de la vallée de l'Ebre: les grottes de Peña Miel et Gabasa. In (E. Carbonell & M. Vaquero, Eds) *The Last Neandertals, The First Anatomically Modern Humans.* pp. 289–313. Tarragona: Universitat Rovira i Virgili.

Burjachs, F. & Julià, R. (1994). Abrupt Climatic Changes during the Last Glaciation Based on Pollen Analysis of the Abric Romaní, Catalonia, Spain. *Quaternary Research*, **42**: 308–315.

Burjachs, F. & Renault-Miskovsky, J. (1992). Paléoenvironnement et paléoclimatologie de la Catalogne durant prés de 30.000 ans (du Würmien ancien au début de l'Holocène) d'aprés la palynologie du site de l'Arbreda (Gérone, Catalogne). *Quaternaire*, **3**(2), 75–85.

Carbonell, E., Giralt, S. & Vaquero, M. (1994). Abric Romaní (Capellades, Barcelone, Espagne): une importante séquence anthropisée du Pléistocène Supérieur. *Bulletin de la Société Préhistorique Française*, **91**(1), 47–55.

Carbonell, E., Cebrià, A., Allué, E., Cáceres, I., Castro, Z., Díaz, R., Esteban, M., Ollé, A., Pastó, I., Rodríguez, X.P., Rosell, J., Sala, R., Vallverdú, J., Vaquero, M. & Vergés, J.M. (1996). Behavioural and organizational complexity in the Middle Palaeolithic from the Abric Romaní. In (E. Carbonell & M. Vaquero, Eds) *The Last Neandertals, The First Anatomically Modern Humans.* pp. 385–434. Tarragona: Universitat Rovira i Virgili.

Gabarró, J.M., Gené, J.M., Mosquera, M., Rosell, J., Vallverdú, J. & Vaquero, M. (1995). Poblamiento paleolítico del Camp de Tarragona y la evolución de las formaciones superficiales del Pleistoceno Superior. In (T. Aleixandre & A. Pérez-González, Eds) *Reconstrucción de paleoambientes y cambios climáticos durante el Cuaternario*, pp. 389–408. Madrid: CSIC.

Geneste, J.-M. (1988). Systèmes d'approvisionnement en matières premières au Paléolithique moyen et au Paléolithique supérieur en Aquitaine. In *L'Homme de Néandertal, vol. 8. La mutation*, pp. 61–70. Liège: ERAUL.

González Echegaray, J. & Freeman, L.G. (1998). *Le Paléolithique inférieur et moyen en Espagne*. Grenoble: Jérôme Millon.

Guilbaud, M. (1995). Introduction sommaire au concept de champ opératoire. *Cahier Noir*, **7**: 121–33.

Hoyos, M., Utrilla, P., Montes, L. & Cuchi, J.A. (1992). Estratigrafía, sedimentología y paleoclimatología de los depósitos musterienses de la Cueva de los Moros de Gabasa. *Cuaternario y Geomorfología*, **6**: 143–55.

Jordá, J.F., Martínez Moreno, J., Mora, R. & Sánchez Casado, F.L. (1994). Modelos deposicionales y ocupación antrópica en el NE de la Península Ibérica durante el Paleolítico Medio. In

Geoarqueología (Actas de la 2ª Reunión Nacional de Geoarqueología), pp. 35–48. Madrid: I.T.G.E.-AEQUA.

Julià, R. & Bischoff, J.L. (1991). Radiometric Dating of Quaternary Deposits and the Hominid Mandible of Lake Banyolas, Spain. *Journal of Archaeological Science*, **18**: 707–22.

Lumley, M.-A. de (1973). *Anténéandertaliens et Néandertaliens du bassin méditerranéen occidental européen*. Marseille: Etudes Quaternaires, mémoire, 2.

Maroto, J. (1984–85). Un jaciment prehistòric a l'interior del massís de l'Alta Garrotxa: la Cova dels Ermitons. *Vitrina*, **1**: 38–48.

Maroto, J. & Soler, N. (1993). Antecedents i problemàtica de l'estudi de la mandíbula de Banyoles. In (J. Maroto, Ed.) *La mandíbula de Banyoles en el context dels fòssils humans del pleistocé*, pp. 35–54. Girona: Centre d'Investigacions Arqueològiques.

Maroto, J., Soler, N. & Fullola, J.M. (1996). Cultural change between Middle and Upper Palaeolithic in Catalonia. In (E. Carbonell & M. Vaquero, Eds) *The Last Neandertals, The First Anatomically Modern Humans.* pp. 219–50. Tarragona: Universitat Rovira i Virgili.

Mellars, P.A. (1996). *The Neanderthal Legacy. An Archaeological Perspective from Western Europe.* Princeton: Princeton University Press.

Montes, L. (1988). *El Musteriense de la cuenca del Ebro.* Zaragoza: Universidad de Zaragoza.

Pettitt, P.B. (1997). High resolution Neanderthals? Interpreting Middle Palaeolithic intrasite spatial data. *World Archaeology*, **29**(2): 208–24.

Soler, N. & Maroto, J. (1987). L'estratigrafia de la cova de l'Arbreda (Serinyà, Girona). *Cypsela*, **VI**: 53–66.

Soler, N. & Maroto, J. (1993). Les nouvelles datations de l'Aurignacien dans la Péninsule Ibérique. In *Actes du XIIe Congrès International des Sciences Préhistoriques et Protohistoriques*, **2**: 162–73. Bratislava: Institut Archéologique de l'Académie Slovaque des Sciences.

Terradas, X., Mora, R., Martínez, J. & Casellas, S. (1993). La Roca dels Bous en el contexto de la transición Paleolítico Medio-Superior en el NE de la Península Ibérica. In (V. Cabrera, Ed.) *El origen del hombre moderno en el Suroeste de Europa*, pp. 247–257. Madrid: UNED.

Utrilla, P. & Montes, L. (1993). El final del Musteriense en el Valle del Ebro. Datos y reflexiones. In (V. Cabrera, Ed.) *El origen del hombre moderno en el Suroeste de Europa*, pp. 219–246. Madrid: UNED.

Vaquero, M. (1997). *Tecnología lítica y comportamiento humano: organización de las actividades y cambio diacrónico en el Paleolítico Medio del Abric Romaní (Capellades, Barcelona).* Unpublished Ph. D. Tarragona: Universitat Rovira i Virgili.

Vilaseca, S. (1952). Mustero-Levalloisiense en Reus. *Archivo de Prehistoria Levantina*, **3**: 31–36.

Yokoyama, Y., Nguyen, H.-V., Quaegebeur, J.-P., Le Hasif, G. & Romain, O. (1987). Datation par la spectrométrie gamma non destructive et la résonance de spin électronique (ESR) du remplissage de la grotte de l'Arbreda. *Cypsela*, **VI**: 137–43.

Yokoyama, Y., Shen, G., Nguyen, H.-V. & Falgueres, C. (1987). Datation du travertin de Banyoles à Gérone, Espagne. *Cypsela*, **VI**: 155–9.

10

Continuity Patterns in the Middle-Upper Palaeolithic Transition in Cantabrian Spain

Victoria Cabrera, Anne Pike-Tay, Mercedes Lloret and Federico Bernaldo de Quiros

Introduction

Views of prehistoric hunter-gatherer societies have changed with time in the minds of both scholars and society in general. In fact, these views have been an expression of the pendulum swings that have taken place in the mentality of contemporary societies. At first, as is recorded by Misia Landau (1991), interest centred on the transformation of anthropoids into human beings, that is to say the ascent from the depths of an animal-like existence to the heights of human civilisation. At this stage the 'myth of the hero' had a considerable influence, with the anthropoids confronting the severest trials only to triumph in the end by reaching the state of *Homo sapiens sapiens*. However, we shall see that this 'myth of the hero' has proved resilient and still appears in theories relating to the origin and dispersal of modern humans.

One of the characteristics of the human species is its ability to make and use tools. Culture is classically defined as the set of extrasomatical adaptations employed to defend against the environment. It may be added that these adaptations are dynamic. While some species close to humans, such as chimpanzees, are well known to be able to use sticks or stones, only the human species is capable of going beyond this use to transform, change, and indeed create tools anew. This dynamism is the basis upon which researchers into prehistory can study the various periods of human culture, because this creativity causes the existence of changing forms in the various sorts of implements used by humans over the course of time. Nevertheless, the archaeological record does not show us the totality of these items, but only those made in lasting materials, which are in the minority. It is only stone items or animal remains such as bone and antler that can constitute a major source of information for us. Yet this is only a fraction of the daily reality of Palaeolithic human groups.

In Europe the appearance of the Upper Palaeolithic has given rise overall to two methodological trends. On the one hand, it is possible to assume that there was a process of change in which industries evolved from the baseline of the local Middle Palaeolithic (as in Laplace 1962; 1968). On the other hand, it could be argued that new human groups (*Homo sapiens sapiens*) arrived, originating in the Near East, where anthropological remains and industries with a blade-tool technique show an earliest presence related to the Middle Palaeolithic. In recent years, discoveries have rendered the model more complex (Otte 1990). In Western Europe during the Hengelo interstadial (Würm II/III) Lower Perigordian, or Châtelperronian, and Aurignacian industries begin to appear. These are the first in which elements characteristic of the Upper Palaeolithic, such as blade technology or bone industry, appear. Both these industries can be related to the Mousterian in its different facies. Thus, Lower Perigordian or Châtelperronian, characterised by Châtelperron points, would be derived from Mousterian of Acheulean Tradition type B, in which backed knives are also found, especially those of the Abri Audi variety. Side-scrapers are also still present in quantity in this industry (Bordes 1958, 1972). A dramatic confirmation of its 'Mousterian' nature was provided by the discovery of remains of *Homo sapiens neanderthalensis* in the Saint Césaire deposit (Lévêque and Vandermeersch 1979), confirming some of A. Leroi-Gourhan's suggestions on the Arcy materials (1958). In this way a connection between the Mousterian of Acheulean Tradition and the Châtelperronian was confirmed and became generally acknowledged.

The Aurignacian has, *a priori*, aspects that could be related to the Mousterian, especially in respect of scale retouching which would link it to Charentian Mousterian of Quina type. However, for a considerable time the existence of a certain chronological *hiatus*, especially in the Dordogne, together with the presence of a bone industry, unknown in the Mousterian, led many authors to propose an origin outside Europe for the Aurignacian. Its geographical extension is greater than that of the Lower Perigordian, since it is found all over Europe from the Balkans to the Iberian Peninsula. It is characterised by a stone industry of large blades, combined with thick flakes transformed into carinated and nosed scrapers, and with a bone industry centred on antler *sagaies*. The confirmation of the late date of the Aurignacian industries of the Near East corrected this and pointed to an origin in the Balkans (Debrosse & Kozlowski 1988).

However, the fundamental problem is the lack of real unity in the early stages of the Aurignacian. Its characteristic elements are not equally present all over Europe. In some places there are *sagaies* already at dates close to 39ka, for instance at Mladec in the Czech Republic, where the rest of the industry is difficult to attribute, having carinated scrapers, Aurignacian blades and blade points (Oliva 1993). This is also the case at Istallosko in Hungary, where the *sagaies* are linked to a hunting site and dated to around 40ka (Desbrosse & Kozlowski 1988). The materials found in the Bulgarian caves of Bacho Kiro and Temnata were also dated at around 40ka, and offered thick end-scrapers and a bone industry. They were at first attributed to the Aurignacian, although later this was revised to include them in a transitional culture termed 'Bachokirian' (Ginter & Kozlowski 1982), from which it was hypothesised that there had been a spread westwards (Desbrosse & Kozlowski 1988). Nevertheless, the new dating for Level 11 at Bacho Kiro means that it is necessary to re-open this question (Hedges *et al.* 1994). The presence of similar dates in Cantabria in Spain also obliges us to review this invasion model. As a consequence, it is possible to suggest that there was a trend more in accordance with the archaeological evidence, and this, as we shall see, would involve the existence not of a single, but rather of several transitional processes in which characteristic features appear in a number of places between 40ka and 35ka, becoming homogenised by about 35ka into the first pan-European culture.

The new and well-defined radiocarbon and ESR dating series obtained from Spanish sites, such as the El Castillo cave, place the first and transitional Aurignacian industries between 40ka and 38ka. This allows the *hiatus* in south west Europe to be eliminated, and lets us postulate a local transition to the Aurignacian, at least, in the Cantabrian region. Moreover, an earlier date for the Aurignacian, as opposed to the Châtelperronian, has been shown at a number of sites, both in France (Roc de Combe, La Piage) and in Spain (El Pendo), where Aurignacian levels are to be found underlying the Lower Perigordian, with a consequently clearer view of their relationship to local Mousterian traditions.

For the study of the changes occurring between the Middle and Upper Palaeolithic in Cantabria, and more especially the origin of the Cantabrian Aurignacian, there is now information available from a number of sites in the region, and this allows a local origin to be proposed for these industries, first noted in Cabrera Valdés & Bernaldo de Quiros (1988). This information is related to the management of basic subsistence behaviour and is linked with game strategies and elements of the *chaine operatoire*.

Faunal and seasonal variation

The monitoring of both long term and short term seasonal changes in land use and resource procurement patterns is recognised as an important line of inquiry into the nature of social and economic change from the Middle to Upper Palaeolithic in Cantabria. We present here the summary of the results of a seasonality study of fauna pertaining to this period of transition from the sites of El Castillo, El Pendo, and Cueva Morín (Pike-Tay *et al.* 1999) (see Figure 10.1). Data concerning season of death and age at death of prey animals from these sites were derived from dental growth mark analysis of their teeth (e.g. Pike-Tay 1991, 1995; Burke & Castanet 1995). The sample selected from El Castillo's recent excavations consisted of 159 teeth; 33 teeth from Cueva Morín, and 31 teeth from El Pendo. In an attempt to balance both under- and over-representation of individual animals from a given archaeological level, 1) qualitative tooth wear assessments were factors in initial sample selection, and 2) teeth showing similar seasonal and age results under the microscope were later linked to one individual; resulting in the modified dental MNI. In order to correctly assess the season of capture and age at death from the recording structures of teeth rates of cementogenesis and/or initiation and cessation times of the 'winter' annulus of known-aged ungulates of the same genera (and species, where possible) living under similar environmental conditions, the Spanish archaeofaunas were used as control references.

For El Castillo, the results suggest year-round hunting episodes throughout the Middle and Early Upper Palaeolithic. However, the seasonal patterning of the Mousterian sample differs somewhat from that of the EUP in that the majority of animals were taken from late autumn through spring in the Mousterian levels and from winter through spring (*i.e.* a slightly more limited seasonal period) in the EUP.

Results from dental annuli analyses of Cueva Morín's fauna suggest that prey was taken during the late autumn and/or winter during the Mousterian and early Aurignacian, with the more recent Aurignacian and Gravettian levels showing a slightly broader seasonality; that of winter/spring/early summer.

El Pendo's entire sample exhibited late growth, complete growth, or slow growth stages of cementogenesis. Throughout the Mousterian and EUP levels at the site, kills are limited to late autumn through winter.

The age distribution of prey animals remains fairly constant throughout both the Mousterian and EUP levels

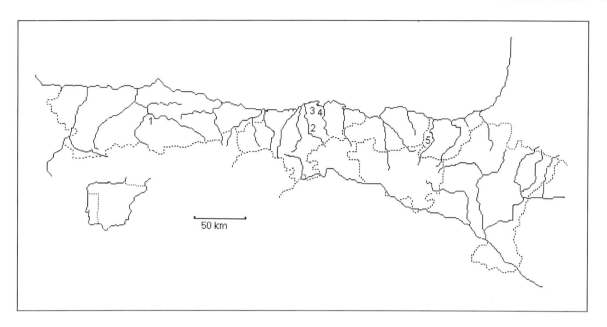

Figure 10.1: Main sites mentioned in text: 1– La Viña; 2– El Castillo; 3–Pendo; 4– Morin; 5– Lezetxiki.

at all three sites with all ages being represented, but prime-aged animals dominating. In this regard at least, there is no evidence that EUP site occupants were targeting a particular age group of animals any more or less "effectively" than their Mousterian predecessors.

Due to the concentration of resources, Cantabria, like much of Southern Europe, probably experienced increasing population densities from the Middle to the Upper Palaeolithic. At the same time, the degree of human mobility and territory sizes appear to have been less than those of areas to the north and north east (e.g. Cabrera Valdés *et al.* 1993; Straus 1995; Cabrera Valdés & Bernaldo de Quirós 1996). The results of the seasonality study of the deeply stratified caves of El Castillo, Cueva Morín, and El Pendo can be viewed in light of this characterisation. During the late Interpleniglacial, as today, these sites were located in a resource-rich zone, within a day's reach of coastal, river valley, forest, and mountain resources. None of the caves show dramatic differences between Mousterian and EUP subsistence practices or site use in terms of season of hunt and age of individual prey animals. Yet each site reveals a unique pattern that may well reflect behavioural choice on the part of its Mousterian and EUP occupants. Both groups appear to have used El Pendo in a similar manner; for small scale late autumn and winter occupations. Both groups also may have used El Castillo in similar ways, but on different scales; *i.e.*, sometimes using the site for short term, sporadic small group stays in summer or autumn; and other times, especially in the spring, for larger group (or regional band) aggregations. The shifts in seasonal hunting patterns and in the duration and nature of occupations at these sites undoubtedly reflect changing land use patterns and resource procurement strategies that are themselves

responding to climatic fluctuations, technological innovations, and a probable increase in regional population densities occurring from *c.* 50ka to 30ka in Cantabria.

The technological processes and *chaînes opératoires* of level 18 at El Castillo

Technological analysis of the reduction of lithic raw materials in level 18 has so far provided us with a conceptual scheme for understanding the manufacture of artefacts in this level. Two lithic reduction processes can be identified: one involving flake production, the other bladelet production (Figure 10.2). The flake production model shows three 'reduction sequences' relying on the centripetal method, the bladelet production model has two 'reduction sequences' involving unipolar methods of exploitation, resulting in Levallois unipolar laminar flakes and unipolar bladelets.

Both reduction processes were employed on a very wide range of raw materials, a feature also observed in the underlying Mousterian of level 20. This indicator of cultural continuity in the selection and acquisition of raw materials extends throughout the Transitional Aurignacian in level 18.

The raw materials primarily consist of quartzite, flint, limestone, ophite, limonite and a fine-grained sandstone. Detailed analysis allows the quartzite to be sub-divided into three classes according to rock grain and homogeneity of texture (Cabrera Valdés *et al.* 1996b). Here we highlight especially the use of quartzite, 'C1', a very fine-grained type on small river pebbles (5cm) and opaque green quartzite, 'C2', on larger river pebbles (10cm), which has a homogeneous texture and is fine-grained. Apart from the quartzite, there is a very compact, smooth black

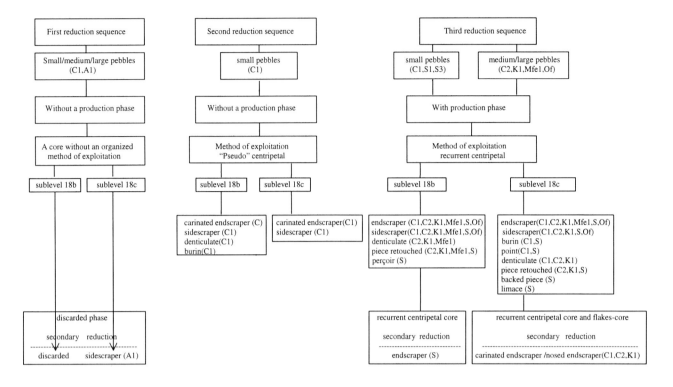

Figure 10.2: Model of flake reduction process in the level 18 of Castillo.

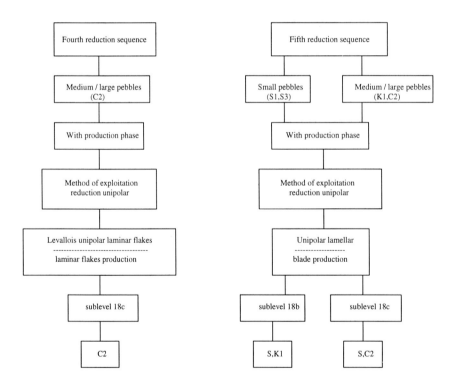

Figure 10.3: Model of blade reduction in the level 18 of Castillo.

limestone with a fine, grey crust occurring in medium to large pebble form of which there is only one variety, termed 'K1'. There are also two types of flint: the first, following the nomenclature of previous authors (Lloret 1995), is flint type 'S1' with a very fine grain and homogeneous texture. Due to variability in its opaqueness, we prefer to sub-divide it into two types 'S1.1' and 'S1.2'. Both sub-types exhibit minute points and lines of manganese. The crust is porous and fine (0.5mm). Type 'S1' occurs as water-rolled pebbles and its quality is very suitable for knapping purposes. The sub-type 28 'S1.1' is a grey, off-white colour while 'S1.2' is brown, beige or dark grey and is noticeably more opaque. The other previously described flint, 'S3', is of mediocre quality, with a fine grain and homogeneous texture and minute points of manganese and silica. It is normally desilicified and has a porous crust. So far we have not discovered its source (Lloret 1995; Cabrera Valdés *et al.*1996). Its colour ranges from beige/off-white with some small red points, to a white flint with a variety of black inclusions and some bright points, and also a white flint with black points.

The ophite is fine-grained and has small pellets of pyroxene, with a fine outer crust (0.5–1mm). There are three sub-types based on colour variation, that range from beige through to grey. The ophite is highly suitable for knapping purposes.

The limonite is the only variety of iron-rich mineral, 'Mfe1'. It is brown in colour, very smooth, with a fine and even crust. The knapping quality of this material is good to mediocre.

There is a fine-grained sandstone 'A1' beige in colour with small black inclusions. It has a fine crust and occurs only in pebble form.

Finally, we include reference to the anecdotal presence of a white microcrystalline quartz, 'Q1', which appears in sub-level 18b.

Continuity in the cultural tradition of raw material acquisition is also reflected in the flaking process which relies on centripetal exploitation. This reduction technique is used for all the above mentioned raw materials and does not seem to have been influenced by size dimensions, as it was employed on small, medium and large pebbles.

The first reduction sequence to be described is the simplest one found in the Transitional Aurignacian level. Although this was not the only method to be used, together with a related sequence it shows the progression to a fully-developed centripetal reduction scheme. As such, it can be classified together with two other reduction sequences which fall within the centripetal scheme. In its simplest form we note that hammerstones, (not only small pebbles of fine grained quartzite 'C1', but also medium and large pebbles of sandstone), were then converted into cores for extracting flakes. The process left no clear signs of discarded knapping debris. This phenomenon explains the existence of a *chaîne opératoire* without an obvious production phase in sub-levels 18b and 18c. However, there does appear to be a difference between the two sub-

levels: sub-level 18c shows some elements of the hammers' discard phase. Here, attempts can be seen to make a sandstone sidescraper and there is an unfinished quartzite end-scraper. This suggests a 'secondary reduction' phase to extend the use of raw material.

The second reduction sequence is characterised by the selection of small pebbles of fine-grained quartzite, type 'C1'. The production phase is also absent in this sequence with the pebbles being worked in a very simple way, quickly and with the purpose of making various tools on core-pebbles and *entames* (in this case decortication flakes). In both sub-levels the presence of carinated end-scrapers shows how the core-pebbles were used in this way. In 18b and 18c we find sidescrapers as end-scrapers on *entames*. The only difference between the sub-levels appears to be the greater variety of tools on core-pebbles in 18b, including sidescrapers, denticulates and burins as well as the end-scrapers mentioned already. This second reduction sequence on quartzite 'C1' is virtually complete yet we regard it as a 'pseudo'-centripetal type which gives rise to a third reduction sequence where the full production phase of the centripetal method is present.

The third reduction sequence is the most complete in the studied series because all the stages of the *chaîne opératoire* are present. The acquisition and initiation phases are the same as in the second sequence, however, in this case a more intensive reduction is achieved with the recurrent centripetal method. Here the 'pseudo'-centripetal method is fully implemented due to the fact that the knapper wanted to make a greater number of blanks and so extended use of the core.

In the pebble quartzite, type 'C1', the products of the initiation phase were preferred for manufacturing end-scrapers in sub-level 18b, while in 18c they were made into end-scrapers as sidescrapers, burins, notches, points and denticulates. In both sub-levels, the thick, wide and short flakes of the production phase were deliberately selected for the manufacture of sidescrapers and end-scrapers.

Recurrent centripetal cores and flake-cores of the final discard phase were sometimes used for the manufacture of carinated and nosed end-scrapers in both sub-levels. The somewhat greater number of these finds in 18c suggests a deliberate secondary reduction strategy for the production of end-scrapers.

In the green quartzite, type 'C2', the products of the initiation phase were deliberately selected for the manufacture of sidescrapers and end-scrapers in 18b, and sidescrapers and notches in 18c. Similarly, the blanks resulting from the production phase of recurrent centripetal cores were used for making sidescrapers, notches and retouched pieces in 18b, and sidescrapers, end-scrapers and retouched pieces in 18c. Some recurrent centripetal cores were then used as blanks for end-scrapers, especially the fine-grained quartzite.

In the limestone, decortication flakes of the initiation stage provided blanks for end-scrapers and sidescrapers.

The by-products of the production stage, based on the recurrent centripetal method, were used for manufacturing sidescrapers, notches and retouched pieces. The use of cores for the manufacture of end-scrapers is also a noticeable feature in this raw material.

In the limonite, tools were only made on blanks from the production phase of recurrent centripetal cores. In 18b, they were used for making an end-scraper, a notch and three retouched pieces, one of which has been reclassified as a sidescraper, following a review of the material which is currently in progress. In addition to the above we would like to add the presence of an end-scraper in 18c. Finally, in the discard phase, there is only one core with evidence of the recurrent centripetal flaking technique.

The treatment of flint is similar to the 'C1' quartzite. Most of the products were intended for the manufacture of end-scrapers, sidescrapers, retouched pieces as well as a borer in sub-level 18b. It also includes a secondary chain in which a discarded centripetal core was made into an end-scraper. In 18c the blanks were used for end-scrapers, sidescrapers and retouched pieces, and to a lesser extent, points, backed pieces and burins.

The ophite was not used as intensively for making tools as in other raw materials but included the manufacture of sidescrapers and end-scrapers. The cores in this material were centripetally flaked.

In short, we would like to emphasise the very great homogeneity which exists between the two sub-levels both in the selection and treatment of raw material as well as in the centripetal flaking methods used. However, it is clear that distinctions can be made, for example in the choice of tool blanks from the initiation phase, as illustrated by the 'C1' quartzite of the third reduction sequence in 18c, where there is a greater diversity in tool-making. Nevertheless, for the rest of the reduction stages there is much clearer homogeneity between the sub-levels, in the production of sidescrapers and end-scrapers.

In relation to the reduction methods, it should be noted that the hard hammer percussion technique was used in the first as well as the second sequences. In both sub-levels there was a noticeable absence of the preparation stages, and only limited evidence of lithic debris. Finally, despite the general trend, seen in the third reduction sequence of both sub-levels, for the sole use of hard hammer, the increase in debris and the production of thick blanks, there is a small difference in the presence of the preparation stage in sub-level 18c, which is not apparent in 18b.

The centripetal flaking technique employed by the Aurignacians at El Castillo was not the only conceptual scheme in evidence because a fourth reduction method relying on the extraction of bladelets from unipolar cores has also been recognised. The method of producing bladelets depended on two conceptually different approaches. The first was a *chaîne opératoire* of 'Levallois' type, which was aimed at producing laminar-flakes (only seen in the green quartzite of sub-level 18c). In the second method the *chaîne opératoire* falls within the pattern of bladelet production seen in the Late Palaeolithic. Our study of the El Castillo sample reveals the presence of plain and plain-punctiform butts on blades and some bladelets of limestone from sub-level 18b and on flint in both sub-levels where Aurignacian blades occur albeit in low number. In addition, we have noted the flank of a blade core (a rejuvenation flake) and a blade core on green quartzite with unipolar bladelet scars. Together they confirm the use of bladelet production and bear witness to a distinctive methodology and a completely new conceptual approach to the volumetric management of nodules. From our point of view, this change takes place only gradually and against a tradition in which flake production was deeply rooted.

In summary, when it comes to interpreting the reduction methods employed in the Transitional Aurignacian at El Castillo, we can be fairly confident about the purpose behind the lithic output of the Aurignacian knappers. We have described five reduction sequences. Two of them utilised the recurrent centripetal technique; the products were generally short, wide and thick blanks and were intended for the manufacture of end-scrapers. The end-scraper can be seen as a special marker distinguishable from the rest of the lithic tools, since, whenever secondary reduction occurs, the tool is found on products of the discard phase of various cores of the main operating chain. The other types of reduction sequences mentioned do not show the same degree of polarisation in tool-making because the finished products, which are also used as supports for other retouched forms, are more diversified.

Concluding remarks

As we have been discussing, in the Cantabrian region there are a number of sites where it is possible to follow the sequence of changes that gave rise to Upper Palaeolithic industries, especially the Aurignacian. First, the characteristic features of the lithic industry show that there is definite proof of the existence of technical and typological continuity between the La Quina Mousterian and the Aurignacian, both in the presence of lithic stereotypes like the carinated end-scapers or burins and in the presence of techonological affinities reported previously (Cabrera Valdés and Bernaldo de Quiros 1988; Cabrera Valdés *et al.* 1993). Similarly we noted a marked continuity in the management of game, both in the mortality patterns and the seasonal use of caves (see also Pike-Tay *et al.* 1999). For El Castillo and Cueva Morín, the results show year-round hunting episodes throughout the Middle and early Upper Palaeolithic, but with an emphasis on different seasons depending on the archaeological level. Seasonal indicators from El Pendo are unchanging from the earliest Mousterian through to the Gravettian where exclusive autumn and winter kills are recorded. The results suggest similar use of the sites and their surrounding landscape by both Mousterian and Early Upper Palaeolithic groups with a possible increase in the size of the occupying group, at least at El Castillo, which may have served as an aggregation site for larger regional groups at various times in the Palaeolithic.

These reflections lead us further into considering the possible authorship of the lithic industries. According to the traditional view *Homo sapiens sapiens* or Anatomically Modern Humans (AMH) were responsible for the changes in the Early Upper Palaeolithic, but there are numerous problems with this interpretation. To begin with, the only well-known fossil human evidence for the time range 40–35 ka is either of Neanderthal or undiagnostic type (see Garralda *et al.* 1992), while the presence of modern human types is not certainly recognized in Europe until about 30 ka (Gambier 1997). The results presented in this work concern the differences in processes of resource management, both lithic and nutritional, between the Mousterian and the earliest Aurignacian. They clearly indicate to us a marked continuity between both cultural entities, and, together with the published typological evidence (Cabrera Valdés & Bernaldo de Quiros 1988) allow us to put forward two rival hypotheses. One interpretation would suggest that the first AMHs to arrive in Europe were indistinguishable from the Neanderthals in a cultural sense, or alternatively, that it was the Neanderthals themselves who were responsible for the earliest Aurignacian. We find the second hypothesis more parsimonious, and, unless and until AMH fossils are found in Europe in this period, we feel this is the most likely explanation. The hypothesis should not seem so surprising given the fact that the same technocomplex is attributable to these two human types in the Near East where Neanderthals co-existed with AMHs (Vandermeersch 1993; 1997). Equally, the evidence from Vindija would seem to support the idea that Neanderthals could be associated with Aurignacian industries (Wolpoff 1996). Whatever eventually turns out to be the case, we recognise the modernity of the Early Upper Palaeolithic.

The bone industry is perhaps one of the features that to some extent can be considered 'new'. Nevertheless, we feel that its 'newness' should be qualified. Throughout the Mousterian sequence at El Castillo and Lezetxiki caves, there is evidence of considerable activity linked with the working of bone, horn, and antler. In both Level 22 and Level 20 at El Castillo there are bones sharpened by polishing (ends and shaft) and also cut (grooved ?) antler. These two types of modification were already recognised by the first researchers of the site (Breuil 1932). The importance of these finds is twofold: first, it provides evidence for the customary working of bone (Gaudzinski 1999), and secondly, it confirms that some of the working techniques 'typical' of the Upper Palaeolithic were probably already known locally during the Middle Palaeolithic. It should not be forgotten in this context that evidence of wood-working is present from the Lower Palaeolithic onwards both as preserved finds e.g. Clacton, Schöningen (Bosinski 1996; Thieme 1997) and indirectly

through wear-traces (Anderson 1980; Keeley 1980). This shows that during the Lower and Middle Palaeolithic wood was regularly worked and the use of bone may simply represent an extension of the same methods but in a different raw material.

In the case of the appearance of art, its 'newness' must again be questioned. The presence of bones with lines, marks, and so forth, showing some sort of patterning is not exclusively Upper Palaeolithic (Kozlowski 1992; Benadrik 1994, 1995; Cremades 1996), as is clear from the spectacular evidence at Berekhat Ram (Goren-Inbar 1986). The same is true for the earliest use of ochre, which is already known in Middle Palaeolithic deposits. The most important change was probably in the appearance of the first naturalistic images. But, interestingly, these seem to be younger in age than the earliest Aurignacian, as shown for example by engraved objects from sites like Geissenklosterle in the Swabian Jura of SW Germany which can be dated to around 35 ka (Hahn 1993) or cave paintings which may be slightly later in date from sites like Chauvet Cave in the Ardèche region of southern France. For portable artwork, it is once again possible to suggest earlier forerunners made in wood (Hahn 1989), which might help explain the absence of 'prototypes' for these items. Accordingly, we would propose an initial period of schematic 'art' based on repeated patterns of lines in the Mousterian and Early Upper Palaeolithic before the first occurrence of classical naturalistic 'art'. The engraving of straight incised lines, such as those from sites like La Viña and El Conde cave, may be related in form to the characteristic incisions made by the groove and splinter technique used in working bone, and dating to the Early Aurignacian (Fortea 1994).

The importance of El Castillo layer 18 and the other Cantabrian sites lies in their intermediate status between the Mousterian and the classic Aurignacian, from the point of view of their chronology, technology and typology. Thus, while the Lower Perigordian or Châtelperronian evolved from the Mousterian of Acheulean tradition, the direct ancestor of the Aurignacian appears to have been the Charentian Mousterian of Quina type. The Cantabrian data would therefore seem to span the chronological *hiatus* which exists in the South of France. Thus, the beginnings of the Upper Palaeolithic must be understood within a multi-level analysis, in which the various European regions show their own lines of evolution.

Acknowledgements

This paper was made possible by a grant from the DGICYT (grant No. PB92–0564) and the support of the Cosejeria de Cultura de Cantabria and the Ayuntamiento de Puente Viesgo for the excavations at Castillo Cave.

References

Anderson, P.C. (1980). A testimony of prehistoric tasks: diagnostic residues on stone tool working edges. *World Archaeology.* 12, 181–194.

Benadrik, R.G. (1994). Art origins, *Anthropos,* 89, 169–180.

Benadrik, R.G. (1995). Concept-mediated Marking in the Lower Palaeolithic, *Current Anthropology.* 36:4, 605–634.

Bernaldo De Quirós, F. & Cabrera Valdés, V. (1993). Early Upper Paleolithic Industries of Cantabrian Spain. In (H. Knecht, A. Pike-Tay, & R. White, Eds) *Before Lascaux,* pp. 57–70. CRC Press.

Bordes, F. (1958). Le passage du Paléolithique Moyen au Paléolithique Supérieur. In *Hundert Jahre Neanderthaler,* 1856–1956, pp. 175–181. Böhlau Verlag : Köln.

Bordes, F. (1972). Du Paléolithique moyen au Paléolithique supérieur: continuité ou discontinuité? In *The origin of* Homo sapiens, pp. 211–218. Unesco : Paris.

Bosinski, G. (1996) *Les origines de l'homme en Europe et en Asie,* Ed. errance.

Breuil, H. (1932). Pointe d'epieu en os du Mousterien de la caverne du Castillo (Santander), *Institut Française d'Anthropologie,* 2, 35.

Burke, A.M. & Castanet, J. (1995). Histological observations of cementum growth in horse teeth and their application to Archaeology, *Journal of Archaeological Science.* 22, 479–493.

Cabrera Valdes,V. & Bernaldo De Quiros, F. (1988). Donnes sur la transition entre le Paleolithique Moyen et le Superieur a la Region Cantabrique; revision critique, *De l'homme de Neandertal a l'homme moderne,* Colloque du C.N.R.S.: Nemours.

Cabrera Valdés, V. & Bernaldo De Quirós, F. (1996). Economic strategies in the Upper Palaeolithic in the Cantabrian Region, *Human Evolution,* 11(2), 121–128.

Cabrera Valdes, V., Hoyos Gomez, M. Bernaldo De Quiros, F. (1993). La transición del Paleolítico Medio/Paleolítico Superior en la Cueva de "El Castillo": características paleoclimaticas y situación cronológica, *El Origen del Hombre moderno en el Suroeste de Europa,* pp. 81–104. UNED, Madrid.

Cabrera Valdes, V., Valladas, H., Bernaldo De Quiros, F. & Hoyos Gomez, M. (1996). La transition Paleolithique moyen-Paleolithique Superieur a El Castillo (Cantabria): nouvelles datations par le Carbone 14, *Comptes Rendues De La Academie Des Sciences De Paris.* 322, IIA, 1093–1098

Cabrera Valdés, V., Lloret Martinez De La Riva, M., & Bernaldo De Quirós, F. (1996b). Materias primas y formas liticas del Auriñaciense arcaico de la cueva Del Castillo Puente Viesgo, Cantabria. *Espacio, Tiempo Y Forma, Serie I,* 9, 141–158.

Cremades, M. (1996). L'expression graphique au Paleolithique inferieur et moyen: l'exemple de l'Abri Suard (La Chaise-de-Vouthon, Chartente), *B.S.P.F.,* 93/4, 494–501.

Desbrosse, R. & Kozlowski, J. (1988). *Hommes Et Climats A L'age Du Mammouth,* Masson, Paris.

Fortea, F.J., (1994). Los "santuarios" exteriores en el Paleolítico Cantábrico. In (T. Chapa Brunet, & M. Menendez, Eds), *Arte Paleolitico, Complutum 5,* pp. 203–220.

Garralda, M.D., Tillier, A.M. Vandermeersch, B., Cabrera, V. & Gambier, D. (1992). "Restes humains de l'Aurignacien archaique de la Cueva de El Castillo, Santander, Espagne", *Anthropologie,* XXX/2, 159–164.

Gambier, D. (1997). Modern humans at the beginning of the Upper Palaeolithic in France, In (G.A. Clark, & C.M. Willwermet, Eds) *Conceptual Issues In Modern Human Origins Research,* pp. 117–131. Aldine De Gruyter.

Gaudzinski, S. (1999). Middle Palaeolithic Tools from the open-air Site Salzgitter-Lebenstedt (Germany). *Journal Of Archaeological Science.* 26:2, 125–142.

Ginter, B. & Kozlowski, J. (1982). Conclusions. *Excavation In The Bacho Kiro Cave,* Pwn, Varsovia.

Goren-Inbar, N. (1986). A figurine from the Acheulean site of Berekhat Ram, *Mi'tekufat Ha'even* 19, pp. 7–12.

Hahn, J. (1989). Las primeras figuras: las representaciones Auriñacienses, *Los Comienzos Del Arte En Europa Central.* Museo Arqueológico Nacional, Madrid, 27–35.

Hahn, J. (1993). Aurignacian Art in Central Europe. In (H. Knecht, A. Pike-Tay & R.White Eds) *Before Lascaux,the complex record of the Early Upper Palaeolithic,* pp. 229–241. CRC Press.

Hedges, R.E.M., Housley, R.A., Bronk Ramsey, C. & Van Klinken, G.J. (1994). Radiocarbon dates from the Oxford AMS System: *Archaeometry* Datelist 18, *Archaeometry,* 36.2, 337–374.

Keeley, L.H. (1980). *Experimental Determinations Of Stone Tool Uses: A Microwear Analysis,* Chicago University Press.

Kozlowski, J.K. (1992). *L'art de la prehistoire en Europe Orientale,* C.N.R.S.

Landau, M. (1991). *Narratives Of Human Evolution,* Yale University Press.

Laplace, G. (1962). Recherches sur sur l'origine et l'evolution des complexes leptolithiques. le probleme des Perigordiens I et II et l'hipothese du synthetotype Aurignaco-Gravetien, essai de typologie analythique, *Quaternaria,* V, 153–240.

Laplace, G. (1968). Les niveaux Aurignaciens et l'hipothese du synthetotype, *L'home De Cro Magnon, Anthropologie Et Archeologie,* Paris, 141–163.

Leroi-Gourhan, A. (1958). Etude des restes humains fossiles provenant des Grottes D'arcy-Sur-Cure. *Annales De Paléontologie.* 44, 87–148.

Leveque, F. & Vandermeersch, B. (1979). Découverte de restes humains dans un niveau Castelperronien à Saint Cesaire (Charente), *Comptes Rendues De La Academie Des Sciences De Paris.* 291, D,187–189.

Lloret, M. (1995). Análisis tecnológico de los núcleos de la Cueva de la Pila (Magdaleniense Superior: Nivel V Y Iv.4). *Espacio, Tiempo Y Forma.* 8, 11–32.

Otte, M. (1990). From the Middle to the Upper Palaeolithic: the nature of the transition. In (P. Mellars & C. Stringer, Eds.) *The Emergence Of Modern Humans,* pp. 438–456. Edinburgh University Press: Edinburgh.

Oliva, M., (1993). Le contexte archeologique des restes humains dans la grotte de Mladec. *Actes Du Xii Congrès International Des Sciences Préhistoriques Et Protohistoriques,* pp. 207–215. Bratislava.

Pike-Tay, A. (1991). *Red deer hunting in The Upper Paleolithic of Southwest France: A study in seasonality.* British Archaeological Reports International Series S569, Oxford: Tempus Reparatum.

Pike-Tay, A. (1995). Variability and synchrony of seasonal indicators in dental cementum microstructure of the Kaminuriak *Rangifer* Population. *Archaeofauna* 4, 273–284.

Pike-Tay, A., Cabrera Valdes, V., & Bernaldo De Quiros, F. (1999). Seasonal variations of the Middle-Upper Palaeolithic Transition at El Castillo, Cueva Morín and El Pendo (Cantabria, Spain). *Journal Of Human Evolution.* 36, 283–317.

Rink, W.J., Schwartz, H.P., Lee, H.K., Cabrera Valdes, V., Bernaldo De Quirós, F. & Hoyos, M. (1995). ESR dating of tooth enamel: comparison with AMS ¹⁴C at El Castillo Cave, Spain, *Journal of Archaeological Science.* 23, 6,1196, 945–952.

Rink, W.J., Schwarcz, H.P., Lee, H.K., Cabrera Valdes, V., Bernaldo De Quiros, F., & Hoyos, M. (1997). ESR dating of Mousterian levels at El Castillo Cave, Cantabria, Spain, *Journal of Archaeological Science.* 24, 593–600.

Straus, L.G. (1995). The Upper Palaeolithic of Europe: an overview. *Evolutionary Anthropology.* 3(1), 1–13.

Straus, L.G. (1996). Continuity or rupture; convergence or invasion;

adaptation or catastrophe; mosaic or monolith: Views on the Middle to Upper Palaeolithic Transition in Iberia. In (E. Carbonell & M. Vaquero, Eds) *The Last Neanderthals, The First Anatomically Modern Humans,* pp. 157–167. Universitat Rovira i Virgili.

Thieme, H. (1997). Lower Palaeolithic Hunting Spears From Germany. *Nature,* **385**, 807–810.

Vandermeersch, B. (1993). Le Proche Orient et l'Europe: continuite ou discontinuite, *El Origen del Hombre moderno en el Suroeste de Europa,* pp. 361–372. UNED: Madrid.

Vandermeersch, B. (1997). The Near East And Europe: continuity or discontinuity? In (G.A Clark, & C.M. Willwermet, Eds) *Conceptual Issues In Modern Human Origins Research,* pp. 107–116. Aldine De Gruyter.

Wolpoff, M.H., (1996). Neanderthals Of The Upper Palaeolithic, In (E. Carbonell & M. Vaquero, Eds) *The Last Neanderthals, The First Anatomically Modern Humans,* pp. 51–76. Universitat Rovira i Virgili.

11

The Middle-Upper Palaeolithic Transition in Portugal

Luis Raposo

Introduction

After the research performed by Henri Breuil and Georges Zbyszewski in the 1940's, which concentrated on the Portuguese coastal areas and the valleys of the main river systems, (especially the Tagus: Breuil & Zbyszewski 1942–45), it has been common to mention the abundance of Lower and Middle Palaeolithic sites in Portuguese territory. This idea has survived through time, especially for older assemblages and particularly the Acheulian, which can be positively identified by a few characteristic tools (e.g. bifaces and cleavers). It is, therefore, easy to find plenty of evidence in Portuguese sites that testifies to the presence of biface industries, despite the difficulty in assigning them to specific chronological periods or in interpreting their historical significance.

In the case of the Middle Palaeolithic, the picture is much more complex. None of the 'fossil-types' traditionally used for identifying these assemblages can be maintained with certainty. Hence, any careful analysis of the database available will dramatically reduce the number of Portuguese sites accurately identified as Middle Palaeolithic. Among these, only a few possess a satisfactory chronological assignment. In fact, only about twenty sites in Portugal exhibit these characteristics; half are located in caves or rockshelters, and the other half constitute open air sites (Raposo 1993a, 1993b, 1995).

A simple observation of the absolute dates available for the Portuguese Middle Palaeolithic (see Figure 11.1) illustrates the potential drawbacks of the available data. The majority of available elements refer to the final stage of that period; the dates for earlier stages are scarce and often inaccurate. The techno-typological characterisation of lithic industries reinforces this pattern: the most numerous assemblages are those from the late Middle Palaeolithic and are clearly different from the Early Upper Palaeolithic sites. The assemblages from the earliest phase

of the Middle Palaeolithic generally consist of small samples and exhibit more significant continuity with those from the late Lower Palaeolithic. In fact, there are enough traces suggesting the survival of Acheulian industries until very late, especially in the Tagus valley, through the so-called 'Micoquian', which, in Alcobaça, survived until less than 100ka (Raposo *et al.*1996).

In this article I will concentrate exclusively on the problems regarding the Middle to Upper Palaeolithic transition. I have, therefore, selected only those sites that exhibit sufficient dates attributable to the latest stages of the first of these periods (<35 ka). Reference to the sites assignable to the early stages of the second phase (>25 ka) will only be used for demonstrating existing (dis)continuities. Hence, I have excluded from my analysis some of the most important sites from the Portuguese Middle Palaeolithic which date from the 60 to 40 ka range, open air sites such as Vilas Ruivas (with habitat structures, including built hearths, dating from *c.* 50 ka) or Santo Antão do Tojal (with associated elephant remains and dating from *c.* 80 ka), and caves such as Escoural and Oliveira-Almonda. The Oliveira site is particularly important, given that its stratigraphic sequence dates from *c.* 61.5 ka at the base (Zilhão and Mckinney 1993) and it has provided Neanderthal remains in a layer dated from *c.* 40 ka. For more recent dates obtained for the site, see Zilhão this volume.

The archaeological data basis

Caves and rockshelters
Columbeira
This cave is located approximately 10 km from the Atlantic coast, in the county of Bombarral in the Portuguese Estremadura, in a valley where other caves and rockshelters had already been identified with human

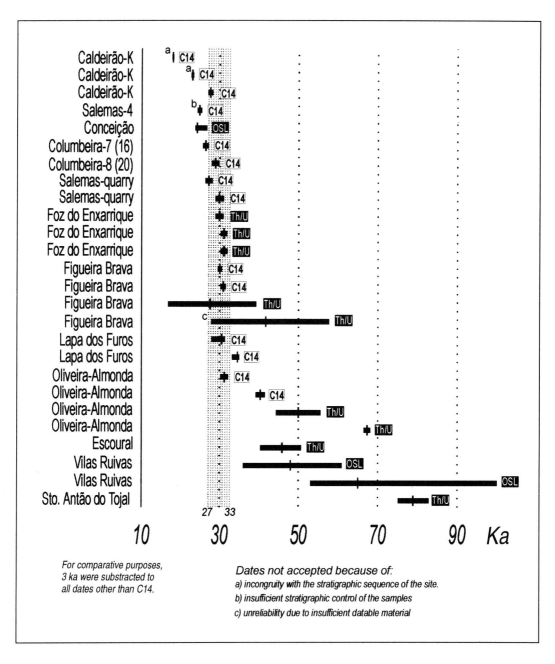

Figure 11.1: Absolute dating framework available for the Portuguese Middle Palaeolithic sites.

prehistoric occupation from different time ranges, including the Middle and Late Upper Palaeolithic.

Immediately after its discovery in 1962 (Ferreira 1993), the site was found to be one of the most important in the Portuguese Middle Palaeolithic. Four factors contributed to this evaluation. The site is well preserved, having been sealed at the time of discovery. It has an important, 2.5 m-thick stratigraphic sequence in which only Mousterian industries were found, and which were especially abundant in the lower layers, according to Ferreira (1984). It contains abundant Pleistocene megafaunal remains (deer, goat, horse, rhinoceros, auroch, hyaena, lynx, etc., Cardoso 1993) and finally, it yielded the lower left molar that Denise de Ferembach identified as *Homo sapiens neanderthalensis* (Ferembach 1964–65).

In the 1970s, Jean Roche obtained two radiometric dates for the most important levels of human occupation which were later considered unreliable, because they were 'too recent' (Table 11.1). They can, however, be accepted today in the framework of the Iberian Late Mousterian, as will be explained further. No extensive monograph has yet been published on the site. Recent reassessment of its lithic industries, however (Raposo & Cardoso 1998a) has confirmed thé initial diagnoses and allowed a higher precision in the definition of the techno-typological characteristics of the assemblages.

Table 11.1: Most important Middle Palaeolithic Iberian sites, dated <35 ka (see map, Figure 11.4).

No.	Site	Region	Stratigraphy	Age	Method	Comments
(Spain)						
1	Ermitons	Girona	lev. IV	33190 +-660	C14AMS	(C14 conventional: 36430 +-1800)
2	Jarama VI	Guadalajara	lev. 2	29599 +-2700	C14	
3	Cova Negra	Valência	lev. 5	<30000		stratigraphy
4	Beneito	Alicante	X (D1)	30160 +-680	C14	(C14 AMS: 38800 +-1900)
5	Perneras	Murcia	A-B	c. 29/30000		stratigraphy
6	Palomarico	Murcia	middle lev.	c. 29/30000		stratigraphy
7	Carihuela	Granada	lev. IV	c. 25000		stratigraphy and microfauna
			lev. V	c. 30000		stratigraphy and microfauna
			?	c. 28000	TL	
			?	c. 32000	TL	
			?	c. 31-35000	TL	
8	Horá	Granada	lev. II-VI	<30000		stratigraphy
9	Zafarraya	Granada	lev. I-3/1	25100 +-1300	Th/U	
			id	26900 +-2700	Th/U	
			id	28900 +-4200	Th/U	
			id	29800 +-600	C14	
			lev. I-8	31700 +-3600	Th/U	
			id	31800 +-550	C14	
			lev. D	33400 +-200	Th/U	lev. with neandertal remains
10	Bajondillo	Torremolinos	botton lev.	25300/26500+-10/15%	ESR	travertine date(wall of shelter)
				27300 +-1700	Th/U	idem
11	Devil's Tower	Gibraltar	lev. 3	>30000	C14	
			lev. 4	c. 29000	C14	
12	Gorham's Cave	Gibraltar	lev. G	45300 +-1700	C14AMS	
			lev. E-F(16-17)	c.30000		stratigraphy
(Portugal)						
13	Foz Enxarrique	Ródão	lev. C	32938 +-1055	Th/U	single Middle Palaeolithic level
			id	34088 +-800	Th/U	
			id	34093 +-920	Th/U	
14	Caldeirão	Tomar	lev. K (top)	27600 +-600	C14	or Initial Upper Palaeolithic
			id (botom)	23040 +-340	C14	disputable, due to stratigraphic considerations
			id (bottom)	18060 +-140	C14	id
15	Lapa dos Furos	Tomar	lev. 4	30570 +-760	C14	residual occupation, not diagnostic
			lev. 4	34580 +1160 -1010	C14	
16	Almonda	T. Novas	lev. 8	31200 +-900	C14	
17	Columbeira	Bombarŕal	lev. 7(16)	26400 +-750	C14	
			lev. 8(20)	28900 +-950	C14	
18	Salemas (algar)	Loures	lev. 2	27170 +1000 -900	C14	
			id	>29200	C14	
			id	29890 +1130 -980	C14	
19	Pêgo do Diabo	Loures	lev. 2-botton	28120 +-860	C14	base of an Upper Palaeolithic level
20	Conceição	Alcochete	lev. C-top	27200 +-2500	TL/OSL	
21	Figueira Brava	Sesimbra	lev. 2	30930 +-700	C14	
			lev. 3	30050 +-550	C14	
			id	30561 +10726 -11759	Th/U	

In the stratigraphic sequence of the cave, I confirm that the human occupation is limited to the lower levels (layers 9 to 4, with a maximum length of 2 meters). The upper levels (layers 3 to 1, 0.5 m deep), are sterile and the faunal remains are limited to birds of prey and hunted fauna. It is not possible to specify the dates of the stratigraphic sequence by geostratigraphic or biostrati-graphic criteria; the lower levels strictly present Middle Palaeolithic occupation levels, but it is possible that the upper layers were contemporaneous with the Upper Palaeolithic, when the cave would have been impossible to inhabit.

In total, about 6,000 artefacts and lithic remains have been collected during the excavations; the possible presence of bone artefacts has also been proposed (Barandiaran & Ferreira, 1971). The results of our analysis, based on a total of 5,500 lithic artefacts of known provenance, confirmed the different occupations of each layer. Some levels, with a high prevalence of carnivore remains over herbivores and an insignificant lithic industry, must represent long-term palimpsests, characterised by occasional use of the cave by human groups. This is the case in layer 6 (approximately 1m thick), with only 445 lithic artefacts. Other layers exhibit the opposite character-istics, including features that the initial excavators called *"long sand* utilised *hearths"*, corresponding to short term occupation palimpsests, similar to the patterns which can be attributed to a 'base camp' regular occupation of the cave. This pattern is particularly visible in layers 7 and 8, the first 20cm thick, with 1,880 lithic artefacts, and the latter 30cm thick, with 2,433 lithic artefacts.

Lithic industries from different layers exhibit a global uniformity, which places them within what in Bordian terms would be assigned to a 'Denticulate Mousterian of Levallois facies, rich in sidescrapers'. Some trend is, however, recognisable in the stratigraphic sequence, not towards an Upper Palaeolithic pattern but, instead, towards what we might characterise as an intensifying Middle Palaeolithic pattern, a sort of 'Mousterianisation' process. In spite of the scarcity of industry in some of the layers, it is possible to verify that these characteristics are expressed in different aspects. With regard to raw material utilisation, I verify that it is clearly opportunistic, without a systematic procurement of any particular rock (namely flint), but the index of artefact production in siliceous rocks (quartz, quartzite) increases through time. Regarding technology, within very stable patterns (principal indices – IL, IF, IFs, ILam – exhibit practically the same values across the entire stratigraphic sequence), I pinpoint a relative increase of the Levallois cores, against the discoidal cores and, in particular, the globular cores, as well as the core preforms. At the typological level, the Upper Palaeolithic type artefacts are merely residual, and the denticulates and notches are dominant; the increase of intensity of the Mousterian Group, in particular the number of scrapers, is visible through time, from bottom to top.

Figueira Brava

Located on the present coastal cliff of the Arrábida Mountain, south of Lisbon, this cave, which was actually a rockshelter at the time of Palaeolithic human occupation, was first mentioned in the early 1980s. It was the object of archaeological field research in the first chamber, whose preliminary results were published (Antunes 1992). A second, interior chamber, was also mentioned but it has not been excavated to date. There are indicators of a possible Middle Palaeolithic occupation in the inner chamber, suggesting that the external area is actually formed by sediments coming from the interior of the cave. In fact, the thickest layer (± 1m), with dense Palaeolithic remains (Layer 2) presents evidence of redeposition of sediments, or at least has been locally disturbed, so that recent historical remains have penetrated to a considerable depth.

Only at the base of this layer and in the one immediately subjacent to it (Layer 3), where the lithic industry is less abundant, is there no apparent intrusion from the levels above. At the base of the cave a marine transgression conglomerate is visible (5–8 m above sea level), ascribed to the Tyrrhenian III. In spite of these limitations, the absence of other prehistoric human occupation renders the individualisation of the Mousterian industries easier. Similarly, it is possible to identify the Pleistocene fauna, given its particular colour and associated sediments.

The complete assemblage recovered at this site renders it particularly important. Firstly, the associated fauna is remarkable, probably constituting the most complete example of all the Iberian Middle Palaeolithic. The faunal assemblage includes molluscs and other invertebrates, fish (rare), reptiles, birds (32 species) and mammals. The latter are represented by 18 species of large mammals (including humans) and 19 species of small mammals. The occurrence of a few species adapted to clear cold water conditions (such as arctic seal, Great Auk and the northern sea ducks) points to a regressive Würmian glacial episode. It is not possible, however, to determine the chronology of this fauna strictly on the basis of biostratigraphic arguments and, consequently, the dating of the associated human occupation cannot be specified. A few samples were dated by radiocarbon (*Patella* shells), and by Uranium-series method (deer tooth enamel), with very satisfactory results (Table 11.1 and Figure 11.1).

Palaeolithic occupation of the cave is directly observ-able by the presence of human remains identified as *Homo sapiens neanderthalensis*, namely one upper premolar, and by an abundant lithic industry. Human activity on some animal bones has also been recorded.

Recently, we (Raposo & Cardoso, in press) have analysed the lithic industry, which comprises a total of nearly 4,000 artefacts, or around 2,500 if the flaking chips are excluded (chips: 36%; debitage: 46%; cores: 9%; tools: 9%). It is an occasional expedient industry, without artefacts of great typological elaboration, mostly due to the poor quality of the locally available raw materials.

Quartz blanks, in the form of small rolled pebbles, mostly flaked *in situ*, are largely predominant. They have been collected directly from the nearby Upper Jurassic conglomerates of Serra da Arrábida, or from the Tertiary deposits. Other raw materials were also used and sometimes collected from up to 10 km away. Among these there are different flint-like rocks, which were, contrary to the quartz, essentially worked elsewhere; at this site, they were only transformed into tools, by secondary retouch of the edges. The flaking procedures – mainly discoidal and Levallois – are characteristic of the Middle Palaeolithic industries. The discoidal procedure largely dominates (20% of the total of cores are discoid cores with preparation of platforms on the reverse side of the core; and 10% are discoid cores without this preparation). This is probably due to the nature of the available raw materials and initial blank supports. Quartz being the most used raw material, fragments and formless cores are common (40% of the total of cores). Among the retouched tools, sidescrapers are predominant (IR: 57), especially those of simple convex forms; they are followed by denticulates (Group IV: 17) and notches (Group IVa: 22,6). According to the traditional Bordes' diagnosic criteria, applied to the Middle Palaeolithic industries, it is possible to state that the industry of Figueira Brava cave corresponds to a 'Typical Mousterian, rich in denticulates, with non-Levallois debitage and a non-Levalloisian facies. 'Upper Palaeolithic type' artefacts (cores and retouched tools) are merely residual.

Caldeirão

Located approximately 140 km north east of Lisbon, close to Tomar, this cave was discovered in 1979 during an archaeological survey of the area aimed at identifying Palaeolithic sites. Since then, and until 1988, the site was excavated by João Zilhão (Zilhão 1997). It is a relatively small cavity – a narrow corridor, 20m long, gives access to a room with around 14 square meters – but it exhibits an important and complex, ± 6 metre sedimentary infill history, with human occupation from historical times down to the Middle Palaeolithic. The lower sequence has two sedimentary blocks (layers Q to L, and K to Fa, from base to top), separated by a marked discontinuity (identified as the Denekamp interstadial by radiocarbon dating). In the lower block, carnivore remains are abundant (in particular, hyaena), and lithic artefacts assignable to the Mousterian are rare (48 artefacts in the all the layers together). In the upper segment, the first layer (K) also exhibits a reduced number of lithic artefacts (98 in total, without cores and only 7 tools: sidescrapers, denticulates, and partially retouched flakes). The adjacent layers (Jb and Ja) exhibit a denser industry (with 176 artefacts), especially with some cores and tools typologically more characteristic (in Layer Jb, for example, we observed the presence of some retouched bladelets and one splintered piece). Zilhão assigns the lithic industry from Layer K to the Mousterian, although mentioning the presence of the

'first artefacts clearly associated with the Upper Palaeolithic, at the top of the layer – a retouched flint blade and two perforated marine shells'. The following layers are assigned to the Gravettian (Jb: Lower Gravettian; Ja: Late Gravettian).

Given the numerical scarcity of the lithic assemblages in the lower segment of Layer K, and its non-diagnostic character, we find it impossible to assign them to the Mousterian with certainty. In Layer K, another difficulty was added: the obscure separation of the Upper Palaeolithic tools recovered at the top of the layer, precisely at the level where a C14 date of 27.6ka±600 was considered consistent, given that the other two dates for the bottom of the same layer were considered inconsistent with the general stratigraphic sequence of the site (Table 11.1 and Figure 11.1). It is important to emphasise that a strict stratigraphic consistency is not sufficient to assign a higher reliability to the mentioned date, especially because it can, in fact, date a Gravettian assemblage, with which it would be, in fact, compatible. We can conclude that, although possible, the dates and the association of the lithic industries from the base of the stratigraphic sequence to the Mousterian are not completely proven, although they constitute feasible working hypotheses for future work.

Other sites

Other caves and rockshelters could be considered in this article. Apart from recently discovered sites, not yet published but of significant importance (e.g. Rio Almonda), others are less relevant, either due to their questionable chronological dating, the scarcity of their lithic assemblages or the absence of recent analyses of their materials. They are, nonetheless, sites that 'make sense' within the general framework of the major sites. In that sense, they acquire some informative value.

Three of them, all very close geographically, are in the area surrounding Lisbon (County of Loures): Salemas Cave, Salemas Quarry and Pêgo do Diabo Cave. The first two were discovered and excavated in the late 1950s. Salemas Quarry is part of a group of karstic fissures, vertically opened to the surface. In one of these openings, Middle Palaeolithic industries were identified at the base of the stratigraphic sequence (level 2), although they have not been thoroughly published or recently studied. This level was dated from *c.* 29 ka (Table 11.1 and Figure 11.1). Immediately below this was a sterile level (level 3) and another level (level 4) which provided lithic industries possibly associated with the Upper Palaeolithic, although these were very scarce and have not been described recently. Salemas Cave is, actually, a diaclasite, with a 30 m long, narrow (1 m wide) corridor. The described sedimentary sequence is quite complex, containing evidence of human occupations from different periods of prehistory. Middle Palaeolithic industries (not yet published extensively) are mentioned for the bottom layer (level 4 or 8, according to the two different stratigraphic notations existing at this site), are discontinuous and are described as *terra rossa* infilling the karstic fissures. They constitute an assemblage composed of several tens of artefacts (flakes, tools and cores) of clearly Mousterian techno-typological aspect. The patina is also intensely yellow, very different from the other levels (personal observation). Human remains (one left mandibular molar) have been found, apparently in this level. Denise Ferembach pointed out some metric analogies with other similar Neanderthal teeth. This level is followed by another (level 3 or 7) with an industry composed by a few bone tools (3 *sagaies*) and about one hundred lithic artefacts, including some prismatic cores with multiple percussion platforms, bladelets, tools (one endscraper, one dihedral burin, some microgravettes, microlithic points, retouched bladelets, denticulates and notches). The original excavators have attributed this assemblage to an evolved Gravettian or Perigordian. More recently, João Zilhão, accepting this attribution for the majority of the assemblage, has proposed the separation from it of only four artefacts (three Dufour bladelets and one hypothetical fragment of split-base bone point), which should, in his opinion, be assigned to the Aurignacian. Dates available for these layers (layer 4: 24.82 ka±500; layer 3: 20.25 ka ±320) cannot be considered reliable, given the inadequate control of the provenance of the faunal samples used for dating. It is, however, possible to establish a comparison between this sedimentary sequence and that from Pêgo do Diabo (Zilhão 1997). In the latter, a lower level (level 3, similar to level 4/8 of Salemas), with rare lithic artefacts, (one quartz flake and six flint flakes, all with the yellow patina characteristic of the Salemas Cave Mousterian assemblage) can be assigned to the Middle Palaeolithic. A higher level (level 2, similar to level 3/7 of Salemas), which produced a sample of 31 lithic artefacts (with no cores and only nine tools, including six Dufour bladelets) and one *sagaie*, has been attributed by Zilhão to the Aurignacian. If the only date (18.63 ka±640) available for level 3 is discarded, the chronological framework for this sequence is given by two dates obtained for level 2: 28.12 ka–780, + 860 (base), 23.08 ka±490 (top).

These typological and chronometric data, although interesting, open the cultural identification and dating of human occupation episodes to discussion. The same is true for other sites: some provide acceptable dates but reduced lithic assemblages, such as Lapa dos Furos, which has two dates from *c.* 30 ka and 34 ka but only seven artefacts (Zilhão 1997:32). Other sites exhibit better-defined Mousterian industries but deficient chronometric dates, e.g. Buraca Escura, which has evidence for Middle Palaeolithic occupation, including one hearth, subjacent to Gravettian levels, (Aubry & Moura 1994).

Open air sites

Foz do Enxarrique

This site was discovered in 1982 (Raposo *et al.* 1985) and has been the object of successive archaeological field seasons, which are still ongoing. It is located in the Ródão region, near the banks of the Tagus River, in the interior of Portugal approximately 10 km from the border. The identified Middle Palaeolithic horizon (the only evidence for prehistoric human occupation in the site) is located near the base of a thick silty clay layer, approximately 6 m deep overall. This horizon, which is approximately 20 cm thick, is visible in stratigraphic profiles and has been excavated, to date, to an area of approximately 150 m². It consists of an ancient riverbank, physically materialised in a thin layer of calcium carbonate, probably accumulated by limestone precipitation in the river waters. The sheets of calcium carbonate are slightly dipping over the concavities of the bedrock. Abundant stratigraphically and spatially associated faunal remains and lithic industry (more than 10,000 artefacts) were recovered from this site.

The faunal assemblage is being analysed by Jean-Philip Brugal, who has provided the information below. From a total of 808 bone fragments, approximately 50% were taxonomically classified, revealing the prevalence of deer (27% of the total number of identified fragments; MN: 3), and horse remains (18%; MNI: 3). Auroch bones are also present, although in a lower percentage (1.2%; MNI: 2). Residual species are also present, such as rabbit and one unknown proboscidean specimen (probably elephant), together with rhinoceros remains. Carnivores are represented by rare fragments of fox, hyaena, and lynx. This association denotes a temperate climate, with open spaces and scattered patches of forest.

The lithic industry of this horizon has not yet been extensively studied. It is, however, possible to state that the majority of the assemblage was knapped *in loco*. Apart from small flint and chalcedony pebbles, transported by the river, and detectable in the surroundings of the site, the abundant quartzite pebbles from the gravel bed were utilised. Preferential choice was given to elements exhibiting better mechanical characteristics (isotropic homogeneity, hardness, etc) and morphology (external surfaces with irregularities predisposed for obtaining the desired core masses). This conscious choice is directly linked to the dominant Levallois technique, whether it was applied in the recurrent pattern (largely centripetal, but also unipolar and bipolar), or used as preferential flaking (flake or point).

Although cores and the debitage resulting from a complete reduction sequence are abundant, Levallois products (especially retouched tools) are, apparently, under-represented. It is possible that they were both removed from the site, which might have represented a 'work camp'. This definition is, however, too reductionistic, as functional classifications of sites across the Lower and Middle Palaeolithic generally are. It also appears evident that numerous debitage products were utilised as 'tools *a posteriori*', without secondary retouching of the edges, but with microdenticulation and wear facets. This feature could be explained by one (or all) of the following:

raw material quality, perfection of the flaking methods and techniques utilised, economy of production, or expedient character of the desired tools.

At present, Foz do Enxarrique constitutes the most important site of its type (open-air) and chronology (Late Middle Palaeolithic) in the whole Iberian Peninsula. Its chronological framework is well-defined by three U-series dates obtained for tooth enamel specimens (two horse teeth and one auroch tooth), which provided very reliable results and an average date of 33.6 ka±500 (or 30 ka in conventional radiocarbon terms).

Conceição
Also located in the Tagus valley, but near the estuary, south of Lisbon, this site was discovered in 1996. This was immediately followed by a rescue excavation, before it was covered by the access structures to the Vasco da Gama bridge. A small monograph of the site has been published (Raposo & Cardoso 1998b). Geological survey work identified the superposition of two transgressive cycles of sedimentation corresponding to the Eemian and the Würmian interpleniglacial periods. The archaeological horizon already studied is situated on the surface of a gravel bed, corresponding to the second period mentioned, which is covered with a thin layer of fluvio-aeolian origin. The absolute dates obtained for the sand layer below the gravel bed (64.5+11.6–10.4 ka), and for the covering thin layer (27.2±2.5 ka), confirm the geochronoclimatic interpretation previously suggested. The date for this last layer establishes, therefore, a *terminus post-quem* for the human occupation and can be validly used as an approximate indicator of its true age.

In the same area, other similar sites are known. In each one of them, their most impressive feature is the great abundance of their respective lithic industries: tens of thousands of artefacts, sometimes dispersed over very extensive areas. Obviously, they constitute a palimpsest corresponding to the accumulation of successive occupation levels, impossible to isolate. The main factor that can explain this pattern is the local abundance of quartzite and quartz pebbles, raw material that becomes scarce further away from the Tagus River valley. Although it is impossible to define a chronology for these occupations, it is interesting to reflect on their historical significance in the framework of an intensification process in the economic systems of Neanderthal communities in the final phase of their existence.

At Conceição, during the short time available for its study, around 8,500 lithic artefacts were identified, of which 1,200 were collected in a 5m² excavated area. Detailed analysis of the collections recovered by different methods (systematic survey in a predetermined area, mechanical testing, and the small excavated area referred to previously) rendered it possible to determine the effect of these methods on the resulting samples. But it also reaffirmed the global integrity of the assemblage, emphasising the 'work camp' character of the site. Although

retouched tools are rare (around 250 specimens, i.e., *c*. 3 % of the total industry), approximately 2,000 core objects were recovered (core preforms: ±500; core fragments: ± 900; organised cores: ±520). Every step of core reduction is perfectly represented, from tested pebbles to the exhausted, residual and broken debris. The dominant patterns of lithic exploitation are based on concepts of core mass volume reduction on two opposite faces (discoidal cores and Levallois cores). Other cores, including globular, as well as the tridimensional volume conception cores, and prismatic ones are all scarce. The recurrent, mainly centripetal, exploitation method is also predominant, although further examples of core configuration might occur (unipolar, bipolar and crossed). In general, a standardisation of the technical procedures is recognisable, based on the development of the most elaborate pattern of gesture economy. Regarding this subject, I should mention the relevance of the discoidal cores on cortical convex pebbles, in which the morphology of the natural block is used for extracting the desired flakes, with no use of formatting or preparation of striking platform preparation actions, translated into flaking scars from the reverse of the core. The extraordinary number of cores in this site, together with their homogeneity, constitute an excellent basis for more detailed technological studies, particularly for testing the distinction between 'discoidal' and 'Levallois' (which in this case does not appear to be established), on the basis of the commonly proposed variables. Considering these technological characteristics, and regardless of the scarcity of retouched tools already mentioned (mostly denticulates and notches), there is no difficulty in assigning this industry to the Mousterian complex, although it is not possible to be more specific about its classification within the traditional Bordes system.

Synthesis

Geographic distribution of sites and raw material procurement
Figure 11.2 shows the most important Middle and Upper Palaeolithic sites in central Portugal – the Tagus River basin and its peripheral areas (Raposo 1995). It includes all the sites mentioned in the previous section, as well as numerous others that were not mentioned, either because they lie outside the chronological framework analysed here, or because they are only of minor importance.

A clear break between the two periods is evident. The Middle Palaeolithic sites are predominantly related to the sedimentary river basins and they do not form clusters that might suggest individual territories, occupied by different human groups. It is an identical situation to that which is observable in mapped Lower Palaeolithic sites. There is one minor difference between the two periods, however: the use of low-altitude peripheral rocky massifs during the Middle Palaeolithic.

This pattern is, as I mentioned, totally distinct from

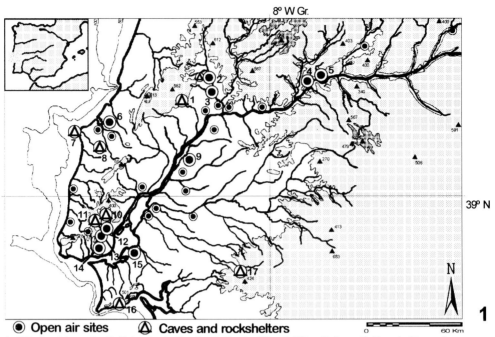

Open air sites   Caves and rockshelters

1: Oliveira-Almonda; 2: Estrada do Prado; 3: Santa Cita; 4: Vilas Ruivas; 5: Foz do Enxarrique;
6: Panascosa;7: Furninha; 8: Columbeira; 9: Vale do Forno; 10: Salemas; 11: Correio-Mór;
12: Santo Antão do Tojal; 13: Casal do Monte;14: Calçada dos Mestres; 15: Alto da Pacheca
and Cascalheira; 16: Figueira Brava; 17: Escoural.

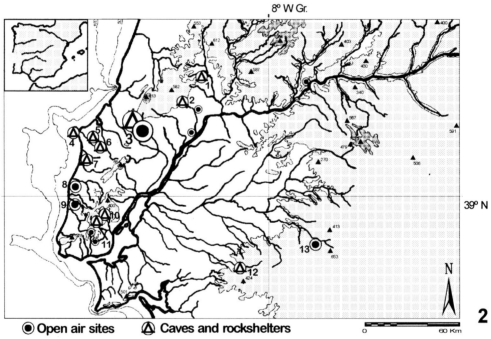

Open air sites   Caves and rockshelters

1: Caldeirão; 2: Oliveira - Almonda; 3: Several sites in the region of Rio Maior; 4: Furninha;
5: Casa da Moura;6: Lapa do Suão; 7: Lapa da Rainha; 8: Vale da Almoinha and Rossio do
Cabo; 9: Vale da Mata; 10: Salemas;11: Correio-Mór; 12: Escoural; 13: Évora-Monte.

Figure 11.2: Most important Middle (1) and Upper (2) Palaeolithic sites in Central Portugal.

that visible in the Upper Palaeolithic. Although I must admit that there are gaps, due to the insufficient survey work performed in some areas, and the sedimentation suffered by the Late Pleistocene formations by Holocene sediments (especially in the lower flood plains) one cannot ignore the fact that during the Upper Palaeolithic the main fluvial valleys appear to have been less intensely occupied, being replaced by the secondary valleys and the peripheral massifs. Other site clusters are seen in areas where food or lithic resources are more abundant, and in strategic circulation areas, giving access to different physical environments. This aspect, together with the functional interpretation of the different sites, renders it tempting (although not always credible) to define the Upper Palaeolithic resource procurement pattern in terms of territories that might have been occupied by different, self-conscious human groups.

It is not by chance that in the caves mentioned above, the presence of the Middle Palaeolithic remains are very discreet, even when the following layers at the same sites indicate important Upper Palaeolithic occupations. On the contrary, the caves with a more significant Middle Palaeolithic occupation were not subsequently utilised in the next phases. Clearly, Neanderthals and modern humans did not share the same requirements, be it the general settling of the territory or the choice of specific settlement places. One exception is the recently excavated Gruta da Oliveira which represents a complex karstic network (an Almonda River spring), with many cave openings and evidence of human occupation during all time periods.

At present, there are no modern zooarchaeological studies to provide information on aspects more directly related to the practices of food procurement. The only available databases list faunal species presented in each site (see, for instance, Cardoso 1996). It is, however, possible to identify Late Mousterian horizons through these kinds of data. For example: the absence of exploration of a particular species (and, most probably, more evidence of scavenging than hunting); the exploitation of marine resources, at least in the case of Figueira Brava; the consumption of turtle (?tortoise), demonstrated in more than one site; etc. These are, however, insufficient data and it is often difficult to distinguish human activity from the bone accumulations resulting from carnivore action, especially in cave sites.

Hence, one factor that can be adopted for explaining this marked rupture between the Late Middle Palaeolithic and the Early Upper Palaeolithic is the different require-ments of both periods for specific lithic sources. In this respect, a clear distinction between the assemblages should be emphasised: Mousterian industries predominantly used locally available raw materials, with a prevalence of quartz and quartzite; Early Upper Palaeolithic industries, how-ever, are predominantly based on siliceous bases and, in some cases, there is a systematic search for flint.

In the few examples where both periods occur (e.g. Gruta do Caldeirão), the difference between the percent-ages of different raw materials is notable. Even in areas where flint is easily collectable, it is rarely used for even half of the total number of artefacts in each Mousterian lithic assemblage. In the case of Columbeira, for example, the flint tools constitute only one-third of the total number, with a correspondingly higher rate of transformation of 'non-flint' materials – this in one area where in the immediate vicinity there exists at least one other cave with Upper Palaeolithic tools predominantly produced in flint. It is difficult to assign a specific cause for this contrast in the use of raw materials. The distinct isotropic needs imposed by the use of blade industry methods are commonly invoked. In fact, these are practically absent in the Late Middle Palaeolithic industries and very common in Early Upper Palaeolithic. If this explanation is plausible, it is, however, insufficient. Perhaps the advantages or disadvantages of different raw materials were mostly related to factors such as the type of actions performed in these periods, and, above all, to the economy of technical gestures in obtaining tools (the *a posteriori* tools are vastly more common in Middle Palaeolithic, and the unretouched edges in quartz or quartzite are more resistant and, therefore, more efficient for applying blunt forces, than the natural flint edges).

Stratigraphic sequences and cultural affiliations

As previously mentioned, the number of sites where a continuity of occupation between the Late Middle Palaeo-lithic and the Early Upper Palaeolithic may be seen is limited. In Figure 11.3, I present the most important sites for both periods for which we have sufficiently reliable dating elements. In approximately half of them (Lapa dos Furos, Figueira Brava, Foz do Enxarrique, Salemas Quarry, Columbeira and Conceição) only Late Middle Palaeolithic occupation levels are recognised. In four of them (Casa da Moura, Vale Comprido-Cruzamento, Fonte Santa and Gato Preto), only Early Upper Palaeolithic horizons occur; only the remaining three caves (Salemas Cave, Caldeirão and Pêgo do Diabo) present stratigraphic sequences with continuity between the two periods. It is therefore problematic to use this database for building large global hypotheses except perhaps the one stated before: the evident rupture between the two periods.

The unsatisfying cultural diagnoses performed are a result of these difficulties. Regarding the sites with exclusively Middle Palaeolithic industries, we have seen how two of them – Salemas Quarry (small and never described) and Lapa dos Furos (3 flakes in flint, 2 notches, 1 undetermined core in flint, 1 denticulate), do not provide guarantees of positive cultural classification. They can be assigned to this period exclusively by the dates obtained. In any case, there is an important set of sites that allow a solid overview of the main characteristics of the industries in this period. Ongoing research will eventually point out variability related to the geological location of the sites (caves or open air sites), the proximity and/or distance

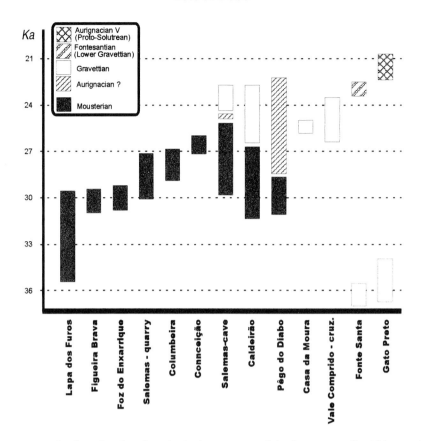

Figure 11.3: Main important absolute-dated archaeological sequences of the Portuguese final Mousterian and initial Upper Palaeolithic.

from the raw material sources, the duration of the occupation and, finally, their function.

Regarding the sites with exclusively Early Upper Palaeolithic industries, we recognise only two Gravettian groups, well-dated and typologically classified (Casa da Moura and Comprido-Cruzamento; Zilhão 1997). Regarding two other sites (Fonte Santa and Gato Preto) TL dates were originally obtained that appeared considerably too old (*c.* 36 ka), and were later rejected on the basis of the techno-typological classification of the respective lithic assemblages, assigned to the Gravettian and Proto-Solutrean (Zilhão 1997).

Finally, each of the sites with occupation from both periods present difficulties in their interpretation. In this case, the assemblages potentially assigned to the Middle Palaeolithic on the basis of stratigraphy are scarce, except for Salemas Cave. The Early Upper Palaeolithic sites, however, raise other questions. In all of these the presence of the Gravettian cultural horizon was originally recognised – which appears to be expected, given its chronology and the fact that it is the technological complex most widely and firmly recognised in the southern and western Iberian Peninsula before the Solutrean. Recently, however, João Zilhão supported the identification of a more or less discreet Aurignacian presence in two of them (Salemas Cave and Pêgo do Diabo). Given the absence of chrono-

logical data to support this hypothesis, it was merely identified by the presence of a reduced number of Dufour bladelets in both sites, used as true *fossiles-directeurs* for the Aurignacian. This procedure is unjustifiable, in our opinion, as the Dufour bladelet is not sufficiently diagnostic, especially in such minor quantities (3 specimens in Salemas Cave; 6 specimens in Pêgo do Diabo) to enable us to use it outside the whole regional context, for identifying that technological complex (Bordes 1984: 262). It should be noted that, apart from these two cave sites, Zilhão only identifies the Aurignacian in two open-air sites with industries resulting from surface collections, whose homogeneity and/or representative character is legitimately questionable.

In conclusion, I note that in Portugal, Middle Palaeolithic industries are followed by an important Gravettian horizon, the presence of Aurignacian being questioned. This evaluation is completely coherent with the present chronological framework, discussed in the next section.

General discussion

Portuguese sites within the Iberian Peninsula
It is widely recognised today that the survival of Mousterian industries until very late (28 or 27 ka) in Portugal was not an isolated event in the Iberian Peninsula.

Portuguese data are however particularly significant in this respect. In fact, when this scenario was first proposed by Vega Toscano (Vega Toscano 1990, 1993) there was some resistance to it: either because the majority of the dates were based on geo/biostratigraphic arguments, or because there were questions raised about the stratigraphic provenance of the few absolute dates available.

It became, therefore, essential to evaluate the degree of confidence in the set of available dates. In Figure 11.1 I presented the set of chronometric dates for the Portuguese Middle Palaeolithic. I then emphasised the fact that they constitute a cluster of results ranging from 33 to 27 ka This fact is solid, and survives the critical presentation of the data for each site in the previous section. It is certain that, in some cases, the lithic assemblages with those dates can only be assigned to the Middle Palaeolithic on the basis of some techno-typological indicators or because they are stratigraphically located below the Early Upper Palaeolithic levels. It is also clear that in other cases the dates obtained only establish *terminus post-quem* limits, as in general is characteristic of the methods themselves. It is also certain that special attention should be paid in confronting the conventional radiocarbon dates with dates obtained by other methods. But, necessary cautions observed, none of these issues significantly challenges the fact that there is a considerable set of dates obtained by different methods, with converging results.

The Portuguese data considerably reinforce the information known for southern Spain. Figure 11.4 and Table 11.1 present the inventory of approximately the twenty most important sites for this subject in the Iberian Peninsula. The occurrence of Mousterian sites dated from <35 ka from the Spanish Levant to the Portuguese Estremadura is notable. The absence of sites in the region between the Guadalquivir river basin and the coast of Alentejo can be attributed either to the nature of the sedimentary sequence or, more likely, to the absence of research in this area. The only two sites located outside this region do not constitute real exceptions; they represent situations for which more interesting interpretations may be made. *Les Ermitons* represents a mountain site, where Neanderthal populations maintained their presence in a marginal way until later when, at a lower altitude, Aurignacian groups must have occupied the region. *Jarama VI* suggests an entirely different interpretation of the settlement patterns of the Iberian interior during this phase, which still remains almost completely unknown.

This territorial pattern needs to be combined with the known occurrence of Aurignacian and Gravettian human occupations in Cantabria and Catalonia, probably since around 40 ka. Zilhão has designated the term 'Ebro frontier' (Zilhão 1993), a somewhat debatable expression, given that it does not take into account the fact that the settlement patterns of intermediate areas such as the Iberian north-west and interior regions are largely unknown. In addition, it suggests a geographical boundary with no ecological basis. In fact the border that, approximately 10

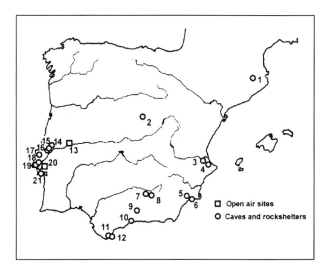

Figure 11.4: Major Middle Palaeolithic Iberian sites, dated <35 ka (see Table 11.1).

ka, ensured the separation between south and west Neanderthal populations and north and northeast modern populations, is exactly the same as that which today distinguishes the Iberian continental landmass and southern coastlines, with its temperate-warm climate (closer to the north African system) from the entirely different Northern Iberia, of temperate-cold climate (closer to the European model).

The Iberian data in the European context

The correct evaluation of the Iberian record must, however, be seen within a wider geographical and historical framework. In fact, observing the maps of Europe during three chronologically successive periods (Figure 11.5), it is possible to envisage the following scenarios:

c. **40 ka or earlier** (Figure 11.5: Map 1), the first Upper Palaeolithic industries (Aurignacian) seem to occupy a rather narrow latitude strip. This consistitutes a 'front' that begins in the east (Bacho-Kiro level 11), occupies central Europe along the Danube River (Istallöskö level 9, Willendorf c+, Geissenklosterle IIIa) and the Alpine arch (Grotta di Fumane, Grotta di Paina), extending possibly as far as the regions of Catalonia (Arbreda BEIII) and Cantabria (Castillo 18C), if one accepts the respective datings, which are not entirely consensual. Peripherally no significant 'transitional industries' are identifiable. The leafpoint industries of Germany are excluded because they represent the development of ancient indigenous traditions. Similarly, the blade industries of northern France and Belgium cannot be included because they date to many thousands of years before the period under consideration.

c. **35 ka** (Figure 11.5: Map 2). The so-called 'transitional industries' multiply, especially in marginal zones, from the previous Aurignacian latitudinal strip. Leaving

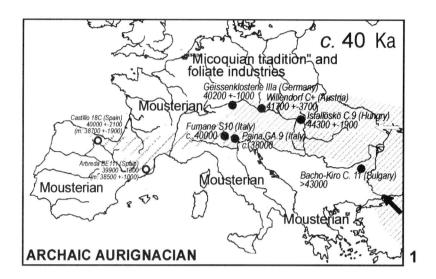

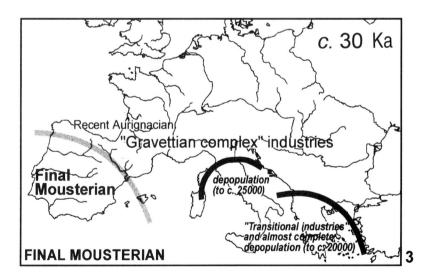

Figure 11.5: Europe between 40 and 30 ka: the passage from Middle to Upper Palaeolithic.

aside the historical significance of such industries and especially one reductionist interpretation which lumps them together as similar, I would emphasise the strong presumption of the effect of acculturation in some of them. In any other way it would be difficult to understand how, lacking immediate local roots, geographically very diverse populations could converge so abruptly towards the techno-typological patterns identified as Upper Palaeolithic. It is important here however to underline that acculturation does not mean a generalised diffusion of people – much less a biological or cultural inferiority. It simply represents the most economic way to interpret existing information, making use of the most universal mechanism through which innovation is spread, which is principally at the tool typological level. It is worth noting, in this chronological strip, the existing situation in the Mediterranean zones, the development of 'transitional industries' in the Balkans (although poorly documented and united vaguely in a concept of 'Moustero-Aurignacian' lithic assemblages) and in the Italian region (Uluzzian), and the continuation of the Mousterian in southern and western Iberia.

c. **30 ka and later** (Figure 11.5: Map 3). The Upper Palaeolithic industries occupy Europe extensively, with the so-called 'transitional industries' practically vanished: only the three meridional peninsulas are atypical. In the two eastern territories a near-depopulation is suggested: however, this pattern is due either to the lack of archaeological research, or to some type of environmental adversity (see the important synthesis presented elsewhere by Margherita Mussi and Catherine Perlés: Mussi & Roebroeks 1996, Mussi *et al.* 1997). In the western peninsula a significant permanence of Mousterian industries is indicated.

Even if the particular distribution of Neanderthals and modern *sapiens* in Iberia can be to a certain extent explained within the peninsula itself, I nevertheless insist that it is crucial in this case to adopt a wider perspective, not only in geographical but especially in conceptual terms. In fact the simple geographic position of Iberia, in the western extreme of Europe, would be insufficient to explain the survival of Neanderthals, even if the east to west 'modern *sapiens* invasion' model is accepted. It could easily be asked, in this case, why Italy and Greece were not occupied by modern *sapiens* extensively until *c.* 25 ka? It would also be interesting to ask why Neanderthals survived so late in south and western Iberia but did not in Italy, for instance, if the generic climatic and latitude constraints were the same.

Clearly, the full understanding of the Iberian data requires a much wider approach, based on a palaeobiogeographic interpretation of the 'Neanderthal entity', their origin, their diversified regional development and ultimately their extinction (*cf.* Hublin 1990).

The survival of Mousterian and Neanderthals in south and west Iberia: a palaeobiogeographic model

At this point, we find ourselves in an area of research where it becomes necessary to verify the diversity of landscape and climatic environments of Europe in the period from the Würmian interpleniglacial to the beginning of the climatic deterioration which lead up to the last glacial maximum. This is a field of interdisciplinary study which should consider mesological factors, the geography of Europe itself, theoretical models and which should evaluate the development of endemisms in Europe and in its different meridional regions, (especially in the three major peninsulas), referred to above. A great deal of work is still to be done in this respect: not only are essential data certainly missing, but also the existing data have yet to be summarised and reviewed using homogenous methodological standards. This is why an investigation project, assembling researchers from different disciplinary fields (palaeontology, palaeobotanic, palaeoclimatology, palaeoecology, and palaeoanthropology) is necessary and should be organised.

Some guidelines can nevertheless be proposed for future research. Working with existing data and using more rigorously dated key anthropological findings, it might be possible to verify the occurrence of an unsuspected biological variety, with potential for adaptation, within what have previously been classified as 'Neanderthals'. It may be possible, for example, to reconstruct the old idea of Sergio Sergi about the existence of a Mediterranean Neanderthal variety – more undifferentiated and gracile than the so-called classic variety – an idea that authors have returned to many times, despite the lack of solid chronological evidence. In 1982, Anne-Marie Tillier concluded her study of the Neanderthal children of Devil's Tower by hinting that the plesiomorphous traces she detected in them might have been only due to their possible pre-Würmian age (an explanation similarly used to interpret identical traces in some Italian and East European fossils). She did, however, admit that "..si par contre les fossiles de Gibraltar sont plus récents (dernière glaciation) comme le suposait Garrod, ils constitueraient les seuls représentants en Europe d'une variété néanderthalienne isolée géographiquement" (Tillier 1982: 147).

In 1991, Silvana Condemi noted that the plesiomorphous characteristics of the Circeo I cranium were similar to the Saccopastore fossils (dated in the last interglacial period), and quite different from the classic Neanderthal populations (dominated by autapomorphous characters). He also concluded that, allowing for the recent dating of Circeo I (Würm), "it would be tempting to interpret this difference in terms of a local continuity particular to each of these two geographic regions" (Condemi 1991: 353). In 1995, Giorgio Manzi and his collaborators, analysing new Neanderthal remains from Mount Circeo (this time from Grotta Breuil), affirmed that the signs of gracile patterns detected in them "are

108 LUIS RAPOSO

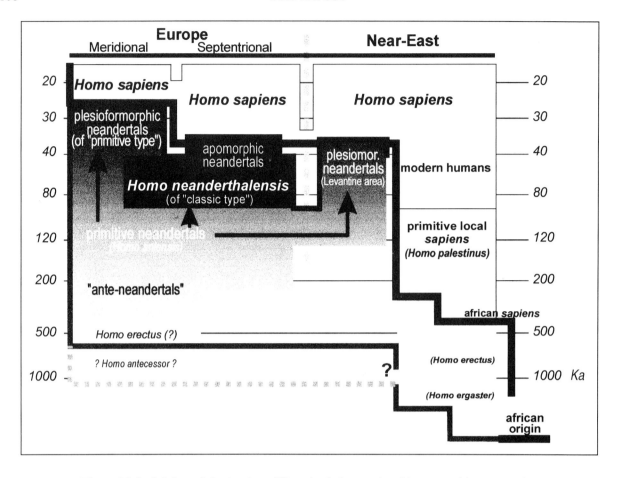

Figure 11.6: Origin and destination of Neanderthals: a palaeobiogeographic perspective.

best considered as the expression of geographic (and adaptative) variation" (Manzi *et al.* 1995: 395).

These suggestions have recently all been confirmed by Anne Hambücken, in her study of Neanderthal postcranial features, especially the morphology of the distal end of the humerus. This author positively identifies a 'Mediterranean variety' of the Neanderthals, with similarities to the Near East variety. Working with more conclusive radiometric dating, she clearly states: "L'hypothèse d'une variabilité due à la disparité chronologique des fossiles peut être écartée lorsque l'on considère l'âge qui leur est accordé" (Hambücken 1997: 116). The existence of such varieties could be put down to different climatic environments, expressed by different functional and behavioural characteristics. At the local level, low population density and mobility would also have some impact: "il est possible qu'une faible mobilité des Néandertaliens, et donc des flux génétiques réduits soient un élément d'explication à retenir pour expliquer la variabilité observée au niveau local".

The data used by Anne Hambücken are still very fragmentary. Many other specimens should be taken into consideration: those from Breuil in Italy, and in particular those from Iberia. The fossils from Devil's Tower, in Gibraltar, if dated from a recent period, and the exceptional finds from Zafarraya, could acquire a crucial importance

in this context. They would definitely confirm the occurrence of a Mediterranean Neanderthal variety, more undifferentiated and potentially progressive than the so-called 'classic' variety, allowing eventually the construction of a model close to that presented in Figure 11.6. If this framework is to be proven valid, then it would open the way to an entire reconsideration of the 'Neanderthal entity'. The so-called 'classic Neanderthals' would, in this case, be viewed as an outcome of an extreme, derived cold adaptation. The real representatives of the Neanderthal population would be placed in meridional Europe, the core territory where more conservative patterns would naturally be maintained and where people would subsist until later.

Iberia, an entire subcontinent by itself, offers the ideal area to study one of the most important Neanderthal homelands. In fact, if we consider the conditions of isolation and the geographical dimensions of each of the three European meridional peninsulas, we might perhaps begin to explain the survival of the Neanderthal populations in Iberia until after 30 ka years, and the apparent near-depopulation of Italy and Greece from the same period until nearly 25 ka. The absence of a precocious occupation by the first biologically modern populations of the centre, south, and west of the Iberian Peninsula, and their discreet presence in the Italian and Balkan peninsulas might be due to the combined action of two factors. First is the possible difficulty of adaptation to their respective natural environments and, secondly, the fact that these environments were actually occupied by biologically progressive populations (not in the sense of an approximation to the morphological modern *sapiens* entity, but in the strictly biological sense, within the Neanderthal framework), even though quite possibly less evolved technologically and culturally.

In these terms, it might be expected that the dimension of the territories in the three southern European peninsulas would play a decisive role. Smaller, geographically accessible territories would create all kinds of phenomena of acculturation and/or rapid population decline and extinction of the less well-equipped population. Less well-equipped, in this context, means a variety of possible adaptive difficulties, some of them strictly biological: reproduction rates, resistance to epidemics, perhaps. Others might be culturally dependent: hunter-gathering practices, technological procedures, tool efficiency, etc.

Larger, geographically inaccessible territories would sustain distinct cultural characteristics and a longer survival of the ancient populations, which would have sufficiently large reproductive spaces at their disposal. This may have been what happened in the east (Greece and Italy) and in the west (Portugal and Mediterranean Spain). Faunal evidence supports this scenario, especially in Iberia, where endemic species, and the survival of an ancient megafauna until later periods, are documented (e.g. the occurrence of *Elephas antiquus*, at nearly 30 ka, at Foz do Enxarrique), afterwards being radically substituted by associations of modern type. After all, Neanderthals were not alone. They must be perceived as only one more element of one particular European biocultural trajectory.

References

Antunes, M. Telles (1992). O Homem da Gruta da Figueira Brava (ca. 30000 BP). *Memórias da Academia das Ciências de Lisboa*, Classe Ciências. **31**, (1990–91), 487–536.

Aubry, Th. & Moura, M.H. (1994). Paleolítico da Serra de Sicó. *Trabalhos de Antropologia e Etnologia*. **34** (3–4), 43–60.

Barandiaran, I. & Ferreira, O. da V. (1971). Huesos labrados en el paleolítico antíguo y médio de Portugal. *Arqueologia e História*. 9(3), 31–54.

Bordes, F. (1984). *Leçons sur le Paléolithique, vol. 2, Le Paléolithique en Europe*. CNRS: Paris.

Breuil. H. & Zbyszewski, G. (1942). Contribuition à l'étude des industries paléolithiques du Portugal et leurs rapports avec la géologie du Quaternaire, Vol. 1. *Comunicações dos Serviços Geológicos de Portugal*. **XXIII**, 1–374.

Breuil. H. & Zbyszewski, G. (1945). Contribuition à l'étude des industries paléolithiques du Portugal et leurs rapports avec la géologie du Quaternaire, Vol. 2. *Comunicações dos Serviços Geológicos de Portugal*. **XXVI**, 1–678.

Cardoso, J.L. (1993). *Contribuição para o conhecimento dos grandes Mamíferos do Plistocénico Superior de Portugal*. Câmara Municipal de Oeiras: Oeiras.

Cardoso, J.L. (1996). *Les grands mammifères du Pléistocène supérieur du Portugal. Essai de synthèse*, GEOBIOS. 29 (2), 235–250.

Condemi, S. (1991). Circeo 1 e la variabilitá dei neandertaliani classici'. *Il Cranio Neandertaliano Circeo I. Studi e Documenti*. 339–355, Roma.

Ferreira, O. da V. (1963). Algumas descobertas importantes da Pré e Proto-história portuguesa nos últimos anos. *Revistas de Guimarães*. **73**, 271–280.

Ferembach, D. (1964–65). La molaire humaine inférieure moustérienne de Bombarral (Portugal). *Comunicações dos Serviços Geológicos de Portugal*. **48**, 185–190.

Ferreira, O. da V. (1984). O mais importante nível de ocupação do caçador neandertal da Gruta Nova da Columbeira (Bombarral). In (Ed.) *Hommage au géologue G. Zbyszewski*, pp. 365–370. Recherche sur les Civilisations. Paris.

Hambücken, A. (1997). La variabilité géographique des Néandertaliens: apport de l'étude du membre supérieur. *Anthropologie et Préhistoire*. **108**, 109–120.

Hublin, J.-J. (1990). Les peuplements paléolithiques de l'Europe: un point de vue paléobiogéographique. *Mémoires du Musée de Préhistoire d'Ile de France*. **3**, 29–37.

Manzi, G. & Passarello, P. (1995). At the Archaic/Modern boundary of the Genus Homo: The Neandertals from Grotta Breuil, *Current Anthropology*, **36**, (2), 355–366, Chicago.

Mussi, M. & Roebroeks, W. (1996). The big Mosaic. *Current Anthropology*. **37**, (4), 697–699.

Mussi, M., Roebroeks, W. & Svoboda, J. (1997). *Hunters of the Golden Age: The Middle Upper Palaeolithic of Europe (30000–20000 BP)*. Univ. of Leiden.

Raposo, L. (1993a). *O Paleolítico Médio. O Quaternário em Portugal – balanço e perspectIvas*, pp.147–161. APEQ & Colibri: Lisbon.

Raposo, L. (1993b). *O Paleolítico ticoî, História de Portugal, Vol. I – O começo*, pp. 21–99. Ediclube: Lisbon.

Raposo, L. (1995). Ambientes, territorios y subsistencia en el Paleolítico Medio de Portugal. *Complutum*. **6**, 57–77.

Raposo, L., Silva, A.C. & Salvador, M. (1985). Notícia da descoberta da estação mustierense da Foz do Enxarrique, *Iª Reunião do Quarternário Ibérico*. **2**, 79–90.

Raposo, L., Salvador, M. & Pereira, J.P. (1996). L'Acheuléen dans la vallée du Tage, au Portugal, *CERP*. **4**, 41–50.

Raposo, L. & Cardoso, J.L. (1998a). Las industrias líticas de la Gruta Nova de Columbeira (Bombarral,Portugal) en el contexto del Musteriense Final de la Península Ibérica. *Trabajos de Prehistória*. **55** (1), 39–62.

Raposo, L. & Cardoso, J. L. (1998b). *O sítio do Paleolítico Médio da Conceição (Alcochete)*. CEMA: Lisbon.

Raposo, L. & Cardoso, J.L. (in press). Breve caracterização da indústria lítica da gruta da Figueira Brava (Setúbal), *Academia das Ciências de Lisboa*.

Tillier, A.-M. (1982). Les enfants néanderthaliens de Devil's Tower (Gibraltar). *Zeitschrift für Morpohologie und Anthropologie*. **73**, (2), 125–148.

Vega Toscano, L.G. (1990). La fin du paléolithique moyen au sud de l'Espagne: ses implications dans le contexte de la péninsule ibérique. *Mémoires du Musée de Préhistoire d'Ile de France*. **3**, 169–176.

Vega Toscano, L.G. (1993). El tránsito del Paleolítico Medio al Paleolítico Superior en el Sur de la Península Ibérica. In (V. Cabrera Ed.)*El origem del hombre moderno en el suroeste de Europa*, pp. 147–170. UNED: Madrid.

Zilhão, J. (1993). Le passage du Paléolithique moyen au Paléolithique supérieur dans le Portugal. In *(V. Cabrera, Ed)* El Origen del Hombre Moderno en el Suroeste de Europa, pp. 127–145. UNED: Madrid.

Zilhão, J. (1997). O Paleolítico Superior da Estremadura Portuguesa, Colibri: Lisbon.

Zilhão, J. & Mckinney, C. (1993). Uranium-Thorium dating of Lower and Middle Palaeolithic sites: in the Almonda karstic system (Torres Novas, Portugal)'. *3ª Reunião do Quaternário Ibérico*, pp. 513–516, Coimbra.

12

The Ebro Frontier: A Model for the Late Extinction of Iberian Neanderthals

João Zilhão

Introduction

The idea that Mousterian industries and, consequently, Neanderthals, survived in Valencia and Andalucia until *c.* 28–30 ka, i.e., significantly later than elsewhere in Western Europe, was first put forward on a sound geoarchaeological basis by Vega (1990) and Villaverde and Fumanal (1990). Confirmation of the concept would soon come from reliable radiometric dates for several Portuguese cave and open air sites (Zilhão 1993; Raposo 1995) and for the Andalucian cave site of Zafarraya (Hublin *et al.* 1995). Meanwhile, however, much earlier results had also been obtained for Aurignacian contexts in Cantabria and northern Catalonya (Bischoff *et al.* 1989, 1994; Cabrera and Bischoff 1989; Maroto 1994; Cabrera *et al.* 1996), suggesting that the establishment of Upper Palaeolithic modern humans in those regions dated to *c.* 38–40 ka.

These facts inspired the formulation of the Ebro frontier model (Figure 12.1), first presented in October 1991, in the Madrid Conference on the origins of anatomically modern humans (Zilhão 1993). From the spatial and temporal aspects of the Iberian situation the proposition was derived that, in Western Europe, the replacement of Neanderthals by moderns had not been the outcome of a gradual geographic progression of the latter but a punctuated process during which stable biocultural frontiers might have lasted for significant amounts of time. One such frontier, largely corresponding to a major biogeographical divide (*cf.* Gamble 1986), would have been located along the Cantabro-Pyrenean mountains: for possibly as long as 10,000 years but certainly for at least some 5,000 years, the Ebro basin would have separated the Mousterian Neanderthals of Iberia from the Aurignacian Moderns of Cantabria, Aquitaine and northern Catalonya (Zilhão 1993, 1995, 1997, 1998, in press).

This hypothesis has since received considerable support from many different lines of evidence. This paper will discuss the archaeological data substantiating the model, focusing on the Portuguese material, and elaborate on its implications for the study of Neanderthal extinction.

The late Mousterian and the Aurignacian of Portugal

Table 12.1 shows an annotated list of all radiometric dates currently available for the Portuguese Middle Palaeolithic. Several sites have results later than 40 ka that cannot be accepted. In most cases, rejection is a consequence of technical problems in the dating procedures. Low collagen or low uranium content, for instance, immediately force us to remove from further consideration all the post-28 ka dates, which are in any case incompatible with the cultural stratigraphy of the Last Glacial (Zilhão 1995, 1997).

The inadequate nature of the dated material also brings into question acceptance of the radiocarbon results for Columbeira (Delibrias *et al.* 1986). The need to reject these results is also suggested by the stratigraphic context. According to Raposo and Cardoso (1998a), the sequence begins with a 0.5 m package rich in archaeological remains: levels 7–9. These are overlain by 1.5 m of deposits which, although poor in artefacts, are still entirely Middle Palaeolithic: levels 4–6. Accepting the radiocarbon age of *c.* 26 ka for level 7 necessarily entails, therefore, accepting that the Mousterian industries in levels 4–6 would have been contemporary with the later Upper Palaeolithic of the rest of Europe. Zbyszewski *et al.* (1977) argued along those lines on the basis of their analysis of foliates recovered at the site of Arneiro. Their hypothesis of a direct transition from the Mousterian to the Solutrean in Portugal is, however, empirically untenable. Not only are Aurignacian and Gravettian sites well described and dated in the region but the Arneiro

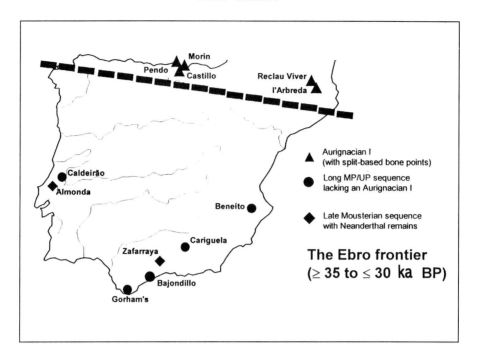

Figure 12.1: The Ebro frontier. For at least 5 ka a stable biocultural frontier separated Aurignacian modern humans living in Cantabria and northern Catalonya from the Mousterian Neanderthals that continued to thrive in the rest of Iberia until c. 20–30 ka.

foliates are neither Mousterian nor Solutrean points but Neolithic-Chalcolithic preforms for bifacial knives and halberds (Zilhão 1995, 1997).

Figure 12.2 gives the location of those sites for which the recent dates obtained are technically acceptable and compatible with regional chrono-stratigraphic patterns. From north to south, these are the open air site of Foz do Enxarrique (Ródão), and the cave sites of Furos and Caldeirão (Tomar), Almonda (Torres Novas), Pedreira de Salemas (Loures) and Figueira Brava (Setúbal). Furos and Pedreira de Salemas, however, yielded very small assemblages, and some of the other sites are not without problems either.

At Figueira Brava, the chaotic nature of the excavated deposit suggests that it may in fact correspond to a redeposition of material eroded from an inner chamber. Given that only Middle Palaeolithic artefacts are present (Cardoso and Raposo 1995), it is clear that the dated *Patella* shells must have been accumulated by Middle Palaeolithic humans. Consequently, the inference that Mousterian technologies survived in the region until *c.* 31 ka is legitimate. To what extent the lithic and mammal assemblages recovered in level 2 are entirely contemporary with the dated shells, or represent instead the mixed product of many different occupations taking place throughout a much longer time span, remains, however, to be seen. It is not certain, therefore, whether the upper left second premolar considered to show Neanderthal affinities by Antunes (1990–91) is indeed as recent as the occupation episode documented by the *Patella* shells (the

two other bones attributed to *Homo* by Antunes – a phalanx and a metacarpal – clearly belong to a carnivore).

Brugal and Raposo (pers. comm) consider that the Foz do Enxarrique bone assemblage represents for the most part a natural accumulation along the river margin. The human occupation coincided topographically but not behaviourally with the bone scatter (except, perhaps, in the case of red deer) and, therefore, the dated horse teeth are not an anthropic component of the sediments. The depositional environment, suggesting a rapid rate of accumulation, however, warrants their geochronological association with the artefacts. The numerous lithic assemblage remains largely undescribed but is unambiguously Middle Palaeolithic. Raposo and Cardoso (1998b) consider that another open air site, Conceição (Alcochete), is broadly contemporary with Foz do Enxarrique, on the basis of a *c.* 27.2 ka OSL date on wind-blown sediments covering the archaeological level. Since the latter is separated from the former by a major geological unconformity, all that can be safely said about the age of the occupation, however, is that it must be dated between *c.* 27 and, given the OSL result for the underlying deposits, *c.* 75 ka (Table 12.1).

The late survival of Mousterian industries in Portugal documented by Figueira Brava and Foz do Enxarrique is clearly confirmed by the radiometric and chronostratigraphic data available for the two key cave sites of Caldeirão and Oliveira (Almonda karstic system). Under a 2.5 m deep Holocene and Tardiglacial sequence, Caldeirão contains 4 m of Mousterian through to Solutrean

Table 12.1: Radiometric results for the Middle Palaeolithic of Portugal. (sources: Antunes 1990–91; Antunes et al. 1989; Zilhão 1995, 1997; Zilhão and Mckinney 1995; Raposo 1995; Mckinney 1996; Raposo and Cardoso 1998).

Site	Level	Sample	Method	Lab Reference	Age BP	Comment
Almonda, EVS	EVS Cone	*Equus* (tooth enamel)	U-Th	SMU-231E1	35,000±2,000	Low 230Th/232Th ratio
Almonda, Gruta da Oliveira	8	Burnt bone	AMS C14	GrA-10200	31,900±200	Alkaline fraction dated
	9	Burnt bone	AMS C14	GrA-9760	38,390±480	Alkaline fraction dated
	9	Burnt bone	AMS C14	Beta-111967	40,420±1,220	
	Mousterian Cone	*Equus* (tooth enamel)	U-Th	SMU-308□247E2	53,000+5,600—5,300	Average of the two determinations, *c.* 62,000
				SMU-247E1	70,250±9,000	
Gruta do Caldeirão	K top (J6)	*Cervus*	AMS C14	OxA-5541	18,060±140	Low collagen content (0,32%N; 3,66%C; 0,53%H)
	K base (K5)	*Capra*	AMS C14	OxA-5521	23,040±340	Low collagen content (0,32%N;2,39%C).
	K top	*Cervus*	AMS C14	OxA-1941	27,600±600	
Conceição	C	Sediments	OSL	QTLS-CNC11	27,200±2,500	Layer C overlies the archaeological level; result is minimum age
	E	Sediments	OSL	QTLS-CNC12	74,500+11,600—10,400	Layer E underlies the archaeological level; result is maximum age
Gruta do Escoural	Test 3a, 90□100	*Bos* (tooth enamel)	U-Th	SMU-248	26,400+11,000—10,000	Low uranium content
	Test 3a, 80□90	*Cervus* (tooth enamel)	U-Th	SMU-249	39,800+10,000—9,000	Low uranium content (3,4%)
	Test 3a, 60□70	*Equus* (tooth enamel)	U-Th	SMU-250	48,900+5,800—5,500	
Gruta da Figueira Brava	2	*Patella* sp. shells	C14	ICEN-387	30,930±700	
	2	*Cervus* (tooth enamel)	U-Th	SMU-232E1	30,561+11,759—10,725	
	2	*Cervus* (tooth enamel)	U-Th	SMU-233E2	44,806+15,889—13,958	
Foz do Enxarrique	C	*Equus* (tooth enamel)	U-Th	SMU-225	32,938±1,055	Average of the three results, 33,600±500
	C	*E'quus* (tooth enamel)	U-Th	SMU-226	34,088±800	
	C	*Equus* (tooth enamel)	U-Th	SMU-224	34,093±920	
Gruta Nova da Columbeira	16 (=7)	Carbonaceous earth	C14	Gif-2703	26,400±700	Inadequate dating material
	7	Tooth enamel	U-Th	SMU-235E1	35,876+27,299—35,583	
	7	Tooth enamel	U-Th	SMU-238E1	54,365+22,240—27,525	
	20 (=8)	Carbonaceous earth	C14	Gif-2704	28,900±950	Inadequate dating material
	8	Tooth enamel	U-Th	SMU-236E1	60,927+27,405—35,522	
					101,487+38,406—55,919	

Table 12.1: continued

Site	Level	Sample	Method	Lab Reference	Age BP	Comment
Lapa dos Furos	4	*Helix nemoralis* shells	C14	ICEN-473	34,580+1,160—1,010	Layer 4 underlies the archaeological level; result is maximum age
Gruta do Pego do Diabo	3	Bone collagen	C14	ICEN-491	18,630±640	Impure collagen
Pedreira de Salemas	1	Bone collagen	C14	ICEN-366	29,890+1,130—980	
Gruta de Salemas	T.V.b	Bone collagen	C14	ICEN-379	24,820±550	Dated level contains a mix of Middle and Upper Palaeolithic artefacts
Santo Antão do Tojal	2	*Elephas* (bone)	U-Th	SMU-305	81,900+4,000—3,800	
Vilas Ruivas	B	Sediments	TL	BM-VRU1	51,000+13,000—12,000	Average of the two results, 54,000/+12,000/-11,000
	B	Sediments	TL	BM-VRU2	68,000+35,000—26,000	

deposits which have been the object of a magnetic susceptibility study (Ellwood *et al.* 1998). The palaeoclimatic curve obtained almost perfectly matches the record from deep-sea sediments off the Portuguese coast, with the LGM around 20 ka, followed by a temperate peak around 18 ka (Figure 12.3). The warm nature of OIS 3 climates in the region inferred from the susceptibility data is supported by other lines of evidence. The *Helix nemoralis* mollusc fauna dated at Furos, for instance, is indicative of an open woodland/maquis environment. The contemporary pollen profiles studied by Diniz (1993a, 1993b), in turn, suggest a landscape of heathland and pine on the coast and on the sandy soils of the interfluves, with oak woodlands covering the low altitude limestone massifs.

The fact that the available palaeoclimatic evidence places the Middle-Upper Palaeolithic divide at Caldeirão in early OIS 2 independently confirms, therefore, the date of *c.* 28 ka obtained at the top of the Mousterian sequence (Table 12.1). The validity of this result is further reinforced by the stratigraphically coherent column of radiocarbon dates obtained for the overlying Upper Palaeolithic levels. Similar results are now available for the Almonda karstic system (Figure 12.4), where work began in the wake of the discovery of a small archaeological deposit in the labyrinth of narrow fossil galleries above the spring of the Almonda river. This 'Mousterian Cone' represented the bottom of the fill of a collapsed cave, sealed by eboulis and breccia, which has already been reopened and is currently under excavation – the Gruta da Oliveira.

Sampling of 0.25m² of the Mousterian Cone yielded some 250 artefacts, about half of them flint, the rest being quartzite (*c.* 30%), quartz (*c.* 20%) and limestone (<1%). The flint material is characterised by the debitage of thin, large flakes and blades and has an important Levallois component. The faunal assemblage included turtle, rabbit, some 150 long bone fragments of large mammals (30% of which were burned), and many teeth (ibex, red deer, rhino and horse). Two early uptake U-series dates were obtained from the enamel of a single horse tooth, suggesting an OIS 4 age for the base of the Oliveira sequence (Zilhão and Mckinney 1995). This result is compatible with the abundance of open space species, almost entirely absent from Oliveira's uppermost archaaeological level (level 8), which is overwhelmingly dominated by red deer and has been radiocarbon dated to *c.* 32 ka (Table 12.1).

During level 8 times, the cave was already almost completely filled up, so the site functioned more like a small rock-shelter, with occupation taking place in a restricted 4m² area of the former porch, at the bottom of a chimney opened to the outside in the framework of a major episode of roof collapse. The lithic assemblage is small – the tools and debitage greater than 2.5cm form a total of 95 items – and made of quartzite (60%) and flint (35%). A preliminary study characterises Level 8 as proportionately poor in retouched pieces (8, mostly notches and denticulates) and featuring a well developed Levalllois flake production, especially on fine-grained quartzites, where ovoid and triangular shapes are dominant and dorsal scar patterns tend to be radial or part radial (Marks pers. comm.). This is also the case at Foz do Enxarrique (Raposo *et al.* 1985) and in Level K of Caldeirão (Zilhão 1995, 1997): there is absolutely no evidence of an autochthonous or externally influenced change towards a blade-based Upper Palaeolithic technology.

Human remains from Oliveira include a hand phalanx in Level 9 and a proximal ulna in Level 10. Although none of these pieces is anatomically diagnostic, their chronology (*c.* 39 ka for Level 9) and associated Mousterian material suggest that these remains are of Neanderthals.

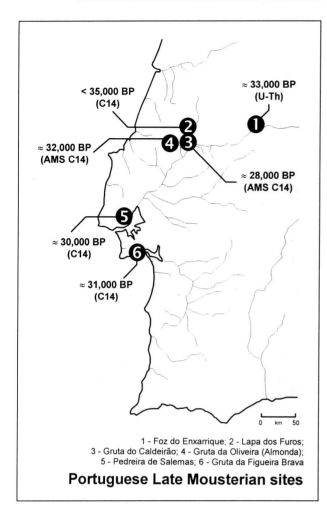

1 - Foz do Enxarrique; 2 - Lapa dos Furos;
3 - Gruta do Caldeirão; 4 - Gruta da Oliveira (Almonda);
5 - Pedreira de Salemas; 6 - Gruta da Figueira Brava

Portuguese Late Mousterian sites

Figure 12.2: Portuguese Mousterian sites reliably dated to less than 35 ka.

The radiometric chronology of the Portuguese late Mousterian is independently confirmed by the fact that the earliest Upper Palaeolithic is represented by Aurignacian industries that are both chronologically and typologically late (Zilhão 1995, 1997). This late Aurignacian is known from small-sized but characteristic assemblages recovered in caves, featuring Dufour bladelets of the Dufour subtype that are non-existent in later Upper Palaeolithic times. At the site of Pego do Diabo, north of Lisbon, one such context was dated to c. 28 ka (Table 12.2). Coupled with the evidence from Caldeirão, this indicates that, in Portugal, the replacement of the Mousterian by the Aurignacian took place between c. 27 and c. 29 ka.

The other known aspect of the Portuguese Aurignacian are the open air workshop sites of the Rio Maior region (Heleno 1944, 1956; Zilhão 1995, 1997). Residential sites of the kind exemplified in France, for instance, by the Castanet rock-shelter, have not yet been found, but their existence is predicted by the features of the lithic production system inferred from the industrial composition

of logistical and workshop sites (Figure 12.5). This system is characteristically Aurignacian, featuring the exploration of large single platform cores for the production of regular, thin blades with abraded platforms that, on average, are almost twice as large as those from later Upper Palaeolithic times. Thick 'burins' and 'scrapers' of different types were used as cores for the extraction of blanks for Dufour bladelets. Those of the Dufour subtype, flat and bilaterally pointed by a combination of marginal direct retouch and invasive, semi-abrupt, ventral retouch, stand out very clearly, by these technological attributes and by their metrics, from the kinds of bladelets with inverse retouch sometimes found in subsequent Gravettian and Proto-Solutrean industries (Figure 12.6). Typological and technological comparison with the Aquitaine sequence indicates that this is late Aurignacian, given the absence of typical 'Aurignacian' retouch on blades and the clear predominance of 'burins', including busked and Vachons forms, over-carinated and nosed 'scrapers'.

The cultural diversity of the latest Neanderthals

A situation similar to that which I have just described for Portugal exists in all Iberian regions located south of the Ebro basin. The survival of Mousterian industries until c. 30 ka, which is documented at Zafarraya, is confirmed in the Meseta by the dates for Level 2 of the Jarama VI cave, in Guadalajara (García 1997): 29.5±2.7ka (Beta-56638) and 32.6±1.86ka (Beta-56639). Furthermore, as confirmed by the recent results for Gorham's (Pettitt, this volume), no dates earlier than c. 30 ka exist for the Upper Palaeo-lithic of southern Iberia and Valencia (those available for Beneito – Iturbe et al. 1993 – clearly come from disturbed contexts). In these regions, the stratigraphic sequences spanning the Middle-Upper Palaeolithic divide, such as Bajondillo (Cortés et al. 1996) and Cariguela (Vega 1990), always lack Aurignacian 0 or Aurignacian I levels.

In Cantabria and northern Catalonya, by contrast, it has been suggested that the earliest Aurignacian is some 10 ka earlier. The archaeological meaning of the available dates, however, is debatable. As exhaustively argued elsewhere (Zilhão and d'Errico 1999a), there are grounds to believe that, in the area of the new excavations, El Castillo's Level 18 is a mostly Middle Palaeolithic palimpsest. At l'Arbreda, the homogeneous nature of the sedimentary sequence, the importance of cave bear denning, and the fact that the site was excavated in artificial horizontal units in spite of the dip that characterised the relevant section of the deposits, may explain the several instances of stratigraphic inversion of results and in any case shed doubt on the assertion that the Aurignacian occupation of the site began c. 38.5 ka. Stratigraphically reliable results have been obtained for other sites in the Franco-Cantabrian region, such as La Viña (Fortea 1995) or Isturitz (Turq pers. comm.) which suggest that, in fact, its earliest Aurignacian dates to no more than c. 36.5 ka.

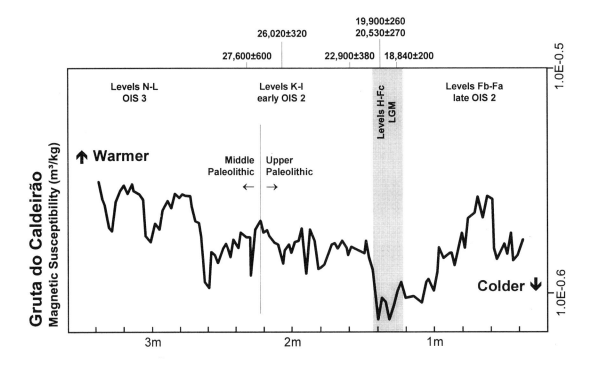

Figure 12.3: The magnetic susceptibility curve for the Mousterian through Solutrean sequence at Gruta do Caldeirão.

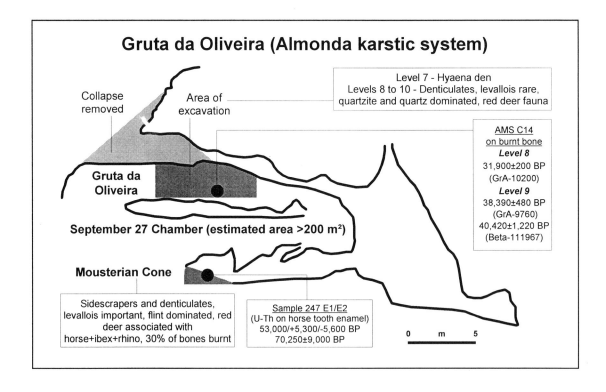

Figure 12.4: Gruta da Oliveira (Almond karstic system, Torres Novas). Schematic profile.

Table 12.2: Radiometric results for the earliest Upper Palaeolithic of Portugal (sources: Zilhão 1995, 1997).

Site	Level	Sample	Method	Lab Reference	Age BP	Comment
Gruta do Caldeirão	Jb	Bone collagen	AMS C14	OxA-5542	26,020±320	Non-diagnostic early Upper Palaeolithic with blades and
Gruta do Pego do Diabo	2b	Charcoal	C14	ICEN-306	2,400±80	Intrusive
(Aurignacian)	2a	Bone collagen	C14	ICEN-490	23,080±490	Contaminated? (level 2 is surface in sampled area)
	2b	Bone collagen	C14	ICEN-732	28,120/+860/-780	
Vale Comprido — Cruzamento	−35	Burnt flint	TL	BM-VCO1	12,400±2,100	
(early Gravettian)	−40	Burnt flint	TL	BM-VCO6	26,700±2,700	Average of the two acceptable results, 27,900±2,200
	profile	Burnt flint	TL	BM-VCO12	30,300±3,900	

Note: experimental TL dates in the range of *c.* 40 ka have been obtained for the open air sites of Fonte Santa and Gato Preto; although the British Museum laboratory could not provide a fully satisfactory explanation for the large error, these dates are totally incompatible with the nature of the archaeological assemblages, which suggest ages of *c.* 23—25 and 21—22 ka for these sites

Even so, this is still significantly earlier than the age of no more than *c.* 30 ka for the end of the Mousterian in Portugal, Andalucia, Valencia and the Meseta.

This upward revision of the values for the age of the earliest Aurignacian that are currently accepted on the basis of l'Arbreda and El Castillo does not affect, therefore, the empirical basis of the Ebro frontier model. By contrast, its impact on models that explain the Châtelperronian as a product of acculturation brought about by Neanderthal contact with the first waves of modern human immigrants is devastating, since it confirms what was already shown by a simple consideration of the chronostratigraphy of the region (there now are some 30 sequences documenting a Châtelperronian under an Aurignacian 0 or an Aurignacian I, and the 'interstratifications' at Le Piage, Roc-de-Combe and El Pendo result from processes of postdepositional disturbance): that the emergence of the Châtelperronian (AMS radiocarbon dated at *c.* 38 ka at Combe-Saunière, Grotte XVI and Roc-de-Combe, and at *c.* 45 ka at the Grotte du Renne) predates the arrival of modern humans and, therefore, can only be considered as an independent, authochthonous Neanderthal transition to the Upper Palaeolithic (d'Errico *et al.* 1998; Zilhão and d'Errico 1999a, 1999b).

The significance of the Châtelperronian to our understanding of Neanderthals cannot be simply dismissed by invoking a process of acculturation inevitably brought about by long-term contact with neighbouring populations of modern newcomers spreading east-west along the 43rd parallel. This is also indicated by the fact that throughout the several millennia of co-existence with Aurignacian

people living north of the Ebro frontier, Iberian Neanderthals did not undergo any significant change in their material culture. Coupled with the fact that Cantabro-Pyrenean moderns did not invade their territories for such a long period of time, this empirical fact alone challenges the notion of an overwhelming, biologically-based, intellectual inferiority of Neanderthals that underlies prevalent explanations of their extinction (*cf.* Mellars 1996, for instance). In the framework of the stratigraphically and radiometrically documented precedence of the Châtelperronian relative to the Aurignacian, the Ebro frontier pattern is one more reason to doubt that such a notion can be used to explain away the bone tools, the body ornaments and the lithic technology of the Châtelperronian as a simple by-product of 'imitating, but not understanding, modern symbolical behaviour' (Stringer and Gamble 1993). The facts, instead, are that most features of the so-called Upper Palaeolithic package are now well documented in Neanderthal Europe at least since last interglacial times; that the Châtelperronian evolved from the local MTA, and its lithic technology shows absolutely no Aurignacian influence; and that the same is true of the rich and diverse collection of bone tools and ornaments recovered in levels VIII-X of Grotte du Renne, at Arcy, where their association with both the Châtelperronian lithics and the human bones recently confirmed by Hublin *et al.* (1996) to be of a Neanderthal child is unquestionable (d'Errico *et al.* 1998).

The implication of these facts is, first, that the 'Upper Palaeolithic package' as defined thirty years ago is a misrepresentation of reality, inspired by a view of human evolution proceeding through 19th century-type universal

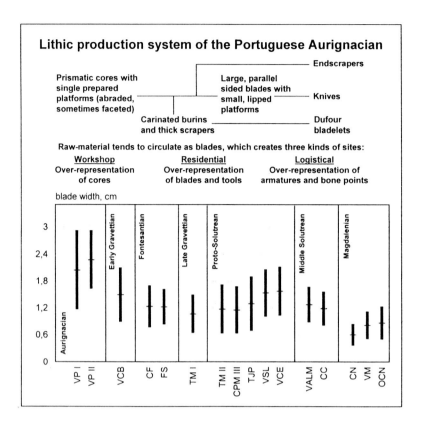

Figure 12.5: The lithic production system of the Portuguese Aurignacian. The large size of elongated products (blades and bladelets) is unmatched in subsequent periods.

stages. As a technologically based subdivision of time, the concept retains its utility only if redefined as the period of Eurasian Prehistory that is characterised by the production of bladelets and the use of microliths. This technological trait should not be taken, however, as in any way correlated with developments in other realms of life, let alone the development of biologically-based intellectual capabilities. It has been demonstrated, in any case, that it takes more intelligence to make an upper Acheulian handaxe than a Levallois point or, for that matter, than to extract a blade from a prismatic core (Wynn 1989). It is also an indisputable fact that symbolic behaviour is present in societies of the ethnographic present that, from the point of view of lithic technology, are 'Lower Palaeolithic'.

In this regard, one should always bear in mind, when attempting to measure intelligence through technology, that fully modern humans, anatomically and behaviourally, such as the Tasmanian Aborigines of two hundred years ago, had a tool-kit comprising no more than a dozen different kinds of quite simple artefacts and did not know how to produce fire (Ryan 1996). In any case, the Châtelperronian assemblages from Grotte du Renne are empirical evidence that there is no necessary link between the cultural features of the so-called 'Upper Palaeolithic package' and anatomical modernity, and that the appearance of personal ornaments must be related instead to the operation of social processes connected with the estab-

lishment of territoriality and ethnicity, which are ultimately dependent on the density of populations and the intensity of social interactions. Adaptationist explanations of the appearance of ornaments, relating it to the need for the social identification of individuals involved in long-distance alliance networks have been put forward in the past, notably by Gamble (1983). Such explanations are strengthened by the fact that, on present evidence, it is among the Neanderthals from northern Europe and the modern humans living in structurally similar environments at the other end of the world, in South Africa, that the use of personal ornaments and the mass utilisation of red ochre are simultaneously documented for the first time in the history of humankind, between 40 and 50 ka.

Uneven development and extinction in Neanderthal Europe

The temporal precedence of the Châtelperronian over the Aurignacian and the evidence from Grotte du Renne indicate that Neanderthal groups in central and western Europe were undergoing their own independent 'symbolic revolution' at the time of contact with Aurignacian modern humans ultimately originating in the Near East. As was the case in the historical trajectory of modern humans, this revolution, however, was a geographically uneven process. At the same time that central and western

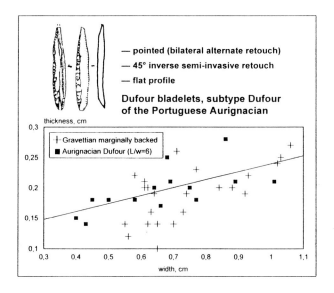

— pointed (bilateral alternate retouch)
— 45° inverse semi-invasive retouch
— flat profile

Dufour bladelets, subtype Dufour of the Portuguese Aurignacian

Figure 12.6: Typology and metrics of Portuguese Aurignacian Dufour bladelets compared with the marginally backed bladelets of the Gravettian and the Proto-Solutrean.

European Neanderthals were becoming technologically Upper Palaeolithic and were starting to experiment with personal ornaments, Iberian Neanderthals continued to be fully 'Middle Palaeolithic' and remained so until the end. At that time, such was also the case with North African moderns, who did not become 'Upper Palaeolithic' until well after 30 ka.

These patterns suggest that the replacement of Neanderthals by modern humans should be looked at simply as another instance of contact between isolated populations with different, albeit largely parallel, cultural trajectories. In this case, as has often been documented in both the historical and the ethnographic records, the long-term outcome of contact was that one of those trajectories was truncated and the corresponding genetic lineage went extinct. This may be explained through the action of a number of factors operating in the realms of immunology, fertility or social organisation. The notion of a biologically based intellectual inferiority is no more required to explain the extinction of Neanderthals than that of Aboriginal Tasmanians or Fueguian Indians. Such an epistemologically primitive notion is based on an a-historical understanding of human behaviour and is flawed at a basic logical level by the systematic practice of anachronistic comparisons.

Examples of these flaws can be found in many otherwise excellent works dealing with the Neanderthal problem. A study of Neanderthal *versus* modern human subsistence practices, for instance, compares Italian Neanderthals with modern human groups from the same region that are 20 or 30 ka younger, not with contemporary modern humans from different regions, such as the Middle East (Stiner 1994). This approach makes sense only if one assumes that the two kinds of humans have fixed behavioural characteristics and that any one group of modern human hunters can be compared with any one group of Neanderthals, regardless of the place they occupy in absolute time or in concrete historical trajectories. This particular instance of anachronistic reasoning is all the more significant since, at the same time, the author clearly states her position in favour of a view of the origins of modern human ecological behaviour as caused by 'selection upon variation in the context of widespread environmental (including social) forces' as opposed to 'diffusion of genius' (p. 387). Often, reductionism has also led, on the other hand, to a double standard in the evaluation of the archaeological record, particularly in regard to the interpretation of faunal remains. While head-dominated or head-and-foot dominated Eurasian Middle Palaeolithic assemblages were attributed to scavenging Neanderthals, the same kinds of assemblages produced by modern humans in the Upper Palaeolithic, or even in the Neolithic, were explained as a product of the operation of taphonomic agents over the remains of actual kills of wild or domesticated animals. As shown by Marean and Kim (1998), it turns out that, when an adequate methodology is applied, Middle Palaeolithic faunal assemblages are shown to be a product of the same kinds of hunting practices that are documented in the Upper Palaeolithic.

Why such reductionist arguments have found so much favour among students of human evolution is all the more difficult to explain since sophisticated models of interaction put forward by leading biologists have been available for a long time, even if published under the unorthodox form of B. Kurtén's pre-historical novels (Kurtén 1980, 1986). In any case, the late survival of Neanderthals in Portugal and southern Spain represents an excellent opportunity to test competing explanatory models of Neanderthal extinction. In fact, unless we go back to 19th century notions of a north-south gradient in human intelligence – i.e., Iberian Neanderthals were even dumber than French ones, which at least were able to imitate – the Ebro frontier pattern cannot be explained at all in the framework of the paradigm of a biologically based intellectual inferiority of Neanderthals.

Geographical/adaptationist models, on the contrary, perform a lot better at explaining why Iberian regions located south of the Ebro were lagging behind in the cultural revolution unfolding further to the north since about 50 ka. Contrary to popular notions, Neanderthals cannot be simply described as a 'cold-adapted species'. Instead, they occupied a wide range of habitats, including the open woodlands that covered extensive regions of Iberia throughout the early last glacial. Thus, while, north of the Ebro, the cultural revolution of Neanderthals may have been unleashed by population packing in steppe environments with large herds of gregarious herbivores, further to the south, a more sparse occupation of a more wooded landscape may have allowed the survival of less stressed, non-ritualised, 'Middle Palaeolithic' life ways.

In the beginning of OIS2, with the onset of the trend towards maximum glacial conditions, the human range was compressed at its northern end and, probably for the first time in the Late Pleistocene, the kinds of environments to which Aurignacian moderns had adapted to expanded southwards into Iberia, and they expanded southwards with them. When this happened, demographic and bio-geographic laws alone *a priori* guaranteed the swift extinction of those last Neanderthals who had continued to thrive in the Iberian regions south of the Ebro basin since moderns first arrived in Western Europe.

Conclusion

Iberian regions located south of the Ebro are probably the only part of the world where traditional views of the transition from the Middle to the Upper Palaeolithic, as a process of population replacement at both the biological and the cultural levels, entailing the replacement of the Middle Palaeolithic by a full package of Upper Palaeolithic biocultural features, are compatible with the empirical evidence.

Paradoxically, the spatial and temporal features of the Iberian process indicate, at the same time, that the link of causality between modern anatomy and so-called modern behaviour proposed by many as the explanation for the symbolic revolution of the Upper Palaeolithic is non-existent. This clarification opens up new perspectives for the understanding of what may have been the rich processes of interaction that occurred when Neanderthals and modern humans established their own 'close encounters of the third kind'.

It may well be true that, as a result of such encounters, the genes of Neanderthals may have been completely or almost completely lost, as suggested by some interpretations of the DNA results obtained by Krings *et al.* (1997). The evidence from Grotte du Renne and other sites, however, indicates that Neanderthals may have been the first humans to wear personal ornaments and to manufacture sophisticated bone tools, i.e., that, in Europe, modern humans may well have been the acculturated, not the acculturators. Thus, regardless of what happened in terms of population biology, in cultural terms Neanderthals must indeed be counted among our direct ancestors. The recent find at the Abrigo do Lagar Velho (Lapedo, Leiria, Portugal) of the buried skeleton of a 25,000 year old modern human child with Neanderthal traits (Duarte *et al.* 1999), however, indicates that Neanderthals may also have contributed, through extensive admixture of anatomically archaic and anatomically modern groups at the time of contact, to the gene pool of the earliest Upper Palaeolithic peoples of Iberia.

References

Antunes, M.T. (1990–91). O Homem da Gruta da Figueira Brava (c.30,000 BP). Contexto ecológico, alimentação, canibalismo. *Memórias da Academia das Ciências de Lisboa. Classe de Ciências.* **XXXI**, 487–536.

Antunes, M.T., Cabral, J.M.P., Cardoso, J.L., Pais, J., Soares A.M. (1989). Paleolítico médio e superior em Portugal: datas ¹⁴C, estado actual dos conhecimentos, síntese e discussão. *Ciências da Terra.* **10**, 127–138.

Bischoff, J.L., Soler, N., Maroto, J., Julià, R. (1989). Abrupt Mousterian/Aurignacian boundary at c. 40 ka bp: Accelerator ¹⁴C dates from l'Arbreda Cave (Catalunya, Spain). *Journal of Archaeological Science.* **16**, 563–576.

Bischoff, J.L., Ludwig, K., Garcia, J.F., Carbonell, E., Vaquero, M., Stafford, T.W., Jull, A.J.T. (1994). Dating of the Basal Aurignacian Sandwich at Abric Romaní (Catalunya, Spain) by Radiocarbon and Uranium-Series. *Journal of Archaeological Science.* **21**, 541–551.

Cabrera, V. (Ed.) (1993). *El Origen del Hombre Moderno en el Suroeste de Europa*, Madrid, Universidad Nacional de Educación a Distancia.

Cabrera, V., Bischoff, J.L. (1989). Accelerator ¹⁴C dates for Early Upper Paleolithic (Basal Aurignacian) at El Castillo Cave (Spain). *Journal of Archaeological Science.* **16**, 577–584.

Cabrera, V., Valladas, H., Bernaldo De Quirós, F. & Hoyos M. (1996). La transition Paléolithique moyen-Paléolithique supérieur à El Castillo (Cantabrie): nouvelles datations par le carbone-14. *Compte-Rendus de l'Académie des Sciences de Paris.* **322–IIa**, 1093–1098.

Cardoso, J.L. & Raposo, L. (1995). As Indústrias Paleolíticas Da Gruta Da Figueira Brava (Setúbal), In *3ª Reunião Do Quaternário Ibérico*, pp. 451–456. Actas, Coimbra: Universidade De Coimbra.

Cortés, M., Muñoz, V.E., Sanchidrián, J.L. & Simón, M.D. (1996). *El Paleolítico En Andalucía*. Córdoba: Universidad De Córdoba.

D'errico, F., Zilhão, J., Baffier, D., Julien, M. & Pelegrin, J. (1998). Neanderthal Acculturation In Western Europe? A Critical Review Of The Evidence And Its Interpretation. *Current Anthropology.* 39, Supplement, S1–S44.

Delibrias, G., Guillier, M.-T., Labeyrie, J. (1986). Gif Natural Radiocarbon Measurements X. *Radiocarbon,* **28** (1), 9–68.

Diniz, F. (1993a). Aspectos Da Vegetação E Do Clima De Formações Quaternárias Entre Óbidos E Peniche, In *El Cuaternario En España Y Portugal, 1.* p. 337–344. Madrid: Asociacion Española Para El Estudio Del Cuaternario.

Diniz, F. (1993b). Aspectos Paleoflorísticos E Paleoclimáticos Do Plistocénico Português. Análise Polínica Da Jazida De Vale Benfeito (Ferrel), In *3ª Reunião Do Quaternário Ibérico, Coimbra, 27 De Setembro A 1 De Outubro De 1993. Programa. Participantes. Resumos,* p. 45.

Duarte, C., Maurício, J., Pettit, P.B., Souto, P., Trinkaus, E., Van Der Plicht, H & Zilhão, J. (1999). The Early Upper Paleolithic Human Skeleton From The Abrigo Do Lagar Velho (Portugal) And Modern Human Emergence In Iberia. *Proceedings Of The National Academy Of Sciences USA,* **96**, 7604–7609.

Ellwood, B.B., Zilhão, J., Harrold, F.B., Balsam, W., Burkart, B., Long, G.J., Debénath, A. & Bouzouggar, A. (1998). Identification Of The Last Glacial Maximum In The Upper Paleolithic Of Portugal Using Magnetic Susceptibility Measurements Of Caldeirão Cave Sediments. *Geoarchaeology.* **13** (1), 55–71.

Fortea, J. (1995). *Abrigo De La Viña. Informe Y Primera Valoración De Las Campañas 1991 a 1994*, In *Excavaciones Arqueológicas En Asturias 1991–94*, pp. 19–32. Oviedo: Servicio De Publicaciones De La Consejería De Educación, Cultura, Deportes Y Juventud.

Gamble, C. (1983). Culture And Society In The Upper Paleolithic Of Europe, In (G. Bailey, Ed.) *Hunter-Gatherer Economy In Prehistory. A European Perspective*. Cambridge, Cambridge University Press.

Gamble, C. (1986). *The Paleolithic Settlement Of Europe*. Cambridge: Cambridge University Press.

García, M.A. (1997). Aproximación Al Paleolítico Medio En La Vertiente Sur Del Sistema Central: Guadalajara. In (R. Balbín, & P. Bueno, Eds.) *Ii Congreso De Arqueología Peninsular. Tomo I – Paleolítico Y Epipaleolítico*, pp. 85–103. Zamora: Fundación Rei Afonso Henriques.

Heleno, M. (1944). *O Problema Capsense. Contribuição Portuguesa Para A Sua Revisão*, Lisboa: Comunicação Ao Instituto De Arqueologia Na Sessão De Abril De 1944.

Heleno, M. (1956). Um Quarto De Século De Investigação Arqueológic. *O Arqueólogo Português, 2nd Series*. 3, 221–237.

Hublin, J.-J., Barroso Ruiz, C., Medina Lara, P., Fontugne, M. & Reyss, J.-L. (1995). The Mousterian Site Of Zafarraya (Andalucia, Spain): Dating And Implications On The Paleolithic Peopling Processes Of Western Europe. *Comptes-Rendus De L'académie Des Sciences De Paris*. 321, Series Iia, 931–937.

Hublin J.-J., Spoor , F., Braun, M., Zonneveld, F. & Condemi, S. (1996). A Late Neanderthal Associated With Upper Palaeolithic Artefacts. *Nature*, 381, 224–226.

Iturbe, G., Fumanal, M.P., Carrion, J.S., Cortell, E., Martinez, R., Guillem, P.M., Garralda, M.D. & Vandermeersch, B. (1993). Cova Beneito (Muro, Alicante): Uma Perspectiva Interdisciplinar. *Recercques Del Museu D'alcoi*. 2, 23–88.

Krings, M., Stone, A., Schmitz, R.W., Krainitzki, H., Stoneking, M. & Pääbo, S. (1997). Neandertal DNA Sequences And The Origin Of Modern Humans. *Cell*. 90, 19–30.

Kurtén, B. (1980). *Dance Of The Tiger. A Novel Of The Ice Age*. Pantheon Books: New York.

Kurtén, B. (1986). *Singletusk. A Novel Of The Ice Age*. Pantheon Books: New York.

Marean, C. & Kim, S.Y. (1998). Mousterian Large-Mammal Remains From Kobeh Cave. Behavioral Implications For Neanderthals And Early Modern Humans. *Current Anthropology*. 39, Supplement, S79–S113.

Maroto, J. (1994). *El Pas Del Paleolític Mitjá Al Paleolític Superior A Catalunya I La Seva Interpretació Dins Del Context Geográfic Franco-Ibéric*, Girona: University Of Girona, Unpublished Ph. D. Thesis.

Mckinney, C. (1996). Datations By Uranium Series, In (M. Otte, & A.C. Silva Eds.) *Recherches Préhistoriques À La Grotte De Escoural, Portugal*, pp. 349–350. Liège: Études Et Recherches Archéologiques De L'université De Liège.

Mellars, P.A. (1996). *The Neanderthal Legacy*. Princeton: Princeton University Press.

Raposo, L. (1995). Ambientes, Territorios Y Subsistencia En El Paleolítico Medio De Portugal. *Complutum*. 6, 57–77.

Raposo, L. & Cardoso, J.L. (1998a). Las Industrias Líticas De La Gruta Nova De Columbeira (Bombarral, Portugal) En El Contexto Del Musteriense Final De La Península Ibéric. *Trabajos De Prehistoria*. 55 (1), 39–62.

Raposo, L. & Cardoso, J.L. (1998b). *O Paleolítico Médio Da Conceição (Alcochete)*. Montijo: Lusoponte.

Raposo, L., Silva, A.C. & Salvador, M. (1985). Notícia Da Descoberta Da Estação Moustierense Da Foz Do Enxarrique, In *Actas Da I Reunião Do Quaternário Ibérico, 1*, pp. 79–89. Lisboa.

Ryan, L. (1996). *The Aboriginal Tasmanians*, 2nd Edition. St. Leonards: Allen & Unwin.

Stiner, M.C. (1994). *Honor Among Thieves. A Zooarchaeological Study Of Neanderthal Ecology*, Princeton: Princeton University Press.

Stringer, C. & Gamble, C. (1993). *In Search Of The Neanderthals*, London: Thames & Hudson.

Vega Toscano, L.G. (1990). La Fin Du Paléolithique Moyen Au Sud De L'espagne: Ses Implications Dans Le Contexte De La Péninsule Ibérique. In *Paléolithique Moyen Récent Et Paléolithique Supérieur Ancien En Europe (Colloque International De Nemours, 9–11 Mai 1988)*, pp. 169–176. Mémoires Du Musée De Préhistoire De L'ile De France.

Villaverde, V. & Fumanal, M.P. (1990). Relations Entre Le Paléolithique Moyen Et Le Paléolithique Supérieur Dans Le Versant Méditerranéen Espagnol. In *Paléolithique Moyen Récent Et Paléolithique Supérieur Ancien En Europe (Colloque International De Nemours, 9–11 Mai 1988)*, pp. 177–183. Mémoires Du Musée De Préhistoire De L'ile De France.

Wynn, T. (1989). *The Evolution Of Spatial Competence*. Urbana: University Of Illinois Press.

Zbyszewski, G., Ferreira, O.V., Leitão, M. & North, C. (1977). Estação Paleolítica Do Olival Do Arneiro (Arruda Dos Pisões, Rio Maior). *Comunicações Dos Serviços Geológicos De Portugal*. LXI, 263–333.

Zilhão, J. (1993). Le Passage Du Paléolithique Moyen Au Paléolithique Supérieur Dans Le Portugal, In (V. Cabrera, Ed.), *El Origen Del Hombre Moderno En El Suroeste De Europa*, pp. 127–145. Madrid: Universidad Nacional De Educación A Distancia.

Zilhão, J. (1995). *O Paleolítico Superior Da Estremadura Portuguesa*. Lisbon: University Of Lisbon, Unpublished Ph. D. Thesis.

Zilhão, J. (1997). *O Paleolítico Superior Da Estremadura Portuguesa*. 2 Vols., Lisbon: Colibri.

Zilhão, J. (1998). The Extinction Of Iberian Neandertals And Its Implications For The Origins Of Modern Humans In Europe, In (F. Facchini, A. Palma Di Cesnola, M. Piperno, & C. Peretto, Eds.) *Xiii International Congress Of Prehistoric And Protohistoric Sciences. Proceedings*, Vol. 2, pp. 299–312. Forlì: Abaco.

Zilhão, J. & D'errico, F. (1999a). he Chronology And Taphonomy Of The Earliest Aurignacian And Its Implications For The Understanding Of Neanderthal Extinction. *Journal Of World Prehistory*. 13 (1), 1–68.

Zilhão, J. & D'errico, F. (1999b). Reply, In The Neanderthal Problem Continued. *Current Anthropology*, 40 (3), 355–364.

Zilhão, J. & Mckinney, C. (1995). Uranium-Thorium Dating Of Lower And Middle Paleolithic Sites In The Almonda Karstic System (Torres Novas, Portugal), In *3ª Reunião Do Quaternário Ibérico. Actas*, pp. 513–516. Coimbra: Universidade De Coimbra.

13

Bajondillo Cave (Torremolinos, Malaga, Andalucia) and the Middle-Upper Palaeolithic Transition in Southern Spain

Miguel Cortés Sánchez

Introduction

Bajondillo Cave is located in the municipality of Torremolinos, on the western side of the Bay of Malaga. Historically, the area has demonstrated great potential for studying the cultural dynamics of the Upper Pleistocene in the southern Iberian peninsula (Figure 13.1). The site was investigated as a rescue excavation carried out over a number of months in 1989. The deposits cover a maximum thickness of about 5 m, in which a total of seventeen layers have been distinguished in the west profile (Figure 13.3), where a major part of the sedimentary sequence survives. The main sedimentary column shows that the layers are sub-horizontal, and that the archaeological industries occur within this well-stratified sequence. The basal 0.8 m of deposits contain Mousterian assemblages and these are overlain by some 3.85 m of deposits with Aurignacian, Gravettian, Solutrean and more recent prehistoric material, as identified by the technological and typological characteristics of the lithic collections in each of the layers (Baldomero *et al.* 1991, Cortés & Simón 1997, 1998).

The Stratigraphic Sequence

Bajondillo rockshelter is situated in the lower levels of the Torremolinos travertine formation. This tufaceous structure was formed at the contact between the karstic aquifer of the Sierra de Mijas and the sea. Various palaeogeographical data from the Bay of Malaga (Figure 13.2) are available and provide evidence for:

a) the dates of the different travertine formation episodes of this littoral edge (Durán *et al.* 1988)

b) the age of marine deposits corresponding to altimetric palaeopositions of the sea level during the Upper Pleistocene (Lario *et al.* 1993)

c) the height above sea level at which Bajondillo opens (10 m).

Together, these seem to indicate that:

1) some of the dates of the Torremolinos travertine appear too recent (ESR and U-Series dates). This is not unexpected given the difficulties in obtaining precise chronological information in these open systems and the lack of agreement between the dated travertine zone and the age of the cave deposit

2) the sedimentary formation of the site could have occurred in a phase following Isotopic Sub-Stage 5c, coinciding with the Tyrrhenian-III phase which, in this part of the Mediterranean, lies at 10 m above sea level.

However we must remain cautious about these interpretations until new, more accurate studies are undertaken to define both the palaeogeographic dynamics of the area and the cycles of sedimentation from the deposits of the cave. Nevertheless, Bajondillo's long sequence of sediments places it alongside other important locations in southern Iberia, including Carigüela, Gorham's Cave, Ambrosio, and Nerja, and allows us to contribute further to the understanding of the chrono-cultural development of this part of the Iberian peninsula.

Bajondillo Level 14: characteristics and parallels

The important sequence, which covers the end of the Middle Palaeolithic and the beginning of the early Upper Palaeolithic, occurs within levels 11 to 14 in the west profile.

Level 14 consists of brownish-yellow sediments, 0.2 m average thickness, with a large number of coarse, small clasts, which could perhaps indicate an episode of climatic deterioration.

The lithic finds recovered in this level mark a distinct

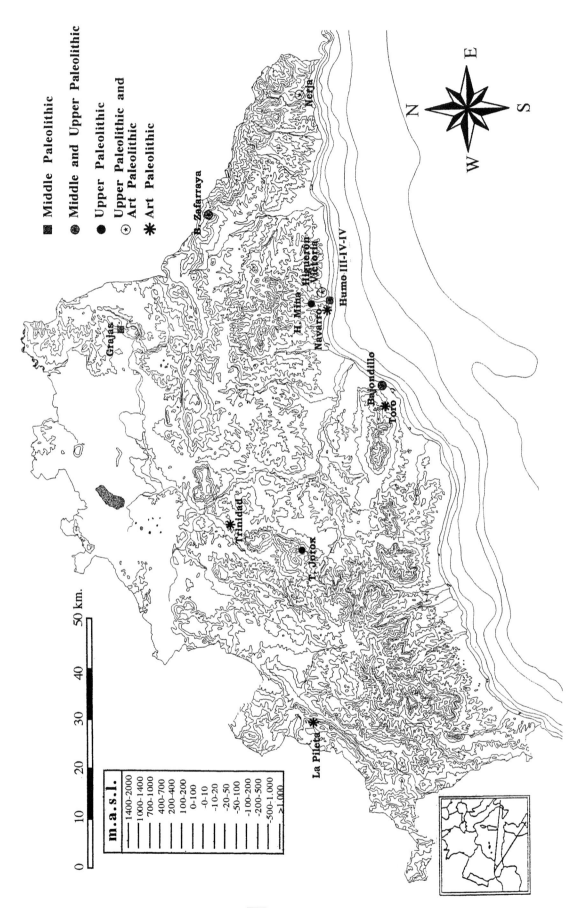

Figure 13.1: Bay of Malaga. Map of Middle and Upper Palaeolithic sites.

	Travertine Building	masl	Age (cal B.P.)			Marine Isotopic	Marine Episode
			E.S.R.	U-Series	Estimate		
Holocene		2	←		6		
P L E I S T O C E N E — Upper (Recent)	Torremolinos	1					Tirreniense IV
		80-0	25.3-26.5+15/20 %	27.3+-1.7			
		10	←		95	5 c	Tirreniense III
Ancien — Middle	Benalmádena	50-200	86.3-109+15/20 %				
		14	←		128	5 e	Tirreniense II
		12	←		180	7 a	Tirreniense I
	Mijas	400-430	217+15/20 %			7	

Figure 13.2: Travertine formation in association with the aquifer of Mijas (age and metres above sea level). Highstands of the sea level during the Middle-Upper Pleistocene in the Bay of Malaga. Elaborated from data of Durán et al. 1988 and Lario et al. 1993.

change in form from those in the underlying assemblages as well as displaying clear differences from the collections in the layers above. Flint is the most commonly occurring lithic raw material, with smaller amounts of quartzite and limestone, which, together make up less than 10% of the total lithic component (Figure 13.4).

The most common manufacturing technique observed in this level is the Levallois recurrent centripetal method; there are also some discoidal cores (Figure 13.6). Plain butts predominate in both the unretouched flakes and retouched flake classes, although there is a slight preference for faceted butts amongst the tools. Cortical examples are also well-represented (Figures 13.4 and 13.5).

Based on the essential index of counted tools (Figure 13.4), Group II is only poorly represented (17%), indicating a loss of tool diversity in comparison to the underlying assemblages. Group III displays a slight but continuous rise throughout the Bajondillo Mousterian sequence. In this level, it reaches 13.8 % and is dominated by perforators and becs. Denticulates make up 14.9 % of the tools and the lm-d contributes 40 % of the retouched material. We have also noted that the blunt edges of naturally backed knives and *éclats débordants* (core edge removal flakes) were probably also used as tools; as indicated by macroscopic wear traces along their edges.

Following this line of reasoning, Bajondillo Level 14 together with Cariguela V-1 (Vega 1988; 1990) can be assigned to a Mousterian facies rich in denticulates. We think these two caves are probably closely linked chronologically. Within the wider context of Western Europe, the rise in Group-IV tools in Middle Palaeolithic technocomplexes seems to be related to ancient phases of the Early Würm Pleniglacial or to the Hengelo Interstadial (beginning of Würm III). A similar observation has been made for Mousterian sites in the Valencian region (Villaverde 1995). If we also add to this the superposition of Aurignacian industries in Levels 12–11 at Bajondillo (see below), it seems logical to situate level 14 in an advanced episode of the Würm (perhaps Würm III).

Apart from Cariguela, the assemblage from Bajondillo Level 14 would seem to have parallels with the site of Beneito (Alicante) (Iturbe *et al.* 1993) where the top of the Mousterian series is typified by a collection rich in notches and denticulates, especially within unit D-2. Analogies exist also with the site of Petxina (Valencia), surface and level 2 (Villaverde 1984). This is based on the decrease in various measurable indexes (Levallois technique, facetted butts, Levallois typology) as well as a reduction in the numbers of scrapers and an increase in notches and denticulates.

Amongst sites dating to the period of the Upper Würm pleniglacial, with a low IR (scraper index) and elevated group III and IV tools we can include Abric Romaní (Barcelona) and Gabasa-a+c (Huesca) (*cf* L.A.U.R.V. 1996; Utrilla & Montes 1989; Simón & Cortés 1996).

The techno-typological characteristics of Bajondillo Level 13 are still being studied and will not be considered here. In the next section we deal with Levels 11 and 12. Level 12 could only be distinguished in the central-south area of the excavation. The lithic industry is identical to that found in Level 11, so it is probably part of the same sedimentary unit.

Bajondillo Level 11/12 and the Aurignacian in the Southern Iberian Peninsula

The industry in Level 11 represents a radical shift from the Middle Palaeolithic according to the evidence of the blade technology and the appearance of Upper Palaeolithic tools (e.g. end-scrapers, burins) (Figures 13.7 and 13.8).

The retouched tool assemblage from Levels 11–12 are characterised by a higher index of end-scrapers than burins. Amongst the end-scrapers are carinated forms and nosed end-scrapers (Figure 13.8). Special mention should be made of examples made on cortical flakes which bear strong similarities to those in the well-established stages of the Aurignacian of the Mediterranean Iberian peninsular.

Also noteworthy are the presence of small bladelets,

Figure 13.3: Bajondillo Cave, 1998 stratigraphy. West profile, central west section.

some retouched and with a sinuous profile (Figure 13.8). Those with alternate retouch, although superficially resembling *dufours* bladelets of the archaic Aurignacian, are in fact much closer in likeness to younger forms (e.g. Arbreda and Beneito), due to the marginality of the retouch or the typometric reduction of the selected support. The presence of other items with *Aurignacian retouch* and related characteristics, seems to correlate closely with advanced chronological moments of the Mediterranean Aurignacian of Western Europe (Sacchi *et al.* 1996).

An important point to bear in mind with regard to the Middle-Upper Palaeolithic transition in the Iberian Peninsula is the noticeable north-south gradient in sites and the delay in the appearance of the leptolithic industries. This is based on sedimentary, climatic and chronological indicators from various Würm III Mousterian sites, for example Cova Negra, Beneito, Carigüela and Zafarraya (Villaverde & Fumanal 1988, Iturbe *et al.* 1993, Fumanal 1995, Vega *et al.* 1988, Barroso & Hublin 1994, Hublin *et al.* 1995). Neither the evidence from the central Spanish plains (Moure *et al.* 1997) nor from Portugal (Raposo this

volume) seems to contradict the late continuation of *Homo sapiens neandertalensis* populations in the eastern zone of the Iberian peninsula.

This point is emphasised by the fact that despite an overlap of ten millennia between the Aurignacian and the late Mousterian (Cantabria/Catalunya *versus* the rest of the Iberian peninsula), as indicated by radiometric evidence, there are still no sites where interstratified Mousterian and Early Upper Palaeolithic levels are known. However, there are a number of underlying problems which complicate current investigation of this period:

a) The lack of research
b) The clear dependence on luck in the location of sites of this age (e.g. Bajondillo)
c) The widespread destruction of deposits and sites caused by anthropic and natural erosion of the Mediterranean environment
d) The paucity of lithic and, especially, bone materials for study
e) The problems arising from the application of different

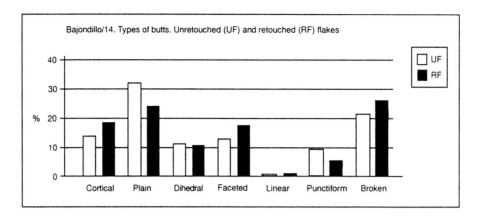

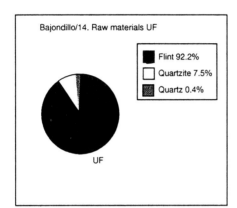 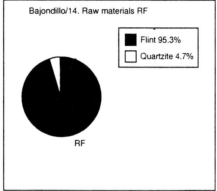

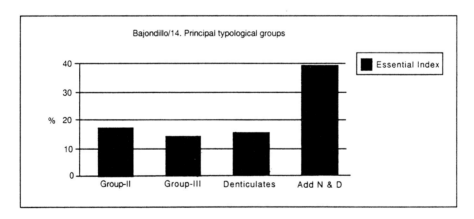

Figure 13.4: Bajondillo Layer 14. Types of butts; raw materials and typological groups.

dating methods (conventional radiocarbon, AMS radiocarbon, TL etc.), as well as the large standard deviations, potential contamination of samples, statistical treatment of the dates and so on.

f) The broad time range over which regional correlations are made. Thus, for example, in Catalunya an overlap in radiometric dates can be demonstrated for various late Mousterian sites and archaic Aurignacian sites, even though there are no verifiable stratigraphic intercalations (Maroto *et al.* 1996).

Based on current knowledge, the Early Upper Palaeo-

lithic appears in southern parts of Iberia in the form of Aurignacian industries, of 'non-archaic' type. In the Spanish Mediterranean region these are associated with what would seem to be sporadic visits (Villaverde 1992; Villaverde *et al.* 1996), which left a distinctive blade technology and *chaîne opératoire* but tools that are unspecific at a typological level. If we exclude Beneito and Bajondillo, the rest of the Aurignacian sites of the Mediterranean south of the Ebro consist of surface scatters, minor occupations, sites lacking extensive stratigraphic series, small collections and so forth, which makes their attribution difficult.

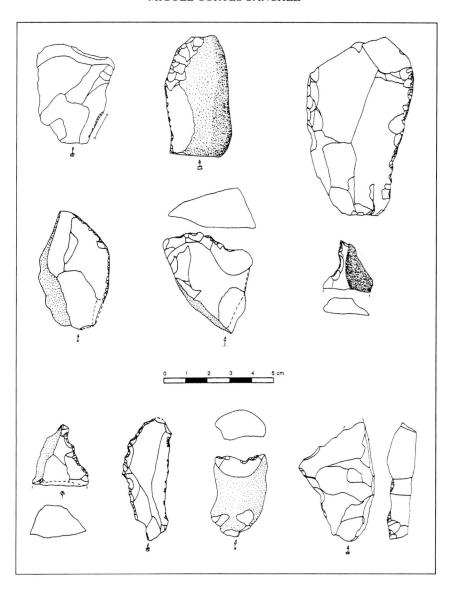

Figure 13.5: Bajondillo Layer 14. Retouched tools. For graphic conventions, see Simón, M.D. & Cortés, M.(1996).

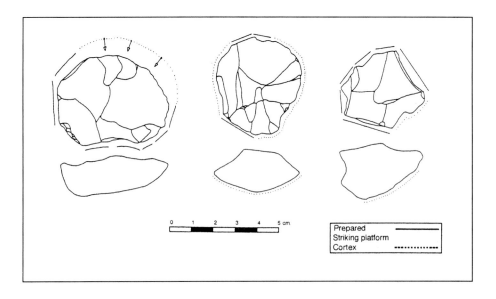

Figure 13.6: Bajondillo Layer 14. Cores.

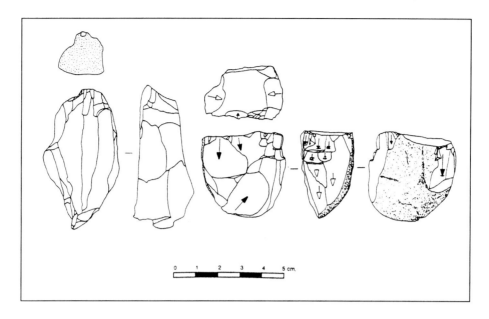

Figure 13.7: Bajondillo Layer 11. Cores.

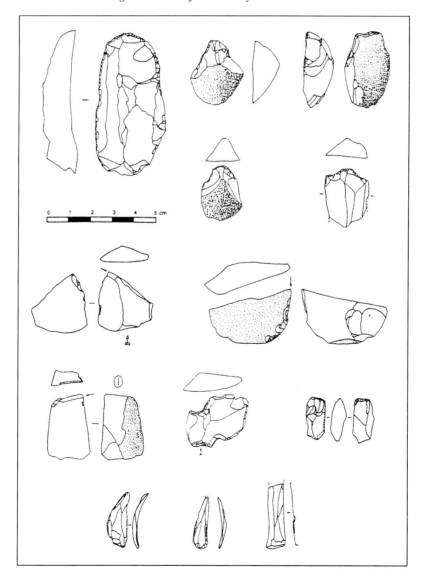

Figure 13.8: Bajondillo Layer 11. Retouched tools.

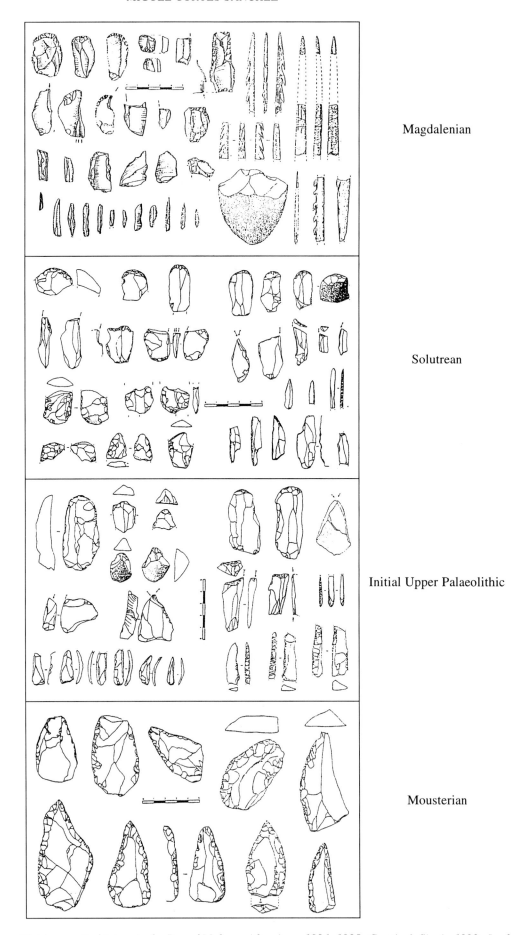

Magdalenian

Solutrean

Initial Upper Palaeolithic

Mousterian

Figure 13.9: The Upper Pleistocene Prehistory in the Bay of Malaga. After Aura 1986, 1995; Cortés & Simón 1998; Jorda 1986; Lopez & Cacho 1979.

If we look at the technological and typological No. 1. differences of the Mousterian and Early Upper Palaeolithic there would appear to be no evidence for cultural continuity. On the other hand, dates from some of the Mediterranean Early Upper Palaeolithic sites (e.g. Mallaetes, Beneito, Nerja, Gorham's Cave) could overlap with Mousterian (although one sample of bone from Bajondillo layer 11 sent to Beta Analytic for a AMS date – Beta-119285 – has not yielded a separable collagen component) and seem to indicate dates of around 30–28ka for the Middle-Upper Palaeolithic transition. A similar pattern has been observed at various Portuguese sites (Zilhão 1993; Zilhão this volume; Raposo this volume).

The economy of the Middle Palaeolithic and Bajondillo Cave

In terms of subsistence evidence, the remains of fauna from Bajondillo are relatively sparse and if we add to this the poorly preserved nature and fragmentary condition of the osteological remains, the possibilities of obtaining relevant data on this aspect of the site are strictly limited.

Marine molluscan remains are fairly common, but even so it is difficult to know their relative importance in the human diet. Nevertheless, as we have stated elsewhere (Sanchidrián et al. 1996, 51; Cortés & Sanchidrián 1998, 34), the evidence is consistent with finds from other coastal locations with Mousterian industries in Gibraltar (Barton this volume) and northwards through the Bay of Malaga to Murcia. These activities and strategies should possibly be understood in terms of a certain degree of seasonality in the movements of people between the coast and the interior. This is clear if we compare data from inland Mousterian sites in the same region above 1000 m, such as Zafarraya and Carigüela.

The data on the overall hunter-gatherer systems of the Spanish Mediterranean sites (Villaverde & Martìnez 1992; Villaverde et al. 1996) are not conclusive enough to be able to test models of continuity versus rupture between the Mousterian and the Early Upper Palaeolithic. Such differences may only be perceptible if there· had been more mobility in the Mousterian or a greater presence of human-modified rabbit bones during the Early Upper Palaeolithic.

It can be argued that the earliest evidence for shellfish collecting in Iberia occurs in the Middle Palaeolithic (Sanchidrián et al. 1996; Cortés & Sanchidrián 1998). However the distribution of these resources from the coast to the hinterland is unequal. It would appear that the Middle Palaeolithic communities only exploited shellfish when it was profitable to do so, according to their proximity to the sea, as can be seen with the sites on Gibraltar and in the Bay of Malaga. References to marine shellfish species at sites further inland are, so far, lacking. In the south of the Iberian peninsula there are also no intermediary stations which would allow us to evaluate the maximum distribution

range of these products in the interior. The pattern that might be deduced from these facts is similar to that presented for other regions (Altuna 1989) whereby resources were exploited in the area immediately around the sites. In contrast, during the Early Upper Palaeolithic, certain molluscs were transported inland as blanks for ornaments, sometimes over distances of more than 35 km from the sea (Beneito-Iturbe et al. 1993). In this context the shoreline sites constitute the starting point for obtaining the marine shell resources and the origin of circulation within the various social networks of the Early Upper Palaeolithic. In southern Iberia this marks a change in the previously limited alimentary rôle of molluscs and may coincide with the commencement of greater socio-cultural complexity.

The Bay of Malaga and the cultural sequence of the Mediterranean region of the Iberian Peninsula

It should be mentioned that although various 'Africanist theories' have been proposed, the characteristics of the Middle Paleaolithic techno-complexes of the Magreb (cf. Débenath 1992, Wengler 1997) do not seem to be present at all in the Iberian peninsula, at least not in the sequences at Carigüela, Beneito or Cova Negra. And in the case of Bajondillo there is nothing in the archaeological record that appears to bear any relation to the North African cultural sequence. In addition to the divergence of the material culture in both areas within these periods, it is necessary to add the differences in human types present in North Africa and southern Europe (Bar-Yosef this volume).

From all that has been said above it is possible to conclude that the archaeological record of the Bay of Malaga (Figure 13.9), including the Middle Palaeolithic series from Bajondillo, is concordant with the characteristics of Mousterian sites in Eastern Andalucia (Vega 1988, 1990). In such cases the final episodes are marked by an enrichment of notches and denticulates, a decrease of Group II tools and an a slight augmentation of Group III tools, as seen also at Carigüela and Beneito. At the same time, sites like Bajondillo and Nerja, the latter with a good climatostratigraphy and faunal succession (Aura et al. 1998), have added significantly to the data on the Upper Palaeolithic and, even though they exhibit certain special peculiarities, they can be shown to fit conformably within the established techno-cultural succession for this central sector of the Spanish Mediterranean.

References

Altuna, J. (1989). Subsistance D´Origine Animale Pendant Le Mousterien Dans Le Region Cantabrique (Espagne), In (M. Otte Ed.): L´Homme De Néandertal, Vol. 6, pp. 31–43. Liège.

Aura, J.E. (1986). La ocupación magdaleniense de la Cueva De Nerja (la Sala de la Mina). Trabajos sobre la Cueva de Nerja, No

1. In *La Prehistoria de la Cueva De Nerja (Malaga). Paleolitico y Epipaleolitio*, pp. 205–268. Malaga.

Aura, J.E. (1995). El Magdaleniense Mediterraneo: la cova del Parpalló (Gandía, Valencia). *Serie De Trabajos Varios.* **91**.

Aura, J.E., Jorda, J.F., Gonzalez-Tablas, J., Becares, J. & Sanchidrián, J.L. (1998). Secuencia Arqueológica De La Cueva De Nerja, La Sala Del Vestíbulo, In (J.L. Sanchidrián, & M.D. Simón, Eds.), *Las Culturas Del Pleistoceno Superior En Andalucía*. Malaga.

Baldomero, A., Ferrer, J.E. & Marques, I. (1991). Excavaciones De Urgencia En El Bajondillo (Torremolinos, Málaga). *Anuario Arqueológico De Andalucía/1989.* **Iii**, Actividades De Urgencia, 357–359.

Barroso, C. & Hublin, J.J. (1994). The Late Neanderthal Site Of Zafarraya (Andalucía, Spain), In (F. Rodríguez, F. Díaz Del Olmo, C. Finlayson & F. Giles, Eds.) *Gibraltar During The Quaternary*, pp. 61–70. Aequa Monografías-2: Seville.

Cortés, M. & Simón, M.D. (1997). Cueva Bajondillo (Torremolinos, Málaga). Aportaciones Al Paleolítico En Andalucía, In *El Món Mediterrani Després Del Pleniglacial (18.000–12.000 B.P.)*, pp. 275–290. Gerona.

Cortés, M. & Simón, M.D. (1998). Cueva Bajondillo (Torremolinos, Málaga), Implicaciones Para El Conocimiento De La Dinámica Cultural Del Pleistoceno Superior En Andalucía, In (J.L. Sanchidrián, & M.D. Simón, Eds.), *Las Culturas Del Pleistoceno Superior En Andalucía*. Malaga.

Cortés, M. & Sanchidrián, J.L. (1998). El Paleolítico Inferior Y Medio En Andalucía. *Arte, Arqueología E Historia* **5**, 19–38.

Debenath, A. (1992). Hommes Et Cultures Matérielles De L'atérien Marocain. *L'anthropologie* **96**, 711–720.

Duran Valsero, J.J., Grün, R. & Soria, J.M. (1988). Edad De Las Formaciones Travertínicas Del Flanco Meridional De La Sierra De Mijas (Provincia De Málaga, Cordilleras Béticas). *Geogaceta* **5**, 61–63.

Fumanal, M.P. (1995). Los Depósitos Cuaternarios En Cuevas Y Abrigos. Implicaciones Sedimentoclimáticas, In *El Cuaternario Del País Valenciano*, pp. 115–124. Valencia.

Hublin, J.J., Barroso, C., Medina, F., Fontugne, M. & Reyss, J.L. (1995). The Mousterian Site Of Zafarraya (Andalucia, Spain): Dating And Implications On The Palaeolithic Peopling Processes Of Western Europe. *Comptes Rendus De L'academie De Sciences De Paris*, Série IIa 931–937.

Iturbe, I., Fumanal, M.P., Carrion, J.S., Cortell, E., Martinez, R., Guillem, M.P., Garralda, M.D. & Vandermeersch, B. (1993). Cova Beneito (Muro, Alicante): Una Perspectiva Interdisciplinar. *Recerques Del Museu D'Alcoi* **2**, 23–88.

Jorda, F. (1986). La Ocupació n más antigua de la Cueva de Nerja.). Trabajos sobre la Cueva de Nerja, No. 1. In *La Prehistoria de la Cueva De Nerja (Malaga). Paleolitico y Epipaleolitico*, pp. 205–268. Malaga.

L.A.U.R.V. (1996). Behavioural And Organizational Complexity In The Middle Palaeolithic From The Abric Romani, In (E. Carbonell & M. Vaquero Eds.), *The Last Neandertals,The First Anatomically Modern Humans. Cultural Change And Human Evolution: The Crisis At 40 Ka BP*, pp. 385–434. Universitat Rovira I Virgili: Barcelona.

Lario, J., Zazo, C., Somoza, L., Goy., J.L., Hoyos, M., Silva, P.G. & Hernandez, F.J. (1993). Los Episodios Cuaternarios De La Costa De Málaga (España). Revista De La Sociedad Geológica De España 6, 41–46.

Lopez, P. & Cacho, C. (1979). La Cueva del Higuerón (Malaga): Estudio de sus materiales. *Trabajos De Prehistoria.* **36**, 11–81.

Maroto, J., Soler, N. & Fullola, J.M. (1996). Cultural Change Between Middle And Upper Palaeolithic In Catalonia, In (E. Carbonell & M. Vaquero, Eds.), *The Last Neandertals, The First Anatomically Modern Humans. Cultural Change And*

Human Evolution: The Crisis At 40 Ka BP, pp. 219–250. Universitat Rovira i Virgili: Barcelona.

Moure, A., Delibes, G., Castanedo, I., Hoyos, M., Cañaveras, J.C., Housley, R.A. & Iriarte, M.J. (1997). Revisión Y Nuevos Datos Sobre El Musteriense De La Cueva De La Ermita (Hortigüela, Burgos). Ii Congreso De Arqueología Peninsular, Tomo-I. *Paleolítico Y Epipaleolítico*, 67–83.

Sanchidrián, J.L., Simon, M.D., Cortes, M. & Muñoz, V.E. (1996). La Dinámica De Los Grupos Predadores En La Prehistoria Andaluza. Ensayo De Síntesis, In (M. Cortés, V.E. Muñoz, J.L. Sanchidrián & M.D. Simón), *El Paleolítico En Andalucía*, pp. 11–94. Cordova.

Sacchi, D., Soler, N., Maroto, J. & Domenech, E. (1996). La Question De L'Aurignacien Tardif Dans Le Domaine Méditerranéen Nord-Occidental. *Xiii Intern. Congress Of U.I.Sp.P, Forlí. The Late Aurignacian*, pp. 23–40. Forli.

Simón, M.D. & Cortés, M. (1996). Cadenas Operativas Líticas. Algunas Aportaciones Al Dibujo Tecnológico. *Complutum*, Extra Ii, 89–102.

Utrilla, P. & Montes, L. (1989). La Grotte Mousterienne De Gabasa, In (M. Otte Ed.), *L'Homme De Néandertal, Vol. 6, La Subsistance*, p. 145–153. Liège.

Vega, L.G. (1988). *El Paleolítico Medio Del Sureste Español Y Andalucía Oriental*. Serie Doctoral Dissertations, Universidad Complutense. Madrid.

Vega, L.G. (1990). La Fin Du Paléolithique Au Sud De L'espagne: Ses Implications Dans Le Contexte De La Peninsule Ibérique, In (C. Farizy Ed.), *Paléolithique Moyen Récent Et Paléolithique Supérieur Ancien En Europe*, pp. 169–176. Nemours.

Vega, L.G, Hoyos, M., Ruiz, A. & Laville, H. (1988). La Séquence De La Grotte De La Carihuela (Piñar, Grenade): Chronostratigraphie Et Paléoécologie Du Pléistocène Supérieur Au Sud De La Péninsule Ibérique, In (M. Otte Ed.), *L'homme De Néandertal, Vol. 2*, pp. 169–180. Liège.

Villaverde, V. (1984). La Cova Negra De Xàtiva Y El Musteriense De La Región Central Del Mediterráneo Español. *Serie Trabajos Varios Del Sip.* **79**.

Villaverde, V. (1992). El Paleolítico En El País Valenciano, In (P. Utrilla, Ed.), *Aragón/Litoral Mediterráneo, Intercambios Culturales Durante La Prehistoria*, pp. 55–87. Saragossa.

Villaverde, V. (1995). El Paleolítico En El País Valenciano: Principales Novedades. *Actes De Les Jornades D'Arqueologia*, pp. 13–36. Valencia.

Villaverde, V. & Fumanal, M.P. (1990). Relations Entre Le Paléolithique Moyen Et Le Paléolithique Supérieur Dans Le Versant Méditerranéen Espagnol, In (C. Farizy Ed.), *Paléolithique Moyen Récent Et Paléolithique Supérieur Ancien En Europe*, pp. 177–183. Nemours.

Villaverde, V. & Martinez, R. (1992). Economía Y Aprovechamiento Del Medio En El Paleolítico De La Región Central Del Mediterráneo Español, In (A. Moure, Ed.), *Elefantes, Ciervos Y Ovicápridos. Economía Y Aprovechamiento Del Medio En La Prehistoria De España Y Portugal*, pp.77–95. Santander.

Villaverde, V., Martínez-Valle, R., Guillem, P.M. & Fumanal, M.P. (1996). Mobility And The Role Of Small Game In The Middle Paleolithic Of The Central Region Of The Spanish Mediterranean: A Comparison Of Cova Negra With Other Paleolithic Deposits, In (E. Carbonell & M. Vaquero Eds.), *The Last Neandertals, The First Anatomically Modern Humans. Cultural Change And Human Evolution: The Crisis At 40 Ka BP*, pp. 267–288. Barcelona

Wengler, L. (1997). La Transition Du Moustérien À L'Atérien. *L'Anthropologie* T. **101**, 448–481.

Zilhão, J. (1993). Le Passage Du Paléolithique Moyen Au Paléolithique Supérieur Dans Le Portugal, In (V. Cabrera Ed.), *El Origen Del Hombre Moderno En El Suroeste De Europa*, pp. 127–145. Madrid.

14

Gibraltar and the Neanderthals 1848–1998

Chris Stringer

The year 1848 saw many momentous events in European politics, but it was also an archaeological watershed, seeing the publication of a number of highly influential works such as those by Layard on Nineveh, Dennis on Etruria, and Squier and Davis on the Mississippi Valley (see *Antiquity*, volume 27, number 278, December 1998). Another momentous event, although unrecognised at the time, was the recognition and curation of a fossilised human cranium found during work at Forbes' Quarry, Gibraltar (Busk 1865; Broca 1869; Sollas 1907). Although, technically speaking, the child's skull from Engis in Belgium was the first known discovery of a Neanderthal fossil, some 18 years earlier, its features were less obviously distinct from those of a modern human, and it was over a hundred years before its importance was recognised. In the case of the Forbes' Quarry discovery, the unusual morphology of the face and vault alone could have been enough to alert an educated observer to its possible significance, but instead fate decreed that today we discuss 'Neanderthal Man' (*Homo neanderthalensis*) rather than 'Calpican Man' ('*Homo calpicus*') (King 1864; Keith 1911).

Recently, as part of his research on George Busk (Gardiner 1999), Professor Brian Gardiner located a review paper by Cook (1997), which referred to two neglected publications of Busk from 1864. These provide further information on the Forbes' Quarry discovery, and show that Busk was remarkably prescient in identifying some key morphological features of the fossil – in fact he was the first to note the midfacial projection and inflated cheekbones which are now considered one of the most distinctive of Neanderthal characters. As these sources were apparently unknown to Sir Arthur Keith when he described what was known of the early history of the specimen (Keith 1911), I will quote some of the pertinent material from these papers. On the 16th July 1864, Busk wrote a short communication in *The Reader* (Busk 1864)

entitled 'Pithecoid Priscan Man from Gibraltar'. Near the end he stated of the Forbes' Quarry cranium "Its discovery also adds immensely to the scientific value of the Neanderthal specimen, if only as showing that the latter does not represent, as many have hitherto supposed, a mere individual peculiarity, but that it may have been characteristic of a race extending from the Rhine to the Pillars of Hercules: for, whatever may have been the case on the banks of the Dussel, even Professor Mayer [a contemporary sceptic regarding the Neanderthal find] will hardly suppose that a rickety Cossack engaged in the campaign of 1814 had crept into a sealed fissure in the Rock of Gibraltar."

In the *Bath Chronicle* Busk (1864) described the fossil in more detail, making morphological comparisons with 'Negro', Australian and Tasmanian crania. He stated "The cranium in question, we understand, was originally deposited in a museum of natural curiosities, which at one time existed at Gibraltar, but which it is to be much regretted has of late years been allowed to fall into a state of confusion and neglect......Its extraordinary peculiarities fortunately struck the notice of Dr Hodgkin in a visit paid by that ethnologist to Gibraltar in the course of last year, in company with Sir Moses Montefiore, and it was at his instance that Captain Browne [Brome?], with his eminent zeal in the cause of science, was induced to procure its being forwarded to us for examination and description. .....it was dug up in the course of some excavations being made in what is termed "Forbes Barrier", which is situated near the entrance into the fortress from the neutral ground or mainland. ....the Gibraltar skull exhibits not only several of the striking peculiarities of the maeanderthal [sic] calvarium but also many others, which from the imperfect condition of that famous specimen, are altogether wanting in it......In general outline the Gibraltar cranium viewed in profile, bears a strong resemblance to that from the Neanderthal, except that the sapraorbital [sic] projection is not quite so great. The forehead is equally receding, and the great depression in the hinder part of the cranium is equally remarkable in both.....One consequence of the great breadth and convexity of the nasal process of the maxillary bone, combined with the increased width of the nasal opening, is, as it were, to throw forward the entire nasal framework, whilst at the same time the canine fossa....is entirely filled up, the central portion of the bone rising in a uniform curve on either side, so that the central part of the countenance projects in a very remarkable manner. "

Today, Forbes' Quarry is nearly stripped of Pleistocene sediments, but there are lingering pockets of a cemented, shelly sand which, to judge from the remaining matrix on the fossil, may relate to the provenance of the cranium. However, it will only be by direct age estimates using techniques such as Electron Spin Resonance on tooth enamel, or Gamma Ray dating on the whole cranium, that we will eventually determine whether the Forbes' Quarry Neanderthal dates from the earlier or later part of the Late Pleistocene. The neighbouring site of Devil's Tower (Figure 14.1) produced the partial skull of a Neanderthal child in 1926 (Garrod et al. 1928; see also Currant, this volume), and has greater potential for further excavation and discoveries. It preserves much more Pleistocene sediment than Forbes' Quarry, and it is possible to relate that sediment to the previous excavations, but the site lies directly beneath the sheer north face of the Rock and it is hence one of the most dangerous places for rock falls in the whole of Gibraltar! Further excavations at Devil's Tower would therefore require major engineering work to ensure the safety of the personnel involved.

Fortunately, however, there are several other sites in Gibraltar which preserve evidence of Neanderthal occupation. One, Ibex Cave, lies high up on the eastern face of the Rock, while four others lie to the south-east, close to the sea near "Governor's Beach" (Figures 14.1–2). The present beach mainly consists of fine limestone blast debris from military tunnelling operations, but there are also cemented remnants of more ancient beaches which presumably accumulated during Oxygen Isotope Stage 5. The caves are named (from the south) Bennett's, Gorham's, Vanguard and Boat Hoist. Three of these caves (Ibex, Gorham's and Vanguard) have been excavated since 1994 as part of the Gibraltar Caves Project, and below I will introduce the sites and some of the results of our excavations, which were presented by myself and my colleagues during the session I chaired at the 1998 Conference.

Although Captain A. Gorham is credited with the discovery of one of these caves in 1907, it was not systematically investigated until after 1945, when access was still only possible by sea from below, or by ropes from above. The British archaeologist John d'Arcy Waechter conducted the first large scale excavations in Gorham's cave from 1947–1954, and established that the cave contained a record spanning perhaps 100,000 years

of Middle Palaeolithic, Upper Palaeolithic and Holocene occupation. Waechter also reported the presence of ancient hearths at various levels in the cave, especially in the Upper Palaeolithic, and of faunal material throughout the sequence, dominated by the remains of ibex, rabbit, and many species of bird. Unfortunately, many aspects of Waechter's excavations were never properly recorded or published, and much of the material he recovered has since disappeared.

Waechter's stratigraphic sequence of layers running approximately horizontally east-west must have been considerably simplified compared with the complex reality which we have since observed (Waechter 1951, 1964; see also Currant, this volume). However, he delineated a series of Layers G, K, M, P, R and S1 as Mousterian, with Layers H, J, L, N, O, Q, S2–3 and T as sterile (by which he meant lacking in artefacts), and reported a "fossil beach" at 9.7m above mean sea level forming his Layer U at the base of the sequence (but see Currant, this volume). He also recognised a number of Upper Palaeolithic Layers (B, D, E and F), capped by the historic "Punic" Layer A. Typologically, Waechter noted the presence of prepared cores throughout the Mousterian levels, even including an example from Layer U. However, he believed that Layer G was separated from the lower levels by an interstadial (represented by Layer J), and was distinctive in having only a few, inferior, prepared cores, but large blades. Regarding the Upper Palaeolithic levels, Waechter also eventually recognised the industries of each Layer B, D and F as distinct, but avoided assigning them to existing categories such as Aurignacian or Solutrean. He was also aware that there was little evidence of true Aurignacian or Chatelperronian industries elsewhere in southern Iberia. Waechter's attempts at dating the archaeological sequence were heavily influenced by Zeuner's assessment of the stratigraphy, and the models underlying this, but some independent chronological control was provided from charcoal samples collected by Topp and Oakley in 1957. Groningen radiocarbon determinations dated the Upper Palaeolithic of Layer D at about 28ka and the Middle Palaeolithic of G at at least 47 ka (Waechter 1964).

Our work at Gorham's since 1995 has concentrated on re-exposing, recording and sampling what survives of Waechter's sections and excavating selected Middle Palaeolithic levels containing lithics, fauna, burnt seeds and charcoal. A range of dating methods are being applied to the stratigraphic sequence, and some of these are discussed in the subsequent papers by Rink et al. and Volterra et al. In addition, there are now a number of radiocarbon accelerator dates on bone and charcoal, as discussed by Paul Pettitt in his paper (Pettitt & Bailey, this volume). Charcoal from one of the highest Middle Palaeolithic levels produced a date of 45.3 ± 1.7 ka (OxA-6075), which might suggest a correlation with the latest of Waechter's Mousterian levels, Layer G. However, as radiocarbon dating demonstrates, and Barton reports (this volume), a Middle Palaeolithic characterised by small disc

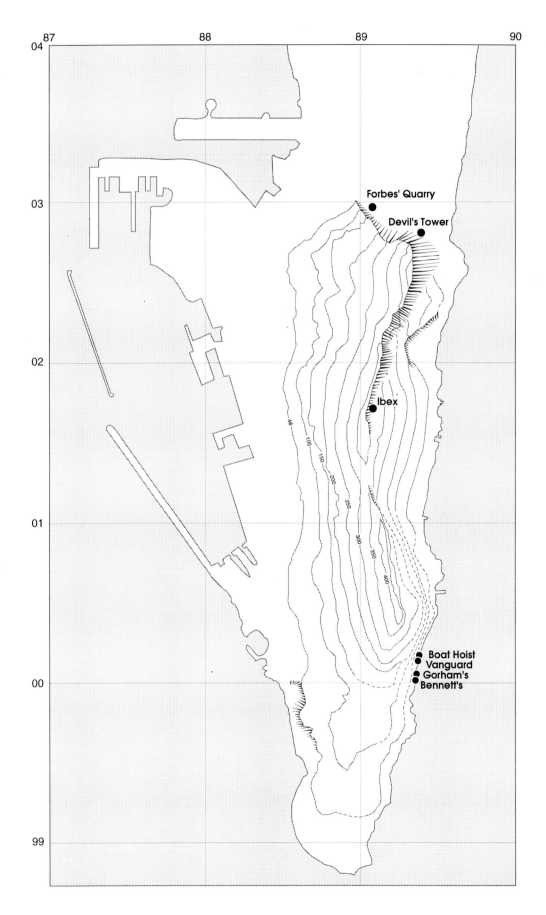

Figure 14.1: Map of Gibraltar, showing location of sites mentioned in text (courtesy of Nick Barton).

Figure 14.2: The caves on Governor's Beach. From left: Bennett's Cave, Gorham's Cave, and the double arch of Vanguard and Boat Hoist Caves (Frank Greenaway, NHM Photographic Unit).

cores continues through several more units, including one dated from charcoal at 32. 28 ka±420 years. This is then succeeded by several levels of Upper Palaeolithic combustion zones which are radiocarbon dated to between about 26 and 30 ka. As Raposo, and Zilhao, report (this volume), these last dates suggest that the arrival of modern humans in Gibraltar may have occurred while Neanderthals still lived in the more mountainous interior of Iberia (see also d'Errico *et al.* 1998; Mellars 1998, this volume).

Up to 1995, the Pleistocene sediments in Vanguard Cave were largely buried under a natural sand slope, although surface finds of artefacts and fauna could be made. However, excavations have since revealed two rich Middle Palaeolithic levels separated by intervening deposits of sand, and a small alcove in the north of the site with evidence of both Neanderthal and hyaena occupation (Barton, this volume; Fernandez-Jalvo & Andrews, this volume). Radiocarbon dating suggests that Vanguard, a smaller site than Gorham's, was virtually full of sand and sediment by about 40 ka and therefore the main chamber is only likely to contain significant evidence of Middle Palaeolithic occupation (Pettitt & Bailey, this volume). A particularly remarkable find from the upper levels of Vanguard appears to provides the strongest evidence yet found that Neanderthals utilised marine food resources.

In 1997, a discrete Middle Palaeolithic layer was excavated containing mussel shells of consistent size, alongside ash, charcoal, coprolites and refitting lithics (see Barton, and Fernandez-Jalvo & Andrews, this volume). The presence of the mussels during the relatively low sea level of Oxygen Isotope Stage 3 (Davies *et al.* and Finlayson & Pacheco., this volume) implies that they were brought to the cave over some distance, perhaps in containers, from their marine or, more likely, estuarine source. Furthermore, in 1998, part of the mandible of a monk seal was recovered from one of the lower stratigraphic levels at Vanguard (Currant, this volume), with apparent cut marks and in association with Middle Palaeolithic artefacts, although it is not known whether its presence is the result of scavenging or hunting.

Micromorphological study of samples from Gorham's and Vanguard Caves have provided valuable data for palaeoenvironmental and taphonomic analyses (Macphail & Goldberg, this volume). These studies show that the neighbouring caves have surprisingly different sedimentological histories, but their records are fortunately complementary rather than conflicting. Both were influenced by the coastal environment which was dominated by sand dunes, and this served to mediate any direct marine influence on sedimentation, *contra* the views of Waechter and Zeuner. While Vanguard shows rather uniform patterns throughout the excavated areas, with only a few relatively undisturbed combustion zones separated by large volumes of sand input, Gorham's shows much more complex depositional and postdepositional processes both vertically and horizontally, and much greater signs of biological influences. While some palaeoclimatic signals may still be deduced from these sequences, they are far from the straightforward reflections of sea level and ice cap fluctuation envisaged in some of the earlier work at Gorham's.

The third site we have excavated, Ibex Cave, is located at about 260 metres above sea level on the East side of The Rock of Gibraltar, at the top of the water catchments. This huge expanse of metal sheeting was mainly constructed at the beginning of this century over a natural slope of Pleistocene breccias and wind-blown sand. The cave was first exposed in 1975, during quarrying operations on the sands and breccias, following the dismantling of one of the highest levels of catchment sheeting. Over 50 artefacts of Middle Palaeolithic character were collected by workmen at the site from the sands filling the cave entrance, and a small excavation was also undertaken at that time in the cave entrance, producing some vertebrate material, and marine and terrestrial mollusca. In 1994, systematic excavations were carried out at the site, with the collection of further artefacts and faunal remains. Many of the tools are made from a dark red chert, local to Gibraltar, but the raw material was probably transported to the site in the form of beach cobbles (Barton, in press). However, taphonomic work on the Ibex Cave faunas suggests that human impact on the faunas was negligible (see Fernandez-Jalvo & Andrews, this volume). Human occupation was probably sporadic, with the main body of Ibex lithics deriving from a single discrete episode of activity during the period of deposition of Unit 2. Tooth enamel from a cervid and ibex excavated from the underlying Unit 3 was dated using ESR (Rhodes *et al.* in press), giving mean age estimates of about 37 ka (Early Uptake) and 49 ka (Linear Uptake). The dates certainly support a mid-last glaciation age for the fauna of Unit 3 and they provide a maximum age for the overlying Unit 2 and its contained Middle Palaeolithic artefacts.

Acknowledgements

I would like to take this opportunity, on behalf of my scientific collaborators in the Gibraltar Caves Project, of thanking the many people who have worked with us on site or post-excavation work, as well as the people of Gibraltar, for their interest and support over five enjoyable and productive seasons of work. I would also like to thank the following funding bodies for their generous support of the project: The National Geographic Society, The Leakey Foundation, The British Academy, The Natural History Museum, The Society of Antiquaries, NERC, Oxford Brookes University, The Gibraltar Heritage Trust and the Gibraltar Earth Sciences and Archaeology Trust, and The Government of Gibraltar. A large team of people were involved in the successful planning, running and publication of the 1998 Conference, particularly Geraldine Finlayson, Director of the John Mackintosh Hall, Peter Cabezutto, staff at Parodytur, and on the editorial side, Jackie Skipper and Veronica Hunt.

References

Barton, R.N.E. (in press). Raw material exploitation and lithic use at the Mousterian site of Ibex Cave, Gibraltar. In (C. Finlayson, Ed.) *Gibraltar during the Quaternary: the southernmost part of Europe in the last two million years.* Gibraltar Government Heritage Publications: Gibraltar.

Barton, R.N.E., Currant, A.P., Fernandez-Jalvo, Y., Finlayson, J.C., Goldberg, P., Macphail, R., Pettitt, P. & Stringer, C. (1999). Gibraltar Neanderthals and results of recent excavations in Gorham's, Vanguard and Ibex Caves. *Antiquity* **73**, 13–23

Broca, P. (1869). Remarques sur les ossements des cavernes de Gibraltar. *Bull. Mem.Soc.Anthropol. Paris* **4**, 146–158.

Busk, G. (1864). Pithecoid Priscan Man from Gibraltar. *The Reader* **4**, 109–110.

Busk, G. (1864). Bath: Report on British Association Meeting. *Bath Chronicle* (special daily edition) 22nd September, 3 pp.

Busk, G. (1865). On a very ancient human cranium from Gibraltar. *Report of the 34th meeting of the British Association for the Advancement of Science, Bath 1864.* 91–92.

Cook, G. (1997). George Busk FRS (1807–1886), nineteenth-century polymath: surgeon, parasitologist, zoologist and palaeontologist. *Journal of Medical Biography* **5**, 88–101

D'Errico, F., Zilhao, J., Julien, M., Baffier, D. and Pelegrin, J. (1998). Neanderthal acculturation in western Europe? *Current Anthropology* **19**, supplement, S1–S44.

Gardiner, B. (1999). Picture Quiz. *Newsletter and Proceedings of the Linnean Society of London* **15**, 6–13

Garrod, D.A.E., Buxton, L.H.D., Elliot Smith, G. and Bate, D.M.A. (1928). Excavation of a Mousterian Rock-shelter at Devil's Tower, Gibraltar. *Journal of the Royal Anthropological Institute* **58**, 91–113.

Keith, A. (1911). The early history of the Gibraltar cranium. *Nature* **87**, 313–314.

King, W. (1864). The reputed fossil man of the Neanderthal. *Quart.J.Sci.* **1**, 88–97.

Mellars, P. (1998). The fate of the Neanderthals. *Nature* **395**, 539–540.

Rhodes, E., Stringer, C., Grün, R., Barton, R.N.E., Currant, A. and Finlayson, C. (In press). Preliminary ESR dates from Ibex Cave, Gibraltar. In (C. Finlayson, Ed) *Gibraltar during the Quaternary: the southernmost part of Europe in the last two million years.* Gibraltar Government Heritage Publications: Gibraltar.

Rose, E. & Stringer, C. (1997). Gibraltar woman and Neanderthal Man. *Geology Today* **13**, 179–184.

Sollas, W. (1907). On the cranial and facial characters of the Neanderthal race. *Phil.trans.R.Soc. London* B, **199**, 281–339.

Stringer, C., Barton, R.N.E., Currant, A.P., Finlayson, J.C., Goldberg, P., Macphail, R. & Pettitt, P.B. (1999). The Gibraltar Palaeolithic revisited: new excavations at Gorham's and Vanguard Caves 1995–7. In (W. Davis & R. Charles, Eds) *Dorothy Garrod and the progress of the Palaeolithic*, pp. 84–96. Oxbow: Oxford.

Waechter, J. D'A. (1951). Excavations at Gorham's Cave, Gibraltar. *Proceedings of the Prehistoric Society* **17**, 83–92.

Waechter, J. D'A. 1964. The excavations at Gorham's Cave, Gibraltar, 1951–1954. *Bulletin of the Institute of Archaeology of London* **4**, 189–221.

15

The Southern Iberian Peninsula in the Late Pleistocene: Geography, Ecology and Human Occupation

Clive Finlayson and Francisco Giles Pacheco

Introduction

Current research suggests that the southern Iberian Peninsula may have been among the last refuges of the Neanderthals where they may have survived beyond 32 ka (Antunes *et al.* 1989; Barroso & Hublin 1994; Hublin *et al.* 1995; Zilhao 1993; 1995; d'Errico *et al.* 1998; Raposo & Cardoso 1998; Pettitt 1999). The Rock of Gibraltar, at the southernmost tip of Iberia, has yielded two Neanderthal skulls (Finlayson 1994; Stringer 1994) and three additional sites of occupation (Barton *et al.* 1999) within an area of 6 km². Recent research (Barton *et al.* 1999; Stringer *et al.* 1999) has produced significant anthracological and osteological evidence to permit an understanding of the environments in which these Neanderthals lived during Oxygen Isotope Stage (OIS) 3 and of the deteriorating conditions towards its end and the onset of OIS 2 (Finlayson *et al.* 1999).

The aims of this paper are to:

(a) model the environmental conditions immediately around the Rock of Gibraltar during the Late Pleistocene;

(b) situate these within the larger spatial context of the southern Iberian Peninsula; and

(c) present an ecological perspective to the Neanderthal-Modern Human spatio-temporal distribution patterns in southern Iberia.

Environmental conditions immediately around the Rock of Gibraltar during the Late Pleistocene

An Oxygen Isotope Stage 3 Model

Physical Geography

During the cool but variable OIS 3 Stage, between 60 and 25 ka (van Andel & Tzedakis 1998), the sea level would

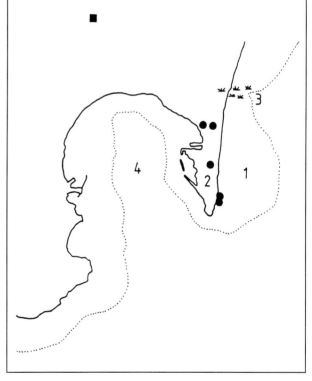

Figure 15.1: The Rock of Gibraltar with the expected increase in land surface with a sea level descent of 80 metres.

Key: ⋯⋯ *Coastal limit at −80m;* • *Location of known Neanderthal sites;* ∎ *Location of furthest known site of raw material utilization (17 km); 1– The east side of sandy plain; 2– The rocky peninsula of Gibraltar; 3– Shallow estuary; 4– Deep estuary/bay.*

have oscillated between −70 and −85m. In Gibraltar, the coastline, on the eastern side in particular, would have been significantly extended. Based on extrapolation of current bathymetric charts we estimate that the surface area of land available outside Gorham's and Vanguard Caves would have been of the order of 35km² and the coastline to the east may have been between 2.5 and 4.5km from the caves (Figure 15.1). The main characteristic of this land area was its sandy nature, with significant evidence of its character remaining in Quaternary dune deposits on the eastern side of Gibraltar (Rose & Rosenbaum 1991; Rose & Hardman 1994; Rodriguez Vidal & Gracia Prieto 1994). Two other topographical features of interest emerge from Figure 15.1: (a) a shallow river estuary opening into the Mediterranean Sea north-east of the Rock; and (b) a deep and narrow bay in the west into which the palaeo-Palmones and Guadarranque rivers would have opened.

The East Side Sandy Plain

The basis of the model which we present was arrived at following the discovery of two specimens of the Azure-winged Magpie *Cyanopica cyanus* in Gorham's and Vanguard Caves during the course of the current excavations (Cooper 1998). The Gorham's Cave specimen was obtained from a level which was older than a radiocarbon horizon dated to 45±1.7 ka (OxA-6075) but younger than an Electron Spin Resonance dated horizon (Early Uptake 56.5±4.9 ka ; Late Uptake 62.4±5.1 ka) (Finlayson *et al.* in prep.; Volterra *et al.* this volume). The Vanguard Cave specimen was obtained from a level which was dated at >44.1 ka (OxA-7078) that was situated above an OSL level dated at <58 ka (Finlayson, *et al.* in prep.). These levels can be therefore correlated with events within OIS 3.

While most bird species are poor indicators of fine-grain environmental conditions, given that many travel over large distances during the course of their annual cycle (Finlayson *et al.* 1997), the Azure-winged Magpie has very specific environmental requirements and is sedentary (Cramp & Perrins 1994). Its current European distribution is largely restricted to the western half of the Iberian Peninsula (Goodwin 1976; Hagemeijer & Blair 1997; Purroy 1997). It is no longer present in Gibraltar (Finlayson 1992). We analysed data which we collected from 680 sites in the south-western Iberian Peninsula (Finlayson *et al.* 1997) from Portugal to Almería (SE Spain), and found the Azure-winged Magpie restricted to 4.1% of the sites. The data from a subset of 18 sandy coastal sites (thought to be the closest to the conditions of Gibraltar) were then extracted to generate a model of the environmental requirements of this species. A total of 32 vegetation structural and qualitative (species composition) variables were analysed. The mean variable data were then subjected to Monte Carlo simulation (1000 trials on normally distributed data) to provide the basis for the quantitative model. Assuming that the environmental requirements of the Azure-winged Magpie had remained unchanged since the Late Pleistocene, the model was used to predict the environmental conditions of (at least a part of) the sandy

plain immediately outside Gorham's and Vanguard Caves in the period 45–60 Uncalibrated Ka of OIS 3.

The results predict that the conditions outside Gorham's and Vanguard Caves were similar to those of a wooded savanna (e.g. Morel 1968). Of particular interest is the high expected probability of grass cover (Figure 15.2a) which would be expected to support a rich herbivore community (Owen-Smith 1988; Sinclair 1995). The expected patchy distribution of shrub and tree cover (Figure 15.2b & 2c) would have further enhanced herbivore diversity (Guthrie 1984). The structural tree characteristics (height, cover, trunk circumference and density) are consistent with an open landscape in which herbivores could be easily detected by by predators (Figure 15.2c-e). If it is correct that the predicted landscape would support a rich herbivore community and that such a landscape would enhance their detection, then it would follow that a rich carnivore community (and associated scavengers) would be expected to thrive in such conditions (Hanby & Bygott 1979; Sunquist & Sunquist 1989; Dayan & Simberloff 1996).

The dominant tree species predicted by the model is the Stone Pine *Pinus pinea* (Figure 15.3) with a high probability of reaching a widespread distribution (Figure 15.4a). Of particular interest also is the presence of Juniper *Juniperus phoenicea* (Figure 15.3) which would be expected to be patchily distributed across the landscape (Figure 15.4b). The generic composition of shrubs would be dominated by Mediterranean-type (Rivas-Martinez 1987) woody species (Figure 15.5). In Table 15.1 we compare the predicted tree and shrub composition with the results obtained from anthracological analyses of charcoal samples from the relevant stratigraphic horizons at Gorham's and Vanguard Caves (Finlayson *et al.* in prep.). We conclude that the predictions of the model are closely matched by the results with two significant exceptions. First, the absence of Oaks (especially Cork Oak *Quercus suber*) could be explained either by predicting a more arid Late Pleistocene climate or by the avoidance of collection of this type of wood by the Neanderthals. Cork Oak is particularly fire-resistant. Secondly, two Mediterranean shrubs (Tutin *et al.* 1968; 1972) which are present in the charcoal samples are either absent (Olive *Olea europaea*) or are predicted to be less frequent (Lentisc *Pistacia lentiscus*) than they really are. We attribute the difference to the edaphological requirements of these species which preferentially grow in rocky areas with alkaline soils (Valdes *et al.* 1987). These two species are characteristic of the maquis of the limestone Rock of Gibraltar even today and we conclude that the Neanderthals collected these woody shrubs from the cliffs and screes above the caves and not from the sandy plain.

The mammalian herbivore community of this sandy plain during the stratigraphic sequence covering OIS 3 appears constant in terms of species composition in spite of the climatic fluctuations of this stage (Bond *et al.* 1993; Dansgaard *et al.* 1993; McManus *et al.* 1994). The

Table 15.1: A comparison of the plant species/genera predicted by the OIS 3 Model and the results obtained from actual charcoal samples.

Species/Genus*	Model	Charcoal
(a) Trees		
Pinus pinea	Present	Present
Quercus suber	Present	Absent
Juniperus phoenicea	Present	Present (sp.)
Pinus pinaster	Present	Present
Quercus rotundifolia	Present	Absent
(b) Shrubs*		
Halimium	Present	Absent
Cistus	Present	Probable
Erica	Present	Probable
Rosmarinus	Present	Absent
Pistacia (lentiscus)	Present	Present
Ulex	Present	Absent
Lavandula	Present	Absent
Dittrichia	Present	Absent
Olea (europaea)	Absent	Present
Rosa	Absent	Probable

* For each category, species/genera are ranked in order or predicted abundance.
** Identified to the species level.
*** Identified to the genus level, but see *Pistacia lentiscus* and *Olea europaea.*

permanent components are Red Deer *Cervus elaphus*, Cattle *Bos* cf. *primigenius* and Rabbit *Oryctolagus cuniculus* (Sutcliffe 1999; Currant this volume). Other herbivores/omnivores include the Rhinoceros *Stephanorhinus* cf. *hemitoechus* which was the last surviving component of the megaherbivore fauna (Currant pers. comm.) and a species which became extinct in Mediterranean latitudes around five thousand years before the end of the last glaciation (Tchernov 1984); Horse *Equus caballus*; and Wild Boar *Sus scrofa.* (Sutcliffe 1999; Currant this volume). The prediction of a diverse herbivore community, albeit of reduced species composition when compared to earlier in the Pleistocene, in the sandy plain outside Gorham's and Vanguard Caves would also appear to be fulfilled.

The mammalian carnivore community for the same sequence is also diverse (Sutcliffe 1999; Currant this volume). The most uniformly spread species across the stratigraphy are Spotted Hyaena *Crocuta crocuta*, Lynx *Lynx pardinus,* and Leopard *Panthera pardus.* Also present in several levels are Wolf *Canis lupus*, Brown Bear *Ursus arctos* and Wild Cat *Felis sylvestris.* A large felid (tentatively ascribed to a Lion *Panthera* cf. *leo*) has also been described (Sutcliffe 1999). The mammalian carnivore community therefore fits well in the predicted scenario of the model.

In addition to hyaenas there is further supporting evidence for the presence of scavengers within the plains. Three of the four contemporary European vultures have been described: Griffon Vulture *Gyps fulvus* in Gorham's Cave (Eastham 1967; Cooper pers. comm.); Bearded Vulture *Gypaetus barbatus* in Ibex Cave in a level ESR-dated between 37.1 ± 3.3 ka (Early Uptake) and 49.4 ± 3.2 ka (Late Uptake), (Cooper 1999); and Egyptian Vulture *Neophron* cf. *percnopterus* from Vanguard Cave (Cooper, pers. comm.). To these we can add the following bird species which regularly scavenge on carcasses: Red Kite *Milvus milvus* and/or Kite sp. *Milvus* cf. *milvus* (Eastham 1967; Cooper pers. comm.); Raven *Corvus corax* (Eastham 1967); Carrion Crow *Corvus corone* (Eastham 1967; Cooper 1999); and Jackdaw *Corvus monedula* (Eastham 1967)

Additional supporting evidence for the environment predicted by the model comes from the presence of Hermann's Tortoise *Testudo hermanni* in Gorham's and Vanguard Cave levels (Currant pers.comm.) and from several species of bird which are characteristic of open woodland or plains environments in southern Europe today: Lesser Kestrel *Falco naumanni* (Cooper 1999); Turtle Dove *Sterptopelia turtur* (Cooper pers. comm.); Roller *Coracias garrulus* (Cooper pers. comm.) and, possibly corresponding to this sequence from Gorham's Cave, Great Bustard *Otis tarda* and Hoopoe *Upupa epops* (Cooper pers. comm.).

Other environments

In order to present as complete a picture of the environments available to the Neanderthals around Gibraltar during the period in question we briefly present in this section the evidence for the other three major environments which appear to have been available and which are not covered by the model, i.e. the rocky peninsula of Gibraltar itself, peripheral wetlands and the coast.

The rocky peninsula of Gibraltar

We have noted above the presence of Wild Olive and Lentisc which we have attributed to this environment. These species are key indicators of the thermo-Mediterranean bioclimatic stage (Rivas-Martinez 1981; 1987) and would have been major components of a dense woodland or matorral such as is found on the Rock today. Among the mammalian herbivores found in Gorham's, Vanguard and Ibex Caves the Spanish Ibex *Capra pyrenaica* is one of the most numerous (Sutcliffe 1999; Currant pers. comm.). This species would have occurred on the rocky peninsula, especially on the cliffs and taluses of the northern and eastern sides along which these caves, and also Forbes' Quarry and Devil's Tower, are situated. Some of the mammals of the plains would have been found in these environments also, judging from their present-day behaviour, but their detection and predation must have been more complicated given the abrupt relief and/or dense vegetation. These would have been Red Deer, Wild Boar and Rabbit. The carnivores would have included Brown Bear, Wild Cat and Lynx. There is considerable evidence for cliff-dwelling bird communities. Finlayson (1992) has

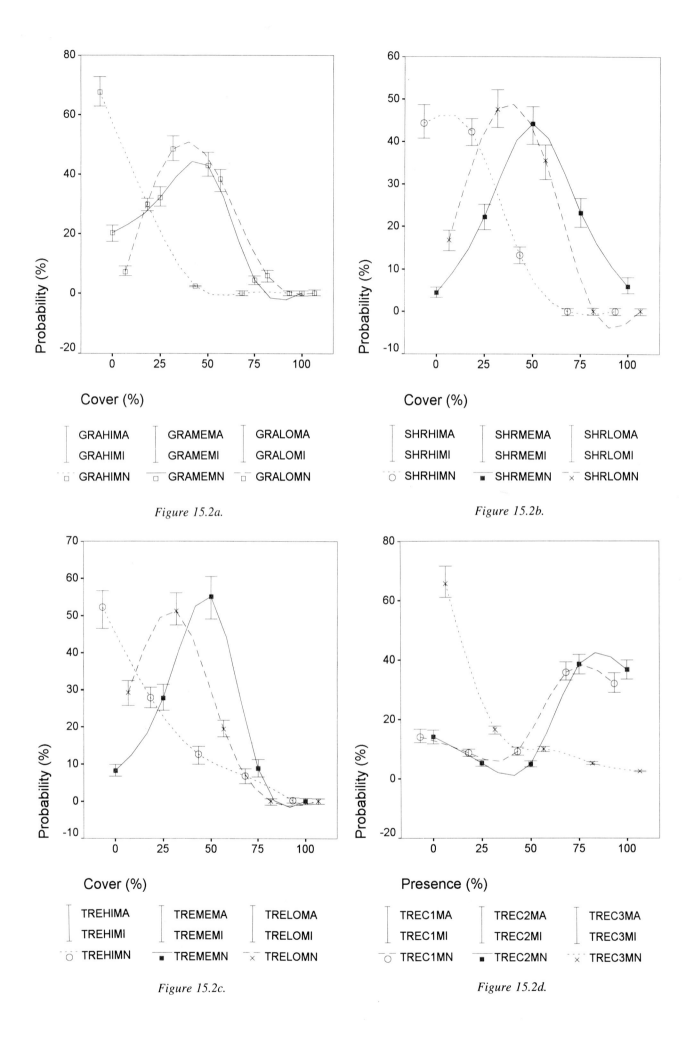

Figure 15.2a.

Figure 15.2b.

Figure 15.2c.

Figure 15.2d.

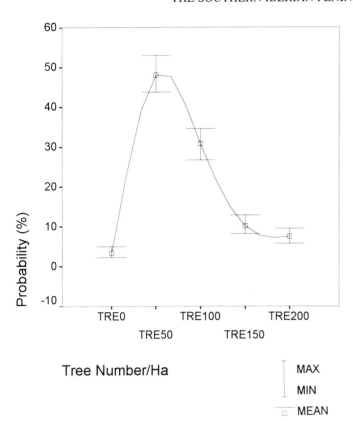

Figure 15.2a-e: Vegetation structure predicted by the model. Five selected components of the vegetation are illustrated. a) Grass Cover (GRAHI = Grass height > 1.5 m; GRAME = Grass height 0.25–1.5 m; GRALO = 0–0.25 m). b) Shrub Cover (SHRHI = Shrub Height >1.5 m; SHRME = Shrub Height 0.25–1.5 m; SHRLO = Shrub Height 0–0.25 m). c) Tree Cover (TREHI = Tree Height >6 m; TREME = Tree Height 1.5–6 m; TRELO = Tree Height 0–1.5 m). d) Tree Circumference (TREC1 = Tree Circumfrence >0.5 m; TREC2 = Tree Circumference 0.5–1.5 m; TREC3 = Tree Circumference >1.5 m). e) Tree Density.

Figure 15.2e.

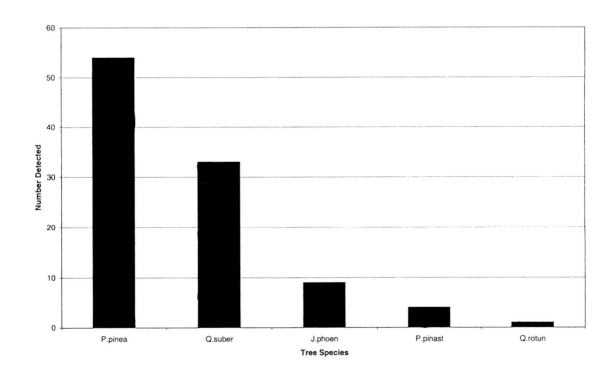

Figure 15.3: Observed ranking of tree species (by number detected) in the sites sampled. Key: P.pinea = Stone Pine Pinus pinea; Q.suber = Cork Oak Quercus suber; J.phoen = Juniper Juniperus phoenicea; P.pinast = Maritime Pine Pinus pinaster; Q.rotun = Round leaved Oak Quercus rotundifolia.

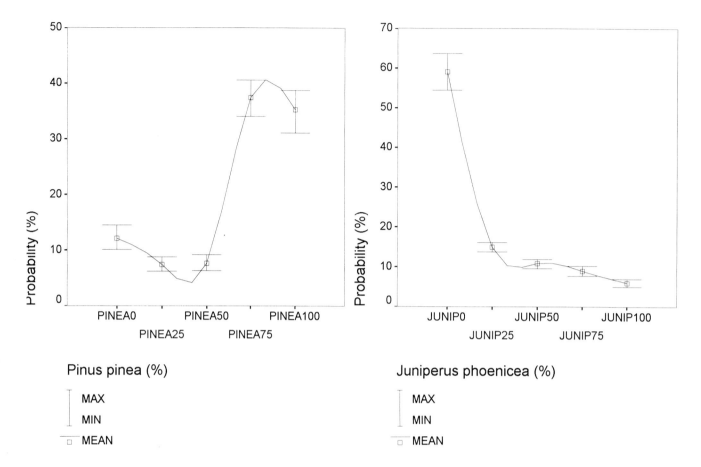

Figure 15.4: Distribution of Stone Pine and Juniper in sites sampled. a) Pinus pinea cover (0 = No cover; 25 = present in 25% of area; 50 = present in 50% of area; 75 = present in 75% of area; 100 = present in all area); b) Juniperus phoenicea cover (scale as for Pinus pinea).

reviewed the cliff-dwelling breeding avifauna of Holocene southern Iberia. In Table 15.2 we compare this avifauna with the species which have been recorded for the relevant late Pleistocene period under discussion. We conclude that the OIS 3 cliff avifauna is identical to that of the Holocene. A number of the scavengers which we have recorded for the sandy plain, i.e. the vultures, the Raven and the Jackdaw, would have nested on these nearby cliffs. Finally, we include here the significant presence of a partridge species (*Alectoris* cf. *rufa*) in the three caves (Eastham 1967; Cooper 1999 and pers. comm.). This sedentary species occurs in a broad range of vegetated environments in southern Iberia today and would be expected on rocky peninsula and the sandy plain.

Wetlands
We have noted the presence of a shallow estuary to the north-east of the Rock. Shallow estuarine conditions, usually with associated lagoons and dense aquatic vegetation, are particularly favourable for waterbirds (Finlayson 1992) and would have attracted most of the mammals from the adjacent sandy plain just as similar conditions do in the Coto Doñana (132km NW of Gibraltar) today.

The presence of a large range of waterbirds in Gorham's, Vanguard and Devil's Tower caves (Eastham 1967; Cooper 1999 and pers. comm.) corresponds, in our opinion, to the existence of this wetland.

The Coast
We include the coast as the final element in the range of environments available around the Rock. The evidence from Gorham's and Vanguard Caves indicates the presence of the Monk Seal *Monachus monachus* (Sutcliffe 1999; Currant pers. comm.) during OIS 3. This species is characteristic of the Mediterranean today where its numbers have been reduced almost to extinction in historical times. Coastal areas would have provided additional resources to Neanderthals, specifically molluscs (Barton *et al.* 1999). We will comment further on the coastal environments later in this chapter.

The larger spatial context of the southern Iberian Peninsula

The environmental conditions within the southern Iberian Peninsula are governed today, and in all probability were

Table 15.2: A comparison of the Holocene cliff-dwelling breeding avifauna of southern Iberia (after Finlayson 1992) with that of the OIS 3 sequence based on results from Gorham's, Vanguard and Ibex Caves (after Eastham 1967; Cooper 1999 and pers. comm.).

Species	Holocene Southern Iberia	OIS3 Gibraltar
Shag *Phalacrocorax aristotelis*	Present	Present
Egyptian Vulture *Neophron percnopterus*	Present	Present
Griffon Vulture *Gyps fulvus*	Present	Present
Bearded Vulture *Gypaetus barbatus*	Present*	Present
Golden Eagle *Aquila chrysaetos*	Present	Present
Bonelli's Eagle *Hieraaetus fasciatus*	Present	Present
Lesser Kestrel *Falco naumanni*	Present	Present
Kestrel *Falco tinnunculus*	Present	Present
Peregrine Falcon *Falco peregrinus*	Present	Present
Yellow-legged Gull *Larus cachinnans*	Present	Present
Rock Dove *Columba livia*	Present	Present
Barn Owl *Tyto alba*	Present	Absent
Eagle Owl *Bubo bubo*	Present	Present
Little Owl *Athene noctua*	Present	Present
Pallid Swift *Apus pallidus*	Present	Present**
Alpine Swift *Apus melba*	Present	Present
Crag Martin *Hirundo rupestris*	Present	Absent
Black Wheatear *Oenanthe leucura*	Present	Absent
Blue Rock Thrush *Monticola solitarius*	Present	Present
Chough *Pyrrhocorax pyrrhocorax*	Present	Present
Jackdaw *Corvus monedula*	Present	Present
Raven *Corvus corax*	Present	Present
Rock Bunting *Emberiza cia*	Present	Absent***

*   Extinct this century
**   Either this species or the Swift *Apus apus*
*** A bunting type is recorded from Ibex Cave

also throughout much of OIS 3, by a longitudinal (west to east) rainfall gradient which is modified by altitude (Finlayson 1998). Altitude has the additional effect of modulating temperature so that the altitudinal mosaic of the region generates a telescopic effect on the bioclimatic stages (Figure 15.6). The presence of typically thermo-Mediterranean plants in Gibraltar during the OIS 3 period under consideration signifies that the annual climatic régime must have been controlled, as today, by a protracted period of summer drought with its consequent effects on productivity (Finlayson 1981).

The only other dated comparative evidence currently available is that of Carihuela Cave in Granada (1020m above sea level) which is currently within the meso-Mediterranean bioclimatic régime (Carrión 1992). During the OIS 3 period comparable to the situation described for Gibraltar the highest ground was covered with Mediterranean montane pines (*P.sylvestris/nigra*) with forests of Round-leaved Oaks (*Q.rotundifolia*) on deeper soils in warm situations, a range of scrub vegetation forms dominated by Mediterranean genera in gullies and slopes and riparian vegetation close to streams (Carrión 1992). The evidence strongly indicates a dominance of Medi-terranean vegetation even into high altitudes inland so that the spatial distribution of the bioclimatic stages would have been very similar to today (Figure 15.6). This being

so the expected climatic régime around the Rock would have been characterised by mean annual temperatures of between 17 and 19°C and the mean minima of the coldest month would not have fallen below zero (Rivas-Martinez 1987). The rainfall régime is more difficult to determine as the tolerance levels of Olive, Lentisc and other species found in the caves could also include more arid conditions than those at present. We would therefore expect the régime to be humid or sub-humid with annual rainfall between 600 and 1600mm. Of particular significance in determining the length of the grass growing season, the emergence of plant resources (e.g. autumn and winter fruit; Finlayson 1981) and the dispersion of the fauna would have been the length of the summer dry season. Thus, for example, mammalian herbivore mortality would have been expected to increase during the course of the dry season and many animals would have been expected to con-centrate around receding pools of fresh water. An additional important feature of these environments is the inter-annual variability of the climate characterised by years of drought and others of heavy rainfall, the effects of which would have become apparent as quantitative changes in resource levels. The situation on the higher ground would have been somewhat different. The effect of altitude would have minimized the effect of the summer drought and conditions would have been cooler.

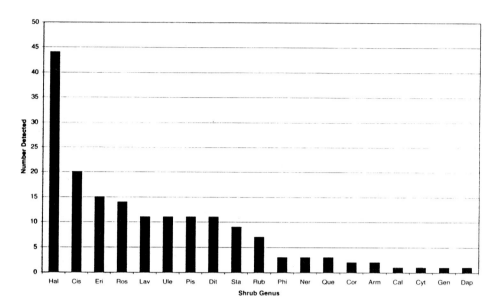

Figure 15.5: Observed ranking of shrub genera (by number detected) in the sites sampled. Key: Hal = Halimium; Cis = Cistus; Eri = Erica; Ros = Rosmarinus; Lav = Lavandula; Ule = Ulex; Pis = Pistacia (=lentiscus); Dit = Dittrichia; Sta = Stauracanthus; Rub = Rubus; Phi = Phillyrea; Ner = Nerium; Que = Quercus (=suber); Cor = Corema; Arm = Armeria; Cal = Calluna; Cyt = Cytisus; Gen = Genista; Dap = Daphne.

Temperature would have played a more important role, especially in reducing the winter growth season, than in the low ground. The conditions on the higher ground would have been complementary to those lower down. These factors would have been critical in the distribution and movement of Neanderthals around their home ranges.

An ecological perspective to the Neanderthal-Modern Human spatio-temporal distribution patterns in southern Iberia

We have compiled a database of all known Middle and Upper Palaeolithic sites in the southern Iberian Peninsula (Appendix 15.1 & 15.2) and these are shown in Figure 15.7. All sites fall within current thermo- and meso-Mediterranean bioclimatic zones. For the Middle Palaeolithic three major spatial regions of occupation may be recognised:

(a) *River Basins*: These are the lower and middle courses of rivers in the west, generally on ground between sea-level and 600m above sea level The sites are related to the exploitation of lithic raw materials and the hunting of fauna. Peripheral sites in the piedmont, between 100 and 600m above sea level appear to be related to movement of groups between river basins. Other sites are related to the exploitation of seasonal faunal resources in lacustrine systems and fall between 50 and 400m above sea level (Giles *et al.* 1999).

(b) *Sub-Betic Range and Intra-Betic Depression*: These are sites of exploitation of lithic raw materials and hunting of fauna and fall between 700 and 2000m

above sea level and many are located in strategic mountain passes which link the previous region from the next one.

(c) *Penibetic Range*: These are characterised by abrupt karstic mountain relief and the narrow coastal strip between Gibraltar and Almería. Altitudes range from sea-level to over 2000m above sea level but not beyond to available heights of over 3000 m above sea level. The majority are cave sites with occupation and evidence of hunting. All known Neanderthal fossils are from this region.

It is not possible without firm dating evidence to precisely correlate these distributions with specific climatic events but we are able to conclude that Neanderthals were widely dispersed across the varied landscapes of southern Iberia. The evidence is indicative of sporadic site occupation (Finlayson *et al.* in prep.) which may well have been seasonal (e.g. in the lakes in the west) or even interannual in cases of severe food shortage. The presence of sites in watersheds would seem to support this view. The Gibraltar Neanderthals, for example, clearly did not confine their activities to the Rock as the nearest source site of one of the raw chert materials used in tool-manufacture was found to be 17km away from the caves. It also seems possible that some of the sites on higher ground were exploited during the summer season through a system of altitudinal migration. Such environments are likely to have been very demanding and were not settled in central Europe before 40ka (Gamble 1993). The mosaic nature of the terrain would have favoured such a régime. The early Neanderthal occupation of the area (as reflected

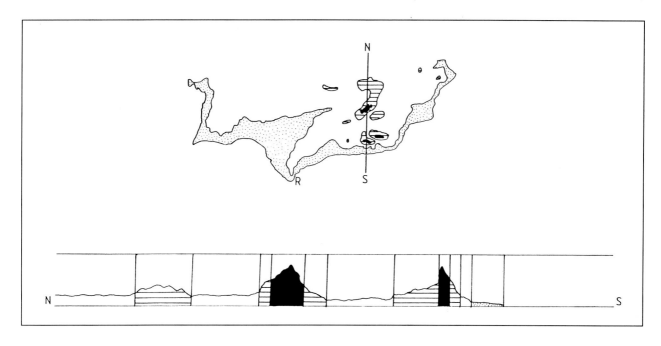

Figure 15.6: Distribution of bioclimatic stages in southern Iberia and a N-S section across the line N-S. Key: R = Rock of Gibraltar; ▢ *= Thermo-Mediterranean;* ▢ *= Meso-Mediterranean;* ▤ *= Supra-Mediterranean;* ■ *= Oro- and Crioro-Mediterranean.*

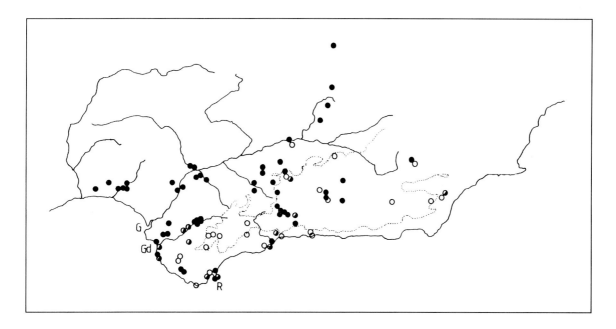

Figure 15.7: Distribution of Middle and Upper Palaeolithic sites in southern Iberia. Key: G = Guadalquivir estuary; Gd = Guadalete estuary; R = Rock of Gibraltar; ● *= Middle Palaeolithic sites;* ○ *= Upper Palaeolithic sites;* ◑ *= Middle and Upper Palaeolithic sites. Note that some points may represent several sites in close proximity. See appendices 1 and 2 for site details.*

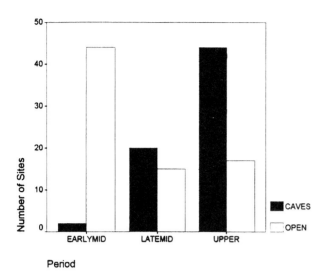

Figure 15.8: Frequency of cave and open-air sites in southern Iberia. Key: EARLYMID = Early Middle Palaeolithic; LATEMID = Late Middle Palaeolithic; UPPER = Upper Palaeolithic.

by an initial type of technology) may be correlated with the last interglacial and is dominated by open air sites (Figure 15.8). Later (Mode 3) Middle Palaeolithic sites show a distinct trend towards the use of cave sites which is presumably connected with the gradual cooling during Isotope Stages 4 and 3. The most extended use of caves occurs in the earliest Upper Palaeolithic which would coincide with the end of OIS 3 and the last glacial maximum (Figure 15.7 & 15.8; Appendix 15.2).

We therefore conclude that the southernmost European Neanderthals were dwellers of open, probably highly seasonal, savanna-type and wetland environments which would be expected to be those with the highest resource yield, combining a large mammal fauna in structurally accessible conditions with a range of alternative potential resources (fruit, seeds, smaller animals and lithic raw materials). They were widely dispersed and probably followed regular seasonal activity cycles related to changing mammalian herbivore biomass. Such activities may have included the exploitation of herbivore concentrations in water holes during the dry season and that of Ibex in the mountains in the summer. Despite often severe and rapid climatic fluctuations their resource world was probably perceived as fairly constant at the human generation timescale, with a very specific range of available prey types. Such environmental constancy, changing only in terms of prey numbers in relation to inter-annual climate fluctuations but not in terms of component species, must have made the Neanderthals seasonal resource specialists capable of hunting large mammals, wildfowl, tortoises, and harvesting plant and marine resources. The evidence from Gorham's and Vanguard Caves supports this view (Barton *et al.* 1999).

Furthermore, the southerly latitudes of these Neanderthals would have permitted a fairly constant year-round activity in response to a relatively uniform daylength pattern, contrasting with the more sharply defined daylength régimes further north.

The situation described is likely to have remained unchanged for much of OIS 3. Towards its end, and coinciding with the onset of colder conditions leading to the last glacial maximum during OIS 2, the environmental conditions in southern Iberia appear to have changed rapidly and dramatically (Finlayson *et al.* in prep.). The bioclimatic belts responded quickly, given their relative spatial proximity along altitudinal gradients, and the open wooded savanna of Gibraltar appears to have been replaced by a denser and less-productive forest of the montane pines (*P. nigra/sylvestris*) characteristic of meso- and supra-Mediterranean stages. At the same time, Mediterranean vegetation practically disappeared from the higher ground which was transformed into an arid steppe (Carrión 1992; Vega-Toscano & Carrión 1993). Such dramatic changes would have significantly altered the resource world of the Neanderthals, only to be partly substituted by the arrival of marine species from the north, e.g. Atlantic Grey Seal *Halichoerus gryphus* and a range of North Atlantic wildfowl, (Finlayson *et al.* in prep.) and may have stressed these last populations beyond recovery. The imminent arrival of modern peoples from the north after a protracted period of entry south of the Ebro River (d'Errico *et al.* 1998) may have exacerbated an already final panorama.

Acknowledgements
The vegetation sampling was conducted by Geraldine Finlayson who also contributed valuable comments to this paper. We are also grateful to the following for their help in the compilation of data and in the field: José María Gutierrez López, Esperanza Mata Almonte, Mario Mosquera, Oscar Prieto, Antonio Santiago Pérez. We thank Professor Stringer, Dr R.N.E.Barton, Andy Currant and all members of the Gibraltar Caves project team for their professionalism and support

References
Antunes, M.T., Cabral, J.M.P., Cardoso, J.L., Pais, J. & Soares, A.M. (1989). *Paleolítico médio e superior em Portugal: Datas* ^{14}C, *estado actual dos conhecimentos, síntese e discussao.* Ciencias da Terra **10**, 127–138.

Asquerino Fernández, M.D. (1988). *Cueva de los Mármoles (Priego de Córdoba). Avance de las campañas de excavación 1.982/ 1.986.* In IFIGEA, **III-IV**, 239–249. Córdoba.

Asquerino Fernández, M.D. (1993). *El Pirulejo (Priego de Córdoba). Informe sobre la campaña de 1991.* Anuario Arqueológico de Andalucía 1991. **II**: 116–119. Actividades Sistemáticas. Sevilla.

Aura Tortosa, J.E. & Villaverde Bonilla, V. (1995). Paleolítico Superior Final y Epipaleolítico en la España mediterránea (18.000–9.000 BP). In (A.Moure & C. Gonzalez, Eds.) *El final del Paleolítico cantábrico,* pp. 313–340 Santander.

Barroso Ruiz, C. & Hublin, J.J. (1994). The Late Neanderthal site of Zafarraya. In (J. Rodríguez Vidal, F. Díaz del Olmo, C. Finlayson, & F. Giles Pacheco, Eds.) *Gibraltar during the Quaternary,* pp. 61–70. Monografías AEQUA, Sevilla.

Barroso Ruíz, C., Hublin, J.J., Medina Lara, F., Rodríguez Vidal, J., & Martín Córdoba, E. (1991). Actuación: excavación arqueológica sistemática. In (C. Barroso, & J.J. Hublin, Eds.) *Proyecto Zafarraya y el reemplazamiento de los neandertales por el hombre anatómicamente moderno en Europa Meridional,* pp. 23–33. Resúmenes de Comunicaciones IV Jornadas de Arqueología Andaluza: Jaén.

Barton, R.N.E., Currant, A.P., Fernandez-Jalvo, Y., Finlayson, J.C., Goldberg, P., MacPhail, R., Pettitt, P.B. & Stringer, C.B. (1999). *Gibraltar Neanderthals and Results of Recent Excavations in Gorham's, Vanguard and Ibex Caves.* Antiquity, in press.

Bond, G.C., Broecker, W.D., Johnsen, S., McManus, J., Labeyrie, L., Jouzel, J. & Bonani, G. (1993). Correlations between climate records from North Atlantic sediments and Greenland ice. *Nature* **365**, 143–147.

Carrión, J.S. (1992). Late Quaternary pollen sequence from Carihuela Cave, southeastern Spain. *Review of Palaeobotany and Palynology* **71**, 37–77.

Castiñeira Sánchez, J.M. & García Rincón, J.M. (1985). Paleolítico Inferior y Medio en la provincia de Huelva. In *Actas I Reunión del Cuaternario Ibérico II*, pp. 61–78. Lisboa.

Castiñeira Sánchez, J.M., Álvarez García, G., García Rincón, J.M., Gómez Toscano, F., Martín Gómez, J & Rodríguez Vidal, J . (1989). Evidencias Paleolíticas en las terrazas de los ríos Tinto y Odiel (Huelva). In (F. Díaz del Olmo, J. Rodríguez, Eds.) *El Cuaternario en Andalucía Occidental. Trabajos de Paleolítico y Cuaternario* pp. 59–66. AEQUA Monografías **1**. Huelva.

Clark. G. (1969). *World Prehistory. A new outline.* Cambridge University Press. 2nd Ed.

Cooper, J. (1998). Cyanopica – a mystery solved. *Bull. Brit. Ornithol. Club* **118**(3), 135.

Cooper, J. H. (1999). A Preliminary Report on the Pleistocene Avifauna of Ibex Cave, Gibraltar. In (J.C. Finlayson, Ed.) *Gibraltar and the Strait during the Quaternary.* Gibraltar Government Heritage Series, Gibraltar. In Press.

Cortés Sánchez, M & Simón Vallejo, M.D. (1995). Cueva Bajondillo (Torremolinos, Málaga). Aportaciones al Paleolítico en Andalucía. In *El món mediterrani després del Pleniglacial (18.000–12.000 B.P.).* Actes du Colloque International: Girona.

Cortés Sánchez, M., Muñóz Vivas, V.E., Sanchidrián Torti, J.L. & Simón Vallejo, M.D. (1996). *El Paleolítico en Andalucía. La dinámica de los grupos predadores en la Prehistoria andaluza. Ensayo de síntesis. Repertorio bibliográfico de 225 años de investigación (1770–1995).* Córdoba.

Cramp, S. & Perrins, C.M. (Eds.) (1994). *Handbook of the Birds of Europe, the Middle East and North Africa. The Birds of the Western Palaearctic.* **VIII**. Oxford University Press: Oxford.

Dansgaard, W., Johnsen, S.J., Clausen, H.B., Dahl-Jensen, D., Gundestrup, N.S., Hammer, C.U., Hvidberg, C.S., Steffensen, J.P., Sveinbjornsdottir, H., Jouzel, J. & Bond, G. (1993). Evidence for general instability of past climate from a 250–kyr ice-core record. *Nature* **364**, 218–220.

Dayan, T. & Simberloff, D. (1996). Patterns of size segmentation in carnivore communities. In (J.L. Gittleman, Ed.) *Carnivore Behavior, Ecology, and Evolution Vol II*, pp. 243–266. Cornell University Press: Ithaca.

d'Errico, F., Zilhao, J., Julien, M., Baffier, D. & Pelegrin, J. (1998). Neanderthal Acculturation in Western Europe? *Current Anthropology* **39** (Suppl.), 1–44.

Díaz del Olmo, F., Vallespí Pérez, E., Baena Escudero, R. & Álvarez García, G. (1991). Bajo Guadalquivir. Terrazas fluviales y secuencia paleolítica. In *Anuario Arqueológico de Andalucía 1989,II*, pp. 17–20. Actividades Sistemáticas: Sevilla.

Díaz del Olmo, F., Vallespí Pérez, E. & Baena Escudero, R. (1992). Formaciones Cuaternarias y Secuencia Paleolítica en el Bajo Guadalquivir. In *Investigaciones Arqueológicas en Andalucía (1985–1992)* pp. 17–20. Proyectos: Huelva.

Eastham, A. (1967). The Avifauna of Gorham's Cave, Gibraltar. *Bull. Inst. Arch. London.* **7**, 37–42.

Finlayson, J.C. (1981). Seasonal distribution, weights and fat of passerine migrants at Gibraltar. *Ibis* **123**, 88–95.

Finlayson, J.C. (1992). *Birds of the Strait of Gibraltar.* T & A D Poyser, Academic Press, London. 534pp.

Finlayson, C. (1994). History of the Gibraltar excavations. In (J. Rodríguez Vidal, F. Díaz del Olmo, C. Finlayson & F. Giles Pacheco, Eds.) *Gibraltar during the Quaternary, 2–5.* Monografías AEQUA: Sevilla.

Finlayson, J.C. (1998). The Role of the Iberian Peninsula in the Palaearctic-African Migration System: Ecological, Evolutionary, Geographical and Historical Considerations at Varying Spatial and Temporal Scales. In (L.T. Costa, H. Costa, M. Araujo, & M.A. Silva, Eds.), *Simpósio sobre aves migradoras na Península Ibérica,* pp. 2–32. Sociedade Portuguesa para o Estudo das Aves: Evora.

Finlayson, C., Mosquera, M. & Finlayson, G. 1997. Birds as Indicators of Climatic and Environmental Change: Current Distribution Patterns in the Iberian Peninsula and Evidence from Pleistocene and Holocene Cave Deposits. In (J. Rodríguez Vidal, Ed.) *Cuaternario Ibérico,* pp. 297–304. AEQUA: Huelva.

Fortea Pérez, F.J. (1986). El Paleolítico Superior y Epipaleolítico en Andalucía. Estado de la cuestión cincuenta años después. *Actas del Congreso Homenaje a Luis Siret (1934–1984).* 67–78.

Fullola Pericot, J.M. (1983). Le Paléolithique Supérieur dans la zone méditerranéenne ibérique. *L'Anthropologie* **87**(3), 339–352.

Gamble, C. (1993). *Timewalkers. The Prehistory of Global Colonization.* Penguin, London. 309pp.

Giles Pacheco, F., Gutiérrez López, J.M., Mata Almonte, E., Santiago Pérez, A. & Gracia Prieto, F.J. (1992a). Secuencia fluvial y paleolítica del río Guadalete (Cádiz). Resultados de las investigaciones hasta 1993. In *Investigaciones Arqueológicas en Andalucía (1985–1992),* pp. 211–227. Proyectos: Huelva.

Giles Pacheco, F., Gutiérrez López, J.M., Santiago Pérez, A., Mata Almonte, E. & Aguilera Rodríguez, L. (1992b). Secuencia paleolítica del Valle del Guadalete. Primeros resultados. *Revista de Arqueología.* **135**, 16–27.

Giles Pacheco, F., Gutiérrez López, J.M., Santiago Pérez, A., Mata Almonte, E., Aguilera Rodríguez, L. & Rodríguez Vidal, J. (1993a). Análisis de la secuencia estratigráfica de la T3 de Majarromaque (cuenca media del río Guadalete, Cádiz). In (M.P. Fumanal, & J. Bernabeu, Eds.), *Estudios sobre Cuaternario. Medios sedimentarios. Cambios ambientales. Hábitat humano.* pp.233–238.Valencia.

Giles Pacheco, F., Mata Almonte, E., Gutiérrez López, J.M., Santiago Pérez, A. & Aguilera Rodríguez, L. (1993b). Secuencia fluvial y paleolítica del río Guadalete (Cádiz). 3a. campaña: Junta de los Ríos-Arcos de la Frontera (1991). In *Anuario Arqueológico de Andalucía 1991, II*, pp.75–82. Actividades Sistemáticas: Sevilla.

Giles Pacheco, F., Santiago Pérez, A., Gutierrez López, J.M., Mata Almonte, E. & Aguilera Rodriguez, L. (1994). Nuevas aportaciones a la secuencia del Paleolítico superior en Gibraltar y su enmarque en el contexto suroccidental de la Península Ibérica. In (J. Rodríguez Vidal, F. Díaz del Olmo, C. Finlayson, & F. Giles Pacheco, Eds.) *Gibraltar during the Quaternary,* pp.91–101. Monografías AEQUA: Sevilla.

Giles Pacheco, F., Santiago Pérez, A., Mata Almonte, E. , Aguilera Rodríguez, L. & Gutiérrez López, J.M. (1999). Prospecciones arqueológicas superficiales en la cuenca del río Guadalete (Cádiz). Análisis geocronológicos y sedimentológicos. 6a. Campaña (1994): Villamartín-Puerto Serrano. In *Anuario Arqueológico Andalúz.*. Junta de Andalucía: Sevilla.

Goodwin, D. (1976). *Crows of the World*. Cornell University Press, Ithaca. 354pp.

Guthrie, R.D. (1984). Mosaics, Allelochemics and Nutrients. In (P.S. Martin & R.G. Klein, Eds.), *Quaternary Extinctions. A Prehistoric Revolution*, pp. 259–298. University of Arizona Press: Tucson.

Gutiérrez López, J.M., Santiago Pérez, A., Giles Pacheco, F., Gracia Prieto, F.J. & Mata Almonte, E. (1994). Áreas de transformación de recursos líticos en glacis de la depresión de Arcos de la Frontera (Cádiz). In (J.F. Jordá, Ed.), *Geoarqueología*, pp. 305–316. Actas 2a Reunión Nacional de Geoarqueología: Madrid.

Hagemeijer, W.J.M. & Blair, M.J. (Eds.). (1997). *The EBCC Atlas of European Breeding Birds. Their Distribution and Abundance*. T & A D Poyser, Academic Press: London. 903pp.

Hanby, J.P. & Bygott, J.D. (1979). Population Changes in Lions and other predators. In (A.R.E. Sinclair & M. Norton-Griffiths, Eds.) *Serengeti. Dynamics of an Ecosystem*, pp. 249–262. University of Chicago Press: Chicago.

Hublin, J.J., Barroso Ruiz, C., Medina Lara, P., Fontugne, M. & Reyss, J-L. (1995). The Mousterian site of Zafarraya (Andalucía, Spain): Dating and implications on the Paleolithic peopling processes of Western Europe. *Comptes Rendus de l'Académie des Sciences de Paris 2*, **321**, 931–937.

Jordá Pardo, J.F. (1986). La Cueva de Nerja en su entorno geográfico. Trabajos sobre la Cueva de Nerja 1. In *La Prehistoria de la Cueva de Nerja (Málaga). Paleolítico y Epipaleolítico*, pp. 21–28. Málaga.

McManus, J.F., Bond, G.C., Broecker, W.S., Johnsen, S., Labeyrie, L. & Higgins, S. (1994). *High-resolution climate records from the North Atlantic during the last interglacial. Nature* **371**, 326–329.

Morel, G. (1968). *Contribution a la synecologie des oiseaux du Sahel Senegalais*. Memoires ORSTOM: Paris. 179pp.

Owen-Smith, R.N. (1988). *Megaherbivores. The influence of very large body size on ecology*. Cambridge University Press: Cambridge. 369pp.

Purroy, F.J. (1997). (Ed.). *Atlas de las aves de España (1975–1995)*. Lynx Edicions: Barcelona.

Raposo, L & Cardoso, J.L. (1998). Las industrias líticas de la gruta nova de Columbeira (Bombarral, Portugal) en el contexto del musteriense final de la Península Ibérica. *Trabajos de Prehistoria*, **55**(1), 39–62.

Ripoll López, S. (1986). *El Solutrense de Cueva de Ambrosio (Vélez-Blanco, Almería): Campaña de 1963*. Excavaciones Arqueológicas en España, nº168: Madrid.

Rivas-Martinez, S. (1981). Les Étages Bioclimatiques de la Végétation de la Péninsule Ibérique. *Actas III Congr. Optima. Anales Jard. Bot. Madrid*. **37**(2), 251–268.

Rivas-Martinez, S. (1987). *Memoria del Mapa de Series de Vegetación de España*. ICONA: Madrid. 268pp.

Rodríguez Vidal, J. & Gracia Prieto, F.J. 1994. Landform analysis and Quaternary processes of the Rock of Gibraltar. In (J. Rodríguez Vidal, F. Díaz del Olmo, C. Finlayson & F. Giles Pacheco Eds.) *Gibraltar during the Quaternary*, pp.12–20. Monografías AEQUA: Sevilla.

Rose, E.P.F. & Rosenbaum, M.S. (1991). *A Field Guide to the Geology of Gibraltar*. The Gibraltar Museum, Gibraltar. 192pp.

Rose, E.P.F. & Hardman, E.C. (1994). *Quaternary geology of Gibraltar*. In (J. Rodríguez Vidal, F. Díaz del Olmo, C. Finlayson & F. Giles Pacheco Eds.) *Gibraltar during the Quaternary*, pp. 21–25. Monografías AEQUA: Sevilla.

Sanchidrian Torti, J.L. (1981). *Cueva Navarro (Cala del Moral, Málaga)*. Corpus Artis Rupestris. I-Palaeolithica Ars, Vol.1. Salamanca.

Sinclair, A.R.E. (1995). Equilibria in Plant-Herbivore interactions. In (A.R.E. Sinclair, & P. Arcese Eds.), *Serengeti II. Dynamics, Management, and Conservation of an Ecosystem*, pp. 91–114. University of Chicago Press, Chicago.

Stringer, C.B. (1994). *The Gibraltar Neanderthals*. In (J. Rodríguez Vidal, F.Díaz del Olmo, C. Finlayson & F. Giles Pacheco Eds.) *Gibraltar during the Quaternary*, pp. 57–60. Monografías AEQUA: Sevilla.

Stringer, C.B., Barton, R.N.E., Currant, A.P., Finlayson, J.C., Goldberg, P., MacPhail, R. & Pettitt, P.B. (1999). *Gibraltar Palaeolithic revisited: new excavations at Gorham's and Vanguard Caves 1995-7*. In (W.Davies & R.Charles Eds.) *Dorothy Garrod and the Progress of the Palaeolithic: Studies in the Prehistoric Archaeology of the Near East and Europe*, pp.84–96. Oxford: Oxbow.

Sunquist, M.E. & Sunquist, F.C. (1989). *Ecological Constraints on Predation by Large Felids*. In (J.L. Gittleman, Ed.) *Carnivore Behavior, Ecology, and Evolution. Vol I*, pp.283–301. Cornell University Press: Ithaca.

Sutcliffe, A.J. (1999). Gorham's Cave, Gibraltar. Faunal Report. In (J.C. Finlayson, Ed.), *Gibraltar and the Strait during the Quaternary*. Gibraltar Government Heritage Series, Gibraltar. In Press.

Tchernov, E. (1984). Faunal Turnover and Extinction Rate in the Levant. In (P.S. Martin & R.G. Klein, Eds.) *Quaternary Extinctions. A Prehistoric Revolution*, pp. 528–552. University of Arizona Press: Tucson.

Toro Moyano, I. & Almohalla Gallego, M. (1985). Descubrimiento de industria del Paleolítico Superior en la provincia de Granada. El yacimiento Solutrense de la "Cueva de los Ojos" (Cozvíjar, Granada). *Actas XVII Congreso Nacional de Arqueología*. 97–104.

Tutin, T.G., Heywood, V.H., Burges, N.A., Moore, D.M., Valentine, D.H., Walters, S.M. & Webb, D.A. (1968). *Flora Europaea. Vol.2. Rosaceae to Umbilliferae*. Cambridge University Press: Cambridge. 455pp.

Tutin, T.G., Heywood, V.H., Burges, N.A., Moore, D.M., Valentine, D.H., Walters, S.M. & Webb, D.A. (1972). *Flora Europaea. Vol.3. Diapensiaceae to Myoporaceae*. Cambridge University Press: Cambridge. 370pp.

Valdés, B, Talavera, S. & Fernández-Galiano, E. (1987). *Flora Vascular de Andalucía Occidental. Vol. 2*. Ketres, Barcelona. 640pp.

van Andel, T.H. & Tzedakis, P.C. (1998). Priority and opportunity: reconstructing the European Middle Palaeolithic climate and landscape. In (J. Bayley, Ed.) *Science in Archaeology – an agenda for the future*, pp. 37–45. English Heritage.

Vega-Toscano, L.G. & Carrión, J.S. (1993). Secuencia paleoclimática y respuesta vegetal durante el Pleistoceno superior de la cueva de la Carihuela (Píñar, Granada, SE de España). *Estudios sobre Cuaternario*, pp.131–138.

Vega Toscano, L.G., Hoyos Gómez, M., Ruiz Bustos, A. & Laville, H. (1988). La séquence de la Grotte de la Carihuela (Píñar, Grenade): Chronostratigraphie et Paléoécologie du Pléistocène Supérieur au Sud de la Péninsule Ibérique. In (M. Otte, Ed.) *L'Homme de Néandertal, 2*, pp.169–180. L'Environnement: Liege.

Waechter, J. d'A. (1964). The excavation of Gorham's Cave. Gibraltar, 1951-1954. *Bull. Inst. Archaeology* **4**, 189–221.

Zilhao, J. (1993). Le passage du Paléolithique moyen au Paléolithique supérieur dans le Portugal. In (V. Cabrera Valdes, Ed.), *El origen del hombre moderno en el Suroeste de Europa*, pp.127–145. UNED: Madrid.

Zilhao, J. (1995). *O Paleolítico Superior da Estremadura Portuguesa*. PhD. Diss., University of Lisbon.

Appendix 1: List of southern Iberian Middle Palaeolithic Sites

Location	Industry
1. Cueva Zájara II (Cuevas del Almanzora, Almería).	Middle Palaeolithic Mode 3*
2. Cueva Umbría de Fuentenueva (Orce, Granada).	Middle Palaeolithic
3. Cueva Horá (Darro, Granada).	Middle Palaeolithic Early
4. Cueva de la Cariguela (Piñar, Granada).	Middle Palaeolithic Mode 3
5. Cueva Colomera (Atarfe, Granada).	Middle Palaeolithic Mode 3
6. Cueva de los Mármoles (Priego de Córdoba, Córdoba).	Middle Palaeolithic Mode 3
7. Cueva de los Murciélagos (Zuheros, Córdoba).	Middle Palaeolithic Mode 3
8. Cueva del Ángel (Lucena, Córdoba).	Middle Palaeolithic Mode 3
9. Cueva de las Grajas (Archidona, Málaga).	Middle Palaeolithic Mode 3
10. Cueva del Boquete de Zafarraya (Alcaucín, Málaga).	Middle Palaeolithic Mode 3
11. Complejo Humo (Málaga).	Middle Palaeolithic Mode 3
12. Cueva Bajondillo (Torremolinos, Málaga).	Middle Palaeolithic Mode 3
13. Gorham?s Cave (Gibraltar).	Middle Palaeolithic Mode 3
14. Devil?s Tower (Gibraltar).	Middle Palaeolithic Mode 3
15. Forbes Quarry (Gibraltar).	Middle Palaeolithic Mode 3
16. Genista 1 (Gibraltar).	Middle Palaeolithic Mode 3
17. Majarromaque (Jerez de la Frontera, Cádiz).	Middle Palaeolithic Early
18. Tarazona 2 (Sevilla).	Middle Palaeolithic Early
19. Alto valle del río Guadalhorce (Villanueva del Rosario, Málaga).	Middle Palaeolithic Early
20. Ventorrillo del Cojo (Villanueva del Rosario, Málaga).	Middle Palaeolithic Early
21. Cuarterones (Villanueva del Rosario, Málaga).	Middle Palaeolithic Early
22. La Dehesa (Escacena del Campo, Huelva).	Middle Palaeolithic Early
23. Río Chanza (Escacena del Campo, Huelva).	Middle Palaeolithic Early
24. El Grillito (Gibraleón, Huelva).	Middle Palaeolithic Early
25. La Barca (Cartaya, Huelva).	Middle Palaeolithic Early
26. La Dehesa (Lucena del Puerto, Huelva).	Middle Palaeolithic Early
27. Gravera del Apeadero (Niebla, Huelva).	Middle Palaeolithic Early
28. El Mentidero (Palos de Moguer, Huelva).	Middle Palaeolithic Early
29. Cueva del Higueral de Valleja (Arcos de la Frontera, Cádiz).	Middle Palaeolithic Mode 3
30. Laguna de los Tollos (El Cuervo, Cádiz).	Middle Palaeolithic Mode 3
31. La Escalera 1 (Arcos de la Frontera, Cádiz).	Middle Palaeolithic Mode 3
32. La Escalera 2 (Arcos de la Frontera, Cádiz).	Middle Palaeolithic Mode 3
33. La Arenosa (San José del Valle, Cádiz).	Middle Palaeolithic Mode 3
34. El Santiscal (Arcos de la Frontera, Cádiz).	Middle Palaeolithic Early
35. Pantano de Bornos (Bornos, Cádiz).	Middle Palaeolithic Mode 3
36. El Tesorillo (Jerez de la Frontera, Cádiz).	Middle Palaeolithic Early
37. Gravera del Torno (El Torno, Cádiz).	Middle Palaeolithic Early
38. Lomopardo (Jerez de la Frontera, Cádiz).	Middle Palaeolithic Early
39. Laguna de Medina. Niveles de suelos rojos (Medina, Cádiz).	Middle Palaeolithic Mode 3
40. Finca de las Yeguas (Puerto Real, Cádiz).	Middle Palaeolithic Mode 3
41. Puente de Hierro (San Fernando, Cádiz).	Middle Palaeolithic Mode 3
42. La Laguna (Villamartín, Cádiz).	Middle Palaeolithic Early
43. Cruce de las Cabezas (Villamartín, Cádiz).	Middle Palaeolithic Early
44. Laguna Estación (Villamartín, Cádiz).	Middle Palaeolithic Early
45. Almendrillo-Cortijo de Picas (Villamartín, Cádiz).	Middle Palaeolithic Early
46. Cortijo de las Gateras (Villamartín, Cádiz).	Middle Palaeolithic Early
47. Soledad (Bornos, Cádiz).	Middle Palaeolithic Mode 3
48. Higuerón (Villamartín-Puerto Serrano, Cádiz).	Middle Palaeolithic Early
49. Carpintero (Puerto Serrano, Cádiz).	Middle Palaeolithic Early
50. Rancho de Gachas (Puerto Serrano, Cádiz).	Middle Palaeolithic Early
51. Glacis de las Cerillas (Puerto Serrano, Cádiz).	Middle Palaeolithic Early
52. Pelarranas (Puerto Serrano, Cádiz).	Middle Palaeolithic Early
53. El Coto (Puerto Serrano, Cádiz).	Middle Palaeolithic Early
54. Hacienda Siret (Puerto Serrano, Cádiz).	Middle Palaeolithic Early
55. Hacienda Siret-Corte de la Carretera (Puerto Serrano, Cádiz).	Middle Palaeolithic Early
56. Cortijo de la Perdíz, Norte (Villamartín, Cádiz).	Middle Palaeolithic Early
58. Cortijo de la Mediana (Villamartín, Cádiz).	Middle Palaeolithic Early
59. Cortijo del Novillero (Villamartín, Cádiz).	Middle Palaeolithic Early
60. Venta Alta (El Puerto de Santa María, Cádiz).	Middle Palaeolithic Early
61. Carretera La Barrosa (Chiclana, Cádiz).	Middle Palaeolithic Mode 3
62. Laguna de la Janda (Tahivilla, Cádiz).	Middle Palaeolithic Mode 3
63. Cerro de las Viñas (Priego de Córdoba, Córdoba).	Middle Palaeolithic Mode 3
64. El Monte (Priego de Córdoba, Córdoba).	Middle Palaeolithic Mode 3
65. Cueva Alma Cholones (Priego de Córdoba, Córdoba).	Middle Palaeolithic Mode 3
66. Cueva de Beida (Cuevas de San Marcos, Málaga).	Middle Palaeolithic Mode 3

Appendix 1: continued.

67.	Abrigo del Pantano de Cubillos (Granada).	Middle Palaeolithic Mode 3
68.	Alto Corbones (Puebla de Cazalla, Sevilla).	Middle Palaeolithic Early
69.	Bajo Corbones (Carmona, Sevilla).	Middle Palaeolithic Early
70.	El Saltillo (Sevilla).	Middle Palaeolithic Early
71.	Arroyo El Rubio (Carmona, Sevilla).	Middle Palaeolithic Early
72.	Morillo (Carmona, Sevilla).	Middle Palaeolithic Early
73.	Arroyo Graneros (Sevilla).	Middle Palaeolithic Early
74.	Arroyo Las Pipas (Sevilla).	Middle Palaeolithic Early
75.	Arroyo Los Espartales (Sevilla).	Middle Palaeolithic Early
76.	Ribera del Huezman (Sevilla).	Middle Palaeolithic Early
77.	San Roque (Guadalquitón?Borondo, Cádiz).	Middle Palaeolithic Mode 3
78.	Punta del Almirante (Algeciras, Cádiz).	Middle Palaeolithic Mode 3
79.	La Barrosa (Chiclana, Cádiz).	Middle Palaeolithic Mode 3
80.	Ibex Cave (Gibraltar)	Middle Palaeolithic Mode 3
81.	Vanguard?s Cave (Gibraltar)	Middle Palaeolithic Mode 3

Sources: Asquerino Fernandez (1988); Barroso Ruiz *et al.* (1991); Castiñeira Sánchez & García Rincón (1985); Castiñeira *et al.*(1989); Cortés Sánchez & Simón Vallejo (1995); Cortés Sánchez *et al.* (1996); Díaz del Olmo *et al.* (1991; 1992); Giles Pacheco *et al.* (1992 a & b; 1993 a & b; 1999); Gutiérrez López *et al.* (1994); Vega Toscano *et al.* (1988).

*Mode 3 follows the nomenclature in Clark (1969).

Appendix 2: List of southern Iberian Upper Palaeolithic Sites.

	Location	Industry
1.	Gorham's Cave (Gibraltar)	Aurignacian?/Solutrean/ Gravettian
2.	Goats Hair Cave (Gibraltar)	Solutrean?/Gravettian
3.	Martin's Cave (Gibraltar)	Solutrean
4.	Sewell's Cave (Gibraltar)	Solutrean?/Gravettian
5.	Cueva Serrón (Antas, Almería)	Solutrean
6.	Cueva de los Morceguillos (Lubrín, Almería)	Solutrean
7.	Cueva Ambrosio (Vélez Blanco, Almería)	Solutrean
8.	Cueva de Almaceta (Lúcar, Almería)	Solutrean
9.	Peñas Blancas (Escúllar, Almería)	Solutrean
10.	Cueva del Morrón (Torres, Jaén)	Solutrean
11.	Pantano de Cubillas (Albolote, Granada)	Solutrean
12.	Cueva de Malalmuerzo (Moclin, Granada)	Solutrean
13.	Cueva de los Ojos (Cozvíjar, Granada)	Solutrean
14.	Peña de la Grieta (Porcuna, Jaén)	Solutrean
15.	El Pirulejo (Priego de Córdoba, Córdoba)	Solutrean
16.	Cueva del Boquete de Zafarraya (Alcaucín, Málaga)	Solutrean
17.	Cueva de Nerja (Nerja, Málaga)	Solutrean/Magdalenian
18.	Cueva del Higuerón o Tesoro (Rincón de la Victoria, Málaga)	Solutrean/Magdalenian
19.	Cueva de la Victoria (Rincón de la Victoria, Málaga)	Solutrean
20.	Complejo Humo (Málaga)	Solutrean
21.	Cueva Navarro (Málaga)	Solutrean
22.	Cueva Bajondillo (Torremolinos, Málaga)	Aurignacian?/Gravettian/Solutrean
23.	Cueva del Toro o Calamorro (Benalmádena, Málaga)	Solutrean
24.	Cueva de Doña Trinidad (Ardales, Málaga)	Solutrean Art
25.	Cueva de las Vacas o del Tajo de Jorox (Alozaina, Málaga)	Solutrean
26.	Cueva de la Pileta (Benaoján, Málaga)	Solutrean/Magdalenian Art
27.	Cueva de las Motillas (Ubrique, Cádiz)	Solutrean
28.	Cueva del Moro (Tarifa, Cádiz)	Solutrean Art
29.	Cubeta de la Paja (Benalup de Sidonia, Cádiz)	Solutrean
30.	Chorrito (Benalup de Sidonia, Cádiz)	Solutrean
31.	Cuevas de Levante (Benalup de Sidonia, Cádiz)	Solutrean
32.	Cueva del Higueral de Valleja (Arcos de la Frontera, Cádiz)	Solutrean
33.	Nacimiento (Pontones, Jaén)	Solutrean
34.	Cueva de los Mármoles (Priego de Córdoba, Córdoba)	Magdalenian
35.	El Pirulejo (Priego de Córdoba, Córdoba)	Magdalenian
36.	Ermita del Calvario (Cabra, Córdoba)	Magdalenian
37.	Cueva del Hoyo de la Mina (Málaga)	Magdalenian
38.	El Duende (Ronda, Málaga)	Magdalenian
39.	Arenosas (San José del Valle, Cádiz)	Aurignacian?/Solutrean
40.	La Escalera II (Arcos de la Frontera, Cádiz)	Solutrean
41.	Barranco Blanco (Puerto Serrano, Cádiz)	Solutrean Art
42.	VR?7 (Villaluenga del Rosario, Cádiz)	Solutrean Art
43.	Llanos de Don Pedro (Arcos de la Frontera, Cádiz)	Solutrean
44.	Los Frailes (Bornos, Cádiz)	Solutrean/Magdalenian
45.	La Escalera III (Arcos de la Frontera, Cádiz)	Solutrean
46.	El Jadramil (Arcos de la Frontera, Cádiz)	Solutrean
47.	El Pinar (Arcos de la Frontera, Cádiz)	Solutrean
48.	La Escalera I (Arcos de la Frontera, Cádiz)	Solutrean
49.	Cueva del Higueral de Motilla (Córtes, Málaga)	Solutrean
50.	Cueva del Quejigo (Córtes, Málaga)	Solutrean
51.	Cueva del Bombín (Córtes, Málaga)	Solutrean
52.	Casa de Postas (Conil, Cádiz)	Solutrean
53.	Tajo de las Figuras (Benalup de Sidonia, Cádiz)	Solutrean Art
54.	La Fontanilla (Conil, Cádiz)	Solutrean/Magdalenian
55.	Torre del Puerco (Chiclana, Cádiz)	Solutrean
56.	Desembocadura del río Palmones (Algeciras, Cádiz)	Gravettian?
57.	Pinar del Rey (San Roque, Cádiz)	Solutrean
58.	VR'15 (Villaluega del Rosario, Cádiz)	Solutrean Art
59.	Torre del Almirante (Algeciras)	Solutrean
60.	Cueva de las Palomas (Facinas, Cádiz)	Solutrean Art
61.	Atlanterra (Tarifa, Cádiz)	Solutrean Art
62.	Cueva Zájara (Cuevas del Almanzora, Almería)	Early Upper Palaeolithic
63.	Tapada (Torremolinos, Málaga)	Magdalenian

Sources: Aura Tortosa & Villaverde Bonilla (1995); Asquerino (1993); Finlayson (1994); Fortea Pérez (1986); Fullola Pericot (1983); Giles Pacheco et al. (1994); Jordá Pardo (1986); Ripoll López (1986); Sanchidrian Torti (1981); Toro Moyano & Almohalla Gallego (1985).

16

AMS Radiocarbon and Luminescence Dating of Gorham's and Vanguard Caves, Gibraltar, and Implications for the Middle to Upper Palaeolithic Transition in Iberia

P. B. Pettitt and R. M. Bailey

Introduction

The Research Laboratory for Archaeology at Oxford University have made luminescence and AMS radiocarbon measurements of samples from recent excavations in Gorham's and Vanguard caves, the AMS dating using the standard Oxford methods of pretreatment and measurement of samples outlined in Hedges *et al* 1989 and 1992. Preliminary dates have been published in interim reports (Barton *et al* 1999, Stringer *et al* 1999). AMS radiocarbon dates are most important for the Gorham's Cave upper section, in which the Middle to Upper Palaeolithic transition occurs, whilst luminescence dating plays a much more important role in dating the Vanguard Cave sequence given that much of this is out of radiocarbon range. This paper presents results to date, and discusses the implications of these in relation to the following issues:

1. Correlation of the current excavations with Waechter's stratigraphy in Gorham's.
2. The latest Middle Palaeolithic at Gorham's and the Middle to Upper Palaeolithic transition.
3. Sedimentation and chronology in Vanguard Cave.
4. Wider implications of the chronological status of the Gibraltar Caves Research Project.

Gorham's Cave

To date, 17 AMS radiocarbon measurements have been made on 15 samples from the upper area (Area 1) of Gorham's stratigraphy. OxA's –7075 and –7076 date the same piece of charcoal as a quality control method – the two results are statistically the same age, and OxA-205 redates the same sample as OxA-8526, again with statistically identical results. In view of the paucity of bone from these contexts the samples are necessarily of charcoal, usually in the form of discrete lumps but occasionally from well within combustion zones of a broad (palimpsest) or discrete (hearth) nature. The results are listed overleaf and noted on a schematic section illustrated in Figure 16.1.

Correlation with Waechter's stratigraphy

Five ^{14}C measurements were made in the late 1950s and reported by Oakley (1964) as an appendix to Waechter's second field report. Two of these samples originate from Waechter's Layer D, three from his Layer G. As Oakley and Topp collected the samples for dating from Waechter's section in 1957 it is conceivable that they had to rely on photographic evidence for Waechter's nomenclature (Stringer pers. comm.), and because of this some caution must be exercised in interpreting the original Groningen dates.

A correlation of current stratigraphy for the Gorham's upper section with Waechter's Layer D may be attempted with perhaps the greatest degree of confidence. In his original report (1951) Waechter subdivides Layer D into two sublayers, D1 (above) and D2 (below). The former he describes as being "...rather compact and slightly clayey in texture and mixed with charcoal. *At the base there are hearths over the whole area. These hearths were apparently lined with flat water-worn pebbles,* but it was not possible to establish any clear arrangement as the majority of stones were not in their original position. Flint flakes, bones and shells were fairly plentiful." (our emphasis). The latter he describes as "...merely a subdivision of D and comprised the hearth level and the *sands immediately below.*" (our emphasis again). Thus, his Layer D may be taken to comprise a continuous combustion zone underlain by "water-worn" pebbles, directly overlain by "clean yellow sands" of his Layer B and underlain by the sands of his Layer E which are described as being "...markedly lighter in colour than D and contains very little

Context *7 combustion zone*

| OxA-6997 | GORC 96 526 | burnt longbone fragment | $\delta^{13}C=-21.2$ per mil | 25680 ± 280 |

Context *15 discrete patch of carbonised material within* Context *7 combustion zone*

| OxA-7792 | GOR97 7 | charcoal | $\delta^{13}C=-24.5$ per mil | 28680 ± 240 |

Context *9 combustion zone*

OxA-7074	GORC96(511)	charcoal, *Pinus* sp	$^{13}C=-24.2$ per mil	30200 ± 700
OxA-7075	GORC96(512a)	charcoal, *Pinus* sp	$\delta^{13}C=-27.3$ per mil	29800 ± 700
OxA-7076	GORC96(512b)	charcoal, *Pinus* sp	$\delta^{13}C=-25.2$ per mil	30250 ± 700
OxA-7077	GORC96(514)	charcoal	$\delta^{13}C=-24.7$ per mil	29250 ± 650
(GrN-1455	28700 ± 200)			
(GrN-1363	27860 ± 300)			

Context *13a discrete combustion zone*

| OxA-7110 | GORC96(528) | charcoal, *Pinus* sp | $\delta^{13}C=-24.4$ per mil | 29250 ± 750 |

Context *24 sandy lens with remnant of combustion zone in* Context *16 sediment*

| OxA-7857 | GOR97 119 | charcoal | $\delta^{13}C=-22.8$ per mil | 32280 ± 420 |

Context *18 brown silts*

| OxA-7791 | GOR97 132 | charcoal | $\delta^{13}C=-23.9$ per mil | 42200 ± 1100 |
| OxA-7979 | GOR97 167 | charcoal | $\delta^{13}C=-21.7$ per mil | 23800 ± 600 |

Context *18/19 contact*

| OxA-8542 | Sample 1099 | charcoal, *Juniperus/Tetraclinis* | $\delta^{13}C=-24.4$ per mil | 42800 ± 2100 |

Context *19 light sands*

OxA-8541	Sample 928	charcoal, dicotyledonous shrub	$\delta^{13}C=-24.9$ per mil	31900 ± 1400
OxA-8525	Sample 951	charcoal, *Juniperus/Tetraclinis*	$\delta^{13}C=-20.9$ per mil	43800 ± 1300
OxA-205	Sample 952	charcoal, *Pistacea* sp	$\delta^{13}C=-23.4$ per mil	47900 ± 2100
OxA-8526	Sample 952	charcoal, *Pistacea* sp	$\delta^{13}C=-23.7$ per mil	46700 ± 1900

Context *22 combustion zone*

| OxA-6075 | GORC93(240) | charcoal, | $\delta^{13}C=-25.2$ per mil | 45300 ± 1700 |

Context *22d dark brown sandy silt*

| OxA-7790 | GOR97 131 | charcoal | $\delta^{13}C=-24.5$ per mil | ,51700 ± 3300 |

archaeological material" (*ibid*, 85). The sequence, therefore, of Waechter's Layers B, D, and E is a clear parallel to the current upper area stratigraphic units of Contexts 8 (a light brown brecciated sand) at the top, 9 (a continuous combustion zone sitting on Context 10a, a continuous layer of brecciated limestone fragments very well-rounded by erosion, possibly by carnivore urine (Currant pers. comm.) and 11 (light sands). It is conceivable that Waechter mistook the layer of brecciated limestone fragments – highly rounded as they were (PBP pers. obs.) for a deliberate lining for the immediately overlying combustion events. While the archaeological material recovered from Context 9 was poor, it is compatible with an Upper Palaeolithic attribution. Why it was so poor is unclear: this may relate to the small area of material excavated, or to the possibility that it lies towards the periphery of the main Early Upper Palaeolithic activity areas in the cave, e.g. those which Waechter excavated or which lie in the unexcavated areas towards the rear of the cave. The new Oxford radiocarbon measurements for Context 9 are statistically identical to the existing Groningen measurements for Waechter's Layer D, which is strong support for such a stratigraphically-based correlation, and one might tentatively conclude a presence of the Aurignacian on site around 31–28 ka at two standard deviations.

A correlation with Waechter's Layer G is more difficult. From Waechter's account (1951, 85) this is a sand matrix "...*streaky and slightly sticky in texture*...[with] ...*little traces of charcoal on the north side*...[in which] ...*Mousterian flakes, bones and shells are plentiful*". The three Groningen measurements indicate an age for this layer of around 56–44 ka:

GrN-1556	49200 ± 3200 BP
GrN-1473	47700 ± 1500 BP
GrN-1678	47000 (humic fraction).

These results, taken at face value, are in accord with the Oxford measurements from Contexts 19 (light sands), 22 (heterogeneous brown organic layer) and 22D (dark brown sandy silt). Contexts 2a to d, in fact, represent subdivisions of an overall geological unit rich in organic material (Goldberg pers. comm.), and lithics of a Middle Palaeolithic nature are found throughout but are particularly abundant in 22d, in which charcoal and bone is also abundant. Tentatively, then, Waechter's Layer G may be related very broadly to the Context 22a-d units, representing one of the later Mousterian occurrences at Gorham's. Archaeological support for this general correlation is apparent but not entirely unambiguous, however: from Waechter's reports it is clear that a number of lithics from layer G are of a Levallois –often laminar– nature

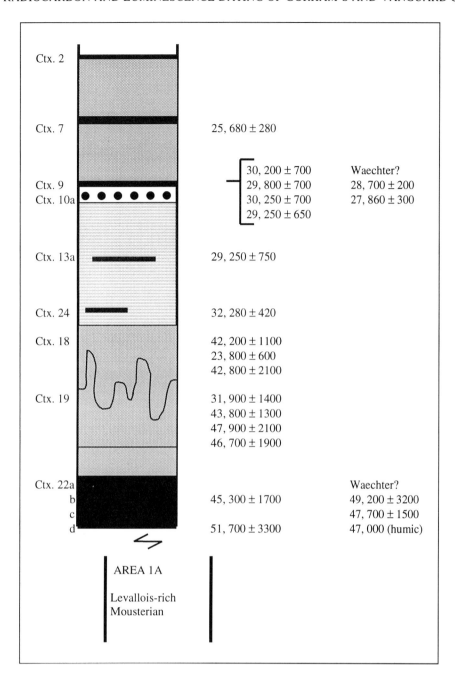

Figure 16.1: Schematic section through Gorham's Cave upper section showing dated contexts and Radiocarbon chronology. Not to scale. Combustion zones expressed as thick black lines, grey shading indicates sand/silt matrices. Note soft sediment loading in Ctx.18/19.

(see for example 1951, Figs. 3, 4, and p.91 where Waechter notes that "...blades seem to be rather characteristic of this level"), the majority of material employed being quartzite, with some chert in evidence (ibid, 87–91), with only a small number of pieces 'finished' (i.e. retouched). Regarding technology, Waechter notes that only one 'tortoise' (i.e. classic Levallois) core was recovered and that most cores were "generally rather shapeless". In addition he found that several quartzite pebbles had been

brought to the area, but were unworked. Context 22 in the recent excavations contained abundant charcoal lumps apparently not clustered in any one area, abundant bones of highly fragmentary nature, and lithics dominated by chert, with quartzite less abundant (PBP pers. obs.). Retouched pieces were certainly rare – a finely worked Mousterian Point being one exception – and techno-logically the discoidal technique seems to be the most commonly employed. In fact, the uppermost occurrence

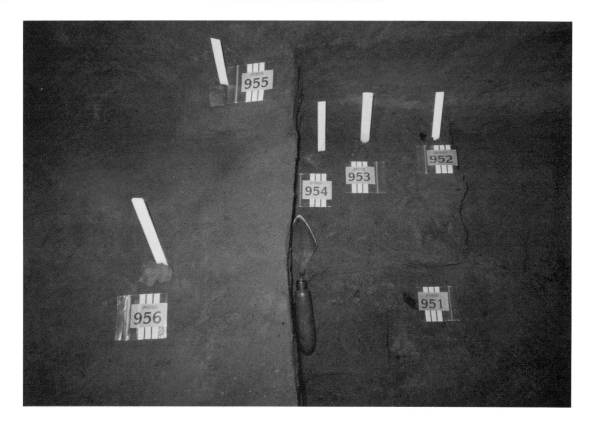

Figure 16.2: Context 19 sediments in Gorham's Cave showing samples taken for radiocarbon dating (author's photograph).

of a Levallois product was found just below the surface of 22d in gridsquare B101 during surface cleaning prior to excavation of the underlying level. Thus, in terms of stratigraphic observations, lithic raw materials, and technology, it is conceivable that Waechter's Layer G equates broadly with Context 22 *sensu lato*, although one cannot eliminate the possibility of a correlation with deposits underlying Context 22 which also contain similar lithic items.

If these correlations are correct, the general picture is of a relatively late Middle Palaeolithic at Gorham's Cave, employing discoidal and occasionally Levallois technology between 56 – 44 ka, and an Aurignacian present between 31 – 28 ka.

The latest Middle Palaeolithic and the transition in Gorham's Cave

The uppermost diagnostically Middle Palaeolithic assemblage was recovered from Context 18 and (mainly) 19. These deposits are of light sand which has clearly been subject to soft sediment loading distortion, and some degree of vertical movement of recovered archaeology seemed inevitable from the outset. Samples taken for AMS radiocarbon dating either took the form of discrete charcoal lumps in apparent association with diagnostic lithics (Figure 16.2), or of charcoal taken from well-within the remnant of a combustion zone ('hearth' – Context 24) at the contact of Contexts 16 and 18. The result for the latter

sample – OxA-7857, provides only a *terminus ante quem* for the Gorham's Cave Middle Palaeolithic of *c.* 33–31 ka, as the only potentially 'securely' associated archaeological find for this dated feature is an undiagnostic quartzite denticulate recovered in gridsquare B97, over a metre from the hearth remnant and in a sand matrix. Taken at face value and in conjuction with the measurements for the Aurignacian of Layer D and (one assumes) Context 9, this would suggest that the Middle to Upper Palaeolithic transition is reflected at Gorham's one or two millennia around 31 ka .

The dating of the uppermost diagnostically Middle Palaeolithic level – Context 18/19 – is problematic but is not inconsistent with this chronology. It can be seen that there is a considerable age range within the seven samples dated from these Contexts, which clearly indicates stratigraphic mobility, as was suspected through stratigraphic observation. This is not surprising given that all of these samples are small, isolated lumps of charcoal which are prone to stratigraphic mobility: these samples were dictated not by choice, but by the lack of any other more suitable samples.

There are two clear outliers in a selection of samples which otherwise demonstrate an age range of *c.* 50 – 40 ka for Contexts 18 and 19. OxA-7791, which dates a charcoal sample from within Context 18 is clearly too young and must therefore be intrusive from above. OxA-8541 from Context 19, dates the charred remains of a dicotyledonous shrub which was associated spatially with samples dated by OxA's -8525 and -8526, all of which were found in close proximity to a pseudo-Levallois flake. That the determinations on the latter two samples are statistically the same is encouraging, but the under-estimation of OxA-8541 demonstrates again the problems of intrusiveness in cave deposits. If one is justified in ignoring these two measurements, the remaining results indicate an age of between 50 – 40 ka for the Context 18/19 archaeology, and were themselves found in close proximity to diagnostically Middle Palaeolithic lithics, specifically a discoidal core and characteristic products of discoidal technology in the case of OxA's -8525 and -8526. The lithic assemblage of this level is dominated by discoidal technology produced overwhelmingly on quart-zite. If one takes the AMS results at face value, then the archaeologically sterile deposits between the Context 13a combustion zone at *c.* 31–28 ka and the uppermost date Middle Palaeolithic represent a radiocarbon-dated age of between 9 and 22 ka. Clearly the archaeological and chronological resolution of the Gorham's Cave upper section is not of a precision as to allow a more informative picture of the Middle to Upper Palaeolithic transition.

Vanguard Cave

AMS radiocarbon dates

It became apparent from a small pilot sample group that most of the sediments in Vanguard Cave were beyond the range of radiocarbon dating. The six AMS radiocarbon results, shown below, for this site therefore relate solely to the uppermost sedimentary units, and luminescence dating plays a far more important role in establishing a chronological scheme than for Gorham's Area 1.

The sedimentary units from which these samples originate remain Middle Palaeolithic, and demonstrate simply that the Middle Palaeolithic at Vanguard persisted to as late as 40 ka, i.e. the time in which the uppermost Middle Palaeolithic at Gorham's was being deposited. In all, the set of results demonstrates that Vanguard Cave had filled to its present level by *c.* 45 ka, and therefore provided little or no overlap with the Upper Palaeolithic

deposits of Gorham's Cave. It can be seen that, given levels of measurement precision in this time/depth the resulting ages for the important archaeological horizons within units 53–55 (Barton this volume) range from *c.* 40 to 55 ka at two standard deviations. In this case these deposits may be said to be broadly 'contemporary' with the later Middle Palaeolithic deposits within Gorham's Cave.

The Alcove

Traces of human activity in the Vanguard Cave Alcove were rare. An exception was a discrete combustion zone (hearth), from which a fragment of charcoal was sampled. The result is as follows:

OxA-7078   VAN-N96 351   charcoal, *Pinus* sp $\delta^{13}C$ =-23.9 per mil   > 44100

This demonstrates that human activity in the Alcove occurred at *very broadly* the same period as that in the uppermost levels dated by the AMS radiocarbon method and discussed above. In addition to this sample, bones of hyaena were pretreated for dating but were found to contain no collagen: it has been speculated that this may be due to the erosional properties of carnivore urine (Currant pers. comm.).

Luminescence dating of Vanguard Cave deposits: Sample collection

Four sediment samples for luminescence dating were taken from the Vanguard Cave deposits. The material sampled was from finely bedded horizons, previously ascribed to aeolian transport. Sample VAN1 is from the upper area of the cave and was estimated, on the grounds of the AMS radiocarbon dates noted above, to be in the range of 45–50 ka. Samples VAN6 and VAN7 are from the middle part of the sequence, estimated (on stratigraphic grounds) to be approximately 80–90 ka. The final sample, VAN2, from the lower deposits of the cave, was estimated to be associated with Oxygen Isotope Stage 5 *sensu lato*. The following sections provide a brief introduction to the basic principals of luminescence dating and describe the luminescence measurement sequence employed and the results obtained.

Top section, base of spit 3.

OxA-7389	VAN-S 96 377	charcoal		$\delta^{13}C$ =-25.5 per mil	45200 ± 2400
Unit 53					
OxA-6891	VAN-S 96 285a	charcoal, *Juniperus* sp		$\delta^{13}C$ =-22.1 per mil	54000 ± 3300
OxA-6892	VAN-S 96 285b	charcoal, *Pistacea* sp		$\delta^{13}C$ =-22.6 per mil	46900 ± 1500
Unit 54					
OxA-7127	VAN-S96 347	charcoal, *Olea* sp		^{TM13}C =-24.4 per mil	> 49400
Unit 55					
OxA-6998	VAN-S 96 245	charcoal, *Olea* sp		$\delta^{13}C$ =-25.1 per mil	41800 ± 1400
OxA-7191	VAN-S96 230	bone, *Sus* sp.		$\delta^{13}C$ =-15.1 per mil	10170 ± 120

NB: OxA-7191 yielded a low amount of collagen and should be treated with caution – it is certainly an underestimate and should therefore be considered to be a minimum age.

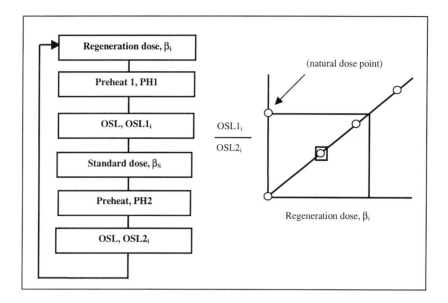

Figure 16.3: The measurement procedure of the Single-aliquot-regeneration method. *Steps 1–6 are repeated n times in order to produce the data points required for interpolation (the first dose â₁ being zero, to give a measure of the natural signal). Typically n=4 (i.e. the natural plus 3 regeneration points). PH1 and PH2 are usually different although Wintle & Murray (1999) report no dependence of Dₑ on either (over the range of 200–280°C). The OSL signal is integrated over the initial part of the decay (to ~10% of initial intensity) and the background is taken as the light level measured either at the end of the OSL measurement or the end of the previous OSL measurement. Two further steps are included to assess the accuracy of the procedure. The first is the re-measurement of the first regenerated data point (indicated by the box in the explanatory figure above). The ratio of the two points (the 'recycling ratio') provides an assessment of the efficacy of the sensitivity correction and the accuracy of the technique (large differences being suggestive of an ineffective technique). The second additional step is a measurement of the regenerated OSL due to zero dose. This value, ideally zero, gives a measure of the degree of thermal transfer (to the trap(s) responsible for OSL) during preheating. The ratio of this value to the natural OSL value (both corrected for sensitivity change) gives the 'thermal transfer ratio' and this is typically in the range of 0.005–0.020. The 'recycling ratio' (ideally unity) is typically in the range 0.95–1.05.*

The luminescence dating: principals and methodology

When ionising radiation (predominantly alpha, beta or gamma radiation) interacts with an insulating crystal lattice (such as quartz), a net redistribution of electronic charge takes place. Electrons are stripped from the outer shells of atoms and though most return immediately, a proportion escape and become trapped at meta-stable sites within the lattice. This charge redistribution continues for the duration of the radiation exposure and the amount of trapped charge is therefore related to both the duration and intensity of radiation exposure.

Even though trapped at meta-stable sites, electrons become 'free' once again under certain conditions (e.g. if the crystal is heated and/or illuminated). Once liberated a free electron may become trapped once again or may return to a vacant position caused by the absence of a previously displaced electron (a 'hole'). This latter occurrence is termed 'recombination' and the location of the hole is described as the 'recombination centre'. As recombination occurs, a proportion of the energy of the electron is dissipated. Depending upon the nature of the centre where recombination occurs, this energy is expelled as heat and/ or light. When the crystal grain is either heated or illuminated following irradiation (the 'dose') the total amount of light emitted (luminescence) is therefore directly related to the number of liberated electrons and available recombination sites. This is the fundamental principle upon which luminescence dating is based. In cases where the duration of dosing is not known (as is the case for dating), estimates can be made from laboratory measurements. The response (the sensitivity) of the sample to radiation dose (i.e. the amount of light observed for a given amount of laboratory radiation, usually α-radiation) must be established. From this relationship the equivalent radiation exposure required to produce the same amount of light as that observed following the environmental dose can be determined, and is termed the 'equivalent dose' (D_e). The D_e (measured in Gy) is therefore an estimate of the total dose absorbed during the irradiation period. When the dose rate (the amount of radiation per unit time, measured in Gy/ka) is measured (or calculated from measured concentrations of radionuclides), the age of the sample can be calculated: Age = D_e / dose rate. Further details of general luminescence theory can be found in a variety of texts (see for example Aitken, 1985; McKeever, 1985; Aitken, 1998).

Sample preparation comprised the extraction of 125–180μm quartz grains (415–500μm grains in the case of one sample, VAN1) from each of the four samples. The bulk material was initially treated in dilute HCl to remove carbonate material. Minerals with a density greater than 2.68 gcm⁻³ were subsequently removed with a sodium polytungstate solution. Following density separation, treatment with 40% hydrofluoric acid, for one hour, was used to remove the outer (naturally α-irradiated) layer of each grain. Sample purity (with regard to feldspar contamination) was monitored using infra-red stimulated luminescence (IRSL).

The environmental dose rate for each sample was calculated using the concentrations of U, Th and K (in each of the samples), as measured by inductively couple plasma mass spectrometry (ICPMS). Luminescence measurements were performed using an automated Risø reader. OSL excitation was provided by a 75W filtered halogen lamp attachment (HA3, 3xGG420 and a broad band interference filter, providing blue-green stimulation between 420 and 560 nm). Luminescence was detected in the UV region, using an EMI 9635Q bialkali photo-multiplier tube, filtered with two Hoya U340 glass filters. Measurement of the equivalent dose (D_e) was made using the Single Aliquot Regeneration (SAR) procedure of Murray & Wintle (1999). The SAR method is a re-generation procedure in which the light level of the natural signal is converted into an equivalent dose via an interpolation between regenerated (i.e. known dose) points. The natural and regenerated signals are measured using the same aliquot. Sensitivity change between each measure-ment cycle is monitored in the SAR method (for each aliquot) following each OSL measurement ($OSL1_i$) using the OSL response to a common test dose ($OSL2_i$). Plots of $OSL1_i/OSL2_i$ provide the necessary (sensitivity change corrected) data for interpolation. The procedure is further outlined in Figure 16.3.

The determination of D_e for each sample was performed using six or more sample aliquots. All OSL measurements were made at 160°C for 100s. The signal in the first 2s (with the stable background count rate from the last 20s subtracted) was normalized using the OSL signal re-generated by a 4.7 Gy beta dose ($β_s$). Preheating (PH1) at 260°C for 10s was used following the regenerative dose ($β_i$). A preheat (PH2) of 220°C for 20s was used following the 4.7Gy standard dose.

Results

The results of the measurement described in the previous section are summarised in Table 16.1. The environmental dose rate for each sample was calculated using the dose rate conversion factors given by Adamiec and Aitken (1998) and the moisture corrections factors of Aitken 1985 (assuming a moisture content of 10±3%). The contribution of cosmic radiation to the total dose rate was calculated as a function of geomagnetic latitude, altitude and burial depth, according to Prescott and Hutton (1994). However,

Table 16.1: Summary of measurement results. U, Th and K measurements were obtained using ICPMS. The total absorbed dose (equivalent dose, De) was calculated from luminescence measurements using the SAR procedure described in the text.

Sample	Dosimetry				De (Gy)
	U (ppm)	Th (ppm)	K (%)	Total dose rate (G/ka)	
VAN 1	1.2	2.2	0.52	0.78±0.05	36.28±1.03
VAN 7	0.9	2.4	0.45	0.74±0.05	68.65±2.54
VAN 2	0.9	2.8	0.60	0.89±0.06	99.67±5.91

Table 16.2: Summary of age calculation results. Ages were calculated using data summarised in Table 16.1.

Sample	Age estimate code	Age (ka)
1	OxL-1029	46.32±3.30
7	OxL-1030	93.38±7.03
2	OxL-1031	111.85±10.02

the depth of overburden (>200m) was such that the contribution of cosmic radiation to the total (terrestrial) radiation field was negligible. A term for cosmic radiation was therefore not included in the final calculation. All calculations were performed using software developed by one of the authors (RMB), within the Oxford laboratory.

The D_e measurements of samples VAN1,2 and 7 yielded extremely consistent results for each sample, with each sample aliquot exhibiting similar behaviour. This is reflected in the relative statistical uncertainty of the D_e estimates (Table 16.1). The internal consistency check of the SAR procedure (the repeated point ratio) yielded consistently good values for these samples. Repeated regeneration points (following Bailey, 1999) show stability and a proportional relationship between regenerated OSL and measured OSL sensitivity (a requirement for the SAR technique). The results for sample VAN6 were not so encouraging however, with estimates of D_e from individual aliquots being varied and imprecise (estimates of D_e ranging from ~20–80Gy at the 1σ level, with the fractional standard deviation of ~30%). Confidence in the mean D_e from sample VAN6 was therefore regarded as low and no age estimate was made.

The dates obtained for samples VAN1,2 and 7 are shown in Table 16.2. It is satisfying to note that the luminescence ages lie within the range expected. These samples showed no signs of deviation from expected quartz luminescence behaviour and the consequently there is no reason to doubt the validity of these age estimates.

Wider Implications: The Middle To Upper Palaeolithic Transition In Iberia

The chronology of the Middle to Upper Palaeolithic transition in Iberia has played a central role in recent discussions of Neanderthal extinction and its potential relation to the spread of anatomically modern humans through Eurasia. Regionally, this relates specifically to a perceived environmental frontier along the Ebro River and its tributaries (d'Errico et al 1998) and to the Lagar Velho 1 'hybrid' burial of Portugal (Duarte et al 1999), the latter which in radiocarbon terms is contemporary with the Context 7 archaeology in Gorham's. Such studies indicate a relatively late persistence of the Middle Palaeolithic – and one therefore assumes Neanderthals – south of the Ebro. The dating of the upper sequence at Gorham's does not contradict such a view, given that the Middle Palaeolithic there may persist as late as c. 31 ka. The appearance of the Aurignacian between 31 and 28 ka would also fit with a relatively late spread of the Upper Palaeolithic south of the Ebro, i.e. in 'Aurignacian II times'. Thus, the Gibraltar chronology, whilst leaving something to be desired in terms of precision, is entirely consistent with the model proposed by d'Errico et al.

Acknowledgements

The authors gratefully acknowledge the Natural Environmental Research Council for funding the AMS radiocarbon determinations through the Oxford National Facility, Robert Hedges and the staff of the Oxford Radiocarbon Accelerator Unit for general support and for undertaking the measurements.

References

Adamiec G. and Aitken M.J (1998). Dose-rate conversion factors: update. *Ancient TL.* **16**, 37–50.

Aitken M.J. (1985). *Thermoluminescence dating.* Academic Press: London.

Aitken M.J. (1998). *Introduction to Optical Dating.* Oxford University Press.

Bailey R.M. (1999). Circumventing possible inaccuracies of the single-aliquot-regeneration method of quartz OSL. (In press, *Radiation Measurements*).

Barton, R.N.E., Currant, A.P., Fernandez-Jalvo, Y., Finlayson, J. C., Goldberg, P., Macphail, R., Pettitt, P.B. & Stringer, C.B. (1999). Gibraltar Neanderthals and results of recent excavations in Gorham's, Vanguard and Ibex Caves. *Antiquity.* **73**, 13–23.

D'Errico, F., Zilhão, J., Julien, M., Baffier, D. and Pelegrin, J. (1998). Neanderthal acculturation in western Europe? A critical review of the evidence and its interpretation. *Current Anthropology.* **39**, Supplement. S1–S44.

Duarte, C., Maurcio, J., Pettitt, P.B., Souto, P., Trinkaus, E. & Zilhao, J. (1999). An earlier Upper Palaeolithic human skeleton from the Abrigo do Lagar Velho (Portugal) and modern human emergence in Iberia. *Proceedings of the Natural Academy of Sciences (USA).* **96**. 7604–9.

Hedges, R.E.M., Law, I.A., Bronk, C.R. & Housley, R.A. (1989). The Oxford accelerator mass spectrometry facility: technical developments in routine dating. Archaeometry. **31** (2), 99–113.

Hedges, R.E.M., Humm, M.J., Foreman, J., Van Klinken, G.J. & Bronk, C.R. (1992). Developments in samples combustion to carbon dioxide, and in the Oxford AMS carbon dioxide ion source system. *Radiocarbon.* **34** (3), 306–311.

McKeever S.W.S. (1985). *Thermoluminescence of Solids.* Cambridge University Press.

Murray A.S. & Wintle A.G. (in press). Luminescence dating of quartz using an improved single-aliquot regenerative-dose procedure. *Radiation Measurements.*

Oakley, K.P. (1964). Appendix V. *Bulletin of the Institute of Archaeology of London.* **4**. 219.

Prescott J.R. & Hutton, J.T. (1994). Cosmic ray contributions to dose rates for Luminescence and ESR dating: large depths and long term time variations. *Radiation Measurements.* **23**, 497–500.

Stringer, C.B., Barton, R.N.E., Currant, A.P., Finlayson, J.C., Goldberg, P., Macphail, R. & Pettitt, P.B. (1999). Gibraltar Palaeolithic revisited: new excavations at Gorham's and Vanguard Caves. In (W. Davies & R. Charles Eds.) *Dorothy Garrod and the Progress of the Palaeolithic: Studies in the Prehistoric Archaeology of the Near East and Europe,* pp. 84–96. Oxford: Oxbow.

Waechter, J. D'A. (1951). Excavations at Gorham's Cave, Gibraltar: preliminary report for the seasons 1948 and 1950. *Proceedings of the Prehistoric Society.* **17**. 83–92.

Waechter, J. D'A. (1964). The excavations at Gorham's Cave, Gibraltar, 1951–1954. *Bulletin of the Institute of Archaeology of London.* **4**. 189–221.

17

Results of the Current Program of ESR Dating of Gorham's Cave Teeth from the Gibraltar Museum

V. Volterra, H. P. Schwarcz and W. J. Rink

The current program of excavation at Gorham's Cave has unearthed several successive cultural layers, a number of which contain Mousterian artefacts. In an attempt to date these layers, several teeth were obtained from the Gibraltar Museum collection for electron spin resonance (ESR) analysis. These samples were originally reported to have been recovered from four different layers in the site during the original excavation by Waechter (1954).

ESR is a particularly effective technique in such cases because it can be applied successfully to tooth enamel, a material that is almost ubiquitous in archaeological sites (Grün 1989; Ikeya 1980; Rink 1997). Tooth enamel consists mainly of hydroxyapatite in crystalline form and, as such, does not change mineral form during burial. Tooth enamel is as sensitive to radiation as photographic film is sensitive to x-rays. Natural radiation in the form of α and β particles and γ rays arises from the uranium absorbed in teeth after burial, and from the presence of uranium, thorium and potassium in the nearby sediment and rock. Another source of natural radiation is cosmic rays. The radiation sensitivity of all tooth enamel seems to be quite similar, and therefore it is well suited for dating by ESR.

The advantage of ESR over thermoluminescence (TL) or optically stimulated luminescence (OSL) is that no shifting of trapped electrons is involved in testing the specimens and therefore tests on the same sample can be repeated. Furthermore, no pre-treatment, such as heating or light exposure is required to zero the signal (Aitken 1990; Grün 1989).

The ESR technique has proven particularly useful when dealing with sites which have suspected ages near to or beyond the practical limits of radiocarbon dating. This is therefore very important for sites containing Mousterian layers.

The accuracy of ESR dates is comparable with TL/OSL and radiocarbon techniques. It depends on a large number of environmental and other variables which can differ between sites. Examples include the effect of moisture in the sediment, the effectiveness of a and b radiation, the attenuation of cosmic radiation, and the escape of radon and thoron gases. Age determinations by ESR are also limited by the difficulties associated with inhomogeneity of radiation levels at some sites (Rink 1997; Rink *et al.* this volume).

Notwithstanding the above, this method has been successfully applied to numerous archaeological sites (Çetin *et al.* 1994; Hewnning *et al.* 1981; Latham and Schwarcz 1992; Rink *et al.* 1994; Rink *et al.* 1996; Rink and Schwarcz 1994; Rink and Schwarcz 1995; Schwarcz *et al.* 1988a; Scwarcz *et al.* 1988b; Schwarcz *et al.* 1991; Yokoyama *et al.* 1988; Zhou *et al.* 1997).

For example, the efforts of Stringer *et al.* were successful in the case of the Es Skhul cave in spite of the fact that all the material analysed came from the British Museum archives and no *in situ* dosimetry was feasible (Stringer *et al.* 1989). The age established for layer B compared favourably with the ESR and TL dates obtained by others for layers at Qafzeh Cave which are considered coeval on the basis of archaeological material.

The case of Gorham's Cave is similar in that the sample provenance was from museum archives. In Gorham's case however extensive site dosimetry was carried out. The sandy nature and the general homogeneity of radiation levels in Gorham's Cave is ideal for ESR determinations on museum samples, although it is far preferable to work with *in situ* materials.

A total of 13 museum samples from Waechter's layers G, K, M and P were prepared for analysis. Aliquots of each sample were irradiated at the McMaster Reactor facility with a cobalt source at a rate of 13.14 rads/sec and subjected to a maximum dose of 24.06 kilorads. The dose response of each aliquot was then measured in a Bruker

Table 17.1: ESR dates for teeth from Gorham's Cave.

Waechter industry	Waechter level	Sample#	EU ka	LU ka
Mousterian	G	1	29.7 ± 4.4	33.1±5.1
"	"	2	23.6±1.9	26.3±2.3
"	K	5	32.7±2.7	36.2±2.3
"	"	6	36.4±3.4	41.3±4.1
"	"	7	32.5±6.7	37.4±7.9
"	"	9	32.8±2.8	6.3±3.3
"	M	15	34.8±3.0	41.3±3.9
"	"	18	29.5±2.6	34.1±3.1
"	"	21	29.0±2.9	33.0±3.5
"	P	24	31.1±2.5	36.1±3.1
"	"	31	20.7±1.2	25.9±1.7
"	"	33	27.5±2.9	32.8±3.6
Average G-P		35±5	30±5	
?	R	7	56.5±4.9	62.4±5.1

EMX EPR Spectrometer and the dates determined by computer fitting of an appropriate algorithm (Brennan *et al*. 1997).

Like all scientific techniques, dating methods must be applied to the resolution of archaeological problems with due consideration to context since, with very rare exceptions, they are not used to date human remains directly. The use of archival material can always prove problematic in this respect.

As shown in Table 17.1, the dates obtained for tooth samples which reportedly were recovered from the uppermost Waechter Mousterian layer [G] from ESR are 30 ± 6 ka LU and 27 ± 5 ka.Combining the results obtained for all the samples as shown in the Table would yield average ages for the upper Waechter Mousterian layer at 35 ± 5 ka LU and 30 ± 5 ka EU. It would thus appear possible that the samples analysed were, in effect, all originally recovered from the same uppermost Mousterian layer. These model ages will be refined by U-series analysis of the samples currently underway. Unless they reveal a very unusual uranium uptake pattern model ages for these deposits would then range between 25 and 40 ka at the 1 s confidence level.

These seem to be at least partly in the same age range as the lower section being currently excavated by the Stringer team, as they appear to overlap the ^{14}C results obtained on charcoal (Pettitt *et al*. this volume). OSL dates for samples from Stringer's excavation and from levels believed to correlate with Waechter's layers have been completed (Rink *et al*. this volume). These dates range from about 30 ka to > 150 ka. Mass spectrometric U-series dates on crystalline calcite pods found in parts of these same layers give ages in close agreement with OSL dates for the same layers (Rink *et al*. this volume).

The linking of the Waechter and Stringer levels involving ESR dates rests on the ongoing research which involves dating of the *in situ* samples and for which we hope to present results in final form at a later date.

References

Aitken, M.J. (1990). *Science-based dating in archaeology.* Longman: New York.

Brennan, B.J., Rink, W.J., McGuirl, E.L., Schwarcz, H.P. & Prestwick, W.V. (1997). Beta dose in tooth enamel by "One Group' theory and the ROSY ESR dating software. *Radiation Measurements*, **27**, 307–314.

Çetin, O. Ozer, A.M. Wieser, A. (1994). ESR dating of tooth enamel from Karaïn excavation, (Antalya, Turkey). *Quaternary Geochronology*, **13**, 661–669.

Grün, R. (1989). Electron spin resonance (ESR) dating.*Quaternary International*. **1**, 65–109.

Grün, R., Schwarcz, H.P., & Zymela, S. (1987). Electron spin resonance of tooth enamel. *Canadian Journal of Earth Sciences*. **24**, 1022–1037.

Henning, G.J., Herr, W., Weber, E., & Xirotiris, N.I. (1981). ESR dating of the fossil hominid from Petralona cave, Greece. *Nature*. **292**, 533–536

Ikeya, M. (1980). ESR dating of carbonates at Petralona Cave. *Anthropos*. **7**, 143–150.

Latham, A.G. & Schwarcz, H.P. (1992). The Petralona hominid site: uranium series re-analysis of 'Layer 10' calcite and associated paleomagnetic analyses. *Archaeometry*. **34**, 135–140

Rink, W.J., Grün, R., Yalcinkaya, I., Otte, M., Taskiran, H., Valladas, H., Mercier, N. & Schwarcz, H.P. (1994). ESR dating of the last interglacial Mousterian at Karaïn Cave, southern Turkey. *Journal of Archaeological Science*. **21**, (839–849).

Rink, W.J., Schwarcz, H.P., Valoch, K., Seitl, l. & Stringer, C.B. (1996) ESR dating of Micoquian industry and Neanderthal remains at Kulna Cave, Czech Republic. *Journal of Archaeological Science*. **23**, 889–901.

Schwarcz, H.P., Grün, R., Latham, A.G., Mania, D. & Brunnaker, K. (1988a). The Bilzingsleben archaeological site : new dating evidence. *Archaeometry*. **30**, 5–17.

Schwarcz, H.P., Grün, R., Vandermeersch, B., Bar-Yosef, O., Valladas, H. & Tchernov, E. (1988b). ESR dates for the hominid burial site of Qafzeh in Israel. *Journal of Human Evolution*. **17**, 733–737.

Schwarcz, H.P., Buhay, W., Grün, R., Stiner, M., Kuhn, S. & Miller, G.H. (1991). Absolute dating of sites in coastal Lazio – *Quaternaria Nova*. **1**, 51–67.

Stringer, C.B., Grün, R., Schwarcz, H.P. & Goldberg, P. (1989). ESR dates for the hominid burial site of Es-Skhul in Israel. *Nature*. **342**, 756–758.

Waechter, J. d'A. (1954). Excavations at Gorham's Cave, Gibraltar. *Procedings of the Prehistoric Society*: 83–92.

Yokoyama, Y., Falgueres, C. & Bibron, R. (1988) Direct dating of Neanderthalian remains and animal bones by the non-destructive gamma-ray spectrometry: comparison with other methods. In (M. Otte, Ed.), *L'homme de Néandertal, 1*: pp.135–141.

Zhou, L.P., McDermott, F., Rhodes, E.J., Marseglia, E.A. & Mellars, P.A. (1997). ESR and mass-spectrometric uranium-seres dates of mammoth tooth from Standton Harcourt, Oxfordshire, England. *Quaternary Geochronology*. **16**, 445–454.

18

ESR, OSL and U-Series Chronology of Gorham's Cave, Gibraltar

W. J. Rink, J. Rees-Jones, V. Volterra and H. Schwarcz

Introduction

With the dating of Neanderthal remains at Zaffaraya Cave in Southern Spain to less than 30 ka by Hublin *et al.* (1995), and the late dates of Mousterian industries in Portugal that were emerging in the 1980's and 1990's (e.g. d'Errico *et al.* 1998), sites hosting Neanderthals and Mousterian industries in Gibraltar and Southern Spain gained renewed importance among anthropologists and archaeologists. It appeared that the Iberian Peninsula became a refugia or last homeland for the Neanderthals. Renewed dating of these sites with modern techniques became important in considering the fate of the Neanderthals, particularly because the ^{14}C and U-series ages (on bone and teeth) probably only provide minimum ages for these sites. Gorham's Cave, with its well-preserved sequence of Mousterian and Upper Palaeolithic Layers offered good opportunites for refining the chronology of the terminal Mousterian in southern Iberia, as did other well-known sites like Carihuela Cave in Andalucía (Vega Toscano 1993) which is currently being dated with ESR and TL at McMaster University by V. Volterra and co-workers. Vanguard Cave (Barton *et al.* this volume), also being dated at McMaster University, is an important new site whose rich Mousterian deposits were only discovered in 1995 by the team from the Natural History Museum and Brookes University during their excavations at nearby Gorham's Cave.

Gorham's Cave is located at present-day sea level on the east side of Gibraltar. At the beginning of Waechter's excavations in 1948, a sequence of windblown sands with some cemented horizons sloped upward into the cave to a maxiumum elevation of 17 m above sea level. Waechter identified (1951 and 1964) a sequence of sterile and occupational horizons extending upward from a fossil beach (Layer U). Layers T through G were characterised as an alternating sequence of sterile and Mousterian layers, the latter containing abundant mammal fauna. Continuing upward, Layers F through B were recognised as Upper Palaeolithic sequence without sterile horizons, and these were surmounted by terminal Layer A of Punic origin. Rewenewed excavations in Gorham's Cave by the British Museum and Natural History Museum in the 1980's included attempts to relate the present day exposures to Waechter's excavation layers, but this task proved difficult because the only reliable datum found in Waechter's descriptions was that the base of the lowermost occupational Layer (S3) was located at 9.70 m above mean sea level.

The main aim of this study was to make a comprehensive dating intercomparison using three methods relevant to archaeological problems: 1) electron spin resonance (ESR) dating of tooth enamel on both newly excavated teeth found *in-situ* and museum teeth available from the Waechter collections stored at the Gibraltar Museum, 2) optically stimulated luminescence (OSL) dating on the sands enclosing archaeological material, and 3) mass-spectrometric uranium series (MSUS) dating on the cave calcites which occur within the stratigraphic sequence. The reported results were also meant for comparison with ongoing AMS ^{14}C dating on bone and charcoal (Pettitt *et al.* this volume), some of which are at the limit of the ^{14}C dating method at circa 40 ka. We also hoped that the Waechter museum samples for ESR dating might produce useful information on the age of the terminal Middle Palaeolithic here, and potentially help to correlate the present excavation area with that of Waechter's from the 1940's and 1950's (Waechter 1951,1964). This latter work is hampered by the difficulty that proxy values for the dose rates experienced by the teeth must be used because they were not excavated by Waechter expressly for the purpose of ESR dating.

ESR dating of tooth enamel is a technique which yields

the burial age of teeth provided that they are not derived from older contexts. The age estimate is obtained from measurements of the radiation exposure received by the enamel portion of the tooth, and requires no assumptions related to zeroing of any previous radiation exposure. In contrast, OSL dating of the quartz grains in sand is a technique that relies on an assumption that light exposure to grains was strong during their last transport into a stratigraphic horizon. If this light exposure is weak, either in its intensity or duration, then incomplete zeroing of the previous radiation dose will result in an age overestimate. The age obtained corresponds to the last light exposure event that the grains experienced, provided that strong light exposure (in its intensity and duration) occurred. OSL dating is also based on the radiation exposure to the sample during burial. MSUS dating of calcite does not rely on any aspect of radiation exposure from the environment, rather the age is a calculation of the ratios of radiogenic isotopes within the sample. These provide an internal clock since the time of crystallisation of the calcite. The archaeologically relevant aspects of these dating methods was recently described by Rink (1999).

The precision of the radiation exposure methods (ESR and OSL) depends upon aspects of the radiation environment. The environment may be fortuitously well-behaved in one site, whereas it may be problematic in others. In some sites, uranium is mobile in the environment, leading to the situation where uranium migrates into the teeth. At Gorham's Cave, some teeth did, and others did not absorb uranium. For those teeth which contain U, one may reasonably assume that the age falls within the EU-LU range, unless the teeth experienced abnormal uranium uptake histories (see Rink 1997). Those which have not absorbed uranium provide the most reliable ages, but still suffer from the problem of uncertainty in the average moisture content over the entire burial history. For cases where uranium was absorbed, we use ESR age models (early and linear uptake) to estimate the range of age that is most likely for the time of burial of the teeth. The early uptake (EU) age corresponds to the assumption that uranium uptake occurred near the beginning of the burial period, and linear uptake is a model which assumes that the uranium was absorbed continuously and constantly from time zero until the day the tooth was retrieved. These models will eventually be refined on the teeth from Gorham's Cave using MSUS dating on the teeth. However, in this paper we report only MSUS ages for calcites, which are assumed to absorb their uranium at time zero (during crystallisation). Therefore the MSUS ages on calcite are analogous to ESR ages on teeth which have not absorbed any uranium, and are similar to those ESR ages on teeth which prove (by later U-series dating) to have absorbed their uranium very early in the burial history.

In contrast to ESR, uranium series dating provides highly accurate age estimates by use of mass spectrometry, that allow highly accurate measurement of the isotope ratios. Its application is only limited by correct interpret-ation of the relationship between the dated archaeological calcite and the cultural material. Of course, ESR and OSL ages (and ^{14}C ages) can only be correctly interpreted in light of a clear understanding of the site formation processes. Site formation processes are the key informants in the interpretation of the various dating results (Rink, in press), as will become clear as the results are presented below. We note that inferences about the site formation processes can sometimes be obtained from the dating work itself, provided that a significant number of different and independent methods are used in concert.

Sample Procurement and Experimental Methods

During the 1995 field season, WJR and VV collected a series of luminescence (JR95 Gor OSL1 and JR95 Gor OSL3) and U-series (JR95 Gor95 MSUS5–1 and JR95 Gor MSUS1–3) datable samples, all located relative to the Stringer and Barton datum used in 1995. The archaeological team had tentatively correlated these positions with some of the sterile and Mousterian levels of the excavations of Waechter between 1948 and 1954 (Waechter 1951 and 1964), but the correlations with Waechter level designations will not be reported here because they remain uncertain. Two additional luminescence dating samples studied at McMaster (GOR OSL1, GOR OSL2) were collected by the excavators in 1995 and these were also dated and reported herein. Finally, two OSL samples collected from older profiles in the very deepest parts of the exposed sequence at +692 cm and +612 cm above datum were also dated, yielding totally saturated dose response curves, which led to infinite OSL ages. Brief mention of these occurs in the results section for completeness, but full analytical data are not reported here.

In-situ teeth (Gor 43 and 49a) were collected by Stringer and Barton 1995 and 1997 respectively. Gor 49a's location was determined relative to a different datum than that used in 1995.

ESR dating was done using the method described in Rink *et al.* (1994 and 1997), except that beta radiation dose rates to enamel were obtained using the results of One-Group Theory incorporated into the ROSY ESR dating software (Brennan *et al.* 1997 and in press). Although gamma scintillometry was carried out for OSL dating positions, gamma doses to tooth enamel were estimated using neutron activation analysis of sediment collected within 5 cm of the teeth (analytical data are given in Table 18.1. The same sediment attached to recently excavated teeth was used for the beta dose calculations to tooth enamel. For museum teeth (Volterra *et al.* this volume), we assumed that sediments collected in areas thought to be correlated to Waechter's inked designations on teeth were appropriate for calculating beta and gamma dose rates to those teeth, those these correlations remain uncertain. Specific samples were also

Table 18.1: ESR Dating Results and Analytical Data for Gorham's Cave Teeth Recovered in 1995 and 1997.

McMaster No.	Site No.	Year Recovered	x	y	z		
Gor ESR 49 (Ibex)	235	1995	36 cm	15 cm	-115 cm		
Gor ESR 43 (Horse)	203	1997	85 cm	40 cm	11.0 m		
McMaster No.	Equivalent Dose (Gy)	γ Dose Rate (Gy/ka)	β Dose Rate (Gy/ka)	α Dose Rate (Gy/ka)	Total Dose Rate (Gy/ka)	ESR Age (EU) (ka)	ESR Age (LU) (ka)
Gor ESR 49 (Ibex) (2% moisture)	14.4 ± 1.0	0.277	0.088 (EU and LU)	0	0.365 (EU and LU)	39.4 ± 5.0	39.5 ± 5.0
Gor ESR 43 (Horse) (2% moisture)	15.8 ± 1.0	0.188	0.236 (EU) 0.147 (LU)	0	0.424 (EU) 0.335 (LU)	35.0 ± 4.0	43.6 ± 5.0
Mean (2% moisture)						37.2	41.6
Mean (15% moisture)						41.1	46.3
Mean (30% moisture)						45.6	51.9
	Sed U (ppm)	Sed Th (ppm)	Sed K (ppm)	Den U (ppm)	Cem U (ppm)	Enam U (ppm)	
Gor ESR 49 (Ibex)	0.71	2.66	3000	<0.1	Not Applicable	<0.1	
Gor ESR 43 (Horse)	0.49	1.90	2700	12.1	16.2	<0.1	

collected for studying the present-day moisture content of the deposit. The cosmic dose rate used for OSL and ESR age determinations was insignificant and near-zero because of the >50 m of overburden in the cave roof.

Gorham's Cave differs strongly from many other European limestone cave sites hosting Mousterian deposits in that its sedimentary fill is not characterised by brecciated layers. Cave breccias composed of limestone with intervening sediment are often very inhomogeneous in regard to their gamma dosimetry because of the relatively lower radioactivity in the limestone blocks relative to the sedimentary matrix. However, the clay-rich layers were considerably more radioactive than the sands, leading to as much as a 70% difference in the gamma radiation dose rates. For example, the sand GOR OSL 2 had a gamma dose rate of only 0.197 Gy/ka, while the stratified brown sand with clay of GOR OSL 3 had a dose rate of 0.347 Gy/ka (Table 18.2) when calculated using the same moisture content. Gamma dose rates to teeth (calculated from the sediment less than 5 cm away) had values of 0.188 and 0.277, effectively in the same range.

OSL dating at McMaster was carried out on 90–150 micrometer-size quartz grains using a narrow stimulation band of 514 ± 17 nm. They were measured on a Daybreak luminescence reader using conditions described in Rees-Jones *et al.* (1997). Beta and gamma radiation dosimetry in the local environment of the sands collected was done using neutron activation analysis of a fraction of the whole sediment collected (before separation of the quartz grains), and using gamma scintillometry in some of the locations (JR95 Gor OSL3 and Gor OSL1). Internal alpha doses were assumed to be negligible.

Mass-spectrometric U-series dating, as described in Li

et al. (1989) was applied to calcitic concretions found embedded within the sedimentary fill of the cave. These included fragments of calcite speleothems enclosed within a brown, clay-rich sand, consisting of thin isolated pods 2–5 cm in width and < 1cm thick, and < 1 cm-size cylindrical forms which exhibited sediment-filled cores characteristic of root casts or fallen stalactites. These calcite deposits may have formed in pools on the cave floor, within the sediment layer after its deposition, or may have fallen into the deposit from the roof or adjacent stalagmites observed along the walls of the cave. The pods and cylindrical forms were found in horizontal orientations. If they were incorporated at the time of deposition as previously formed calcite objects, they would provide a maximum age on the sedimentation. If they were formed after deposition, then they would provide a minimum age on the sedimentation events that formed the layers. If they were formed as discontinuous layers of calcite in pools on the cave floor and subsequently buried, they would provide the approximate age of sedimentation of the overlying unit, provided the time was short between crystallisation and burial.

ESR Dating Results

Table 18.1 gives the results for the only two teeth recovered *in-situ.* The individual tooth ages were calculated using a moisture content value for sediment of 2%, and two additional ages for GOR 43 are reported for 15% and 30% sediment moisture respectively, to show the effect of variation in moisture content on the ages. Ages for both teeth calculated at 2% (the value measured in the sediments) range from 35 ka (EU) to 45 ka (LU). Sediment

Table 18.2: OSL Dating Results for Gorham's Cave.

Area	Unit	Level	Elevation Above Datum (cm)	Field Sample Name	Lithology	Moisture (%)	Gamma Dose Rate (Gy/ka)	Beta Dose Rate (Gy/ka)	Equivalent Dose (Gy/ka)	Age (ka)
I	A98/B98		1398	Gor OSL 2 *	Soft Sand	2	0.197	0.367	28 ± 5	50 ± 9
						15	0.177	0.325	28 ± 5	56 ± 10
						30	0.158	0.288	28 ± 5	62 ± 11
	4d	7	1235	JR95 Gor L3 **	Stratified Brown	2	0.347	0.545	21 ± 4	24 ± 5
					Sand with Clay	15	0.311	0.484	21 ± 4	26 ± 5
						30	0.278	0.428	21 ± 4	30 ± 6
III	D108		1092	Gor OSL 1 *	Soft Sand	2	0.258	0.443	40 ±15	57 ± 21
						15	0.231	0.393	40 ± 15	64 ± 24
						30	0.206	0.348	40 ± 15	72 ± 27
			819	JR95 Gor L1 **	Friable Orange	2	0.335	0.634	42 ± 11	43 ± 14
					Sand, 5cm above	15	0.300	0.563	42 ± 11	49 ± 16
					Hard Yellow	30	0.268	0.498	42 ± 11	55 ± 18
					Lens					

attached to these teeth and from within 5 cm of the teeth were used to determine the beta and gamma dose rates for each of the teeth. Tooth Gor ESR 49 contained almost no uranium (U), providing an age estimate essentially free of the problem of U uptake in teeth, whereas tooth GOR ESR 43 had 12.1 and 16.23 ppm in the dentine and cementum respectively. This suggests that the latter tooth had been buried where more water was moving through the sediments. The ages of this tooth range from 37.2 ka EU to 46.3 ka LU, suggesting that the age of deposition of these sediments was about 41–42 ± 4 ka. The maximum ESR age values of about 37 to about 52 ka are consistent with minimum uncalibrated ^{14}C time ages of about 40 ka as found by Pettitt *et al* (this volume) for the levels under current excavation. However, if the moisture content was considerably higher in the past than the values measured for samples collected in 1995 and 1997, the ESR dates would be considerably older, ranging from 41 ka (EU) to 52 ka (LU), as shown for moisture content values of 15 and 30 % in Table 18.1.

Radiation Dosimetry and Results for OSL Samples

The annual radiation dose received by the OSL samples was determined by *in-situ* gamma scintillometry measurements to give the gamma dose for two samples, and neutron activation analysis of sediment for U, Th and K to give the beta dose and additional estimates of the gamma dose for all four samples. The ages in Table 18.2 were calculated using beta dose attenuation factors (Mejdahl 1979) using a range of assumed moisture contents (the average from samples that were collected within 30 cm of drying profiles

was <3%). The true moisture content over the burial history is not known, but for each 1% increase in the assumed moisture content, the ages increase by about 1%. Table 18.3 shows a comparison of the *in-situ* gamma dose rates measured by gamma scintillometry and those measured by NAA. They are in close agreement.

These results differ considerably from those previously presented in the abstracts of the Gibraltar conference. The reason they are so much younger is that the potassium results used in the previous dose rate calculations were in error, leading to errors in the beta and gamma radiation dose rate estimates. We apologise for this previous error and urge that the results in the abstract not be further quoted.

The new results are in broad agreement with the ESR dating of the *in-situ* teeth. OSL ages for samples from elevations of +1235 and +1398 cm above datum were 56 and 26 ka respectively, yielding a mean age of about 40 ka. If we do not accept that such large differences in the OSL ages allow a meaningful average to be considered, then it would appear that the stratigraphically higher sample was not completely reset during deposition, and that the lower OSL sample dated to 25–30 ka underestimates the burial age for an unknown reason (given as about 41–42 ka by ESR using sample GOR ESR 49 and 43).We believe the ESR ages are better constrained because of the large errors in the OSL ages, and hence are probably more reliable. One possible reason that the younger age is obtained for the OSL sample is the fact that it is a brown sand, whose radiation dose rate may have increased over time due to authigenic (*in-situ*) crystallisation of new minerals such as potassium-rich siliceous aggregates. This has been observed in Hayonim

Table 18.3: Comparison of Gamma Dose Rates Obtained by in-situ *scintillometry* v. *Neutron Activation Analysis (NAA).*

Sample Name	NAA Gamma Dose Rate (Gy/ka)	Scintillometry Gamma Dose Rate (Gy/ka)
JR95 GOR OSL 3	0.311	0.265
JR95 GOR OSL 1	0.300	0.296

and Kebara caves in Israel (Schiegl *et al.* 1996) and similar processes may have occurred here. As to the older age for the overlying sand, that can be explained by deposition without complete zeroing, not an unlikely circumstance for a sample located deep in a cave like this. Cave sands can be remobilised and redeposited entirely within the dark confines of the cave, and hence not receive sufficient light exposure to produce overestimates of the burial time.

The two OSL samples at +1092 and +819 cm above datum yield older ages than those just described, and therefore are stratigraphically consistent with ages in the higher levels, although they are stratigraphically out of order (the deeper sand appears to be slightly younger). The average age obtained from these lower OSL samples of about 50 ka is consistent with their stratigraphic position some 4–5 meters lower in the section than the samples yielding ESR ages of about 40–50 ka.

Sample JR95 GOR OSL2 came from an elevation of +692 cm above datum in a brown clay/sand unit with some shell and stone which was characterised by local areas of harder cemented sand with curvate forms and strong relief. Its OSL age was infinite because it did not respond to doses of laboratory radiation (saturated). Sample JR95 GOR OSL4 came from an elevation of +612 cm above datum in a loose, brownish yellow sand, some 27 cm below a cemented sand layer. The OSL age was also infinite. We suppose that these samples may be > 200 ka in age, which corresponds to the time needed for saturation of OSL signals in quartz at the observed dose rate. Alternatively, they may not have been completely bleached before deposition.

MSUS Dating Results

The MSUS ages for two calcite samples collected within the lower sand levels are reported in Table 18.4. The ages are entirely consistent with trends seen in many other caves because their ages fall within a range expected for Stage 5c of the last interglacial. An increase in the rate of cave calcite (speleothem) formation occurs throughout Europe and North America during Isotope Stage 5 (Baker *et al.* 1993). The ages we obtain are older than the age found with OSL dating for the underlying sediment at +819 cm above datum, and for the sample some 2m higher at +1092 cm above datum. However, if we consider the rather large errors on the latter, the U-series ages agree with the OSL

ages at the ± 2σ confidence interval, and only with the overlying sample at the ± 1σ level.. On the other hand it is possible that these are fragments of earlier speleothem deposits that fell into the sediments as they were being deposited.

ESR ages of samples from Waechter: comparison with other dates

The ESR samples collected *in-situ* are in broad agreement with the ages of museum teeth collected from Waechter's Mousterian levels G, L, M, and P (Volterra *et al.* this volume), which gave a mean ESR EU age of about 30 ± 5 ka and an LU age of 35 ± 5 ka (calculated with 2% moisture content). Considering the variability of gamma and beta dose rates found for OSL samples, this agreement is quite good because we had to assume the gamma and beta dose rates for most of the ESR ages of museum samples (only a few samples had sediment attached which could be used for the beta dose rate estimate). The average OSL age from the upper part of the dated section (at 1235 and 1398 cm above datum) is slightly older than the Waechter ESR ages regardless of the moisture content used for determining the OSL ages.

The OSL ages from the lower part of the dated sequence at +819 and +1092 cm above datum are in broad agreement with the ESR dates from Waechter's level R (Volterra *et al.* this volume) of 56.5 ± 4.9 ka EU and 62.4 ± 5.1 ka LU. This level was reported by Waechter to have been about 4 to 4.5 meters lower than level G. Notably, the elevation difference between the ESR age at +1235 cm above datum and these OSL ages at +819 and 1092 cm above datum is 1.5 to 4 meters, suggesting that Waecter's Level R may have been in the vicinity of the lower part of the OSL sequence.

Discussion and Conclusions

Only two of the samples collected for luminescence dating came from within the Stringer and Barton excavation area. Sample JR95 Gor OSL3 comes from Unit 7 in Area I, adjacent to square C101. Its elevation in the archaeological log was z = 118 to -125, which corresponds to +1235 cm above datum. Its OSL age of 26 ± 5 ka is much younger than an AMS radiocarbon date of 45.3 ka ± 1700 yrs BP (OxA-6075) from this area and elevation (pers. comm. C. B. Stringer). However, GOR ESR 49 was collected in a position very close to the ^{14}C sample, and its ESR ages of 44.4 ± 5.6 ka (EU and LU, 15% moisture) and 50.8 ± 5.6 ka (EU and LU, 30% moisture) are entirely consistent with the ^{14}C AMS age, as is the ESR age of 39.4 ± 3.2 ka (EU and LU, 2% moisture) at the ±2σ confidence level.

Three other luminescence dating samples came from considerably lower positions in the deposit. Sample JR95 Gor OSL1 came from within the same unit but slightly lower than the enclosed calcite samples used for U-series dating. It would appear that the older ages of the enclosed

W. J. RINK, J. REES-JONES, V. VOLTERRA AND H. SCHWARCZ

Table 18.4: MSUS Dating Results for Gorham's Cave.

Sample	Elevation above datum (cm)	Shape	$^{234}U/^{238}U$	$^{230}Th/^{234}U$	$^{230}Th/^{232}Th$	U (ppm)	Age (ka)
JR95 GOR MSUS5?1	844	Tabular	1.031 ± 0.008	0.593 ± 0.005	88 ± 0.4	0.657 ± 0.003	97.1 ± 1.3
JR95 GOR MSUSU1?3	838	Cylindrical	1.052 ± 0.003	0.591 ± 0.003	20 ± 0.1	0.646 ± 0.002	96.1 ± 0.9

calcites may be taken as maximum ages for these units. The calcites probably fell into the sand and were subsequently buried. If we assume that they were formed *in situ* as root casts (cylindrical) or formed in small pools as small lenses of calcite (tabular), then the OSL ages must be seen to be strongly underestimating the true age of the deposit. However, recall that the large uncertainty in the OSL age of sample GOR OSL1 from +819 cm (about 20–25 cm lower than the U-series sample is consistent with that of the calcite at the ± 2ó level range of the OSL age.

In summary, the ESR ages provide a more secure range of ages for the sequence than the uppermost two OSL ages. The problems of the OSL ages are not particularly surprising given that deposition occurred deep within the confines of a cave. The MSUS ages seem to provide maximum ages for the enclosing sand that are consistent with the OSL ages on samples deposited closer to the front of the cave (the lowermost two OSL ages). These ages are also consistent with the ESR ages for Waechter's Level R (Volterra *et al.* this volume), and hence seem to delineate a region of the stratigraphy below +1092 m above datum that may correspond to Waechter's level R. If Waechter's level R was as low as +819 cm above datum, as suggested by the corroborating ESR dates for this level, then Waechter's level G (Uppermost Mousterian) would correspond to a position around +12m above datum and would be dated securely by ESR to about 40–50 ka.

Acknowledgements

We would like to thank J. Johnson, K.Goodger, N. Barton, A. Currant, P. Goldberg, R. North and N. Haziza for assistance with various parts of the sample collection and dating work. This research was funded with grants from the Natural Sciences and Engineering Research Council of Canada, and from the Social Sciences and Humanities Research Council to WJR and HPS, travel grants from the North Atlantic Treaty Organization to HPS and WJR and V. Cabrera-Valdés and F. Bernaldo de Quíros.

References

Baker, A., Smart, P.L. & Ford, D.C. (1993). Northwest European palaeoclimate as indicated by growth frequency variations of secondary calcite deposits. *Palaeogeography, Palaeoclimatology and Palaeoecology*, **100**, 291–301.

Brennan B.J., Rink, W.J., McGuirl, E.L., Schwarcz, H.P. & Prestwich, W.V. (1997). Beta doses in tooth enamel by "One-group" theory and the ROSY ESR dating software. *Radiation Measurements* **27**, 307–314.

Brennan, B.J. Rink, W.J., Rule, E.M., Schwarcz, H.P. & Prestwich, W.V. *et al.* (1999, in press). The ROSY ESR dating software. Ancient TL.

Mejdahl, V. (1979). Thermoluminescence dating: beta-dose attenuation in quartz grains. *Archaeometry* **21**, 61–73.

Li, Wang-Xing, Lundberg, J., Dickin, A. P., Ford, D. C. and Schwarcz, H. P. & Williams, D. (1989). High-precision mass-spectrometric U-series dating of cave deposits and implications for paleoclimate studies. *Nature*, 339: 534–536.

Rees-Jones, J., Hall, S.J.B. and·Rink, W.J. (1997). A laboratory inter-comparison of quartz optically stimulated luminescence (OSL) results. *Quaternary Science Reviews/Quaternary Geochronology* **16**, 275–280.

Rink, W.J. (1997). Electron spin resonance (ESR) dating and ESR applications in Quaternary science and archaeometry. *Radiation Measurements* **27**, 975–1025.

Rink, W.J. (1999, in press). Beyond ^{14}C dating: A user's guide to long-range dating methods in archaeology. In (P. Goldberg, R. Ferring, & V. Haynes, Eds) *Earth Sciences and Archaeology*, Plenum Press.

Schiegl, S., Goldberg, P., Bar-Yosef, O. and Weiner, S. (1996). Ash deposits in Hayonim and Kebara Caves, Israel: macroscopic, microscopic and mineralogical observations and their archaeological importance. *Journal of Archaeological Science* **18**, 763–782.

Vega Toscano, L.G. (1993). La transicíon de Palaeolítico medio al Palaeolítico superior en el sur de península ibérico. In (V. Cabrera Valdés Ed) *El Orígen del homre moderno en el Suroeste de Europa* pp. 147–170. Madrid: Univ. Nacional de Educacion a Distancia.

Waechter, J. d' A. (1951). Excavations at Gorham's Cave, Gibraltar. *Proceedings of the Prehistoric Society* **17**, 83–92.

Waechter, J. d' A. (1964) The excavation of Gorham's Cave, Gibraltar, 1951–1954. *Bulletin of the Institute of Archaeology* **4**, 189–221.

19

The Taphonomy of Pleistocene Caves, with Particular Reference to Gibraltar

Yolanda Fernández-Jalvo and Peter Andrews

Introduction

The discoveries of the Forbes' Quarry Neanderthal skull and especially of the Devil's Tower Neanderthal child, the latter associated with Mousterian artefacts and faunal remains, have provided evidence of a late Neanderthal occupation in Europe. These discoveries together with the site at Zafarraya (Malaga) suggest that the southern part of the Iberian Peninsula provided refuge to the last Neanderthals.

In addition to Forbes' Quarry and Devil's Tower, the Rock of Gibraltar contains many caves, some of them currently under investigation, for example Ibex Cave, Vanguard Cave and Gorham's Cave. None of these sites has provided human fossil bones yet, but human occupation levels and evidence of human activity have been recovered.

All of these sites are on the eastern side of the Rock. Ibex Cave is a small shelter site that is located at about 260 metres above sea level (Figure 19.1) at the bottom of the limestone cliff of the Rock and at the top of the extensive fossil sand dunes that mantle much of the eastern face of Gibraltar. Gorham's and Vanguard Caves are situated at the south east part of the Rock (Figure 19.1). They are wave-cut caves just above the present sea level. These sites have been excavated since 1994 as part of the Gibraltar Caves Project.

Gorham's Cave, previously dug by John Waechter in the middle 1950's, contain deposits which cover the Upper and Middle Palaeolithic transition (~26 ka to ~50 ka AMS radiocarbon dates) reaching a maximum age at the bottom of the section of 80 to 100 ka estimated by Uranium series. Vanguard Cave covers similar ages although the upper part of the series (>45 ka, the Upper-Middle Palaeolithic transition) has neither palaeontological nor archaeological record. This site was not previously excavated and was covered by a wind-blown sand that protected the previously partly eroded edges of the stratified deposits.

Predation is the main source of bone accumulation observed at the Gibraltar sites, most of it effected by Neanderthals but sometimes also by other carnivores. It is our aim here to show the results of taphonomic analyses initiated in the three sites at Gibraltar currently investigated by the research team directed by Chris Stringer. All three sites have abundant large and small mammal remains, sometimes in direct association with stone tools.

Methods

Digging at Gorham's has the principal aims of recovering fossil and archaeological remains and distinguishing stratigraphic units. The attempt was also made to find correlations with previous excavations done by John Waechter. Distribution of fossil bones, lithics, shells, cave stalactites/stalagmites, hearth ashes and any other organic or inorganic remains of interest are recorded on plans, with co-ordinates taken using an EDM (electronic distance measurer).

The collections from Gibraltar have been analysed using a variable magnification (x8 to x40) light microscope. Observations were backed with detailed images derived from a scanning electron microscope (SEM), operating in the back-scattered electron (ISI ABT55) imaging mode under relatively low vacuum (10^{-1} torr) in an environmental chamber (Taylor 1986). This enables uncoated specimens to be viewed directly thus facilitating the collection of a large database for both recent and fossil specimens.

Taphonomy of Pleistocene caves

The main feature of cave environments that differentiates them from other environments is a three dimensional spatial limitation (floor, walls and roof). As a result, cave structure and sedimentary infilling may change spatially in just few metres (Figure 19.2). Another important trait of caves is that they may rapidly change in geomorphology, and a consequence of this is that the taphonomic conditions may

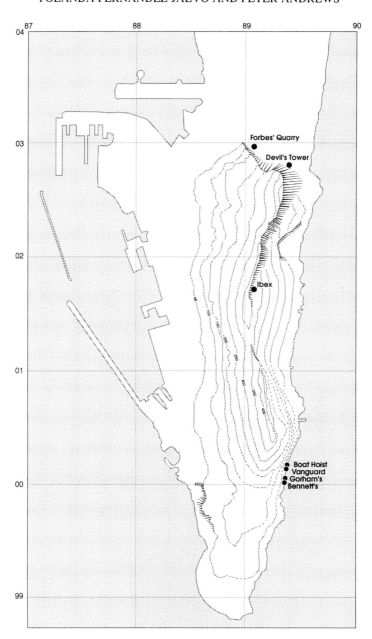

Figure 19.1: Gibraltar Rock and location of the sites.

also change due for instance to sudden roof collapse (that is, opening direct contact between inner cave and open-air environments) or cave entrance blocking (that is, seal or reduction of previous connection with open-air environments). This seems to have happened in a site named Gran Dolina, a cave infilling that belongs to the Sierra de Atapuerca karstic complex in Burgos in northern Spain. This site has yielded human remains at unit TD6 of the infilling (Carbonell *et al.* 1995) with an age of around 780 ka (Parés & Pérez-González, 1995), at a time when the cave had an entrance with direct connection to the open air. The cave was then receiving sediments through the entrance as well as bones brought in by humans (Fernández-Jalvo, *et al.* 1996) who were temporarily

inhabiting the cave (Díez *et al.* 1999). In the same deposit, small mammals were provided by raptors (Figure 19.3a) by deposition of pellets containing these small mammal bones (Fernández-Jalvo 1995). This cave dramatically changed around 200 ka later (TD8–TD9), when the cave entrance was blocked and sediment accumulation was reduced as the cave became isolated from the exterior of the cave (Figure 19.2b). These conditions lasted almost other 200,000 years until the cave environment of Gran Dolina rapidly changed again due to sudden roof collapse (TD10–TD11). This event again provided direct contact between the cave and the open air, with sediments gravitationally coming from the exterior into the cave. Humans took advantage of this direct contact and used

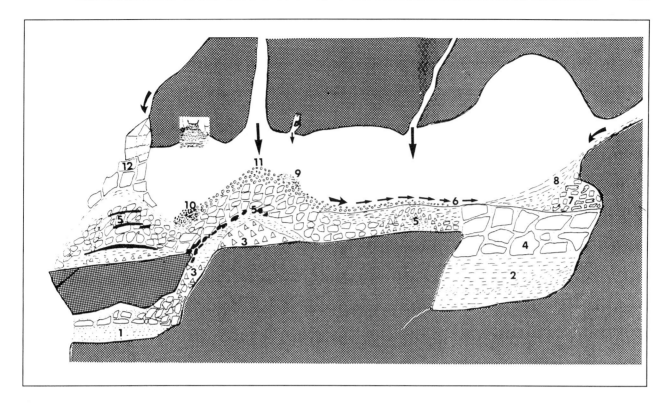

Figure 19.2: Generalised section of a cave (Sutcliffe et al. 1973, modified by Andrews, 1990). Talus cones are accumulating at the cave entrance, beneath a large aven (3, 11), beneath a smaller aven (5) and from a passage way (7,8). Some of the cave sediments in the main chamber have fallen through into a lower chamber (3). The cave sediments are depicted as accumulating in the order indicated by the numbered sequence 1–12, as follows: 1. accumulation of cave earths in the closed environments of the lower chamber; 2. waterlain silts and sands; 3. accumulations of breccias in the upper chamber, and the loss of some of this material into the lower chamber; 4. roof fall on top of waterlain deposits sealing the source from whence they came; 5. the accumulation of breccia at the entrance and beneath the two avens, with fire hearths from earlier human occupations near the entrance; 6. flattened areas of breccias caused by large mammal trampling; 7. den accumulation of bears together with breccia formation; 8. transport of mud-flow through a passage connecting to another part of the cave; 9. bat guano and bones from bat colony in roof above; 10. accumulation of owl pellets from beneath roost site on cave wall; 11. inflow of soil and pellets and scats from the surface above through the aven; 12. closing off of the entrance by partial collapse of the cliff face.

the cave as a shelter camp site, and the bones abandoned by the hominids show the effects of open-air taphonomic agents such as weathering and plant root marks (Díez 1992; Fernández-Jalvo 1995).

Caves are used seasonally over long periods of time by animals such as bears for hibernation or amphibians for aestivation. At Draycott Cave, a present day cave chamber in Somerset, there are several layers of silt, and amphibians have been discovered in great numbers, having died there as a result of periodic catastrophic effects probably during successive aestivations (Pinto and Andrews 1999). Foxes used the other end of this small cave and brought in small mammals as prey (Andrews 1990). Bear hibernation behaviour provides high numbers of bear bones resulting from death during hibernation and intra-specific killing of the weakest individuals (old and cubs). This is seen in several stratigraphic levels in the middle Pleistocene cave at Westbury-sub-Mendip in Somerset (Andrews, Cook, Currant and Stringer 1999) (Figure 19.4), Sima de los

Huesos, one of the Atapuerca caves near Burgos, Spain (Andrews and Fernández-Jalvo 1997) and Yarimburgaz Cave in Turkey (Stiner *et al.* 1998).

Another method of bone accumulating in caves is through transport by geological agents. Streams or mud-flows can carry animals dying near caves or within a catchment area of a cave into the interior of the cave. This is the case of Sima de los Huesos, another of the caves at Atapuerca (Burgos, Spain), where bones were derived from at least two origins. These consist of the bear remains resulting from hibernation within the cave, and humans accumulated elsewhere by humans and then eaten by lions. The latter were transported from a different but still unknown part of the cave system and brought to their present resting place that acted as sink hole, the present-day cave chamber of Sima de los Huesos (Andrews and Fernández-Jalvo 1997). At another of the Draycott caves, the remains of an animal that died within a few metres of the cave entrance were transported into the cave by the

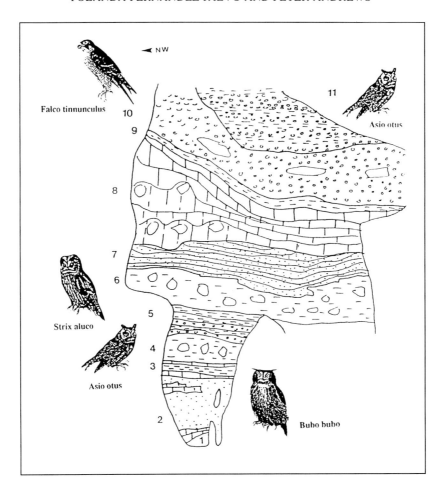

Figure 19.3a: Predators inferred in Gran Dolina according to taphonomic alterations observed on the small mammal fossil bones. **European eagle owl** *(Bubo bubo) TD3 and part of TD4;* **long eared owl** *(Asio otus) TD4 and TD11;* **tawny owl** *(Srix aluco) TD5 and TD6;* **kestrel** *(Falco tinnunculus) TD10. Units TD7, TD8 and TD9 have no small mammal content (Figure from Fernández-Jalvo, 1995).*

joint effects of gravitation and trampling (Andrews and Cook 1985). In general, however, our experience of caves leads us to conclude that transport of large mammal bones into or within a cave system acts more to disperse bones in the cave than to accumulate them in rich bone assemblages.

In contrast to all this, predation is a common source for animal accumulation in caves, of both large and small mammals. Hyaenas are especially important for carrying bones into caves (Sutcliffe 1973; Maguire *et al.* 1980, Brain 1981). Humans are also an important agent of accumulation during the Pleistocene. Their activity can be differentiated from other predators, although sometimes human accumulations may be subsequently scavenged by other carnivores, disturbing the original distribution and erasing the signs left on the bones by these humans. Sometimes humans are the ones that disturb and scavenge food abandoned by other carnivores, and in such cases it is possible to observe cutmarks covering previous toothmarks on the bone (Moreno 1993).

Ibex Cave

Ibex Cave site is a small shelter site high up in the on the eastern face of Gibraltar (Figure 19.1). Ibex Cave contains stone tools and the fossil bones of ibex (hence the site name) and also the remains of rabbits, red deer, gastropods, wolf, birds, voles and abundant remains of tortoise.

No evidence of human activity was found on any of the fossils, large, medium or small mammal remains. Large vertebrate fossil bones are fragmentary, in part due to falling blocks of cave material and sediment compaction, and also due to carnivores. Spiral fractures and splinters, chewing and puncture marks are frequent, and the toothmark size and morphology indicates the action of a carnivore the size of a wolf. Apart from tooth marks, the mandible of a wolf recovered from this site supports the evidence of this predator in the area.

No evidence of predation has been seen on the tortoise remains and gastropods. In contrast to this, the remains of rabbits and birds, and especially voles and murines, are strongly digested. Degrees of digestion and percentages

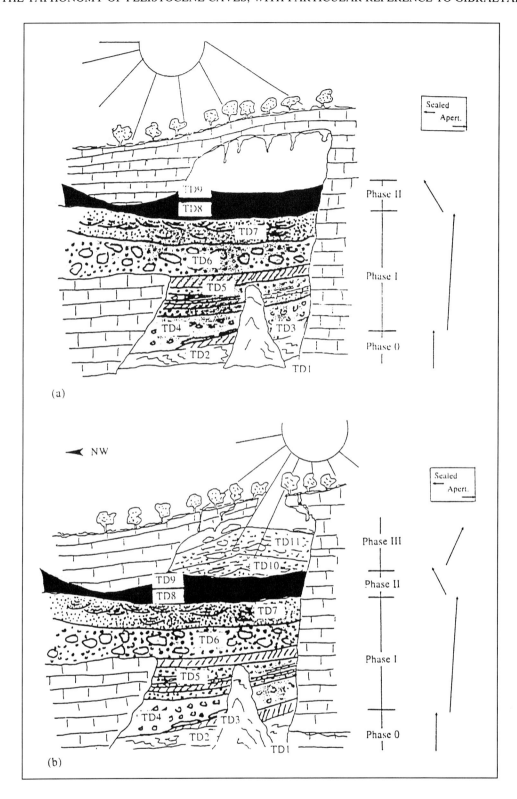

*Figure 19.3b: Interpretation of the infilling sequence of Gran Dolina obtained from the taphonomic results from the small mammals (Fernández-Jalvo 1995), and the succeeding taphonomic phases. **Below** = Phase 0: TD1 and TD2; Phase I: TD3–TD7; Phase II: TD8 and TD9 (when the cave was sealed and isolated from the exterior). **Above** = Phase III: TD10 and TD11 (when the cave roof collapsed and direct connection with the open-air environment occurred). Right hand columns show the cave tendency to sealing or opening to the outside environments.*

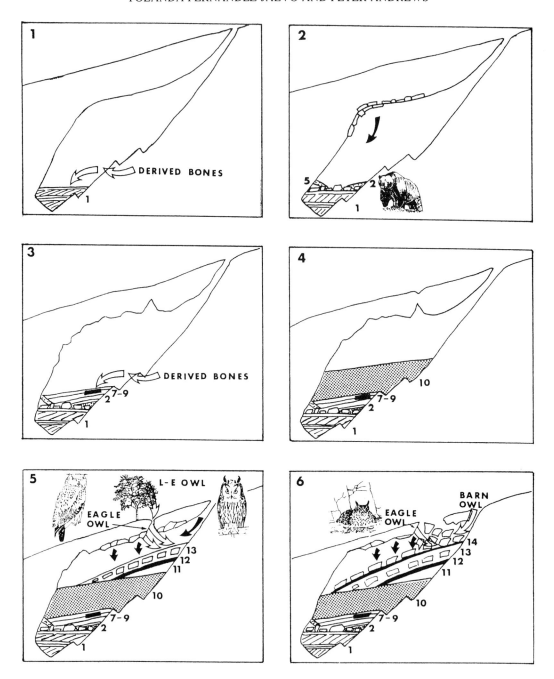

Figure 19.4: Schematic sections from Westbury Cave, showing the proposed model of accumulation of sediments and bones (see Andrews 1990. Pg. 160–161). Black arrows indicate direction of accumulation of sediments, and open arrows indicate sources of animal remains, whether bear hibernation (2), water transport (1, 3) or from predators (5, 6: eagle owl Bubo bubo, long-eared owl Asio otus, barn owl Tyto alba).

of elements affected by digestion are high on the rodent bones and teeth. Most of the postcranial elements are heavily digested and rounded which is typical of mammalian carnivore digestion. Most of the incisors are digested over their whole surface, indicating that they were detached already from the jaws during digestion. Breakage before digestion in small mammal bones is characteristic of mammalian carnivores, the breakage being due to chewing. All features described above are consistent with canid prey assemblages, more specifically with fox (*Vulpes vulpes*). On the other hand, the presence of a raptor pellet indicates a third predator involved at the site. Traits of the bones preserved in this pellet suggest an eagle owl such as European eagle owl (*Bubo bubo*) as predator.

The high diversity of predators and prey and the postdepositional features observed on these fossils are consistent with a shelter cave site, a mixture between open air and inner cave (Jennings 1985; Fernández-Jalvo 1995).

Figure 19.5: Excavations at Gorham's cave. The ancient stratigraphy described by John d'Arcy Waechter, has been exposed again in order to recover his descriptions and layers. The excavations have been extended for about 4m².

All the predators identified are opportunistic hunters, though individual hunting preference and size restriction due to the predator size and behaviour can be expected (e.g. poor representation of diurnal animals, Jaacksic and Marti 1984). Apart from this, the prey assemblages obtained by these predators can be considered to be a relatively accurate representation of the animals living in the habitat.

Some fossil bones of large mammals have gnawing marks by rodents, indicating that there were bones exposed on the ground before burial. Most of the fossils are weathered in stages 1–3, and some reaching stage 4 (Behrensmeyer, 1978). This indicates variable conditions of humidity, temperature, and exposure to UV rays for about 5 to 15 years following modern comparative studies of Behrensmeyer (1978) and Andrews (1990). Root marks are also abundant, indicating vegetated ground cover. A few fossils are stained by oxide of iron (giving a reddish or yellowish colour to the fossils). Others are locally or completely stained black by manganese oxides, suggesting wet conditions during sedimentation. Water transport is absent. Reworking processes have not been noticed at this assemblage.

The absence of indicators of human activity on the bones recovered from this site suggests that humans were not involved in the bone accumulation in the cave. The shelter is not deep, and many of the bones evidently

accumulated outside the cave where they were weathered and modified by plant roots. Both these bones and others inside the cave were scavenged by canids, probably wolves and foxes, and it is likely that these carnivores brought many of them into and to the cave. At times human presence at the site is indicated by the presence of stone tools, some of which may be refitted (Barton this volume), and this suggests that knapping took place inside the cave. It has to be kept in mind that at this stage of the late Pleistocene the sea level was lower and the environment of the area today covered by the sea was a flat plain similar to the marismas of the nearby Doñana Natural Park (Finlayson this volume).

Gorham's and Vanguard Caves

John d'Arcy Waechter, a British archaeologist, conducted large scale excavations in Gorham's Cave from 1951–1954. As a result of these excavations Waechter established that the cave had archaeological records of Middle Palaeolithic, Upper Palaeolithic, Neolithic and later occupation (Figure 19.5).

The fossil distributions have shown that bones are associated with stone tools and hearths at various levels in the cave. In general, the main modifications to the bones observed at Gorham's and Vanguard fossil bone assemblages consist of cutmarks made by stone tools as a result

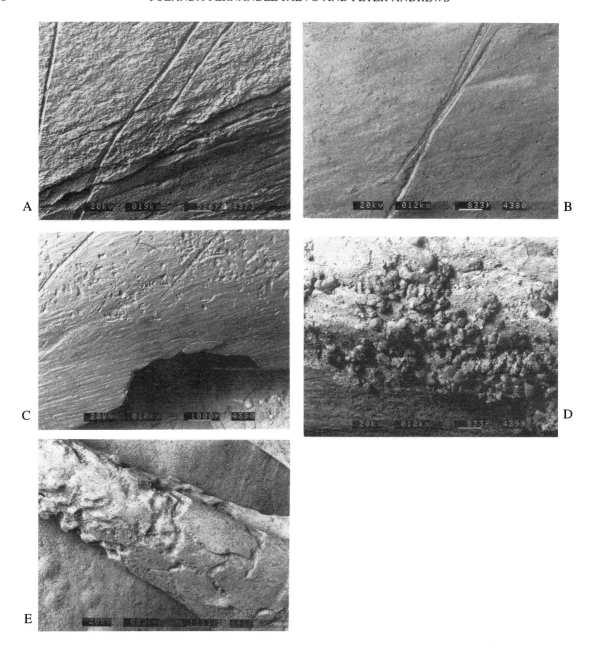

Figure 19.6: A– SEM microphotograph of cut marks on a fossil bone from Gorham's Cave (G'218). The incision was made with a stone tool flake on the muscle attachment area of an ibex bone fragment. The regular and thin shape of the incision indicates that it was made with a non-retouched flake; B– SEM microphotograph of a Gorham's fossil bone (G'275) cut mark made with a flake retouched on both sides indicated by the X shape obtained in a single motion (see Schick and Toth 1993); C– SEM microphotograph of a Vanguard fossil bone (V'200) with conchoidal breakage and a small adhered flake at the edge of the fracture suggesting that this fracture was intentional; D– SEM microphotograph of a Gorham's fossil bone (G'223) extensively covered by massive stains of manganese of tarry aspect that have entrapped sand grains on its surface; E– SEM microphotograph of a Vanguard fossil bone (V'44) of small mammal extensively covered by root marks.

of human butchering, and breakage due both to the butchering processes and to natural processes. These alterations suggest several activities performed by early humans at the site. Incisions on muscle attachment areas (Figure 19.6a) on the bone suggest dismemberment, and other cutmarks on the bone surface suggest filleting or defleshing activities. Most of the cutmarks are simple incisions, indicating they were made by a non-retouched flake (see Figure 19.6a), but sometimes, as seen in Figure 19.6b, cutmarks have the typical shape formed by double retouched flakes (Schick and Toth 1993). Scraping marks are also present on a few bones indicating periosteum removal or grease extraction. Conchoidal scars, some having adhered flakes (Figure 19.6c), provide evidence

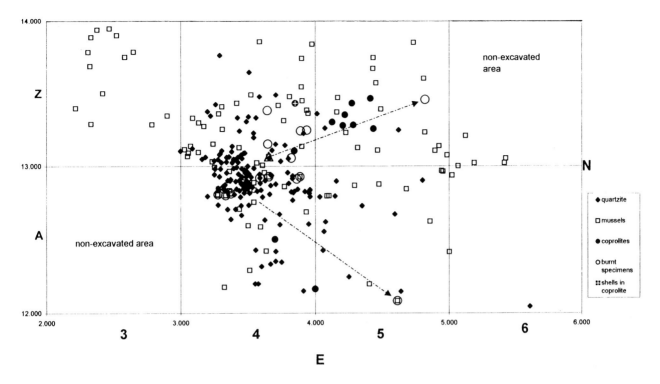

Figure 19.7: Plan of finds from Vanguard cave (top series). The black triangle at the centre area (southern part of square Z4) indicates the only mussel shell that is trampled and burnt. The arrows indicate the possible displacement of the two burnt shells that appear farther from the hearth domain possibly due to trampling (scale in metres). One of the coprolites at square Z4 has been distinguished with a white cross to indicate the inclusion of mussel shells.

for bone fracture and indicate marrow extraction. Evidence of most stages of butchering is therefore present on fossil bones from these sites. Some bones have been partially or completely burnt, suggesting direct exposure to fire. Ibex bone remains are the most abundant at these assemblages and this is the species that represents the most complete sequence of butchering.

Black stains due to manganese oxides are frequent on the bones in both caves, and sometimes these stains are very extensive. In such cases, sand grains are entrapped in a form that looks like tar (Figure 19.7d), but chemical analyses carried out on these regions confirm that it is manganese oxide.. Both manganese oxide formation and cementation suggest periods of damp in the interior of the cave shelter.

Less than a 10% of the bones show superficial weathering on the surface, and only a few reach high stages (3/4, see Behrensmeyer 1978). Root marks are frequent and abundant on the bone surfaces of this assemblage, both on large and small mammals (Figure 19.7e). This is in agreement with the type of site, a shelter cave near open air environments.

Both Vanguard and Gorham's Cave show similar types of activities performed at the sites by hominids, possibly more intense at Gorham's than at Vanguard. It can therefore be said that the human population could exploit most food resources available in the surrounding environment, including seafood, as will be described below. Periods of occupations, however, seem to have been relatively short, maybe seasonal and sometimes as short as one day.

Vanguard Cave North

In a small alcove situated to the north side of the major series at Vanguard Cave, a small and sub-circular hearth provides evidence of human activity (Barton *et al.* 1999). No cutmarks or intentional breakage has been observed, however, on any of the bones associated with the hearth, suggesting that humans were not responsible for this bone accumulation. Although the presence of fossil bones of *Crocuta crocuta* suggests denning activities (Barton *et al.* 1999), none of the herbivore bones recovered from this area of excavation have modifications compatible with hyaenas or humans as agents of accumulation. Tooth marks affect around 10% of these fossil bones, but the size of the animal was no bigger than a common red fox or even smaller. There is not enough evidence to identify the predator with a higher level of accuracy.

Vanguard Cave South (top series excavation)

An exceptional layer was excavated in the top series of

S   **North-South section**   **N**

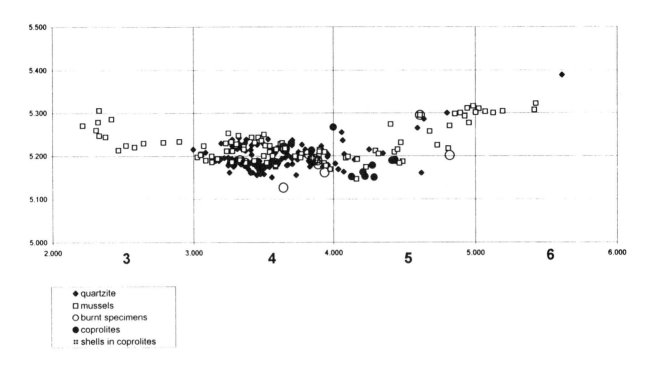

Figure 19.8: Section of finds from Vanguard Cave (top series). Vertical scale has been exaggerated (scale in metres). Notice the wide lateral distribution of shells (squares) and the relatively limited lateral concentration of the quartzite knapping debris (black diamonds), though vertically the quartzite debris is present through the whole level thickness.

Table 19.1: Species of molluscs identified at Vanguard cave, upper series, with numbers of specimens recorded at the site (P.Jeffery pers.comm.).

Common name	Genus/species	n.specimens	MNI
limpets	*Patella vulgata*	11	11
limpets	*Patella caerula*	2	2
mussels	*Mytilus galloprovincialis*	~100	~50
barnacles	*Balanus* sp.	8	8
cockles	*Acanthocardia tuberculata*	1	1
veneracean bivalve	*Callista chione*	1	1

MNI – Minimum Number of Individuals

the Vanguard sedimentary succession, corresponding to Layers 53–55 (Goldberg and MacPhail this volume). This is a hearth, and radiocarbon dating of the hearth ashes gives an age of 50 ka–40 ka (Barton *et al.* 1999). The types of wood identified at the hearths are mainly *Juniperus*, *Pistacea* and *Olea* (Barton *et al.* 1999). The results from this 6m² excavation greatly increase our knowledge of behaviour, food availability and living strategies of the Neanderthals occupying the cave. In particular it shows that the hominids of this period included seafood in their diet, for the human occupation floor consists of a layer of molluscs associated with the hearth

and with knapping debris (Figure 19.7). The most abundant types of mollusc at this layer are mussels, as well as a few specimens of barnacles and limpets and one fragment of cockle shell (Table 19.1).

The large size of the mussels and the advanced age of some of these individuals suggest that the colony being predated had to be in sheltered conditions, away from waves, probably in a estuary (P.Jeffery *pers.comm.*). The MNI of mussels has been calculated to be 50 from the excavated area. There is only one cockle (*Acanthocardia tuberculata*) shell and one veneracean (*Callista chione*). These two specimens are broken and are the only abraded shells, so that they were probably brought by the sea and not eaten by the hominids. Both species live in low intertidal environments at depths of around 100–180 metres (Jeffery *pers.comm.*), and although they are perfectly edible, these species were too difficult to be collected and they surely did not form part of the hominid diet. Barnacles could possibly come attached to the mussels.

Experimental work has been carried out in order to understand the resistance of the mussels to being opened and whether it was necessary to burn the shells to open them. The results of the experiment showed that when the mussels were placed around a low fire on the floor, two to three minutes were necessary to get the shells opened and

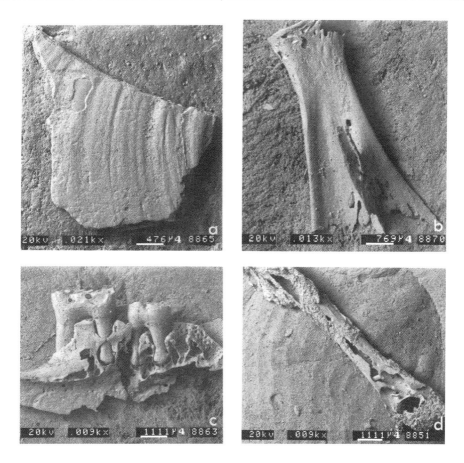

Figure 19.9: A– Shell fragment recovered from coprolite Van-U'97 343; B– Small mammal scapula heavily digested recovered from coprolite Van-U'97 394; C– Small mammal mandible heavily digested and broken from coprolite Van-U'97 367; D– Small mammal humerus very heavily digested recovered from coprolite Van-U'97 394.

ready to be eaten. In some instances when the shells were still too tight, they had to be opened with a knife, and in these cases the shells were frequently flaked. To avoid the use of knives, mussels were left exposed to the fire for longer, but under these conditions the shells dried out and the animal was burned and became uneatable. It was observed that shells thrown into the fire took several hours to be completely burnt, and a lot of smoke came out from the burning shells. After six hours in the fire, most shells were still complete, unless the ashes were turned over. In this case, the shells started to break, though always in identifiable pieces; shells did not disintegrate or become powdered.

The hearth sediment from Vanguard Cave North was analysed under a light microscope. Rounded grains of sand formed the hearth sediment, but no fragments of burnt shell were observed. No shell debris was found in the Vanguard hearth, and therefore we can then say that few or no shell were thrown into the hearth. A few shells, however, appear burnt, (Figure 19.7) and most of these were found close to the hearth except for two shells from further away, possibly kicked away by trampling. Flake refitting following the same direction (Barton this issue) could support this hypothesis.

Two types of stone industry assemblages have been found associated with the hearth. One type consists of lithics in limestone and sandstone (Barton this issue), and since no flake refitting of these materials has been found, this suggests that these stone tools were brought to the site already made. In particular, two pieces of broken flint and red chert tools have been discovered, both of them with similar shape and being perfect knives to open shells. The second type is evident from a well defined area of quartzite "debris", which was found near and in the hearth. This forms a strong concentration in the vicinity of the hearth (Figure 19.7). Most of the debris is on top of the hearth, but some of the biggest quartzite flakes appear at the bottom of the hearth and are burnt or have ashes attached to the surface (see Figure 19.8). Several.of these flakes refit (Barton this issue) and the way the debris is dispersed suggests much of it was produced by a single individual, perhaps knapping a single quartzite nodule (Figure 19.7).

Several coprolites have been recovered from the top and middle area of the hearth. At least one of these coprolites contains shell fragments (Figures 19.7 and 19.8), and since there is nothing to scavenge from mussel shells, it is likely that these coprolites could be human. Apart from shell fragments (Figure 19.9a), the coprolites also contain small mammal remains that have been very heavily digested (Figures 19.9b, 9c and 9d). Rabbit bones are also present. These high degrees of digestion show that it was probably produced by a mammalian carnivore, and although not conclusive the evidence is in agreement with previous experimental studies of human digestion (Crandall & Stahl 1995). The species content of the food remains in these coprolites suggests a diverse diet and further may indicate human predation on small mammals as seen in much older stages of human evolution (Fernández-Jalvo et al. 1999).

Post-depositional processes have not been destructive and all remains would have been rapidly buried as they were abandoned by the hominids. This is indicated by several of the shells resting in unstable positions such as lying laterally or on the convex side of the shell.

Bone remains are almost absent from the area of the hearth (Figure 19.7). This absence distinguishes this area from other human occupation levels at the Gibraltar caves. The relatively low nutritional content of mussels (compared with meat from vertebrates), and the relatively low number of individuals recovered from this site, seem to be insufficient to cover dietary needs for any length of time. The absence of disturbance of the shell assemblage, the absence of bone remains as food discard, the sequential distribution of hearth and knapping, and the distribution of knapping debris all suggest that this could have been a one day occupation. The sequence of activities interpreted from this unit, therefore, is as follows: hominids (perhaps a single individual) obtained mussels from a colony nearby the site; branches were collected to prepare a fire in the cave; the fire was used to open and cook the shellfish; and finally, when the fire was almost extinguished, one of the hominids started knapping next to the embers to make a quartzite tool. After the cave was abandoned these remains were rapidly buried.

Acknowledgments
The authors are grateful to Paul Jeffery for taxonomic identification of marine molluscs and information about their living environments. Thanks are extended to Chris Stringer, Nick Barton and Clive Finlayson for organising this special volume, as well as for their help during excavation and discussions. Andy Currant provided many helpful comments on the manuscript for which we are grateful. We are also very grateful to the whole excavation team for assistance and constant collaboration with taphonomic analyses. This taphonomic project is part of a funded project to YFJ by the European Community ENV4–CT96–5043.

References

Andrews, P. (1990). *Owls, Caves and fossils.* London: Natural History Museum.
Andrews, P., Cook, J., Currant, A. & Stringer, C. (1999). *Westbury Cave, the Natural History Museum Excavations 1976–1984.* Bristol: Western Academic and Specialist Press.
Andrews, P. & Fernández-Jalvo, Y. (1997). Surface modifications of the Sima de los Huesos fossil humans. *J. hum. Evol.* **33,** 191–217.
Barton, R.N.E. Currant, A.P. Fernández-Jalvo, Y. Finlayson, J.C. Goldberg, P. Macphail, R. Pettitt, P.B. and Stringer, C. (1999). Gibraltar Nenaderthals and results of recent excavations in Gorham's, Vanguard and Ibex Caves. *Antiquity* **73,** 13–23
Brain, C.K. (1981). *The Hunters and the Hunted.* Chicago: University of Chicago Press.
Beherenmeyer, A.K. (1978). Taphonomic and ecologic information on bone weathering. *Paleobiology* **4,** 150–162.
Carbonell, E. Bermúdez de Castro. J.M. Arsuaga, J.L. Díez, J.C. Rosas, A. Cuenca-Bescós, G. Sala, R. Mosquera, M. & Rodríguez, X.P. (1995). Lower Pleistocene hominids and artefacts from Atapuerca-TD6 (Spain). *Science,* **269,** 826–830.
Crandall, B.C. & Stahl, P. (1955). Human digestive effects on a micromammalian skeleton. *J. Archaeol. Sci.* **22,** 789–797.
Dart, R.A. (1957). The osteodontokeratic culture of *Australopithecus prometeus. Transvaal Museum Memoirs,* **10.**
Díez, J.C. (1992). *Zooarqueología de Atapuerca (Burgos) ye Implicaciones Paleoeconómicas del Estudio Tafonómico de Yacimientos del Pleistoceno Medio.* PhD. Thesis.Universidad Complutense de Madrid.
Díez, J.C. Fernández-Jalvo, Y. Rosell, J & Cáceres I. (1999). The site formation of "Aurora Stratum" TD6 Gran Dolina (Atapuerca, Spain) *J.hum.Evol.* 37, 623–652.
Fernández-Jalvo, Y. (1995). Small mammal taphonomy at La Trinchera de Atapueca (Burgos, Spain). A remarkable example of taphonomic criteria used for stratigraphic correlations and palaeoenvironment interpretations. *Palaeogeography, Palaeoclimatology, Palaeoecology* **114,** 167–195.
Fernández-Jalvo, Y., Andrews, P. & Denys, C. (1999). Cutmarks on small mammals at Olduvai Gorge Bed-I. *J. Hum. Evol.* **36,** 581–589.
Fernández-Jalvo, Y., Díez, J.C., Bermúdez de Castro, J.M., Carbonell, E. & Arsuaga, JL. (1996). Evidence of Early Cannibalism. *Science* **271,** 277–278.
Jaaksi, F.M. & Marti, C.D. (1984). Comparative food habits of *Bubo* owls in Mediterranean-type ecosystem. *The Condor* **86,** 288–296.
Jennings, J.N. (1985). *Karst geomorphology* New York: Basil Blckwell Inc.
Maguire, J.M. Pemberton, D. & Collett, N.H. (1980). The Makapansgat Limeworks grey breccia: hominids, hyaenas, hystricids or hillwash. *Palaeont. Afr.* **23,** 75–98.
Moreno, V. (1993). Estudio Arqueológico de la fauna del nivel 10A de Galería, Sierra de Atapuerca, Burgos, MA Thesis. Univ. Complutense de Madrid.
Parés, J.M. & Pérez-González, A. (1995). Paleomagnetic age for hominid fossils at Atapuerca archaeological site, Spain. *Science* **269,** 830–832.
Peringuey L. (1911). The Stone Ahges of South Africa as represented in the collection of the South African Mueum *Ann.S.Afr. Mus.* **8,** 1–218.
Pinto, A. & Andrews, P. (1999). Amphibian taphonomy and its application to the fossil record of Dolina (middle Pleistocene, Atapuerca, Spain). *Palaeogeog. Palaeoclimat. Palaeoecol.* 149, 411–429.
Taylor, P.D. (1986). Scanning electron microscopy of uncoated fossils. *Paleontology* **29,** 689–690.
Schick, K.D. & Toth, N. (1993). *Making Silent Stones Speak. Human Evolution and the Dawn of Technology.* Indiana: Simon and Schuster.
Stiner, M. Achyutan, H. Arsebuk, G. Howel, F.C. Josephson, S.C. Juell. K.E. Pigati, J. and Quade J. (1998). Reconstructing cave bear paleoecology from skeletons: a cross-disciplinary study of middle Pleistocene bears from Yarimburgaz Cave Turkey. *Paleobiology,* **24,** 74–98.
Sutcliffe, A.J. (1973). Caves of the East African rift valley . *Trans. Cave Res.Gp.* **15,** 41–65.

20

Geoarchaeological Investigation of Sediments from Gorham's and Vanguard Caves, Gibraltar: Microstratigraphical (Soil Micromorphological and Chemical) Signatures

Richard I. Macphail and Paul Goldberg
with a contribution by Jöhan Linderholm

Introduction

Gorham's and Vanguard Caves are enlarged karstic joints situated along the south eastern part of Gibraltar, overlooking the Mediterranean Sea. Gorham's Cave, was originally excavated by Waechter (1951: p.83) who noted that the deposits are comprised of locally cemented wind-blown sand which sloped seaward, and also recognized a number of light and dark sandy and clayey units, interbedded with stalagmitic layers. Vanguard Cave had never been excavated.

Recent excavations at both neighbouring caves have significantly increased the vertical and lateral exposures of the deposits since they were abandoned by Waechter over 45 years ago (Goldberg and Macphail in press). These exposures have permitted detailed microstratigraphic examination of the sediments that were either non-existent in the case of Vanguard, or the observation of sediments further toward the interior of the cave in Gorham's Cave. These observations revealed details on a number of depositional and post-depositional processes that previously were either not evident or were poorly documented. Vanguard Cave contains Mousterian (Middle Palaeolithic) artifacts; AMS radiocarbon dates range from 41 to 54 ka (Barton *et al.*. 1999). Gorham's Cave includes both Middle and Late Palaeolithic remains, and appears to post-date the last interglacial high sea level; radiocarbon dates range from 25 to 51 ka (Barton *et al.* 1999; see Pettitt this volume).

Since 1989, we have examined more than 130 thin sections, combining soil micromorphological observations with 70 chemical and microchemical analyses. Our aim has been to employ a microstratigraphic sedimentological approach to elucidate the geological dynamics and history of the site. These inquiries serve to complement other environmental and artifactual investigations conducted by our colleagues at Gibraltar, which are focused upon reconstructing lifestyles and environments of Late Pleistocene hominids, with specific focus on the Middle and Upper Palaeolithic boundary, an important period during the history of the human species.

Field and Laboratory Methods

Fieldwork and sampling were carried out during an early excavation season in 1989, and in a series of seasons that lasted from 1995 through to 1998. The sampling and laboratory studies at Gorham's were specifically aimed:

a) to compare the Lower, Middle and Upper sediment sequences in terms of chronology/climate, site formation processes and faunal/human use of the cave (Figures 20.1–20.2),

b) to identify the influence of humans on cave sedimentation, by investigating, for example, the microstratigraphy of combustion zones and associated post-depositional sedimentological effects. Knowledge of these process will permit us

c) to attempt, with other disciplines, to compare Middle Palaeolithic (Neanderthal?) and Upper Palaeolithic occupations (combustion zones and reworked combustion zones from the Middle and Upper Levels) and associated behaviour (Figure 20.2).

At Vanguard Cave the focus of thin section, chemical and magnetic susceptibility analyses was the assessment of site formation processes operating at the cave, specifically relating to the preservation of activity areas as

*Figure 20.1: Gorham's Cave 1997: field photo illustrating the dry, sandy Middle Level,
and the charcoal spreads within them.*

*Figure 20.2: Gorham's Cave 1997: field photo illustrating
the Middle/Upper Palaeolithic transition at the Upper Level,
including the layers with Upper Palaeolithic combustion
zones.*

exemplified by washed silts, black humic clays, and both *in situ* and modified combustion zones (Figures 20.3 – 20.5).

This study utilizes a selected portion of all the samples collected and studied from both caves. Table 20.1 presents the samples, locations, sediment types, and bulk analytical results discussed here.

Soil micromorphology

Undisturbed samples collected in the field were oven-dried at 60° C and then impregnated with a crystic polyester resin diluted with styrene or acetone (Murphy 1986). After curing for several weeks they were then placed overnight in an oven at 60° C. Slices from these blocks were manufactured into large-format thin sections (about 3.5 x 7 cm observable area) by Spectrum Petrographics (Winston, Oregon), or at the thin section laboratory of the Natural History Museum, London. In all, 95 thin sections have been made from Gorham's Cave and 42 from Vanguard Cave. Thin sections were described according to Bullock *et al..* (1985) and Courty *et al..* (1989). They were viewed at a number of magnifications from x1, up to x400 under a polarising microscope, employing plane polarised light (PPL), crossed polarised light (XPL), oblique incident light (OIL), and ultra-violet (blue) light (UVL) (*cf.* Stoops 1996). The combined use of these different types of illumination permit a large number of optical examinations, for example, forms of apatite (bone, guano and coprolites) which are autofluorescent under UVL. The authors made extensive use of their own thin section reference collections and material from other cave studies (e.g. Meignen 1989; Schiegl 1996; Weiner 1993; Weiner 1995).

Table 20.1: Samples, elevation, sediment type, micro-facies, chemistry and magnetic susceptibility.

SAMPLES	Relative Elevation	Sediment Type	Micro-facies present	pH (H$_2$O)	Tot. P$_{nitric}$ ppm	MS 10^{-8} Si/Kg	% LOI	P^{o} citric (ppm)	P$_{citric}$ tot (ppm)	P ratio
Vanguard Cave										
51a	*6.9*	**CZ**	*A/S*			76	*nd*	*220*	*nd*	
51b	*6.8*	**CZ**	*A/B/S*			31	*0.3*	*460*	*480*	*1.0*
52a	6.6	**S**	*S*		1880		2.5			
52b	6.5	**S**	*S*		850		1.1			
52c	6.4	**G**	*G/OM/S*		18000		3.9			
52d	6.3	**S**	*S*		760		1.3			
54a	*6.3*	**CZ**	*S/OM (G, C, A)*			234	*2.4*	*340*	*530*	*1.5*
54b	*6.29*	**CZ**	*S/A/OM (B, C)*			223	*3.8*	*270*	*440*	*1.6*
54c	*6.28*	**CZ**	*S/A*			128	*2.5*	*390*	*570*	*1.5*
54d	*6.27*	**S**	*S*			90	*1.8*	*750*	*700*	*0.9*
52e	6.1	**S**	*S*		2300		1.2			
Van-96–13	5.65	**Si**	*S/Si/OM*	8.1		98	2	740	520	*0.7*
Van-96–16	-0.67	**Si**	*Si (OM)*	8.1		99	2.6	750	730	*1.0*
Van-96–17	-0.77	**Si**	*Si/S (OM)*	7.8		63	1.3	1090	710	*0.6*
Van-96–18	-0.88	**Si**	*S/Si (OM)*	8.3		93	1.8	690	610	*0.9*
19a	-0.93	**CZ**	*S/OM (G, C, A)*		3210		3.3			
19b	-0.98	**CZ**	*S/A/OM (B, C)*		4860		2			
19c	-1.03	**CZ**	*S/OM (G, C, A)*		2300		3			
19d	-1.08	**CZ**	*S/OM (A, B)*		2060		1.6			
Van-98–100	-1.09		*C*	7.8		72	2.6	1290	1000	*0.8*
19e	-1.13	**CZ**	*S/OM (G, C, A)*		3060		2			
53	-4	**Si**	*Si*		1740	107	*0.55*	*520*	*470*	*0.9*
Van-98–101	-5	**S**	*S/Si*	8.6		22	0.7	350	470	*1.3*
Van-98–102	-5.25	**S**	*S/Si*	8.7		14	0.8	640	630	*1.0*
Van-98–103	-6.15	**Si**	*S/Si (A?)*	7.8		22	1.3	750	690	*0.9*
Gorham's Cave										
Gor-98–164	?			7.5		29	1.1	3380	3140	*0.9*
68	15.75	**CZ**	*S/C (B/G)*		7860		2.6			
67	15.65	**CZ**	*G/B/C*		31000		6.3			
Gor-96–52 ash	15.55	**CZ**	*B/C/G*	7.8		418	8.1	4080	2190	*0.5*
Gor-97–66a	15.3	**S**	*S*		810		0.1			
Gor-97–66c pale brown "hearth"	15.3	**CZ**	*S*			24	5	3870	4260	*1.1*
Gor-97–66b bedded brown under hearth	15.3	**G**	*S/G/OM*	8.0		23	4.1	4350	4200	*1.0*
66b	15.25	**G**			32800		2.8			
66c	15.2	**CZ**			41800		2.5			
Gor-89–28/29 "sands"	14.4	**S**	*S*	9.1		14	0.6	270	570	*2.0*
Gor-89-28/29 "lower silts"	14.38	**Si**	*S/Si/OM*	7.8		167	5.9	610	410	*0.7*

Table 20.1: continued.

SAMPLES	Relative Elevation	Sediment Type	Micro-facies present	pH (H$_2$O)	Tot.P$_{nitric}$ ppm	MS 10^{-8} si/Kg	% LOI	P$^{o}_{citric}$ (ppm)	P $_{citric}$ tot (ppm)	P ratio
69a	14.25	G	G/Om/s		10300	38	4.7	4110	3870	0.9
69b	14.1	G	G/Om/s		990	24	0.6	700	1020	1.4
69c	13.95	G	G/Om/s		7150	36	2.3	3950	3890	1.0
65a	13.9	G	Om/G/B/S		1890	17	0.5	1720	1350	0.8
69d	13.85	S	S/C		7420	56	2.6	3840	3590	0.9
65b	13.7	G	S/OM/G		14700	22	4.5	4350	4330	1.0
65c	13.51	G	S/OM/G		7270	16	4.3	3930	3610	0.9
71a	13.5	S	S/C		410		0.4			
71b	13.4	S	S (OM)		2660		1.3			
70a	13.3	S	S (OM)		1960		0.2			
70b	13.15	S	S (OM)		580		0.1			
70c	13	Si	Si (OM)		1970		1			
70d	12.9	S	S (OM)		2010		0.8			
64a	12.8	G	G/S/B		21980		5			
72a	12.7	G	G (S,B)		10050	32	5.7	4300	4340	1.0
Gor-89–11	12.65	S	S/G(OM)	8.0		47	2.3	4950	4530	0.9
64b	12.65	G	G/B		18500		5.9			
Gor-89–9b	12.6	G	G/OM		EDAX					
63a	12.6	G	G/Om/s		24000		2.9			
72b	12.55	G	G/C (S)		9160	21	3.2	4140	4090	1.0
63b	12.52	G	G		72100		3.1			
64c	12.5	S	S (G)		5020		1			
63c	12.44	G	G/Om/s		24500		5.3			
63d	12.36	S	S/C		17800		1.3			
63e	12.28	G	G/S/B		15400		0.9			
Gor-96–54	12.12	S	S (OM/B)	8.5		41	0.9	2880	2610	0.9
Gor-98–166	11.56	S	S/B	8.4		39	0.9	3260	2730	0.8
Gor-96–58	11.4	S	S (OM)	8.6		25	0.5	810	850	1.1
62	10.7	S	S/Ca/B		2630	67	1.4	1883	1631	0.8
60	10.5	S	S (Om)		1700		0.2			
Gor-96–59 upper	9.1	S	S/OM//Ca	8.4		72	2	1020	720	0.7
Gor-89–12	8.78	S	S (Om)	8.1		100	2.5	1210	810	0.7
Gor-89–13	8.7	Si	Si/Om (C)	7.8		302	7	2540	540	0.2
Gor-89–14	8.65	Si	Si/G/B	7.2		128	6.9	4380	4020	0.9
Gor-89–15	8.5	S	S/OM	7.8		271	8.7	350	90	0.3
Gor-98–152	8.44	G	G/Om/s/C	7.9		230	5	3380	1380	0.4
Gor-89–18	8.29	S	S/Ca	8.2		50	3	310	660	2.1
Gor-98–153	8.29	CZ	C/OM	7.9		247	7.1	360	120	0.3
Gor-98–151	7.44	S	S/OM	8.1		82	4	540	550	1.0

Key to Sediment (Facies) type:
CZ – Combustion Zone, G – Guano, S – Sands, Si – Silts,
and micro-facies types present:
A – ash, B – burrows (biological activity), C – charcoal, Ca – secondary calcium carbonate, G – guano, OM – organic matter, S – sands, Si – silt,

Figure 20.3: Vanguard Cave 1997: field photo of Vanguard North and the interbedded sands and silt (sample 53).

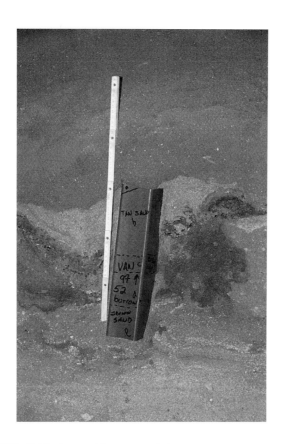

Figure 20.4: Vanguard Cave 1997: field photo of long monolith sample 52, across sands and a possible transformed combustion zone.

Figure 20.5: Vanguard Cave 1997: field photo of Mousterian combustion zone set in dark silts (samples 19 and 104).

During 1990–91, the constituents of 35 thin sections from the Gorham's Cave excavation of 1989 were systematically analysed (e.g. quartz sand, charcoal, organic matter, bone, coprolitic remains) and recorded on an abundance scale of 1 to 5. Other elements (e.g. microfabric type and related distribution) were also noted for each sample/context. A number of typical sediment examples were then studied by SEM/EDXRA (see below)(Goldberg and Macphail, unpublished data).

During the 1995–1997 excavations at Gibraltar, sediments from Vanguard Cave and new deposits from Gorham's Cave were studied in thin section, thereby enlarging the previous database from the latter. Excavation benefitted from microstratigraphic data recovered from the previous year's sampling. For example, in 1997, a microscope and thin sections from the 1989–1996 excavations were taken to Gibraltar in order to aid in the understanding and excavation of partially exposed features and sediments, and to provide insights into future sampling strategies. The present soil micromorphology database allows the identification of several types of sedimentary signatures and microfacies (see Results). Thin sections from the 1998 excavation have yet to be examined.

Microchemistry

Micromorphological thin section data and bulk chemical findings from both caves were supplemented by SEM/EDXRA and microprobe analyses. Sediments from the 1989 excavations at Gorham's Cave, were analysed by SEM/EDXRA. From Vanguard Cave three layers (layers a, b and c) of typical microfabric types were selected from an uncovered thin section (Van-96–11–6) for microprobe (line and elemental map) analyses. These studies were carried out at University College London, using a Jeol JXA8600 EPMA microprobe.

Soil chemistry (by Jöhan Linderholm)
Bulk chemical analyses

Samples were analysed both at UCL, Institute of Archaeology, and at Umeå University, Sweden. Bulk samples (<0.5 mm) from the 1989 and 1995–1997 excavations were analysed for total phosphorus (P) employing ignition, HCl pretreatment and 2N nitric acid extraction (UCL). Some of these and samples from the 1998 excavation were further subjected to chemical and magnetic susceptibility analysis using methods that have been successfully developed at Umeå University, Sweden (Arrhenius 1934; Arrhenius 1955; Engelmark 1996; Arrhenius 1934; 1955; Engelmark and Linderholm 1996; Macphail and Cruise in press). Only a brief outline is provided here.

All samples were homogenised, passed through a 0.5 mm sieve, and then subsampled. Measurements were made of LOI (loss-on-ignition; 550° C), volume magnetic susceptibility (MS), MS after ignition at 550°C (MS550), 2% soluble citric acid soluble phosphate ($P°_{citric}$, represented as P_2O_5), and 2% soluble citric acid soluble phosphate after ignition at 550°C ($P_{citric}tot$). Two percent (2%) citric acid is a weaker extractant of P than is nitric acid, but the research cited above has shown that successfully differentiates inorganic phosphate (e.g., bone and mineral phosphate, including cemented guano and coprolites) from organic phosphate (e.g., plant material, bird and animal dung). Dominantly mineral/inorganic phosphate measurements achieve low P ratios (1.0), while the presence of organic phosphate raises the P ratio (1.0). Phosphate and magnetic susceptibility data are reported in ppm and SI-units (SI^{10-8} Si/Kg), respectively. As a caveat, it is stated that the fractional conversion MS data gained during the ignition of the soil at 550°C is only a qualitative guide to fractional conversion (%MS_{conv})(*cf.* Tite and Mullins 1971; Crowther and Barker 1995). In short, this measure is an indication of how much of the potential magnetic susceptibility is recorded in the sediment. These studies were carried out at the Centre for Environmental Archaeology, Umeå University, Sweden.

These multidisciplinary investigations permit the detailed characterisation of sediment types according to a number of broadly defined attributes, such as microfacies (included components, grain size and sorting, microfabric type), and chemical and magnetic signature.

Results

Field

Gorham's Cave

The current excavations have produced for the first time since Waechter's excavations a continuous stratigraphic section in the Middle Palaeolithic and the Upper Palaeolithic deposits from the Middle and Upper stratigraphic levels of the cave. Primarily for functional purposes, we subdivided the stratigraphic sequence into a number of thick units which from bottom to top are:

Lower Levels – These sediments correspond roughly to Waechter's layers S1 through S3 (elevations of ~800–880 cm; Middle Palaeolithic). They are composed of interbedded and irregularly-bedded bright red and reddish brown clayey sand with abundant charcoal and tan/pink sands (fine to medium). Abundant limpets, shells and coarse travertine roof fall occur within the lighter pink, calcareous sands.

Middle Levels – These units correspond roughly to Waechter's layer P (elevations of ~1250–1265 cm; Middle Palaeolithic), and are similar to those in the Lower Levels but are slightly less sandy and show more lithologic variability (Figure 20.1). They include (1) dark brown, organic-rich silty clay, with light and dark stringers; (2) grey sand and irregularly bedded yellowish brown sand containing coarse charcoal fragments and yellow inclusions; (3) brown black organic-rich clay with whitish gritty phosphatic lenses; and (4) interbedded massive homogeneous coarse brown clayey sand.

Upper Levels – These sediments coincide approximately with Waechter's layers F through K (elevations of ~1400 to 1580 cm) (Figures 20.1 and 20.3). They contain predominantly Middle Palaeolithic artifacts, but include the transition to the Upper Palaeolithic. These sediments are composed of a number of different lithological types:

(1) dry, brown, crumbly silty clay lenses with charcoal flecks and hyaena coprolites;
(2) soft to very hard cemented ashes with fine flecks of charcoal associated with dark brown, organic-rich combustion zone-like accumulations; (3) soft, pink sand with charcoal flecks on soft darker pinkish brown sand containing mussel shells. Good exposures between the Middle and Upper Levels (Sq. B/C 99 to B/C 101) near the Upper/Middle Palaeolithic transition show distinct lateral differences in sediment types:

toward the exterior massive sandy units are calcareous, with some ashy bands and charcoal, but no evidence of *in situ* burning is present; there is good preservation of bone, shell and limestone (Figure 20.2). Two meters toward the rear of the cave, laterally equivalent sediments are generally softer, finely bedded, finer grained and apparently much richer in organic matter and phosphorous. Bones or shells are absent, and limestone clasts are weathered and commonly phosphatised.

Vanguard Cave

Excavation at Vanguard Cave revealed Middle Palaeolithic artefacts and combustion zones in generally massive, coarse sands interfingered with tabular to lenticular units of brown silts and silty sands (Figures 20.3 – 20.6). In the 'Vanguard North' section massive sands are punctuated with numerous reddish-brown clay and silt stringers that thin in a direction away from cracks in the bedrock walls suggesting that the brown silty units (e.g., sample 53, Figure 20.3) were washed in to the cave along joints and fissures.

Additional observations at Vanguard show that the present-day surface slopes at about 40% from the back of the cave to the entrance. Also, most of the Vanguard sediments are calcareous with little diagenesis, except for phosphatisation at the very top of the cave. Here, interdigitated sands and black humic clays occur. The paucity of karstic cave ornamentation (e.g., stalactites) suggests relatively dry conditions within the cave throughout most its history.

Laboratory

Soil Micromorphology

Sediment types from both caves are grouped according to their facies and sub-facies characteristics, namely,

S – Sands: clean fine- to medium-size sands; massive to very coarsely bedded, commonly well-sorted, with few charcoal, and very few humic and excremental inclusions (Figures 20.7 and 20.8). Variants at Gorham's Cave include moderately sorted sands containing few bone, guano, limestone and travertine/flowstone (speleothem) fragments, and at Vanguard Cave, moderately sorted sands containing land snail shell fragments.

Si – Silts: calcitic and non-calcitic silts; finely bedded, commonly well-sorted with few fine sand, charcoal and few humic fragments. Variants at Gorham's Cave include, non-calcitic silty humic clay, with fine inclusions of guano and bone (sample Gor-89–14; Table 20.1), and at Vanguard Cave, a calcitic, in places ashy (?) fine fabric, and planar pseudomorphs of plant fragments (sample Van 53; Table 20.1).

G – Guano: the guano facies is composed dominantly of two sub-facies. Subtype *Gi* is heterogeneous, reddish brown, porous, highly humic and excremental (burrowed) in character, and may contain inclusions of bone, charcoal

Figure 20.6: Vanguard Cave: cross section showing the location of combustion zones, silt and sand beds, and samples.

Figure 20.7: Gorham's Cave: macro-photograph of thin section Gor-89–9, showing pale guano layers over bedded, likely burned guano/combustion zone material over sands containing bone (e.g., left corner). (Frame 7.5cm).

and plant fragments. Irregular-shaped, amorphous material, sometimes containing plant material and autofluorescent under UVL, may also occur as inclusions (sample Van52c; Gor-65b; Table 20.1). The second type, *Gii*, is homogeneous, pale grey, massive/bedded, non-birefringent, and is highly autofluorescent under UVL (sample Van52c; Gor-69a; Gor-63b;Table 20.1; Figure 20.7). It is similar to secondary phosphates observed in other prehistoric caves in the Mediterranean region (Weiner 1995; Schiegl 1996).

CZ – Combustion zone: variants include – at Gorham's Cave – rubefied and similar to Gi, with coarse wood charcoal fragments, coarse burned bone, charred fine organic matter and burned guano; an Upper Palaeolithic example (sample Gor-97–68; Table 20.1) is coarsely bedded with much included sand and a blackened/charred

Figure 20.8: Gorham's Cave: macro-photograph of thin section Gor-89–31, an example of interbedded sand and brown silts. (Frame 7.5cm).

excremental and charcoal-rich fine fabric; below this (sample Gor-97–67; Table 20.1), the combustion zone is dark yellow to red (rubefied) and guano rich (Gi). Towards the cave wall the uppermost combustion zone (samples Gor-97–68/Gor-89–23B) is cemented by secondary calcite. At Vanguard Cave, rubefied, finely bedded silts (Si) contain sand, fine charcoal, charred organic matter, burned bone and ash crystals (e.g., sample Van 54). In the case of sample Van 51, weakly rubefied sands (S) occur, sometimes with a 10–20 mm thick ash layer composed of micritic remains of wood ash (no phytoliths). This ash exhibits pseudomorphs of very thin burrows and broad excrements (including biogenic calcite). Bedding and welding of micrite and the increasing abundance upwards of sand testify to exposure and weathering of the combustion zone.

In Table 20.1, more information on the micro-facies that are present and make up the sediment/facies types, are listed as A – ash, B – burrows (biological activity), C – charcoal, Ca – secondary calcium carbonate, G – guano, OM – organic matter (plant fragments and amorphous organic matter), S – sands and Si – silt.

Chemical and Magnetic Susceptibility Characteristics (with Jöhan Linderholm)

Chemical and magnetic susceptibility characteristics are presented in Table 20.1 and Figures 20.9 – 20.15. Most sediments are alkaline (Gorham's Cave, mean pH 8.0, range pH 7.2–9.1; Vanguard Cave, mean pH 8.1, range

pH 7.8–8.6). Scattergrams have been employed to compare the sediments of the two caves. Figures 20.9 and 20.10 demonstrate the comparison of the chemical and magnetic susceptibility characteristics of the sediments from both caves. Generally, the sediments from Gorham's Cave have higher amounts of phosphate, but a similar range of MS values, as compared to those of Vanguard Cave (Figures 20.9 and 20.10). Similarly, sediments at Gorham's Cave (mean 3% LOI; max. %LOI 6.9) are generally more organic than those at Vanguard Cave (mean 2% LOI; max. % LOI 3.9)(Table 20.1; Figure 20.9).

Qualitative values for $\%MS_{conv.}$ are high throughout the sediments at Gorham's and Vanguard Caves, but with some values >100% because of a drop in MS after ignition. (This last phenomenon is currently under investigation.) Some high MS and $\%MS_{conv.}$ values are coincident with known combustion areas ("combustion zones") at both caves (Figure 20.10).

When MS values are plotted against elevation at Vanguard Cave, the scattergram is obviously skewed by the sampling of known "combustion zone" samples (Figures 20.9 and 20.11), and no particular trend is visible. On the other hand, at Gorham's Cave, the scattergram points to some enigmatically high MS values in the "Lower Levels" (Figure 20.12).

Analyses of total nitric acid extractable phosphorus at Gorham's Cave suggests that there is a general trend for increasing amounts of P from the Lower to the Higher Levels (Tot. P_{nitric} ppm in Table 20.1):

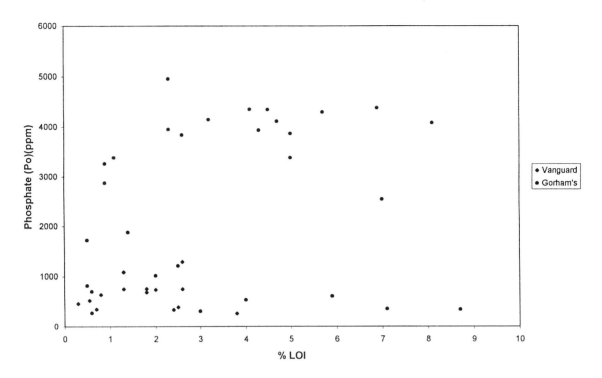

*Figure 20.9: Scattergram; Gorham's and Vanguard Cave – % LOI (loss on ignition) versus ppm Phosphate (P*o*).*

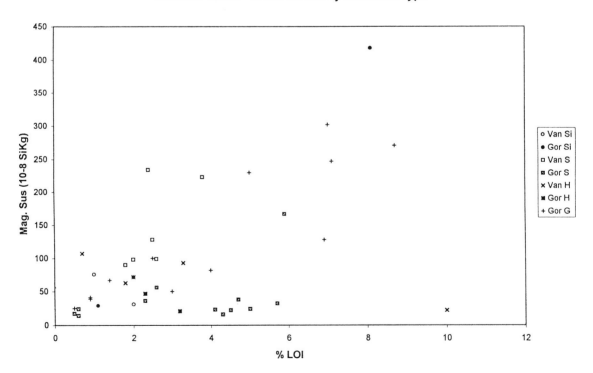

Figure 20.10: Scattergram; Gorham's and Vanguard Cave – %LOI (loss on ignition) versus MS (magnetic susceptibility SIKg[10–1]).

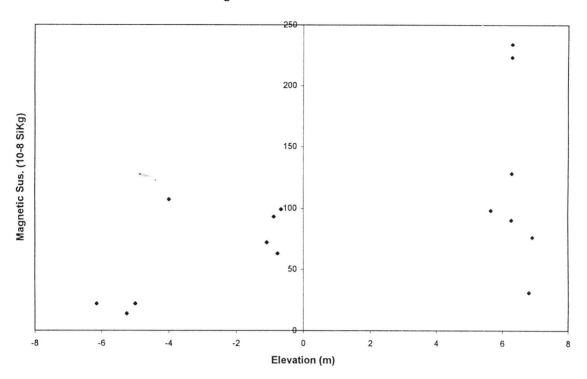

Figure 20.11: Scattergram; Gorham's and Vanguard Cave Figure 14: Scattergram; Vanguard Cave – Elevation versus MS (magnetic susceptibility SIKg$^{10-1}$).

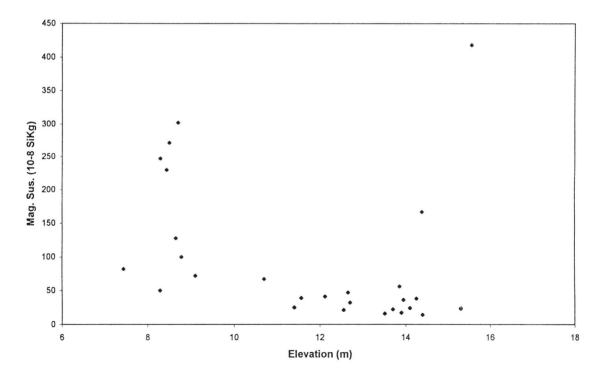

Figure 20.12: Scattergram; Gorham's Cave MS – Elevation versus MS (magnetic susceptibility SIKg$^{10-1}$).

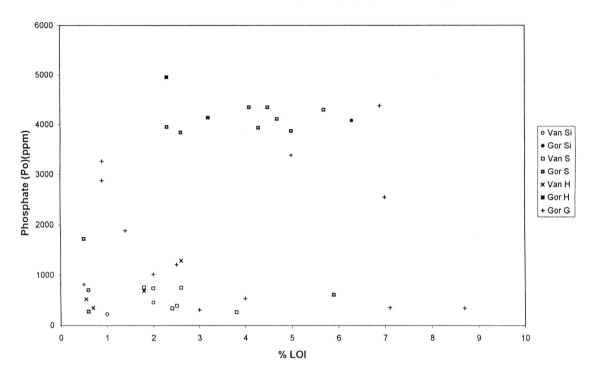

Figure 20.13: Scattergram; Gorham's and Vanguard Cave – %LOI (loss on ignition) versus ppm P⁰ (citric acid extractable phosphate).

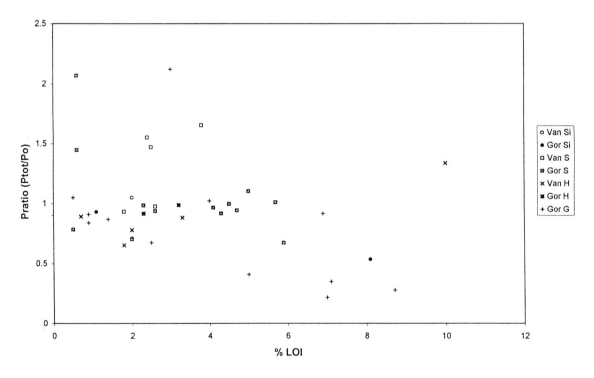

Figure 20.14: Scattergram; Gorham's and Vanguard Cave – %LOI (loss on ignition) versus P ratio (Ptot/ P⁰).

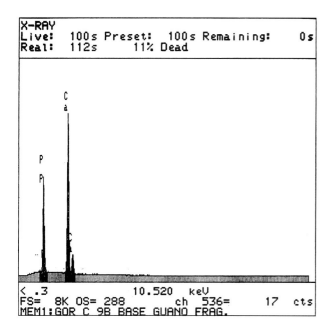

```
X-RAY
Live:   100s Preset:   100s Remaining:    0s
Real:   112s      11% Dead

        C
        a

    P
   Pl



<  .3          10.520  keV
FS=   8K OS= 288      ch  536=      17  cts
MEM1:GOR C 9B BASE GUANO FRAG.
```

Figure 20.15: Gorham's Cave; sample Gor-89–9b; SEM/ EDXRA (peaks of P and Ca in guano – Gii).

a)   Lower Levels – These are moderately phosphatic (2,000–5,000 ppm phosphorous – P).

b)   Middle Levels – Here, the sands are poorly phosphatic (400–2,000 ppm P), with bands richer in phosphorus (2,000–10,000 ppm P).

c)   Higher Levels – Again, the sandy layers have the least phosphatic values (e.g., 600–7,000 ppm P), although the darker, more humic layers are extremely phosphate rich (20,000–70,000 ppm P).

At Vanguard Cave, a maximum of 18,000 ppm P is recorded from sample 52c, a dark fill-feature, while the associated sands (max. 2,000 ppm P) and silts (2300 ppm P) are far less rich in P (Figure 20.3). (At the microscale, microprobe analysis shows that up to 14% P or 140,000 ppm P, is present; see below).

Field observations and micromorphological analyses show that the deposits can be divided into broad sediment types (see soil micromorphology, above)(Table 20.1). This subdivision is substantiated by the analytical data, which shows that at Gorham's Cave the sediments are commonly more phosphatic than at Vanguard Cave, and that combustion zones and guano at Gorham's Cave are likely to be more organic compared to those of Vanguard Cave (Figure 20.13). Sands and silts at both caves are the least humic. Measurement of P° and Ptot by citric acid extraction (P$_{citric}$) permits a nuanced chemical separation of the sediment types by comparing ratios of these values ("P ratio") (Figure 20.14). Low (1.0) P ratios dominate for burned areas (CZ- combustion zones) and those with likely secondary calcium phosphatic (see microchemistry) mineral deposition (G – guano); these sediments generally

contain inorganic phosphate in the form of bone (apatite). It is therefore intriguing to note the presence of combustion zones and sandy deposits with enhanced (1.0) P ratios at both caves. Such ratios (1.5–2.0) imply inputs and non-mineralisation of organic phosphate (organic matter, bird dung).

Microchemistry
Non-quantitative SEM/EDXRA confirmed initial ideas of the elemental makeup of several micro-facies types. These include,

1)   peaks of Ca indicating calcite in layers without P (i.e., not calcium phosphate/apatite);
2)   dominant associations of Si and Al with smaller quantities of P and Fe, pointing to the presence of iron and phosphate enriched clays; and
3)   layers containing only Ca and P, confirming the occurrence of guano in the form of calcium phosphate (Figure 20.15).

Quantitative microprobe analysis was performed on three layers (a, b and c) within sample 52 from Vanguard Cave (Table 20.1). These three examples from a microfabric within a "guano" (G) type sediment were analysed by elemental mapping and by line analysis. In broad terms, these layers contain mean values of 9% Si, 7% Ca, 2.9% P, 1.8% Al, 1.5% Fe, and 0.8% Mn (n=227), with maximum values of 41% Si, 36% Ca, 14% P, 35% Al 27% Fe and 42% Mn, respectively. Layer a (type Gi) is dominated by an association of Ca/P with a crack infilled with Mn (Figures 20.16 –20.18). In contrast, layer b (type Gii) – although containing Ca/P – is much richer in Fe, Al and Si (Figure 20.19 and 20.20). Layer c (type Gii) is heterogeneous and contains patches again rich in Ca/P (Figure 20.21).

Discussion

Microstratigraphical (soil micromorphological and chemical) signatures (with Jöhan Linderholm)
The identification and recognition of microstratigraphic signatures permit us to extend our interpretations of site formation processes and human activities at both sites. These are discussed in terms of the major sediment (facies) types.

S – Sands: At both caves, clean, well-sorted, fine to medium sands are likely to reflect episodes of dry conditions and wind blown deposition of sands from coastal dunes present along the coastline when sea levels were lower than today (Finlayson and van Andel this volume). This origin and mode of deposition is reflected in their low LOI, phosphate content and MS values.

Sands can contain rounded sand-size shell, limestone and fossil fragments from these putative dunes. The sands can also include sand-size bone, non-rounded limestone and stall fragments, and charcoal, some of which have

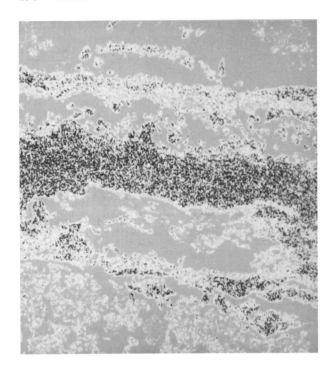

Figure 20.16: Microprobe elemental map: Van-52–11–6a – P in guano – Gii. Frame length ~ 4.5mm.

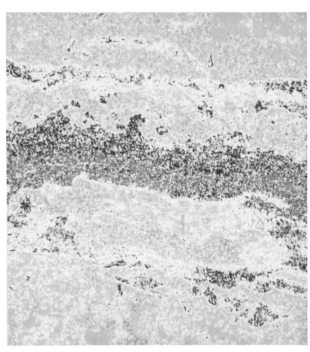

Figure 20.17: Microprobe elemental map: Van-52–11–6a – Ca in guano – Gii. Frame length ~ 4.5mm.

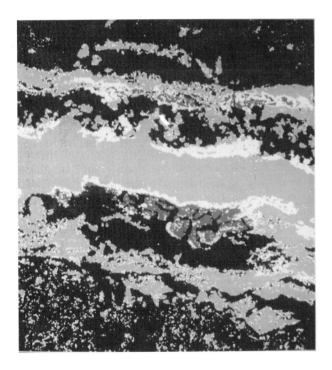

Figure 20.18: Microprobe elemental map: Van-52–11–6a – Ca/P in guano – Gii. Frame length ~ 4.5mm.

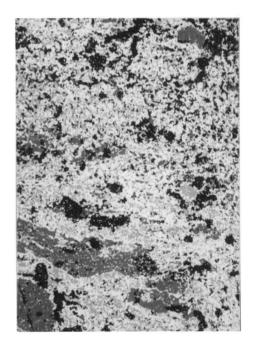

Figure 20.19: Microprobe elemental map: Van-52–11–6b – P in guano – Gi. Frame length ~ 9mm.

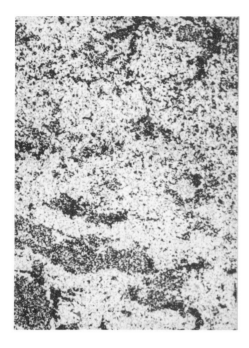

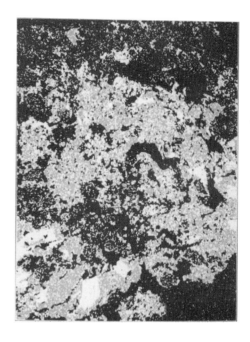

Figure 20.20: Microprobe elemental map: Van-52–11–6b – Fe/P/Ca in guano – Gi. Frame length ~ 9mm.

Figure 20.21: Microprobe elemental map: Van-52–11–6c – Mn/P/Ca in guano – Gi. Frame length ~ 8mm.

been penecontemporaneously reworked within the caves. Charcoal may occur in broadly bedded layers within the generally massive sand bodies, or in thinner layers produced by occasional wash events, as for example from a reworked Mousterian combustion zone in the Middle Level at Gorham's Cave (Gor-97–71)(Figure 20.1). Of particular interest are some sand bodies in the Lower Levels of Gorham's which have enhanced (>2.0) P ratios that are indicative of unexpectedly high proportions of organic phosphate (samples Gor-89–18, Gor-98–151; Table 20.1; Figure 20.14)(see Silts, below). At Vanguard Cave, massive sands are typically interbedded with silts, and may well represent cyclical/seasonal climatic/weather (i.e., wetter/drier) fluctuations (Figures 20.3 and 20.8).

Si – Silts: At Gorham's Cave, silts are best expressed in the Lower Levels, and like the sands, they display similarly unexpected characteristics in the form of enigmatically high MS values (samples Gor-89–13/14; see also sand samples Gor-89–12/15; Table 20.1). One possible explanation is that washed sediment from Mousterian combustion zones – not yet exposed – have produced these high MS values, confirming field and thin section hypotheses that these beds are colluvial and contain burned clay. The soil micromorphology of these silts is also consistent with their high LOI and occasional highly phosphatic character (sample Gor-89–14; Table 20.1). We suggest that these silts result from the colluvial wash of fine surface sediment enriched in bird guano and organic matter brought in by birds for nesting material: Gibraltar caves being well-established roosts and nesting places for migratory birds throughout the Pleistocene to the present

(Finlayson and Pacheco, this volume). The importance of birds in some Mediterranean coastal caves cannot be over-emphasised. At Arene Candide, Liguria, Italy, for example, late Pleistocene climatic reconstructions are based upon recovered bird and small mammal bones, and complementary soil thin section studies (Macphail *et al.* 1994; Wattez *et al.* 1990). Raptors also deposited guano and bone fragments (cf. Andrews 1990). The cave was also occupied by hominids roughly at the same time that the these guano and organic-rich deposits were accumulating, since most combustion zones (discussed below) at Gorham's Cave characteristically contain charred and rubefied guano material (Gi; see below).

At Vanguards Cave, silts are finely bedded, and may contain planar voids that are presumably pseudomorphs of plant remains. The origin of these silts (e.g. Van-53) – as derived from surface soils washed through fissures in the karstic system – is supported by their relatively low LOI values (even compared to the sands), and high MS and MS$_{conv}$ values As burned sediments are not present, they therefore are the likely result of in-wash of long-weathered and strongly oxidised Red Mediterranean (terra rossa) soils (Collins *et al.* 1994). The occasional fine bone and charcoal content, ultimately represents the influence of fauna and humans within the cave (see Vanguard combustion zones).

G – Guano: Organic, phosphate-rich and biologically-worked guano layers (Gi), which commonly contain fragments of bone, charcoal and individual bird droppings (Figures 20.19 – 20.21), result from the surface accumulation of biological remains from bird activity (Finlayson and Pacheco, this volume). Other animals, such as hyenas and hominids, also contribute to these biological deposits, as shown by numerous hyaena coprolite fragments and the results of faunal analyses (Barton *et al.* 1999). Many guano deposits are also associated with combustion zones (see below).

Studies of guano show it to be composed of inorganic forms of calcium phosphate, such as apatite (Horwitz 1989; Wattez *et al.* 1990). The highly burrowed nature and excremental character of these deposits testify to the intensity of biological activity, the likely cause – along with oxidation – of pollen destruction in these sediments. (Despite the high quantities of phosphate and numerous attempts, no pollen has been found in any of the deposits.)

Massive, homogeneous grey coloured guano layers, (Gii), are very pure (Figures 20.7 and 20.15 – 20.17). They result from the deposition of secondary calcium phosphate. (Weiner *et al.* 1995b), that is ultimately derived from bird guano (Gi). There are numerous examples of recent studies of cave phosphates that span the temperate regions of Europe (Yellow Breccias of Middle Pleistocene Westbury-sub-Mendip; Macphail and Goldberg, 1999; Andrews 1990), down to the Mediterranean region (Courty *et al.* 1989; Goldberg and Macphail 1990; Macphail and Goldberg in press; Weiner *et al.* 1995). In the latter region, bone, ashes and other sediments in Pleistocene caves have been replaced by a variety of secondary·phosphates, and it is possible that at Gorham's Cave some examples of Gii result from the similar replacement of ash here (Figure 20.7) and at Vanguard Cave (Figures 20.4 and 20.16 – 20.17).

CZ – Combustion zones: As discussed above, many combustion zones at Gorham's Cave appear to be rubefied, and contain charred guano layers, rich in organic matter and phosphate (samples Gor-97–66/67/68, Table 20.1; Figure 20.2). At Vanguard Cave, combustion zones occur as barely disturbed ash layers overlying rubefied sediments (e.g. sands – sample 51, Table 20.1), or as layered, rubefied and charcoal-rich "silts" (e.g., sample 54, Table 20.1; Figure 20.5). These findings show that human occupation and burning activity took place on both sandy and silty substrates, implying no preference for either. It is also worth noting that the 50 mm thick sequence of combustion zone–>silts–>sand in sample 54, clearly demonstrates the repeated use of the same locality as a fireplace. This inference is further indicated by the MS values of the washed CZ deposits which increase upwards, implying final heating of this multi-laminated combustion zone deposit (sample 54, Table 20.1). Phosphate analysis of the combustion zone sediments shows that levels of heating were low (<550° C) and not sufficiently high to convert organic phosphate (organic bird dung) into inorganic forms.

The presence of charcoal in sample 52 (Figure 20.3) also indicate that the reddish brown guano deposits (Gi; Figures 20.19 – 20.20) likely result from rubefication by heating. On the other hand, the Gii layer mentioned above

(Figures 20.16 – 20.18) constitutes the phosphatised remains of an earlier ash layer (*cf.* Schiegl 1996).

At Gorham's Cave, combustion zones have the same values of $MS_{conv.}$ of 70%, even whilst their MS values clearly differ: from 23–24 $^{10-8}$ SiKg to 418 $^{10-8}$ SiKg (samples Gor-97–66b/66c; Gor-96–52; Table 20.1). This difference in MS probably relates to the different amounts of iron that are present, with pale layers such as Gor-97–66c likely being leached of iron. Microprobe analysis at Vanguard Cave showed that sediments can be influenced by the mobilisation, leaching and redeposition of iron and manganese (e.g. Hill and Forti 1997). The local cement-ation of the uppermost Upper Palaeolithic combustion zone by sparitic calcite is another example of a secondary process that can affect combustion zones. Commonly, ash is not preserved in the combustion zones at Gorham's Cave, because of decalcification and dispersal by aeolian reworking. In some areas (e.g. sample Gor-71), prominent accumulations of charcoal are present, but ashes are not obvious. Apart from these chemical taphonomic changes, some combustion zone layers at Gorham's appear to be reworked by fauna, wash and wind. Hence Middle Palaeolithic combustion zones are not particularly well-defined (although, some scattered decimeter size *in situ* hearths were observed in the field).

Sediment deposition at the two caves

Our present thinking substantiates the thoughts of (Waechter 1951) by postulating a coastal environment dominated by a large dune system. At Vanguard Cave, for example, the entire accumulation of >18 m is, overall, inclined toward the rear of the cave suggesting that the bulk of the sand mass is situated further seaward where sea levels were lower. Furthermore, sand is interspersed with silty washed accumulations, which gave rise to the interbedding of the sands and silts. Aeolian and sheet wash processes removed and reworked many of the sediments associated with Middle Palaeolithic occupation, resulting in redistribution of artefacts and combustion zone material. In fact, within Vanguard Cave, only three, clearly recognizable *in situ* areas tied to use of fire were recognized.

In Gorham's Cave, on the other hand, site formation processes are more complex, and they are considerably more influenced by organic and phosphatic inputs and biological activity; the sediments are volumetrically less mineralogenic. Unlike at Vanguard Cave, where sediments are overall more uniform throughout, those at Gorham's Cave exhibit greater vertical and lateral variation. In the rear of the cave, where the stratigraphically highest sediments are exposed, the deposits are quite damp and extensive diagenesis (e.g. calcification, decalcification, leaching and phosphatisation) is common. In contrast, at the front of the cave – and comprising stratigraphically older deposits – dry sandy calcareous sands are more dominant, associated with guano-rich silty deposits. In general, Upper Palaeolithic combustion zones are massive, and generally represent *in situ* features, whereas Middle Palaeolithic ones show a greater degree of dismantling, as outlined above.

Conclusions

This detailed microstratigraphic study – including soil micromorphology and chemistry – has brought to light a number of depositional and post-depositional processes linked to geogenic, biogenic and anthropogenic activities in these two caves. These major findings can be summarized within two broad categories:

Cave Sedimentation:

Sedimentological history differs between the two caves, although both were subjected to substantial inputs of windblown sand derived from the plains in front of the caves. Sediments at Vanguard Cave are less phosphatic and organic, and generally have undergone few diagenetic changes. Remarkably, *in situ* combustion zone ash layers are preserved at Vanguard Cave. Although at both caves sedimentation is affected by likely seasonal/climatic fluctuations in cave water, karstic activity (e.g. speleothems) is absent from Vanguard Cave, despite the evident occurrence of waterlain silts. Animals, especially birds, have contributed substantially to organic and phosphatic sedimentation, especially at Gorham's Cave, and ephemeral surfaces were subjected to intense biological activity, including the presence of humans.

Hominid Activity:

As evidenced by the microstratigraphic nature of the combustion zones (and artefacts), hominids were influential in modifying sediment at both caves, as shown by the presence charred guano. There is also compelling evidence of the presence of combustion zones or combustion areas being reused at Vanguard Cave; as yet this situation is less demonstrable at Gorham's Cave. We also noted that Neanderthals occupied both sandy and silty substrates.

Acknowledgments

The authors wish to thank the National Geographic Society for funding this research, the Natural History Museum for its support, and Nick Barton (who also supplied Figure 20.7) of Oxford Brookes University, Clive Finlayson of Gibraltar Museum and Chris Stringer of the Natural History Museum, for collaboration and discussion. Also thanked are Sandra Bond (SEM/EDXRA, UCL), Cyril Bloomfield (phosphate analysis, UCL), Jöhan Linderholm (phosphate and magnetic susceptibility analysis, Centre for Environmental Archaeology, Department of Archaeology, University of Umeå), Kevin Reeves (microprobe, UCL), and the Natural History Museum and Spectrum Petrographics for thin section manufacture. We also acknowledge the many other contributors to the Gibraltar Cave Project, who aided this paper – Peter Andrews, Andy Currant, Lorraine Cormish, Jo Cooper, Yolanda Fernandez-Jalvo and Frank Greenaway of the Natural History Museum, Gerry Black (Oxford Brookes University) and Paul Pettitt (Oxford Dating Laboratory).

References

Arrhenius, O. (1934). Fosfathalten i skånska jordar. *Sveriges Geologiska Undersökningar. Ser C, no 383*. Årsbok 28, no 3.

Arrhenius, O. (1955). The Iron Age settlements on Gotland and the nature of the soil. In (M. Stenberger, Ed.) *Valhagan II*, pp.1053–64. Copenhagen: Munksgaard.

Andrews, P. (1990). *Owls, Caves and Fossils*. British Museum, London.

Barton, R.N.E., Current, A.P., Fernandez-Jalvo, Y., Finlayson, J. C., Goldberg, P., Macphail, R., Pettitt, P.B., and Stringer, C.B. (1999). Gibraltar Neanderthals and Results of recent excavations in Gorham's, Vanguard and Ibex Caves. *Antiquity* **73**, 13–23.

Bullock, P., Fedoroff, N., Jongerius, A., Stoops, G., Tursina, T., and Babel, U. (1985). *Handbook for Soil Thin Section Description*. Waine Research, Wolverhapton.

Collins, M.B., Gose, W.A., and Shaw, S. (1994). Preliminary geomorphological findings at Dust and nearby caves. *Journal of Alabama Archaeology* **40**, 35–56.

Courty, M.A., Goldberg, P., and Macphail, R.I. (1989). *Soils and Micromorphology in Archaeology*. Cambridge University Press, Cambridge.

Crowther, J. and Barker, P. (1995). Magnetic susceptibility: distinguishing anthropogenic effects from the natural. *Archaeological Prospection* **2**, 207–215.

Engelmark, R. and Linderholm, J. (1996). Prehistoric land management and cultivation. A soil chemical study. In *6th Nordic Conference on the Application of Scientific Methods in Archaeology, Esjberg 1993, P. A. C. T.*, pp. 315–322.

Goldberg, P. and R.I. Macphail (in press). Micromorphology of Sediments from Gibraltar Caves: Some Preliminary Results from Gorham's Cave and Vanguard Cave. In (C. Finlayson, Ed.), *Gibraltar during the Quaternary: the southernmost part of Europe in the last two million years*. Gibraltar Government Heritage Publications, Gibraltar.

Hill, C., and Paolo Forti (1998). *Cave Minerals of the World*. Huntsville, National Speleological Society.

Horwitz, L.K. and Goldberg, P. (1989). A Study of Pleistocene and Holocene Hyaena Coprolites. *Journal of Archaeological Science* **16**, 71–94.

Macphail, R.I. and Goldberg, P. (1999). The soil micromorphological investigation of Westbury Cave. In (P. Andrews, J. Cook, A. Currant and C. Stringer, Eds.) *Westbury Cave. The Natural History Museum Excavations 1976–1984*, CHERUB, Bristol, 59–86.

Macphail, R.I. and Cruise, G.M. (in press). The soil micromorphologist as team player: a multi-analytical approach to the study of European microstratigraphy. In (P. Goldberg, V.T. Holliday and C. Reid Ferring, Eds.) *Earth Sciences and Archaeology*. Plenum Press, NY.

Macphail, R.I., Hather, J., Hillson, S., and Maggi, R. (1994). The Upper Pleistocene Deposits at Arene Candide: Soil Micromorphology of Some Samples from the Cardini 1940–42 Excavation. *Quaternaria Nova* **IV**, 79–100.

Meignen, L. B.-Y., Bar-Yosef, O. and Goldberg, P. (1989). Les Structures de Combustion Moustériennes de la Grotte de Kébara (Mont Carmel, Israël). *Mémoires Du Musée de Préhistoire d'Ile de France* **2**, 141–146.

Schiegl, S.G., Goldberg, P., Bar-Yosef, O. and Weiner, S. (1996). Ash Deposits in Hayonim and Kebara Caves, Israel: Macroscopic, Microscopic and Mineralogical Observations, and Their

Archaeological Implications. *Journal of Archaeological Science* **23**, 763–781.

Tite, M.S. and Mullins, C.E. (1971). Enhancement of magnetic susceptibility of soils on archaeological sites. *Archaeometry* **13**, 209–219.

Waechter, J.D.A. (1951). Excavations at Gorham's Cave, Gibraltar. *The Prehistoric Society* **15**, 83–92.

Wattez, J., Courty, M.A., and Macphail, R.I. (1990). Burnt organomineral deposits related to animal and human activities in prehistoric caves. *In* (L. A. Douglas, Ed.) *Soil Micromorph-ology: A basic and applied science,* pp. 431–441. Elsevier: Amsterdam.

Weiner, S., Schiegl, S., Goldberg, P., and Bar-Yosef, O. (1995). Mineral assemblages in Kebara and Hayonim Caves, Israel: Excavation strategies, bone preservation, and wood ash remnants. *Israel Journal of Chemistry* **35**, 143–154.

Weiner, S. Goldberg, P. and Bar-Yosef, O. (1993). Bone Preservation in Kebara Cave, Israel Using On-Site Fourier Transform Infrared Spectrometry. *Journal of Archaeological Science* **20**, 613–627.

21

A Review of the Quaternary Mammals of Gibraltar

Andrew P. Currant

Introduction

From region to region across the Earth's surface there are clearly great differences in the scale of faunal response to Quaternary climatic changes. Much of the author's experience of Quaternary mammal faunas comes from the richly fossiliferous cave and river deposits of the British Isles, one of the regions of the world where the extent of faunal change in response to past climatic fluctuations is at its most extreme. At different times during the Late Pleistocene Britain has been home to the hippopotamus *Hippopotamus amphibius* and the reindeer *Rangifer tarandus*. In Britain and adjacent parts of continental Europe the last populations of Neanderthals shared their environment with an animal community dominated by mammoth *Mammuthus primigenius*, woolly rhinoceros *Coelodonta antiquitatis*, horse *Equus ferus* and spotted hyaena *Crocuta crocuta*. This fauna is quite unlike that found in the region today or at any time since the last glacial maximum.

While the southern Iberian peninsula also contains evidence for significant changes in mammalian faunal composition through time, these changes seem to be relatively subdued during the period corresponding to the Last Cold Stage and the present Interglacial. This observation lends support to the idea that the southern parts of the Iberian peninsula were to some extent sheltered from the changes which had such a major impact on the biotas of other parts of Europe. South of the Andalusian upland belts, away from the major terrestrial migration routes and environmentally buffered by the proximity of the Mediterranean, the southern Iberian coastal region may well have been an ecological oasis for the late Neanderthals.

Over the last ten years, a team from the Natural History Museum, London and Oxford Brookes University has been extending and reviewing the evidence for human occupation of the caves on Gibraltar in close collaboration with the Gibraltar Museum and other institutions. During the course of this work it has been possible to examine most of the surviving mammalian material previously recovered from the Rock and to visit nearly all of the localities from which significant Quaternary faunal collections have been made, with the notable exception of Genista Cave no.1 in the Windmill Hill Flats which have not been accessible for many years. We have also visited a number of Quaternary sites in Andalusia and had the opportunity to observe at first hand much of the modern mammal fauna of the region.

Although the record of vertebrate faunas on Gibraltar undoubtedly extends back to a very ancient date, the fragmentary nature of the sequences and the clear evidence for major tectonic modification of the topography of the Rock currently make it extremely difficult to construct a biostratigraphic framework extending back much beyond the end of the last phase of high sea level. This high sea level event is believed to correspond to the end of the Last Interglacial, now more widely known as Oxygen Isotope Stage 5 (OIS 5). One of the primary observations arising from examination of the mammal faunas of the later Pleistocene of Gibraltar is how little they seem to vary through time and how many of the principal species found as fossils in the Gibraltar caves can still be found living in the region today or are known to have occurred there in the comparatively recent past. This forms a very stark contrast with the huge changes observed in NW Europe during the same period. Since the final disappearance of the Neanderthals, the major losses to the Southern Iberian megafauna have been the larger carnivores – leopard *Panthera pardus*, spotted hyaena *Crocuta crocuta* and brown bear *Ursus arctos* – along with the larger species of herbivore, notably the narrow-nosed rhinoceros *Stephanorhinus hemitoechus*. Several other elements of the fauna, like the aurochs *Bos primigenius* and horse *Equus ferus,* are now represented solely by domesticated or feral populations. Excavations by W.L.H. Duckworth in Sewell's Cave suggest that the leopard may have survived on Gibraltar well into the Holocene (Duckworth 1912).

In common with the Quaternary mammal faunas of Spain and Portugal, those recovered from the caves and fissures on Gibraltar are composed of species which are either indigenous to the Peninsula or which have arrived from the north. Even in the north there seems to have been some kind of natural barrier roughly corresponding with the valley of the R. Ebro which acts as a partial filter limiting the immigration of a number of otherwise widespread European species into the rest of the Iberian peninsula. Among the mammals which have not crossed this particular frontier we must include European mole *Talpa europaea,* common shrew *Sorex araneus,* Alpine shrew *Sorex alpinus,* northern water shrew *Neomys fodiens,* fat dormouse *Glis glis,* harvest mouse *Micromys minutus,* yellow-necked mouse *Apodemus flavicollis,* bank vole *Clethrionomys glareous,* water vole *Arvicola terrestris,* stoat *Mustela erminea* and pine marten *Martes martes.* Many of these Post-Glacial recoloniser species would probably have been effectively excluded from the region south of the Ebro by the presence of ecologically similar southern European endemics which had been able to remain on their home territory throughout the Last Cold Stage.

The Rosia Bay Breccias

Gibraltar has long been famous for its Pleistocene 'bone breccias'. The Rosia Bay Breccias were described in some detail by John Boddington (1770), and fossil mammals from this locality were commented on by the great French comparative anatomist Baron Georges Cuvier (1823). The site was briefly described by William Buckland (1823) in his *Reliquiae Diluvianae* and Rosia Bay and other 'ossiferous' sites on the Rock were mentioned by John Smith (1846) in the first comprehensive account of the geology of Gibraltar. Many hundreds of tons of bone-bearing breccia were removed from the Rosia Bay exposure during military engineering work conducted to improve the defences of the Fortress. Although most of this material was destroyed, a few pieces of the breccia found their way into museum collections around Europe. The small fragment of stalagmitic breccia containing the holotype lower jaw of the extinct lagomorph *Prolagus calpensis* Forsyth Major, 1905 which is labelled "Pleisto-cene, from Gibraltar" almost certainly comes from this locality. Charles Forsyth Major (1905) also records seeing a breccia fragment from Rosia Bay collected by John Smith in the museum of the Geological Society of London (now in the NHM, London) which contained the characteristic anterior premolar of *Prolagus,* confirming the earlier record from Rosia (under the name *Lagomys*) by Cuvier (1823).

The Rosia Bay Breccia is still visible today in the cliff and foreshore just south of the Rosia Mole. The deposit is complex and difficult to interpret, but it appears to be an old cave or fissure filling in which successive phases of debris flow have deposited and redeposited muds, breccias and stalagmite. Bone is still quite common in places. On a recent visit, a unit of hard, dark red breccia with scattered cervid teeth and bones was traced from the foot of the cliff down into the sea. Another heavily cemented unit contained fairly common remains of a small lagomorph which compares very well with *Prolagus calpensis.* The age of the breccias is currently unknown, but further sampling and mapping of this site is in progress. There appear to be related deposits extending through the brecciated limestone into Camp Bay, the site of a recent major collapse, though whether these are directly con-nected to the Rosia Bay Breccias is uncertain.

Genista Cave no. 1

In their preliminary account of Captain F. Brome's excavations in the Genista Cave no.1, discovered beneath the military barracks on the west side of Windmill Hill, George Busk and Hugh Falconer (1865) gave the first real idea of the range of mammal species that were represented in the Quaternary deposits on Gibraltar. A full account of the Genista Cave mammal fauna was published by Busk (1877) and the plates of this work remain the definitive illustrations of the more abundant Quaternary mammals of Gibraltar. Most of the published material from Genista Cave no. 1 is now in the Natural History Museum, London.

In all of the faunal lists given in the present paper the original material has been re-examined, identifications confirmed and the taxonomy updated. Records considered to be dubious are noted.

Table 21.1: List of Quaternary Mammals from the Genista Caves, Gibraltar (based on Busk 1877).

Lepus sp.	hare
Oryctolagus cuniculus (Linnaeus, 1758)	rabbit
Ursus arctos Linnaeus, 1758	brown bear
Felis sylvestris Schreber, 1777	wild cat
Lynx lynx (Linnaeus, 1758)	lynx
Panthera pardus (Linnaeus, 1758)	leopard
Crocuta crocuta (Erxleben, 1777)	spotted hyaena
Equus ferus Boddaert, 1758	horse
Stephanorhinus hemitoechus (Falconer in Gaudin, 1859)	narrow-nosed rhinoceros
Sus scrofa Linnaeus, 1758	wild boar
Cervus elaphus Linnaeus, 1758	red deer
Bos primigenius Bojanus, 1827	aurochs
Capra ibex Linnaeus, 1758	ibex

Busk notes that rhinoceros was common and the remains of rabbit were extraordinarily abundant. The age of this site is not known with any certainty. Comparison of its mammal remains with other European material would suggest that it falls somewhere in the Middle Pleistocene. Efforts are being made to relocate this important locality and some of the natural cave passages cut into by the old military hospital tunnels do match quite well with nineteenth century descriptions of the lower cave passages. No fossils have been found so far.

Devil's Tower

Our understanding of the nature and age of the later Pleistocene Gibraltar mammal fauna was greatly extended by the description of a sequence of deposits near Devil's Tower discovered by the Abbé H. Breuil in 1917 (Breuil 1922). This deposit, which lay at the foot of the North Front, was subsequently excavated by Dorothy Garrod and the mammals further described by D.M.A. Bate (in Garrod *et al.* 1928). For the first time, it was possible to put a well excavated faunal assemblage from Gibraltar into a stratigraphical context which gave some direct evidence as to its age and the conditions under which it accumulated. The vertebrate remains were interpreted as representing a period during which Neanderthal people were in occupation following on from the high sea level event of the Last Interglacial. These finds were believed to be significantly younger than those reported from Genista Cave. At Devil's Tower, species like the horse and spotted hyaena were still present, but narrow-nosed rhinoceros was not recorded at all. The dominant elements of the fauna were rabbit *Oryctolagus cunniculus*, wild boar *Sus scrofa*, red deer *Cervus elaphus* and ibex *Capra ibex*, all living forms and mostly animals that are still common in adjacent parts of Spain today. The Devil's Tower mammalian remains are now in the Natural History Museum, London.

Table 21.2: List of Quaternary Mammals from the Devil's Tower Mousterian site (based on Bate 1928).

Talpa caeca Savi, 1822	Mediterranean mole
Crocidura russula (Hermann, 1780)	greater white-toothed shrew
Myotis cf. *myotis* (Borkhausen, 1797)	mouse-eared bat
Tadarida teniotis (Rafinesque, 1814)	European free-tailed bat
Oryctolagus cuniculus (Linnaeus, 1758)	rabbit
Arvicola sapidus Miller, 1908	water vole
Terricola sp. [formerly *Pitymys* sp.]	pine vole
Microtus brecciensis Giebel, 1847	extinct vole
Apodemus sylvaticus (Linnaeus, 1758)	wood mouse
Eliomys quercinus (Linnaeus, 1766)	garden dormouse
Hystrix cristata Linnaeus, 1758	crested porcupine
Canis lupus Linnaeus, 1758	wolf
Ursus arctos Linnaeus, 1758	brown bear

Table 21.2: continued.

Meles meles (Linnaeus, 1758)	badger
Felis sylvestris Schreber, 1777	wild cat
Lynx lynx (Linnaeus, 1758)	lynx
Panthera pardus (Linnaeus, 1758)	leopard
Crocuta crocuta (Erxleben, 1777)	spotted hyaena
Monachus monachus (Hermann, 1779)	Mediterranean monk seal
cf. *Palaeoloxodon antiquus* (Falconer in Murchison, 1868)	straight-tusked elephant
Equus ferus Boddaert, 1785	horse
Sus scrofa Linnaeus, 1758	wild boar
Cervus elaphus Linnaeus, 1758	red deer
Bos primigenius Bojanus, 1827	aurochs
Capra ibex Linnaeus, 1758	ibex

Gorham's Cave

A similar fauna to that found at Devil's Tower was later recovered from deposits in Gorham's Cave on Governor's Beach by John Waechter (1951; 1964) and studied in some detail by Antony Sutcliffe of the Natural History Museum, London. Although an abbreviated account appeared as an appendix to Waechter (1964), a very substantial part of Sutcliffe's report was left unpublished (Zeuner and Sutcliffe 1964). It is hoped to publish a version of his original manuscript at some future date.

A few words need to be said about Waechter's excavations. Recent work at the site directed by Christopher Stringer of the Natural History Museum, London and Clive Finlayson of Gibraltar Museum, shows major discrepancies between Waechter's recorded stratigraphy and the surviving deposits. His sections seem to have been drawn up from notes, possibly after he had left the site. In the longitudinal section represented by Figure 1 of his 1964 report, about 10 metres of cave sediments are entirely missing. One must assume that Waechter's finds do actually represent some kind of sequence, and that the discrepancies in his account result from mis-correlation from one area of the cave to another. His longitudinal section of the Gorham's Cave sediments shows roughly horizontal stratigraphy. Even a brief examination of the remaining sediments show this to be seriously in error. The deposits at the mouth of the cave dip back into the interior, while post-depositional slumping and localised solution of the carbonate fraction have created steeply sloping unit boundaries in the sediments further back inside the cave. Some of these features can clearly be seen on published photographs of the site. For these reasons, no attempt is made here to relate the fauna identified by Sutcliffe to Waechter's recorded stratigraphy.

We must also discount Waechter's claim to have discovered a "raised beach" deposit at the base of his recorded sequence at the cave mouth somewhere around 6 to 7 metres above above present sea level. There is unquestionably a fossil beach at or just above modern high sea level which is associated with the deposits lying immediately on top of the present rock platform, but in spite of cutting a continuous section right through the deposits at the cave entrance we have found nothing resembling beach deposits any higher in the sequence. Although these observations cast doubt on the exact stratigraphic assignment of the finds from Waechter's excavations, it would appear that nearly all of his vertebrate faunal material came from deposits which we would now associate with the Middle Palaeolithic (Mousterian) occupation of the cave. Recent excavations have shown the Upper Palaeolithic levels to contain very little well preserved fauna. Waechter did not specifically sample for small vertebrate remains and examination of the spoil from his excavations indicate that even his recovery of larger finds was to some extent haphazard, but the scale of his work was so great that the faunal remains he did manage to recover still constitute a very important record. This material is now in the Gibraltar Museum.

Table 21.3. List of Quaternary mammals from Gorham's Cave, Gibraltar (based on Sutcliffe 1964, and unpublished mss.)

Talpa cf. *caeca* Savi, 1822	Mediterranean mole
Lepus cf. *timidus* Linnaeus, 1758	mountain hare
Oryctolagus cuniculus (Linnaeus, 1758)	rabbit
Rodentia	undetermined rodents
Canis lupus Linnaeus, 1758	wolf
Ursus arctos Linnaeus, 1758	brown bear
Felis sylvestris Schreber, 1777	wild cat
Lynx lynx (Linnaeus, 1758)	lynx
Panthera pardus (Linnaeus, 1758)	leopard
Panthera leo? (Linnaeus, 1758)	lion [a very uncertain record]
Crocuta crocuta (Erxleben, 1777)	spotted hyaena
Monachus monachus (Hermann, 1779)	Mediterranean monk seal
Halichoerus grypus (Fabricus, 1791)	grey seal
Cetacea	undetermined small cetacean
Equus ferus Boddaert, 1785	horse
Stephanorhinus cf. *hemitoechus* (Falconer in Gaudin, 1859)	narrow-nosed rhinoceros
Sus scrofa Linnaeus, 1758	wild boar
Cervus elaphus Linnaeus, 1758	red deer
Bos primigenius Bojanus, 1827	aurochs
Capra ibex Linnaeus, 1758	ibex

Recent work and future research

Much of what is known about the vertebrate fauna of Gibraltar still remains in unpublished form. Many finds were made during the extensive tunnelling and scaling operations which have taken place over the last two centuries. A large amount of this material is now untraceable, but some significant finds do survive in museum collections. Current research on the Gibraltar mammal faunas includes locating and verifying provenanced material in old collections, tracking down archival information relating to these discoveries, sampling from both old and new localities and attempting wherever possible to reconstruct some kind of biostratigraphic framework for the Quaternary terrestrial sequences based on their vertebrate faunas.

Even amongst the published material there are still a number of enigmatic finds which require further detailed investigation. Not least of these is the extraordinary deer skull from deposits at Farringdon Battery some 190 metres up the Rock which was described as a new species, *Cervus taricus* by Dorothea Bate (1943). Bate speculates that *Cervus taricus* may be the deer noticed by earlier writers in the Rosia Bay Breccias, but the material which would confirm or refute this suggestion is no longer available and needs to be collected afresh. There is also a breccia block figured by Busk (1877) from Poca Roca high on the western slopes which contains the only published record of fallow deer (*Dama dama*) from Gibraltar. The absence of this species from the Late Pleistocene fauna suggests that this site would be worth further investigation. Although the cliffs at Europa Point have been almost cleared of superficial deposits by scarping, some of the sequence, including what may be remnants of the two raised beaches described by Smith (1846), still survives. It was from the higher of these beach deposits (21 metres) that he recovered the tooth of an elephant, described by Falconer as *Elephas antiquus* (= *Palaeoloxodon antiquus*). This remains the only unequivocally identified fossil elephant from Gibraltar and it would be very useful to know more about its age. The straight-tusked elephant appears to have disappeared from the region before the narrow-nosed rhinoceros, which is still represented in the Late Pleistocene fauna by rare finds from Gorham's Cave.

Recent excavations have produced detailed information about the fauna of Ibex Cave at the top of the old water catchments on the east side of the Rock [UTM grid ref. approximately TF 89050172] and human use of both Vanguard Cave [TF 89360021] and Gorham's Cave [TF 89340007]. Almost all of the archaeological material in Vanguard Cave appears to relate to occupation by Neanderthal humans, while Gorham's Cave contains deposits which cover much of the period from the Last Interglacial high sea level event, through the transition from use by Neanderthals to anatomically modern human populations and on into the early historical period. The Mousterian horizons at the latter two sites show the same pattern seen in most other contemporary central and southern Iberian localities. The dominant larger prey animals, where these can be identified, are ibex (*Capra ibex*), red deer (*Cervus elaphus*), wild boar (*Sus scrofa*) some large bovines (cf. *Bos* sp.), and a background noise of other species. Both adult and juvenile specimens of monk seal *Monachus monachus* are included in the human predation assemblage. Remains of large carnivores, notably leopard *Panthera pardus*, also appear to be an integral part of the human catch. Some bones have been used to retouch stone tools, but this usage appears to be casual and we have found no evidence of bone hammers being retained for prolonged use. Much of the mammalian material shows clear signs of human modification in the form of deliberate bone breakage (presumably for marrow extraction), cut marks and localised burning or scorching. Detailed examination of the human activity is outside the remit of this discussion, but there is a strong impression that the Neanderthals occupying Gibraltar during the Last Cold Stage were doing exactly the same range of things to their prey as much later populations of modern humans were doing during the Upper Palaeolithic and Mesolithic.

The new work has also resulted in the assembly of important collections of small vertebrate material which are currently being studied. Samples from all sites have produced large quantities of fish, amphibians, reptiles and birds, and teeth and bones of a range of small mammals including bats, shrews, dormice, mice, voles and rabbits. This material will greatly extend our knowledge of the Pleistocene fauna of the area and permit much more precise analysis of the effects of changing conditions through time.

Conclusions

The later Pleistocene mammalian record from Gibraltar displays quite extraordinary stability in terms of its species composition throughout a period in which other parts of Europe, particularly those north of the Pyrenean – Alpine mountain belt, saw the coming and going of several quite distinct animal communities. Drawing on the material from nearly two centuries of collecting, this paper provides a synopsis of where we have got to in understanding the composition of this fauna in order to provide a foundation and point of reference for future work.

Acknowledgments
As a member of the Gibraltar Caves Project team I would like to thank all of my fellow team members and the Government and People of Gibraltar for their support and encouragement throughout our work.

References

Bate, D.M.A. (1943). A new Pleistocene Deer from Gibraltar. *Annals and Magazine of Natural History*, 11th series, **10**, 411–426.

Boddington, J. (1771). Account of some Bones found in the Rock of Gibraltar, in a Letter from John Boddington, Esq; to Dr. William Hunter, F.R.S., with some Remarks from Dr. Hunter in a Letter to Dr. Matthew Maty, M.D. Sec.R.S. *Philosophical Transactions of the Royal Society of London.* **60**, 414–416, tab. 10. [read Feb. 1770; dated "Tower" 17 Dec. 1769.]

Breuil, H. (1922). Palaeolithic Man at Gibraltar: new and old facts. *Journal of the Royal Anthropological Institute of Great Britain and Ireland*, **52**, 46–54.

Busk, G. (1877). On the Ancient or Quaternary Fauna of Gibraltar, as exemplified in the Mammalian Remains of the Ossiferous Breccia. *Transactions of the Zoological Society of London.* **10**, 53–136, plates 1–27. [received and read 2 May 1876.]

Busk, G. & Falconer, H. (1865). On the fossil contents of the Genista Cave, Gibraltar. *Quarterly Journal of the Geological Society of London.* **21**, 364–370

Cuvier, G. (1823). *Ossemens Fossiles.* **4**, 174. Paris.

Duckworth, W.L.H. (1912). Cave exploration at Gibraltar in 1911. *Journal of the Royal Anthropological Institute of Great Britain and Ireland*, **42**, 515–526.

Forsyth Major, C.I. (1905). Pleistocene rodents of the Western Mediterranean Region. *Geological Magazine*, Decade 5, **2**, 462–467; 501–506.

Garrod, D.A.E., Buxton, L.H.D., Elliot Smith, G. & Bate, D.M.A. (1928). Excavation of a Mousterian Rock Shelter at Devil's Tower, Gibraltar. *Journal of the Royal Anthropological Institute of Great Britain and Ireland.* **58**, 91–113.

Smith, J. (1846). On the Geology of Gibraltar. *Quarterly Journal of the Geological Society of London.* **2**, 41–51.

Waechter, J. d'A. (1951). The Excavation of Gorham's Cave, Gibraltar – preliminary report for the seasons 1948 and 1950. *Proceedings of the Prehistoric Society*, (for 1951) n.s. **18**, 83–92.

Waechter, J. d'A. (1964). The Excavation of Gorham's Cave, Gibraltar 1951–54. *Bulletin of the Institute of Archaeology.* **4**, 189–221; plate 13 (p.269).

Zeuner, F.E. & Sutcliffe, A.J. (1964). Preliminary report on the Mammalia of Gorham's Cave, Gibraltar. Appendix I, pp. 213–216, in Waechter, J. d'A., The Excavation of Gorham's Cave, Gibraltar, 1951–54. *Bulletin of the Institute of Archaeology.* **4**, 189–221; plate 13 (p.269).

22

Charcoal and Charred Seed Remains from Middle Palaeolithic Levels at Gorham's and Vanguard Caves

Rowena Gale and Wendy Carruthers

Introduction

Prior to the current excavations little was known of the vegetation and ecology in this region of the Iberian Peninsular during the Mousterian, Middle and Upper Palaeolithic eras. Hominid use or occupation of the caves may have been sporadic or seasonal but appears to have occurred on a fairly continuous basis over several millennia. The remains of charcoal and charred seeds from combustion zones and other contexts occurred in both caves in Upper Palaeolithic and earlier levels. The identification of the plant remains has provided both environmental data on the character of the local woodland and ethnological evidence of the use of woodland resources for fuel and food. The analyses presented here are from charcoal samples collected in 1996 and 1997, and charred plant macrofossils from the 1996 samples; both relate to levels associated with the Middle Palaeolithic (*c.* 50–40ka).

Materials and Methods

A total of 88 charcoal samples were examined (39 from Gorham's Cave and 49 from Vanguard Cave). The charcoal consisted of small fragments, mostly <5mm in the longest axis which were extremely fragile and difficult to handle. They were prepared for examination using standard methods, by manually fracturing to expose fresh transverse (TS), tangential (TLS) and radial (RLS) surfaces. The fragments were supported in sand and examined using a Nikon Labophot incident light microscope at magnifications of up to x400. The anatomical structures were matched to thin sections of wood (microscope slides) in the reference collection at the Jodrell Laboratory, Royal Botanic Gardens, Kew (Figure 22.1, 1–5).

Thirteen samples included charred plant macrofossils (8 from Gorham's Cave and 5 from Vanguard Cave). These were examined under a dissecting microscope at magnifi-

cations from x10 to x100. Comparisons were made with reference material from the herbarium of the National Museum of Wales, Cardiff.

Results

Charcoal

Gorham's Cave

In general the charcoal was more abundant in the samples from Gorham's Cave than from Vanguard Cave. The charcoal mostly consisted of pine (*Pinus*) wood although a few narrow stems from unidentified broadleaf shrubs were also present. Slight anatomical differences in the wood structure of pine species allow differentiation into distinct groups (Phillips 1948) and it was evident that at least two groups were represented in the charcoal. In the Mediterranean landscape of today these include:

Black pine (*P. nigra*)
Maritime pine (*P. pinaster*)
Stone pine (*P. pinea*)
Aleppo pine (*P. halepensis*)

Vanguard Cave

Although charcoal deposits in this cave were sparser than in Gorham's, a wider range of taxa was recorded. Coniferous wood included similar pines (*Pinus*) to those from Gorham's Cave and, in addition, juniper (*Juniperus*) and/ or alerce (*Tetraclinis articulata*). The wood structure of juniper and alerce is almost indistinguishable particularly in archaeological material. Broadleaf taxa matched olive (*Olea*), lentisc and/ or terabinth (*Pistacia lentiscus, P. terabinthus*) and other shrubby species. Fragments from the latter were too degraded to identify with certainty but some were superficially similar to members of the Ericaceae (e.g. heathers), Cistaceae (e.g. rock-rose) and Rosaceae (e.g. hawthorn *etc*).

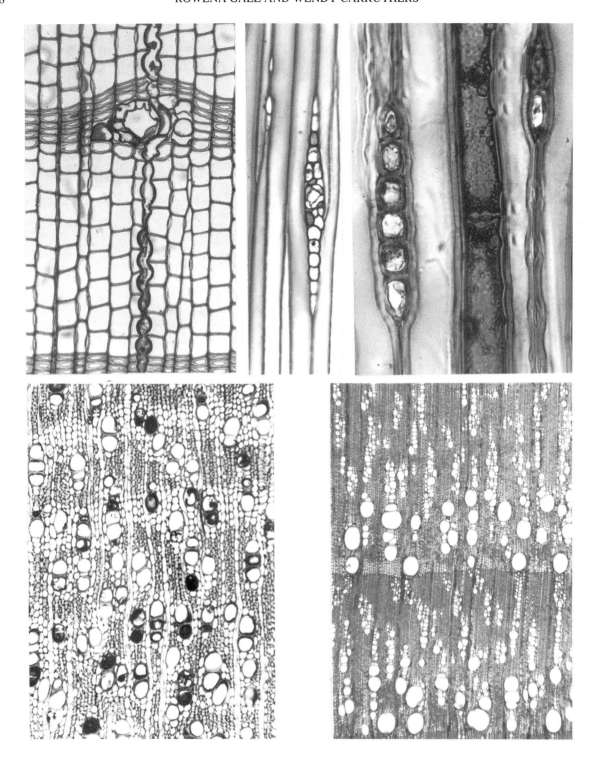

Figure 22.1: 1) Pinus nigra *TS x150, showing resin canal; 2)* P. nigra *TLS x150, showing radial resin canal in ray; 3)* Juniperus communis *TLS x384, showing rays and axial parenchyma; 4)* Olea europaea *TS x150; 5)* Pistacia lentiscus *TS x25, showing ring porous arrangement of vessels.*

Plant macrofossils

Gorham's Cave and Vanguard Cave

Herbarium specimens from all of the *Pinus* species native to the area were examined, and the charred remains were confirmed as comprising stone pine (*P. pinea*) cone scale fragments and stone pine nutshell fragments.

The cone scales of stone pines are large, thick and have five or six characteristic ridges radiating from a prominent rounded apex (Figure 22.2). The oblong, wingless nuts contained within the cones have thick, dense shells that are difficult to crack. In cross-section, the nutshell has small, rounded, thick-walled cells.

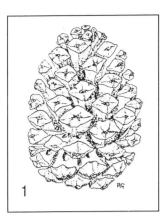

Figure 22.2: Stone pine (P. pinea) cone, approx. half actual size.

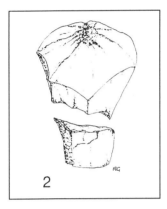

Figure 22.3: cone scale, x2 from Gorham's Cave identified as stone pine (P. pinea).

These were clearly visible on the broken surfaces of the fragments.

Some of the cone scale fragments were quite large (e.g. max. width 14mm, length 18mm) and a whole scale was recovered from one sample (Figure 22.3). The nutshell fragments were small, but all of the material was well preserved and showed no signs of weathering. Both caves produced cone scale remains, but nutshell fragments were only recovered from Gorham's Cave. A few fragments of parenchyma from Vanguard Cave remain unidentified, and these might be the remains of charred stone pine kernel.

Environmental Implications

Precise dating of some contexts and the inter-relationship of the stratigraphy between the two caves is still unresolved. The significance of the wider range of broad-leaved shrubs identified from Vanguard Cave hinges on the secure dating of these sequences. At present, possible scenarios include:

A) That localised ecological zones existed close to each cave and supported distinct and differing plant communities. This seems a real possibility since the soils in front of the caves (now raised beach) were sandy and acid while the cliffs housing the caves and rising above them are calcareous.

B) That the results reflect preferential selection of species for fuel or food preparation.

C) That changing environmental conditions influenced and altered woodland composition between the periods of occupation.

The identification of useful 'indicator' species has proved to be very interesting. For example, black pine (*P. nigra*) and other members of this group (e.g. Scots pine, *P. sylvestris*) are characteristic of cold montane regions, whereas stone pine (*P. pinea*) grows in mild, humid, coastal areas. In the charcoal the black pine group occurred in samples from the earlier sequences, while charcoal and cone/ seed fragments from stone pine occurred in the later samples, thereby indicating a warming of the environment in the later phase. Olive (*O. europaea*) in particular, and lentisc and terabinth (*P. lentiscus* and *P. terebinthus*) slightly less so, are considered to be 'indicator' plants of Mediterranean conditions (Polunin and Walters 1985). Many heathers (e.g. tree heather, *Erica arborea*) and rock-rose (*Cistus*) are also typical components of Mediterranean *maquis* (Polunin and Walters 1985).

With the exception of black pine, *P. nigra* group, the taxa identified typify the Mediterranean flora of the present day. Although stone pine (*P. pinea*) does not grow in Gibralter today (a marked rise in sea-level has probably eradicated its previous habitat), dense stone pine woodland still flourishes on coastal sand dunes, not far away, to the north of Tarifa, Spain. Communities of lentisc (*P. lentiscus*) and wild olive (*O. europaea*) grow on The Rock above the caves.

The Ecology of Stone Pine and Ethnographic Evidence for its use

Stone or umbrella pine is a large tree native to the western Mediterranean, and is often found in coastal locations. It can form three types of woodland, depending on the extent of management and grazing; grass-rich, *maquis*-type and woods on damper soils.

Stone pine seeds, pine nuts or pignolia nuts have been valued as a food source for thousands of years, to the extent that they were imported into areas where they were not native, for example the British Isles in the Roman period (Willcox 1977). In the past they were often considered to be an aphrodisiac, according to classical authors such as Apicius (Flower and Rosenbaum 1958). In Italy and Spain stone pine trees are cultivated or preserved in large stands, and the nuts are still an important commercial food. The heavy, 10x10cm globose cones are gathered in winter and stored until summer, when they are laid out in the sun to ripen in order to remove the nuts (de Rougement 1989). Pine nuts can be difficult to crack because of their thick, hard shells, but the kernels are rich in oils and proteins making the effort worthwhile. Because of the thick shells and low water content, unshelled nuts have a long storage life.

Ethnographic evidence for the extraction of the pine nut kernels by North American Indians using various different species of pine suggests that, whilst some cones would be left to ripen on the tree, others would be knocked down when still green (Opler 1941). Unripe cones were either left to ripen in the sun, or held on their branches over a fire or in the ashes (Vestal 1952). Some tribes would heap the cones up before setting light to them. Once the pitch burnt off, the scales partially opened allowing the nuts to fall out (Dixon 1905). Others roasted the cones for an hour or more in an earth oven in order to facilitate the removal and shelling of the nuts (Kelly 1931). Ethnographic evidence suggests that roasting can also make the nuts more palatable and prolong storage life. For nomadic people, shelled nuts would have been less bulky for transportation purpose.

The recovery of charred cone and nutshell fragments from Gorham's and Vanguard Caves suggests that fire may have been used to help to open the cones, and this would have also made the nutshells brittle and easier to crack. Alternatively, the remains could represent fuel and waste from people feasting around the fire. The recovery of large beach cobbles with signs of percussive damage from amongst the charred remains gives further evidence for the processing of nuts in the caves. Further studies may provide evidence for the use of other gathered plant foods, and indicate the scale and duration of these activities.

Acknowledgements

The authors are grateful to the following people for their help, advice and the loan of reference material:
Tony Tipper and other staff of the Herbarium, National Museum of Wales; the Director of the Royal Botanic Gardens, Kew; Julie Jones; and Sarah Mason.

References

Flower, B. & Rosenbaum, E. (1958). As the Roman Cookery Book.

Dixon, R.B. (1905). The northern Maidu. *Bull. of the American Mus. of Nat. Hist.* **17**, 119–381

Kelly, I.T. (1931) Ethnography of the Surprise Valley Paite. *University of California Publications in American Archaeology and Ethnology* **31**, 67–210

Opler, M.E. (1941). *An Apache Lifeway: The Economic, Social and Religious Institutions of the Chiricahua Indian.* Chicago: University of Chicago Press.

Phillips, E.W.J. (1948). *Identification of soft woods by their microscopic structure,* Dept. of the Environment Building Research Establishment, Forest Products Research Bulletin No. 22. HMSO, pp. 34–35.

Polunin, O. and Walters, M. (1985). *A guide to the vegetation of Britain and Europe.* Oxford University Press.

De Rougement, G.M. (1989). *A Field Guide to the Crops of Britain and Europe.* Collins.

Vestal, P.A. (1952). Ethnobotany of the Ramah Navaho: Reports of the Ramah Project Report No. 4. *Papers of the Peabody Museum of American Archaeology and Ethnology* **40**, (4).

Willcox, G.H. (1977). *Exotic plants from Roman waterlogged sites in London.* J.A.S.**4**, 269–282

23

Mousterian Hearths and Shellfish: Late Neanderthal Activities on Gibraltar

Nick Barton

Introduction

Palaeolithic sites in which artefacts and other residues are well-preserved in thin occupation layers are extremely uncommon in the archaeological record. The significance of such deposits for providing direct insights into past human behaviour has been widely reported in the archaeological literature e.g. Bordes 1975, Roe 1980, Connard *et al.* 1998. In particular, over recent years the study of hearths associated with occupation surfaces has proved an extremely instructive and rewarding area for Middle and Upper Palaeolithic research (Perlès 1975, Bar-Yosef *et al.* 1992, Rigaud *et al.* 1995, Mellars 1996, Henry 1998). Hearths are widely regarded as key elements in the structuring of human activities within sites (Binford 1983, Gamble 1991). Apart from identifying the nature of activities needing heat and light, studies have also indicated how human social behaviour, including language capacity, actively influenced the configuration of artefacts and debris surrounding these structures. Interest in hearths and the spatial arrangement of finds associated with them continues to intensify because of the current controversy surrounding the behavioural capabilities of archaic humans (Stringer & Gamble 1993, Rigaud *et al.* 1995)

In this paper preliminary information is given on a number of Middle Palaeolithic Mousterian hearths discovered in two adjacent caves on Gibraltar. The hearths sampled, and in some cases totally excavated, have been subjected to a range of analytical techniques, including thin-section study for soil micromorphology, magnetic susceptibility and charcoal analysis. The detailed results of these analyses will be presented in the definitive site publication, but instead this paper considers some of the initial findings on the spatial analysis of the hearths and resulting inferences concerning patterns of human behaviour.

Vanguard and Gorham's Caves

The two sites under study are large caves situated on the east side of the Rock of Gibraltar, close to the sea near 'Governor's Beach'. One of the caves, Vanguard Cave, had not been dug previously, the other, Gorham's Cave, had been examined on a number of occasions since the last century (Waechter 1951, 1964).

Our excavations at both sites began in 1995 and are continuing. In Vanguard Cave work has so far been conducted in the main chamber and a smaller alcove or antechamber on the north side of the cave (Figure 23.1). The cave was evidently favoured for occupation in the Mousterian but, conversely, there is surprisingly little evidence of Upper Palaeolithic activity except in the uppermost area of the cave. A potential explanation for the scarcity of Upper Palaeolithic remains, supported by AMS dating results, is that the cave was largely infilled by sand deposits by about 45 ka. A different situation exists at Gorham's Cave, where there is extensive evidence for successive Middle and Upper Palaeolithic occupation layers. The work at this site has concentrated on deposits towards the back of the cave where archaeological levels are well-preserved. A large sample of Mousterian artefacts has so far been recovered, however, due to problems of access, relatively limited sampling of the Upper Palaeolithic horizons has so far proved possible. Gorham's Cave nevertheless provides an exceptionally well-dated archaeological sequence which spans the so-called Middle-Upper Palaeolithic transition (Barton *et al.* 1999). Inter-comparison of the deposits of both caves suggests that there is a considerable chronological overlap between Mousterian activities at Gorham's and Vanguard Caves.

The Mousterian hearths at Vanguard Cave

A number of discrete and well-stratified Mousterian

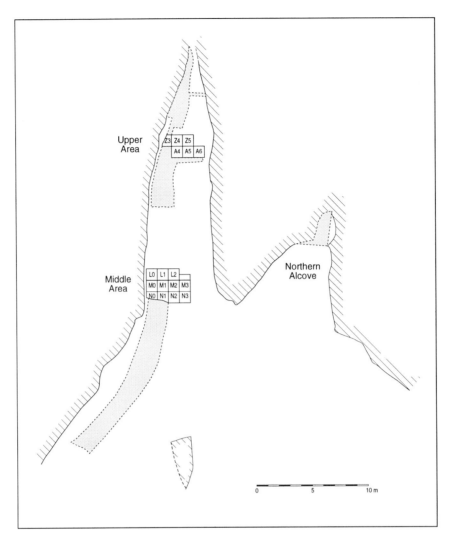

Figure 23.1: Location of excavations trenches in Vanguard Cave.

occupation horizons containing hearths have been located within the 17m of cave deposits in Vanguard Cave. For convenience the excavations within the cave can be divided into the upper area, the middle area and the northern alcove (Figure 23.1). The main occupation layers are more or less horizontal, only dipping slightly towards the back of the cave. They cover fairly extensive areas of the interior and can be traced laterally across the whole width of the cave. Near the entrance the sequence has been truncated and the archaeological sediments are covered by a more recent deposition of dune sands.

Vanguard Upper Area

The youngest Mousterian layers to be investigated are situated near the top of the cave sequence within about 5 m of the roof. The archaeological horizon occurs as a more or less continuous layer only truncated on the side facing the cave mouth. It is unclear how far the deposits originally extended towards the entrance but we estimate

the area of human activities was quite localised. The occupation zone lies about 30 m inside the cave dripline and approximately 13–14 m above the present storm beach. It thus occupies a relatively sheltered position well away from the entrance.

The archaeological level consisted of a thin white ashy deposit interstratified with a shallow midden of marine shells, lithic artefacts and a number of well-preserved coprolites (Figure 23. 2). No large vertebrate remains were found in the deposit. The highest concentration of ash was recorded near the south wall of the cave. It rested on heavily rubified (burnt) sands indicating the position of an *in situ* hearth. The occurrence of ash and burned sand, together with the very fresh appearance of the associated archaeological remains suggests the deposits were probably buried by relatively low energy sedimentation processes (Macphail and Goldberg this volume). This appears to be one of the rare cases of a high integrity deposit where no major post-depositional disturbance has occurred (*cf.* Galanidou 1997, 1). No direct dates are yet

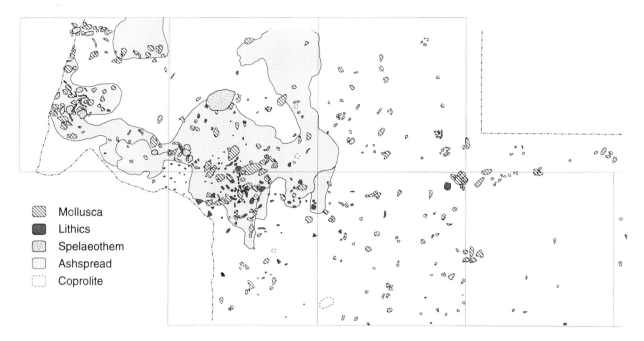

Figure 23.2: Vanguard Cave upper area. Hearth and midden distribution.

Mollusca
Lithics
Spelaeothem
Ashspread
Coprolite

available for this level but radiocarbon dates on the overlying horizons and an OSL date from the same horizon imply an age for the hearth level of about 45 ka to 49 ka.

The upper hearth conforms to a simple, flat open type. The core of the hearth zone covered a sub-circular area of about 80 x 80 cm although its edges were somewhat diffuse and partly obscured by separate lobes of ash which extended beyond the limits of the main combustion zone (Figure 23. 2). Preliminary analysis of the ashy deposits by Rowena Gale and Wendy Carruthers has revealed small quantities of charcoal attributable to lentisc (*Pistacia* sp.), juniper (*Juniperus*) and/or alerce (*Tetraclinus articulata*). Closely associated with this deposit was a dense scatter of marine shells which were concentrated principally in the central zone of burning but also extended outwards beyond this area in the form of a diffuse scatter. Although some of the shells showed signs of discolouration and had adhering patches of ash or charcoal, they appear to have been remarkably unaffected by the heat. It therefore does not appear likely that the shells were left for any length of time in the hot ashes of the fire. The shells were of marine species, mainly mussel (*Mytilus galloprovincialis*) but also with two species of limpet (*Patella vulgata, Patella caerula*), cockles (*Acanthocardia tuberculata*), a veneracean bivalve (*Callista chione*) and some barnacles (*Balanus sp.*) (Table 23.1). The mussel shells were of a uniformly large size untypical of a naturally accumulated deposit.

The presence of shellfish is of interest because it throws light on two particular aspects of Neanderthal behaviour. First, it provides rare evidence for the early exploitation of these foods, a subject which, up until now, has received only minimal attention in the archaeological literature (but

see Stiner 1994). Secondly, the size of the mussels allows us to say something about the collecting methods employed. In relation to the latter, due to the noticeably large size of the mussels, it seems very likely that they were harvested from a river estuarine environment rather than the sea shore (Paul Jeffreys pers. comm.). This is a slightly surprising observation given the fact that the evidence from submarine contours suggests that the rocky shoreline, with numerous opportunities for collecting shells, lay relatively close to the caves (< 2 km). The nearest available estuarine source of the shells would either have been in Algeciras Bay or possibly in the lowlying isthmus that joins Gibraltar to Spain. In either case, the total distance would have been perhaps 3–4 kilometres. It is also clear from the uniformly large size of the mussels that only the bigger valves were selected for consumption. Selective harvesting of shellfish by Neanderthals may also explain the presence of exceptionally large mussel shells reported in the Mousterian levels of Devil's Tower rockshelter (Garrod *et al*. 1928, 112), a site which lies at the base of the northern end of the Rock of Gibraltar and faces the isthmus.

Overlapping with the shell accumulation in the upper area was a well-defined scatter of lithic artefacts which, unlike the shells, was almost entirely confined to the central hearth zone (Figure 23.3). The Mousterian industry consisted mainly of quartzite flakes struck from discoidal cores, with virtually the whole of the *chaîne opératoire* represented. The lithic raw material was almost exclusively on beach pebbles. An extremely short-term occupation episode seems to be indicated by the restricted numbers of artefacts recovered. Moreover, based on the close spatial relationship of the finds and refitting flakes to cores,

Table 23.1 Identification of marine mollusca from the upper level hearth at Vanguard Cave

Common name	Genus/species	n.specimens	MNI
limpets	*Patella vulgata*	11	11
limpets	*Patella caerula*	2	2
mussels	*Mytilus galloprovincialis*	~100	~50
barnacles	*Balanus* sp.	8	8
cockles	*Acanthocardia tuberculata*	1	1
veneracean bivalve	*Callista chione*	1	1

MNI – Minimum Number of Individuals

it is clear that the artefacts were knapped in one place on top of the hearth zone. The location of *in situ* knapping is further identified by the recovery in the ash of millimetre-size quartzite debris, typical by-products of the flaking process. In the event of disturbance by natural processes these are invariably the first items to be removed (Barton 1992) and their presence here thus demonstrates the *in situ* nature of the lithic scatter. Despite the close association of flakes with the hearth, few if any of the quartzite artefacts displayed any obvious outward signs of thermal damage. Apart from the quartzite flakes and cores, two artefacts made of chert were recovered from this horizon. They were the only retouched tools found in this area and consist of a heavily edge-damaged flake and a fire-cracked double side-scraper (Figure 23.4). Since there was no associated debitage in this material, it seems very likely that they were both introduced to the site as pre-manufactured tools. Our experiments have shown that such objects make ideal shucking knives for mussels. Microwear analysis on the tools unfortunately proved inconclusive in this respect (John Mitchell pers. comm.).

The shallow midden deposit also contained a number of small coprolites, which were unburned and appear to have been deposited after the fire had died down. The coprolites contained millimetre pieces of shell and could be of human origin. From their diminutive size it has been suggested they may have been produced by a young child (Fernandez-Jalvo and Andrews pers.comm.).

Observations on the condition and quantity of shells and the presence of artefacts have allowed us to reconstruct a possible sequence of events for the midden. Based on the information described above it seems likely that a small number of Neanderthals, maybe one or two adults accompanied by their young, arrived at the cave from a nearby estuary carrying a few armfuls of shellfish. Perhaps dusk was falling or maybe due to the inclement weather conditions, the Neanderthals settled in the dark interior of the cave and lit a small fire using lentisc and juniper brushwood collected from the dunes outside. After the fire had burned down a little, the mussels were gently stacked on a bed of leaves or seaweed in the ashy embers of the hearth, the heat allowing the shells to open. Then,

with the knives they were carrying, they levered the meat out of the half-opened shells, eventually discarding the implements in the warm ashes. Perhaps they slept awhile in the space between the fire and the cave wall. In any event, the cave's occupants did not stay long. Before leaving, they knapped a fresh set of sharp flakes from quartzite collected from the beach, and pausing to select the most useful pieces, they set off again. As they departed, a child stopped briefly to defecate in the ashes. While the details of this reconstruction are necessarily sketchy and speculative, they nevertheless describe a plausible sequence of events that fits the available evidence. They illustrate, for example, how a thin palimpsest of archaeological material can be analysed and understood as a series of separate but inter-related events closely circumscribed in space and time.

Vanguard Middle Area

A number of Mousterian occupation levels have also been recorded lower down in the sequence and nearer the entrance overhang. Here, in the middle section of the main cave, thin well-defined hearth deposits consisting of bone remains and lithic artefacts are concentrated on the south side of the chamber near the cave wall (Figure 23. 1). This part of the cave is rarely in direct sunlight but lies 15 m within the main dripline, approximately 8 m above the present storm beach, and therefore within easy reach of the entrance platform.

The deposits in this part of the cave comprise a series of finely bedded brown silty sands and clays each associated with evidence of human occupation. The sands and clays form more or less continuous horizons that can be followed across the cave and are separated from one another by intervening thin sterile layers of coarse and medium grained pale yellow sands (see Macphail and Goldberg this volume). Individual, charcoal-rich hearth horizons have been recorded within the brown silty sands and clay layers, the most completely excavated example being in contexts 157/158 (Figures 23.5 and 23.6). The hearth in question is a flat, open structure marked by a sub-circular charcoal spread covering an area of approximately 1.5 x 1.2 m and 2–3 cm thick. From thin-section analysis by Paul Goldberg and Richard Macphail it can be seen that successive fires were built in the same location. At least three separate episodes of burning can be distinguished, each marked by successive bands of rubified sand, charcoal and ash. The absence of ash coating on the topmost hearth surface may be explained by small-scale post-depositional processes, such as sheetwash or aeolian action, which are known to have been active in the cave (Goldberg and Macphail pers. comm.). Although potentially responsible for displacing the smallest debris, there is no evidence of major sorting processes having affected the overall integrity of the bone and artefact concentrations.

Examination of the charcoal in the different individual hearth horizons reveals a common predominance of

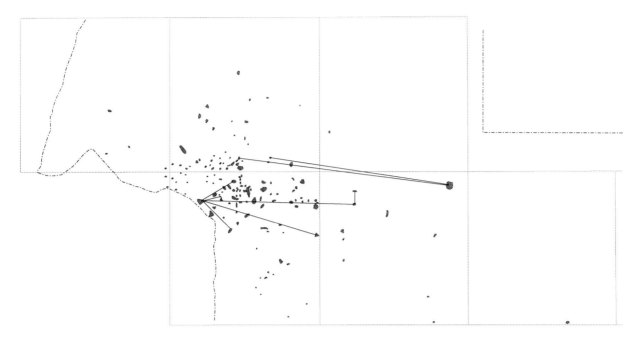

Figure 23.3: Vanguard Cave upper area. Spatial distribution of lithics and refitting artefacts.

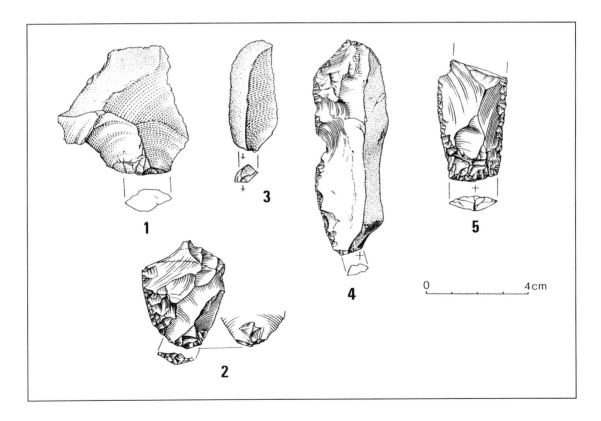

Figure 23.4: Vanguard Cave. Mousterian artefacts from middle (1–3) and upper (5–6) areas. 1 – 95/168 quartzite flake; 2 – 95/169 éclat débordant (chordal flake) in red chert; 3 – 96/155 naturally backed flake in quartzite; 4 – 97/20 naturally backed chert flake with edge damage; 5 – 96/114 double side scraper in chert.

Vanguard South Artefacts

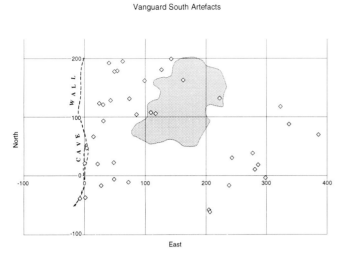

Figure 23.5: Vanguard Cave middle area. Spatial distribution of lithic artefacts in relation to the hearth in contexts 157/ 158.

Vanguard South Fauna

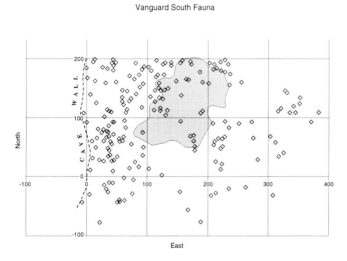

Figure 23.6: Vanguard Cave middle area. Spatial distribution of faunal remains in relation to the hearth in contexts 157/ 158.

pinewood belonging to the groups including stone pine (*Pinus pinea*) and maritime pine (*Pinus pinaster*). Amongst the wood charcoal identified by Rowena Gale were also recorded pine cone scales and nut fragments of the same species, as well as the wood of lentisc (*Pistacia* sp.) and fragments of charcoal resembling oak (*Quercus*) but too degraded to be certain of its identification (Rowena Gale pers. comm). An OSL determination of 93 ka on sands overlying the hearth gives the likely minimum age of the archaeological deposits.

Preliminary work on the artefacts from contexts 157/ 158 reveals that a high proportion of flakes were made

according to the same discoidal techniques observed in the upper levels of the cave (Figure 23.4). Amongst the relatively few retouched tools recovered were scrapers and naturally-backed knives, although the latter could well be incidental by-products of the discoidal *chaîne opératoire*. The lithic raw materials utilised appear to be dominated by locally obtained pebbles, in the same range of fine-grained red cherts and quartzites that occur naturally in the beach deposits outside the cave today. There were no cherts. The presence of hammerstones in the archaeological contexts implies that the pebbles were knapped inside the cave near the hearth. Initial results of spatial analysis show a fairly dispersed distribution of lithics and bones scattered around and partly overlapping with the hearth zone. The largest concentration of bones and artefacts appears on south side of the hearth between this feature and the cave wall (Figures 23.5 and 23.6). The associated bone consists of smashed and cut-marked examples of red deer (*Cervus elaphus*) and ibex (*Capra ibex*) with smaller quantities of tortoise (*Testudo* sp.). Most of the bones and artefacts can be shown to be lying horizontally and with no preferred orientation. An exception is near the cave wall where the bones showed a tendency to lie perpendicular to the wall and with a marked angle of dip (Figure 23.7). As the sediments were inclined at a similar angle, it appeared to us that the area around the hearth may have been deliberately cleared and the debris pushed against the wall. Clearly, such an observation will need further testing to examine the possibility of size sorting or the influence of erosive processes, but for the moment it does imply that Neanderthals at this site emptied and re-used hearths in much the same way recorded in both the Upper Palaeolithic of Europe (Gamble 1993) and the Mousterian of the Near East (Bar-Yosef *et al.* 1992).

Vanguard Northern Alcove

A separate niche on the north side of the main chamber had further evidence of human activities in the form of scattered lithic artefacts and a small, oval hearth. The hearth was exceptionally well-preserved, probably due to its protected position within the side alcove. It was situated in relatively unconsolidated sands about 18m within the main dripline and approximately 7–8 m above the storm beach.

The hearth was flat and measured 50 x 25 cm in overall dimension (Figure 23.8). It consisted of a 1–2 cm thick layer of laminated ash overlying a further 2 cm of burnt sand and charcoal with underlying patches of rubified sand. Charcoal within the hearth gave a direct AMS age determination of >44.1 ka (OxA-7078). As in the hearths of the middle area, the pine charcoal was exclusively of the stone and maritime pine grouping typical of the present day Mediterranean zone.

One of the surprising features of this hearth was the very low level of human activity recorded associated with

Figure 23.7: Vanguard Cave. Photograph of bones close to the south wall.

it. With the exception of a few isolated flakes in the surrounding sand there were no signs of the intensive occupation evidence recognised elsewhere in the cave. The only large vertebrate material recovered in this area were a few dentary and post-cranial remains of spotted hyaena (*Crocuta crocuta*), but significantly not from the same level as the hearth. Furthermore, the absence of cutmarks or burning on the hyaena bones would appear to rule out human accumulation. In our view, the simplest explanation is that the hearth represents an ephemeral human presence, perhaps amounting to no more than an overnight stay. This part of the cave may also have been used for animal denning when humans were not present.

Gorham's Cave hearths and activity areas

Work on the upper part of the cave sequence has uncovered a series of charcoal-rich horizons associated with Upper Palaeolithic artefacts. These directly overlie horizons containing large quantities of Mousterian finds also with combustion zones. Due to problems of access, the upper area has been excavated in a series of stepped sections and consequently there is relatively little information yet forthcoming on the overall spatial extent of the hearths or related artefact distributions. The uppermost level with Mousterian artefacts is context 16 which has an associated AMS date of 32,280 ± 420 BP (OxA-7857). The date is on charcoal from a remnant hearth or combustion zone in context 24, contained within context 16. Unfortunately, these contexts and the immediately adjacent sedimentary units have been affected by minor slumping or bioturbation (Macphail and Goldberg this volume), which, for the moment, makes any further interpretation difficult.

Below this upper, stepped sequence lies a much more thickly developed series of Mousterian deposits which contain artefacts, shellfish and bone remains. These appear to be less distorted and offer a record of multiple hearth use, probably representing a palimpsest of numerous occupation episodes. The exceptional preservation of burnt organic materials in these levels provides some added detail of the nature and type of activities undertaken by Neanderthals. An example of this kind has been recorded in layers dated to before 51,700 ± 3300 BP (OxA-7790). Here charred hulls and shell fragments of stone pine nut (*Pinus pinea*) were recovered from a palaeosurface in amongst a scatter of beach cobbles. The existence of percussive damage on the extremities of the cobbles, and even in some cases adhering charcoal, suggests they had been used for processing the pine nuts for consumption. The preparation method may also have entailed first heating the pine cones and kernels in order to help release the nuts before smashing them with the cobbles (Carruthers and Gale this volume).

As at Vanguard Cave, the lithic artefacts recovered from the Middle Palaeolithic levels conform to a Mousterian tradition characterised by the use of discoidal core technology and its variants (*cf.* Bordes 1950, 1961; Boëda 1988, 1993). The raw materials used are highly diverse but are mostly pebbles of apparently local origin (Barton *et al.* 1999).

Although this paper is not strictly concerned with the Upper Palaeolithic levels, several observations may be made which reveal similarities and contrasts with the underlying Middle Palaeolithic hearth units. In the Upper Palaeolithic units various hearth zones have been identified by dense concentrations of charcoal, in some cases with burnt bone and artefacts. One of the richest of these combustion horizons is in context 9 for which AMS dates

Figure 23.8: Vanguard Cave. Photograph of hearth in the northern alcove.

now provide an age range of 31–28 ka (Pettitt and Bailey this volume). John Waechter, who excavated in the same levels several decades earlier, described the remains of hearths 'apparently lined with flat water worn cobbles' in his layer D.I (Waechter 1951, 85). Our work has confirmed the existence of a band of small rounded limestone cobbles in context 9 and this appears to provide a stratigraphical link with Waechter's layer D.I. However since the cobbles form part of the cave's geological substrate, this seems to offer a natural explanation for the pebble accumulation and we could see no reason for invoking the existence of stone-lined hearths, at least in this part of the observed sequence.

So far, then, within the constraints of our limited excavations, it is difficult to see much variation in the morphology of the different hearth units. One exception, however may be in the wood charcoal component of the various combustion zones. Whereas there is an observed tendency for charcoal of the stone pine and maritime pine to be preserved in the Middle Palaeolithic hearths in both caves, the Upper Palaeolithic combustion zones in Gorham's Cave have produced evidence of mainly pine of the black pine (*Pinus nigra*) group. The latter is a montane species which occurs today at elevations only above 1500 m. As it seems unlikely that this contrast in wood species can be attributed solely to cultural prefer-ences in fuel selection, Finlayson and Pacheco (this

volume) have proposed that the presence of the montane pine group in the Upper Palaeolithic levels may signify the existence of cooler climatic conditions than the present. One of the implications is that the Neanderthals were operating in Mediterranean environments very similar to those of today, while the Upper Palaeolithic occupation occurred during a cooler climatic episode.

Concluding discussion

Until recently any discussion of shellfish exploitation by Neanderthals or other archaic humans would have been restricted to just a few exceptional examples. However, following publication of work on the Italian Mousterian by Mary Stiner and others, there are now a growing number of instances where evidence has been documented for deliberate harvesting of marine shellfish resources by Neanderthals. These include cave sites and rockshelters in the Ligurian Riviera (Costa dei Balzi Rossi, Riparo Mochi, Barma Grande), further south in Latium (Grotta dei Moscerini) and in the southern Italian province of Puglia (Grotta dell'Alto, Grotta del Cavallo, Grotta Uluzzo C, Grotta Mario Bernadini, Grotta dei Giganti) (Stiner 1994, fig 6.9). Further afield in Africa similar occurrences have been reported from Middle Stone Age deposits at Blombos Cave in the southern Cape (Henshilwood and Sealy 1997) and at the Haua Fteah in Cyrenaica (Klein and Scott 1986). To these can now be added the localities of Vanguard and Gorham's Caves and the Devil's Tower, Gibraltar. The Gibraltar examples indicate that mussels and other shellfish probably contributed regularly to the Neanderthal diet. Furthermore they show that selective use was made of the larger shells collected from estuarine habitats and these small packages of food were carried up to four kilometres to the caves to be prepared and consumed. Much larger accumulations of shellfish in association with the Mousterian deposits are also known from unpublished sites north of Gibraltar near Torremolinos, in the Spanish Costa del Sol (Miguel Cortés Sánchez pers. comm.).

The presence of thin *in situ* ashy hearth horizons in Vanguard Cave has helped establish that the use of the site by Neanderthals was generally episodic with individual occupation events usually being short-lived. Ephemeral use of this cave is exemplified by the upper hearth and midden which probably represented a single episode of use of no more than a few hours duration. Further down the sequence more intensive evidence of occupation is indicated by accumulations of butchered bones of ibex and red deer but here too the data are consistent with short-term occupational use. In both the upper and middle section of this cave it was noticeable that the hearths were positioned in proximity of the southern cave wall. Similar juxtapositions have been noted at other Mousterian sites (e.g. Tor Faraj, south Jordan; Henry 1998), but unlike Tor Faraj there is no suggestion of multiple individually spaced hearths. Indeed it is noteworthy that the single hearth in the middle section of Vanguard was re-used at least three times. This may reflect the generally lower density of human groups occupying the site at one time. The position of the hearths near the cave wall and the extensive ash spread in the upper part of the cave may also have been partly connected with sleeping or resting activities. For example in ethnographic contexts, it has been noted that ashy spreads between the hearth and the rock wall may coincide with places where bedding was laid down (Parkington and Mills 1991). Equally, the choice of location of the hearths may simply have been dictated by the direction of the prévailing wind or to factors of air circulation and draughtiness of the cave interior.

Whatever the eventual outcome of further interpretative work on the Mousterian hearths, it is clear that even where some post-depositional disturbance is recorded, as at Gorham's Cave, these structures offer considerable scope for identifying repetitive patterns of human behaviour. They may in due course allow us to pinpoint further aspects of cultural variability in site structure for the Middle and Upper Palaeolithic. The preservation in Gorham's Cave of apparently thicker palimpsests of material, accumulated over longer periods, also provides an opportunity of comparing low-resolution spatial patterns of cultural activity with short-term, high integrity events represented by some of the hearth distributions in Vanguard Cave.

Acknowledgements

I would like to thank the following for their help: Gerry Black for the mapped illustrations, Alison Roberts for producing the computer-generated spatial plots, Hazel Martingell for the artefact drawings, and Paul Jeffrey for his assistance in identifying the species of marine mollusca. Paul Goldberg, Alison Roberts and Yolanda Fernandez-Jalvo are also thanked for commenting on an earlier draft of this paper.

References

Barton, R.N.E., Currant, A.P., Fernandez-Jalvo, Y, Finlayson, J.C., Goldberg, P., Macphail, R., Pettitt, P.B. and Stringer, C.B. (1999). Gibraltar Neanderthals and results of recent investigations in Gorham's, Vanguard and Ibex Caves. *Antiquity* **73**, 13–23.

Bar-Yosef, O., Vandermeersch, B., Arensburg, B., Belfer-Cohen, A., Goldberg, P., Laville, H., Meignen, L., Rak, J., Speth, J., Tchernov, E., Tillier, A.-M. and Weiner, S. (1992). The excavations at Kebara Cave, Mt Carmel, *Current Anthropology* **33**, 497–550.

Binford, L. R. (1983). *In Pursuit of the Past*. London: Thames and Hudson.

Boëda, E. (1988). Le concept Levallois et évaluation de son champ d'application. In (Otte, M., Ed), *L'Homme de Néandertal, Vol. 4: La Technique*. pp. 13–26. Liège: Etudes et Recherches Archéologique de l'Université de Liège.

Boëda, E. (1993). Le débitage discoïde et le débitage Levallois récurrent centripète. *Bulletin de la Société Préhistorique Française* **90**,(6), 392–404.

Bordes, F. (1950). Principes d'une méthode d'étude des techniques et de la typologique paléolithique ancien et moyen. *L'Anthropologie* **54**, 19–34.

Bordes, F. (1961). *Typologie du Paléolithique Ancien et Moyen*. Bordeaux: Delmas.

Bordes, F.(1975). Sur la notion de sol d'habitat en préhistoire paléolithique. *Bulletin de la Société Préhistorique Française* **72**, 139–44.

Connard, N.J., Prindiville, T.J. and Adler, D.S. (1998). Refitting bones and stones as a means of reconstructing Middle Palaeolithic subsistence in the Rhineland.*Economie Préhistorique: les comportements de subsistance au Paléolithique*, pp. 273–290. XVIIIe Rencontres Internationales d'Archéologie et d'Histoire d'Antibes. Editions APDCA: Sophia Antipolis.

Galanidou, N. (1997). *Home is where the hearth is*. Oxford: British Archaeological Reports International Series 687.

Gamble, C. (1991). An introduction to the living spaces of mobile peoples. In (Gamble, C.S. and Boismier, W.A., Eds), *Ethnographical Approaches to Mobile Campsites*, pp. 1–24. Ann Arbor, Michigan: International Monographs in Prehistory.

Gamble, C. (1993). *Timewalkers. The prehistory of global colonisation*. Stroud: Alan Sutton Publishing.

Garrod, D.A.E., Buxton, L.H.D., Smith, G. Elliot and Bate, D.M.A. (1928). Excavation of a Mousterian Rock-shelter at Devil's Tower, Gibraltar. *Journal of the Royal Anthropological Institute* **58**, 33–113.

Henry, D.O. (1998). Intrasite spatial patterns and behavioral modernity. Indications from the Late Levantine Mousterian Rockshelter of Tor Faraj, Southern Jordan. In (Akazawa, T., Aoki, K. and Bar-Yosef, O., Eds), *Neanderthals and Modern Humans in Western Asia*, pp. 127–142. New York: Plenum Press.

Henshilwood, C. and Sealy, J. (1997). Bone artefacts from the

Middle Stone Age at Blombos Cave, Southern Cape, South Africa. *Current Anthropology* **38**, (5), 890–895.

Klein, R.G. and K, Scott (1986). Re-analysis of faunal assemblages from the Haua Fteah and other Late Quaternary archaeological sites in Cyrenaican Libya. *Journal of Archaeological Science* **13**, 515–542.

Mellars, P. (1996). *The Mousterian Legacy*. Princeton: Princeton University Press.

Parkington, J. and Mills, G. (1991). From space to place: the architecture and social organisation of Southern African mobile communities. In (Gamble, C.S. and Boismier, W.A., Eds) *Ethnographical Approaches to Mobile Campsites,* pp. 355–370. Ann Arbor, Michigan: International Monographs in Prehistory.

Perlès, C. (1975). L'homme préhistorique et le feu. *La Recherche* **60**, 829–839.

Rigaud, J-P., Simek, J.F. and Ge, T. (1995). Mousterian fires from Grotte XVI (Dordogne, France). *Antiquity* **69**, 902–12.

Roe, D.A. (1980). Introduction: precise moments in remote time. *World Archaeology* **12** (2), 107–108.

Stiner, M.C. (1994). *Honor among thieves. A zoological study of Neandertal ecology*. Princeton University Press.

Stringer, C. and Gamble, C. (1993). *In search of the Neanderthals*. London: Thames and Hudson.

Waechter, J. D'A. (1951). Excavations at Gorham's Cave, Gibraltar. *Proceedings of the Prehistoric Society* **17**, 83–92.

Waechter, J. D'A. (1964). The excavations at Gorham's Cave, Gibraltar, 1951–1954. *Bulletin of the Institute of Archaeology of London* **4**, 189–221.

24

Provenancing of Mousterian cherts

V. Volterra, R. G. V. Hancock, C. B. Stringer, R. N. E. Barton and L. G. Vega Toscano

A number of archaeological layers which contain stone tools have been unearthed during the current cycle of excavations at Gorham's Cave. All the material recovered from the site is the subject of extensive multi-disciplinary studies including the analysis of artefacts and debitage. In addition to the more conventional typological sorting we decided to investigate the possibility of determining the potential sources of the raw materials employed in the production of such tools. Accordingly, several samples of cherts of Mousterian manufacture were made available for study employing Instrumented Neutron Activation Analysis (INAA). Additional samples recovered from the Mousterian layers of Carihuela Cave in Andalusia were also obtained to provide a basis for comparison.

The determination of provenance of materials through the identification of their trace elements composition via INAA is a well established procedure (Pavlish *et al.* 1985; Hancock *et al.* 1989; Volterra and Hancock 1994; Volterra 1994; Volterra 1997). Determination of provenance of cherts by this method has been carried out already for other Iberian sites.

At times, some general conclusions on the provenance of materials can be drawn based on the identification and quantification of major chemical constituents (Mahaney and Hancock 1991). However, all types of chert consist mainly of SiO_2 and tend to have similar concentrations of major elemental constituents (Hancock *et al.* 1989). Therefore there are limitations to discrimination by gross chemical analysis of major chemical components. To ensure that a clear differentiation can be achieved, the analysis must be carried out at the trace element level. INAA permits the rigorous determination of the chemical composition of materials, beyond their surficial attributes, at the parts per million level.

Neutron activation relies on the bombardment of samples with neutrons, resulting in the transformation of natural elemental nuclei into radioactive nuclids and allowing the subsequent measurement of the γ-radiation which emanates from them. The radiation spectra are converted into meaningful digital results by detecting apparatus.

The original procedure involved a purely radiochemical analysis using Geiger or scintillation counters after separation of components into radio-chemically pure forms (Hoste *et al.* 1971). This is very cumbersome, particularly since a large number of sub-samples have to be analysed serially and because short-lived isotopes often cannot be separated readily after irradiation.

The current approach uses nuclear reactors with high, reliable neutron fluxes and advances in high resolution γ-ray spectrometry, with detecting apparatus close-coupled to computer-driven counters run with sophisticated software. Such instrumented analysis permits the automatic conversion of the radiation spectra into meaningful digital results, making INAA a most productive archaeometric technique for the measurement of a wide spectrum of trace element compositions when a large number of archaeological samples are involved. Another advantage is that only very small samples are required to obtain a positive identification and quantification of elemental compositions.

In the procedure we followed in our research, slow thermal neutrons, produced by a SLOWPOKE reactor, were utilised. The neutrons were captured by the nuclei of stable isotopes present in the sample. The resulting compound nuclei have the same atomic numbers but a larger mass than before bombardment. This renders them unstable. These radioactive nuclids de-excite by emitting β-particles followed by γ-rays which have characteristic energy levels for each element contained in the sample. The amount of γ-ray decay product is proportional to the quantity of each element present. By measuring the former

Table 24.1: INAA results for the sites of Carihuela and Gorham's cave. The elements tested ranged from the more common aluminium, calcium and sodium to rare earths such as dysprosium and europium. They were chosen as the elements most likely to display clear differences between samples.

Sample	Al	Ca	Cl	Dy	Mg	Mn	Na	Ti	U	V	Eu	K	Sr	Si
33	0.04	0.42	0.0	0.0	0.08	1152.0	1006.0	0.0	0.00	4.65	0.00	1959.0	0.0	0.00
34	0.83	12.95	822.0	1.2	0.69	108.0	756.0	0.0	0.00	18.00	0.34	2040.0	152.0	42.1
35	0.48	0.16	211.0	0.6	0.19	79.0	390.0	211.0	0.00	4.52	0.16	772.0	0.0	0.00
36	0.09	0.69	302.0	0.0	0.29	30.90	394.0	0.0	0.64	1.93	0.00	261.0	0.0	40.4
37	0.38	0.27	1540.0	0.4	0.10	7.360	1461.0	0.0	0.00	0.00	0.16	777.0	0.0	45.8
38	0.17	2.00	273.0	0.0	0.63	87.20	471.0	0.0	1.19	4.29	0.00	550.0	77.8	53.0
39	0.13	1.05	78.6	0.2	0.00	51.50	386.0	0.0	0.61	3.62	0.08	319.0	0.0	40.5
40	0.25	0.99	121.0	0.0	0.08	33.10	363.0	0.0	0.67	3.53	0.00	360.0	0.0	57.1
41	0.13	1.61	65.6	0.0	0.00	115.00	151.0	0.0	0.71	0.00	0.00	535.0	0.0	44.4
42	0.27	3.05	0.0	0.0	0.00	426.00	185.0	0.0	0.00	0.00	0.00	2068.0	0.0	53.7
43	0.11	2.59	91.0	0.3	0.00	44.10	134.0	0.0	0.00	0.00	0.10	282.0	0.0	39.9
44	0.24	0.13	154.0	0.0	0.00	1.13	239.0	0.0	0.30	1.31	0.00	671.0	0.0	60.6
45	0.16	0.28	46.8	0.1	0.00	15.00	142.0	0.0	0.44	2.10	0.07	308.0	0.0	46.5
46	0.23	1.27	50.5	1.3	0.05	15.40	270.0	0.0	1.15	2.15	0.32	452.0	0.0	61.0
47	0.36	1.13	70.1	0.6	0.09	28.20	631.0	154.0	0.00	2.77	0.18	1283.0	0.0	39.8
48	0.19	0.50	49.6	0.0	0.04	5.91	114.0	105.0	1.43	2.15	0.07	306.0	0.0	53.7
49	0.24	0.18	24.6	0.0	0.05	8.55	328.0	93.4	0.41	2.21	0.00	558.0	0.0	46.6
50	0.34	0.48	59.6	0.0	0.00	129.0	180.0	0.0	0.00	0.00	0.00	736.0	0.0	61.7

we can identify and quantify the elements composing the samples. The basic activity equation is:

$$A = Nf\sigma(1-e^{-\lambda t})$$

where:

A = the number of disintegration per second
N = the number of atoms of the target element present in the sample
f = the neutron flux of the reactor
σ = the cross-section of the target sample
λ = ln2/half life of the isotope
t = the time duration of the bombardment

Materials & Methods

Eight samples from Gorham's Cave and ten samples from Carihuela were analysed via instrumental neutron activation analysis (INAA) using the University of Toronto's SLOWPOKE Reactor Facility. All the materials studied had the visual appearance of standard chert as is found widely in the Iberan peninsula.

Samples were washed in distilled water and sub-samples for analysis were removed from the artefacts using a cold chisel. All materials were then further reduced in size and subdivided so that samples of each could be retained as duplicate reference for additional testing, if necessary. Analysis aliquots were crushed to a coarse size, oven-dried and weighed. They were then placed in individual polyethylene containers, each with separate identification, for analysis.

Samples were subjected to an irradiation carried out at a flux of 1.0x10" n.cm-2.s-1 (at a nominal reactor power of 5 kW) for a period of one minute. This was followed by a 5 minutes count with a Ge(Li) γ-ray detector after approximately 16 minutes. Results are tabulated in Table 24.1

After the first analysis a number of samples were soaked in water and then re-irradiated and their γ-emissions remeasured. The procedure was then repeated in order to test for sodium/chlorine ratio changes due to leaching.

Results and Discussion

Elements examined for were sodium, aluminium, manganese , magnesium, potassium, barium, titanium, chlorine, calcium, uranium, dysprosium, vanadium, europium, strontium and silicate. The most useful of these elements proved to be calcium, sodium, potassium, chlorine and aluminum. The results of the analysis confirmed that all the material was siliceous. While samples from both sites fell clearly within typical sodium/potassium *versus* aluminium parameters for chert, some of the material is quite "clean" and some contains significant quantities of impurities. This should make it easier to identify the source of the chert.

Two of the units from Gorham's stand out clearly from the bulk of the sample and are also considerably different from each other (Figures 24.1 and 24.2). Given their outstanding chemical compositional markers, sources for these cherts should be easily identifiable once a chemical database is established for potential southern Iberian coastal deposits.

The single Gorham's chert which appears to have been sourced from an inland site seems to be tantalizingly similar

Al vs. Na

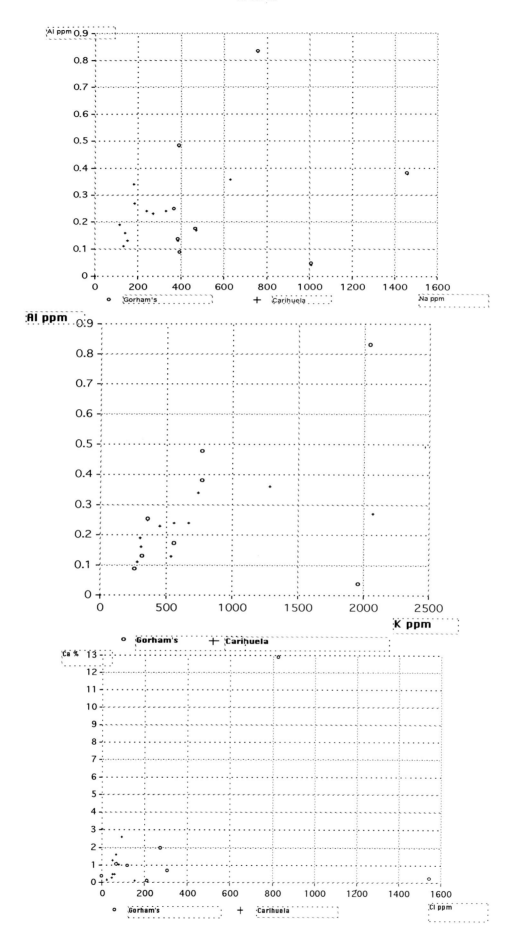

Figure 24.1: Discriminating diagram for chosen trace elements. Note the two outlier samples at the right hand side of the diagrams (particularly noticeable in the bottom diagram). The supply source for these samples should be traceable once a chemical database is established for southern Iberian chert deposits.

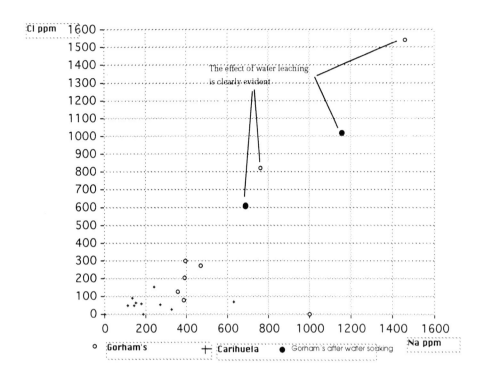

Figure 24.2: Discriminating diagram for chlorine and sodium. Differentiation between inland and coastal chert deposits based on sodium/chlorine ratios is clearly demonstrated. This is the result of sea water percolating into coastal deposits and eventually diffusing into chert. Sodium chloride was leached out in the laboratory for two of the Gorham's cave samples (a and b on the right hand side of diagram); the sodium chloride diffusion is clearly evident.

to some of the Carihuela samples and it is possible that it might have been extracted from the same type of geological deposit.

A detailed analysis of potential sources of easily accessible chert in the southern end of the Iberian peninsula is required to ascertain the actual provenance of the samples we analysed. However even without further assessments it would appear that at both sites several deposits of raw material were exploited during the Mousterian period.

Differentiation between inland and coastal chert deposits based on sodium/chlorine ratios has been clearly demonstrated already with material from other Iberian sites. This discrimination is possible because sea water percolates into coastal deposits and eventually diffuses into the chert. Such an analysis was carried out on the Gorham's and Carihuela cherts and the results show that 75% of the former came from coastal deposits (Figure 24.3). This is not unexpected given the location of the site. The Carihuela cherts were all found to come from inland deposits.

Since the number of samples provided for analysis was small, it is impossible to determine how representative each sub-sample was of the respective site. It should also be noted that samples, although culturally uniform, were

recovered from several different layers at each site. However the results indicate that in general the material from Carihuela seems to be more homogeneous in terms of chemical composition than that from Gorham's. This does not signify that all the chert from Carihuela was obtained from the same deposit. It just points to the fact that the lithic resources exploited by the Neanderthals living at the latter site were more scattered than those exploited by those living at the Carihuela Cave.

Analysis of material recovered from different living floors at each site would allow for the discrimination of diachronic changes in chert source utilisation. This would be an interesting line of study to pursue, but unfortunately the limited number of samples made available for analysis was not sufficient to yield adequate data.

References

Hancock, R.G.V., Grynpas, M.D. & Pritzker, K.P.H. (1989). The abuse of bone analysis for archaeological dietary studies. *Archaeometry.* **31**, 169–179.

Hostes, J., op De Beek, R., Gijbels, R., Adams, S., Van Den Wikel, P., & De Soete, D. (1971). *Instrumental and radiochemical activation analysis.* CRC Press: Cleveland.

Mahaney, W.C., & Hancock, R.G.V. (1991). Geochemistry of Holocene and late Pleistocene soils in the Rouge River and

Scarborough Bluffs area, South- Central Ontario, Canada. *Journal of Radioanalytical and Nuclear Chemistry*. **148**, 1, 167–178

Pavlish, L.A., Sheppard, P.J., & Hancock, R.G.V. (1985). NAA method for determining feldspar types and their mixtures in fine grained rhyolites. *Workshop on Analytical Tools in Archaeometry.*

Volterra, V. (1994). *Dating and provenancing of sherds from five Balsam Lake area sites.* Unpublished Master's degree thesis, McMaster University.

Volterra, V. (1997). Provenancing of ancient Roman millstones. In (C.J. Simpson, Ed.)*The Excavations of San Giovanni di Ruoti*, pp. 75–82.Vol. **2**,

Volterra, V., & Hancock, R.G.V. (1994). Provenancing of ancient Roman millstones. *Journal of Radioanalytical and Nuclear Chemistry*. **180**, 37–44

25

The 'Robusticity Transition' Revisited

Erik Trinkhaus

'We have not succeeded in resolving all of our problems. The answers we have found only serve to raise a whole new set of questions. In some ways we are as confused as ever, but we believe that we are confused on a higher level and about more important things' (graffito, author unkown)

Introduction

In the 1980s, I published several review articles and a monograph (1983a,b, 1984, 1986) which proposed a major decrease in human paramasticatory and appendicular robusticity across the transition from late archaic to early modern humans. This was interpreted as indicating a significant increase in human cultural adaptations and a commensurate decrease in the loads placed upon human biology. This led Isaac (1984) to refer to this period of human evolution as the 'loss of robusticity transition', and Stringer et al. (1984) to list a gracile postcranial skeleton as a 'probable autapomorphy' of modern humans.

Paleoanthropologists have continued to investigate robusticity across the Late Pleistocene late archaic to early modern human transition. Some of these studies (e.g. Rak 1986; Trinkaus 1987; Trinkaus & Churchill 1988; Trinkaus & Villemeur 1991; Vandermeersch 1991; Churchill 1994; Villemeur 1994; Vandermeersch & Trinkaus 1995; Niewoehner et al. 1997; Stefan & Trinkaus 1998a) have reinforced the notion of a significant change in hypertrophy with the emergence of modern humans, whereas others have either failed to document such a shift or have noted only subtle shifts between late archaic and early modern humans (e.g. Ruff et al. 1993; Anton 1994; Hambücken 1995; Abbott et al. 1996; Lieberman 1996; Trinkaus & Hilton 1996; Trinkaus 1997; Trinkaus et al. 1998; Trinkaus

& Ruff, 1999a,b; Kallfelz-Klemish & Franciscus n.d.; Trinkaus & Rhoads n.d.).

As part of these analyses, there has been increasing emphasis on more precise quantification of reflections of masticatory and appendicular hypertrophy and on the appropriate scaling of those reflections. This has led to a more complex perception of the nature of changes in 'robusticity' with the emergence of early modern humans. In light of this, it is appropriate to present here, on the anniversary of the discovery of one of the specimens which started the scientific investigation of modern human emergence, a reconsideration of the 'Robusticity Transition.'

Robusticity and Scaling

We (Ruff et al. 1993) have defined robusticity as 'the strength or rigidity of a structure relative to the mechanically relevant measure of body size.' This can be generalised to: *the ability of a structure to withstand habitual physiological loads placed upon it, scaled to the appropriate measure of body size and/or its functional unit.*

For weight-bearing structures, the relevant 'measure of body size' is body mass or body mass times the relevant beam length for structures subjected to bending and torsional loads. For normally non-weight-bearing structures, such as the human upper limb, some measure of limb or bone length appears to be most appropriate, although it remains unclear to what extent body mass may play a role in human upper limb scaling (Ruff et al. 1993; Churchill et al. n.d.; Ruff, n.d.); it is assumed here that the role of body mass as a baseline for loading the human upper limb is minimal.

For other structures, such as the dentition (subjected to both bite force and attrition) and the mandible (modelling

Table 25.1: Patterns of change in reflections of robusticity across the late archaic to early modern human transition. Features in parentheses are qualified in the text, and the arrow indicates the direction in which it might be moved.

	Stasis	**Shift**	**Contrast**
Mastication			
	mandible corpus		anterior dentition
Diaphyses			
	left humerus	right humerus	
	femur	pedal phalanges 2-4	
	tibia		
Articulations			
	femur head	distal humerus	
	talar trochlea		
Articular Orientation			
	tibial retroversion	$\Leftarrow$(femur neck angle)	
Moment Arms			
	(tibia condyle)$\Rightarrow$		radius neck length
	(patella thickness)$\Rightarrow$		radius curvature
			hamulus projection
			pollical phalanges
Muscular Reflections			
		biceps brachii	pectoralis major
		gluteus maximus	
		(apical tufts)$\Rightarrow$	

the corpus as a bent beam), the baseline is less clear. Body mass ultimately scales the dentition, especially the postcanine dentition, through dietary requirements. However, the issues here are anterior dental hypertrophy related to paramasticatory use of the dentition and mandibular corpus rigidity related to facial hypertrophy. It consequently becomes appropriate to use the dimensions of the cheek teeth (as a masticatory baseline) to scale the anterior teeth, and mandibular length (as a beam length) to scale corpus rigidity.

Materials and Methods

The number of relevant comparisons for assessing late archaic to early modern human 'robusticity' is almost endless. As a result, a selection was made of those features which have received specific attention, are represented on a reasonable number of specimens on either side of this transition, and have the relevant data available. The set of 22 comparisons should characterise the range of both patterns of change and functional units of interest. The comparisons include elements that are likely epigenetic (e.g., dental dimensions) and highly developmentally plastic (e.g., diaphyseal hypertrophy). The issue

is not how plastic these features might have been, but whether they accurately reflect changes (or stasis) in robusticity.

To the extent possible, measures that closely approximate the limb structures of interest and appropriate scaling measures were employed. In some cases, however, fossil preservation, limited associated remains, available data and/or the current state of analysis make the measures employed less than ideal. Nonetheless, these data include a number of measures (diaphyseal cross-sectional parameters, appropriate moment arms, etc.) which permit more accurate assessments than were possible a decade ago.

The primary data consist of linear and angular osteometrics and diaphyseal cross-sectional second moments of area. The majority of the cross sections were reconstructed from subperiosteal contour moulds and biplanar radiography; the remainder are from natural breaks. They were digitised and parameters were computed using SLICE (Nagurka & Hayes 1980; Eschman 1992). In addition, 'polar moments of area' were computed for the mandibular corpus and the proximal pedal phalangeal shafts modeling them as solid beams and using ellipse formulae (Runestad *et al.* 1993); both assumptions limit the precision of the assessments, but they are mechanically significant improvements for assessing hypertrophy over raw external diameters.

Comparisons are done graphically, and the results are categorised as 'stasis', 'shift' or 'contrast', reflecting respectively no meaningful change, a modest shift in the distributions, and largely complete separation of the distributions. The comparisons have been categorised (Table 25.1), but a few of the comparisons may fall between two of these categories.

The remains have been assigned *a priori* based on other morphological criteria to one of three samples: Late Pleistocene late archaic humans (Neandertals), Near Eastern Middle Paleolithic Qafzeh-Skhul early modern humans, and earlier Upper Paleolithic (=18 ka) early modern humans. All derive from Europe and the Near East. With the exception of destroyed material (i.e., Pøedmostí), postcranial data are from personal study of the material supplemented by data from Formicola (1990), Churchill (1994), Holliday (1995) and Holt (1998); mandibular and dental data are to a greater extent from the literature (see Stefan & Trinkaus 1998a,b).

The need to scale weight-bearing elements to body mass requires its estimation for these fossil hominids. This was done using a geometric technique based on stature and bi-iliac breadth (Ruff *et al.* 1997). Body mass estimation is essential to these comparisons, given the marked contrasts in body proportions across these samples (Trinkaus 1981; Ruff 1994; Holliday 1997a,b), with the Neandertals exhibiting hyperarctic proportions and the early modern humans having tropical to warm temperate ones. Use solely of long bone lengths to scale weight-bearing articulations and diaphyses confounds the effects of body proportions and structural hypertrophy and does not permit any conclusions about robusticity.

Paramasticatory and Masticatory Hypertrophy

There have been numerous attempts to explain Neandertal dental size and facial morphology as a response to high levels of paramasticatory loading of the anterior dentition. This has been based on perceptions of their large, shovel-shaped anterior teeth, high levels of anterior dental attrition and midfacial prognathism.

Dentally, it has been shown that Neandertals do not have particularly large teeth, taken one-at-a-time, vis-à-vis early modern humans, with ranges of variation overlapping and only the incisors being significantly larger on average (Stefan & Trinkaus 1998a). However, when summed anterior versus posterior teeth are compared for sufficiently complete mandibular dentitions (Figure 25. 1), cheek tooth ranges are similar but the Neandertals have relatively larger anterior teeth, with only Dolní Vìstonice 13 creeping into the Neandertal range and the large Qafzeh 9 teeth approaching it.

In contrast, a plot of mandibular lateral corpus (M_1/M_2) 'polar moment of area' versus mandibular (mid-condyles to infradentale) length shows no meaningful

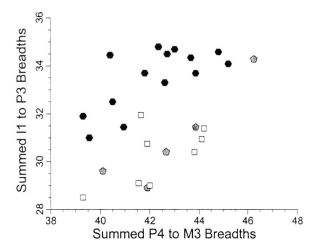

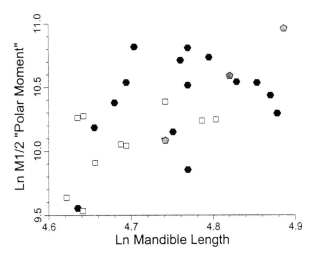

Figure 25.1: Dental and mandibular hypertrophy. Summed anterior versus posterior dental breadths (above) and mandibular corpus (M_1/M_2) 'polar moment of area' versus length (below). Solid hexagons: Neandertals; gray pentagons: Qafzeh-Skhul; open squares: earlier Upper Paleolithic.

difference between the samples. The Neandertals show more variation and exhibit the highest and lowest relative values. This supports previous assessments of a reduction in overall facial massiveness among the Neandertals relative to their predecessors (Trinkaus 1987) and is in agreement with recent biomechanical analyses (Anton, 1994; Kallfelz-Klemish & Franciscus n.d.) demonstrating the inability of Neandertal faces to generate high anterior bite forces. It also implies that the reduction in anterior dental dimensions was primarily related to paramasticatory attrition and not bite force *per se*.

Diaphyseal Hypertrophy

The Neandertals have been noted for the hypertrophy of their diaphyses, especially those of the humerus, femur,

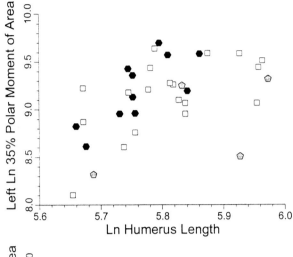

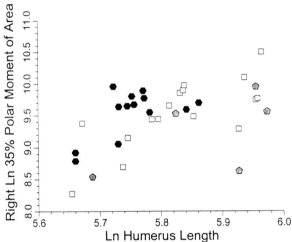

Figure 25.2: Humeral shaft hypertrophy. Left (above) and right (below) humeral mid-distal polar moment of area versus length. Symbols as in Figure 25.1.

tibia and pedal phalanges (Trinkaus 1976; Lovejoy & Trinkaus 1980; Trinkaus & Hilton 1996), although the degree of change between them and early modern humans has been questioned (Ruff *et al.* 1993; Bridges 1995; Churchill & Formicola 1997; Trinkaus 1997; Trinkaus & Ruff 1999a,b; Trinkaus *et al.* n.d.). Diaphyses are ideal for robusticity assessments, since they can be modeled as beams, assessed biomechanically, and remain plastic in response to habitual loads throughout life (Ruff *et al.* 1993; Trinkaus *et al.* 1994; and references therein).

Humeral mid-distal diaphyseal rigidity was assessed separately for the right and left bones, given consistent and sometimes marked asymmetry in these bones in Late Pleistocene humans (Trinkaus *et al.* 1994; Churchill & Formicola 1997; Trinkaus & Churchill 1999). The left humerus, which provides more of a baseline assessment given near universal right side dominance among these humans (Weaver *et al.* n.d.), shows little difference

between these samples (Figure 25.2). The Neandertals fall on average slightly higher than the early modern humans (even if one ignores the low values for Dolní Vìstonice 14 and Skhul 2 & 5), but there is little difference between the cores of the samples. The right humerus, however, shows more of a shift, with a couple of Neandertals (Amud 1 and La Ferrassie 1) being modest and one early modern specimen (Krems-Hundssteig 1) being more robust.

If one were to incorporate body mass into the scaling of humeral diaphyseal strength, it would eliminate any difference in the right humerus. However, it would also make the Neandertal left humeri appear more gracile than those of most of the early modern humans. Given the low probability of the latter conclusion, it is best that these and other upper limb reflections of robusticity (see below) be scaled to limb lengths alone.

In the femoral and tibia midshafts there is little difference between the samples, once body mass and bone length are taken into account (Figure 25.3). There are a couple of relatively gracile early modern tibiae (Dolní Vìstonice 3 & 14) and one robust Qafzeh-Skhul femur (Qafzeh 9), but the majority of the remains from all three samples fall within a modest range of variation. This implies little change in locomotion-related loading of the legs across this transition.

In contrast, assessments of pedal middle proximal phalangeal diaphyses (from digits 2 to 4) show an interesting pattern (Figure 25.3). The Neandertals have generally higher values, with the Middle Paleolithic Qafzeh-Skhul remains falling among the more gracile of them. The earlier Upper Paleolithic remains, however, are largely more gracile than either of the Middle Paleolithic samples. Given the similarities in femoral and tibial diaphyseal hypertrophy, this implies more of a difference in anterior foot loading patterns than in overall locomotor levels and that the real contrast is Middle versus Upper Paleolithic rather than late archaic versus early modern human.

Articular Hypertrophy

Neandertals have been described as having large articulations in both upper and lower limbs (Rhoads & Trinkaus 1977; Trinkaus 1980; Churchill & Trinkaus 1990). Yet, it has been shown at least for the femoral head that weight-bearing joints scale to body mass similarly across the genus *Homo* (Ruff *et al.* 1993). This was reassessed for these Late Pleistocene samples for humeral distal articular breadth, femoral head diameter and talar trochlear 'area' (length x breadth). The first is scaled to humeral length (as an indicator of arm size), the second to estimated body mass (representing lower limb axial loading) and the third to talus length (as a general body size indicator).

The resultant comparisons (Figure 25. 4) show a modest decrease in relative humeral articular size, stasis in relative femoral head with a suggestion of an increase with early

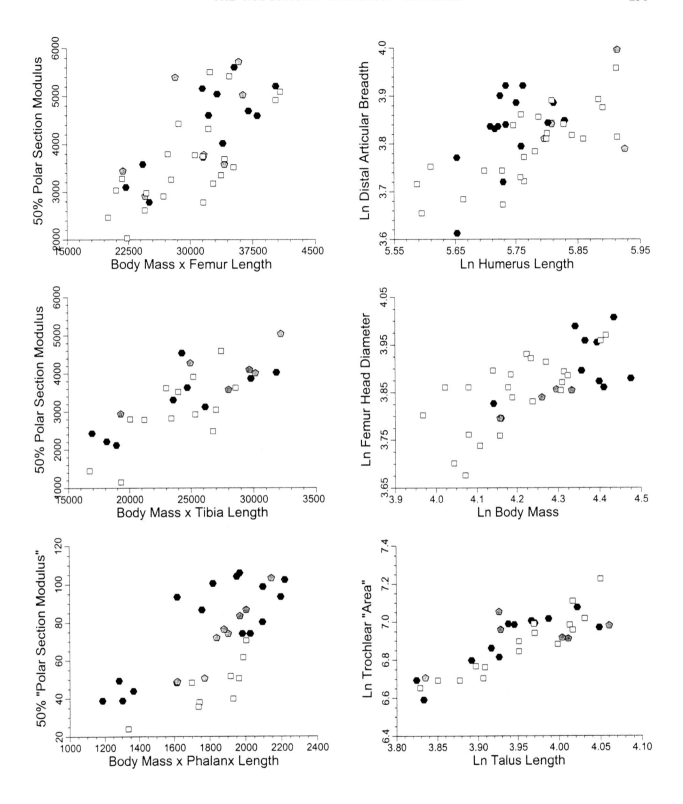

Figure 25.3: Lower limb shaft hypertrophy. Midshaft polar section modulus versus bone length times body mass for the femur (top), tibia (middle) and middle pedal proximal phalanges (bottom). Symbols as in Figure 25.1.

Figure 25.4: Articular hypertrophy. Humeral distal articular breadth versus length (top), femoral head diameter versus body mass (middle), and talar trochlear 'area' versus length (bottom). Symbols as in Figure 25.1.

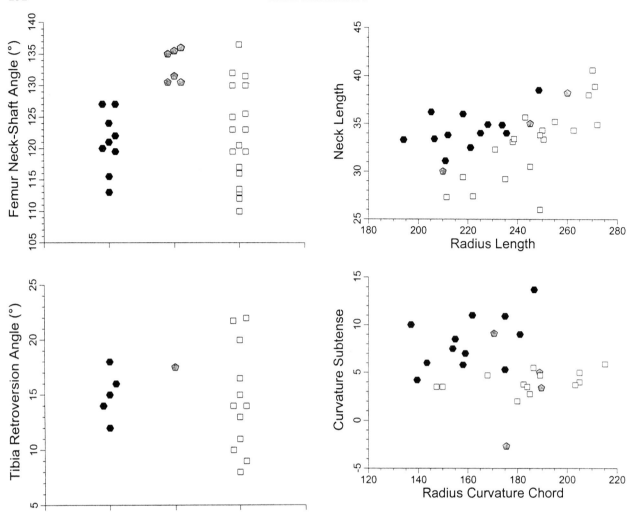

Figure 25.5: Articular orientation. Femur neck-shaft angle (above) and tibial retroversion angle (below). Symbols as in Figure 25.1.

Figure 25.6: Radial muscle moment arms. Relative neck length (above), and shaft curvature (below). Symbols as in Figure 25.1.

modern humans (the three low Neandertal values are Amud 1 and Shanidar 4 & 5), and stasis in relative talar trochlear size.

Articular Orientation

In addition to articular size, loading regimes can affect articular orientation, in particular femoral neck-shaft and tibial retroversion angles (Trinkaus 1975; Anderson & Trinkaus 1998). Both of these reflect developmental changes as a result of activity levels, with lower neck-shaft angles and higher retroversion angles associated with increased lower limb loading during ontogeny. The Qafzeh-Skhul sample is unusual for its high femoral neck-shaft angles (Trinkaus, 1993), but there is little difference between the samples in tibial retroversion and between the Neandertals and earlier Upper Paleolithic remains in femoral neck-shaft angles. Pooling the early modern human samples, one would have to categorise the femoral neck-shaft angle comparison as a shift, but the Neandertals are

still well within the earlier Upper Paleolithic range of variation.

Muscle Moment Arms

The moment arms for muscles are hard to determine precisely from skeletal remains, but reflections of them can be measured for several muscles in the cubital, antebrachial, carpal and pollical regions and across the knee.

The elbow flexion moment arm for *M. biceps brachii* is close to the radial neck length (proximal head to mid-tuberosity), and the associated load arm (forearm plus hand length) should correlate closely with radial length given similar relative hand size across these samples (Trinkaus 1983a). A plot of the two variables largely separates these samples, with Skhul 7 and Shanidar 1 providing slight overlap (Figure 25.6).

Radial lateral curvature provides an assessment of the

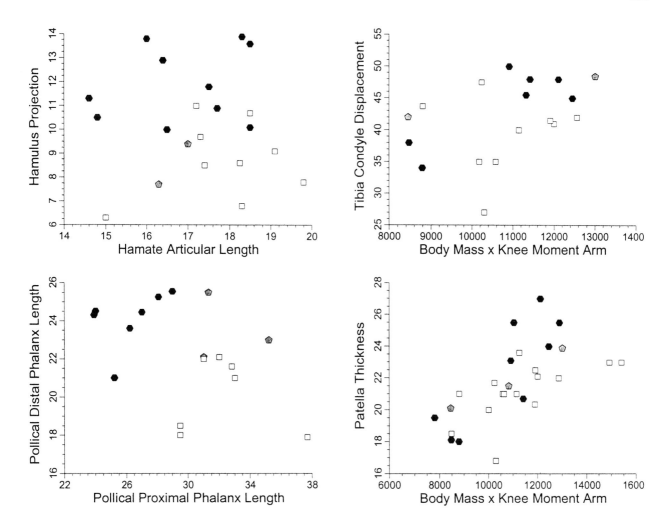

Figure 25.7: Hand moment arms. Relative hamulus projection (above) and thumb phalangeal proportions (below). Symbols as in Figure 25.1.

Figure 25. 8: Knee moment arms. Tibial condyle displacement (above) and patellar thickness (below) versus body mass times its moment arm. Symbols as in Figure 25.1.

moment arms of *M. pronator teres* and *M. pronator quadratus* relative to the pronation-supination axis of the forearm. Similarly, there is little overlap between the samples, with Régourdou 1 and Shanidar 1 being more modest among the Neandertals and Skhul 7 having a high value (Figure 25.6).

Within the hand, the palmar projection of the hamulus provides leverage for *M. flexor carpi ulnaris* for wrist flexion and stabilisation, as well as affecting the dimensions of the carpal tunnel and providing leverage for intrinsic hypothenar muscles. There is only modest overlap in distributions of the Neandertals and early modern humans in relative hamulus projection (Figure 25.7), due in part to variation in relative hamate length, the best available indicator of hand size given the incomplete nature of most Pleistocene hand remains.

It has been shown (Trinkaus & Villemeur 1991) that the relatively short proximal phalanx of the thumb and associated long distal pollical phalanx provided the

Neandertals with an increased mechanical advantage in power grips relative to recent humans. When early modern human thumb phalanx lengths are compared to those of the Neandertals, the samples are largely separate, with only Qafzeh 8 approaching the Neandertal distribution, especially with respect to La Ferrassie 2 (Figure 25.7).

At the knee, the load arm is the perpendicular from the line of weight support (hip to ankle) to the joint axis of rotation, which can be calculated from femur and tibia lengths for given angles of flexion (Trinkaus & Rhoads n.d.). The power arm for *M. quadriceps femoris* is from the same axis of rotation to the patellar ligament, and it is influenced by tibial condyle displacement (posteriorly relative to the tibial tuberosity) and patellar thickness. Assuming static equilibrium, the proportions of tibial condyle displacement and patellar thickness can be compared to the load arm times body mass (Figure 25.8). The result is a suggestion of a decrease in *M. quadriceps femoris* relative mechanical advantage, but there is complete overlap in the tibial comparison and only two Neandertals (Kiik-Koba 1 and Shanidar 4) stand out in the patellar comparison. All of these values fall well within the ranges of variation of recent non-industrial humans (Trinkaus & Rhoads n.d.). Therefore, these are considered as qualified stasis.

Muscle Attachment Hypertrophy

Inferences regarding muscular hypertrophy are difficult to make from skeletal remains, given the generally diffuse and/or indistinct attachment areas for individual muscles. However, a few cases with discrete insertions serve to evaluate patterns of muscle hypertrophy, given that enlargement of one muscle requires hypertrophy of its antagonists and synergists to maintain joint stability.

M. pectoralis major forms a distinct tuberosity on the proximal humerus, whose breadth can be reliably measured. When that dimension is plotted against humeral length (as a load arm for the muscle), the Neandertal and early modern human samples are largely separate (Figure 25.9). The pattern is more pronounced than this illustrates, since all of the Neandertals have highly rugose tuberosities, whereas a number of the early modern human tuberosities are smooth and barely discernible against the subperiosteal bone.

One of the major forearm flexors as well as a primary supinator, *M. biceps brachii*, inserts (with a bursa) into the radial tuberosity. Comparison of tuberosity 'area' (length x breadth) versus forearm length provides a clear shift, with overlap, between these samples. This implies a decrease in average tendon insertion size. The effect of this reduction on supination is more pronounced, given the shift from a medial orientation of the tuberosity to a more antero-medial one (Churchill 1994), which decreases the moment arm for *M. biceps brachii* in higher degrees of supination (Trinkaus & Churchill 1988).

Although it is not strictly a muscle insertion area, the apical tufts of the terminal hand phalanges provide attachments for the volar pad and are hence related to force generated across the terminal fingers. The large size of the tuft in Neandertals has been noted (e.g. Trinkaus 1983a), and comparison of its breadth for the three middle fingers to bone length (Figure 25.9) supports the contention of a major shift between the samples. However, there is some overlap between the samples.

Finally, one lower limb reflection of muscular hypertrophy is gluteal tuberosity enlargement (Trinkaus, 1976, 1983a). It is assumed that the same proportions of *M. gluteus maximus* inserted into the proximal femur versus the iliotibial tract across these samples, so that the size of the tuberosity (its breadth) reflects muscle size and hip musculature hypertrophy generally. Since it crosses a weight-bearing joint, it should be scaled against its load arm (femoral length) times body mass (Figure 25.10). Even though the Neandertals generally have the largest tuberosities, most of them fall well within early modern

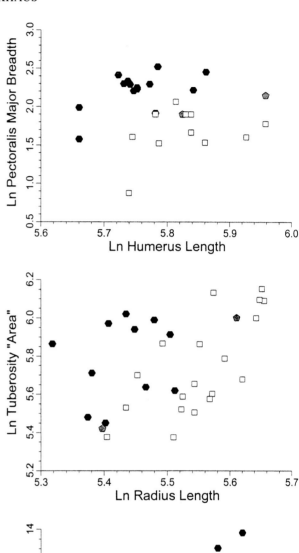

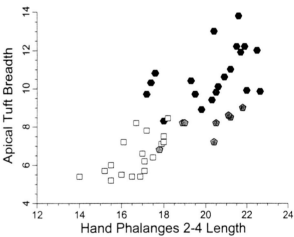

Figure 25.9: Upper limb muscle attachment areas. M. pectoralis major tuberosity breadth versus humeral length (top), radial tuberosity (for M. biceps brachii) 'area' versus radial length (middle), and terminal hand phalanx tuft breadth versus length (bottom). Symbols as in Figure 25.1.

human ranges of variation once body size and proportions are taken into account. The three outliers are all small females, La Ferrassie 2, Shanidar 6 and Tabun 1, indicating

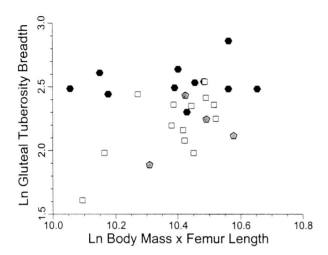

Figure 25.10. Gluteal tuberosity breadth (for M. gluteus maximus) versus body mass times femur length. Symbols as in Figure 25.1.

that there is little size scaling in this feature among the Neandertals, despite a general increase in tuberosity size with stature and body mass among early modern humans.

Conclusions

These comparisons are summarized in Table 25. 1. A few patterns emerge. In the lower limb, there is predominantly stasis in locomotor related robusticity. The only shifts are in the pedal phalangeal shafts, the gluteal tuberosity, and possibly femoral neck-shaft angle. All of the contrasts are related to manipulation, either in the upper limb or the anterior dentition. Yet, the structural characteristics of these regions, the mandibular corpus and the humeral diaphyses, show stasis or a shift. This implies that the changes related to manipulation may reflect either attrition with moderate force levels or occasional peak forces with little repetitive loading.

In any case, what becomes apparent here is that the Late Pleistocene 'Robusticity Transition' was a mosaic. There is a general dichotomy between the degree of changes related to manipulation versus locomotion. However, additional consideration of these and other anatomical reflections of musculo-skeletal hypertrophy will probably further complicate the picture, but hopefully direct us more towards understanding the nuances of the evolutionary transition associated with the emergence of early modern humans.

Acknowledgments

I would like to thank Chris Stringer & Clive Finlayson for inviting me to participate in this symposium and providing an opportunity to pull these thoughts together. This work has been possible through the generosity of curators too numerous to mention, support from N.S.F. L.S.B. Leakey Fdtn., C.N.R.S., Wenner-Gren Fdtn., and Academy of Sciences (CR), and it has benefitted from conversations and collaborations with many colleagues and students. T.L. Estenson provided the graffito. To all of them I am grateful.

References

Abbott, S., Trinkaus, E., & Burr, D.B. (1996). Dynamic bone remodeling in later Pleistocene fossil hominids. *Am. J. Phys. Anthropol.* **99**, 585–601.

Anderson, J.Y. & Trinkaus, E. (1998). Patterns of sexual, bilateral and inter-populational variation in human femoral neck-shaft angles. *J. Anat. (Lond.)* **192**, 279–285.

Anton, S. (1994). Mechanical and other perspectives on Neandertal craniofacial morphology. In (R.S. Corruccini & R.L. Ciochon, Eds) *Integrative Paths to the Past*. pp. 677–695. Englewood Cliffs: Prentice-Hall.

Bridges, P.S. (1995). Skeletal biology and behavior in ancient humans. *Evol. Anthropol.* **4**, 112–120.

Churchill, S.E. (1994). *Human Upper Body Evolution in the Eurasian Later Pleistocene*. Ph.D. Thesis, University of New Mexico.

Churchill, S.E. & Formicola, V. (1997). A case of marked bilateral asymmetry in the upper limb of an Upper Palaeolithic male from Barma Grande (Liguria), Italy. *Intl. J. Osteoarcheol.* **7**, 18–38.

Churchill, S.E., & Trinkaus, E. (1990). Neandertal scapular glenoid morphology. *Am. J. Phys. Anthropol.* **83**, 147–160.

Churchill, S.E., Wall, C.E. & Schmitt, D. (n.d.). Bone strength to body size scaling in non-weight bearing structures: Constraints on size and relative strength of the human humerus. *Journal of Morphology*. (in press).

Eschman, P.N. (1992). *SLCOMM Version 1.6*. Albuquerque: Eschman Archeological Services.

Formicola, V. (1990) The triplex burial of Barma Grande (Grimaldi, Italy). *Homo* **39**, 130–143.

Hambücken, A. (1995) Étude du degrée de robustesse des os longs du membre supérieur des Néandertaliens. *Bull. Mém. Soc. Anthropol. Paris* **ns7**, 37–47.

Holliday, T.W. (1995). *Body Size and Proportions in the Late Pleistocene Western Old World and the Origins of Modern Humans*. Ph.D. Thesis, University of New Mexico.

Holliday, T.W. (1997a). Body proportions in Late Pleistocene Europe and modern human origins. *J. Hum. Evol.* **32**, 423–447.

Holliday, T.W. (1997b). Postcranial evidence of cold adaptation in European Neandertals. *Am. J. Phys. Anthropol.* **104**, 245–258.

Holt, B. (1998) *Biomechanical Evidence of Decreased Mobility in Upper Paleolithic and Mesolithic Europe*. Ph.D. Thesis, University of Missouri – Columbia.

Isaac, G.L. (1984). The loss of robusticity transition. *Quart. Rev. Archaeol.* **2**, 12–13.

Kallfelz-Klemish, C.F. & Franciscus, R.G. (n.d.). Bite force production capability and efficiency in Neandertals and modern humans. *Am. J. Phys. Anthropol.* (in press).

Lieberman, D.E. (1996). How and why humans grow thin skulls: Experimental evidence for systemic cortical robusticity. *Am. J. Phys. Anthropol.* **101**, 217–236.

Lovejoy, C.O. & Trinkaus, E. (1980). Strength and robusticity in the Neandertal tibia. *Am. J. Phys. Anthropol.* **53**, 465–470.

Nagurka, M.L. & Hayes, W.C. (1980). An interactive graphics package for calculating cross-sectional properties of complex shapes. *J. Biomech.* **13**, 59–64.

Niewoehner, W., Trinkaus, E. & Ward, C.V. (1997). Pliocene and

Pleistocene hominid hamulus size and robusticity (abstract). *Am. J. Phys. Anthropol. Suppl.* **24**, 178–179.

Rak, Y. (1986). The Neanderthal: A new look at an old face. *J. Hum. Evol.* 15, 151–164.

Rhoads, J.G., & Trinkaus, E. (1977). Morphometrics of the Neandertal talus. *Am. J. Phys. Anthropol.* 46, 29–44.

Ruff, C.B. (1994). Morphological adaptation to climate in modern and fossil hominids. *Yrbk. Phys. Anthropol.* 37, 65–107.

Ruff, C.B. (n.d.). Body size, body shape, and long bone strength in modern humans. *J. Hum. Evol.* (in press).

Ruff, C.B., Trinkaus, E. & Holliday, T.W. (1997). Body mass and encephalization in Pleistocene *Homo. Nature.* **387**, 173–176.

Ruff, C.B., Trinkaus, E., Walker, A. & Larsen, C.S. (1993). Postcranial robusticity in *Homo*, I: Temporal trends and mechanical interpretations. *Am. J. Phys. Anthropol.* **91**, 21–53.

Runestad, J.A., Ruff, C.B., Nieh, J.C., Thorington, R.W. & Teaford, M.F. (1993). Radiographic estimation of long bone cross-sectional geometric properties. *Am. J. Phys. Anthropol.* **90**, 207–213.

Stefan, V.H. & Trinkaus, E. (1998a). Discrete trait and dental morphometric affinities of the Tabun 2 mandible. *J. Hum. Evol.* **34**, 443–468.

Stefan, V.H. & Trinkaus, E. (1998b). La Quina 9 and Neandertal mandibular variability. *Bull. Mém. Soc. Anthropol. Paris.* (in press).

Stringer, C.B., Hublin, J.J. & Vandermeersch, B. (1984). The origins of anatomically modern humans in western Europe. In (F.H. Smith & F. Spencer, Eds), *The Origins of Modern Humans.* pp.51–135. New York: Alan R. Liss.

Trinkaus, E. (1975). Squatting among the Neandertals: A problem in the behavioral interpretation of skeletal morphology. *J. Archaeol. Sci.* **2**, 327–351.

Trinkaus, E. (1976). The evolution of the hominid femoral diaphysis during the Upper Pleistocene in Europe and the Near East. *Z. Morphol. Anthropol.* **67**, 291–319.

Trinkaus, E. (1980). Sexual differences in Neanderthal limb bones. *J. Hum. Evol.* **9**, 377–397.

Trinkaus, E. (1981). Neanderthal limb proportions and cold adaptation. In (C.B. Stringer, Ed.), *Aspects of Human Evolution.* pp. 187–224. London: Taylor & Francis.

Trinkaus, E. (1983a). *The Shanidar Neandertals.* New York: Academic Press.

Trinkaus, E. (1983b). Neandertal postcrania and the adaptive shift to modern humans. In (E. Trinkaus Ed), *The Mousterian Legacy.* Oxford: British Archaeological Reports. *S164*, 165–200.

Trinkaus, E. (1984). Western Asia. In (F.H. Smith & F. Spencer Eds), *The Origins of Modern Humans.* pp.251–293. New York: Alan R. Liss.

Trinkaus, E. (1986). The Neandertals and modern human origins. *Annu. Rev. Anthropol.* **15**, 193–218.

Trinkaus, E. (1987). The Neandertal face: evolutionary and functional perspectives on a recent hominid face. *J. Hum. Evol.* **16**, 429–443.

Trinkaus, E. (1993). Femoral neck-shaft angles of the Qafzeh-Skhul early modern humans, and activity levels among immature Near Eastern Middle Paleolithic hominids. *J. Hum. Evol.* **25**, 393–416.

Trinkaus, E. (1997). Appendicular robusticity and the paleobiology of modern human emergence. *Proc. Nat. Acad. Sci. USA.* **94**, 13367–13373.

Trinkaus, E., & Churchill, S.E. (1988). Neandertal radial tuberosity orientation. *Am. J. Phys. Anthropol.* **75**, 15–21.

Trinkaus, E. & Churchill, S.E. (1999). Diaphyseal cross-sectional geometry of Near Eastern Middle Paleolithic humans: The humerus. *J. Archaeol. Sci.* (in press).

Trinkaus, E., Churchill, S.E., & Ruff, C.B. (1994). Postcranial robusticity in *Homo*, II: Humeral bilateral asymmetry and bone plasticity. *Am. J. Phys. Anthropol.* **93**, 1–34.

Trinkaus, E., & Hilton, C.E. (1996). Neandertal pedal proximal phalanges: diaphyseal loading patterns. *J. Hum. Evol.* **30**, 399–425.

Trinkaus, E. & Rhoads, M.L. (n.d.) Neandertal knees: Power lifters in the Pleistocene? *J. Hum. Evol.* (in review).

Trinkaus, E. & Ruff, C.B. (1999a). Diaphyseal cross-sectional geometry of Near Eastern Middle Paleolithic humans: The femur. *J. Archaeol. Sci.* (in press).

Trinkaus, E. & Ruff, C.B. (1999b). Diaphyseal cross-sectional geometry of Near Eastern Middle Paleolithic humans: The tibia. *J. Archaeol. Sci.* (in press).

Trinkaus, E., Ruff, C.B., Churchill, S.E., & Vandermeersch, B. (1998). Locomotion and body proportions of the Saint-Césaire 1 Châtelperronian Neandertal. *Proc. Nat. Acad. Sci. USA.* **95**, 5836–5840.

Trinkaus, E., Stringer, C.B., Ruff, C.B., Hennessy, R.J., Roberts, M.B. & Parfitt, S.A. (n.d.). Diaphyseal cross-sectional geometry of the Boxgrove 1 Middle Pleistocene human tibia. *J. Hum. Evol..* (in press).

Trinkaus, E., & Villemeur, I. (1991). Mechanical advantages of the Neandertal thumb in flexion: A test of an hypothesis. *Am. J. Phys. Anthropol.* **84**, 249–260.

Vandermeersch, B. (1991). La ceinture scapulaire et les membres supérieures. In (B. Vandermeersch & O. Bar-Yosef, Eds) *Le Squelette Moustérien de Kébara 2.* pp.157–178. Paris: C.N.R.S.

Vandermeersch, B., & Trinkaus, E. (1995) The postcranial remains of the Régourdou 1 Neandertal: The shoulder and arm remains. *J. Hum. Evol.* **28**, 439–476.

Villemeur, I. (1994). *La Main des Néandertaliens.* Paris: C.N.R.S.

Weaver, A.H., Holliday, T.W., Ruff, C.B. & Trinkaus, E. (n.d.) The fossil evidence for the evolution of human intelligences in Pleistocene *Homo*. In (A. Nowell, Ed) *Archaeology of the Human Mind.* Cambridge: Cambridge University Press. (in press).

26

Investigation of Neanderthal Morphology with Computer-Assisted Methods

M. S. Ponce de León, C. P. E. Zollikofer, R. D. Martin and C. B. Stringer

Introduction

The accidental discovery of a fossilised human cranium, blasted out during work at Forbes' Quarry, below the North Face of the Rock, nearly placed Gibraltar in the forefront of prehistoric studies 135 years ago. In September 1864, sixteen years after its discovery, this cranium was exhibited at the British Association for the Advancement of Science meeting in Bath by George Busk (Busk 1865), and Hugh Falconer suggested in a letter to Busk that it be made the type of a new human species *Homo calpicus*, named after Mons Calpe, the ancient name for Gibraltar (Keith 1911). But this proposal was overtaken by the publication in the same year of the species name *Homo neanderthalensis*, by William King (King 1864), based on the Neander Valley (Feldhofer) skeleton from Germany, the first time a new species of human had been properly and scientifically proposed. The German skeleton thus received most of the scientific attention, and such famous scientists as Thomas Huxley, Rudolf Virchow and Charles Darwin commented on the Neanderthal find, but ignored the equally important Gibraltar specimen. Although it lacked an associated skeleton, the Forbes' Quarry find possessed the more complete cranial vault, and also had the face preserved, which we now know is one of the most informative and distinctive of Neanderthal anatomical complexes.

Even though the French anthropologist Broca provided a brief description in 1869, the Forbes' Quarry cranium had to wait nearly 50 years before it got the attention it deserved, from the next generation of scientists, such as William Sollas (1907), Arthur Keith (1911, 1915) and Marcellin Boule (1921).

Although it could not be (and still has not been) accurately dated, comparative studies of its anatomy soon showed that the Forbes' Quarry specimen was similar to other western European Neanderthals from sites such as the Neander Valley, Spy (Belgium) and La Chapelle-aux-Saints and La Ferrassie (France). These remains derive from an ancient Eurasian population which was often associated with cold-adapted Pleistocene animals such as reindeer and mammoth, and with Middle Palaeolithic (Middle Old Stone Age, or Mousterian, from the site of Le Moustier in France) stone tools (Stringer & Gamble 1993). These early humans had large brains, housed in relatively long, broad and low braincases, and long faces dominated by a voluminous nasal aperture and surmounted by a double-arched brow ridge. The prominent nose may have acted to warm and moisten inhaled air. The body skeleton, where preserved, suggests a relatively short, stocky physique, reflecting adaptation to cold environments, and a powerful musculature. The evolutionary lineage of the Neanderthals of Europe and western Asia probably separated from that of modern humans (*Homo sapiens*) at least 300 ka.

This interpretation of anatomical distinctiveness and relatively early divergence, originally based on the fossil evidence alone, has received strong support from the recent recovery of mitochondrial DNA from the actual Neander Valley skeleton. Its DNA is distinct from that of all living people so far sampled, and the degree of difference suggests that the Neanderthal lineage could have begun its separation from our own as far back as 600 ka ago (Krings *et al.* 1997). The best known ("classic") Neanderthals are those from 100 ka to 35 ka, who were adapted to the climatic and physical rigours of life in Ice Age Europe.

A second significant Neanderthal find was made in Gibraltar in 1926, at the Devil's Tower site, surrounding a cleft in the North Face limestone, not far east of Forbes' Quarry (Garrod *et al.* 1928). This find was excavated systematically, and was associated with animal bones, stone tools, and charcoal from ancient fires. The fossil remains consist of parts of the upper and lower jaws and braincase of a Neanderthal infant. The original assumption that they represented a single child about five years old at death (Buxton, in Garrod *et al.* 1928) was challenged by Tillier (1982), who suggested that these bones might actually represent two children, one aged about three years at death (the temporal bone) and the other about five (the rest of the bones). However, more extensive comparative studies of cranial ontogeny and of incremental lines in the teeth reaffirmed the unity of the Devil's Tower bones, but suggested that the individual might have been about four years old at death (Dean *et al.* 1986; Stringer *et al.* 1990). Most recently, the Devil's Tower remains have been the subject of Computer-Assisted Palaeoanthropological (CAP) studies which have revealed new anatomical data, and have allowed a three-dimensional reconstruction of the whole skull (Zollikofer *et al.* 1995, 1998). This reconstruction confirmed the interpretation that all fragments were derived from a single skull.

In this paper, we report on the principles, methods and technologies of computer-assisted palaeoanthropology and applications in the investigation of the Neanderthals.

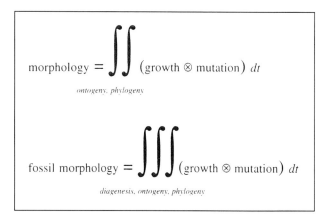

Figure 26.1: Morphologies of living and fossil organisms. The morphology of a living organism can be understood as the double integral of morphogenesis over phylogeny and ontogeny. In the genesis of fossil morphology, diagenetic alteration acts as an additional integrator that obscures the original morphology.

Investigating Neanderthal morphology

One of the major difficulties that commonly arises in the analysis of fossils is the lack of extensive samples and the incompleteness of individual specimens. In the particular case of the Neanderthals, however, a comparatively large sample of both immature and adult specimens spread over geological time and space is available (Stringer & Gamble 1993). Among these fossils, those from Gibraltar – Forbes' Quarry and Devil's Tower – occupy a special position. Thanks to the good conservation of external and internal structures in these remains, it was possible to characterise anatomical key features by applying novel techniques and to derive valuable information about the life history of this unique species.

Prior to undertaking any morphological analysis of a fossil specimen, it is imperative to take into account all potential processes that might have contributed to its present morphology. Following the course of a fossil's history, we have to consider three different time scales and their effects:

- On the ontogenetic time scale, we consider the interaction between genes and environment that basically lead to the fundamental morphology of the living organism.
- On the phylogenetic time scale, we need to focus on changing ontogenetic patterns.
- On the diagenetic time scale, most of the original morphology (e.g. soft tissue) becomes degraded and what remains becomes distorted through taphonomic events.

Separation of the respective contributions of ontogeny and phylogeny to the morphology of a living organism is itself an intricate task, but interpretation of fossils is even

more complex, since fossilised morphological evidence is altered and blurred by the additional effects of diagenesis (Figure 26.1). It is therefore of primary importance to devise methods that help to identify the distorting effects of post-mortem changes. Furthermore, we need methods for the exploration, analysis and quantitative evaluation of morphological features in three dimensions. Ultimately, these methods will help us to recognise and interpret the ontogenetic and phylogenetic signals that are contained in fossil specimens.

A methodological framework for computer-assisted palaeoanthropology

Palaeoanthropological research typically involves physical preparation of the fossil fragments, their reconstruction, description and morphometric analysis, and replication by casting. These procedures are highly invasive, and at the same time their effectiveness is limited. For example, physical preparation cannot reveal the morphology of internal structures without destroying them, and data sampled with conventional morphometric tools such as calipers are essentially confined to linear or angular measurements between landmark configurations.

To tackle these difficulties, we designed and developed a methodological framework of computer-assisted palaeo-anthropology that combines 3D data acquisition techniques with computer graphics procedures and rapid prototyping technology (Figure 26.2; Zollikofer & Ponce de León 1995).

Data acquisition
To obtain a more coherent apprehension of the spatial geometry of fossils, an array of 3D data-acquisition

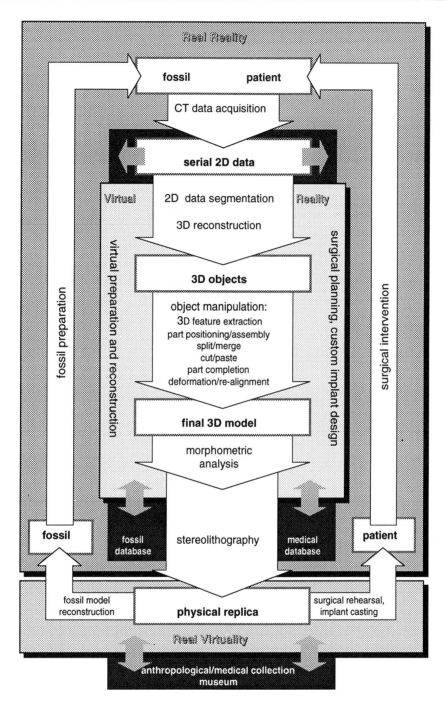

Figure 26.2: Computer-assisted anthropology and medicine. Data acquisition with Computerised Tomography (CT) yields serial 2–dimensional sections which are stored in a database. All subsequent data-processing steps are performed in Virtual Reality (VR), i.e. with graphical representations of the data, utilising interactive computer graphics tools. Exploiting parallelisms between computer-assisted fossil reconstruction and surgical procedures, fossil/patient data are processed with a uniform graphics toolkit: Fossil/matrix separation and hard tissue extraction is based on similar 2D image data segmentation procedures. Preprocessed 2D data are then transformed into 3–dimensional object representations. 3D objects can then be manipulated in various ways on the computer screen to plan and perform reconstructive and interventional tasks in both fossils and patients. Once a final model has been generated, extensive morphometric analyses can be performed in 2 or 3 dimensions, using comparative data from the database. Rapid prototyping technology such as stereolithography is used to create Real Virtuality (RV) objects, i.e. physical models of computer-generated or modified objects. Stereolithographic replication of fossils represents a non-invasive alternative to conventional casting techniques. Physical models are also used extensively for surgical rehearsal and implant casting. Note the iterative and interconnected character of the procedure as a whole. At any stage, data from "real" reality, Virtual Reality, and Real Virtuality can be compared and combined with information from the database.

techniques have been developed in recent years. These techniques range from sampling 3D coordinates of predefined morphometric landmarks (using 3D pointers) through surface data sampling (with a laser scanner) to volumetric data acquisition. Among these latter techniques, Computer Tomography (CT) deserves special mention. This X-ray-based method has become an important tool in medical diagnostics, mainly because CT permits acquisition of cross-sectional images from patients – as well as from fossils.

It is worth noting here that the rapid appreciation of the potential value of classical X-ray technology for palaeontological applications soon after Roentgen's pivotal discovery in 1895 is paralleled by an equally rapid spread of CT imaging technology into palaeoanthropology since the development of medical CT in the seventies (Zonneveld & Wind 1985).

Scanning an average-sized fossil fragment using a medical CT device yields a stack of cross-sectional images representing $10-100 \times 10^6$ 3D data points (volume elements = voxels) per specimen. The information content of this data volume can only be explored exhaustively with the aid of computer graphics hardware and software tools whose capacities go beyond those of standard medical CT consoles tuned to medical diagnostics. First, because of mineralisation, fossils generally exhibit a much larger range of physical densities than living patients. With respect to data acquisition and image reconstruction, the correction of density-induced image distortions (artefact removal) poses a specific challenge. Second, while medical CT imaging is mainly concerned with visualisation of data volumes, analysis of fossil CT data requires special-purpose algorithms and tools that permit non-invasive preparation, reassembly and quantitative comparative analyses of fossil fragments.

Virtual Fossils

Virtual Reality (VR) denotes a computer graphics-based setting in which a user interacts with graphical representations of real or model objects, utilising tools and performing manipulations and movements that emulate physical tools and actions. Working in VR has one salient feature which is of immediate practical benefit for palaeoanthropological applications: any manipulations are absolutely non-invasive. It is possible to free fossil fragments embedded in matrix with the electronic chisel and to disassemble/reassemble fossils previously reconstructed with conventional methods.

Using VR models of fossils, morphometric characteristics can be determined in one, two and three dimensions. The spatial positions of classical landmarks can be established and inter-landmark·distances and angles can be derived. Features that are easy to define but difficult to measure conventionally – such as surface areas, object thickness and object volumes – can be determined. Further, complex parameters such as characteristics of surface curvature can be evaluated. Deformational procedures can

be used to re-align fossils that suffered from taphonomic deformation, and similar procedures can be used to simulate growth processes or to compare homologous morphologies by transforming one object into another.

Many recent studies aim at an essentially explorative approach to morphometrics, using the computer as a visualisation instrument. With the aid of special-purpose morphometric tools, it is possible to visualise and quantify morphological features that are only qualitatively accessible with conventional methods, for example surface curvature or mechanical stiffness. This is especially important for the analysis of fragmentary fossil specimens, since harvesting a maximum of quantifiable data can greatly facilitate evolutionary interpretation.

Real Virtuality

Virtual fossils prepared and reconstructed on a computer can be transferred back to physical reality. As opposed to Virtual Reality, we use the term Real Virtuality (RV) to denote an environment where a user interacts with physical models of 3D objects generated or modified by computer-assisted procedures. Physical objects convey touch-and-feel information and can therefore be handled, explored and assembled under much more realistic conditions than virtual objects on a computer screen.

Currently, the most accurate automated replication technology available is laser stereolithography, an industrial technology that was originally devised for rapid prototyping (i.e. physical modelling) of computer-aided design (CAD) parts. Objects are built through consecutive polymerisation of thin layers of a photosensitive liquid resin by a computer-guided UV laser beam (this process resembles that of building topographical models through piling layers of cardboard). Stereolithographic replication of fossil specimens represents a valuable non-invasive alternative to traditional moulding and casting techniques. Once polymerised, stereolithographic resins exhibit virtually no shrinkage. For these reasons, the accuracy of stereolithographic models matches or even surpasses that of conventional casts.

It is interesting to note that there are close methodological links between virtual palaeoanthropology and virtual surgery (see Figure 26.2) leading to intensive interaction and mutual benefit across the boundary separating these two disciplines.

Following this brief outline of methods, we report on the application of CAP in the analysis of Neanderthal cranial remains from Gibraltar and Le Moustier (France).

New evidence from Neanderthal skulls

Gibraltar 1 (Forbes' Quarry)

The 3–dimensional reconstruction derived from CT scans of the Forbes' Quarry (Gibraltar 1) skull showed that, during the process of fossilisation, the upper jaws had been bent out of shape and internal structures had been crushed. It emerged that, during earlier reconstructions,

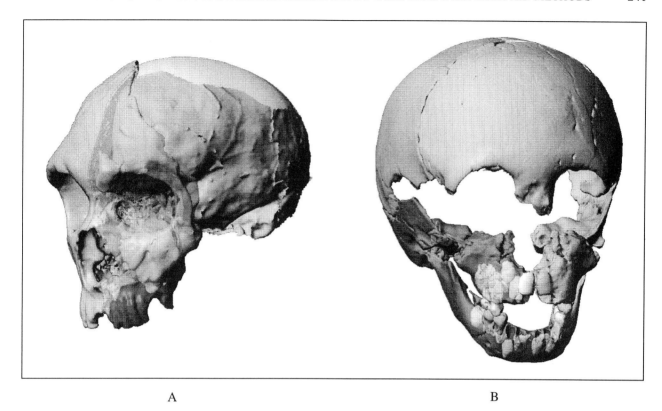

A   B

Figure 26.3: Computerised reconstruction of the Gibraltar Neanderthal skulls (A: Forbes' Quarry; B: Devil's Tower). In both specimens, missing parts on one side of the skull were completed by mirror-imaged regions from the contralateral side. Moreover, computer-assisted methods permit to examine hidden structures such as the size and shape of the paranasal sinuses and the endocranial cavity (A) as well as the anatomy of the inner ear and of teeth buds (B).

fragile regions of the internal facial skeleton had been protected with plaster fillings and are therefore inaccessible to direct observation. Having removed the fillings in Virtual Reality, mirror images from the right side were used to restore missing parts on the left side. The resulting reconstruction was then complete apart from a region of the skull roof. We were able to complete the braincase by building in an approximate replacement for the missing bone. This allowed us to produce a relatively complete endocast and to determine a fairly precise cranial capacity of 1230–1250cc. Moreover, it was possible to extract internal structures such as the paranasal sinuses and the cavities of the right bony labyrinth (see Zollikofer *et al.* 1998, and Figure 26.3A).

Gibraltar 2 (Devil's Tower)

Five individual fragments represent the Devil's Tower (Gibraltar 2) Neanderthal child skull: an incomplete mandible, the right maxilla, the right temporal, the frontal, and the left parietal (Garrod *et al.* 1928). To establish regions of anatomical contact between the isolated fragments, we completed missing parts through mirror-imaging of existing fragments. After rebuilding the right mandibular premolars using mirror imaging of the existing left teeth, dental occlusion with the upper jaw fragment could be established. At this stage, stereolithographic

copies of the jaws were generated to check the accuracy of dental occlusion. In the next reconstructive step, the semicircular canals of the preserved right inner ear cavities served as an anatomical compass to orient the temporal bone along the sagittal plane of the skull, defined by an angle of 45° relative to the planes of the superior and posterior semicircular canals. The oriented temporal bone and its mirror copy were then placed on the mandibular condyles. Finally, the temporoparietal suture between the mirrored temporal and the original parietal bone was used to determine the anatomically appropriate position of the cranial vault bones (Figure 26.3B).

To check on the general reliability of the Devil's Tower reconstruction, notably because of potential deviations from bilateral symmetry, parallel reconstructions were conducted using complete skulls of modern human children of comparable dental age and exhibiting a normal degree of bilateral asymmetry. In these reconstructions, only the parts corresponding to the fragments preserved in the fossil were utilised, following exactly the same procedures as for the Neanderthal child. Comparison of the original modern human skulls with the resulting reconstructions showed relatively little deviation. Measurements taken on different versions of reconstructions suggest that reconstructive errors are in the same range as anatomical departures from bilateral symmetry. This confirms the

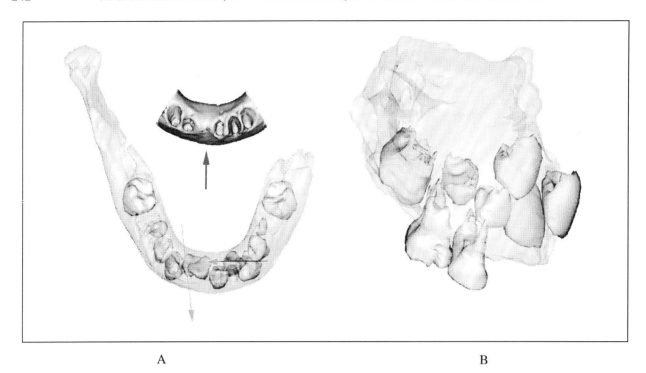

A   B

Figure 26.4: Visualisation of the developing permanent mandibular (A) and maxillary (B) dentition of the Devil's Tower Neanderthal child. Note the deviation in the orientation of the right incisors and the corresponding lack of an alveolar cavity in the associated alveolar bone (scale bar is 10 mm).

essential reliability of the virtual fossil reconstruction.

Visualisation of the hidden elements of the developing permanent dentition (Figure 26.3B) reveals considerable asymmetry in the front teeth of the Devil's Tower mandible. This condition had already been identified as pathological using conventional radiography. Close inspection of the 3D reconstruction in this region (Figure 26.4) leads to a more confident palaeopathological diagnosis. The right lower permanent incisors are normal in shape but show considerable misorientation, whereas the bone above the incisor buds lacks any trace of alveolus of the right deciduous I_2. The associated structures indicate bone resorption following an injury in early childhood. It is likely that the traumatic event also affected development of the permanent dentition, causing the observed distortion of the tooth row underneath.

Le Moustier 1

The Le Moustier 1 fossil represents the most completely preserved adolescent Neanderthal skeleton recovered to date, although much of the original material had been lost during World War II. Restoration and reconstruction of this specimen faced a number of difficulties that are intimately connected to its convoluted history. The present state of the cranial remains is the result of at least four earlier reconstructions during which the original fragments were repeatedly disassembled and recomposed (Weinert 1925). In its current physical reconstruction, the skull exhibits considerable overall deformation and anatomical inconsistencies that need correction. Moreover, the original

fossil components are camouflaged with filling material, but actual physical disassembly would subject the specimen to unnecessary risk. We therefore applied our non-invasive procedure to the skull in order to generate a new reconstruction and to extract additional information (Ponce de León & Zollikofer 1999).

Our virtual reconstruction of Le Moustier 1 proceeded as follows: Using CT-based 3D data, the specimen was freed from heterologous material, disassembled into its almost 100 original fragments (Figure 26.5A). Following similar criteria to those established for the Gibraltar 2 reconstruction, the fragments were recomposed on the computer screen, starting with the isolation of the well-preserved inner ear cavities that served as anatomical compasses to re-establish bilateral symmetry in the heavily distorted cranial base. On top of the re-adjusted base, the cranial vault could be reconstructed, using mirror-imaged parts as placeholders for missing fragments where necessary. During this process, distortions present in the current reconstruction could be eliminated by re-establishing correct anatomical correspondences between adjacent fragments. However, once completed, the virtual reconstruction still exhibited overall deformation. The slanted appearance of the cranium clearly reflected taphonomic effects that resulted in plastic deformation, notably of the cranial vault bones. Since fossil bones that had undergone plastic deformation cannot be re-aligned just by repositioning isolated fragments, we used virtual procedures to correct for this type of deformation. We performed a detailed analysis of the skewed 3D geometry

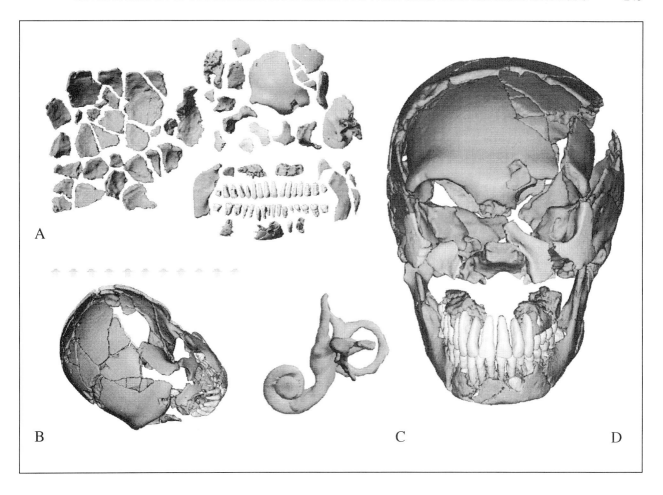

Figure 26.5: Reconstruction of the Le Moustier 1 adolescent Neanderthal skull. The isolated fragments (A) were recomposed on the computer screen, and distortion caused by vertical compression was corrected (B) to obtain a re-aligned reconstruction (D, scale bar is 50 mm). Using micro-CT analysis, it was possible to isolate the left anvil from the middle ear cavity (C, dark grey) and to visualise a virtual endocast of the inner ear cavities (C, light grey).

of the skull to determine the directions of minimum/ maximum stress bringing about the present shape. In a second step, we used historical photographs to determine the taphonomic *in situ* position of the skull. Combining morphometric and taphonomic evidence, it turned out that the skull had undergone vertical compression along an axis leading from the left frontal to the right occipital poles. This effect could be reversed on the computer screen by positioning the virtual skull in situ and applying appropriate decompression (Figure 26.5B, D).

Industrial micro-CT techniques were used to analyse structures of special interest at high resolution (0.1mm slice thickness, 0.05mm within-slice resolution). During reconstruction of the jaws and dentition, detailed 3D models of the dental occlusal surfaces showing the cusps and wear facets were utilised to reconstruct the occlusion between the lower and upper dentition. Micro-CT analysis was extended to the otic regions. After removal of matrix fillings, a dislocated but virtually complete incus could be recovered from the left middle ear cavity (Figure 26.5C). A morphometric analysis of the cavities of both inner ears

showed that these structures deviate substantially from the condition reported to be typical for Neanderthals and fall within the range of modern human variability (Hublin *et al.* 1996).

As with Gibraltar 2, computer-assisted methods were used to assess the palaeopathological status of the Le Moustier 1: The marked deformation of the left mandibular joint can most probably be attributed to a healed condylar fracture.

Computer-assisted morphometrics

The new computerised methods permit quantitative analysis of novel 2D and 3D morphometric features. For example, determination of cranial vault bone thickness has long been restricted to sampling data at a few landmarks. Likewise, assessment of cranial vault curvature was limited to approximations. On the basis of 3D CT data, it is possible to quantify these parameters by generating thickness and curvature maps that reveal complex patterns of fluctuations (Figure 26.6). Comparisons of juvenile Neanderthals and juvenile modern

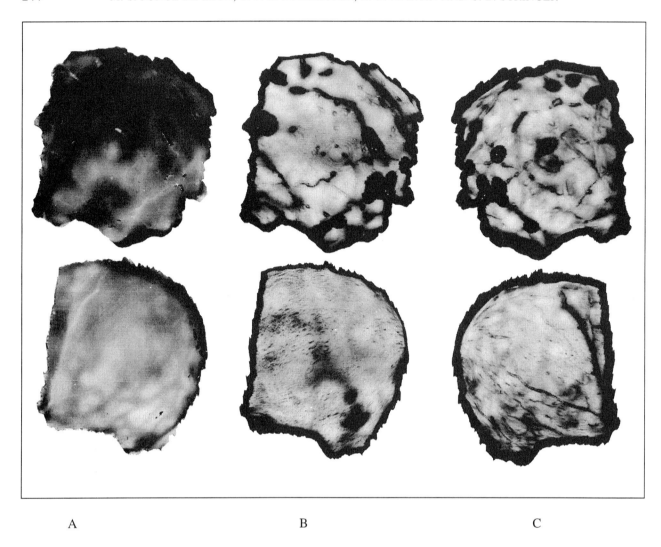

A   B   C

Figure 26.6: New morphometric characters of cranial bones (top: Devil's Tower left parietal fragment; bottom: left parietal bone of a modern human child of comparable dental age): bone thickness (A), external bone curvature (B) and internal bone curvature (C).

humans have demonstrated that bone thickness in relation to bone size is markedly greater in the former.

An additional possible application of computer-assisted procedures is extrapolation of missing anatomical structures on the basis of comparative data from more complete fossil specimens and/or modern human data sets. To assess cranial capacity of the Gibraltar 1, 2 and the Le Moustier 1 specimens, we attempted to reconstruct missing parts by adjusting complete endocasts of modern human skulls of comparable individual age (Figures 26.3A and 26.7). For this purpose, a series of landmarks was identified on the preserved endocranial parts of the Neanderthal skulls, and homologous landmarks were determined on the modern counterparts. Applying the 3D thin plate splines morphing technique proposed by Bookstein (1991), the modern landmark constellation was transformed into the Neanderthal constellation and the modern endocranial volume was deformed accordingly. The resulting cranial capacities are 1230–1250cc, 1370–1420cc and 1550–1600cc for Gibraltar 1, Gibraltar 2, and Le Moustier, respectively. It is worth noting that cranial capacities have also been determined in this way for two additional Neanderthal skulls from immature individuals comparable in age to the Gibraltar 2 skull: 1440cc for the Engis specimen and 132cc for the Roc de Marsal specimen (Zollikofer *et al.* 1995, 1998).

Discussion

Entirely new possibilities for palaeoanthropology have been opened up by recent advances in medical imaging technologies, in computer graphics technology and in rapid prototyping technology (notably laser stereolithography). In combination, these advances have permitted development of a 3–phase procedure in which fossil specimens are scanned using computed tomography followed by 3–dimensional reconstruction on the computer screen (Virtual Reality) and then by production of physical replicas of

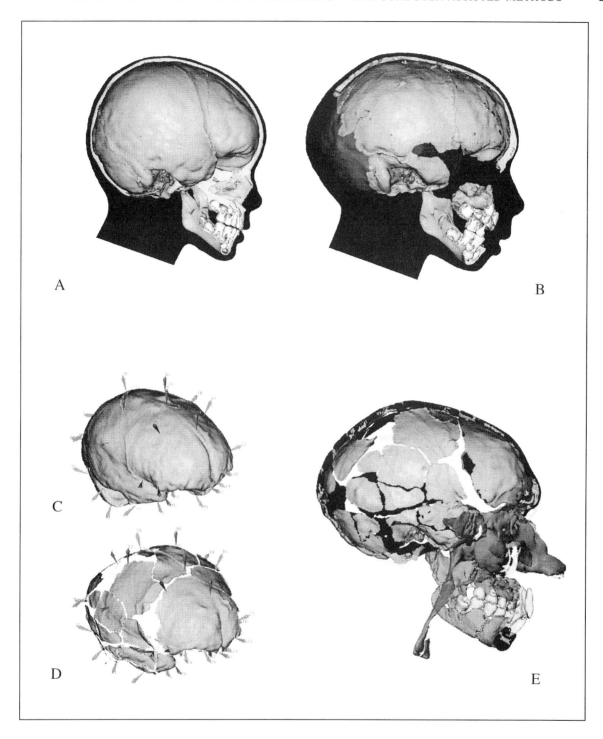

Figure 26.7: Extrapolation of Neanderthal soft tissue structures by morphing data from modern humans. Modern human child soft tissue and endocast (A) morphed to the Devil's Tower reconstruction (B); equivalent landmarks on the endocasts of a modern human adolescent (C) and of Le Moustier 1 (D); extrapolation of the upper airways of Le Moustier 1 (E).

computer-generated reconstructions (Real Virtuality; see Figure 26.2). With computer-assisted palaeoanthropology, it is now possible to return to long-known fossil specimens, subjecting them to re-examination and extracting extensive additional information, hopefully leading to more securely based interpretations. Celebration of the 150th anniversary of the discovery of the Gibraltar 1 Neanderthal skull provides a very appropriate context for this report on applications of such a 3–phase procedure to both the adult and infant skulls from Gibraltar and to the juvenile Le Moustier 1 specimen.

Before considering the advantages of this new approach

and the novel findings that have emerged, it is perhaps as well to note some of the technical requirements and problems. In the first place, there is a practical problem posed by the relatively high density that is typical of fossil specimens and the accompanying matrix. When dealing with palaeontological material, it is therefore usually necessary to adapt medical scanners by modification of parameters or recalibration (Zonneveld & Wind 1985). It should also be emphasised that interactive pre-processing of individual images by an appropriately trained investigator is obligatory. As noted by Zollikofer et al. (1998): "The live anthropologist is still an essential part of the procedure." Direct inspection of CT images is an essential first step. Separation of a fossil from the matrix is based on 2D image data segmentation procedures. In some cases, this can be achieved through automatic "thresholding", exploiting any difference in density between fossil bone and matrix, but in many cases it has to be user-guided, with the investigator sitting at the screen and applying an "electronic chisel" to individual images in turn. 3D object representations can only be generated in a subsequent stage. At this stage, too, considerable interactive control is necessary. For instance, new reconstruction of previously assembled skulls requires decomposition of the specimen into individual parts. Cross-checking of reconstructions through production of intermediate-stage stereolithographs is often necessary. Further, mirror-image copies may be used as "placeholders" during virtual reconstruction on the computer screen. Valuable aids for checking reconstructions are a 3D computer mouse and stereo glasses in combination with a stereo screen. In fact, interactive work is particularly revealing and clearly shows the need for continuous quality control. The problem of reconstructive error propagation is particularly acute, but also particularly evident. Production of multiple alternative reconstructions graphically shows how a relatively minor difference at an early stage of reconstruction can lead to a major difference in the end product. This is especially obvious in reconstruction of the braincase and subsequent determination of cranial capacity.

A central problem associated with fossil specimens is distortion arising from taphonomic processes. It is possible to test for the presence of such distortion by comparison of mirror images of left and right halves, and certain possibilities exist for objective correction of deformation ("virtual decompression"), as in the case of the Le Moustier 1 skull (Ponce de León & Zollikofer 1999). Last but not least, there is a potential problem associated with mirror imaging during reconstruction of incomplete skulls. With the Gibraltar 2 skull, for example, straightforward articulation of the original fragments was only possible between the left parietal and fused frontal bones. By means of mirror imaging, it proved possible to generate a fairly extensive reconstruction of the skull in which original and mirror-imaged parts fitted together very well (Zollikofer et al. 1995). However, we have to consider that natural

skulls do not show perfect bilateral symmetry. Interestingly, this question has not generally been raised with respect to hand-made reconstructions, probably because it is extremely difficult to make them reasonably symmetrical in left and right halves. Indeed, part of the work reported here depended on prior correction of previous errors in the reconstructions of the Gibraltar 1 and Le Moustier 1 skulls. The fact of the matter is, however, that reconstructive errors are in the same range as that of natural departures from bilateral symmetry (±6%; Zollikofer et al. 1998).

The advantages of the new approach to palaeontological specimens are numerous. One general practical benefit of the method is that it provides tools for non-invasive, non-destructive investigation of specimens that may be very fragile. Beyond this, it is important to emphasise novel applications permitted by the new approach, rather than dwelling upon replication of findings that were possible (even if more time-consuming) with previous techniques. One obvious new benefit is the potential for quantitative evaluation of extremely large data volumes. This is accompanied by novel possibilities for interactive and highly accurate recording of linear, areal and volumetric measurements. There are also more specific benefits and three major areas of application can be identified: (1) 3D-visualisation of hidden anatomical structures; (2) computer-assisted reconstruction of fragmentary fossils and stereolithographic replication of computer-generated reconstructions; (3) morphometric/biomechanical analysis of morphological structures. These will be considered in turn.

The new approach makes it possible to investigate and quantify complex internal structures that would otherwise remain inaccessible to study. Although classical radiography has long permitted some work on internal structures, it does not permit reliable interpretation of three-dimensional structures. Good examples for new applications are provided by visualisation of the bony labyrinth of the ear region, of developing teeth still enclosed in the jaws and of cranial sinus cavities. It should be noted, incidentally, that use of the bony labyrinth as an "anatomical compass" during reconstruction has proved to be a very valuable asset.

Turning to reconstruction, it is possible to conduct in Virtual Reality procedures that would pose a considerable risk if conducted through direct intervention on a fossil specimen itself. A particularly good example is provided by the disassembly and reassembly of fragments to produce alternative reconstructions. Earlier reconstructions of fossil specimens were commonly carried out using the actual fossil fragments and it was common practice to bind the fragments together in an almost definitive fashion using hard-setting materials. Any attempt at physical disassembly of such a reconstruction in order to correct previous errors would therefore be fraught with risk. Apt examples of such early constructions requiring correction are provided by the skulls of Gibraltar 1 and Le Moustier 1. In the case of Gibraltar 1, plaster filling made delicate parts inaccessible to direct observation. Furthermore, the shape of the reconstructed skull was distorted when fragments were fitted into place at its rear end. In the case of Le Moustier 1, a further problem of a similar kind was encountered in that the glue used in reconstruction had penetrated the cavities of the labyrinth system. It was necessary to "extract" this filling through laborious examination of individual images in order to produce an error-free reconstruction. In this connection, it should be noted that the new approach will also permit virtual extraction of fossil specimens from matrix, for example as an aid to subsequent preparation.

The availability of large bodies of accurate 3–dimensional data for fossil specimens will, in the long term, probably prove to the most significant advantage of the new approach. Extensive sampling of measurements on continuous morphological structures is in itself of considerable value. This is, for example, the case with measurement of thickness of cranial bones or cross-sectional areas of the mandible or long bones. In fact, measurement of such continuous structures is commonly hindered by the absence of clearly definable landmarks. Here, too, computer-assisted palaeoanthropology can offer new solutions, for example with respect to the general paucity of landmarks on the cranial vault. Concepts of computational geometry can be applied to the large volumes of 3–dimensional data that are generated and it is, among other things, possible to evaluate complex features such as surface curvature. It should also be noted that computer-assisted palaeoanthropology permits a number of additional applications, including the following: (1) Use of deformation procedures to compare homologous structures by transforming one into the other (e.g. using thin plate spline analysis; Bookstein 1991). (2) Simulation of growth processes. (3) Generation of hypothetical intermediates and inferred ancestral stages. (4) Perfectly scaled magnification or reduction of structures or entire specimens.

Some of the new possibilities have already been explored using the existing data set for Neanderthal skulls, including extensive sampling of cranial vault thickness and of cross-sectional profiles of the mandible, determination of mandibular volume and determination of cranial capacity. In comparison with modern humans, skulls of infant Neanderthals show a relatively thick cranial vault and a relatively large mandibular volume. More significantly, there is no evidence of the development of a chin, the largest cross-sectional area of the mandible being located between the canine and the anterior premolar (in stark contrast to the condition in modern humans). Overall, the marked differences found between Neanderthals and modern humans at such an early age reinforces the interpretation that an ancient separation occurred and that we should recognise two species: *Homo neanderthalensis* and *Homo sapiens*.

Acknowledgements

Special thanks are due to P. Stucki, Director of the MultiMedia Laboratory at the University of Zurich, whose invaluable support and collaboration have accompanied our work from the onset. We are grateful to the staff of the Natural History Museum, London, for supporting us in CT scanning the Gibraltar specimens. We thank Almut Hoffmann and G. Menghin of the Museum für Vor- und Frühgeschichte in Berlin for kindly loaning us the Le Moustier skull for micro-CT analysis. Our research was supported by Swiss NSF grants #31–32360.91 and #31–42419.94.

References

Bookstein, F.L. (1991). *Morphometric Tools for Landmark Data.* Cambridge: Cambridge University Press.

Boule, M. (1921). *Les Hommes Fossiles.* Paris: Masson.

Broca, P. (1869). Remarques sur les ossements des cavernes de Gibraltar. *Bull. Mem. Soc. Anthrop. Paris* **4**, 146–158.

Busk, G. (1865). On a very ancient human cranium from Gibraltar. *Report of the 34th meeting of the British Association for the Advancement of Science, Bath 1864*, 91–92.

Dean, M.C., Stringer, C. & Bromage, T. (1986). Age at death of the Neanderthal child from Devil's Tower, Gibraltar and the implications for studies of general growth and development in Neanderthals. *Amer. J. phys. Anthrop.* **70**, 301–309.

Garrod, D.A.E., Buxton, L.H.D., Elliot Smith, G & Bate, D.M.A. (1928). Excavation of a Mousterian Rock shelter at Devil's Tower, Gibraltar. *J. Roy. Anthrop. Inst.* **58**: 33–113.

Hublin, J.-J., Spoor, F., Braun, M., Zonneveld, F. & Condemi, S. (1996). A late Neanderthal associated with Upper Palaeolithic artefacts. *Nature, Lond.* **381**, 224–226.

Keith, A. (1911). The early history of the Gibraltar cranium. Nature **87**, 313–314.

Keith, A. (1915). *The Antiquity of Man.* London: Williams & Norgate.

King, W. (1864). The reputed fossil man of the Neanderthal. *Quart. J. Sci.* **1**, 88–97.

Krings,M., Stone,A., Schmitz,R.W., Krainitzki,H., Stoneking,M. & Pääbo,S. (1997). Neanderthal DNA sequences and the origin of modern humans. *Cell* **90**, 19–30.

Ponce de León, M.S. & Zollikofer, C.P.E. (1999). New evidence from Le Moustier 1: Computer-assisted reconstruction and morphometry of the skull. Anat. Rec. *in press.*

Sollas, W. (1907). On the cranial and facial characters of the Neanderthal race. *Phil. Trans. Roy. Soc. Lond. B*, **199**, 281–339.

Stringer, C. & Gamble, C. (1993). *In Search of the Neanderthals.* London: Thames & Hudson

Stringer, C., Dean, M.C. & Martin, R.D. (1990). A comparative study of cranial and dental development within a recent British sample and among Neandertals. In (C.J. de Rousseau,Ed.) *Primate Life History and Evolution*, pp. 115–152 New York: Wiley-Liss.

Tillier, A.M. (1982). Les enfants néanderthaliens de Devil's Tower (Gibraltar). *Z. Morph. Anthrop.* **73**, 125–148.

Weinert, H. (1925). Der Schädel des eiszeitlichen Menschen von Le Moustier in neuer Zusammensetzung. Berlin: Springer.

Zollikofer, C.P.E., Ponce de León, M.S., Martin, R.D. & Stucki, P. (1995). Neanderthal computer skulls. *Nature.* **375**, 283–285.

Zollikofer, C.P.E. and Ponce de León, M.S. (1995). Tools for rapid prototyping in the biosciences. *IEEE CG&A* **15**, 48–55.

Zollikofer, C.P.E., Ponce de León, M.S. & Martin,R.D. (1998). Computer-assisted paleoanthropology. *Evol. Anthrop.* **6**, 41–54.

Zonneveld, F.W. & Wind, J. (1985). High-resolution computed tomography of fossil hominid skulls: a new method and some results. In (P.V. Tobias, Ed.) *Hominid Evolution: Past, Present and Future* pp. 427–436. New York: Alan R. Liss.

27

CT Reconstruction and Analysis
of the Le Moustier 1 Neanderthal

J. L. Thompson and B. Illerhaus

Introduction

Le Moustier 1, an adolescent Neanderthal dating to *c.* 40 ka provides an important example of a late western European Neanderthal (Bilsborough & Thompson 1996; Thompson & Bilsborough 1994; 1996; 1997; 1998a; b) and is the only adolescent Neanderthal specimen to preserve associated cranial, dental, and skeletal elements. Work on the description, analysis, and reconstruction of this specimen was initiated in 1992 (Thompson 1993; Thompson & Bilsborough 1994). In early 1994, the Museum für Vor- und Frühgeschichte in Berlin, Germany invited the authors of this paper to make a reconstruction of the skull using Computed Tomography data, to ensure that the original specimen was not damaged or changed in any way. We proposed, at this time, to make a reconstruction of the skull using CT data and to investigate the internal structures of the skull (Hoffmann *et al.* 1994). Aspects of this work will be presented in this paper, especially those that expand our knowledge of Neanderthal ontogeny and variation in Neanderthal morphological features.

Other analyses of the Le Moustier 1 specimen have included a detailed anatomical description of the specimen (Bilsborough & Thompson 1996 unpublished; Thompson & Bilsborough 1997; Thompson & Nelson 1997a, b); a reassessment of its age at death, sex, and stature (Thompson 1995; 1998; Thompson & Nelson 1997a, b, submitted; Nelson & Thompson 1998 in press); and a preliminary assessment of where it falls within the range of Neanderthal variability (Thompson & Bilsborough 1996, 1998a, b). We are pleased to have the opportunity to draw attention of Neanderthal specialists to work that has already been completed and is in now progress on the anatomy and morphology of the Le Moustier 1 Neanderthal and aspects of Neanderthal ontogeny.

The Le Moustier 1 Specimen

In 1908 Otto Hauser discovered the Le Moustier 1 specimen in the Lower Cave at the site of Le Moustier in the Dordogne of France (Hauser 1909; Klaatsch 1909a-d; Klaatsch & Hauser 1909). Hauser allowed the skull to be covered and recovered several times between March 7th and the 12th of August (e.g. Schott 1989) and so the exact provenience of the specimen remains unclear. Bordes (1959) maintains, however, that the specimen was most likely from layer J, which has been dated to *c.* 40 ka using thermoluminescence and electron spin resonance dating techniques (Mellars 1986; Mellars & Grün 1991; Valladas *et al.* 1986).

The Le Moustier 1 skull has been reconstructed several times; the first two reconstructions were made by Klaatsch (1909a). In 1910 the skeletons of Le Moustier 1 and Combe Capelle were sold to the Museum für Volkerkunde, Berlin for 160,000 gold marks (Hesse 1966). The third reconstruction of the skull was carried out by E. Krause, a museum preparator in collaboration with H. Klaatsch and E. Kallius (Schuchhardt 1912). W. Dieck, a dentist, who worked on the placement of the teeth in this and the subsequent reconstruction, positioned the third molars as if they were erupting. In the early 1920's Hans Weinert (1925) undertook the fourth major reconstruction of the cranial and dental remains of Le Moustier 1. Unfortunately over the years several bones had been lost, including the zygomatic bone, the left coronoid process, the maxilla, and hard palate.

Hoffmann (1997) reports on the history of the specimen in some detail. The skull was moved to Russia at the end of the second World War, but was returned to the DDR in 1958, where it was "rediscovered" in 1965 (Hesse 1966; Hesse & Ullrich 1966). By 1990, it was returned to its present location in the Museum für Vor- und Früh-

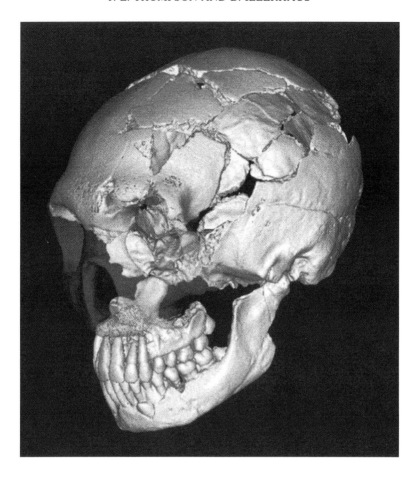

Figure 27.1: New virtual reconstruction of the Le Moustier 1 skull.

geschichte in Berlin. The anatomy and diagnostic features of the skull (including intracranial anatomy), dentition, and postcranial bones have been discussed elsewhere in some detail (Bilsborough & Thompson 1996; Hermann 1977; Thompson 1995; Thompson & Bilsborough 1994 1996 1997 1998a b; Thompson & Nelson 1997a, b).

The New CT Reconstruction of the Le Moustier 1 Skull

We are using this opportunity to announce the new CT reconstruction of the Le Moustier 1 skull. However, readers should note that a full description of the reconstruction process using microcomputed tomography data is outlined elsewhere (Thompson & Illerhaus 1998). The micro-computed tomography data were collected for this analysis using the 3–D micro-tomograph housed at Bundesanstalt für Materialforschung und -Prüfung (BAM), Berlin using methods established in the literature (e.g. Illerhaus *et al.* 1994; Illerhaus *et al.* 1997 a, b).

Computerised tomography (CT) data have contributed to our knowledge of the internal morphology and overall dimensions of incomplete or fragmentary fossil skulls (Tate & Cann 1982; Conroy & Vannier 1984 1986; Wind 1984;

Zonneveld & Wind 1985; Zonneveld *et al.* 1989; Conroy *et al.* 1990; Spoor *et al.* 1993; Spoor & Zonneveld 1994 1995; Spoor *et al.* 1994; Hublin *et al.* 1996). This technique can be used to reconstruct skulls from their various fragments without damaging the original specimen (Kalvin *et al.* 1992; Zollikofer *et al.* 1995, 1998). It has also been used to investigate internal structures of the skull like the labyrinth of the inner ear and the frontal sinus of fossil hominids (e.g. Spoor & Zonneveld 1995; Hublin *et al.* 1996; Seidler *et al.* 1997).

Using the non-destructive technique of microcomputer tomography, we have completed a new, virtual reconstruction of the Le Moustier 1 skull, which corrects defects found in the earlier reconstruction attempts (Thompson & Illerhaus 1998). This analysis had several objectives. The first was to remove the false material (as instructed by the museum in discussions that began in 1992) since several cranial and gnathic fragments are made from a compound painted to match the colour of the fossilised bone. The second objective was to correctly realign the cranial and gnathic fragments that were incorrectly positioned in previous reconstruction attempts and to correct for distortion caused during the fossiliation process. Our third objective was to make a new reconstruction of the cranial vault, jaws, and dentition. We also investigated the frontal sinus and labyrinth of the inner ear to assess the Neanderthal status of these internal structures of the skull. The dentition was also examined to assess dental formation, eruption, and extent of taurodontism.

The main areas affected by false material and glue included the palate, the area surrounding many of the teeth, the left part of the frontal bone, and the right parietal and temporal bones. The removal of this false matrix was achieved by editing each CT slice, "cutting out" the false material when necessary.

Previous attempts at reconstructing the Le Moustier 1 skull failed to correct the distortion of the cranial vault caused by taphonomic processes during the fossilisation process. Much of the distortion was corrected by separating and realigning fragments of the occipital, parietal, temporal, and sphenoid on the right side of the vault. Manipulation of other bones and the teeth was also carried out to correct for inaccuracies made in the earlier reconstructions. The overall effect is a much less distorted cranium, allowing a better articulation with the condyles of the mandible at the mandibular fossae, and a more accurate reconstruction of the skull (see Figure 27. 1).

Neanderthal Features

There are a number of morphological traits commonly found in adult Neanderthal specimens, which may be regarded as characteristic of this population. Most of these traits relate to the external morphology of the skull and postcrania. With regard to Le Moustier 1, these external morphological traits have already been reported on in some detail elsewhere, and we direct interested readers to those publications for further information (Thompson & Bilsborough 1996, 1998a, b; Thompson & Nelson 1997a, b; Nelson & Thompson, in prep.).

The use of CT data has allowed us to expand the list of Neanderthal features associated with this specimen and to reveal details of ontogenetic as well as phylogenetic importance. Work by Vlcek (1967 1969), Tillier (1974), and Heim (1978) has demonstrated that the Neanderthal sinus fills much of the supraorbital torus in the glabellar region, extending laterally to about mid orbit but does not extend up into the frontal squamous as in modern humans. Our results demonstrate that the frontal sinus cavities of Le Moustier 1 are large, but they do not extend up the frontal bone as seen in modern humans (Thompson & Illerhaus 1998). They also extend laterally, as in adult Neanderthals (Trinkaus 1993), but unlike many adults they do not extend to the midline of the orbit. Given that this individual was immature at death (Thompson 1995; Thompson & Nelson 1997, submitted; Nelson & Thompson, in press), further growth of the sinuses would have been likely had this individual survived to adulthood (Thompson & Illerhaus 1998).

The morphology and dimensions of the hominoid labyrinth have been studied in great detail and the significance of these features for Neanderthals has been reported elsewhere (e.g. Spoor et al. 1993; Spoor & Zonneveld 1994 1995; Spoor et al. 1994; Hublin et al. 1996). This previous work demonstrates that Neanderthals have smaller anterior and posterior semicircular canals than those of modern humans and a posterior canal placed inferiorly relative to the plane of the lateral canal. The dimensions of the radii of curvature of the anterior, lateral, and posterior semicircular canals of Le Moustier 1 were measured using the commercial software AVS (Advanced Visualization Software, version 5.3). The actual metric values are reported elsewhere (Thompson & Illerhaus 1998). Our analysis reveals that Le Moustier 1 follows the Neanderthal pattern of having an inferiorly positioned posterior semicircular canal relative to the plane of the lateral canal, adding yet another feature to the impressive list of Neanderthal features already possessed by this specimen.

Metric comparisons between the new CT reconstruction and that of the last reconstruction, carried out by Weinert in 1925, reveal several interesting differences that shed light on craniofacial growth in the adolescent period. New measurements, along with those measuring facial height (NA-PR, NA-GN) and facial projection (BA-PR) indicate that between the age represented by the Teshik Tash 1 individual (dental age: 9.9) and that of Le Moustier 1 (dental age: 15.5), it is upper facial height that expands most significantly. Facial prognathism would likely have increased had Le Moustier 1 lived to adulthood, by lengthening of the jaws to accommodate the eruption of the third molars, but at present his BA-PR measurement differs little from that of Teshik Tash 1 (details are given in Thompson & Illerhaus 1998).

The use of CT data allows information concerning dental formation and eruption and the extent of tauro-dontism to be visualised (see Figures 27.2a-g). Removal of false material revealed the crypt for the upper left M3 and indicates that this tooth, and presumably its antimere, should be positioned higher than at present. Dieck, who assembled the upper dentition in the last two reconstruction attempts, removed the teeth from the jaws. This new information confirms that he placed the M3's as if they were erupting, not in their position at death (see Figure 27.2a). Figure 27.2b indicates that the impacted lower canine was fully developed. Figures 27.2c-e illustrate that the root of both lower M3's appears to be about 1/4 complete. The full thickness of the enamel of the lower right M3 (Figures 27.2c-d) could not be shown since that tooth is tilted in the jaw. Figures 2f and 2g demonstrate that the root of the upper M3's is also 1/4 complete. Figures 27.2d-g demonstrate the extent of taurodontism of the first and second molars of the upper and lower jaws, another morphological feature associated with Neander-thals. The CT data confirms that all the teeth were erupted and/or had completed their formation. The exceptions are the impacted left permanent canine and the 3rd molars

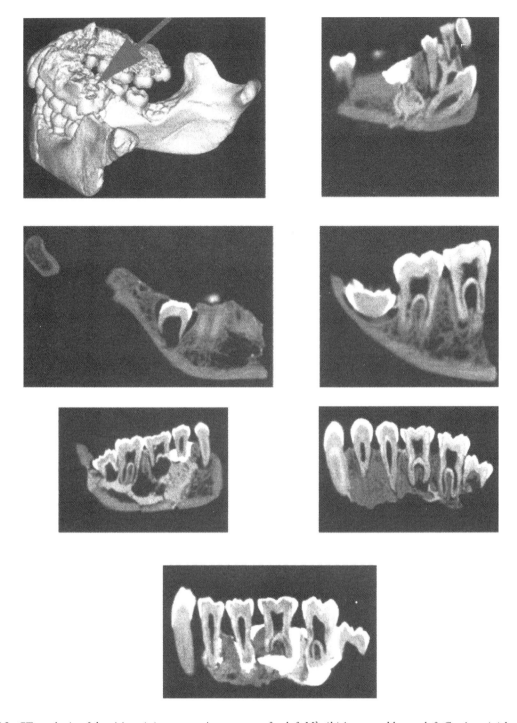

Figure 27.2: CT analysis of dentition. (a) arrow points to crypt for left M³; (b) impacted lower left Canine; (c) lower left M₃; (d) lower right molars demonstrating extent of taurodontism; (e) right side of mandible showing extent of M₃ development; (f) upper left dentition; (g) upper right dentition.

which are unerupted and have only 1/4 of their root completed, supporting a dental age estimate of 15.5 years of age (Thompson 1995, 1998).

The intracranial anatomy of the Le Moustier 1 specimen has already been described in some detail (Thompson & Bilsborough 1997) and readers are directed to that publication for information regarding preservation of sulci

and meningeal vessels, etc. A virtual endocranial cast of this individual was made using CT voxel images (a full report on the endocast will be published elsewhere). Details, as revealed by our CT reconstruction of the endocranium (see Figures 27.3a & 27.3b), demonstrate that Le Moustier 1 possesses the right frontal/left occipital petalia of more recent *Homo*. Unfortunately, while the

Figure 27.3: Brain endocast of the Le Moustier 1 skull. (a) superior view; (b) posterior view.

groove for the superior sagittal sinus is evident superiorly, its intersection at the cruciform is lost because of breakage and loss of internal tabular bone (Figure 27. 3b). Thus it is not possible to tell if the superior sagittal sinus turns infero-laterally to become the left or the right transverse sinus or bifurcates to end in both. However, the left transverse sulcus appears wider and deeper than that on the right and so this may indicate that the superior sinus diverged left to become the left transverse sinus.

Neanderthal Growth and Development

One area of Neanderthal ontogeny that is not well understood is the adolescent period. This is mainly due to the fact that infant and child remains are more numerous than are older juveniles. The recent availability of the Le Moustier 1 adolescent for study has meant that this period of Neanderthal growth and development can be examined in more detail, especially postcranial development that is relatively unknown for this age group.

The Le Moustier 1 specimen has a dental age of approximately 15.5 years (based on modern human

standards) (Thompson 1995, 1998). Skeletally, none of the long bones seems to have fused which indicates that this specimen is younger than 14 years. Further analysis, by Thompson & Nelson (1997, submitted) and Nelson & Thompson (1998, in press) based on the length of the long bones, indicates an age of 11 for this individual (also based on modern human standards). This lack of agreement between the dental and skeletal ages indicates that growth and development in Neanderthals differed somewhat from our own. This work has led to an investigation of the relationship between dental and skeletal developmental fields in modern humans to establish models against which to compare juvenile fossil hominids.

Recent work, in collaboration with Dr. A. J. Nelson (University of Western Ontario), has involved the collection of data from an archaeological sample of Inuit who represent a similarly ecologically adapted population to Neanderthals. Comparison of the relative development of postcranial growth against dental age demonstrates that Neanderthals and *Homo erectus* were following different growth trajectories to modern humans, including early modern humans from the late Pleistocene of Europe. This finding makes a new and significant contribution to our understanding of Neanderthal ontogeny and has implications for our interpretation of hominid phylogeny (Nelson & Thompson 1998, in press; Thompson & Nelson 1997 submitted).

As part of an analysis of Neanderthal growth and development, Nelson & Thompson (in press) estimated the stature of the Le Moustier 1 specimen. Using the age specific femur/stature ratios (Feldesman 1992), the femoral length of 380mm for Le Moustier 1 (Klaatsch & Hauser 1909) yields a stature estimate of 138.5cm. This figure contrasts with earlier published estimates of 145–150cm (Klaatsch & Hauser 1909; Hrdlicka 1930). However, we note that this estimate is likely somewhat generous given the shortening of the tibia already present in the Le Moustier 1 specimen (Thompson & Nelson 1997a, b) and its low vault height, relative to the modern humans in the comparative sample. Certainly, this individual had not yet reached adult stature given an average European Neanderthal adult male value of 168.2cm (Nelson & Thompson, in press).

Conclusions

This paper reviews the work completed and in progress on the Le Moustier 1 specimen. The use of CT data has allowed several internal features to be examined such as details of the intracranial anatomy, internal morphology of the skull and teeth, as well as the extent of dental development. Analysis of the extent of dental development confirmed a dental age estimate of 15.5 years (based on modern human standards). By this dental age, Le Moustier 1's labyrinth had already reached adult proportions (adult size is achieved very early in development) and its dimensions align it with the adult Neanderthal sample.

However, it is unlikely that the frontal sinus had yet reached its adult size and form. Measurement of the new skull reconstruction and comparison with younger individuals demonstrates that upper facial height expands significantly between late childhood and adolescence in Neanderthals. However, during the same period, mid-facial prognathism does not seem to change. It is likely that expansion of the jaws to accommodate the eruption of the third molars would have resulted in both an increase in mid-facial prognathism and the appearance of a retromolar space, but this series of events had not yet begun in this individual.

Although dentally an adolescent, postcranial development of Le Moustier 1 indicates an individual in the later stages of the childhood period and comparative analysis reveals interesting contrasts in the pattern of growth and development between Neanderthals and early modern and recent modern humans (Nelson & Thompson 1998, in press; Thompson & Nelson 1997, submitted). With an estimated stature of 138.5cm, it is unlikely that the Le Moustier 1 individual had yet launched into the adolescent growth spurt typical of modern human children of similar dental age, assuming that Neanderthals experienced this phenomenon. Work on the full extent of growth achieved in this individual by adolescence is in preparation (Nelson & Thompson in prep.).

Aspects of Neanderthal growth and development have been well studied by a number of workers, but little is known about the final stages of the growth period. The new CT reconstruction and analysis of internal features of the Le Moustier 1 skull has not only expanded our knowledge of aspects of this specimen's morphology, it has contributed information pertinent to our understanding of the Neanderthal adolescent period of growth and development.

Acknowledgements
We would like to thank Professor W. Menghin, Director of the Museum für Vor- und Frühgeschichte, Berlin for permission to undertake this new reconstruction of the Le Moustier 1 skull. We thank Mrs. A. Hoffmann for her assistance at each stage of this project. Special thanks should go to Professor H. Czichos, the President of the Bundesanstalt für Materialforschung und -prüfung (BAM), for use of their 3–D Microtomograph and software. We are grateful to Dr. J. Goebbels, T. Wolk, and D. Meinel, for their expertise and support throughout the course of this project. Particular thanks should go to Dr. Fred Spoor for his advice and expertise in measuring the labyrinths of the Le Moustier 1 specimen and to Nathan Jeffery for technical assistance. J. L. Thompson is grateful to Prof. Chris Stringer, Natural History Museum, for permission to measure comparative cast material and to Mr. R. Kruszynski for his assistance during each of her visits. Thanks to A. J. Nelson for comments on the manuscript.

References

Bilsborough, A. & Thompson, J.L. (1996). Dentition of the Le Moustier 1 Neanderthal. *American Journal of Physical Anthropology. Special Supplement* **21,** 69.

Bordes, F. (1959). Le Context Archéologique des hommes du Moustier et de Spy. *L'Anthropologie* **63,** 154–7.

Conroy, G.C. & Vannier, M.W. (1984). Noninvasive three dimensional computer imaging of matrix filled fossil skulls by high resolution computed tomography. *Science.* **226,** 457–458.

Conroy, G.C. & Vannier M.W. (1986). Three-dimensional computer imaging: some anthropological applications. In (J.G. Else & P. C. Lee, Eds) *Primate Evolution,* pp. 211–222. Cambridge: Cambridge University Press.

Conroy, G.C., Vannier, M.W., & Tobias, P.V. (1990). Endocranial features of *Australopithecus africanus* revealed by 2– and 3–D computed tomography. *Science* **247,** 838–841.

Feldesman, M.R. (1992). Femur stature ratio and estimates of stature in children. *American Journal of Physical Anthropology* **87,** 447–459.

Hauser, O. (1909). Découverte d'un squelette du type du Neandertal sous l'abri infériur du Moustier. *L'Homme Préhistorique* **7,** 1–9.

Heim, J-L. (1978). Contribution du massif facial à la morphogénése du crâne Néanderthalien. In *Les Origines Humaines et les Époques de l'Intelligence,* pp. 183–215. Paris: Masson et Cie.

Hesse, H. (1966). Zum Shicksal des Neandertaler-Fundes von Le Moustier (Homo mousteriensis Hauseri). *Forchungen und Fortschritte* **40,** 347–8.

Hesse, H. & Ullrich, H. (1966). Schädel des "Homo mousteriensis Hauseri" wiedergefunden. *Biol. Rundschau* **4,** 158–160.

Hoffmann, A. (1997). Zur Geschichte des Fundes von Le Moustier. *Acta Praehistorica et Archaeologica* **29,** 7–16.

Hoffmann, A., Goebbels, J., Illerhaus, B. (1994). Virtual reconstruction of the skull of Le Moustier – project proposal. Berichtsband 45, Teil 1. *Deutsche Gesellschaft für Zerstörungsfreie Prüfung e.V. 4th Int. Conf. NDT of works of Art.*

Hublin, J-J., Spoor, F., Braun, M., Zonneveld, F., & Condemi, S. (1996). A late Neanderthal associated with Upper Palaeolithic artefacts. *Nature* **381,** 224–226.

Hrdlicka, A. (1930). The skeletal remains of early man. *Smithsonian Miscellaneous Collections* **83,** 297–303.

Illerhaus, B., Goebbels, J., & Riesemeier, H. (1997). Computerized tomography and synergism between technique and art. In (D. Dirksen & G. von Bally, Eds) *Selected Contributions to the International Conference on New Technologies in the Humanities and Fourth International Conference on Optics Within Life Science OWLS IV, Münster, Germany, 9–13 July 1996,* pp. 91–104. Heidelberg: Springer Verlag.

Illerhaus, B., Goebbels, J., Reimers, P., & Riesemeier, H. (1994). The principle of computerized tomography and its application in the reconstruction of hidden surfaces in objects of art. *4th Inter. Conf. NDT of works of Art DGZFP, Berichtsband 45,* 41–49.

Illerhaus, B., Goebbels, J., Riesemeier, H., & Staiger, H. (1997). Correction techniques for detector systems in 3D-CT. *Proceedings of SPIE* **3152,** 101–106.

Kalvin, A.D., Dean, D., Hublin, J-J., & Braun, M. (1992). Visualization in Anthropology: Reconstruction of Human fossils from multiple pieces. In (A. E. Kaufman & G. M. Nielson, Eds) *Proceedings of IEEE Visualization '92,* pp. 404–410.

Klaatsch, H. (1909a). Der primitive Mensch der Verganenheit und der Gegenwart. In (A. Wangerin, Ed) *Verhandlungen der Gesellschaft Deutscher Naturforscher und Ärzte,* pp. 95–108. Leipzig: Verlag von F.C.W. Vogel.

Klaatsch, H. (1909b). Die neueste Ergebnisse der Paläontologie der Menschen und ihre Bedentung für das Abstammungsproblem. *Z. Ethnol.* **41,** 537–584.

Klaatsch, H. (1909c). Die Fortschritte der Lehre von der Neandertalrasse (1903–1908). *Ergebn. Anat. Entw.-gesch.* **17**, 431–462.

Klaatsch, H. (1909d). Preuves que l'Homo Mousteriensis Hauseri appartient au type du Néandertal. *L'Homme Préhistorique* **7**, 10–16.

Klaatsch, H. & Hauser, O. (1909). Homo mousteriensis Hauseri. *Arch. fr. Anthrop.* **35**, 287–289.

Mellars, P. (1986). A new chronology for the French Mousterian period. *Nature* **22**, 410–11.

Mellars, P. & Grün, R. (1991). Comparison of the Electron Spin Resonance and Thermoluminescence Dating Methods: Results of ESR Dating at Le Moustier (France). *Cambridge Archaeological Journal* **1**, 269–76.

Nelson, A.J. & Thompson, J.L. (In Press). Growth and Development in Neandertals and other Fossil Hominids: implications for hominid phylogeny and the evolution of hominid ontogeny. In (R.D. Hoppa & C.M. FitzGerald, Eds.) *Growth in the Past: Studies from Bones and Teeth*. Cambridge Studies in Biological Anthropology. Cambridge: Cambridge University Press.

Nelson, A.J. & Thompson, J.L. (In prep.) Neanderthal Adolescent Postcranial Growth. In (N. Minugh-Purvis & K. McNamara, Eds.) *Human Evolution Through Developmental Change*. Baltimore: John Hopkins University Press.

Schott, L. (1989). Bergung und Rekonstruktion des "Jünglings von Le Moustier". *Ethnogr. Archäol. Z.* **30**, 548–554.

Schuchhardt, C. (1912). Die neue Zusammensetzung des Schädels von Homo Mousteriensis Hauseri. *Amtl. Ber. aus den Königl. Kunstsammlungen, Beil. z. Jahrb. d. Königl. Preuss. Kunstsammlungen* **34**, 4–10.

Seidler, H., Falk, D., Stringer, C., Wilfing, H., Müller, G.B. zur Nedden, D, Weber, G.W., Reicheis, W. & Arsuaga, J-L (1997). A comparative study of stereolithographically modelled skulls of Petralona and Broken Hill: implications for future studies of middle Pleistocene hominid evolution. *J. hum. Evol.* **33**, 691–703.

Spoor, C.F., Zonneveld, F.W., & Macho, G.A. (1993). Linear measurements of cortical bone and dental enamel by computed tomography: applications and problems. *American Journal of Physical Anthropology* **91**, 469–484.

Spoor, C.F. & Zonneveld, F. (1994). The bony labyrinth in Homo erectus; a preliminary report. *Courier Forschungs-Institut Senckenberg* **171**, 251–256.

Spoor, C.F. & Zonneveld, F. (1995). Morphometry of the primate bony labyrinth: a new method based on high-resolution computed tomography. *Journal of Anatomy* **186**, 271–286.

Spoor, C.F., Wood, B., & Zonneveld, F. (1994). Implications of early hominid labyrinthine morphology for evolution of human bipedal locomotion. *Nature* **369**, 645–648.

Tate, J.R. & Cann, C.E. (1982). High-resolution computed tomography for the comparative study of fossil and extant bone. *American Journal of Physical Anthropology* **58**, 67–73.

Thompson, J.L. (1995). Terrible teens: the use of adolescent morphology in the interpretation of Upper Pleistocene human evolution. *American Journal of Physical Anthropology. Special Supplement* **20**, 210.

Thompson, J.L (1998). Neanderthal Growth and Development. In (S.J. Ulijaszek, F.E. Johnston & M.A. Preece, Eds.). *The Cambridge Encyclopedia of Human Growth and Development*, pp. 106–107. Cambridge: Cambridge University Press.

Thompson, J.L. & Bilsborough, A. (1994). Piecing together the past: the Neanderthal from Le Moustier. *American Journal of Physical Anthropology. Special Supplement* **18**, 195.

Thompson, J.L. & Bilsborough, A. (1996). Le Moustier 1: characteristics of a late western European Neanderthal. *American Journal of Physical Anthropology. Special Supplement* **21**, 229.

Thompson, J.L. & Bilsborough, A. (1997). The current state of the Le Moustier 1 skull. *Acta Praehistorica et Archaeologica* **29**, 17–38.

Thompson, J.L. and Bilsborough, A. (1998a). Time for one of the last Neanderthals. In (F. Facchini, A. Palma di Cesnola, M. Piperno, & C. Peretto, Eds.) *Proceedings of the XIII Congress of the U.I.S.P.P.- Forlì (Italia, 8/14 September, 1996),Volume 2*, pp. 289–298. Forlì: Abaco.

Thompson, J. L. & Bilsborough, A. (1998b). Time for one of the last Neanderthals. *Mediterranean Prehistory Online* **0**, http://www.med.abaco-mac.it/.

Thompson, J. L. & Illerhaus, B. (1998) A new Reconstruction of the Le Moustier 1 and investigation of internal structures using 3–D-µCT data. *Journal of Human Evolution* **35**, 647–665.

Thompson, J.L. & Nelson, A.J. (1997a). Relative Postcranial Development of Neanderthals. *Journal of Human Evolution* **32**, A23–24.

Thompson, J.L. & Nelson, A.J. (submitted) The Place of Neandertals in the Evolution of Hominid Patterns of Growth and development. *Journal of Human Evolution*.

Trinkaus, E. (1993) *The Shanidar Neandertals*. New York: Academic Press.

Valladas, H., Geneste, J.M., Joron, J.L., & Chadelle, J.P. (1986). Thermoluminescence dating of Le Moustier (Dordogne, France) *Nature* **322**, 452–4.

Vlcek, E. (1969). *Neandertaler der Tschechoslowakei*. Prag: Verlag der Tschechoslowakischen Akademie der Wissenschaften.

Vlcek, E. (1967). Die Sinus frontales bei europäischen Neandertalern. *Anthrop. Anz.* **30**, 166–189.

Weinert, H. (1925). *Der Schädel des eiszeitlichen Menschen von Le Moustier in neuer Zusammensetzung*. Berlin: Springer.

Wind, J. (1984). Computerized X-ray tomography of fossil hominid skulls. *American Journal of Physical Anthropology* **63**, 265.

Zollikofer, C.P.E., Ponce de León, M.S., & Martin, R.D. (1998). Computer-assisted paleoanthropology. *Evolutionary Anthropology* **6**, 41–54.

Zollikofer, C.P.E., Ponce de León, M.S., Martin, R.D., & Stucki, P. (1995) Neanderthal computer skulls. *Nature* **375**, 283–285.

Zonneveld, F.W. & Wind, J. (1985). High-resolution computed tomography of fossil hominid skulls: a new method and some results. In (P.V. Tobias, Ed.) *Hominid Evolution: Past Present and Future*, pp. 427–436. New York: Alan R. Liss.

Zonneveld, F.W., Spoor, C.F., & Wind, J. (1989). The use of CT in the study of the internal morphology of hominid fossils. *Medicamundi* **34**, 117–128.

28

Heterochrony and the Human Fossil Record: Comparing Neandertal and Modern Human Craniofacial Ontogeny

Frank L'Engle Williams

Heterochrony, or how ontogenies evolve, provides a conceptual framework upon which to compare how adults of different taxa come to be. Indeed, changes in growth and development rates, as well as changes in the timing of maturational events may be largely responsible for the differences seen in Neandertal and modern human adults. In this study, the craniofacial ontogeny of Neandertals and modern humans is compared by analysing the patterns and strengths of their growth allometries, and by comparing changes in shape reflected in Euclidean distances in multidimensional shape space and Principal Component Analysis (PCA). Differences in allometric growth provide information about the relative deviations of traits during ontogeny. However, it is the similarity of proportions (here measured by Euclidean distances and by PCA) that can address whether shape differences between adults are already present during infancy, as well as whether the degree of departure from infant morphologies is the same. Moreover, by comparing shape differences, it is possible to evaluate the degree to which adult modern humans can be described as paedomorphic, or juvenilised, *vis-à-vis* Neandertal infants and juveniles, and whether this paedo-morphosis (to the extent to which it exists) can be attributed to neoteny (slow rate of shape change with respect to size and age at maturation).

Although the first Neandertal discovered was that of a child (Engis 2; Figure 28.1), the study of adults has dominated research on Neandertals since the 19th century (Trinkaus and Shipman 1992; Stringer and Gamble 1993; Wolpoff and Caspari 1997). Fewer researchers have tried to understand how Neandertal adult morphology emerged from juvenile forms (Minugh-Purvis 1988; Tillier 1989; Williams 1996; 1997; Krovitz *et al.* 97). At the same time, investigators proposing heterochonic models for human evolution have largely ignored the human fossil record in arguments for and against the presence of neoteny and

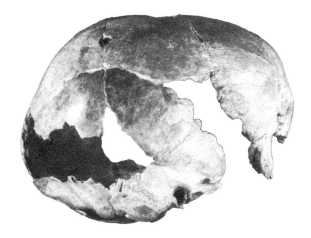

Figure 28.1: Engis 2. This fairly complete infant cranium, associated with a small anterior palatal fragment, was found in Belgium in 1829. It was not identified as a Neandertal until after several adults were discovered later in the 19th century. Engis 2 had its deciduous dentition completely erupted, although the decidous molars and M1 are isolated. M1 was either unerupted or only recently erupted in Engis 2. Photo courtesy of the Laboratoire de Paléontologie, Université de Liège and the Institut Royal des Sciences Naturelles de Belgique.

paedomorphosis (Gould 1977; Montagu 1989; Shea 1989; McKinney and McNamara 1991).

Heterochrony relies on fairly complete ontogenetic sequences to compare relative growth patterns, changes in shape and life history parameters. While *Australopithecus* and *Homo erectus* offer few juvenile remains, Neandertals are represented by a much more complete ontogenetic series. To the extent that Neandertals preserve

Table 28.1: Neandertals by life cycle stage used in variable selection.

Age Category	Infant	Juvenile	Subadult	Adult
Age Range	2.5–4.5 Yrs.	6–11 Yrs.	14–16 Yrs.	19–45 Yrs
Dental Stage	Pre-M1	Post-M1/ Pre-M2	Post M2/ Pre M3	Post M3
Site	Pech de L'Azé Roc de Marsal Subalyuk 2 Engis 2 Devil's Tower Archi 1 Châteauneuf Amud 7 (4 Mths)	La Quina 18 Teshik-Tash Krapina - Maxillas B, C, & E, & Mandible C Sclayn	Malarnaud Krapina- Maxilla D & Mandibles D,E & F	La Ferrassie La Quina 5 Krapina C3, Mandibles H,G & J & Rami 63 & 66 La Chapelle- aux-Saints Tabun C1 Forbes Quarry Spy 1 & 2 Guattari Circeo 2 & 3 Amud 1 Kebara 2 Subalyuk 1
Totals	N=8	N=7	N=5	N=19

the patterns of craniofacial ontogeny of Middle Pleistocene hominids (Stringer *et al.* 1990), ontogenetic data from Neandertals must be consulted to assess neoteny and paedomorphosis in modern humans.

Materials and methods

The Neandertal sample (Table 28.1) was obtained from original fossils and one cast (Teshik-Tash) located at museums in Europe and Israel (Table 28.2). Of the total (n = 39), 22 individuals are represented by whole or partial mandibles or maxillas, while 17 are more complete. The modern human sample (n = 272) covers a wide range of temporal and geographic variability, and was obtained at museums in Europe and the United States. The modern human specimens originate from Europe (n = 60), Southeast Asia (n = 18), the Americas (n = 20), the Middle East (n = 14), sub-Saharan Africa (n = 14), Papua New Guinea (n = 24) and Medieval Belgium (n = 54). Two groups of undocumented infants and children (n = 60), and eight undocumented adults were also included. To check the effects of population variability, craniofacial traits by age for the Papuan and Medieval Belgian populations were compared to the larger mixed population sample. These two populations represent extremes of human variability; Papuans are small in overall body size, whereas the Medieval Belgian population from Koksijde (a 14th to 15th century Flemish abbey) is largely composed of robust males. The variability of these populations rarely exceeds that present in the larger mixed sample. Figures 28.2a, 28.2b, and 28.2c demonstrate the concordance of the modern human sample.

Age was estimated for immature modern humans according to dental eruption patterns, sequence of bone development (e.g., tympanic ring), and whenever possible, epiphyseal plate closure (Buikstra and Ubelaker 1994). Ages for dental adults were estimated on the basis of basilar, palatal and cranial suture closure in combination with the degree of tooth wear. In ageing the Neandertals sample, the same procedures and developmental schedules used to age modern humans were followed. However, according to Dean *et al.* (1986) and Stringer *et al.* (1990) who used perikymata counts, and Wolpoff (1979) who examined relative tooth wear patterns, Neandertals may have followed an accelerated pattern of tooth eruption (but see Skinner 1997).

Two criteria were used in selecting traits to compare. First, traits showing little post-natal growth in size (such as foramen magnum breadth and length) were excluded. Second, the trait had to be present on many original Neandertal fossils at various ages in order to be included in the analysis. From these two criteria, twelve craniofacial traits were selected following Bass (1987) and Buikstra and Ubelaker (1994). These twelve variables originate from three regions of the skull (calotte, face and mandible). The three regions were analysed separately to increase the representation of fragmentary Neandertal fossils. Regional overall size was constructed by summing all linear measurements comprising a region (Gould 1977; Godfrey and Sutherland 1996) such that calotte size consisted of four traits, face size three traits and mandible size five traits (Table 28.3). To calculate growth allometries, all 12 craniofacial variables were log-transformed and regressed against their respective log-transformed regional size. The null hypothesis of isometry was tested using 95% confidence limits.

Shape variables were derived from the 12 craniofacial traits described in Table 28.3 by taking each raw measure-

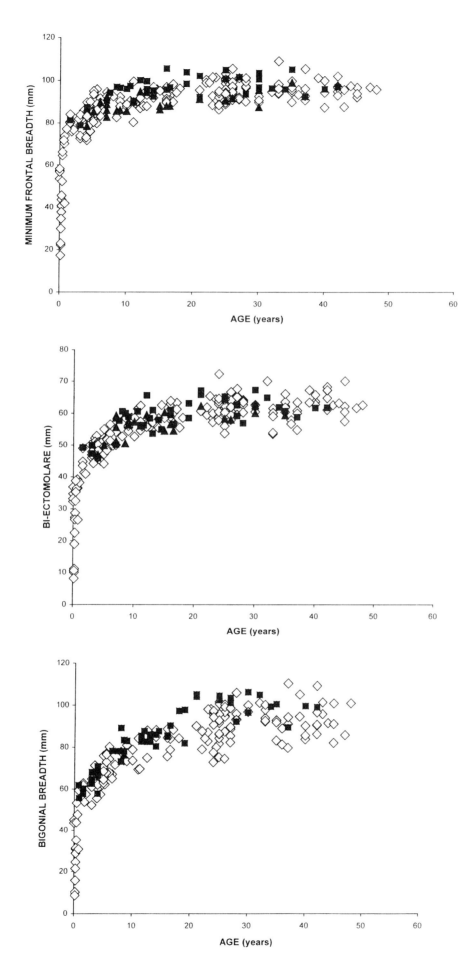

Figure 28.2a, b, c: Scatterplots of (a) Minimum Frontal Breadth, (b) Bi-Ectomolare, and (c) Bigonial breadth. Three modern human growth trajectories are shown here to demonstrate the concordance of the sample using a large mixed population sample (open diamonds), and two more distinct populations: Papua New Guinean (closed triangles) and Medieval Belgian (closed squares).

Table 28.2: List of institutions where Neandertal fossils and modern human remains were examined.

Country	Institution
England	Natural History Museum (Forbes Quarry, Tabun C1, Devil's Tower)
France	Musée de l'Homme (La Chapelle-aux-Saints, La Ferrassie, La Quina 5, Pech de l'Azé, Malarnaud)
	Musée de Antiquities Nationales-Saint Germain-en-Laye (La Quina 18)
	Museum National de Préhistoire-Les Eyzies de Tayac (Roc de Marsal)
	Université de Poitiers (Châteauneuf-sur-Clarente)
Belgium	Institut Royal des Sciences Naturelles de Belgique (Spy 1 and 2; modern humans, n=54)
	Direction de l'Archéologie, Région Wallonne (Sclayn)
	Université de Liège (Engis 2)
Hungary	Termeszettudomanyi Museum (Subalyuk 1 and 2)
Israel	Tel Aviv University (Amud 1 and 7, Kebara 2, cast of Teshik-Tash)
Italy	Pigorini Museum (Guattari)
	Instituto di Paleontologia Umana (Circeo 2 and 3, Archi 1)
Croatia	Croatian Natural History Museum (Krapina maxillas B, C, D, E; mandibles C, D, E, F, H, G, J; rami 63, 66)
Netherlands	Rijksuniversiteit Groningen (modern humans, n=24)
	Rijksuniversiteit Leiden (modern humans, n=86)
	Nationaal Natuurhistorisch Museum (modern humans, n=36)
	Rijksinstituut voor Ouderheidskunde Bodemonderzoek (modern humans, n=5)
United States	American Museum of Natural History (modern humans, n=47)
	Johns Hopkins University (modern humans, n=24)

Table 28.3: Description of traits.

Calotte	Face	Mandible
Maximum Cranial Length (Glabella-Opistocranion)	Bi-Ectomolare (Breadth Across the Most Lateral Points on the Alveolar Margin of the Maxilla)	Bigonial Breadth
Maximum Cranial Breadth (Bi-Parietal)		Mandibular Length (Gonion-Gnathion)
Minimum Frontal Breadth (Maximum Postorbital Constriction)	Palatal Length (Prosthion-Staphylion)	Mandibular Symphyseal Height (Infradentale-Gnathion)
Biorbital Breadth (at Fronto-Maxillary Suture)	Maximum Nasal Aperture Breadth (Bi-Alare)	Height of Mandibular Corpus (at Mental Foramen)
		Thickness of Mandibular Corpus (at Mental Foramen)

ment and dividing it by its respective regional size such that each shape was a proportion of the overall size of a specific region. Euclidean distances were then calculated for each region using a resámpling technique wherein 100 randomly generated inter-individual distances were calculated. The statistical significance of these distances was evaluated using T-tests. When the number of inter-individual pairs was too low to provide 100 trials, only 30 randomly generated trials were used to limit an artificial inflation of the degrees of freedom. This resampling technique is explained in greater detail in Williams *et al.* (in review) where the Euclidean distances separating modern human and Neandertal life cycle stages are compared to those obtained for chimpanzees and bonobos. The shape differences separating the life cycle stages of Neandertals and modern humans are comparable to those separating chimpanzees and bonobos.

For the Euclidean distance analyses, samples were drawn from modern human "infants" ranging in age from 2.75 to 3.75 years, and similarly aged Neandertals (Pech de l'Azé, Roc de Marsal, Archi 1 and Subalyuk 2). The "juvenile" Neandertal group consisted of La Quina 18, Teshik-Tash, Krapina maxilla C and Sclayn, aged between 7–11 years. Both modern human (n=113) and Neandertal (n=19) "adults" included all individuals with M3 in full occlusion. For the PCA (axes 1 and 2), centroids (means) for infants (2.5–5.5 years), juveniles (6–11 years), and adults were calculated for each taxon. Due to the extreme scarcity of subadult Neandertals, centroids were obtained for modern human subadults (12–17 years) only.

Growth allometries

Patterns of allometric growth are different for Neandertals and modern humans in a variety of ways (Tables 28.4, 28.5 and 28.6). Patterns of modern human allometric growth differ from those exhibited by Neandertals in the calotte and face. For example, cranial breadth is negatively

Table 28.4: Comparison of growth allometries of the calotte and the significance of allometric coefficients between taxa.

	Modern humans			Neandertals			
Trait	K	SE	Allometry	k	SE	Allometry	Signif.
Max. Cranial Length	1.05	.009	Positive	.931	.083	Isometry	NS
Max. Cranial Breadth	.977	.012	Isometry	.724	.087	Negative	p<0.05
Min. Frontal Breadth	.917	.007	Negative	.952	.086	Isometry	NS
Biorbital Breadth	1.03	.011	Positive	1.54	.109	Positive	p<0.05

Table 28.5: Comparison of growth allometries of the face and the significance of allometric coefficients between taxa.

	Modern humans			Neandertals			
Trait	K	SE	Allometry	K	SE	Allometry	Signif.
Bi-Ectomolare	.822	.012	Negative	.784	.097	Negative	NS
Palatal Length	1.31	.020	Positive	1.21	.160	Isometry	NS
Nasal Breadth	.922	.026	Negative	1.19	.134	Isometry	p<0.05

Table 28.6: Comparison of growth allometries of the mandible and the significance of allometric coefficients between taxa.

	Modern humans			Neandertals			
Trait	k	SE	Allometry	k	SE	Allometry	Signif.
Bigonial Breadth	.979	.009	Negative	.750	.078	Negative	p<0.05
Mandibular Length	.994	.008	Isometry	1.12	.077	Isometry	NS
Symphyseal Height	1.04	.016	Positive	1.30	.115	Positive	p<0.05
Corpus Height	1.19	.013	Positive	1.41	.181	Positive	NS
Corpus Breadth	.783	.024	Negative	.562	.161	Negative	NS

allometric for Neandertals while for modern humans it is isometric. Similarly, nasal breadth in modern humans grows with negative allometry while for Neandertals it is isometric. The patterns of allometric growth for the mandible are the same in both taxa, although the strengths differ (Figure 28.3).

Modern human craniofacial growth can largely be described as weakly allometric or isometric. In general, Neandertals exhibit stronger growth allometries with respect to modern humans. When patterns of allometric growth coincide, Neandertals exhibit stronger, frequently much stronger, allometric signals than those exhibited by modern humans. For example, both Neandertals and modern humans exhibit negative allometry of bigonial breadth and symphyseal height, as well as positive allometry of biorbital breadth, but Neandertals are significantly stronger for each of these.

In general, Neandertals achieve larger sizes for most craniofacial traits by growing at a faster rate. Neandertal infants differ markedly from Neandertal adults in the shape and size of the frontal bone, particularly in the form of the supraorbital torus, reflected in the strong positive allometry of biorbital breadth (Table 28.4; Figure 28.3). Additionally, Neandertal infant and adult symphyseal heights differ dramatically as reflected in the relative strong positive allometry of this trait (Table 28.6). Occipital shape also differs (Figures 28.4 and 28.5).

An expectation of neoteny (paedomorphosis *via* reduction of shape change with respect to size and maturation schedules) is that allometries weaken, i.e., positive allometries become less positive while negative allometries become less negative (Shea 1989; Godfrey and Sutherland 1995, 1996). In this way, modern humans appear to follow the allometric expectations of neoteny (and therefore paedomorphosis) with respect to Neandertals whose allometries tend to be much stronger, particularly for the calotte and mandible.

Euclidean distances

Table 28.7 compares differences between infants of the two taxa with those present between adults to determine whether the disparity between adults is already reflected in the morphology of infants. Using the resampling technique with 30 randomly generated trials of pairs of individuals, the distance separating modern human and Neandertal infants is not significantly different from the distance separating adults for both the calotte and mandible (Williams *et al.* in review). For the face, Neandertal and modern human infants are closer to each other than are their adults suggesting that the facial differences expressed in adults develop largely after infancy.

Within taxon differences using 100 randomly generated infant to adult pairs (Table 28.8) suggest that modern

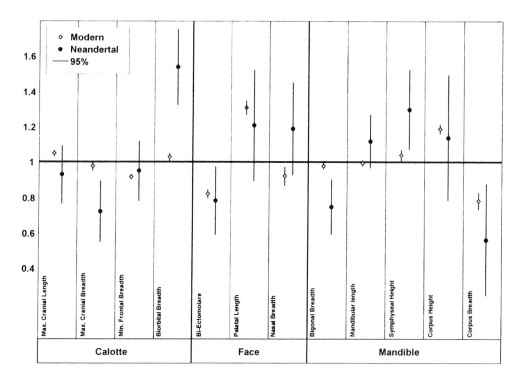

Figure 28.3: Schematic representation of growth allometries for modern humans and Neandertals: Modern humans (open diamonds) and Neandertals (closed circles) are depicted with 95% confidence intervals. When confidence intervals overlap 1, the null hypothesis of isometry cannot be rejected. The confidence intervals (and thus standard errors around the slope, k) for Neandertals are much wider than for modern humans. The shading represents increasingly stronger growth allometries (darker intervals = stronger allometries).

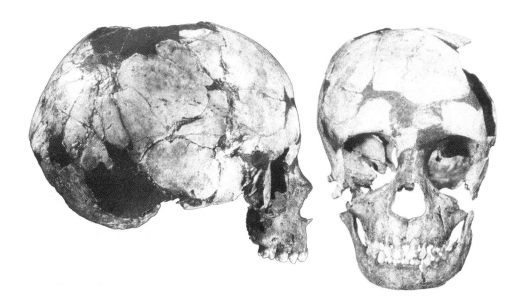

Figure 28.4: Roc de Marsal: Roc de Marsal (found in the Dordogne region of Southwest France) is the most complete infant Neandertal known. This fossil infant has a complete set of deciduous teeth and M1 is far from eruption. The mandible is anteriorly squared-off like many adult Neandertals, and the neurocranium is oriented posteriorly-a feature present in most Neandertals (and very young humans) regardless of age. Some supraorbital relief is already present in this infant anticipating the robustness of this feature found in Neandertal adults (see photograph of Spy). Photo courtesy of the Musée National de Préhistoire, Les Eyzies de Tayac.

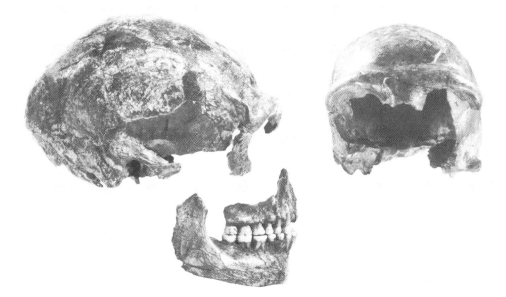

Figure 28.5: Spy 1: This robust male (found in Belgium) displays craniofacial traits which are similar to many Neandertal adults including a robust supraorbital torus, an occiput and posterior elongation of the calvarium. Neandertal adult mandibles are similar in some aspects of shape to those of Neandertal infants, but are much more robust (particularly in the corpus region), with increased mental symphyseal heights, and decreased gonial angles. Photo courtesy of the Institut Royal des Sciences Naturelles de Belgique.

human infant and adult calottes differ more in shape than do those of infant and adult Neandertals. However, Neandertals depart more from their infant morphologies in the face and mandible than do modern humans. The face changes more in both taxa than the other regions, but more for Neandertals than for modern humans.

One hundred randomly generated Euclidean distances were used to test for paedomorphosis in adult modern humans by comparing the distance between Neandertal infants and modern human adults, as well as between Neandertal juveniles and modern human adults, to the distance separating the adults of the two taxa. The distance separating modern human adults and Neandertal infants in the calotte is the same as that between the two adult forms. However, modern human adult mandibles are more similar to those of Neandertal adults than they are to Neandertal infants (Table 28.9). There is no significant difference in the distance separating modern human and Neandertal adult faces and the distance separating those of modern human adults and the infant Neandertals. Thus, modern human adults are not more similar to Neandertal infants than they are to Neandertal adults; in this sense they are not paedomorphic.

Table 28.10 however shows that the distance separating modern human adults and Neandertal juveniles is significantly less than that separating adults of both taxa for all craniofacial regions. Thus modern humans can be classified as slightly paedomorphic in all craniofacial regions when compared to Neandertal juveniles.

Principal Component Analyses

Calotte
PCA axis 1 clearly separates modern humans and Neandertals (Figure 28.6). Yet Neandertal juveniles are quite close to modern human adults, and Neandertal adults are farthest away from modern infants reflecting the Euclidean shape distances presented above. As PCA axis 1 shows, modern human calottes do not change much after the juvenile stage.

The distance traversed ontogenetically by each taxon on PCA axis 2 is different; modern humans travel less than do Neandertals. PCA axis 2 fails to separate the two taxa. On this axis, all modern human life cycle stages overlap with those of juvenile and adult, but not infant Neandertals. The negative loading of relative cranial breadth projects modern human adults in a negative direction, while the positive loading of relative minimum frontal breadth projects Neandertal infants in a positive direction on this axis.

Face
Both modern humans and Neandertals follow parallel patterns of shape change, but PCA axes 1 and 2 fail to separate taxon and developmental stage (Figure 28.7). Modern human adults and Neandertal infants are dispersed on PCA axis 1. Similarly, modern human infants and Neandertal adults are widely separated on PCA axis 2.

Table 28.7: Euclidean distances between Neandertal and modern human infants and adults: Do differences in adults arise during ontogeny or are they present during infancy?

	Calotte	Face	Mandible
Modern Infants & Neandertal Infants	.022	.051	.047
Modern Adults & Neandertal Adults	.024	.069	.047
Significance	NS	p=.01	NS

Table 28.8: Euclidean distances within taxa: Which taxon departs from its infant morphology?

	Calotte	Face	Mandible
Modern Infants & Modern Adults	.035	.057	.038
Neandertal Infants & Neandertal Adults	.029	.078	.068
Significance	p=.00	p=.00	p=.00

Table 28.9: Euclidean distances across taxon and life cycle stage: Are modern humans very paedomorphic?

	Calotte	Face	Mandible
Modern Adults & Neandertal Infants	.025	.077	.060
Modern Adults & Neandertal Adults	.024	.069	.047
Significance	NS	NS	p=.00

Table 28.10: Euclidean distances across taxon and life cycle stages: Are modern humans slightly paedomorphic?

	Calotte	Face	Mandible
Modern Adults & Neandertal Juveniles	.019	.037	.011
Modern Adults & Neandertal Adults	.023	.066	.047
Significance	p=.01	p=.00	p=.00

PCA axis 1 shows overlap between modern humans and Neandertals up to the juvenile stage where modern humans continue farther in a negative direction stemming from the negative loading of relative palatal length. Modern humans traverse only a small distance on PCA axis 2 reflecting their limited degree of departure from infant morphologies (Table 28.8). Modern human and Neandertal infants are very close together on PCA axis 2, while Neandertal adults are strikingly farther away. Neandertal adults are separated from other life cycle stages of both taxa by the very strong negative loading of nasal breadth that may have been adaptively significant for withstanding anterior dental loading in Neandertal adults (Rak 1986, Trinkaus 1987, Demes 1987).

Mandible

PCA axis 1 fails to separate the two taxa whereas PCA axis 2 does (Figure 28.8). The positive projection of both Neandertal and modern human adults on PCA axis 1 stems from the strong positive loading of relative mandibular length that tends to increase as M3 erupts. The projection of Neandertal adults is even more positive on this axis which may reflect the retromolar space present in many adult Neandertals (Fransicus and Trinkaus 1995). The strong negative loading of relative bigonial breadth pulls infants of both groups (Neandertal infants more so) in a negative direction; it reflects the relatively wide and short jaws of infants of both taxa. PCA axis 2 places Neandertal and modern human infants very close to one another. PCA axis 2 additionally contrasts modern human and Neandertal adults. Modern human adults are projected in a negative direction by the negative loading of relative corpus height, and Neandertal adults are pulled in a positive direction via relative corpus breadth; i.e., Neandertal adults tend to have relatively thicker and more shallow mandibles than their modern human counterparts.

For all first and second axes in PCA, both Neandertals and modern humans follow strong ontogenetic signals, despite the *a priori* elimination of size in this reduced shape space. However, Neandertals travel a greater distance on all PCA axes than do modern humans. PCA axis 1 (explaining the largest amount of variance) separates taxon in the calotte and developmental stage in the mandible. PCA axis 2 (explaining less variance) separates developmental stage in the calotte and taxon in the mandible. PCA axes 1 and 2 of the facial region separate neither taxon nor development stage. Instead, modern human adults and Neandertal infants are dispersed on PCA axis 1, while on PCA axis 2, it is modern human infants which are separated from Neandertal adults.

Discussion

Neandertal infants become Neandertal adults via strong positive and negative allometric growth patterns. Generally, shape change during ontogeny is much greater for Neandertals as measured on PCA axes 1 and 2. Modern human adults preserve their infant morphology more than Neandertals in the face and mandible, but for the calotte, it is Neandertals that preserve more of their infant morphology. Before age six there is much shape change in modern human calottes, afterwards there is little change in shape (PCA axis 1, Fig. 6). However, much of the difference observed between modern human and Neandertal adults appears to be present during infancy in the calotte and mandible; much of the difference seen in adult faces arises after infancy.

Neandertal infants are decidedly unlike modern human adults in shape. However, when compared to Neandertal

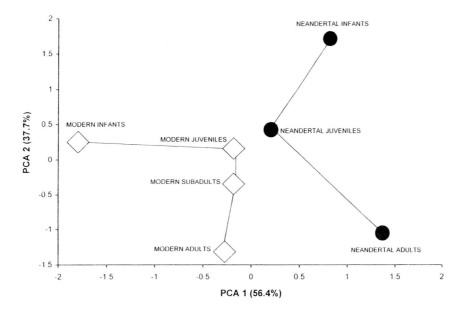

Figure 28.6: PCA of the calotte with lines drawn to connect the developmental stages of each group. Neandertals = closed circles, modern humans = open diamonds.

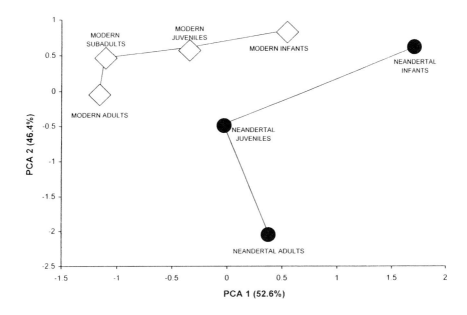

Figure 28.7: PCA of the face with lines drawn to connect the developmental stages of each group. Neandertals = closed circles, modern humans = open diamonds.

juveniles, modern human adults are in the realm of paedomorphosis for all regions compared. This may stem from the limited degree of shape change in modern humans between juvenile and adult stages combined with the similarity of juveniles of both taxa. It may also be an artifact of sampling (Table 28.10) influenced by the comparatively heavy weight attributed to La Quina 18, a gracile and relatively complete Neandertal child cranium (without mandible). However, it is noteworthy that modern

human adults are more similar to the relatively robust juvenile Neandertal mandibles from Sclayn and Teshik-Tash than they are to those of Neandertal adults.

Conclusions

Although modern human adults depart less from their infant morphologies, and have weaker allometries than do Neandertals (two predictions of neoteny), a central

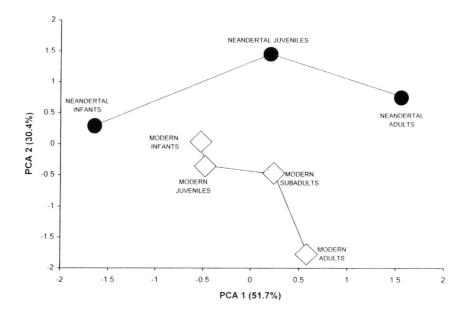

Figure 28.8: PCA of the mandible with lines drawn to connect the developmental stages of each group. Neandertals = closed circles, modern humans = open diamonds.

stipulation of neoteny is violated; the two taxa follow different shape paths to reach adult proportions (Godfrey *et al.* 1998; Williams *et al.* in review). Thus these results suggest that humans are not neotenic with respect to Neandertals. Moreover, Neandertals are larger for most but not all craniofacial traits in relation to modern humans (thus the adult forms are not the same in size). Also, most of the differences between adults are generated early in ontogeny. Fewer of the shape differences that characterise adults emerge after infancy, and these involve mostly changes in the masticatory apparatus. Each taxon remains on its own shape path rendering neoteny *sensu* Gould (1977) untenable.

Modern humans are in the realm of paedomorphosis relative to Neandertals when juvenile Neandertals are compared to adult modern humans. This paedomophosis is probably not stemming from neoteny, but instead probably corresponds to the relatively close phylogenetic relationships present within genera that produce similar juvenile forms before reaching adult termini (combined with the limited amount of modern human craniofacial shape change after late childhood). The dissimilarities in form that typify adult Neandertals and modern humans are largely derived and manifested early in ontogeny.

Acknowledgements
This research was generously supported by a US Fulbright Fellowship to the Netherlands and a Belgian American Education Foundation Graduate Fellowship for study in Belgium. Travel grants were received from the Netherlands-America Commission for Educational Exchange, the Faculteit der Medische Wetenschappen (Rijksuniversiteit Groningen) and Sigma Xi. Many thanks to the Muséum National Préhistoire (Les Eyzies de Tayac), Institut Royal des Sciences Naturelles de Belgique, (and family of Prof. Max Lohest), and Université de Liège for photos of Roc de Marsal, Spy 1 and Engis 2 respectively. Thanks also to Patrick Semal, Laurie Godfrey and Mike Sutherland for their assistance with various aspects of this research.

References
Bass, W. (1987). *The Human Skeleton*. Knoxville TN: University of Tennessee Press.
Buikstra, J.E. & Ubelaker, D.H. (1994). *Standards for Data Collection from Human Skeletal Remains*. Fayetteville, AR: Arkansas Archeological Survey.
Dean, M.C., Stringer, C.B. & Bromage, T.G. (1986). Age at death of the Neandertal child from Devil's Tower, Gibraltar and the implications for studies of general growth and development in Neandertals. *Am. J. phys. Anthrop.* **70**, 301–309.
Demes, B. (1987). Another look at an old face: Biomechanics of the Neandertal facial skeleton reconsidered. *J. hum. Evol.* **16**, 297–303.
Franciscus, R.G. & Trinkaus, E. (1995). Determinants of retromolar space presence in Pleistocene *Homo* mandibles. *J. hum. Evol.* **28**, 577–595.
Godfrey, L.R. & Sutherland, M.R. (1995). What's growth got to do with it? Pattern and process in the evolution of ontogeny. *J. hum. Evol.* **29**, 405–431.
Godfrey, L.R. & Sutherland, M.R. (1996). Paradox of peramorphic paedomorphosis: Heterochrony and human evolution. *Am. J. phys. Anthrop.* **99**, 17–42.
Godfrey, L.R., King, S. & Sutherland, M.R. (1998). Heterochronic approaches to the study of locomotion. In (E. Strasser, J. Fleagle, A. Rosenberger & H. McHenry) *Primate Locomotion: Recent Advances*, pp. 277–307. New York: Plenum Press.
Gould, S.J. (1977). *Ontogeny and Phylogeny*. Cambridge MA: Belknap Press.

Krovitz, G., Cole, T.M. III & Richtmeier, J.T. (1997). Three-dimensional comparisons of growth patterns in Neandertals and modern humans. *Am. J. phys. Anthrop.* **24**, 147.

McKinney, M.L. & McNamara, K.J. (1991). *Heterochrony: The Evolution of Ontogeny*. New York: Plenum Press.

Minugh-Purvis, N. (1988). *Patterns of craniofacial growth and development in Upper Pleistocene hominids*. PhD dissertation, University of Pennsylvannia, Philidelphia, PA.

Montagu, A. (1989). *Growing Young*. New York: McGraw Hill.

Rak, Y. (1986). The Neanderthal: A new look at an old face. *J. hum. Evol.* **15**, 151–164.

Shea, B.T. (1989). Heterochrony in human evolution: The case for neoteny reconsidered. *Ybk. phys. Anthrop.* **32**, 69–101.

Stringer, C.B., Dean, M.C. & Martin, R. (1990). A comparative study of cranial and dental development in a recent British population and Neanderthals. In (C.J. DeRosseau. Ed.) *Primate Life History and Evolution*, pp. 115–152. New York: Wiley-Liss.

Stringer, C.B. & Gamble, C. (1993). *In Search of the Neandertals*. New York: Thames and Hudson.

Tillier, A-M. (1989). The evolution of modern humans: Evidence from young Mousterian individuals. In (P. Mellars & C. Stringer, Eds.) *The Human Revolution: Behavioural and Biological Perspectives on the Origins of Modern Humans*, pp. 286–297. Princeton, NJ: Princeton University Press.

Trinkaus, E. (1987). The Neandertal face: Evolutionary and functional perspectives on a recent hominid face. *J. hum. Evol.* **16**, 429–443.

Trinkaus, E. & Shipman, P. (1992). *The Neandertals: Changing the Image of Mankind*. New York: Alfred A. Knopf, Inc.

Skinner, M. (1997) Age at death of Gibraltar 2. *J. hum. Evol.* **32**, 469–470.

Willliams, F.L. (1996). The use of non-linear models to map craniofacial heterochronies in Neandertals and modern humans. *Am. J. phys. Anthrop.* **22**, 244.

Williams, F.L. (1997). Multivariate analysis of craniofacial heterochrony in Neandertals and modern humans. *Am. J. phys. Anthrop.* **24**, 241.

Williams, F.L., Godfrey, L.R. & Sutherland, M.R. (in review) Heterochrony and the evolution Neandertal and modern human craniofacial form. In (N. Minugh-Purvis & K. McNamara, Eds.). *Human Evolution through Developmental Change*. Johns Hopkins University Press.

Wolpoff, M.H. (1979). The Krapina dental remains. *Am. J. phys. Anthrop.* **50**, 67–114.

Wolpoff, M.H. & Caspari, R. (1997). *Race and Human Evolution*. New York: Simon & Schuster.